EXPECTATIONS, FORECASTING AND CONTROL:

A Provisional Textbook of Macroeconomics

Volume I

Monetary Matters, Keynesian and other Models

William Frazer
University of Florida

William Frazer

University Press of America, Inc.

4720 Boston Way, Lanham, MD 20801

Printed in the United States of America

ISBN: 0-8191-1144-9 (Case)
0-8191-1145-7 (Perfect)

Library of Congress Catalog Card Number: 80-1361

To

Floyd Gillis, Joe Dorfman,

and

Howard Raiffa

Contents

Volume I
Monetary Matters, Keynesian and Other Models

Part I. Introduction

Part II. Theoretical Classifications and Monetary Matters

Part III. Demand Management: The Income and Expenditure Model (with and without Financial Trappings), Statics and Dynamics

Volume II
Prices, Markets and Turning Points

Part IV. Expectations, Supply Side Considerations, and Business Conditions

Part V. An Overview

Appendixes

Preface

A recurring theme in economics since Keynes's time is that of the integration of monetary and general economics. Keynes moved to achieve such an integration with his seminal work, The General Theory (1936).[1] However, in the hands of the emerging Keynesians the economics of output and of money and finance generally were again separated (sect. 4.3), and there evolved in the work of Don Patinkin a synthesis of Keynesian and pre-Keynes economics that has been referred to as "neo-classical."[2] In essence--like in the widely influential Keynesian economics--money and finance did not mean very much. For the most part, money was without the essential store of value property, as defined in chapter 1. It was devoid of the means of dealing with uncertainty about future economic events and of its role in speculative activities.

There was, as many have recognized, a crisis in Keynesian economics, in its inability to explain observable

---

[1]See Donald E. Moggridge, ed., The General Theory and After: Part I. Prepartion, Vol. XIII, "The Collected Writings of John Maynard Keynes," (London: The Macmillan Press, Ltd., 1973), chapter 5; William Frazer, "Review Article: Keynes and Feiwel's Intellectual History of Kalecki," Southern Economic Journal, October 1976, pp. 1163-1166; Hyman P. Minsky, "The Financial Instability Hypothesis: An Interpretation of Keynes and An Alternative to 'Standard' Theory," Nebraska Journal of Economics and Business, Winter 1977, pp. 5-16; and Dudley Dillard, "Revolutions in Economic Theory," Southern Economic Journal, April 1978, pp. 705-724; and Don Patinkin and J. Clark Leith, Keynes, Cambridge and "The General Theory" (Toronto: University of Toronto Press, 1978).

[2]See Minksy, op. cit., and Don Patinkin, Money, Income, and Prices (Evanston, Ill.: Row Peterson, 1956; 2nd ed., New York: Harper and Row, 1965).

reality.[3] This inability was brought into focus by the simultaneous occurrence of inflation and recession and more generally by the overwhelming outpouring of empirical results in the first decade of the widespread use of the modern computer, roughly delineated as the 1960s in the United States.

Monetarist economics emerged in that decade, especially as guided by the work of Milton Friedman, and other disturbances impinging on the economy and the body of economic theory were soon to follow with the Arab oil embargo of 1973. With a strong empirical orientation, monetarist economics benefited from the computer period and served to do three things: (1) challenge Keynesian orthodoxy, (2) provide some redirection, and (3) again suggest important interrelations between general economics, money and finance.

Continuing along the foregoing lines of thought, this book combines discussion of important topics in the theories of price and general economics with the related topics of money and finance. The entire theory becomes more dynamic, with empirical orientation. This is for the most part along lines initiated by Milton Friedman and symbolized by his attention to empirical economics (sect. 7.1) and the interrelations between economic theory and economic policy. His economics was to become in his lifetime an economic theory with facts, and economic facts with theory.

These leads from Friedman were taken unwittingly at first and with more awareness in the end. There is, however, more, and much that one wouid not recognize from reading Friedman's work. The influence of Friedman's writings on the text at hand, though significant, is not the only source. It extends to a philosophy of science and an empirical/policy orientation with respect to economic analysis.[4]

The accomodation of Friedmanesque thought, as presently seen, does not require the abandonment of traditional, mechanical constructions in economics and possibly not even the arrangement of their treatment. The present organization of the topics taken up, in any case, is not radically different from that found in the widely reviewed, 1966 textbook with William Yohe.[5]

---

[3]Journal articles aside, book titles dealing with the condition referred to as the "crisis in economic theory" include the following: William Fellner, Toward a Reconstruction of Macroeconomics (Washington, D.C.: American Enterprise Institute for Public Policy Research, 1976); William Frazer, Crisis in Economic Theory (Gainesville: University of Florida Press, 1973); John R. Hicks, The Crisis in Keynesian Economics (New York: Basic Books, Inc., Publishers, 1974); Robert Skidelsky, ed., The End of the Keynesian Era (New York: Holmes & Meier Publishers, Inc., 1977); and Sidney Weintraub, Capitalism's Inflation and Unemployment Crisis (Reading, Mass.: Addison-Wesley Publishing Company, 1978).

There has been afield for some time the notion that there is something scholarly about narrowing the focus of study, by a careful examination of a set of details in isolation (in a laboratory, as it were) and by a distinction between partial equilibrium as a study of parts and something else as the study of the economy overall. Indeed, it is hard to dispute such a notion as a valid way to proceed in many cases, and no special attempt is made to dispute it. On the other hand, such narrow focus has seemed misleading in economics, all too often, and to give rise to three interrelated practices: one of simply adding additional variables in a least-squares regression equation; a second of adding partial derivatives of a given variable with respect to others in a theory; and a third of scanning the results from analyses of time series data until presumed defensible results are obtained.

The encompassing methodological problems in analysis of economic matters have been threefold: that the whole often appears as more than a sum of parts; that the detailed parts and sectors are highly interrelated; and that changes occurring outside of the usual economic model are having impact upon the parameters of the model. Thus, to deal with these matters we are proceeding most often to view details in the context of a larger body of economics (to view at times, in a sense, an entire economy), and to set a basis for dealing with changes that are impacting upon but occurring outside of the usual economic model, as viewed historically.

Taking leads from M. Friedman, we are interested in the role of independent evidence (the achievement of consistence with evidence that may appear remote at times to the matter immediately at hand) and in dealing with numerous concepts in economic theory indirectly rather than directly. For example (app. to chap. 1; and sect. 7.1), rather than confronting directly the isolation of motives (as in J. M. Keynes's theory) or "economic man concepts" (such as the measurement of utility as found in Alfred Marshall's work) we proceed indirectly to achieve empirical discussion.

Apart from methodology, social philosophy, and the point of view that one is constantly working with a total system of economic analysis and occasionally politics, the specific pillars of a Friedmanesque economics are: (1) the treatment of money in the fullest sense, both as introduced by Keynes's store of value property for money and in relation to fiscal policy, (2) the special use of price theory to address some empirical matters for the economy as a whole, (3) the presence of a

---

[4]See Milton Friedman, Essays in Positive Economics (Chicago, Ill.: University of Chicago Press, 1953), and Lawrence A. Boland, "A Critique of Friedman's Critics," Journal of Economic Literature, June 1979.

[5]See Frazer and Yohe, Introduction to the Analystics and Institutions of Money and Banking. Princeton, N. J.: D. Van Nostrand Company, Inc., 1966.

system of foreign exchange rates, even as one confronts domestic economic policy matters, (4) the liquidity preference demand for money with overshooting, (5) the permanent income consumption function, (6) federal taxes and expenditures with reference to transfers of wealth, and (7) an expectations analysis of the Phillips curve. The first three of these pillars get introduced in chapters 1, 2, and 10. The fourth pillar comes up for consideration in chapters 5 and 6. The fifth pillar comes in the lay out for the conventional Keynesian apparatus in chapters 7 through 9. The seventh pillar comes in chapter 17. However, it calls for some background in the work of the 1970s on rational expectations, and it has underpinnings in some conventional and not-so-conventional topics of the theory of price (including evolutionary change and the pricing of exhaustible resources). This background in prices and markets comes up in the course of chapters 14, 15, and 16.

The energy crisis itself, as brought into focus by the Arab oil embargo, had several disturbing consequences for the theory of aggregative economic behavior and control.[6] For one, it gave rise to a greater urgency for the theory to address the issues of shortages, environmental concern, and supply side matters generally (chaps. 15, 16, and 17), whereas the theory of macroeconomic control had previously been mainly a theory of demand management. For another, the urgency of energy concerns made the laws of thermodynamics seem to bear more heavily on our considerations of production. For still another thing, aspects of shortages and production called to our attention with greater clarity than before aspects of evolutionary change. The awareness of this need has also been reinforced by the experience growing out of the crisis in economic theory. Together the experiences lead us to give attention to the nonrepetitive nature of many changes as they bear on economic theory, forecasting, and control. The nonrepetitive nature of many changes adds to the uncertainty of economic forecasts and calls special attention to the roles of money and liquidity as means of coping with uncertainty.

Other characteristics of the book--viewed as a reaction to the crisis in Keynesian economics and drawing on new, emerging topics--include the following: the enlarged role for expectations, with attention to market efficiency in the use of new information, rational expectations, and forecasting (chaps. 5, 13, and 17); and the greater attention to equilibrium time paths and the time frame of stabilization policy, and the time dimension for the economic theory, as a means of enlarging upon and unifying the theory (chaps. 3, 4, 9, 11, 17, and 18).

---

[6]William Frazer, "Evolutionary Economics, Rational Expectations, and Monetary Policy," Journal of Evolutionary Economics, June 1978.

Viewed differently, the book brings into the author's teaching of macroeconomics, topics that have been excluded and that also appear necessary as a means of moving the economic theory in a more policy oriented direction.[7] In this respect the book could be viewed as being complementary to what has been called a third generation of the large-scale forecasting models.[8] These come about with the expansion of the large structural equations models of the U.S. economy to an 800-equation size. They include expanded roles for financial factors, expectational factors and uncertainty, and inflation forecasting, on the one hand, and they recognize the importance of "agent" sensitivity to speculative prospects and the presence of "major exogenous elements which are very difficult, if not impossible, to forecast."

The present orientation, in any case, is different from that of the large models that require up to 25 or more full-time professionals to develop and operate on a continuing basis. In fact, it is the provisional product of classroom teaching and some writing and research.

Theory, analyses of data, and explicit uses of analysis get interspersed with policy, political, and bank-newsletter discussions at times. The idea from the author's point of view is to convey a relationship between the topics. This takes on importance with regard to students who may be thought of as reading explicit uses of analysis (in the sense of calculus) for the last time and as embarking upon a lifetime of reading newspapers and newsletters.

The overall objective and unifying theme of the diverse topics in the book is an introduction to the two sides of macroeconomic policy above the levels of principles of economics, and beginning calculus and statistics courses. The two interrelated sides of policy are of course the behavioral side and the control side. On the behavioral side we have the workings of the economy, the auxiliary social and institutional arrangements accompanying behavior. We seek explanations of the behavior that is observed in the economic sphere. It appears purposive and adaptive in response to past and anticipated

---

[7]The recognized need for such a move on the part of the author goes back to two works, sometimes referred to by the author as works on the first and second generation of empirical research in the early presence of the modern computer--namely, William Frazer, The Demand for Money (Cleveland, Ohio: The World Publishing Company, 1976); and Frazer, Crisis in Economic Theory, op. cit.. In particular the Crisis book could be viewed as an assessment of the sources of instability in the parameters of the distributed lag and structural equations model of the vintage of the Federal Reserve-MIT model (about 1966-68).

[8]Otto Eckstein, The Great Recession (New York: North Holland Publishing Company, 1978), pp. 191-205.

conditions. This is the focus of expectations, their formation, and actions directed toward the fulfillment of purposes.

On the control side there are the arrangements for controlling economic behavior ("economic agents"). The markets for goods, services, money balances, financial and instruments play roles, but we are especially interested in general controls operating through government--notably, interrelated monetary and fiscal policies. They may be thought of as being directed toward the achievement of national economic goals--the stabilization of economic conditions and employment, production, and purchasing-power goals. Fiscal policymakers share these concerns but the concerns get intertwined with social goals, problems of capital accumulation and productivity, transfers of wealth by the government, and the like. Operating through government, conflicts arise on the parts of the monetary and fiscal officials over the achievements of the stated goals and other goals--the election and reelection of officials, the control of a part of the people by another part. The occasional political behavior of officals (the uses and misuese of controls) gives rise to a call by some for rules and constitutional amendments to limit the potential and occasional misuses of power in the hands of the policymaking officials. The uses and misuses of controls, of announced policies and the like, enter into expectations (indeed, the forecasts on the parts of economic "agents" as well as the forecasting services).

Many have contributed something to the present project. In this respect the author wishes to express his appreciation to Victoria LaPlaca, whose persistence and typing skill brought the project to its present state, and to Cathy L. Cruse, who served as the author's assistant in the 1979-80 period. In addition: Denise Frank, Marjorie Summers, and Anne Nelson brought the art work to a presentable state; Scott G. Saunders kindly reviewed portions of the manuscript (appendixes to chap. 9, and sect. 16.6); and Phillip L. Martin of the University Presses of Florida helped keep the author buoyed up for an extended period. All are absolved from any responsibility for the final product.

William Frazer
Gainesville, Florida
June 1980

Part I

Introduction

Chapter 1

Prices: A Focal Point

1.1. Introduction

Ours is an economic system of money and prices. In such a system there are m-1 prices and m-1 goods and services, exclusive of money (where m is the total number of goods and services, including money). The mth good is money. Quoted in terms of itself money has a price of one (hence, the m-1). Such a price system would not be possible without money. There would be in its place barter--a direct exchange of goods and services for goods and services. This barter system would consist of $(m \times m) - m$ barter prices.

A barter system today would be enormously complicated and inefficient. From a seller's point of view there would be a continuous search to establish numerous prices that would permit him to produce for numerous markets and then clear his goods and services from the markets, on the one hand, or that would permit him to price himself out of the market, on the other, as in the case of shortages of goods or simply the desire to withdraw. From a buyer's point of view, there would be a continuous search to directly satisfy wants in every exchange, to establish the best bargain, or to determine the quality of goods. Even in the presence of money, which permits the indirect satisfaction of wants in exchanges, and gives rise to enormous economies, there is still a good bit of uncertainty, requiring buyers to search for the best price and to compare qualities. This uncertainty--with other characteristics of our economic system, as enumerated later--gives rise to what has been called "sticky" prices.

The economy-providing function as just attributed to money is called its unit of account function. It arises simultaneously with some good being accepted as a medium of exchange, that is as a means of facilitating exchange without a simultaneous satisfaction of wants occurring from the exchange. This acceptance of money in exchange becomes identifiable with another quality too: the accepted medium does not excessively deteriorate from storage or lose in purchasing power (as in the presence of a rise in prices). Following the receipt of income, money balances tide one over from one pay period to the next (say, as checks are drawn against deposits at the bank), among other things. Further, the quality of being relatively free from loss of principal or purchasing power combines with ease of disposal and gives rise to what we call liquidity (that is, ease of disposal on short notice without loss of principal or purchasing power). It is also identified with the store of value function of money. This function concerns money's role in dealing with foreseen and unforeseen events and to prospects for speculation--as in the choice of holding additional bonds or money balances, in one instance, and that of holding additional real goods or money, in another (as defined and set forth initially in section 3.3, and later in chapters 5 and 6).

It is not sufficient in addressing the role of money to say that somewhere at sometime there was barter--the exchange of goods and services for one another--and now there is money. Nor is it sufficient, as far as insights into workings of the real world are concerned, to say--as textbooks in the theory of price and numerous economists have said for years--that we have money only as a numéraire (as a bookkeeping way of reckoning) and then to exclude from consideration its other functions. In the first case, early forms of money were goods --beans, iron nails, wampum, cattle, corn liquor, silver and gold. In fact, the English word "pecuniary" means money and its Latin cognate word means cattle. The evolution of money is from the early forms to a very modern and efficient system of money and banks, with a very low cost for the production of and hence creation of money balances (currency and deposits payable on demand at banks), as should become clear in later chapters. In the second case, the bookkeeping function of money does not arise independently of the medium of exchange and store of value functions.

The acceptance of some good as a medium for exchange is identified with the transactions motive for holding money and it parallels money coming to fulfill the speculative and precautionary motives for holding money. Working through these motives, the demand for money is related to the current output of goods and services as emphasized in chapters 5 and 6.

There is more on this as the definition of money is restated more concisely below.[1] We simply recall, again, that there are $\underline{m}$-1 prices in a money-using economy. We can from these construct price indexes or averages, usually for smaller sets of goods and services. Hence, we have in detail a number of prices to consider in relation to one another, and overall averages of prices. The separate prices on the goods and services comprising the total output may rise and fall absolutely, in relation to one another, and as an average, but mostly the prices will rise, more so at some times than at others, judging from historical circumstances. The changes in the price averages give rise to current and prospective changes in the purchasing power of money balances and, at times, to speculative activity as described and defined on a number of subsequent occasions throughout the book. Viewing the economy as open, as in an international setting as in chapter 2, the price averages of respective countries provide an additional and broader system of relative prices and relative price averages.

At the level of the domestic economy, changes in relative prices perform allocative functions concerning resources for use in production and the composition of total output; and changes in the averages of prices concern allocative effects with respect to the distribution of income among various classes of assets, as introduced in chapter 3 and on numerous other occasions. On the international level, as in chapter 2, the relative prices and price averages perform allocative functions by determining the balance and composition of international trade and monetary reserves.

The flow of goods and services and the stock of assets overall yield utilities to households as introduced in chapters 3, 6, and 16. These flows and stocks include dollar flows in some cases, psychic returns (such as security and convenience), and combinations of dollar and psychic returns. Where there are such returns and prices of goods and services, there are factors of proportionality, so to speak, that relate the two. These concern very special prices, namely, rates of interest or return. Especially these emerge in considering financial instruments and purchases of capital goods, plants, equipment and productive facilities, as introduced in section 3.3. and later discussed in chapter 8.

Indeed, the system of prices becomes very broad. Among the special effects resulting from changes in respective prices are substitution effects, e.g., the effect of holding or purchasing more of one good or asset in relation to another. In fact, as we discuss in chapter 15, substitution effects appear to predominate for the system as a whole over the income effects of relative price changes. These income effects are treated initially in the appendix to this chapter and, as treated there, they are later related to the subject of indexation (sects. 6.4 and 17.2).

The substitution or allocative effects would appear to be among the most dependable predictors in economic theory, at least as to the direction of the changes in the variables being predicted. But as we consider broader classes of assets, the effects become complicated by the introduction of expectations, particularly anticipations about price level changes and the purchasing power of money.

The foregoing presentation of topics up to this point may seem a bit forebearing. It is simply a way of introducing a lot of interrelated and substantive subject matter in a very general way. All of the topics introduced here are treated more fully in subsequent chapters; thus our goal in mentioning them in this chapter is not complete elucidation. Rather, throughout part one and in some measure in chapter 4 our objective is to lay a broad foundation of subject matter on which we can construct an empirical, policy-oriented body of economic theory. Prices and the monetary reality underlying them are treated in the remaining sections of this chapter and in the next. The concept of money as defined in the next section makes the quotation of prices feasible and hence makes possible the construction of price indexes. The function of money as a medium of exchange is stressed in these sections; its other functions loom in importance in later chapters. A brief introduction to sticky prices contains some observations that even the uninitiated should be able to relate to, namely, that quantities sold may be influenced by advertising as well as by prices and, therefore, that the taste of buyers as revealed by their purchases is neither innate nor independent of the influences surrounding them. Consumers vulnerability to this form of manipulation, may be one source of reduced flexibility in prices, and of changes in taste and social values (other possible sources will be considered in later chapters). The topic is rich with behavioral and empirical implications, but it is one that has been suppressed in the mainstream of the economic theory of prices and the theory of an exchange economy. Those theories posit autonomous spending units with homogeneous tastes and expectations, and consequently describe price behavior somewhat remote from reality. One must recognize, however, that abstract constructions may be remote from reality and still serve a function in economic writing, although such a use of abstractions is not a primary objective of this work.

1.2 The Definition of Money

As already indicated, money is a medium of exchange, a standard of value, and a store of value (Frazer 1973, 439-42; Friedman 1970, 110-26). This list of its functions constitutes a definition. These functions, furthermore, can be related to the motives for holding money, which Keynes first enumerated in 1936 as the transactions, precautionary, and speculative motives.

The medium of exchange property has to do with the use of money and its acceptance in exchange. This means that it provides for an indirect exchange of goods or an exchange without the need for the coincidence of wants (that is the coincidence whereby the seller and buyer both get the good they want). The medium of exchange function is related to the transactions demand for money whereby a stock of balances may be used to make transactions and tide one over from one pay period to another, as when income is deposited in the bank and checks drawn against the deposit to tide one over. Thus, the transactions demand is viewed as a function of income, with the quantity demanded (M) increasing in proportion to income (Y).

This transactions-income relationship is thought to be relatively stable, but there are prospects of changes occurring in it. These may occur especially in response to any changes in the payments mechanism such as may occur with the electronic transfer of money balances, with the greater use of credit cards and the related overdraft facilities made possible by them.[2] On occasion, prospective changes in the payments mechanism have been implied by references to a "checkless" society, checks, of course, being the traditional means of transferring deposits payable on demand.

The role of money as a standard of value permits it to be used as an accounting and bookkeeping unit. Thus, the prices of the $\underline{m}$-1 goods and services in each country are expressed in terms of the accepted valuation unit: the dollar in the United States, the pound in the United Kingdom, the franc in Belgium, the yen in Japan, the krona in Sweden, and so on.

The store of value property of money is related to the precautionary and speculative motives for holding money (as sketched in note 1). Here the emphasis is on holding a stock of money balances rather than using it as in the case of exchange. Some have spoken of money at rest rather than in flight to draw this distinction between holding balances and spending them. We have here the idea of the demand for money in relation to income and changes denoted by the ratio of income to money balances, or the velocity ratio, Y/M. There are not necessarily distinct pools or balances set aside to satisfy the various motives, but changes in the total demand for money may be ascribed to changes in strength of these motives. Such becomes one instance, and there are numerous others, where direct measurement and identification are impossible in economics and where some empirical orientation is achieved by going about matters in an indirect way.

The precautionary demand for money arises out of a need to cope with an uncertain future, with foreseen and unforeseen developments and opportunities. Such a store of money balances may be said to lull one's disquietudes, to calm one's disposition in the face of uncertainty. The greater (less) the uncertainty, the more (less) the need for a store of balances to satisfy the precautionary motive.

The speculative motive for holding money concerns especially classes of assets. In the one case, there is the prospect of a loss or gain from changes in bond prices and, in another, there is the prospect of a loss or gain from changes in the purchasing power of money (e.g., from changes in the level of prices). Expectations of change in the purchasing power of money influence the strength of the motive for holding a store of balances for speculative purposes.

1.3. Sticky Prices

Prices were viewed as being fully flexible (and hence not sticky) in response to changes in quantities of goods and services supplied or demanded in the economic theory before

J.M. Keynes's classical and revolutionary work, The General Theory of Employment, Interest and Money (1936). In that tradition those on the buyers' side have utility functions and given incomes, and these provided the basis for demand curves, and those producing for the market had costs and, as shown in chapter 15, these provided the basis for supply curves. After some aggregation, as mentioned in greater detail in the appendix to chapter 1, the concepts of supply and demand relate more naturally to commodities traded in markets. These together determine the market price and--with minor qualifications in this section, the appendix to chapter 1, and elsewhere--we will treat prices as being so determined.

The supply and demand curves are largely "iffy" concepts. The supply curve is generally upward sloping and relates the quantity (q) of a commodity that will be supplied "if" different prices (p's) prevail for it, other things being equal. The other things include a host of factors such as taste, income, known prices on other goods, known quality

Figure 1-1.
A Marshallian Cross

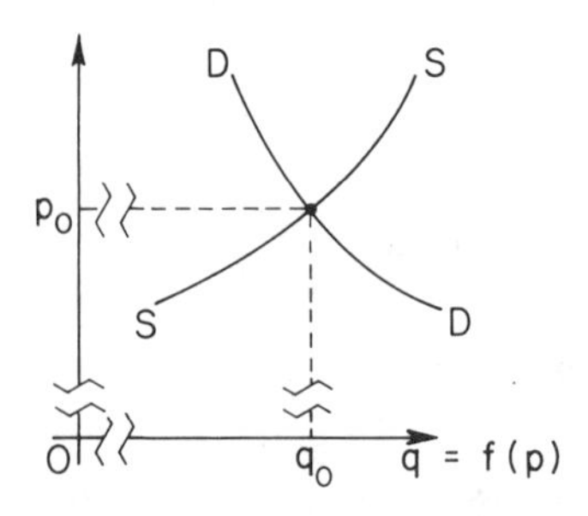

and constant expectations about the future. A commodity is anything the economic entity prefers more of rather than less. The curves and solution values (p_o, q_o) are illustrated in figure 1-1, where they are referred to as a Marshallian cross, after Alfred Marshall (1842-1924) who gave impetus to their use in economics (Friedman 1949; and Viner 1931).[3] The present use of these curves (as elucidated in the appendix to chapter 1, appendix A to chapter 6, and in chapters 15 and 16) however, does not irrevocably commit us to two important assumptions made by Marshall, namely: we do not assume (1) the measurement of utility or (2) declining marginal utility of additional consumption and income.[4] Our use of the curves will be against the backdraw of them from a statistical point of view (app. to chap. 1) and on other occasions it will be in terms of an ordinal ("more" or "less" than) rather than cardinal (exact measurement) utility analysis. Further, we will be more interested, as Milton Friedman was (1953), in using the system of analysis to indirectly get at some empirical notion that may apply for the economy as a whole and not simply in terms of what has come to be called microeconomics.

As stated, the supply and demand curves in figure 1-1 depict rather hypothetical concepts, because they are constructed under such highly static conditions (assuming zero time conditions and holding other influencing variables constant). Efforts at empirical identification of such curves with real world data have met with only modest success and, even then, mainly in the highly specialized case of agriculture.[5] Later we introduce these curves in more dynamic contexts, where one or both are shifting, often at different rates.

In the neoclassical (pre-1936) theory, prices are set in the respective markets consisting of numerous buyers and sellers, so that no one buyer or seller dominates any market. There is freedom of entry and exit of firms, partly because capital requirements for entry are small; thus ensuring that commodities are produced at minimum cost. The consuming or household unit reigns supreme in that it exerts a free choice, maximizes its utility, and determines by its purchases what will be produced (ignoring, for the moment, the effects of advertising and persuasive strategies). The consumer maximizes his utility by distributing his income so that the utilities derived from one additional dollar of spending on the different commodities are equal.

Aspects of the neoclassical model have been widely publicized and still permeate economic thought; especially they did so in the 1950s and 60s when, one might say, Keynes's revolution of the 1930s had to be renewed in some respects. A part of Keynes's special contribution (and there have been others since) was to reverse the order of adjustments in response to changes in the supply and demand conditions. In the neoclassical model, prices adjusted initially and primarily. For Keynes and later the Keynesians, output adjusted and prices were said to be "sticky." The reversal of a downward output adjustment (for example, as called for after a leftward shift in the demand schedule of figure 1-1) is said to be impeded by "sticky" prices (including wages as a special price) and the stickiness in the prices (including in the wages that preclude an outward shift in the supply schedule) is said to contribute to unemployment. One class of explanations for sticky prices has given special attention to the use of money as a medium of exchange, to uncertainty, and to expenditure on research as a means of reducing uncertainty. Another class has emphasized the market structure (whether of a few or many firms), the rise of the large corporation, and the resulting emergence of a planning system as distinct from a market system. Both classes of explanations recognize that the pricing system is primarily a communications system. The system of prices, in other words, communicates to the sellers what and how much to produce, and whether prices are too high or too low. Where the desires of the consumers are weak and the demand low, the decline in demand signals a cutback in production, and the need for lower prices (including wages) to restore the level of production.

Transactions Cost, Uncertainty, and the Price System

As stated, the neoclassical theory of price is rather static and assumes that sellers know where to set prices to achieve their profit maximizing positions. It assumes, further, that buyers have complete knowledge of a host of prices on alternative goods and services, and of their quality. Not surprisingly, analysts have come to question these assumptions, although the abstract model may play a role, apart from its being viewed outright as an explanation of empirical reality.

Karl Brunner and Allan Meltzer introduce uncertainty about the range of prices and the qualities for alternative goods. Even so, their framework is still a relatively static one, where the uncertainty (the variance of an expected value) is characterized by an uneven distribution of information in the economic system rather than by a change in the degree of belief over time. This sort of distinction is drawn more formally in the discussion of risk and uncertainty in chapter 6.

Even in their relatively static framework, two important tendencies of an economic system are illuminated: first, that a society tends to settle on a narrow range of assets to serve as a medium of exchange and, second, that traders tend to specialize and thereby gain from acquiring experience and storing special information about their products or services. Thus, instead of uncertainty, Brunner and Meltzer assume:

1. For each transactor the extra cost of acquiring information about prices on goods or services depends on the goods or services selected.

2. The extra cost of acquiring this information varies systematically within the society and declines as the society tends to narrow its selection of media of exchange.

This second assumption leads to the conclusion that society will settle on a narrow range of media of exchange as a means of reducing uncertainty about the wide range of prices. Thus, because it reduces uncertainty, the medium becomes more valuable (i.e., the demand for money increases).

The Brunner-Meltzer utility function (U) for an individual may be denoted

$$U = f\ [E(Y),\ C] \text{ for } var(Y) = \text{constant}$$

where $\underline{E}(Y)$ is the expected value of goods to be acquired in trading, var (Y) is the variance (or uncertainty) surrounding that value, and $\underline{C}$ is a bundle of resources. The latter can be held or exchanged. Thus, total utility can be increased for any exchange if the variance of the expected value of goods to be acquired can be decreased (i.e., if uncertainty can be reduced). The individual can reduce his uncertainty by investing in information about prices and quality and by using a dominant medium of exchange.

The Planning System

The large corporation, according to J. K. Galbraith (1973), is characterized first by a separation of ownership from management and second by its planning system. The management is "a collective and imperfectly defined entity," embracing officers and department heads, engineers and scientists, especially those who contribute information and bring specialized knowledge, talent, or experience to group decision-making. The technostructure, as Galbraith has called this group, has its own interests, particularly with regard to the growth of the firm and to national economic goals. The national focus follows from the dependence of the firm's sales and growth on the growth of the economy and on the assurance of a market for its product.

There is a long lag between the initial development or modification of a product and its ultimate production and employment, during which time salaries and income are at stake. Management, because of its responsibility for this process, fills a role analogous to that of neoclassical model's entrepreneur (the single owner-manager, promoter, and innovator).

Planning ensures stability and serves other goals of the technostructure. For example, financial planning is conducted to ensure the availability of funds for capital spending. Planning is also necessary to ensure the availability, cost, and quality of factor supplies and to maintain control and stabilize product markets, too. The need to guarantee factor inputs, coupled with the coincidence of the interests of management, organized labor, and government in full employment, leads to our later definition and consideration of "cost push" inflation and "bail out." The need to control the market leads to efforts to influence the public's will, especially with persuasion in the form of advertising. Both lead to the prospect of price setting independently of traditionally emphasized market forces.

The large corporations that make up the planning system are only a thousand or so in number, but they account for most of the production in the manufacturing sector. For this reason especially they are of interest as we attempt to deal with the overall problems surrounding the stabilization of prices, output, and employment. In the first quarter of 1971, the 333 industrial corporations with assets of over $500 million accounted for a full 70 percent of the assets for all manufacturing firms. According to Galbraith's thesis and to others, as well, the numerous smaller firms still produce and function as a market system, more or less as envisioned in the neoclassical model. Galbraith mentions here the "world of the farmer, repairman, retailer, small manufacturer, plumber, television repairman, service station operator, medical practitioner, artist, actress, photographer and pornographer."

Two aspects of Galbraith's thesis require attention. First, the planning system transcends national boundaries. Pricing in even national labor markets can be transcended and circumvented when Ford Motor Company manufactures its "Fiestas" in Europe, for example, or when General Motors and others produce abroad, or when Volkswagen operates plants in the United States. These and other aspects of the modern industrial state lead us to consider the international character of price level changes and control.

Second, Galbraith's approach recognizes that advertising is in a large measure a way of manipulating the public's will and, therefore, of influencing sales independently of price changes.

Advertising, Persuasion, and Social Values

In considering the role advertising plays in separating control over price from the volume of sales, Galbraith makes a number of points. Others extend the notion of influence through advertising to encompass influence over social values (Bartlett 1978), as well as consumer choice (Lancaster 1978) and the marginal propensity to consume out of permanent income (Reza 1978). Bartlett and Lancaster touch on persuasive strategies from the area of social psychology. These strategies may be used as public policy tools (sect. 12.5 and app. to chap. 12) and as a means of influencing social values such as those affecting attitudes about future generations and the conservation of man's natural environment (sect. 16.4). Lancaster argues, however, that advertising cannot change stable underlying attitudes in the short run, although persistent advertising may have some impact.

Several points made by Galbraith about the use of advertising to influence sales may be listed:

> The large firm must have designs that will lend themselves to long and economical production runs. Artistic sense must also yield to the will of those who, on the basis of instinct, experience or market research, are knowledgeable on what the public can be persuaded to buy. (1973, 65)

> The performance of the economy in relation to need is, indeed, unequal. This is because the power to organize resources and to persuade consumers and the government as to need is unequally distributed between the market and the planning systems. (1973, 199)

> The obvious counterpart to the control of prices is an effort to control the response of buyers to those prices. (1973, 135)

> The management of the private consumer has two dimensions: There is the preference or non-preference of the consumer for the producer's product or service. This must be favorably influenced. (1973, 135)

> In the planning system...the firm has power over its prices. An important purpose of this power...is to allow wage costs to be passed on to the public. (1973, 187)

> The technostructure not only controls prices; it seeks to ensure the response of consumers to those prices. Prices must be so set that they are consistent with the need to persuade the consumer. (1973, 116)

> But persuasion is by its nature imperfect. To those who are unpersuaded or insufficiently persuaded, the arbitrary nature of the system is fully seen or sensed. (1973, 209)

> All planning seeks to win control of belief--to have people conform in thought and action to what, for the planners, is convenient....One does not prohibit advertising; one resists its persuasion. (1973, 229-230)

On another aspect of pricing and competition among the few, Galbraith may be quoted thus:

> The power to set the price means that any other major firm or industry--Ford or Chrysler in the case of automobiles or Bethlehem or Inland in the case of steel--can, by fixing a lower price, force an alteration in the level first established. This may happen. But there is also a general recognition that such action, should it lead to further and retributive action by the firm originally establishing the price, could lead to general price-cutting. This would mean a general loss of control--a general sacrifice of the protective purposes of all the technostructure involved. The danger is recognized by all. In the planning system there is, accordingly, a convention that outlaws such behavior. It is almost perfectly enforced. No contract, no penalties and usually no communication are involved. There is only an acute recognition of the disadvantage of such competitive

> and retributive action for all participants. It is a remarkable example of the capacity, where money [vested economic interest] is involved, to recognize and respect a community of interest. (1973, 114-115)

This approach to the behavior of prices, apart from the emphasis on advertising and prices, of course, may or may not be the best one for explaining observed behavior. The matter is debatable. A main point, in any case, however, is that the large firms of Galbraith's thesis receive special attention for the sorts of reasons Galbraith enunciates when the government gets into the matters of price and wage controls, voluntary or involuntary (secs. 17.2 and 17.3).

1.4. Price Indexes

The presence of m-1 prices in the economy has been pointed out, and the theory of separate market price fluctuations has been introduced. Now, however, we move from consideration of market prices and their many changes in relation to one another to a different, broader level of analysis. This movement is sometimes described as that from the micro to the macro level. The price index (or average) is the statistical artifact that facilitates a discussion of "the price level"--of whether prices as a whole, the current output of goods and services, are on balance rising or falling.

The three price indexes considered here are the producer price index (PPI, formerly the wholesale price index, WPI), the consumer price index (CPI), and the GNP deflator. The first is the oldest index, the second was initially published in 1921, and the third is more recent in origin. Data for the PPI and CPI are available on a monthly basis and for the GNP deflator on a quarterly basis. The indexes generally show movements in the same direction though differences in them do arise. The respective series of prices (and selected components of wholesale prices, namely, industrial, and farm products and processed foods and feeds) are shown in figures 1-2 and 1-3 for the decade of the 1970s. On the average, the price level was fairly stable for the period from 1952 through the early 1960s; thereafter it accelerated until 1974 and then decelerated. In 1974 the inflation rate was in the double-digit range.

There are three reasons for the observed deviations in the direction and magnitude of changes in the three series: (1) the producer price index has somewhat greater volatility due to the degree of competitive market pricing in the items covered; (2) price changes in primary markets may get pushed forward in terms of higher costs (an upward shift in the supply schedule in figure 1-1) in consumer product markets; and (3) the price deflator reflects a broader range of prices with a changing weighting scheme.

The Producer Price Index

The PPI measures changes in prices of nearly two thousand commodities sold in primary markets in the United States. Its construction is based on Laspeyres's formula, which is to say that the total value of some base year package of goods (q_1, q_2, . . . , q_n) as measured in current prices (p_1, p_2, . . . , p_n) divided by the total value of the same package of goods as measured in base year prices:

$$WPI = \frac{\sum_{i=1}^{n} p_i^t \; q_i^o}{\sum_{i=1}^{n} p_i^o \; q_i^o} X \; 100$$

where

o = base year
t = current year.

The Consumer Price Index

The CPI is constructed by the same formula as the PPI, only the number of items considered is smaller, consisting of about 300 items. The items considered are those typically consumed by urban wage-earner and clerical-worker families. These families comprise about 64 percent of the urban population, and 40 percent of the total population. The CPI is the measure of price changes used in many wage contracts where cost of living clauses are included. Indeed, the CPI was designed for just such a purpose.

The CPI is generally recognized to have two shortcomings. The first is its failure to measure quality changes over time in the items considered. The presumption has been that quality improves, but there has been increasing dissent from this position. For example, the services attached to the purchases of goods have declined in quality, noticeably so in the period of inflation and high employment beginning in the 1960s. Evidence is found in the increased servicing of automobiles, in waiting lines, and in other inconveniences. Another reason is that the alleged quality improvements have not been improvements at all, but simply the illusion of improvement, as Galbraith asserts in these passages:

> In the case of consumers' goods a change that is without function may be as serviceable for selling a product as a change that has function--it may lend itself as well or better to commercials or salesmanship suggesting sexual fulfillment, sexual or social prowess, personal beauty, lessened obesity, personal

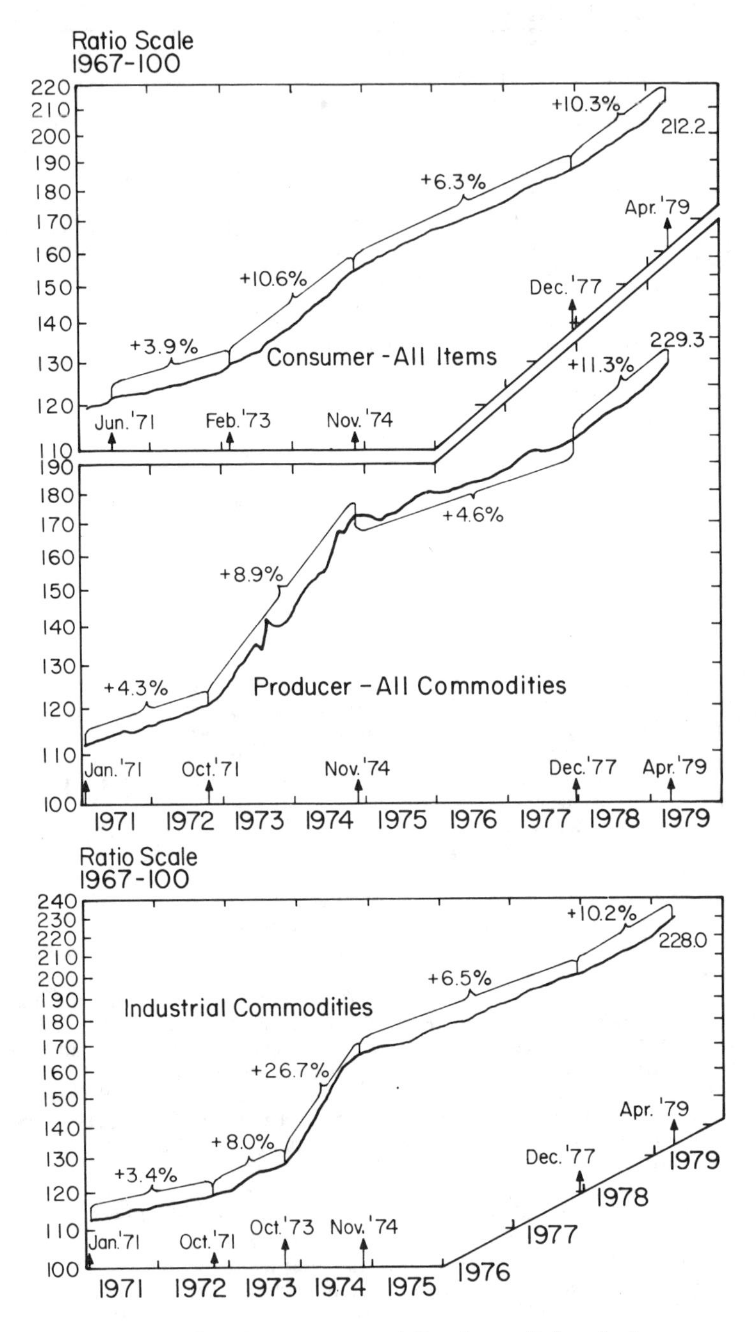

Figure 1-2. Consumer and Producer Price Indexes

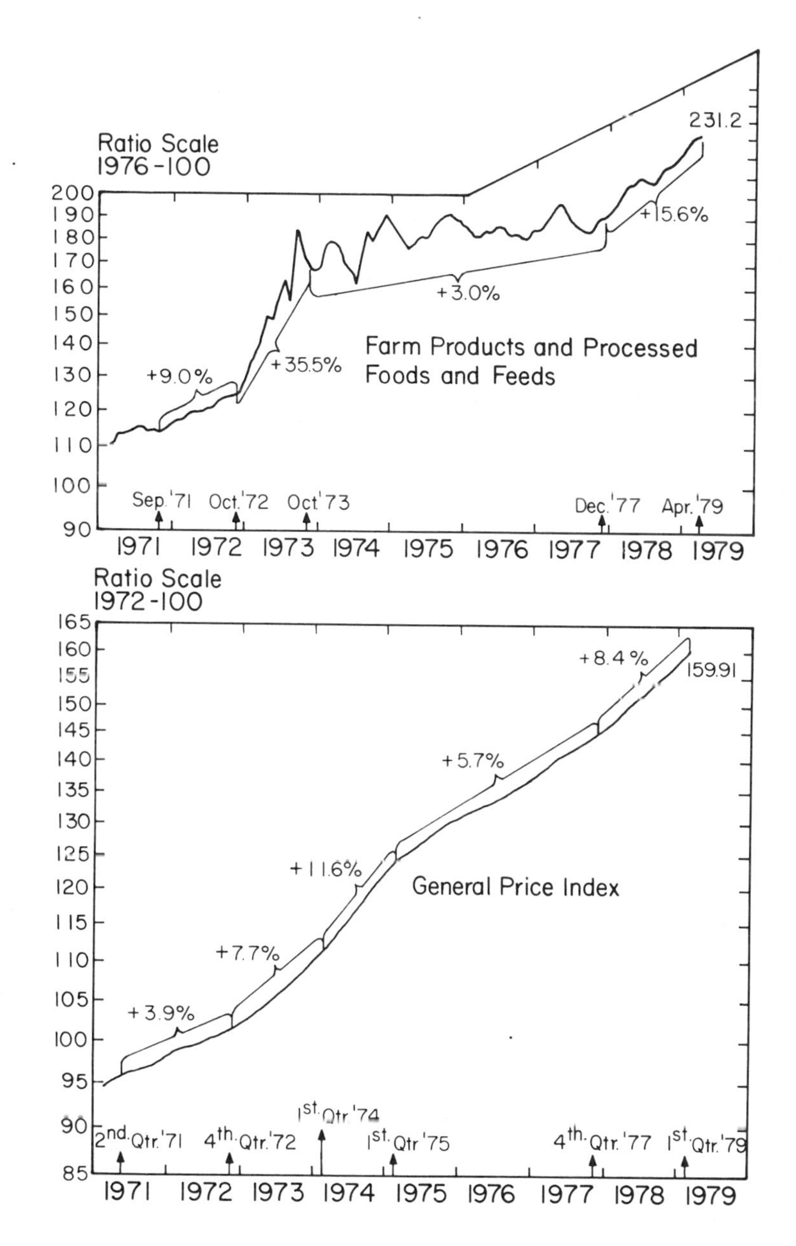

Figure 1-3. Producer Price Index (continued) and GNP Deflator (or General Price Index)

or family prestige, preservation of youth or more efficient peristalsis.

> In the case of its products, persuasion [advertising and public relations expertise] as to the reality is the substitute for the reality. So also with pollution. Instead of eliminating it, the natural recourse is to urge the public that it is imaginary or benign or is being eliminated by actions that are imaginary.

The second deficiency of the CPI is that it does not reflect changes in the importance of selected items in the budget; that is, the CPI has not undergone frequent shifts in its weighting scheme to take into account the substitution effect due to relative price changes. Along this line, some critics pointed out in early 1980, that the fixed-weight index was giving "too great a weight to items like gasoline and meat whose prices have risen faster than average and whose consumption had been cut back." Following the post-World War II record jump in prices of 13.3 percent (CPI) in 1979, the Labor Department had reported that the cost of housing and energy-fueled transportation accounted for about three-quarters of the entire rise in the CPI for that year.

The GNP Deflator

Gross national product (GNP) is the total output of goods and services produced in a period, usually a quarter of a year. The quarterly data may be converted to an annual rate for the given quarter by multiplying the quarterly figures by four. Such measures are provided by national income accounting, which is considered in sections 3.1 and 3.2. One by-product of these national income accounts is a measure of the price level for the output of goods and services. This occurs when GNP in current price or nominal money terms (Y) is divided by GNP in constant price terms (Q), thus:

$$\frac{Y}{Q} = P$$

where P is the GNP deflator (or Y/P = Q where Q is real output).

The weights in this present measure of the price level turn out to be current year quantities rather than base quantities as in the WPI and the CPI. Hence a difference exists between the indexes other than in the breadth and type of the goods and services they cover.

1.5. Summary

Key points made in chapter 1 may be listed as follows:

1. An economic system with money has m-1 prices for the m goods and services exclusive of money. In comparison, barter economy has m (m-1) barter prices. There is, consequently, an enormous increase in convenience and economy and a reduction of computations and mental anguish resulting from the transition to a monetary economy.

2. Money may be defined with reference to the various functions it performs, as a medium of exchange, a standard of value, and a store of value. The first, which permits an indirect exchange of goods, is related to a transactions demand for money. The standard of value relates to the unit of account and bookkeeping aspects of money. And, finally, the store of value function concerns the holding of money balances to satisfy precautionary and speculative demands.

3. In analysis that stresses the precautionary and speculative demands, the emphasis is on the demand side of the market for money. The money stock in some statistical sense (such as currency in circulation plus deposits payable on demand at banks) is given and the public adjusts this to its desired level (in relation to expenditures) by spending more or less, thus causing a change in the price level and a rise in the dollar value of expenditures. As we will see later, nevertheless, changes in the money stock may influence spending and the price level.

4. The precautionary motive concerns the holding of money as a means of dealing with generalized uncertainty --uncertainty about the future and anticipated and unanticipated developments. But uncertainty may be more narrowly defined to refer to uncertainty with respect to the inflation rate.

5. Establishing a medium of exchange (i.e., money) helps reduce uncertainty about prices, but even with money there is still some uncertainty about prices and qualities of goods and services. This may be reduced by spending income (or drawing down money balances) to acquire new information through expenditures on research. Here the role of money in satisfying aspects of precautionary or speculative motives is transferred to its role as a medium of exchange, but the transfer is mainly a gymnastic that sheds light on the interrelated roles of money.

6. The enormous convenience and economy in having the entities of an economic system settle upon a small range of assets to serve as money may explain why the given assets persist in being accepted as a medium of exchange even in the presence of a fairly continuous and rapid inflation.

7. In the system of money and prices, prices on the average tend to be sticky (not flexible), especially with respect to downward adjustments in response to a downward shift in demand. The uncertainty about prices--where to set them from a sellers viewpoint and what they reflect about the actual value and quality from a buyers viewpoint--may account

for some of the stickiness. The role of advertising and possibly monopoly and cost aspects help explain other aspects of sticky prices. Common experiences suggest that firms seek some control over prices and over the quantities that may be sold at the given prices. Advertising is one means of influencing the public's purchases.

8. The notion of advertising, as commonly encountered, may be extended and related to the use of persuasive strategies to influence belief, attitude changes, and social values. In this extension persuasion becomes a tool of public policy.

9. The market for a typical good in a system of money and prices may be represented by means of a Marshallian cross. There a supply schedule is one arm of the cross and a demand schedule the other. The first reflects a cost condition and the other utility, as elaborated later. These schedules, though useful, are rather "iffy" constructions. Except for the intersection points, the schedules themselves are rarely identifiable in any empirical sense.

10. The quotation of up to m-1 prices in a system of m goods and services (including money) is only possible in an economic system that has come to be based on money. Once we have these prices, the construction of price indexes readily follows. With these we can speak of and measure the level of prices, and detect movements in the average of prices, as distinct from the movements of prices of separate goods and services.

FOOTNOTES

1. In the broad overview, however, what we have said thus far may be sketched thus:

Functions of money	Demand for money	Motives for holding money
Medium of exchange ➡	Transactions demand ➡	Transactions motive
Standard of value (bookkeeping entry)		
Store of value ➡	Speculative precautionary demand ➡	Speculative and precautionary motives

2. In most respects the rise in the use of credit cards may simply be a substitute for traditional trade credit. To have an effect on the transactions-income relation the use

of credit cards would have to more than compensate for the decline in trade credit.

3. On Marshall's method and the demand curve in particular, see Ekelund et al. (1972), particularly chapters 2, 9, and 13 on Marshallian demand theory and the demand curve.
4. The notion of cardinal utility in relation to the demand curve is illustrated in the sketch below. There, demand for a single consumer is shown in terms of the price= quantity coordinates, with a separate scale for utils (five utils equal $1.00) parallel to the price axis. As the quantity purchased increases from one to three, the utility from each additional quantity declines from 20 utils to 9, and then to 7. The area under the demand curve depicts, in this cardinal case, the utility acquired, for example, for q =2,

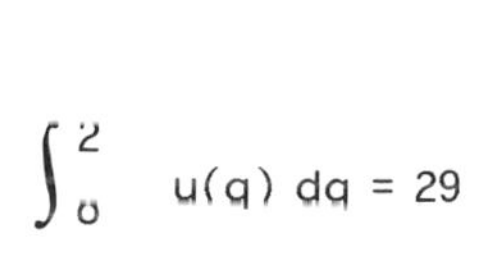

$$\int_0^2 u(q)\,dq = 29$$

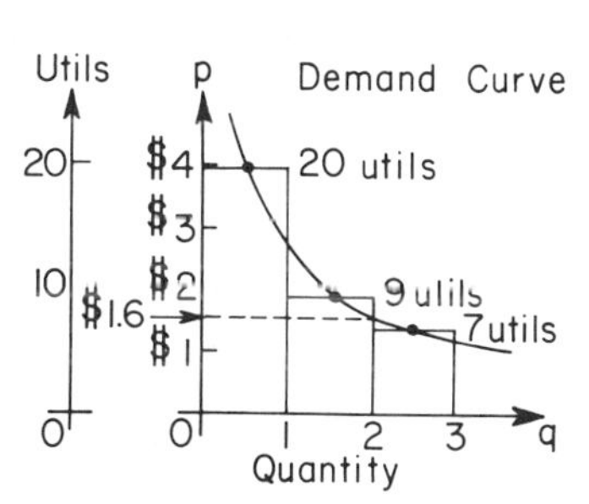

Assuming the marginal utility per unit of income ("money," some would say) is constant, the product of the price ($1.60) for a quantity of two, the five utils per dollar, and the quantity (e.g., 1.6 X 5 X 2 = 16) is the utility given up in the purchase. The difference between the utility acquired and the utility given up is said to be the consumer's surplus.

5. The agricultural case is specialized because the demand for basic food is thought to be inelastic in relation to price and because the quantity produced is "fixed" at the time of planting, acts of nature aside. To oversimplify, in such a context weather conditions may cause supply to vary and thus provide movements along a demand curve. In other cases, what one observes in the real world is a scatter of points consisting of quantity and price coordinates. These are not clearly points on either curve considered separately, and indeed may simply be a reflection of movements in the curves in response to unspecified forces. (See app. to chap. 1)

SELECTED READINGS AND REFERENCES

Allen, R. G. D. 1975. Index Numbers in Theory and Practice. Chicago: Aldine Publishing Company.

Afriat, S. N. 1977. The Price Index. Cambridge: Cambridge University Press.

Bartlett, Randall. 1978. "Marketing Ideologies: The Influence of Social Values." Presented at the Annual Meetings of the American Economic Association (August).

Brunner, Karl, and Allan H. Meltzer. 1971. "The Uses of Money: Money in the Theory of an Exchange Economy." American Economic Review (December).

Cooley, Charles Horton. 1918. "Part VI: Valuation," in Social Process. New York: Charles Scribner's Sons.

Copeland, M. A. 1974. "Concerning the Origin of a Money Economy" American Journal of Economic and Sociology (January).

Cramer, J. S. 1971. Empirical Economics. Amsterdam: North-Holland Publishing Company.

Ekeland, R. B., Jr., E. G. Furubotn, and W. P. Gramm, eds. The Evolution of Modern Demand Theory. Lexington, Mass.: Lexington Books: D.C. Heath and Company.

Frazer, William. 1973. Crisis in Economic Theory. Gainesville, Fla.: University of Florida Press. Appendix to Chapter 7.

Friedman, Milton. 1949. "The Marshallian Demand Curve." Journal of Political Economy (December). Reprinted in Friedman 1953 and in Ekelund et al. 1972.

_________. 1953. Essays in Positive Economics. Chicago: University of Chicago Press.

_________. and Anna Jacobson Schwartz. 1970. Monetary Statistics of the United States: Estimates, Sources, Methods. New York: Columbia University Press for the National Bureau of Economic Research.

Galbraith, John Kenneth. 1973. Economics and the Public Purpose. Boston: Houghton Mifflin Company.

Keynes, John Maynard. 1936. The General Theory of Employment, Interest,and Money. New York: Harcourt, Brace and Company.

Lancaster, Kevin. 1978. "Advertising and Consumer Choice." Presented at the Annual Meetings of the American Economic Association (August).

Reza, Ali M. 1978. "Advertising's Effect on the Permanent Income." Presented at the Annual Meetings of the American Economic Association (August).

Viner, Jacob. 1931. "Cost Curves and Supply Curves." Zeitshcrift für Nationalökonomie Vol. III, 23-46.

Chapter 2

Prices: The Open Economy (A First Approximation)

2.1. Introduction

"Open economy" refers to the United States in its international setting rather than in isolation from other countries and international financial institutions. This chapter is an introduction to price considerations in that broader setting, and to the U.S. balance of international payments. Its subject matter is embellished more fully in a later chapter of the book. This and the later chapter warrant consideration partly because of the increased recognition of the multinational character of U.S. manufacturing firms and the international character of business and price level movements, but especially because of the added perspective given to domestic operations and policy when viewed in their international setting. Evidence of the increasingly multinational character of U.S. manufacturing firms is found in a 1977 study conducted by the nonprofit National Industrial Conference Board. This report states that among U.S. manufacturing firms with sales of $20 million or more, 54 percent owned at least one manufacturing facility abroad, while 46 percent owned such facilities in two or more countries. As reported, firm size and the extent of foreign activity are closely related.

Given the proportion of manufactured products in the U.S. supplied by large firms (as considered in greater detail in chapter 8), the relationship between size and the extent of operations enables these firms to be somewhat more independent of labor and governmental policies and controls of a particular national economy. Production (and hence employment) may be shifted from one economy to the other, depending on the efficiency of the labor force and the stability and other inducements provided by governmental policies. Of course, this does not mean that the wages and efficiency of managers and workers must everywhere be reduced to the same level, because the amount and quality of real capital also contributes to the productivity of labor, as elucidated in chapter 15 and as illustrated in a review of energy and agriculture (Duncan and Webb 1978).

The international character of business and industrial economies in the 1970s and beyond is dramatized by considering the automotive industry, the pricing of crude oil (and the dependence of industry on scarce natural resources and energy in particular), and the importance of foreign exchange rates as they bear on the import and export positions of countries. In the case of automobiles, manufacturing facilities cross national boundaries and foreign imports have come to account for a sizable share of the U.S. market for automobiles. In the case of the pricing of imported oil, as stressed later, imported oil enters as a cost of manufacturing and hence as a major determinant of the U.S. trade position vis-à-vis the rest of the world. And, finally, a declining exchange rate from the U.S. point of view means lower prices for U.S. products in foreign markets and higher prices for foreign products in the U.S. As we shall see, the internationalization of prices and business is interrelated with domestic goals and policies bearing on inflation and unemployment rates. Moreover, the flows of international monetary reserve, as considered in this chapter, are an important determinant of commercial bank reserves for the domestic economy (as considered in chapter 6), while differences in interest rates in the U.S. and abroad (chap. 19) are possible causes of short-term capital movements into and out of the United States.

There are several dimensions to the internationalization of the price levels of the major non-Communist countries involved in international trade. There is both a form of price competition (or its absence) in specific product markets as well as an indirect form of competition for international monetary reserves. Next, there is an international monetary mechanism that potentially imposes more or less restraint on inflation (i.e., a rise in the average of prices on current output) in the respective countries, especially inflation in one country in relation to others or the rest of the world. There is also a role for the internationalization of economic doctrine that may more or less influence national policies of participating countries. The Keynesian doctrine of the 1950s and 1960s (as elucidated in later chapters) is sometimes pointed to as having been biased toward inflationary policy and thus exerting considerable impact on countries. And, finally, there is a role for international monopoly, with some features of competition. The Arab oil cartel is a major example of monopoly on an international scale. Coffee pricing emerges as another, less significant example. The Arab oil cartel is pointed to below as a dramatic example of a foreign influence on domestic prices; it has had considerable impact on the U.S. balance of international payments (as defined in section 2.3).

2.2. Exchange Rates, Payments, and Reserve Flows

In chapter 1 we introduced money, prices, and price levels in terms of the domestic economy. With the rise of the multinational corporation and private multinational financial institutions, with the presence of some monopoly pricing, and with the evolution of the international control and financial mechanism, however, the determinants of the price levels in the various countries--and especially the phenomena of inflation and deflation--have become more international in character.

Traditionally, the international gold standard served as a regulatory device particularly with respect to price levels. Under the gold standard, in which gold was the principal reserve underlying a number of important domestic monetary systems, countries competed with one another for the gold reserves and in order to obtain a favorable balance of trade (that is, an excess of exports of goods and services over imports). In fact, a favorable balance meant an inflow of gold. There was in effect price competition among the producers of competing goods produced in the major industrial countries. An inflow of gold provided the basis for the expansion of money and bank credit (total loans and investments of commercial banks), which would push prices upward in the gold-receiving country, thus weakening its export position while favoring that of another.

There is more, however. Some would call this description of the adjustment process with rising and falling prices a Hume version, after an eighteenth century Scottish skeptic.[1] We will pursue it further as a first approximation to illustrate the forces at work. Later, we will view the price levels and adjustments as having greater complexity: we will allow exchange rates (as defined below) to change and the respective price levels to increase at the same or different rates.

International systems have permitted tariffs (taxes on imports) to reduce competition, cartel pricing, and political negotiations between countries to obtain trading concessions, but the thrust of argument in support of sound international relations has been to view competition and the impersonal regulatory mechanism (as once provided by the gold standard) as a good thing. The gold standard system never worked too well after 1914 and World War II, and there were efforts to repair and modify the mechanism, but it managed to stay intact, modifications and all, until the early 1970s. Then, surprisingly--after all the wars, the isolationism of the 1930s and the post-World War II reconstruction--very special changes occurred. More surprising however, is that the discipline many countries sought to avoid by implementation of the changes of the early-to-mid 1970s still operates in some measure. Under the new arrangements, countries have greater independence in choosing the exchange rate system thought best for them (if not the world as a whole). That some measure of discipline still imposed is illustrated by a review of the classical mechanism, in combination with the changes that have occurred.

The movement that occurred mainly in the early 1970s was away from a fixed exchange rate system, as described shortly, to a mixture of fixed and fully flexible (or floating) exchange rates, as far as the international system as a whole is concerned (Coombs 1977, Heller 1977, Solomon 1977). Since there is no straightforward way to set forth this mixed, managed float system, we will proceed with the fixed exchange rate system, introduce the fully floating one, and present the existing exchange rate system as containing elements of the two extremes, with different countries falling more or less in one category or another.

A combination of factors caused the gold standard to be modified and the exchange system to break down. First, the supply of gold was limited and thus unable to grow with the needs of world trade for a monetary base under the existing system. Second, the national powers wanted to follow their own inclinations toward domestic monetary policies, without the predominance of the guidelines from the international scene, as the gold standard and the system of fixed exchange rates required. As governments pursue the expedient policies of the short run and forgo the statesmanship of the long run, and as transnational corporations and financial institutions try to neutralize the uncertainties of price competition, foreign exchange, and domestic monetary policies, they set the scene for the internationalization of price level changes in an upward direction and for the simultaneous occurrence of inflation and recession worldwide, as in 1973-75.

The scenario quickly becomes complicated. Perhaps we may best prepare to understand the scenario by reviewing the traditional mechanics of fixed exchange rates. The exchange rates introduce another sort of price into our m-price world: the price of foreign currency (e.g., the British pound) in terms of U.S. dollars. Briefly, if the pound will buy $2 worth of U.S. goods, then the pound is worth $2, but if it will buy the equivalent of $1, then it is worth only $1. Such a devaluation of the pound would most likely occur in response to a higher inflation rate in Britain than in the U.S. Actually, there would be two means of achieving adjustment in the balance of payments (or some combination of the two means). They include: (1) the devaluation just outlined, or (2) a reduction in the quantity of goods exported by Britain and hence some possible unemployment in Britain. The first action would make the inflation rate inconsequential as far as the international economy is concerned. Britain would simply export goods at lower value and import goods at higher value. However, a reduction in exports and or the prospect of unemployment would put pressure on the British to alter the governmental policies causing the high inflation rates in the first place.

The following discourse proceeds with a system of fixed exchange rates. Where appropriate, modifications are provided to introduce flexible ("floating") exchange rates.

Exchange Rates and International Monetary Reserves

At an earlier time, tying the value of the monetary unit to gold gave a world value to the unit itself. This value could only be made effective, however, through the foreign exchange market. In that market currencies could be exchanged for each other, or they could be exchanged for gold. By 1977, however, currencies were being exchanged for one another and for monetary reserves (including the new "paper gold," or standard drawing rights), but not for gold. The paper gold was introduced in January 1970, and the IMF was returning some of the original contributions of gold (sect. 2.3).

As the key agency for cooperation in such matters, the International Monetary Fund (IMF) moved toward a demonetization of gold, and the SDR has since become the international numéraire (or unit of account, as in appendix to chapter 1). Many currencies are tied to the SDR for official purposes, just as they were tied to gold at an earlier time, and the paper gold plays virtually the same role as gold, as far as international monetary reserves and the mechanism are concerned. The need for paper gold was not great in the early years of its introduction, but its role has expanded, following the almost simultaneous recessions in many countries in the 1973-75 period.

Under the traditional system, two currencies in forms other than gold (e.g., in bank deposits or paper currency) would exchange for each other as long as the rate at which one exchanged for the other remained within narrow limits. These limits were called "gold points" under the functioning of a more classical form of the gold standard and, for most currencies until the early 1970s, they came to be the buying and selling rates set by a central agency or government exchange stabilization fund. Such an exchange rate system is called a fixed rate or adjustable peg system, where the pegged limits may be changed from time to time. In such a system, gold or international monetary reserves flow into (out of) the country that has a surplus (deficit) and whose currency is at its upper (lower) value. Changes in value occur in such a way as to reestablish a rate of exchange within narrow limits. The limits may still be thought of as the gold points, although individual countries have more freedom in setting the points than they did through agreement with the IMF prior to the changes of the early 1970s.

In figure 2-1 the limits to a fixed exchange rate are shown approximately as they existed for the British pound in relation to the U.S. dollar in 1974, only under a fixed rate system. In point of fact, the British moved toward a managed system with extensive floating in the early-to-mid 1970s; under that system the limits are not fixed. Even so, intervention to stabilize fluctuations still occurs, and when it does monetary reserves still flow as depicted under the fixed rate system, only with more moderation. The system is depicted for the United States vis-à-vis the United Kingdom (U.K.), but with slight modification it could as easily be the U.S. vis-à-vis Japan or West Germany.

International Payments and Interbank Balances

The majority of payments for business transactions between countries are made with bank balances. Generally, there are banks in financial centers that have "correspondent" relationships with banks in other centers; today these may even include foreign branches of domestic banks. A foreign seller of goods or services will typically want payment in currency of his own country, though a store of special currencies (such as the dollar) may be desired by some countries. Even so, the domestic purchaser of foreign items may obtain the means of payment through his bank. The bank credits the account of its foreign correspondent, which will in effect make the payment to the foreign seller. As long as the purchases of goods, services, I.O.U.s, and other items in one country equal those purchases in another, the claims cancel out. However, when country A begins to purchase more items from country B (or the rest of the world) than B purchases from A, then the supply of credits (say, deposits) at banks in country B available for exchange into A's currency decreases relative to the large supply of A's currency available for exchange into B's currency. B's currency may be said to be in short supply. Its price or exchange rate rises in terms of A's currency, and country A's exchange rate declines in terms of country B's monetary unit. These prices are made by dealers in the foreign exchange markets, which are generally the banks transacting in money balances with one another.

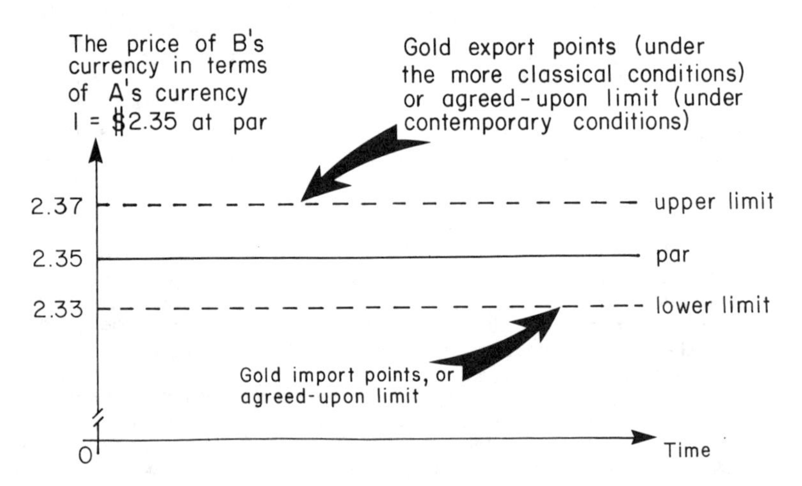

Figure 2-1. A Hypothetical Rate on Foreign Exchange Between Country A and Country B under Fixed Exchange Rates: The Domestic (or Country A's) Point of View

the pound at $2.37 and $2.33, respectively. They can do this by buying all dollars offered at $2.37 and by selling dollars in exchange for pounds for authorized transactions when the price of the pound falls below $2.33. With the move toward floating rates for the pound in the early 1970s, its price has actually been below $2.00, whereas its price was over $4.00 in the 1947-48 period. These facts alone convey a lot about what has happened to the British society.

The proper functioning of the gold flows mechanism or its modified post-World War II counterpart tended to confine fluctuations in the prices of foreign exchange within limits as depicted. Under the more classical conditions, these limits were set by the gold points: the gold export points, the rate of exchange at which the export of gold was worthwhile, and the gold import points, the rate that favored the import of gold from the foreign country. However, over most of the post-World War II years where fixed rates have existed, these rates were set for most countries through agreement with the IMF. Fixed exchange rates served the same purpose as gold points. The idea is that the cooperating countries established par values for their currencies, and then agreed to limit exchange rate fluctuations on either side of par value. Under the old system the spread between the limits was twice the shipping cost of gold; under the system in effect from the late 1940s through the early 1970s, the spread was simply negotiated.

Under freely fluctuating rates, in contrast, the cost of B's currency in terms of A's currency must rise so high as to discourage the purchase of imports from country B when A's price level rises relative to B's, and the rate must fall so low as to stimulate purchases when A's price level falls relative to B's. Under this system, valuation changes occur such that there need be no residual in the balance of claims for exports by the respective countries to be met by a payment with international monetary reserves. Instead, the exchange rates simply fluctuate in sufficient extremes to force the balance called for. No such system was tried by major industrial countries as a whole before the early 1970s.

Monetary Reserve Flows

The operations in the foreign exchange markets and the earlier practice of confining exchange rate changes within prescribed limits, in particular, give rise to a somewhat mechanical system that regulates monetary reserve flows and price level changes in the various countries. As a first approximation, the system may be viewed as operating so as to adjust prices and generate price level changes as a means of correcting imbalances in a country's payments position. Some details and additional complications are added in chapter 19.

The type of price level changes envisioned are those that result as some function of the stock of money, after allowance for changes in output. These are suggested by the previous statements about the relationship between money and income and about income as the product of the average of prices and the real output. But here as well as later we stress that, in comparing price measures for the respective countries, we are especially interested in price levels for the goods and services entering into international trade and for the quality of those goods. Specifically, we will consider prices of goods that are somewhat competitive or can be easily substituted for one another, such as an average of prices for steel, automobiles, motorcycles, TV sets, electronic devices generally, bicycles, foodstuffs, fibers, wearing apparel, cameras, and travel and tourism in the U.S., denoted $P^{(US)}$ versus $P^{(Japan)}$, denoting an average of prices for similar goods. This means we will not be thinking strictly of the price indexes for wholesale goods, a consumer's market basket, and the GNP deflator (as in chapter 1). And it also means that a Japanese price index may be rising rapidly because of increases in the prices of foods they import, while the prices of the goods they export are rising less rapidly.

Prices and the Reserve Flows Mechanism

The acceptance of an international reserve mechanism with fixed exchange rates by several important countries provided in effect an automatic regulator of prices. In such a framework--with the proviso just introduced about the average of prices in U.S. versus the average in Japan--the levels of prices in country A and country B may be related thus:

$$P^{(A)} - P^{(B)} + \text{constant} = 0.$$

Monetary reserves would be attracted toward country A when

(1) $P^{(A)} - P^{(B)} + \text{constant} < 0$ (flow toward country A),

and toward country B when

(2) $P^{(A)} - P^{(B)} + \text{constant} > 0$ (flow toward country B).

In effect, the more favorable prices in country A implied by inequality (1) would attract reserves to A because of an increase in A's exports to B and a decrease in A's imports from B. The relatively more favorably prices in country B, as implied by inequality (2), would induce an outflow of reserves from country A because of a decrease in A's exports to B and an increase in A's imports from B.

In the framework thus far introduced, the flows of international monetary reserves may be viewed as regulating the respective levels of prices, where

$P^{(A)}$ is the average of prices of current output in country A (or, more specifically, the average of prices of exportable goods entering into foreign trade),

$P^{(B)}$ is the average of prices of current output in country B (i.e., the average of prices of exportable goods entering into foreign trade),
$P^{(A)}$ is a function of the money supply in country A,
$P^{(B)}$ is a function of the money supply in country B,
ΔM is an increase in the money supply,
M is the equilibrium stock of money prior to the flow of monetary reserves,
ΔR_o is an initial increase in domestic reserves,
r is a fraction of reserves to note and deposit liabilities.

The regulatory mechanism may be illustrated, as a first approximation, as follows:

PERIOD 1

$[P^{(A)} - P^{(B)} + \text{const.} < 0$ (flow toward Country A)$]$

Country A (Inducement for inflow)		*Country B* (Inducement for outflow)
$\Delta M = \left(\frac{1}{r}\right)(\Delta R_0)$	$\longleftarrow$	$(-\Delta R_0)\left(\frac{1}{r}\right) = (-\Delta M)$
$\downarrow$		$\downarrow$
$\Delta P^{(A)} = f(\overline{M} + \Delta M)$		$f(-\Delta M + \overline{M}) = -\Delta P^{(B)}$

Terms of trade now favor Country B as shown at the outset of period 2.

PERIOD 2

$[P^{(A)} - P^{(B)} + \text{const.} > 0$ (flow toward Country B)$]$

Country A (Inducement for outflow)		*Country B* (Inducement for inflow)
$-\Delta M = \left(\frac{1}{r}\right)(-\Delta R_0)$	$\longrightarrow$	$\Delta R_0\left(\frac{1}{r}\right) = \Delta M$
$\downarrow$		$\downarrow$
$-\Delta P^{(A)} = f(\overline{M} - \Delta M)$		$f(\Delta M + \overline{M}) = \Delta P^{(B)}$

Terms of trade now favor Country A as shown at the outset of period 3.

PERIOD 3

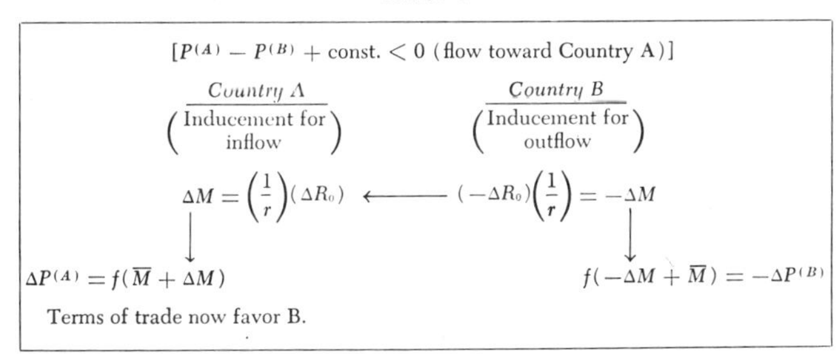

The mechanism just illustrated was assumed to provide a certain discipline that would constrain inflation and contribute to efficiency in production in the respective domestic economies. The constraint on prices was to be provided by competition among trading countries, by a country's payments position, and by limits on the supply of international monetary reserves. With some exceptions, gold worked very well as a reserve in this respect, and the mining of new gold seemed to meet the needs of trade over long periods of time.

Simultaneity of Recessions

In the mechanism just described, the movement of reserves and price levels between the countries would seem to suggest an expansion of business conditions in a country when reserves flowed in, and a contraction as reserves flowed out. Such was a common, early experience, but in more modern times we find governments and central banks, such as the Federal Reserve in the United States, moving more aggressively to control total spending in their respective countries by setting requirements for bank reserves, by controlling the money stock, and by enacting fiscal policy (as considered in chapters 10 and 11). With this control over the broadened range of domestic reserves, it becomes possible for the business conditions of trading partners to move more in phase with one another. A contemporary view is that the accelerated growth of bank reserves and monetary aggregates may influence total spending in an economy, not just for domestically produced goods and services, but for imports as well. Thus, many central banks and governments will react to expand simultaneously, as in response to the same doctrine.

Difficulties in the simultaneous expansion arise from two interrelated sources: (1) when some countries pursue less inflationary policies (i.e., smaller increases in the price level) than others, possibly in reaction to the Keynesian view of the Phillips curve, and (2) when the public starts to react unfavorably toward government because of increasing inflation rates. The Keynesian view of the Phillips curve embodies the idea of a trade-off of a higher inflation rate for a reduction in the unemployment rate, irrespective of the state of business conditions. It concerns us in chapter 4 and later in chapter 17.

The Exchange Rate System Since the Early 1970s

A mixed peg-float system of exchange rates emerged during the early 1970s. Under it, the IMF is still the vehicle for the cooperation of its member countries, including the U.S. and its trading partners, but members are allowed more freedom in deciding on the system that is best for them if not the rest of the world (Heller 1976). An amendment to the Articles of Agreement of the IMF recognizes each member's sovereignty in the choice of its own system, and explicitly prohibits a peg in terms of gold.

The choice of an exchange rate system confronting individual IMF member countries as of mid-1976 is presented as a tree diagram in figure 2-2. The figure shows that a country may elect to peg its currency, as under the old fixed rate system, or to float its currency. Other choices flow out of the decision to peg or float. If the decision is to peg, the peg may be to a single currency such as the dollar or to a basket (index) of currencies such as those providing a measure for the SDR. If the decision is to float the currency, the options are an independent float, one undertaken with a group of countries,[2] or a "crawl." The crawl is simply a pegged rate system, as illustrated in figure 2-1, but the par rate (tied with SDR since mid 1970s) and limits are subject to being changed. Figure 2-2 also gives some indication of the complexity of the system in operation. Among major countries, Saudi Arabia's currency is pegged to the SDR, the U.S. currency crawls, and the British currency floats with a good bit of intervention in exchange markets to simply stabilize the pound's value at times and to influence it at others. What emerges from an examination of the mixed system is a recognition that much of the discipline of the old fixed rate system is still at hand despite the changes in the early-to-mid 1970s. At least this seems to be the case during the period in which countries have had a chance to react to two events: (1) the new-found freedom in selecting of an exchange rate system, and (2) the widespread influence of the idea of a trade-off between inflation and unemployment.

The case of discipline under the new sovereignty among IMF member countries in the choice of an exchange rate is discussed in section 2.5. First, however, we consider the balance of international payments and scarce natural resources (oil, in particular).

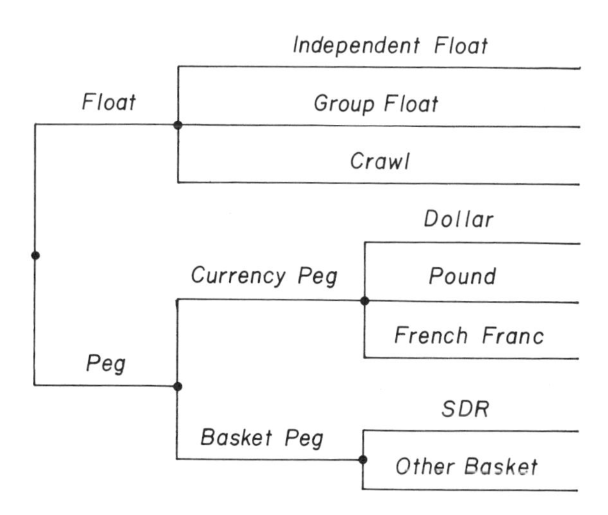

Figure 2-2. The Choice of an Exchange Rate System for an IMF Member Country

Source of figure: H. Robert Heller, "The Choice of an Exchange Rate System: Theory and Practice." An unpublished IMF Staff Paper.

2.3. Balance of International Payments and Monetary Reserves

The balance of international payments is a statement of transactions (or more accurately net amounts arising from transactions) between a country such as the United States and the rest of the world. In a sense it is an accounting statement, but without some of the common features of such a statement. On the one hand, there must be a balance overall (adding to zero in the case of the balance of payments), credits must equal debits, and so on. On the other hand, only flows per period of time are recorded rather than accumulated amounts as on a balance sheet, and, in addition, credits are additions to the various accounts and debits are deductions, with net credits denoted by positive amounts and net debits by a minus sign (-).

Following the use of the term "favorable" as explained in the introduction to the payments mechanism, what we give up (i.e., export) is recorded as a credit and what we receive (i.e., import) is recorded as a debit. From a financial point of view, the credits mean that dollars were obtained from the foreign exchange market, and debits mean that they were supplied.

Table 2-1

U.S. Balance of Payments

SUMMARY EXPLANATION OF U.S. BALANCE OF PAYMENTS

(To be used in conjunction with Table I)

The U.S. balance of payments is a summary record of all international transactions by the Government, business, and private U.S. residents occurring during a specified period of time.

As a series of accounts and as a measure of economic behavior, balance of payments transactions are grouped into seven categories: merchandise trade, services, transfer payments, long-term capital, short-term private capital, miscellaneous, and liquid private capital. We successively add the net balances of the above categories in order to obtain:

- Merchandise Trade Balance
- Goods and Services Balance
- Current Account Balance
- Basic Balance
- Net Liquidity Balance
- Official Settlements Balance

Below the dashed line there are two additional categories, U.S. liabilities to foreign official holders and U.S. reserve assets. These serve to finance the transactions recorded above the dashed line.

There are interrelationships between these accounts. For example, the credit entry associated with an export of goods could result from the debit entry of a private bank loan, a Government grant, a private grant, or an increase in U.S. holdings of foreign currency or gold.

Merchandise Trade: Exports and imports are a measure of physical goods which cross U.S. boundaries. The receipt of dollars for exports is recorded as a plus and the payments for imports are recorded as a minus in this account.

Services: Included in this account are the receipt of earnings on U.S. investments abroad and the payments of earnings on foreign investments in the U.S. Sales of military equipment to foreigners and purchases from foreigners for both military equipment and for U.S. military stations abroad are also included in this category.

U. S. BALANCE OF PAYMENTS, 1974p

(Billions of Dollars)

		Net Balance	Cumulative Net Balance
Merchandise Trade:			
Exports	+ 97.1		
Imports	−103.0		
Merchandise Trade Balance		− 5.9	**− 5.9**
Services:			
Military Receipts	+ 3.0		
Military Payments	− 5.1		
Income on U. S. Investments Abroad	+ 29.9		
Payments for Foreign Investments in U. S.	− 16.7		
Receipts from Travel & Transportation	+ 10.2		
Payments for Travel & Transportation	− 12.7		
Other Services (net)	+ 0.3		
Balance on Services		+ 9.1	
Goods and Services Balance			**+ 3.2**
Transfer Payments:			
Private	− 1.1		
Government	− 6.1		
Balance on Transfer Payments		− 7.2	
Current Account Balance			**− 4.0**
Long-term Capital:			
Direct Investment Receipts	+ 2.3		
Direct Investment Payments	− 6.8		
Portfolio Investment Receipts	+ 1.2		
Portfolio Investment Payments	− 2.0		
Government Loans (net)	+ 1.0		
Other Long-term (net)	− 2.4		
Balance on Long-term Capital		− 6.7	
Basic Balance			**−10.6**

Transfer Payments: Private transfers represent gifts and similar payments by Americans to foreign residents. Government transfers represent payments associated with foreign assistance programs and may be utilized by foreign governments to finance trade with the United States.

Long-term Capital: Long-term private capital records all changes in U.S. private assets and liabilities to foreigners, both real and financial. Private U.S. purchases of foreign assets are recorded as payments of dollars to foreigners, and private foreign purchases of U.S. assets are recorded as receipts of dollars from foreigners. Government capital transactions represent long-term loans of the U.S. Government to foreign governments.

Short-term Private Capital: Nonliquid liabilities refers to capital inflows, such as loans by foreign banks to U.S. corporations, and nonliquid claims refers to capital outflows, such as U.S. bank loans to foreigners. These items represent trade financing and cash items in the process of collection which have maturities of less than three months. The distinction between short-term private capital and liquid private capital is that the transactions recorded in the former account are considered not readily transferable.

Miscellaneous: Allocations of special drawing rights (SDRs) represent the receipt of the U.S. share of supplemental reserve assets issued by the International Monetary Fund. SDRs are recorded here when they are initially received by the United States. The category errors and omissions is the statistical discrepancy between all specifically identifiable receipts and payments. It is believed to be largely unrecorded short-term private capital movements.

Liquid Private Capital: This account records changes in U.S. short-term liabilities to foreigners, and changes in U.S. short-term claims reported by U.S. banks on foreigners.

Short-term Private Capital:			
Nonliquid Liabilities	+ 1.7		
Nonliquid Claims	– 14.7		
Balance on Short-term Private Capital		–13.0	
Miscellaneous:			
Allocation of Special Drawing Rights (SDR)	*		
Errors and Omissions	+ 5.2		
Balance on Miscellaneous Items		+ 5.2	
Net Liquidity Balance			–18.3
Liquid Private Capital:			
Liabilities to Foreigners	+ 15.7		
Claims on Foreigners	– 5.5		
Balance on Liquid Private Capital		+10.3	
Official Settlements Balance			– 8.1
The Official Settlements Balance is Financed by Changes in:			
U. S. Liabilities to Foreign Official Holders:			
Liquid Liabilities	+ 8.3		
Readily Marketable Liabilities	+ 0.6		
Special Liabilities	+ 0.7		
Balance on Liabilities to Foreign Official Holders		+ 9.5	
U. S. Reserve Assets:			
Gold	0.0		
Special Drawing Rights	– 0.2		
Convertible Currencies	0.0		
IMF Gold Tranche	– 1.3		
Balance on Reserve Assets		– 1.4	
Total Financing of Official Settlements Balance			+ 8.1

*There was no SDR allocation for 1974.
P – Preliminary
NOTE: Figures may not add because of rounding.

Source: Donald S. Kemp. 1975. "Balance-of-Payments Concepts --What Do They Really Mean?" Review, Federal Reserve Bank of St. Louis (July).

Balance of payments accounting is not as well established as ordinary public accounting, although it is quite old. Even so, it has evolved mainly since the 1930s, and there are special problems in the accounting by the Department of Commerce, as reviewed in some detail by Pippenger (1973). Transactions are sometimes only estimated or missed entirely. Hence there is a category "errors and omissions." This is a residual that makes the books balance in a final sense, but rather than varying randomly over time, the category appears to behave like short-term capital flows.

A summary of the standard U.S. Balance of Payments statement is shown in table 2-1.[3] There are six broad categories that have characterized such statements in recent years. One may emphasize any or several of the accounts shown, depending on the purpose. We will examine four divisions, including the current account and three others of the six accounts shown. The last three divisions determine whether there is a surplus (favorable balance) or deficit in the balance of payments. To emphasize these dimensions, a horizontal line may be drawn through the groups of accounts with the idea of accounts being "above the line" or "below the line," and with the below-the-line items showing how the balance is financed. The entries above the line must equal those below the line, though with the opposite sign.

All of the transactions recorded above a line drawn under "Current Account Balance" represent the transfer of real assets (goods and services) between the United States and its trading partners, with the exception of unilateral transfers (gifts and similar payments by American govermental units and private citizens to foreign residents). The current account balance of $4.0 billion represents what we may think of traditionally as the balance of trade. In the present case it is in deficit (-), which means the United States imported more goods and services in 1974 than it exported. Another way of viewing this deficit is as a net foreign disinvestment, in the sense that it must be financed by liquidating U.S.-held securities of foreign countries or by exporting securities to foreign owners. Had the current account balance been positive it would represent "net foreign investment" and an excess of exports over imports. This balance is a component of the nation's GNP accounts, as reviewed in the next chapter.

In the three cases concerning whether there is a surplus or deficit in the balance of payments, a line may appear immediately after the boldfaced listing "Basic Balance" (deficit of $10.6 billion), after the listing "Net Liquidity Balance" (deficit of $18.3 billion), or after the listing "Official Settlements Balance" (deficit of $8.1 billion). In case one, we would have the balance on current account plus long-term capital; in case two, the net liquid balance; and in case three, the official reserve transactions balance. The line is drawn for the purpose of determining whether there is a balance of payments surplus (+) or deficit (-). The means of financing the deficit and thus of obtaining the dollars in the foreign exchange market are shown below the line. For the 1974 summary shown, the deficit was made up primarily by having foreign official agencies hold more U.S. liabilities designated in dollars. It could also have been made up by exporting U.S. reserve assets.

The foregoing feature whereby foreign official agencies hold more dollar liabilities is a very tentative means of financing a deficit. In a sense it is backed by the underlying strength of the U.S. economy, by a desire on the part of foreign official agencies to cooperate with the U.S., and by a store of official reserve assets. It is an expedient that is less available to many of the countries of the world where deficits are incurred.

For most countries it is this balance in official reserve transactions, and primarily official reserve assets, that we view as favorable or unfavorable, as under gold standard conditions. In that tradition a favorable balance would be a credit balance, with negative amounts for the entries below the line. These negative amounts would signify imports of official reserve assets and thus increases in holdings of gold and SDRs primarily.

We are especially interested in the monetary reserves for two reasons: (1) they reflect additions or subtractions to the various countries accumulations of "high-powered monies" or bank reserves, and (2) growth in these reserves is thought to be necessary to generate the foreign exchange required by increased foreign trade. This international growth problem is analogous to the domestic problem considered in later chapters whereby the money stock must grow to accommodate the growth of GNP in real terms. Continuing the analogy, we are also interested in defining equilibrium in the balance of payments in a way that is compatible with our use of the term in the analysis of domestic affairs.

The stock of international monetary reserves and its composition is shown for the majority of the non-Communist countries--mainly, the hundred-odd member countries of the IMF--in figure 2-3. The stock for the United States is shown in figure 2-4. The overall growth shown in the first of these figures, when not excessive, is desirable as a means of accommodating foreign trade. Figure 2-3 illustrates that the growth in reserves consists mainly of increases in gold substitutes; this trend is likely to continue due to limited gold resources and efforts by the IMF and the United States to deemphasize gold as a monetary reserve. The effort at demonetization of gold was brought into perspective in January 1977, when the IMF started returning part of the IMF-held gold to its original contributing members.[4] The disparate and negative growth of reserves for the United States (figure 2-4) reflects the unfavorable balance of payments position of the United States from the late 1950s through the early 1970s. In addition, figure 2-4 mirrors the existence of several forces that lead to the two-step devaluation of the dollars in terms of the dollar price of gold during the early 1970s and ultimately to the floating of major currencies against the dollar. These nominal devaluations of the dollar (in December 1971 and in February 1973), are shown in figure 2-5, along with a measure of the effective devaluation of the dollar. The effective devaluation shown is measured against the appreciation in an index of exchange rates for eleven major currencies. One may note that effective devaluation preceded nominal devaluation until the February 1973 action.

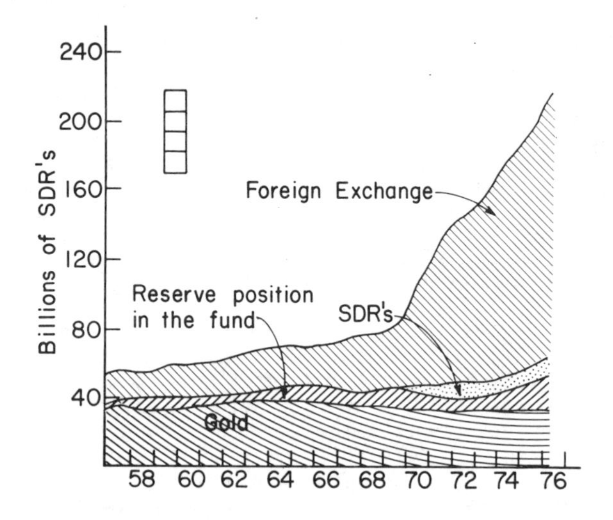

Figure 2-3. International Monetary Reserves of IMF Member Countries

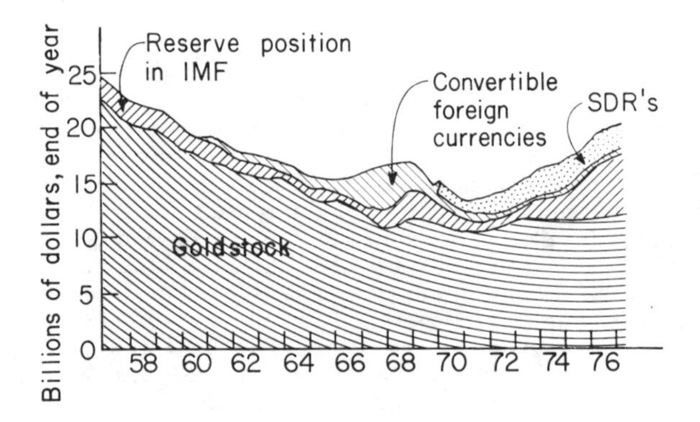

Figure 2-4. International Monetary Reserves of the United States

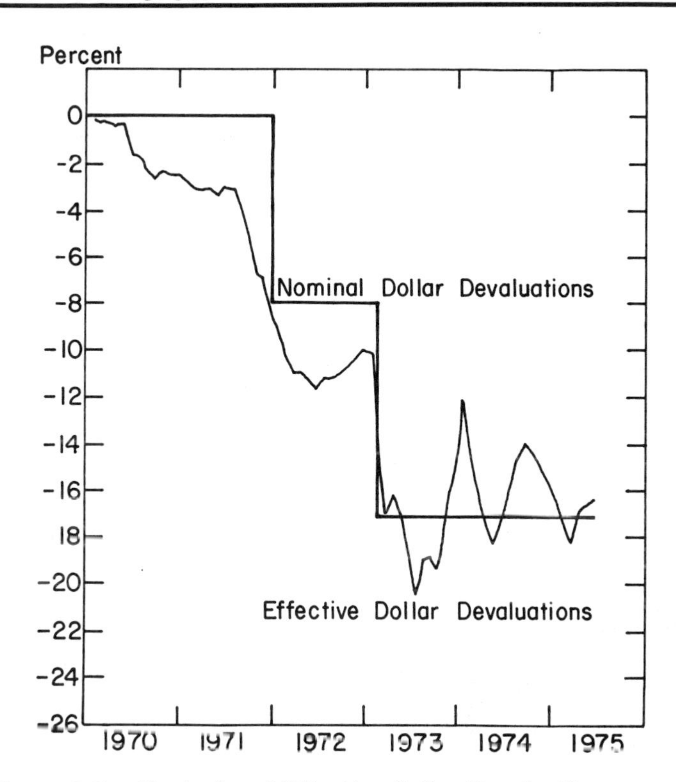

Figure 2-5. Nominal and Effective Dollar Devaluation

Source: IMF and the Federal Reserve Bank of New York

Note: Nominal devaluation is measured by the change in the dollar price of gold. Effective devaluation is measured by the appreciation of eleven major currencies relative to the par values which prevailed as of May 1970. The appreciation is then weighted by separate export and import shares with the United States based on 1972 trade data.

Implicit in the decline of U.S. reserves and dollar devaluations are the domestic policies of the United States, as treated throughout much of the text, and complexities resulting from the role of the dollar as a key international currency. The U.S. played a major role, particularly in the post-World War II years, and in large measure its currency is still a key international currency. But a main point is that the U.S. could not continue to attract the foreign balances (via increases in U.S. liabilities held abroad) in sufficient volume once it started losing gold reserves as shown in figure 2-4, and once speculation set in against the dollar. In an effort to solve some balance of payments problems and demonetize gold as an official reserve, the U.S. broke the official tie to gold (i.e., the commitment to exchange gold for dollar claims by foreign central banks against the United States) as part of President Nixon's New Economic Policy in the early 1970s. What we have instead of the dollar serving as the major monetary reserve is the new paper gold or SDRs of the IMF, and a broader role for foreign exchange balances as shown in figure 2-3. The partial abdication of the role of the dollar as a key currency relieved the U.S. of some of its responsibility for maintaining stable prices and the purchasing power of the returns and principal on its fixed claim liabilities held abroad. In a later chapter we examine further the scenario of international inflation under the "controlled float" or flexible exchange rate arrangement.

2.4. Natural Resources and Domestic Inflation

In mid-1973, omens of the deepest and longest decline in economic activity in the post-World War II U.S. economy began to appear, despite continued inflation. Inflation was indeed a complicating factor--and in later chapters much is said about economic theory and the unusual 1973-75 recession in the United States--but the inflation and the recession were compounded by what has come to be called the energy crisis. Winter induced fuel shortages, and rising gasoline prices have since served as continuing reminders of the crisis and of the pricing of scarce natural resources. The pricing of coffee in 1975-77 another, though less pervasive, example of the pricing of scarce natural resources on an international scale, and of the impact of that pricing on domestic prices in the United States.

The Problem of Scarce, Easily Accessible Energy

The problem of inadequate energy over the foreseeable future concerned the industrial countries and the oil consuming nations prior to the autumn of 1973, but it took an embargo on the shipment of oil by Arab countries and a subsequent fourfold increase in the dollar price of oil by OPEC (Organization of Petroleum Exporting Countries)[5] to bring into focus the reality of the limits of global resources. The energy crisis precipitated by these events has implications for economic growth and for some economics of shortages in addition to that of demand management, as considered in later chapters. The present concern, however, is to introduce some inflationary adjustment and consider the balance of payments aspects of the crisis. The U.S. economy is the focus of the introduction, but the implications apply to the oil consuming nations of Europe and for Japan as well.

The obvious importance of oil to industrialized countries and the almost virtual inelasticity of demand for it over short periods of time is easily recognized, but there are less obvious dimensions to the importance of oil and to the initial success of OPEC in raising revenues. For one, energy is contained in much of the fertilizer used in agriculture, especially in the U.S., and nitrogen, a most important fertilizer, comes mainly from natural gas and petroleum. Consequently, many domestic products are affected, especially when we consider the cost of energy as an underlying cost of production.

Arab oil pricing and the initial success of OPEC brought attention to the vulnerability of Western nations and Japan in their reliance on natural resources, and it set an example for the pricing of scarce resources by other Third World countries (Pindyck 1979, 154-158). These countries--nations for the most part unaligned with big East-West political and economic blocks --are said to be encouraged by the possibility of using natural resources to alter the balance of wealth between the industrialized and less industrialized nations. On the one hand, they have increasingly scarce resources, yet the implementation of their plans for development requires Western technology, equipment, and managerial know-how.

When the OPEC oil cartel (defined as a number of firms or producing units combining with the view to limiting competitive forces within a market) took its first actions, some economists and others gave strong weight to the prospect of a break in the price line. Cartels, they said, break up when disgruntled members seek to get a larger share of revenues by cutting prices. However, the prospect of the cartel breaking through conservation measures in the U.S. and through reduced oil imports soon faded. Instead, the cartel pointed to the need for further increase in the price of oil, especially in response to the depreciation of the purchasing power of the dollar, as illustrated in figure 2-5. Cartel spokesmen pointed to the desire to stabilize the price of oil in relation to the prices of the goods and services their countries imported.

Prior to a September 1975 meeting, OPEC economic experts recommended that OPEC offset further weakening of the U.S. dollar by quoting its prices in terms of some index. One index suggested was that used by the IMF, where the value of SDRs is tied to the average value of sixteen major currencies. Another mentioned was that for the appreciation of eleven major currencies relative to the par values that prevailed as of May 1970, as shown in figure 2-5. In spite of these speculations, no further changes in OPEC prices were announced until December 1976, by which time the U.S. demand for oil had reached a record high (an average of more than 19 million barrels a day during the four weeks ending December 17); the United States by this time relied on imported oil to meet 42 percent of its total petroleum needs. The announced oil price increases went into effect on January 1, 1977. Saudi Arabia, the oil producing giant of the OPEC countries, and the United Arab Empires announced a 5 percent increase in the "light-crude reference price"; the remaining 11 OPEC members announced increases amounting to 10.4 percent, with plans for an additional 5 percent increase to take place on July 1, 1977.[6] These plans were later abandoned.

The Saudi Arabians gave several explanations for their restrained action: they were trying to protect the world's fragile economic recovery from the 1973-75 recession; they wanted to ensure that the rich nations give new concessions to the world's poor countries; and they wanted to enlist the full support of the West, and especially the United States, in bringing a new calm to the troubled Middle East. By its action Saudi Arabia took considerable leadership among OPEC countries and in encouraging ties with the U.S., and it seemed to be in a position to enforce the action. The Saudis not only had the capacity to pump more oil and thereby increase exports, but they were in the process of further increasing that capacity.

Meeting later in December 1978, in Abu Dhabi, United Arab Emirates, the OPEC oil ministers decided to further raise oil prices during 1979 by 14.5 percent (from $12.70 per 42-gallon barrel to $14.54). This was to occur in four steps, beginning with a 5 percent hike, January 1. The plan at the time was undertaken with reference to the West's failure to control inflation and reduce the use of oil. However, by late March, the U.S. had recorded a 15.4 percent jump (at an annual rate) in the consumer price index for February, U.S. daily oil consumption had reached a record 21 million barrels a day, and a revolution had occurred in Iran that resulted first in a total cutoff of oil production and then in long-range plans by Iran for a sizable percent reduction in oil exports. Reacting to these events at a late March meeting, the OPEC oil ministers approved the price of $14.54 a barrel as of the March date and authorized individual member countries to tack on surcharges. Throughout debate among the members, Iraq, Iran, and Libya sought higher increases, and Saudi Arabia and Abu Ahari (later joined by Ecuador, Gabon, and Qater) took more moderate positions. In June, 1979, increases in crude oil prices rose to the $18 to $23.50 a barrel range, and continued to point toward a continuation of reminders of scarce energy and the consequences of inflation in the United States.

The OPEC countries and Saudi Arabia have seemed well advised by economic experts in their price setting. Economists recognize that the cartel price cannot exceed the cost of generating Btu's (British Thermal Units) from other energy sources such as nuclear energy and coal.[7] However, apart from unforeseen technological breakthroughs, this so-called long-run monopoly price of oil rises with increases in the cost of producing substitute sources of energy, and the economics of exhaustible resources may play a special role as introduced later (sect. 16.6). As it would appear later (sect. 16.6), the price of oil may be expected to accelerate in the absence of technological breakthroughs, as the supply in the ground is exhausted.

The Domestic Price Level: the Push Effect

The United States was a major exporter and commercial producer of oil before World War I, but in modern times has not extended a free market price to its residents. As World War I and the advent of the gasoline powered automobile sparked some fears of a shortage, the large companies acted to restrict production and maintain prices, ostensibly on grounds of conservation pursuant to the Interstate Oil Compact.

Domestic production came to be controlled by regulatory commissions at state levels and by oil import quotas at the national level. These quotas continued in effect through the 1960s, when they were relaxed to permit rising imports. In April 1973 President Nixon removed the import quotas. Shortly after, the cartel price became a negotiated one, and the domestic price a partially controlled price. In 1975 President Ford considered decontrolling the price of old oil (oil from domestic wells in existence prior to 1972 and producing less than their 1972 output) by vetoing an extension of price controls on domestic oil. These controls had limited the price of approximately 60 percent of domestically produced oil to $5.25 a barrel, at a time when oil was selling at around $12 a barrel in world markets.

In early April 1979, with the world price of crude oil scheduled to rise above $14 per barrel, President Carter announced a gradual decontrol of prices on U.S. produced crude oil by 1981. Mandatory ceilings on the domestic crude oil prices were scheduled to expire June 1. After that date the President had been authorized to act on his own until the terminal date (September 1981) for the control program.

OPEC prices and domestic price control on crude oil came to mean higher costs to refineries, electrical power plants, gasoline stations, firms in the transportation business and in agribusiness, as well as a host of other energy-using firms and households.

On the international side (and exclusive of the United States), serious competition among oil companies developed in the 1950s and 1960s with the entry of independent oil companies into foreign production. Prices declined, surpluses resulted, and oil exporting countries lost revenues. From this emerged the logic of pricing that led to OPEC.

Some effects of these higher costs on the domestic economy can be illustrated by a brief consideration of the Marshallian cross in chapter 1, the price index, and the U.S. balance of payments. First, the market supply curve in the Marshallian cross is derived from cost curves for producing firms, as shown in chapter 15 in our more formal consideration of costs, prices, and demand. A rise in costs causes an upward shift in the supply curve, say, from S_1 to S_2 in figure 2-6. Now, if this rise is extended to many goods and

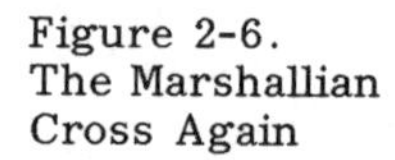
Figure 2-6.
The Marshallian
Cross Again

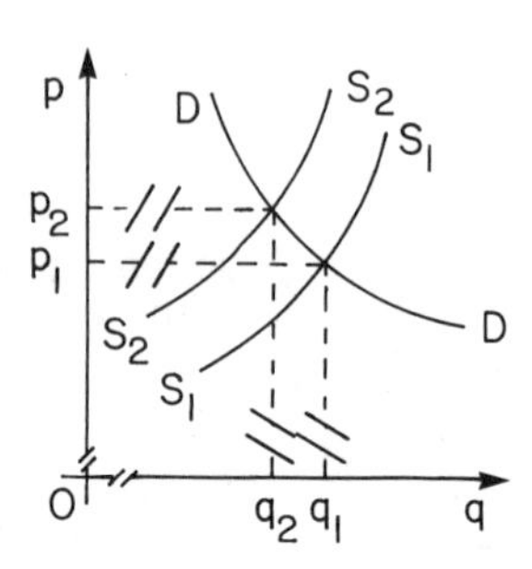

services relying on oil- and gas-based energy sources, then many separate prices are affected. In terms of a price index for country A,

$$p^{(A)} = w_1p_1 + w_2p_2 + w_3p_3 + \ldots + w_np_n$$

many prices rise, with an ultimate impact on the price level. Individual commodity prices may become a source of inflation, unless they are offset by declines in the prices of other index items. Since this decline may require a long period of time, output must adjust downward, causing unemployment. Thus, higher energy prices ultimately may result in inflation and unemployment.

Balance of Payments Impact

The balance of payments is also affected. First, with reference to table 2-1, debits to the merchandise trade balance increase substantially as the dollar price of oil imports increases, even with a contracted flow of the barrels of oil imports. Next, these produce surplus foreign exchange for the oil exporting countries. This surplus has been called "petro-dollars." These were initially invested in short-term securities, and later in short- and long-term securities and other property.

When these funds are invested in U.S. securities and property, they appear as exports of capital (and credits) from the U.S. point of view, as in table 2-1. The capital flows mean a sale of securities representing loans to, or ownership in, private businesses in the United States. The other alternative is to seek cooperation in maintaining dollar balances in the U.S. (e.g., U.S. liquid liabilities) or to transfer official reserves, including gold. In the first instance, the ownership and debt have many implications for future business and political relationships. These are left to the readers' imagination for the time being. In the second instance--reserve and gold losses--there are implications too, which will be enlarged on later, but mainly there is the recognized growth in the financial (and hence diplomatic) strength of oil producing nations.

The Coffee Episode

Coffee prices in 1975-76 serve as another example of the pricing of resources on an international level, with impact on domestic prices and the balance of payments. Although the impact was less pervasive and without the dire proportions of the energy crisis, even so, the coffee episode illustrates another dimension of international pricing. Specifically, changes in coffee prices came about from shifts in expectations about future supply and demand conditions rather than from current shortages and quantity flows to and from the market. In this respect, we have a forerunner of numerous other examples of pricing and supply and demand phenomena.

As is the case with most oil, coffee beans are produced or exported by Third World nations, with about eighteen of them accounting for 80 percent of world exports. Brazil is the largest exporter; Colombia, the second. Other producers include Peru, Angola, and Venezuela. Over the years there have been attempts to organize a cartel of coffee producers, but several factors operate against cartelization, including the ease of entry for producers and the desire of producing countries to enlarge their share of the export market. Brazil and Colombia, however, because of their unique climates, produce the highest quality coffee. Moreover, coffee bean prices are controlled in Brazil at the domestic level and through a controlled tax (called a contribution quota) on exported coffee at the international level. Otherwise the pricing of Brazilian and other coffee in dollars in the New York market works through the usual system of exchange rates. (Brazil's system may be described as a "crawling peg." This has reflected their mixed desires to stabilize their exchange rate while avoiding the necessity of slowing their inflation rate.)

Against this background, the coffee episode began with two events: first, the efforts at the cartelization of coffee pricing and, second, the Antarctica wind that brought frost to Brazil's major coffee producing states in July 1975. The freeze was the more significant of the two events cutting Brazil's 1976 harvest by about 60 percent (or 9.5 million bags), according to U.S. estimates. The 1975 harvest was unaffected, however, since it was already in, and Brazil had a stockpile of 25 million bags to draw on during the three years needed for newly planted trees to start bearing beans.

In the U.S., retail prices for coffee rose from an average of $1.27 a pound before the frost to over $3 in some places by early 1977. Factors cited as causing the rise have included speculation over possible shortages (including a possible build-up of inventories), and a boost in Brazil's export tax on coffee beans from $21 a bag to over $100 by early 1977. On the demand side, estimated coffee consumption in the U.S. was virtually unaffected in 1976, despite price increases of 44 percent.

Under flexible exchange rates the entire adjustment for payment imbalances, as just described, may occur initially in the exchange rate with export and import changes in physical quantities occurring later. Under fixed or adjustable peg rates, the adjustments beyond certain limits occur in the international monetary reserves. At any one time there is a fixed supply, which is being distributed and redistributed among the trading countries.

Export and Import Points for Reserve Flows

Under practices pertaining to the fixed rate system, a move in the price of B's currency above the range bounding the fixed rate (called a "par" rate) would stimulate country A to export foreign reserves to replenish its own foreign credits. And, again at the most general level of abstraction, the movement in B's price would quite likely lead the managers of country B's exchange account to offer to sell their currency at the upper limit in such a way as to give effect to that limit. Then any resale of A's currency in exchange for A's monetary reserves would still cause monetary reserves to flow into the stronger currency country. During most of the post-World War II years (and even where it still exists today), this upper limit has usually been the par value of B's currency in terms of A's currency, plus a given percent of that value.

In either instance--the more classical case or the more contemporary one--gold or other monetary reserves have been used to offset the difference between the value of the imports of goods, services, and other items, and the value of the exports of goods, services, and other items. The export of reserves also tends to offset a rise in the price of country B's currency in terms of A's currency. Conversely, if the price of B's currency in terms of A's currency declines below the lower limit (such as the par exchange rate less the shipping cost or the agreed-upon limit), then gold or other monetary reserves tend to flow into country A, offsetting the decline in the price of B's currency.

The upper and lower limits on the price of B's currency in terms of A's currency are shown in figure 2-1 from the viewpoint of the domestic or country A and in terms of the exchange rate for B's currency. The illustration is set up so that it can be interpreted in terms of the more classical or contemporary condition, as well as in terms of a particular numerical example. The numbers used in the example pertain to a hypothetical par value for the pound in terms of dollars as might have existed about 1974, only under a fixed rate system. The limits on either side of par value are those that the United Kingdom and the U.S. Federal Reserve have presumably been able to maintain since the early 1960s. In the figure the United Kingdom has a par value of $2.35 for the pound, and the Bank of England acting as an agent stands ready to effect an upper and lower limit on the dollar price of

Viewed broadly, the coffee episode concerns (1) the Marshallian cross as it would apply to the retail coffee market in the U.S., (2) the consumer price index, and (3) the U.S. balance of payments. In the first instance, we have an upward-shifting demand schedule for coffee, with some possible inelasticity built into the demand curve itself.[8] Also we have an upward shifting supply curve. This is not because of actual shortages, or altered cost of production, but because of the Brazilian export tax and fears of shortages. In the case of the consumer price index, coffee prices increase total food costs, and hence impact on the domestic price level. Finally, in the case of the balance of payments, the value of U.S. imports rises in relation to exports.

2.5. Discipline under a Mixed Peg-Float System

Under the mixed peg-float system of exchange rates for IMF member countries, countries have the option of pegging their currencies or floating them. The main advantage of floating has been that greater freedom to pursue domestic policies concerning inflation rates. In the presence of the Keynesian view of the Phillips curve, as considered in section 17.4, this was a powerful argument. Another argument for allowing a currency to float has been that it facilitates exchange rate adjustments without requiring the approval of the IMF. This was an especially strong incentive in the case of the United States, since requests for approval from the IMF would precipitate widespread speculation against the dollar, which served as an international currency. Under such conditions, it was virtually impossible for the United States to adjust its peg.

Devaluation is possible, in any case, to bring a currency's nominal exchange rate value more in line with its real value, where there is some prospect of maintaining a real value. But no major country wants its currency simply to float without some intervention to stabilize it and to counter speculation favoring or reacting against it, and no major country wants its currency to continue undervalued in the market, as may result from adverse speculation against a currency (for example, where the market expects it to purchase less in real goods and services). These facts suggest that the old balance of payments mechanism--with its flows of monetary reserves and with countries intervening to support their exchange rates--is still a viable way of viewing economic relationships between trading partners. This is so, despite all the hoopla about floating exchange rates and individual country autonomy (freedom) in the early-to-mid 1970s, as touched off, first, by Milton Friedman's advocacy (Friedman 1953; and Frazer 1973, chap. 18) and, second, by adherence to Keynesian tradition in pursuit of autonomous domestic (mainly inflationary) policies.

The British pound, the Italian lira, and the U.S. dollar illustrate the point about the workings of the payments mechanism. In the early 1970s these countries chose to float their currencies, but later relied upon intervention to support their respective currencies. As a consideration of these cases will illustrate, some discipline from the peg-float system, analogous to that under the fixed rate system with gold flows, is still present. In addition, as these cases will illustrate, there is still the need for some sort of efficiency in production on the part of oil importing countries (and those with scarce natural resources generally), as may be brought about through the payments mechanism and the discipline associated with it. The need for this efficiency in response to the imposed-discipline will be even greater in the presence of increasingly scarce resources.9 The opiate of Keynesian economics offers less hope for the reduction of unemployment rates, and environmental constraints impose still higher standards on efficiency and workmanship in production, as chapter 16 suggests.

The British Example

The British pursued their inflationary policies and the dollar/pound rate declined in the early-to-mid 1970s, as shown for the United Kingdom in figure 2-7. The British were giving up more and more material goods for fewer and fewer imports. In such a context, the British government decided in 1976 that the pound was undervalued, due in part to speculation against it, and recognized that they faced either (or some combination) of two prospects: (1) admit the failures of domestic policies and check domestic inflation with possible adverse political consequences for the party in power or (2) temporarily try to support the currency. The latter has come in the past at a high price to the people of Britain because the government has often used borrowed funds to buy pounds (say, at $1.80 per pound) and later has had to sell them (say, at $1.60 per pound) to buy dollars. Ultimately, reserves have been lost and the support of the pound has required the cooperation from others, such as the IMF. In the 1976 case, however, revenues from the development of North Sea oil reserves saved the day. In addition, the IMF was called in to evaluate the British economy, just as under a fixed rate system. The IMF recommended an "austerity" program designed to qualify Britain for a loan. The main features of the program included a reduction in the government spending and restraint on monetary growth. The loan was to be made in three annual installments, presumably to assure that the government was committed to the announced policies; the first installment was released in January 1977. Cooperating countries carried Britain over with loans of short-term funds until IMF funds became available, and there was other "agency" cooperation to facilitate the orderly liquidation of sterling balances held by foreign monetary authories.

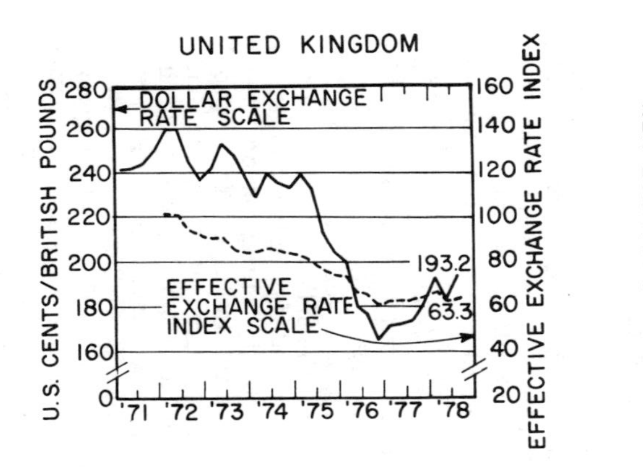
UNITED KINGDOM
U.S. CENTS/BRITISH POUNDS
EFFECTIVE EXCHANGE RATE INDEX
DOLLAR EXCHANGE RATE SCALE
EFFECTIVE EXCHANGE RATE INDEX SCALE
193.2
63.3
280 260 240 220 200 180 160 0
160 140 120 100 80 60 40 20
'71 '72 '73 '74 '75 '76 '77 '78

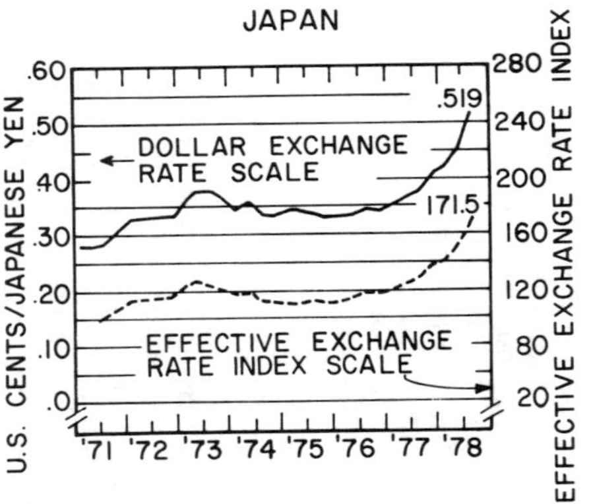
JAPAN
U.S. CENTS/JAPANESE YEN
EFFECTIVE EXCHANGE RATE INDEX
DOLLAR EXCHANGE RATE SCALE
EFFECTIVE EXCHANGE RATE INDEX SCALE
.519
171.5
.60 .50 .40 .30 .20 .10 .0
280 240 200 160 120 80 20
'71 '72 '73 '74 '75 '76 '77 '78

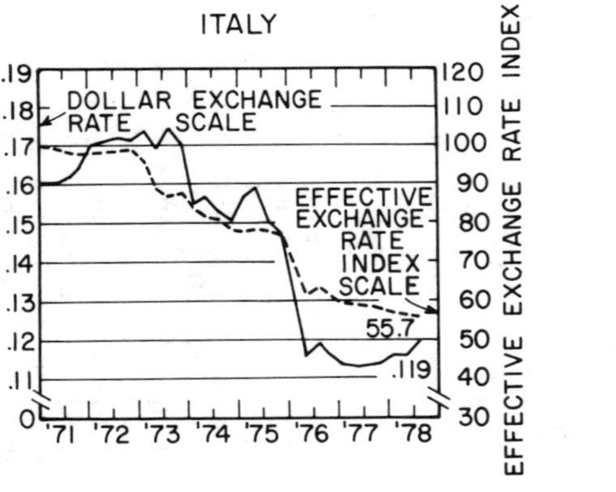
ITALY
U.S. CENTS/ITALIAN LIRA
EFFECTIVE EXCHANGE RATE INDEX
DOLLAR EXCHANGE RATE SCALE
EFFECTIVE EXCHANGE RATE INDEX SCALE
55.7
.119
.19 .18 .17 .16 .15 .14 .13 .12 .11 0
120 110 100 90 80 70 60 50 40 30
'71 '72 '73 '74 '75 '76 '77 '78

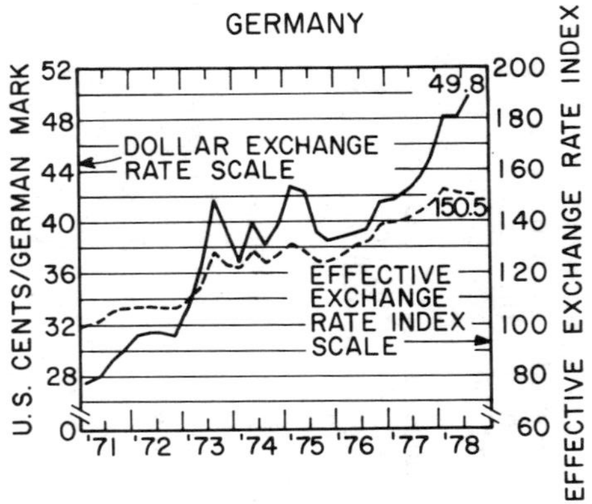
GERMANY
U.S. CENTS/GERMAN MARK
EFFECTIVE EXCHANGE RATE INDEX
DOLLAR EXCHANGE RATE SCALE
EFFECTIVE EXCHANGE RATE INDEX SCALE
49.8
150.5
52 48 44 40 36 32 28 0
200 180 160 140 120 100 80 60
'71 '72 '73 '74 '75 '76 '77 '78

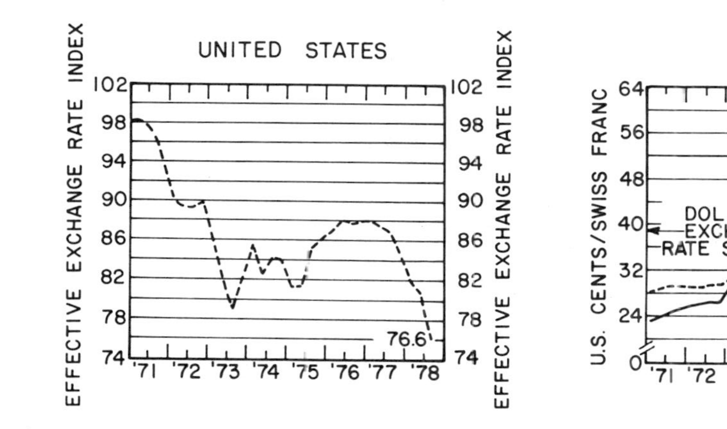

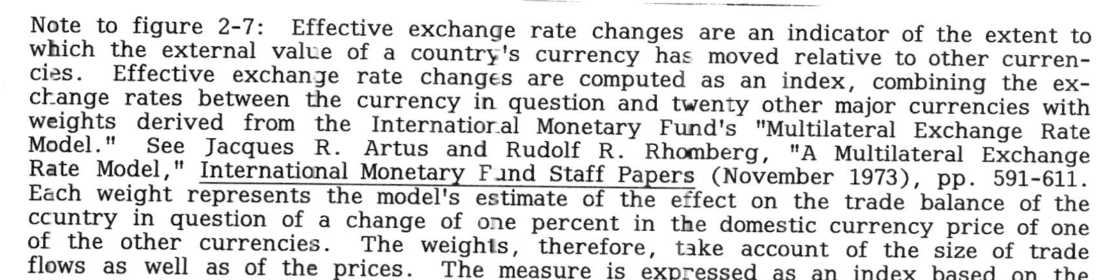

Figure 2-7. Movements in Exchange Rates

Note to figure 2-7: Effective exchange rate changes are an indicator of the extent to which the external value of a country's currency has moved relative to other currencies. Effective exchange rate changes are computed as an index, combining the exchange rates between the currency in question and twenty other major currencies with weights derived from the International Monetary Fund's "Multilateral Exchange Rate Model." See Jacques R. Artus and Rudolf R. Rhomberg, "A Multilateral Exchange Rate Model," International Monetary Fund Staff Papers (November 1973), pp. 591-611. Each weight represents the model's estimate of the effect on the trade balance of the country in question of a change of one percent in the domestic currency price of one of the other currencies. The weights, therefore, take account of the size of trade flows as well as of the prices. The measure is expressed as an index based on the par values in May 1970. Source of figure: F.R.B. of St. Louis.

The Italian Example

Italy, like Britain, continued in the early 1970s to experience losses of monetary reserves in response to inflationary policies and efforts to support its currency (the lira) as its value declined in the foreign exchange markets (see figure 2-7). One reaction to the monetary losses and the declining value of the lira was for Italy to seek further aid from the IMF, and to submit to IMF-imposed constraints on domestic policies in order to qualify for the aid. In April 1977, SDR 450 million ($530 million) was forthcoming under expanded facilities for borrowing from the IMF, as outlined in chapter 19. The draw on the IMF under these new arrangements was necessary, because Italy had already borrowed to its SDR 1,000 million limit.

In order to qualify for the draw under the extended facility, Italy agreed to a comprehensive austerity program with the following main points (Federal Reserve Bank of Chicago, International Letter, April 29, 1977):

> (1) reduction of the budget deficit and limits on governmental spending; (2) reduction in the country's inflation rate from about 22 percent at present to 13 percent by March of next year; (3) restrictions on the growth of bank credit; (4) improvement over the 1976 current account deficit of Lit 2,380 billion. In addition, the Italian government has pledged to refrain from new exchange controls for the duration of the stand-by agreement, and to reform the wage indexation system that has been viewed as inflationary.

In order to assure itself an adequate supply of currencies under the agreement with Italy, the IMF activated the General Agreement to Borrow (GAB). This is a standing arrangement between the IMF and 11 major industrial countries, which allows the IMF to borrow up to SDR 6.6 billion in the participating countries' currencies. Further, the European Community (EC) gave approval on a $500 million line of credit to Italy. The extension of this line had been delayed, apparently contingent upon Italy's commitment to economic policies similar to those required by the IMF.

The U.S. Example

As the United States faced persistent and increasing payments deficits and as the dollar began to slide in 1977 in the foreign exchange markets, almost all of the topics of price competition (as through the balance of payments, sect. 2.2), controls and free trade on an international level, monopolistic practice (as in the cases of oil and coffee prices, sect. 2.4), and doctrinaire conflicts (as in the Keynesian and Friedmanesque views) introduced thus far appeared in the news media.

As figures 2-5 and 2-7 show, the dollar declined against the effective exchange rate index and against the Japanese yen, the German mark, the Swiss franc, and even the British pound. A factor was the growing oil imports by the U.S., but oil imports alone were by no means the principal cause (Mudd and Wood 1978). The improvements in the British position and the long-maligned British pound were traceable to revenues from the development of North Sea oil and natural gas reserves. These were to continue, and to be reinforced by the policies of Britain's Prime Minister Margaret Thatcher following her May 1979 election. For the first time in years, Britain was earning more abroad than it was spending, and its inflation rate was declining. In fact, the new oil fields in the North Sea and on the north slope of Alaska, and the discovery of major reserves in Mexico (along with the politics of Arab oil pricing) may well have contributed to the stable prices for oil and gas confronted by Americans in 1977 and 1978. The situation was much more complicated in relation to trade and competition with Japan and West Germany.

The reappearing topics of 1977-78 were still apparent in the 1979-80 period, after four years of the Carter Administration in the U.S.. The 1977-78 topics may be listed thus:

1. Confronted with the declining dollar, and desiring to lessen the role of the dollar as an international currency, the U.S. appeared hesitant to support the dollar through direct purchases in the foreign exchange markets. Japan and West Germany, however, had been supporting the dollar through currency purchases at year-end 1977. In some respects, they were the most adversely affected from a balance-of-trade point of view, because the declining dollar in relation to the yen and mark had meant higher dollar prices in the U.S. market, most visibly for German Volkswagens and Japanese Datsuns and Toyotas. Even Ford Motor Company's foreign-built Fiesta underwent a price increase after having been on sale for only four months.

In the first week of January 1978--against the above background and in combination with a failure to produce a comprehensive energy plan and uncertainties about a new Chairman at the Federal Reserve--there was the announcement that the Treasury and the Federal Reserve would take steps to protect the dollar. The immediate reaction was improvement in the performance of stock market prices and in the value of the dollar. Some saw the dollar support as purely a cosmetic action, and preferred that the dollar be left to float. One spokesman noted, "The reason we went off fixed exchange rates in the early 1970s was precisely because the market rate the Treasury wanted to maintain wasn't the rate the market thought was appropriate."

2. The initial hesitance to support the declining dollar had been referred to as a policy of benign neglect (good-natured, favorable for U.S. exports), but others began to see it as a policy of malign neglect (malicious and harmful) because the weaker dollar meant American goods were cheaper and

foreign products less competitive, in a contrived, financial sense. Said differently, the weaker dollar meant the U.S. was giving up more physical goods to get less. This was especially the case where the exchange did not reflect an improved value in the products exported, but a contrived value.

A mixed position encountered in the controversy surrounding fears of renewed inflation in the U.S. was that Germany and Japan should stimulate their economies more and improve world growth in output, and that under these conditions the dollar would look better. The difficulties encountered in this argument are twofold: (1) as addressed in section 17.4, the acceptance of a higher inflation rate may be nothing more than a temporary trade-off for increased output (and thus reduced unemployment), and (2) the question arises about what happens to the price of OPEC and Saudi Arabian oil when the inflation rate starts to rise in the U.S..

3. In the presence of a strong favorable trade position for Japan vis-à-vis the U.S., charges arose that Japanese steel manufacturers were dumping carbon steel plate on the U.S. market and thereby affecting employment and production in the U.S. steel industry (International Letter, Federal Reserve Bank of Chicago, October 7, December 8, and December 23, 1977). An unfair trade practice, "dumping" is traditionally defined as charging a lower price for an exported item in a foreign market than a similar item sells for in the exporter's domestic market. These accusations led to investigation and to a proposed system of "reference" prices for steel imports, which went into effect on January 1, 1978. The reference price for steel imports is based on the cost of production plus a margin for profit. The system subjects imports priced below the reference price to import duties by the importing countries.

Also, in early 1978, the U.S. negotiated trade concessions with Japan. These were to the effect that Japan would place export quotas on some of its goods entering the United States, and that it would import more from the United States.

2.6. Summary

In this chapter we consider special price indexes for competitive goods being exported by countries A and B, respectively:

$$P^{(A)} = w_1p_1 + w_2p_2 + w_3p_3 + \ldots + w_np_n$$

$$P^{(B)} = w_1p_1 + w_2p_2 + w_3p_3 + \ldots + w_np_n$$

Other price indexes for the respective countries may include (1) prices for some imported goods (as in the case of imported foodstuffs and automobiles stated in domestic currency prices under partially floating exchange rates) and (2) monopoly prices (such as the price of crude oil and other scarce natural resources). In the case of some of the lower-case p's, we recognize that some form of price competition can occur between the producers of competitive products in the respective countries. Good examples are foreign- and domestic-made automobiles, bicycles, motor bikes, and small electrical appliances. Next, looking at $P^{(A)}$ and $P^{(B)}$, we recognize the existence of another form of competition, exemplified by the competition for the total stock of monetary reserves held by countries A and B.

Under a system of fixed exchange rates, an initial position for $P^{(A)}$ in relation to $P^{(B)}$ may be denoted,

$$P^{(A)} - P^{(B)} + \text{constant} = 0.$$

After a rise in the price level $P^{(A)}$, however,

$$P^{(A)} - P^{(B)} + \text{constant} > 0$$

and imports of merchandise from country B increase. The imports by country A are debits in A's balance of payments. These must be met by credits to other accounts. The main ones we consider are (1) the capital accounts and/or (2) the monetary reserves. In the first case, country B buys the securities (stocks and bonds) representing ownership in or debt by country B's corporations. In the second case, country A loses monetary reserves. Under the older gold flow mechanism, country A's loss of reserves could affect its commercial bank reserves and thus exert downward pressure on its price level, while country B's gain in reserves would have the reverse effects in country B.

Considering again the price indexes $P^{(A)}$ and $P^{(B)}$, the separate prices in the respective countries and their price levels are related through the fixed exchange rate. At times this rate may be changed under administrative arrangements, where we would have a so-called adjustable pegged rate system of exchange rates. Here an increase in the price of B's currency (a decrease in A's) is a revaluation for B (devaluation for A), and consequently the effective prices for B's commodities in terms of A's currency are higher.

Under the system of fully flexible or floating exchange rates the entire adjustment to any balance of payments difficulty is in the exchange rate. This is in lieu of transfers of securities and/or monetary reserves. Rather, values change so that a country with a rising exchange rate simply gives up more goods and services in exchange for less. Consequently, there is no unemployment effect from the contraction of markets, but recessions of international dimensions may result as many countries pursue inflation simultaneously. This corresponds to the Phillips curve trade-off (sect. 17.1), but on an international scale.

Under floating rates any discipline from the competition for monetary reserves is, in effect, lost. Countries are free to pursue domestic policies concerning inflation and employment without regard to their effects on the balance of payments. This same sort of freedom from international considerations is obtained when there is a sort of collusion between countries, for example, where they agree to follow the same inflationary policies. The opportunity to take a particular doctrinaire stand, such as with Keynesian economics, comes in here.

In contrast to the prospects for such freedom, however, countries sometimes want the assurance of the terms of trade provided by a system of fixed exchange rates. Thus, most countries choose floating rates only as a temporary means of having a currency's nominal exchange rate value brought more in line with its actual value (where there is some prospect of maintaining a value). No major country wants its currency simply to float without some intervention, nor does it want its currency to continue undervalued in the market, as may result where speculation occurs in anticipation of inflationary monetary and fiscal policies. Eventually, large-scale intervention and the cooperation of others are needed to rectify the situation. Help may be forthcoming only with assurance of corrective domestic policies. Thus, old discipline of the fixed (peg) rate system is present in the mixed peg-float system, which emerged in the 1970s for the U.S. and its major trading partners. This mixed system of exchange rates also allows greater recourse to the use of fully fluctuating exchange rates.

The case of Arab oil pricing since 1973 illustrates some balance of payments phenomena that cannot be circumvented by floating exchange rates. Indeed, oil is priced directly. As a result of higher oil prices, domestic price levels are affected. When the U.S. imports a higher dollar volume of oil, it offsets this primarily by selling securities to the oil exporters, having them maintain deposits in the U.S. balance of international payments. As the dollar price of oil increases, the costs of energy and energy-related materials to U.S. manufacturers also increase. In terms of analysis surrounding the Marshallian cross, this means higher domestic prices for many products, and thus a source of inflation and the need for downward price adjustments in some products. This source of price level and adjustment problems is temporary, provided the oil price stabilizes. Its stability, however, depends on inflation rates and international relations extending beyond strict economic matters. The adverse flows in the balance of payments from the U.S. point of view, as just described, will continue in the presence of a constant dollar price of oil as long as oil imports remain at the given level.

The coffee episode of 1975-77 is another example of the pricing of natural resources on an international scale that had an impact on the domestic price level. Although the price impact is insignificant by comparison to the energy crisis, it nonetheless contains some speculative features and calls attention to price changes and possible shortages. These are related to the Marshallian cross, and to the otherwise static analysis where price is related to a quantity demanded by one arm of the cross and to a quantity supplied by the other arm.

FOOTNOTES

1. David Hume (1711-1776) gained immortality as a skeptical philosopher, some would say "as a philosophical empiricist," and for his contributions to economics. The latter appeared in the essays of Political Discourses (1752), especially it is said (Citibank 1979, 10), in those titled "Of Money" and "Of the Balance of Trade." His performance is described as impressive and as one "in which Hume 1) distinguishes between the short-run and the long-run impacts of an increase in the money stock on income, employment and prices; and 2) expounds the elements of the gold-flow, price-adjustment mechanism in international trade."
2. An example of the joint float has centered about a group of several European countries. The reference has been to the "snake" monetary arrangements, started in 1972. In early 1979, however, the earlier snake arrangements emerged as a new European Monetary System (EMS). At the outset, seven of the nine members were full participants. These included Belgium, Denmark, France, Germany, Ireland, Luxembourg, and the Netherlands. The other two members are Italy and the United Kingdom.

   The newer EMS system is a more comprehensive monetary system. There are a number of features to this newer system, as outlined in the International Letter (No. 391) of Federal Reserve Bank of Chicago, March 16, 1979. The motivation behind the EMS, however, has been the belief "that stable exchange rates between the member countries will encourage international trade and investment in Europe, as well as provide a step toward a common currency unit." Such stable exchange rates constitute a fixed exchange rate system and require the sort of support of currencies and discipline in dealing with inflation that has been associated with a larger international, fixed exchange rate system.
3. Correct interpretation of the standard balance of payments table (see, for example, table 2-1) requires some familiarity with balance of payments accounting. In addition, the particular categories in which transactions are arranged in the standard table under the concept of a balance may not be useful for some purposes; for example: the concept of an imbalance in trade would be meaningless under a system of fully floating exchange rates; investments by OPEC countries in the U.S. may lead to a desire to distinguish between "direct" and "portfolio" investments; and there may be special interest

in isolating those balance of payments changes that directly affect domestic monetary reserves (or the "monetary base" as defined in section 6.2). Consequently, a table of international transactions has evolved since the mid-1970s in which no balances are drawn, and in which some alternative categories of data are presented.

Such a table and explanatory notes are periodically reported by the Federal Reserve Bank of St. Louis in their publication, International Economic Conditions. The headings for which data are reported are as follows:

I. Merchandise Exports and Imports: the current dollar value of physical goods which are exported from and imported into the United States.

II. Service Exports and Imports: receipts of earnings on U.S. investments abroad and payments of earnings on foreign investments in the United States (interest, dividends and branch earnings), sales and purchases of military equipment, expenditures for U.S. military stations abroad, and payments and receipts associated with foreign travel and transportation.

III. Unilateral Transfers: private transfers representing gifs and similar payments by Americans to foreign residents and government transfers representing payments associated with foreign assistance programs.

IV. Direct Investment Abroad: capital transactions of U.S. enterprises with foreigners in which the U.S. residents by themselves or in affiliation with others own 10 percent or more of the voting securities or other ownership interests of a foreign enterprise.

V. Direct Investment in the U.S.: capital transactions of U.S. enterprises with foreign owners who control 25 percent or more of the voting securities or other ownership interests.

VI. Portfolio Investments: net transactions between U.S. and foreign residents in foreign and U.S. equities and debt securities, other than U.S. Treasury issues, with no contractual maturities or with maturities of more than one year; excludes transactions recorded as Direct Investments.

VII. Deposits Abroad (demand and time): a measure of claims on foreign banks reported by U.S. banks and large nonbanking concerns.

VIII. Deposits in U.S. (demand and time): a measure of the short-term liabilities to foreigners reported by U.S. banks.

IX. Monetary Base Effect: changes in the monetary base which are attributable to international transactions. Included are changes in the U.S. primary reserve assets (foreign currency balances) and foreign deposits at Federal Reserve Banks. Since deposits at Federal Reserve Banks enter the monetary base as a negative item, increases in these deposits decrease the bas and vice versa for decreases in these deposits.

4. Members were able to acquire 6.25 million ounces of gold in amounts proportional to their quotas at the official price of SDR 35.00 (about $40.40 at the December 1976 U.S. $/SDR rate). The SDR 35.00 figure reflects the value of the SDR as being equivalent to the value of the dollar at the time of the initial adoption of the SDR. The dollar price of gold for official purposes was $35.00 per ounce from 1934 until 1971.
5. OPEC was founded in 1960 to unify and coordinate petroleum policies of its members. The members, as of 1979, are Algeria, Ecuador, Gabon (associate member), Indonesia, Iran, Iraq, Kuwait, Libya, Nigeria, Qatar, Saudi Arabia, United Arab Empire, Venezuela. The man behind OPEC has been cited as Perez Alfonso, an unassuming oil economist.
6. The Saudi's main producing company is called Aramco (Arabian American Oil Co.). It accounted for an estimated 98 percent of Saudi Arabia's oil production in 1976. The company was founded and owned by four U.S. oil companies (Exxon, Texaco, Standard Oil of California and Mobil). However, the plan as of the mid-1970s has been for the four companies to continue to run Aramco, and for the Saudi government to completely own and control the company's assets.
7. A Btu is the quantity of heat required to raise the temperature of one pound of water one degree Fahrenheit at or near its maximum density.
9. Elasticity (η), the reader will recall, depends on the slope of the demand curve evaluated at point (p_o, q_o) on the curve. Stated differently, it is the percentage change in quantity called forth by a given percentage change in price, evaluated at a point <u>ceteris</u> <u>paribus</u>,

$$\eta = (\Delta q/q_o)/(\Delta p/p_o) = (\Delta q/\Delta p)/(p_o/q_o) \sim (dq/dp)/(p_o/q_o)$$

Demand is inelastic if $\eta < 1$, i.e., if almost no change in quantity is called forth by a change in price (a large change in the case of coffee).

9. Two sorts of efficiency are commonly recognized: economic efficiency and engineering efficiency. They are mentioned in chapter 15 where the roles of the economists and the engineer in relation to production functions are considered, and they are addressed by Duncan and Webb (1978, 3-14). Economic efficiency has to do with selecting production processes that are the most energy efficient (or that provide the most output for the energy input). The two sources of efficiency are not independent, however, in that high relative energy costs will likely stimulate new technology and hence greater energy efficiency. In the long run, plant and equipment will be engineered for greater efficiency, but even this new

technology may come only at a continuously higher price and as a result of using larger amounts of capital and labor. The presence of a new scarce factor causes us to reconsider (chap. 16) the old law of diminishing returns as it once applied to agriculture.

SELECTED READINGS AND REFERENCES

Adams, Richard K. 1980. "International Trade Flows Under Flexible Exchange Rates." Economic Review, Federal Reserve Bank of Kansas City (March).

Behravesh, Nariman. 1977. "The World Business Cycle: Is It Here To Stay," Business Review, Federal Reserve Bank of Philadelphia (September/ October).

Chase/Manhattan. 1974. "The New SDR." International Finance, The Chase Manhattan Bank's biweekly service (July 29).

Christelow, Dorothy B. 1980. "National Policies toward Foreign Direct Investment." Quarterly Review, Federal Reserve Bank of New York 4 (Winter): 21-32.

Citibank. 1977. "Brelton Woods: The Alamo of the 70s." Monthly Economic Letter, Economics Department, Citibank (January). This article is a review of the Coombs and Solomon books listed below.

Citibank. 1979. "David Hume: The Man of Independent Mind." Monthly Economic Letter, Economics Department, Citibank (February): 9-12.

Coombs, Charles A. 1977. The Arena of International Finance. New York: John Wiley & Sons.

Duncan, Marvin, and Kerry Webb. 1978. "Energy and American Agriculture," Economic Review, Federal Reserve Bank of Kansas City (April).

Francl, Terry. 1975. "Fertilizer Outlook," Business Condition, Federal Reserve Bank of Chicago (May).

Frazer, William. 1973. Crisis in Economic Theory. Gainesville, Fla: University of Florida Press. Chapter 18.

Friedman, Milton. 1953. "The Case for Flexible Exchange Rates." Essays in Positive Economics. Chicago, Illinois: University of Chicago Press.

Kruger, Rovert B. 1975. The United States and International Oil. New York: Praeger Publishers. Chapter 1.

Kuwayama, Patricia Hagen. 1975. "Measuring the United States Balance of Payments," Monthly Review, Federal Reserve Bank of New York (August).

Lee, Moon H. 1976. Purchasing Power Parity. New York: Marcel Dekker, Inc.

Mudd, Douglas R., and Geoffrey E. Wood. 1978. "Oil Imports and the Fall of the Dollar," Review, Federal Reserve Bank of St. Louis (August).

Pindych, Robert S. 1979. "The Cartelization of World Commodity Markets." American Economic Review (May).

Putnam, Bluford H., and D. Sykes Wilford, eds. 1980. The Monetary Approach to International Adjustment. New York: Praeger Publishers.

Rippenger, John. 1973. "Balance of Payments Deficits: Measurement and Interpretation," Review, Federal Reserve Bank of St. Louis (November).

San Francisco Federal Reserve. 1977. "Banking in the World Economy." Economic Review, Federal Reserve Bank of San Francisco (Fall).

Solomon, Robert, The International Monetary System, 1945-1976, An Insider's View. New York: Harper & Row, 1977.

Chapter 3

Analysis, National Income and Other Data

3.1. Introduction

Thus far money and prices have been introduced with both domestic and foreign dimensions. Money was introduced as a way of reckoning, as a means of coping with uncertainty about economic magnitudes and with foreseen and unforeseen events. The existence of money makes possible an economic system of m-1 prices, and permits the construction of price indexes. These indexes provide a means of proceeding from a consideration of the separate markets comprising the economy to a consideration of the overall behavior of the economy. Indeed, price averages in one country vis-à-vis another were shown in chapter 2 to concern price competition for shares of international trade and for the distribution of international monetary reserves, with some qualifications. The extent of the modification was said to depend upon the degree of reliance upon floating exchange rates and economic doctrine broadly viewed. Economic doctrine underlying domestic economic policies was also said to be relevant.

The economic theory prevailing in the public's mind--especially in the minds of the public's elected representatives--in textbooks, and in the minds of the legions of economists in and out of government was introduced as being relevant to a consideration of national economic policies and, through them, to one country's economic position relative to another. A satisfactory and reasonably valid economic theory may also be thought of as contributing to an understanding of the behavior of the economy and to the capacity to forecast--and in some measure to control--the behavior of that economy.

In the not-too-distant past, as we show in later chapters, economic theory has influenced the nation's responses to economic problems, including unemployment, inflation, simultaneous unemployment and inflation, instability, and incentives and disincentives to work. Economic theory too has changed, and not just through the replacement of one doctrine for another. There is an apparent evolutionary quality and empirical study has come to make a difference. In any case, an understanding of government policies, and economic theory itself, is aided by a consideration of some recent developments with respect to economic theory, and its influence in Washington, D.C.

Proceeding along these lines, chapter 4 sets forth a number of the attributes of classes of economic theory. These are labeled as Keynes's economics, Keynesian economics, monetarist economics (as identified with Milton Friedman in large measure), and empirical economics. The monetarist economics is said to have been advanced by virture of its empirical orientation, which lent itself to modern computer techniques (Frazer 1973).

As a point of fact, some aspects of all of the foregoing bodies of economics are synthesized in any reasonably valid theory of the real world, as judged by results from analyses of data and observations. The fourth category above, "empirical economics," is suggested as that body of economics that emerges when empirical criteria are introduced into the judgmental process with respect to whether one or another attribute of a theory is the most valid, the most relevant in explaining the real world.

The empirical orientation gives rise to the theme of expectations, forecasting, and control. Forecasters in modern times as considered in chapter 13, have had some such orientation. We encounter the concept of "rational expectations," also in modern times, as elucidated in chapter 14. It is forecasting ("the formation of expectations") on the basis of the best economic theory. The "best" is that which is the most valid, the most useful in prediction, the theory with the most stable relationships ("parameters"). In some measure, in an ever-changing ("evolving") world, the values for these parameters must always be viewed with uncertainty, as we attempt to introduce presently and demonstrate later (chs. 13, 14, and 17).

To arrive at these larger goals (a body of an empirically oriented economic theory with attention to the formation of expectations, forecasting and control), this chapter starts with introductory aspects of Keynes's economics and its related mechanics. Almost immediately, however, these introductory aspects are extended as a means of anticipating the larger goals of the present study. For example, output adjustments and the measurement and behavior of total output are considered as we touch upon secular time frames, disequilibrium states, time rates of change, and turning points in business conditions.

Keynes's Basic Model

Keynes's basic model centers on the choice of households to spend on consumption or in some measure to refrain from doing so. The act of refraining results in savings and provides a source of funds for capital expenditures. Income, saving, and investment are flows, but all give rise to accumulated amounts or stocks. The flow of income (Y), when discounted by the appropriate rate of interest (i) is wealth (W), namely W = Y/i. Counterparts to these stock and flow magnitudes at the firm level are assets and net sales (or income net of all costs but the cost of funds). In any case, the economic agents (households or firms) are confronted with spending decisions (ranking preferences) and with the management of accumulated amounts (primarily savings in the case of households and assets in the case of firms).

These situations depicting economic decision making are encountered as household consumption subject to an income constraint, and as portfolio management subject to a wealth (or asset) constraint. Both are introduced in this chapter, with some attention to assets classes as fixed or contractual claim assets (such as money and bonds) and as residual claim assets (including real capital, and equities such as those traded on the organized securities exchanges). In this context, money balances and liquidity are given special dimensions for further consideration. The classification of assets and other introductory topics presented in this chapter provide some background necessary for the discussion of classes of economic theory in chapter 4, and for the more in depth consideration of the demand for money and money control in chapters 5 and 6.

As stated, Keynes's basic model brings us to the flow of saving into investment and to financial "intermediation," the process by which financial institutions link both savers and investors. Keynes himself did not get into all of this, and certainly Keynesian economists (as defined in chapter 4) did not, but there is a basis in work since Keynes's time for considering these matters. The introduction of financial flows here enables us to integrate the "real" and financial sectors of the economy in later chapters.

Output in Nominal and Real Terms

The arithmetic of the GNP deflator was said earlier (sect. 1.4) to facilitate a discussion of output in real terms. Furthermore, in the consideration of money, there was the prospect that shifts in the demand for money in relation to income could cause instability in spending and possibly in prices and output. In the Marshallian cross context (figures 1-1 and 2-5), a stronger demand for money translates into downward shifts in the demand schedules for the various product markets and hence into less production (q_1, q_2, . . ., q). In the context of Keynes's theory, with product prices sticky in the downward direction and with money wage units constant, unemployment bears the main brunt of adjustment in response to the stronger demand for money as output declines. Keynes's theory stresses aggregation, however, as in the GNP accounts introduced in this chapter. As we shall see, there are the problems of double counting when aggregating over the product markets and of adding diverse, heterogenous units (such as apples and oranges) that comprise current output. At best, as we proceed from a consideration of the separate markets for the output to the behavior of the overall economy, we have the measure of total output and an index of quantities in the various separate markets.[1]

A special concern in this chapter is focused upon the accounting for total production and the introduction of concepts subsequently bearing on its analysis (including rates of change, logarithmic transformations of data, financial intermediation, the choice between saving and investment, and the classification of assets) and the closely related analysis of employment and the roles of money. Quite specifically the ultimate goals are twofold: (1) to provide an explanation of observed instability in the domestic economy and (2) to present an introduction to the control of that economy via monetary and fiscal policies, with the view to achieving the national economic goals (namely, maximum employment, production, and stable purchasing power).

These goals have been translated to mean that the overall national economic goal is the stabilization of the economy about some optimal sustainable growth path for real output. For example, maximum employment and production are usually taken to mean levels that are sustainable for some period of time, and not simply extreme values temporarily achievable at the price of less than sustainable values in other periods. The purchasing power goal is usually taken to mean a stable and constant price level. So what we have, on the domestic side, are maximum employment and growth in real physical production consistent with price stability--goals that certainly would lead to a favorable balance of international payments on the foreign side, as considered in chapter 2. There is the possibility envisioned in some portions of theory of trading off a little on the attainment of one goal for attainment in another. This trade-off is discussed in later chapters.

Output and Instability

As can be seen in figure 3-1, the time path for total output varies about an upward-sloping trend line. This may possibly be called permanent output, or quasi-permanent output in that the trend line itself may vary. In the figure there are overall trend line and three for shorter, separate periods. These respective lines are defined thus:

(1) overall period, 1954:I through 1974:IV

$$\ln Q = 1.79 + 0.035t, \quad r^2 = 0.98$$
$$(64.93)$$

(2) subperiod 1954:I through 1960:IV

$$\ln Q = 1.82 + 0.027t, \quad r^2 = 0.95$$
$$(15.73)$$

(3) subperiod 1961:I through 1970:IV

$$\ln Q = 2.02 + 0.042t, \quad r^2 = 0.97$$
$$(34.33)$$

(4) subperiod 1971:I through 1975:IV

$$\ln Q = 2.42 + 0.0185t, \quad r^2 = 0.45$$
$$(3.814)$$

(values in parentheses are *t* statistics)

where ln denotes the natural logarithm, data before transformation are quarterly data for GNP per annum in 1972 prices, r^2 is the unadjusted coefficient of determination, and where t is time (t = 0.00, 0.25, 0.50, 0.75, 1.00, ..., n years).

The difference between the time paths for total output and the trend line reflects instability. This is overall for a 22-year period, in the one case, and for the separate time periods of 7, 10, and 5 years respectively. The more precise measures, and those allowing for secular shifts, are those for the shorter periods. The particular way of transforming the data yields average growth rates in output for the respective periods and linear time paths, rather than the exponential or upward-sweeping paths that we will examine later. In the present cases, where the data for annual rates of change were analyzed quarterly, the growth rates as percent per annum are 3.5 (or 0.035 x 100), 2.7 (or 0.027 x 100), 4.2 (or 0.042 x 100), and 1.85 (or 0.0185 x 100).

We seek on various occasions some explanations for both the instability in the shorter time frames, and for the separate and distinct shifts in the underlying time paths themselves. In the former case we will encounter especially changes that are repetitive (that reoccur) over time, and in the former and especially the latter cases we will encounter some changes that are non-repetivie over time. These distinctions between the shorter and longer time frames are partly with the view to understanding the possible use of government spending to eliminate the instability in the shorter time periods, and partly with the view to understanding other possible control measures as they may affect the secular shifts. The shorter run goal, from a policy point of view, would be to merge the fluctuations into the trend lines. We seek guidance from economic theory in doing this.

Figure 3-1 also shows independent measures of turning points in business conditions, and hence recessionary and expansionary phases (peaks, the beginning of such shaded area, and troughs, the ending of each shaded area). These turning points are computed and reported by a national non-profit organization, and this reporting is largely independent of the specific output measures shown in figure 3-1.

The values on the vertical axis in figure 3-1 are natural logarithms. As such, changes measured on the axis reflect percentage changes denoted $(\Delta Q/Q)$ 100, where Q is the output for one time period and ΔQ the increment in output over the previous time period.[2] The continuous counterpart to the ratio measure $\Delta Q/Q$ is $(1/Q)/(dQ/dt)$, $d \ln Q$ (100) is a percentage change and $d \ln Q \cong \Delta Q/Q$.

A similar construction to that in figure 3-1 can be shown with the nontransformed data plotted against a ratio scale on the vertical axis, as is quite common in economics. This presentation is possible because of the special growth property of much economic data and because the natural logarithms and the incremental ratios interchange, with both handling the growth property.

The time path characteristics underlying growth may change, as we have indicated. If growth in the United States changes measurably--e.g., because of the energy crisis (Rasche and Tatom 1977), or because the natural rate of unemployment (as defined later) is higher than what it was in the 1950s and 1960s--then the trend line may take on a smaller slope at a given point in time. (A smaller slope is a slower rate of growth, and a larger slope is a faster rate.)

The overall trend line in figure 3-1 is for the period 1954:I through 1975:IV. However, if one envisions the line that is obtained for the output series for 1954:I through 1960:IV, then one detects a slower trend of growth; whereas, for 1961:I through 1970:IV, one detects a faster trend rate of growth, and so on. The trend rate from the peak of business conditions in 1975 to some future peak in business conditions for another decade may be expected to reflect the emergence of shortages in natural resources (and oil in particular), as well as the continuous entry of women into the labor force. An oil shortage would contribute to a smaller slope in the trend line for output, while the entry of women would contribute to a higher slope, as far as total production is concerned (as distinct from productivity per employed member of the labor force, section 17.2). On the subject of women entrants, declining growth in productivity, and the inflation rate, following the 1973-75 recession, Irwin Kellner of New York's Manufacturer's Hanover Trust (Economic Report, February 1980) proceeds thus:

> The percentage of women in the labor force has gone up from 47 to 52 per cent, while the percentage of teenagers in the labor force has risen to 60 per cent from 55 per cent. By contrast, the percentage of

Figure 3-1
The Trend
of Output

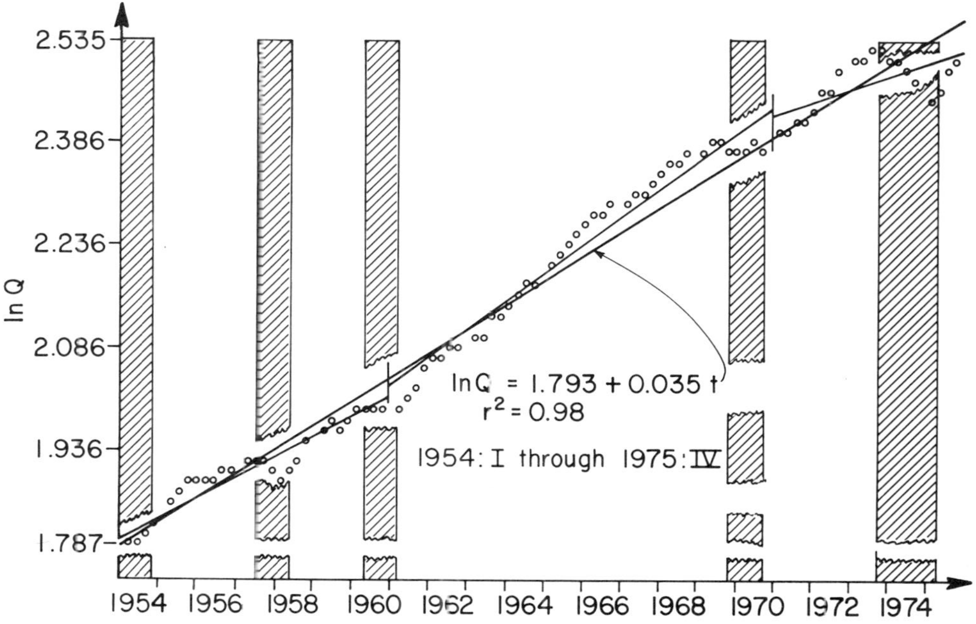

Note: The shaded areas are recessions as identified by turning points reported by the National Bureau of Economic Research. The National Bureau's turning points for the post-World War II years are November 1948 (peak), October 1949 (trough), July 1953 (peak), August 1954 (trough), July 1975 (peak), April 1958 (trough), May 1960 (peak), February 1961 (trough), November 1969 (peak), November 1970 (trough), November 1973 (peak), and March 1975 (trough). In addition to these there is the widely recognized mini-recession of 1966-67.

Ln Q denotes the logarithmic transformation of GNP per annum in 1972 prices. The data are quarterly.

> men in the labor force has held constant at about 80 per cent. Plainly, these numbers mean that the average family now has at least two people working, if not more.
>
> The point I am making here is that many families in the United States have undergone a significant change in their life-styles. What else can you call it when both husband and wife work (and maybe teenage son or daughter as well)? I would bet that the decisions for these additional family members to seek and obtain work were not taken lightly. I would also guess that, in many cases, they were made with an eye towards obtaining an extra luxury: a new car, major appliance, vacation, etc. But it seems to me that, in view of the average family's inability ot keep pace with inflation ..., what may have started out as an option is now a necessity.
>
> How much longer this can go on is anybody's guess. At the moment there are close to 60 million people over the age of 16 who are not in the labor force but could be. I would guess that many of them may well decide to consider looking for work, if inflation doesn't cool off soon.

Rates of change in GNP in real terms can also be presented and the sets of estimates one may use at different times are not always the same. For example, since the 1950s sets of data are available that rely upon 1958 and 1972 prices respectively. Revised 1972 estimates were released in early 1976. The revisions do not alter our reading of the overall picture (and indeed the respective series behave in the same way), but the revised estimates do incorporate into GNP data some notable features.[3]

The Income Accounts and Keynes's Work

The national income accounts that provide the GNP data were in their infancy in 1936 when Keynes wrote his revolutionary work, The General Theory of Employment, Interest and Money (1936). Professor Simon Kuznets, who in 1971 would receive the Nobel prize for his work in this accounting area, had done only pioneering work (Kuznets 1937, 1938, 1941). It was not until the late 1930s and during World War II that official estimates of national income were developed in the U.S. Department of Commerce. As these estimates became available they shed light on Keynes's work, and Keynes's work, on them.

Keynes's theory, as introduced further in chapter 7, is called a general theory of employment because it encompassed the less-than-full employment state (a state varying with production) and viewed the economic theory before 1936 as dealing only with the case of full employment. (In the overall tradition before Keynes, prices were assumed to adjust downward to restore full employment in the presence of inadequate demand.) Keynes's theory was also concerned with instability --changes in output and employment, and shifts in the demand for money--and with the control of instability. His theory, however, was not a theory of business conditions themselves, or the "trade cycle," to use the British term.

In the absence of income accounting, Keynes's measure of income was in terms of the wage bill (a product of labor units, as a measure of employment, and wage units, as a measure of the money wage of a labor unit, in constant prices). In working with wage units--as the 1972 Nobel Laureate Sir John Hicks stresses--Keynes was influenced by the British experience. With some perturbations aside, the situation in Britain in Keynes's day and through most of the 1920s was one of sticky real wages and, one might add, an extremely static state. Movement in the price level was roughly paralleled by movement in money wages, resulting in sticky real wages.

In view of the parallel movement in prices and wages, Keynes's wage bill would seem to stress covariation in labor units (employment) and output. Prices did not seem to matter very much. Viewed in terms of modern GNP, output--GNP measured in constant prices--and employment changed. However, given Keynes's accounting system, sticky real wages did not mean an absence of price changes, as often claimed and taught, but rather parallel movement in money wages and in the price level (Fellner 1976, 27-32).

As time passed and as GNP estimates became available, they facilitated a discussion of Keynes's work, and the two illuminated each other. Keynes's concepts of saving and investment and equilibrium in the aggregate demand for and supply of goods were compatible with the accounting concepts. However, the Federal Reserve's flow-of-funds accounts, which also helped to illuminate the role of financial intermediaries in expediting the flow of saving into investment were not available until the late 1950s; specifications for nonfinancial corporate sources and uses of funds and balance sheets were not incorporated in large forecasting models until the mid 1970s (Eckstein 1978, 192-194).

To obtain a measure of income roughly equivalent to Keynes's income concept, several aspects of the measure were of basic importance. For example, apples and oranges were being combined to obtain an aggregate measure in real terms, whereas, as we know, these cannot be added; expressed in terms of the monetary unit, however, their values can be added. In addition, it was important to avoid double counting, as where goods may be counted as a part of the production process (steel or fabrics, for example) and as a part of the final product (say, automobiles), exclusive of intermediate goods.

The income accounts are indeed complicated. Introductory texts devote chapters and appendices to them (Samuelson 1976) and books are written on the subject (Powelson 1960).

We will not focus on such detail, but will consider certain broad features that stand out in relation to the discussions of the 1970s. For one, the accounts purport to measure the total output of goods and services, yet they exclude the services of housewives. This is because such services are difficult to value. But if the housewife becomes a fashion model, a masseuse, or a cook in a local restaurant, her contribution then becomes a part of the output of goods and services. This suggests issues about the taxation of income for working couples vis-à-vis couples with only one spouse employed outside the home in that the implicit income from the services of the homekeeper, masseuse, and so on go untaxed (sect. 11.3). In addition, the failure to treat the services of the housewife becomes potentially troublesome from an analytical point of view, mainly when the number of women (or their male counterparts) entering the labor force as taxpayers changes in relative importance.

Another issue surrounding GNP is that of economic growth. We are concerned especially with GNP as a measure of instability and growth in this and later chapters. Since the industrial revolution, the assumption has been that GNP increases over time as labor and productivity grow, although it may be influenced by trends in the social and political setting and by the ready availability of natural resources. Even with zero growth in the labor force, productivity is expected to increase because of technological changes, especially as a result of scientific innovation and improvements in the tools at the disposal of workers (sect. 15.2). However, shortages in natural resources, as in the case of the energy crisis of 1973, may influence the trend rate of growth measurably in the years ahead and alter prospects for the living and housing conditions for the average family. The shortages may influence growth in several ways, as later chapters will indicate in more detail. For one thing, as we move from readily available sources of energy, such as oil, to other sources requiring more labor units and other costs, such as natural gas from water hyacinths, then the final product per labor unit declines (as elucidated in sections 15.4 and 16.1).[4] For another thing, the shortages put upward pressure on prices (as in sect. 2.4), induce some inflation and possibly destabilizing speculation in real and financial assets, and otherwise complicate the policy goal of attaining economic stability (as elucidated in chaps. 16 and 17).

Given the setting of society, politics, and natural resources, positive economic growth must occur along with the employment of a given labor force. The growth issue as a social one is separate from this concept. It is concerned with the separate matters of population growth and the forms real output assume--whether in providing medical and educational services, or in meeting the basic material needs of life.

The income accounts and the flow-of-funds accounts are introduced further in this chapter along with basic Keynesian concepts. Related questions of aggregation arise as we further introduce the consumption function, and income (sales), wealth (assets), and substitution effects. Numerous sources of national income data, in addition to those presented already, are introduced as the book proceeds. Although the accounting techniques underlying measures of the money supply are integral to its measurement, they are outside the scope of this book. The interested reader is encouraged to review some of the references at the end of this chapter.

3.2. Keynes's Basic Model and Some Additional Definitions and Concepts

Keynes's basic model and the national accounts tracing the flow of income and the flow of funds through financial intermediaries and between the various sectors of the economy are interrelated. First, both of the accounting systems are based on identities, and, conceptually, data for the many entries can be presented in both systems as either stocks or flows. Second, the stocks or quantities in existence may be thought of as functions of time, and changes in the quantities thus become flows or rates of change with respect to time at a moment in time. These flows, then, can be combined by addition and netted by subtraction until data are obtained that correspond to some crucial variables in the basic model.

The fundamental accounting identity (assets equal liabilities plus capital accounts) is one such identity, on which algebraic operations of addition (subtraction), multiplication (division), and removal (or insertion) of parentheses may be performed. This means that the separate accounts relating to two sides of the balance sheet may be regrouped in various ways so as to permit an expression of one item in terms of all the others. Balance sheets, furthermore, record stocks or a historically accumulated amount up to some moment in time. Changes in such accounts from one period to the next are flows. The income generated by the stock of assets is also a flow and changes may occur in the flow too.

Actually, we have no accounting of national wealth, although it is thought of as generating the GNP (a flow concept). The discounted value of GNP (GNP divided by the interest rate) is total wealth. Milton Friedman, the revolutionary in economics in the 1960s, uses such an approach, and we develop it later in the book. He makes the distinction between human and nonhuman, distinguishing primarily between the discounted value of wages and salaries, on the one hand, and the discounted value of real capital, on the other. The counterpart to wealth at the firm level would be total assets, and a counterpart to GNP would be sales.

The Basic Model

The basic model comprises two equations and a behavioral postulate. The two equations are:

$$Y_d = C(Y) + I, \; 0 < dC/dY < 1 \qquad (3.1)$$

$$Y = C(Y) + S(Y) \qquad (3.2)$$

where

Y_d = aggregate demand
$C(Y)$ = consumption (C) as some function of income (Y)
I = the flow of investment (I = constant),
Y = the aggregate of payments received as income for current output (or supply)
$S(Y)$ = saving (S) as some function of income

The postulate is as follows:

> As the flow of income changes, consumption changes directly by a smaller amount, i.e., $0 < dC/dY < 1$.

Given the postulate, the slope implied by equation (3.1) is less than one, and, by the rule for a derivative with respect to itself (i.e., $dY/dY = 1$), the slope implied by equation (3.2) is one. Clearly, a solution exists, and this condition may be represented at a moment in time as either of the following:

$$Y_d = Y \qquad (3.3)$$

$$I_{constant} = S \qquad (3.4)$$

Now, let us note some features of this model.

1. The postulate has an empirical counterpart. We consider it in this chapter and later as an empirical law.
2. The constants of an equation defining the consumption function may shift. The hypothesis $dC/dY < 1$ holds in the *ceteris paribus* sense, in which other changes are impounded.
3. The expenditures represented by the right-hand member of equation (3.1) may be broken down into various subclasses. This may be done, for example, in order to permit a special consideration of government expenditures and foreign expenditures for the net export of goods and services, or to permit a consideration of expenditures by the various sectors of the economy. Similarly, the right-hand member of equation (3.2) could be presented so as to reflect saving by the various sectors or groups. In later chapters we consider separately the nonfinancial business sector, the consumer sector, and the public sector.

The National Income Accounts

The national income accounts are reported by the U. S. Department of Commerce. In them, the gross national product represents the total of expenditures for consumption, government, and private investment in real capital, as well as foreign expenditures for the net exports of goods and services.[5] The total of these expenditures may also be shown in terms of goods (durable and nondurable) and services. The total expenditures are sometimes called aggregate demand (Y_d). In the same accounts, the gross national product can be variously computed as the value of all the factor services rendered for the goods and services produced. This income generated for the factors of production is sometimes called aggregate income (Y), and it may be stated in both current and constant prices. The data for these payments are published in different forms, such as wages, salaries, interest, rent, and profits, and as gross income originating in manufacturing, agriculture, and so on. As one may say, the demand and supply sides of GNP are basically the same physical quantity measured in two different senses. In effect, there exists a double-entry bookkeeping system in which the total of expenditures is (except for certain nonincome charges) identical to the income generated. This we summarize, along with the several ways of viewing income generated, in table 3.1.

The Flow of Funds

The flow-of-funds accounts are reported by the Board of Governors of the Federal Reserve System. These accounts record both the financial and nonfinancial aspects of transactions, whereas the national income accounts indicate the flow of the current output of goods and services and its distribution in the form of consumption and investment. The Board of Governors' accounts show sources and uses of funds for current transactions, as well as provide estimates of outstanding amounts of assets and liabilities. The accounts are comprehensive and show a standard classification of all transactions for five major sectors in the economy and for subsectors of these major sectors. The major classification consists of (1) the consumer and nonprofit sectors, (2) the nonfinancial business sectors, (3) the government sectors, (4) the financial institutions sectors, and (5) the rest of the world sector. The nonfinancial business sectors are further classified as farm, noncorporate, and corporate sectors. The government sectors are further divided into Federal, state, and local government sectors.

Each transaction is viewed in effect, as being recorded on a balance sheet for the parties or sectors to the two sides of a transaction. Each payment by one unit is also a receipt of another: for the payment something is received, and for the receipt something is given up. In terms of the fundamental accounting identity above, there are four entries to every transaction: a debit and a credit to both of the units involved in the transaction. As one may gather, a credit, whether to an asset or a liability account, is a source of funds, whereas a debit, whether to an asset or a liability account, is a use of funds.[6] Hence, the terms "sources" and "uses" with reference to funds and the fundamental accounting identity carry over to an identity between sources and uses of funds.

What, then, are funds, and what are flows in the present context? Funds are simply accounting entries. They correspond to our employment of the unit of account or monetary unit encountered earlier whereby one reckons wealth and calculates credits and debits. The notion of funds is broader than that of money: funds are money only when bookkeeping entries involve the cash account and demand deposits of the commercial banking system. A flow of funds, then, is a rate of change in any account at a moment in time, whereas the historic accumulation of such flows constitutes a stock (or assets and liabilities).

The value of the sources of funds is always identical to the value of the uses of funds. Nevertheless, one can deal with particular groups of accounts, such as those for financial assets including inventories, plant, and equipment. Such examination can reveal the flows from the financial markets into the expansion of real capital assets, as well as the flows between different sectors. It is thus possible to determine where the funds arise and where they go.

Table 3-1. The Demand and Supply Sides of GNP

Demand			Supply		
Expenditures for:	or	Expenditures for:	Gross income in the forms of:	or	Gross income originating in:
Consumption		Goods output final sales	Wages and salaries		Agriculture
Investment (including additions to inventories)		Inventory change Construction	Profits, interest, and rent		Mining
Government		Services	Capital consumption allowances		Manufacturing
Next exports of goods and services			Sales and other indirect taxes		Trade, finance, insurance real estate, transportation, etc.
Aggregate Demand		Aggregate Demand	Aggregate Supply		Aggregate Supply

Source: U.S. Department of Commerce.

The Flows of Expenditures, Income, and Funds

The aggregate of expenditures recorded in the national income accounts may be classified as consumption and investment. These expenditures may also include the services of the financial institutions sectors. The consumption expenditures may be interpreted to include purchases for private consumption and purchases for public consumption (or government expenditures). Investment may be interpreted to mean effective expenditures for increases in inventory items, fixed capital goods, and the net export of goods and services. The precise classification may be arranged to accommodate a particular analysis.

In this context, the portion of the aggregate income not consumed is, by definition, saving. In the national income identity, then, all counterparts correspond to equations (3.3) and (3.4), although saving and investment in the model are performed by different behavioral units. The portion of household income not spent on consumption flows into insurance and other forms of institutionalized saving. Capital outlays, on the other hand, are primarily made by business units, and require some funds to be obtained outside the units. In order to obtain funds externally, deficits are incurred. Financial claims or assets come into existence to represent these deficits in the form of bank notes, debt instruments, or shares of stock and the like. The extent of such financing is indicated by the sum of the deficits incurred by spending units.

In a world where there is a separate identity between savers and investors, intermediaries have arisen to expedite the flows of portions of income into expenditures. In 1800, insurance companies were in their infancy, only a few commercial banks were in operation, and other present-day financial intermediaries were nonexistent. After 1850, however, the assets of insurance companies increased on an average of 6.7 percent a year. Banks, too, continued to grow, but after 1900 the assets of nonbanking institutions, such as life insurance companies, mutual savings banks, and savings and loan associations (S&Ls), grew somewhat more rapidly. The advantaged offered by financial intermediaries is that, in terms of the separate behavioral units, the units (i.e., the savers and investors) need not always formulate complementary plans and act upon them at precisely the same time. Imbalances between aggregate demand and aggregate supply, or between saving and investment, occur. These imbalances give rise to changes in income and prices, and financial intermediaries play a crucial role.

In fact, when selected intermediaries are receiving a contracted portion of income (for example, when households and others slow the flow of saving directed toward them), bank newsletters and the press have come to refer to the process of disintermediation. It is likely to occur as the economy expands at an excessive rate, and when market interest rates (or, more specifically, rates on government securities and commercial paper) rise above regulated rates on time deposits at commercial banks and on share accounts at S&Ls.[7] The reverse process, intermediation, occurs when savings shift back to the selected intermediaries, as they often do in a recession.

The notion of partial flows of income through financial intermediaries is shown schematically in figure 3-2, along with the classification of total spending on the one side and an allocation of income received on the other. The class of spending labeled "net export of goods and services" is of secondary importance in the evolving analysis of aggregate demand, as far as the United States is concerned. For one reason, its share is small in relation to the total and, for another, the important aspects of the U.S. economy in its open setting concern mainly the bank reserve equation in chapter 6, the concept of an international system imposing some constraint on domestic matters, and the analysis of shortages (particularly, of natural resources).

In figure 3-2 a time slice or a view of the flows at an instant in time is depicted, namely:

$$\lim_{\Delta t \to 0} \frac{\Delta(\text{gnp})}{\Delta t} = \frac{d(\text{gnp})}{dt} = \text{GNP}$$

where gnp is a previously accumulated stock of gross national product, and GNP is the flow or gross national product per annum at a moment in time. Moving clockwise from the top right of the figure, flows are shown as payments to the factors of production. Part of the income received by the factors of production flows directly into consumption and investment outlays without external financing and part into savings in the form of insurance payments, the purchase of savings and loan shares, funds extended to investment banks, bank time deposits, and others. The institutions receiving these funds provide them to expenditure units that are in need of external

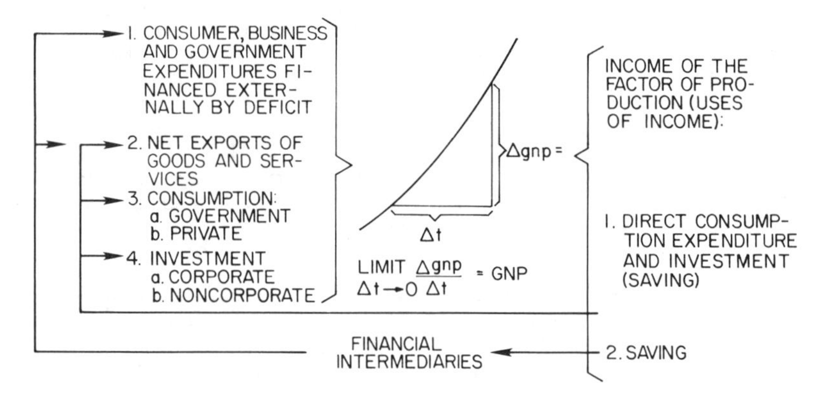

Figure 3-2. The Circular Flow of Funds

financing. These financial institutions have an intermediate position between savers, on the one hand, and investors and consumers financing externally, on the other. The monetary system, however, must be included as a special case in this context because of its capacity to expand the supply of credit (and thus add to the volume of expenditures financed externally) and contract the supply (and thus effect a contraction of the expenditures financed externally). The role of the monetary system in effecting a balance or imbalance between the output of goods and servies and aggregate expenditures becomes of central importance in later chapters.

Imbalances in Supply-Demand Relationships

The two types of imbalances referred to thus far give rise to valuation changes. The imbalance between the aggregate supply and the aggregate demand for goods and services gives rise to changes in the average of prices for current output. These were introduced in chapter 1 and receive more intensive consideration later.

Friedman and his supporters in of the 1960s made special use of this sort of adjustment in dealing with money and prices and imbalances in "desired" and "actual" money balances. The imbalance could correct itself quickly, through pulling prices and/or output upward until the amount of balances held was the amount desired in relation to nominal income. The other imbalance--the imbalance between the supply of funds and the demand for funds--gives rise to changes in the prices of financial instruments and consequently, in interest rates. These changes will also receive further consideration in later chapters.

An Overall View

What we have introduced so far is an enormously complicated view. On the one side, there are accumulated amounts comprising wealth (W), and a flow of returns from this wealth (Y), with the flow being viewed both as total spending (E) and as a payment (Y, $Y = PQ$) for the constant output (Q) of goods and services. On the other, there is the flow of saving (S) into investment (I) in part through financial intermediaries, with assets representing accumulations from past saving, and with the financing of capital spending (investment) by business firms. In the first case, wealth is related to income by a factor i, namely $W = Y/i$; in the second case, there are analytical notions concerning the choice between saving and investment and, more particularly, the classes within which assets may be held.

The development of this complicated view has had a varied history since Keynes's major work in 1936. At times, complicated monetary and financial trappings for the simple physical processes of consumption and investment have been recognized and, at the other times, they have been overlooked for the sake of simplicity (often a desirable goal). Keynesians of the 1950s and 1960s, as distinguished in chapter 4, overlooked the complexities. The result was devastating for the assessments of the impact of a variety of government policies. In contrast, our goal here is to create an awareness of the complexity and interrelatedness of the matters at hand. Thus we proceed immediately to introduce the more complex monetary and financial issues, although an elaboration of them awaits later chapters.

One way of anticipating where this approach leads is to consider the meaning of two latin terms--*ceteris paribus* (other things being equal) and *mutatis mutandis* (let those things change that do in fact change). An impoundment of the financial trapping in *ceteris paribus* would simplify the discussion considerably, but by admitting other things, even if only in an introductory way, we encourage the vision of a complex, interrelated system, from the outset. Otherwise the vision may elude the unawary.

3.3. Income, Wealth, and Substitution Effects

Proceeding with aspects of Keynes's basic model--with the flow of income and wealth as the discounted value of income--we encounter decisions: first, with respect to the distribution of income between saving and consumption and, second, with respect to the "portfolio" (assets and wealth). Proceeding further, we recognize that these decisions are made at the agent (or household) level and thus introduce the need for aggregation. In particular, for consumption and income, as in Keynes's simple consumption function, we have

$$C = c_1 + c_2 + \ldots + c_n \quad \underline{\text{and}} \quad Y = y_1 + y_2 + \ldots + y_n$$

after the elimination of double counting. However, each individual's consumption is a function of his own income. So, as aggregate income changes, the distribution of income among individuals may change, and this distribution may itself influence consumption. Consequently, in addition to having introduced financial institutions and the prospect of spending more than income, as we introduce aggregation, we now make a simplifying assumption: As income changes, any effects from changes in the distribution of income are of secondary importance to the influence of the income changes on consumption.

A Utility Function (with an Income Constraint)

As stated, in the aggregate the discounted value of income (Y) is wealth (W); at the agent level, wealth ($\underline{w}$) is also equal to the flow of income ($\underline{y}$) discounted by the appropriate rate of interest ($\underline{i}$). In the latter case, moreover, the agent (household, firm, or other behavioral unit) exercises

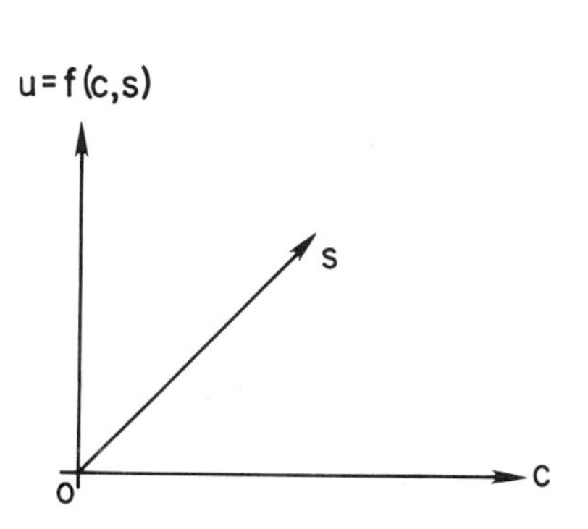

Figure 3-3a. Three Dimensional Utility Space

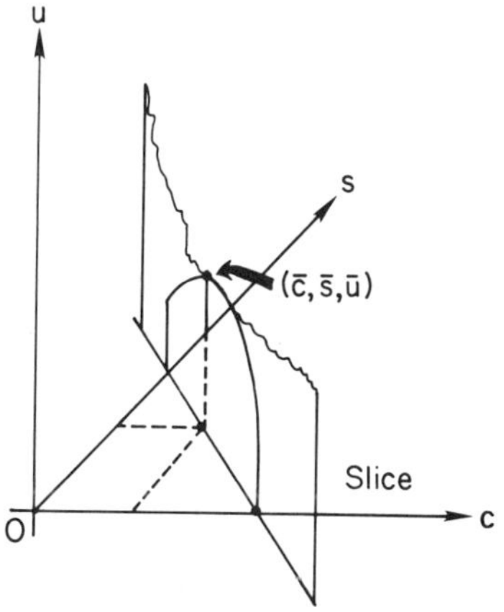

u
s
$(\bar{c}, \bar{s}, \bar{u})$
Slice
O
c

Figure 3-3b. A Slice Through Utility Surface: A Constant Income

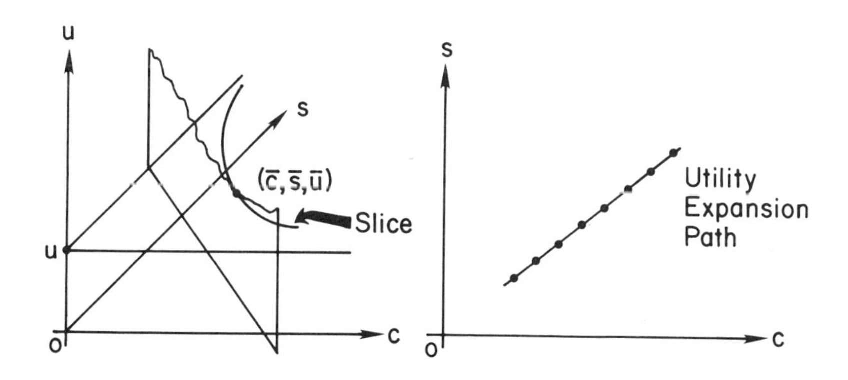

Figure 3-3c. A Slice Through the Utility Surface: A Constant Utility

Figure 3-3d. Combination's of Consumption and Saving at Different Income Levels.

preferences in disposing of income in exchange for various commodities.[8] Income (y) in this context is a constraint on the expenditures for the commodities. Preferences are usually considered in pairs. The first pair we consider consists of consumption and saving, where the general dollar amounts are denoted c and s respectively.

Framing the art of decision making in these terms permits a representation of it in the three dimensional space of figure 3-3a and figure 3-3b, with coordinate axes for the variables c and s and for the function f(c,s).[9] The function is a surface that rolls out from the origin (O) of the 3-space coordinate system, and rises as it rolls out, but also drops off toward the c and s axes. It is left imaginary for the present, but some surfaces are shown later in the appendix to chapter 9.

The constraint, or income plane, in the present case is readily drawn. If all income were spent on consumption, one would have a point on the c axis, and if all income were saved, one would have a point on the s axis. A line would then go through these points as in figure 3-3b. The maximum utility subject to the constraint is the highest point on the slice. The coordinates of this point may be denoted (c, s, u).

If u is viewed as a fixed value, a plane cuts the u axis parallel to the (c, s) coordinate plane, and then makes another slice through the utility surface, as in figure 3-3c. Again, the highest point on the surface and in the constraint plane is the point (c, s, u). But this new slice is a contour and represents a constant elevation or an indifference curve (that is, a slice through points along the utility surface where the behavioral unit--the consumer or household--is indifferent about exchanging some consumption for some saving, and vice versa).

If the constraint plane varies, as when income varies, then a locus of points (c, s, u) on the surface is obtained. All this movement may be projected downward onto the floor or (c, s) coordinate plane of the three dimensional figure. This projection on the floor is shown in figure 3-3d, as the utility expansion path. It is a locus of combinations of consumption and saving yielding the highest utilities at different income levels.

The utility u is actually the utility of income (y) in the present case, because of the way we define saving ($s = y - c$). The utility of income is discussed in the appendix to chapter 6 and in chapter 11.

Utility Flows and Equilibrium (with a Wealth Constraint)

As stated earlier, when funds flow in (income), they may be allocated to consumption expenditures or to assets, such as capital goods (inventories, plants, and equipment) or financial instruments and trappings (money balances and noncash financial holdings such as government bonds and negotiable time certificates of deposit). Liabilities may be affected too, as in the case of bank loans and other outstanding debt (mortgages or bonds). Indeed, in the case of nonfinancial corporations the issuance of capital stock may provide an additional source of funds if retained earnings and the write-off of depreciation are not sufficient for the desired capital expansion. In the case of major firms, these stocks are most often those being traded on the organized securities exchanges, especially the New York Stock Exchange.

For the present, let us consider mainly assets, the allocation of funds, and utility. In this case, we wish to think of the allocation of some funds to the various asset classes, where the optimal allocation occurs when the various utilities (pecuniary and/or psychic returns) derived from the additions to the various classes are equal for each additional dollar of spending. Where these ratios of marginal utility to the last dollar spent are viewed as interest rates (where psychic premiums are introduced along with the pecuniary rate), a criterion that emerges is that the flows of returns from assets are maximum when the rates of return on additions to each class are equal.

A tangible representation of this allocative analysis for wealth (or total assets) may proceed with the classification of assets as fixed and residual claim. The formulation in question gives rise to statements with the Lagrangian function, as in footnote 9, and in the appendix to chapter 9. Again the decision involves ranking and exercising preferences, only this time in the form of the management of assets.

Using the asset constraint and recognizing of two classes of total assets (A)--fixed and residual claims (denoted A_F and A_R for units of the assets such as one bond or one share)--the Lagrangian function (L) may be denoted:

$$L\,(A_F, A_R, r) = f\,(A_F, A_R) + r[g(A_F, A_R) - A]$$

where the function $g(A_F, A_R) = A$ and $A = A_F\,P_{AF} + A_R\,P_{AR}$, where r is the Lagrangian factor of proportionality, and where P_{AF} and P_{AR} are the prices of the asset units. Now to proceed with obtaining equilibrium conditions, the Lagrangian function is differentiated, first with respect to A_F, then with respect to A_R, and finally with respect to r. Each derivative is then set equal to zero, and the following conditions for an extreme value are obtained:

$$\frac{\partial L}{\partial A_F} = \frac{\partial f}{\partial A_F} - rP_{AF} = 0$$

$$\frac{\partial L}{\partial A_R} = \frac{\partial f}{\partial A_R} - rP_{AR} = 0$$

$$\frac{\partial L}{\partial r} = g(A_F, A_R) - A_F\,P_{AF} - A_R\,P_{AR} = 0$$

Rearranging the first two equations comprising the conditions yields:

$$\frac{\partial f}{\partial A_F} = r \, P_{AF}$$

$$\frac{\partial f}{\partial A_R} = r \, P_{AR}$$

Dividing the equations by the respective prices results in equivalent ratios:

$$\frac{\frac{\partial f}{\partial A_F}}{P_{AF}} = \frac{\frac{\partial f}{\partial A_R}}{P_{AR}} = r$$

This is another way of stating the first order conditions for a maximum, since the utility surface in question is said to increase.

In words, the utility from the assets is maximized when the ratios of the marginal (extra) utilities to their respective supply prices are equal. As it turns out these ratios are also equal to the Lagrangian factor of proportionality. In this remarkable case, the factor is the rate of return or interest rate on the assets.

Utility is rather broadly construed and its flow may consist of dollar amounts from the assets or intangible rewards such as security and convenience obtained from holding them. In the narrow sense of dollar amounts we may think of a fixed claim asset such as a bond or note

$$\text{Value} = \frac{R_1}{(1+r)^1} + \frac{R_2}{(1+r)^2} + \ldots + \frac{R_n}{(1+r)^n}$$

where R is the annual flow or dollar return expressed in a contract (the bond certificate). If such a bond is of long maturity (say as $n \to \infty$ or thirty years), then:

$$\text{Value} = \frac{R}{r}$$

Rearranging terms

$$\frac{R}{\text{Value}} = r$$

This is precisely the result obtained with the Lagrangian function, except the returns are narrowly construed to be only dollars. Note that if the value of the bonds is less, the rate of return is higher. This might suggest the substitution of bonds for other assets until the price of bonds rises and the rate of return declines to the equilibrium position (the first order conditions).

By broadly defining utility to encompass such subjective and intangible matters as security and convenience, we lay the groundwork for dealing with liquidity and uncertainty. At the same time, by being specific about the dollar flows as in the case of the bond, we note that elements of the broad notion may be pinned down precisely and that a concrete reality is close at hand. The concreteness is a part of something broader.

If we align the assets on a balance sheet in the order of their increasing dollar returns and decreasing liquidity, a sketch such as the following may be obtained:

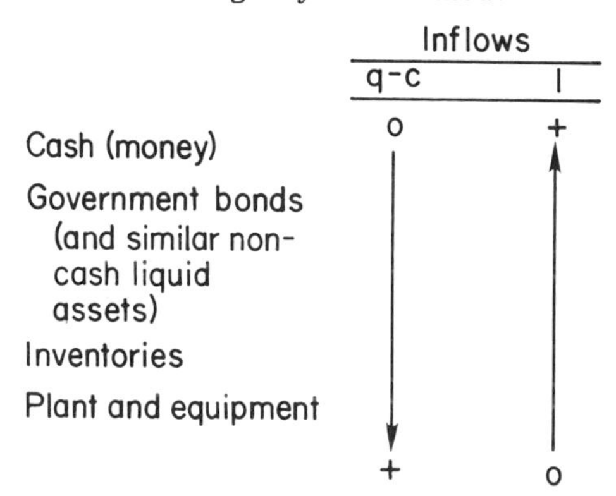

Here (q - c), yield less carrying cost, denotes the tangible or dollar component making up the rate of return, while l denotes the liquidity (security and convenience) and hence an intangible component.

Substitution Effects

The foregoing topics are counterparts to the optimal allocation of income to the consumption budget as introduced with the neoclassical theory in chapter 1. The main difference is simply that income is the constraint to the maximization of utility in the one case and total assets or wealth is the constraint in the other.

In thinking of the traditional neoclassical allocation, we encounter substitution effects that result from the price change of one item in relation to the other in those cases where the goods are substitutes for one another. Commodities that do not compete or substitute are either complementary or bear no relation to one another. A commonly cited example of complementary goods is beer and pretzels. The substitution effects, in any case, are among those easiest to predict in economics, except for some complications mentioned below. For example, at the time of initial, widespread recognition the energy crisis, the Wall Street Journal (December 6, 1973) noted a possible rise in the cost of electricity and thus in the price of electric lighting. This led them to anticipate some substitution effects, for example:

Products that promise to save energy stand to benefit. "Sales of our energy saving bulbs have tripled in the last week or so," says G. Raymond McFruther, president of Duro-Test Corp., a North Bergen, N.J., light-bulb maker.

Apex Aluminum Sales Co., New York, says its storm-window sales are running five times last year's level.

Substitution effects can also be thought of in terms of classes of assets. Consider the two broad classes with subclasses:

I	Fixed, contactual claim assets (so-called monetary assets)	(1) Money balances (2) Noncash liquid assets such as government bonds
II	Residual claim assets (so-called nonmonetary assets)	(1) Common stocks (2) Plant and equipment (or real goods generally)

The first class is fixed dollar claims against future income. If dollar prices on goods and services rise, the purchasing power of the future income is diminished. After the fulfillment of this first class of claims the rest of future income goes to residual claims. For example, think of income (Y) and the product of the average of prices (P) and the current output (Q), (Y = PQ). Now, if the price level increases, less real income can be claimed as a result of cashing in on fixed claims.

In the anticipation of price inflation, economic entities such as firms and households may anticipate a loss of purchasing power from fixed claim assets and an increase in the value of other assets. This might lead to marginal adjustments out of money balances and bonds in relation to income or total assets. This would also result in a rise in the turnover of money balances in relation to the current output of goods and services, that is, it would result in a rise in income velocity of money, Y/M. Some institutions such as banks, moreover, are restricted by law from holding as a part of their securities portfolio anything but debt instruments (loans, mortgages, bonds), so in the presence of an expected loss in purchasing power they may simply increase the interest rates they charge on loans.

Two examples of substitution effects related to changes in the interest rate immediately come to mind:

1. the substitution of bonds for money holdings (in relation to income or total assets) as interest rates on the bonds increase,

2. the substitution of short-term bonds for long-term bonds as the yield on the short-dated instruments exceeds that on the long-dated instruments.

However, complications arise concerning the alleged substitution effect of the interest rate change. The first complication is this: things other than adjustments from cash holdings to bonds may cause the turnover of money and interest rates to rise. The second complication is the liquidity hedging motive. This motive for holding assets manifests itself in the selection of assets of a certain time to maturity such that the repayment or maturity date coincides with some future need for funds. This motive may override any substitution effect from changes in the yields on short-dated relative to long-dated securities.

In presenting the foregoing complications, we have illustrated an aspect of the speculative demand for money and purchasing power risk. In chapter 5 we encounter these concepts again, as we introduce and bring into question the Keynesian model with money, which is a two-asset (money and bond) model with interest rates. The substitution of bonds for money as interest rates rise is a crucial ingredient in this model.

3.4. Summary

Key points in this chapter may be summarized as follows:

1. The stock of wealth (human and non-human) generates a flow of income, which may also be viewed as current output. At the level of the individual behavioral units receiving this income, the income may be viewed narrowly as simply a dollar flow, or broadly as also including convenience, security, and psychic elements. In this broader sense the flow is maximized when the rates of return (also broadly reviewed) on additions to the various classes of assets are equal.

2. The income received by the separate behavioral units may be allocated to consumption. What is not consumed during the present period is called saving. Both are functions of income. The choice between allocating income to consumption or saving may be viewed in a relatively unembellished utility framework, and an expansion path depicting the allocation may be shown as income increases for a single behavioral unit.

3. Keynes offered an aggregate consumption function that represented, as he said, a fundamental psychological law. The law amounted to the prospect that "men are disposed, as a rule and on the average, to increase their consumption as their income increases, but not so much as the increase in their income." Cross-section data from household budget studies have shown a consistency with the simple consumption function. A constancy in the saving to income ratio over time calls for a more dynamic theory, such as presented in chapter 9.

4. Several sorts of analytical problems emerge as we move from the expansion path of the binary relation for an unembellished utility analysis to behavioral laws about consumption and Keynes's aggregate consumption function. For one, there are financial trappings. As income declines consumption may decline, but at a less than proportionate rate. In the extreme case there may be dissaving, which is facilitated by the drawing down of previously accumulated savings. For another, at the level of individual consumption, each unit's consumption is a function of its own income, but as income increases generally, the distribution among individuals may change, influencing spending (e.g., the distribution may shift from rich to poor or vice versa). Thus, as aggregate income changes, the distribution of income is of secondary importance to the effect of the aggregate income on consumption spending.

5. The assumption associated with the slope of the consumption function is of immense importance to the basic aggregate spending building block. It assures an intersection (a solution) for the aggregate income--aggregate spending relationships elucidated in chapter 7. The first is assumed to have a slope of one, the second a slope of less than one; hence, an intersection.

6. In national income accounting, the total income received is equal to the total spent. The two are simply different sides of the same transactions. We have an accounting identity in contrast to the solution following from an assumption about behavioral relationships.

7. The act of saving by households is separate from that of spending on capital goods by business firms. The flow of funds from the household to the business sector is expedited by financial intermediaries, so called because of their intermediate position. Financial instruments and markets arise in this context, as do the concepts of financial intermediation and disintermediation.

8. Aggregate output in real terms may be expected to grow at a constant level of employment. The increased productivity results mainly from technological improvements in the tools and organization of production.

9. The growth in aggregate output may be depicted by a trend or growth path. Movements in output about this path may occur as the growth of total spending and the level of employment change. These movements are related to peaks and troughs in business conditions. One objective of stabilization policy, as we shall observe later, is to eliminate the fluctuations in output about its trend path.

10. The growth path for output and variations about it suggest that income (simply another way to view output) is constantly changing, contrary to the assumption of the elementary expenditure model, which is static, yielding a solution for income at a level (Y). Thus, we have an ambiguity that must be resolved by introducing differential rates of spending (aggregate demand), equilibrium growth paths, and a dynamic role for the simple consumption function and investment spending.

FOOTNOTES

1. By analogy to the wholesale price index of section 1.4, a quantity index (Q_I) could be denoted,

$$Q_I = \frac{\sum_{i=1}^{n} p_i^o q_i^t}{\sum_{i=1}^{n} p_i^o q_i^o} 100$$

where p^o_i is the price of the ith quantity in the base period, q^o_i is the quantity produced in the base period, and q^t_i is the quantity produced in the current period.

2. The rate of change is computed thus:

$$\frac{Q_t - Q_{t-1}}{Q_{t-1}} \approx \frac{1}{Q} \cdot \frac{dQ}{dt}$$

where differentials (dQ, and dt) express continuous (not simply discrete) change and provide the standard notation for a time rate of change. To convert to an annual percentage rate from a computation using quarterly data, we multiply the quarterly changes by four:

$$\frac{Q_t - Q_{t-1}}{Q_{t-1}} \times 4 \times 100$$

The continuous time rate of change actually follows from differentiation. For example, where quantity is a function of time, Q(t),

$$\frac{d[1n\ Q(t)]}{dt} = \frac{1}{Q} \cdot \frac{dQ}{dt}$$

by logarithmic differentiation and the composite function rule. If dt = 1, then the rate of change is dQ/Q.

3. These features are listed by the Federal Reserve Bank of New York, Monthly Review, February 1976. First, the revisions include the regular updating of the estimates for 1972 to 1974 that was postponed until July 1975. Second, they incorporate new "bench-mark" information based on a

number of recent censuses. Third, the new estimates reflect numerous definitional and classificational changes. The most important is the new estimate of economic depreciation which is designed to measure the loss in productive services of the existing capital stock, valued in both current-dollar and constant-dollar terms. Previously, the current estimates of depreciation in the national income accounts had been based on allowable depreciation charges as defined by the United States tax code and tabulated by the Internal Revenue Service from business tax returns. As a result, these estimates were affected anytime the tax code was changed, and they were valued on a historical cost basis, i.e., in terms of the prices of the capital goods prevailing at the time they were purchased. Fourth, improvements were made in certain statistical surveys of inventory accounting methods used by businesses in estimating inventories. Fifth, the base for the constant-dollar estimates of GNP was updated from 1958 to 1972, and additional information has been used to improve the constant-dollar estimates of construction, producers' purchases of durables equipment, and government purchases of goods and services.

4. Water hyacinths are primarily found in the southern part of the United States. They can plug otherwise navigable waterways, but they have the desirable properties of extracting and storing chemicals from polluted water at a fast rate and of being convertible to methane, a natural gas.

5. Gross domestic product (GDP) is still another measure obtained from the national income assets accounts. It is the result of adjusting GNP for the net flow of income coming into or going outside of the United States. The idea is to obtain a special measure of output from factors of production owned by U.S. citizens, including factors located, say, outside of the United States.

   The distinction between GNP and GDP was of no special importance for the United States before 1974 because of the relative insigificance of foreign investment compared to total U.S. production and because the two measures moved together anyway. The GDP series was first released by the Department of Commerce in August 1974 to coincide with the growing importance of U.S. investment abroad, and especially the investment in the U.S. of the "petroleum exporting countries." Much additional wealth began accuring to the Arab oil producing countries in 1974, following the fourfold increase in the dollar price of oil described in sections 2.4 and 15.4. Further, as this wealth on the part of oil producers continues to grow and as the so-called petro-dollars get recycled in the United States, the GDP measure may take on more significance. The recycling of these dollars takes the form of bank deposits and the purchase of land, stocks, and bonds (including U.S. government bonds). As the earnings from these sources increase, the flow of income out of the United States will increase. This is conjecture, however, and for the post World War II years through 1980 we will continue to stress GNP as a key measure.

6. Stated differently, any increase (decrease) in a liability account is a source (use of funds), and any increase (decrease) is an asset account is a use (source) of funds.

7. One such account (Eleanor Erdevig, "1974 Disintermediation--District Impact," Business Conditions, Federal Reserve Bank of Chicago, February 1975) is introduced thus: "The distortions in savings flows that result when high market interest rates attract funds away from financial intermediaries has become a familiar phenomenon. In late 1966 and again throughout 1969, time and savings deposits left commercial banks and thrift institutions only to return at a record-breaking pace when interest rates subsequently dropped. Early in 1973 efforts to restrain excessive credit expansion in the face of accelerating business credit demands again drove market interest rates to levels that threatened disintermediation. To allow more effective competition for funds, the regulatory authorities modified the rules relating to time and savings deposits. Ceiling rates were suspended on large denomination time deposits ($100,000 or more) and were raised on smaller deposits and longer maturities. Although these changes did not prevent disintermediation in the summer of 1973 and for several months during 1974, they undoubtedly reduced its magnitude and facilitated a quicker reversal of the process."

8. A commodity is defined in the formal presentation of utility analysis as something the agent prefer more of rather than less.

9. All of this could be framed in terms of the Lagrangian function (sects. 8.3 and 17.6, and appendixes to chaps. 9 and 16), as stated later for total assets but for one complication, namely: c and s have been defined as dollar amounts. To use the function in its traditional way and to generate a statement of first-order conditions at the same time, c and s would have to be treated as products of prices and their corresponding quantities in physical units. Without attempting any statement of first-order conditions, the Lagrangian function could be written:

$$L(c,s,\lambda) = f(c,s) + \lambda[y - c - s]$$

where $f(c,s)$ is the function to be maximized, where the constraint is income ($y = c + s$), and where λ is the Lagrangian factor of proportionality.

SELECTED READINGS AND REFERENCES

Eckstein, Otto. 1978. The Great Recession, Data Resources Series, Vol. 3. New York: North-Holland Publishing Company.

Fellner, William. 1976. Towards a Reconstruction of Macroeconomics: Problems of Theory and Policy. Washington, D.C.: American Enterprise for Public Policy Research.

Frazer, William. 1973. Crisis in Economic Theory: A Study of Monetary Policy, Analysis, and Economic Goals. Gainesville, Fla.: University of Florida Press.

__________, and William P. Yohe. 1966. Introduction to the Analytics and Institutions of Money and Banking. Princeton, N.J.: D.Van Nostrand Company, Inc. Chapter 10.

Hicks, John R. 1974. The Crisis in Keynesian Economics. New York: McGraw-Hill Book Company, Inc.

Introduction. 1975. Introduction of the Flow of Funds. (Washington, D.C.: Board of Governors of the Federal Reserve System.

Kuznets, Simon. 1937. National Income and Capital Formaton, 1919-1935: A Prelimary Report. New York: National Bureau of Economic Research.

_________. 1938. Commodity Flow and Capital Formation, Volume I. New York: National Bureau of Economic Research.

_________. 1941. National Income and Its Composition, 1919-1938, two volumes. New York: National Bureau of Economic Research.

Powelson, John P. 1960. National Income and Flow-of-Funds Analysis. New York: McGraw-Hill Book Company, Inc.

Rasche, Robert H., and John A. Tatom. 1977. "Energy Resources and Potential GNP." Review, Federal Reserve Bank of St. Louis (June).

Samuelson, Paul A. 1976. Economics, tenth edition. New York: McGraw-Hill Book Company. Appendix to Chapter 10.

von Furstenberg, George M. 1977. "Flow-of-Funds Analysis and the Economic Outlook." Annals of Economic and Social Measurement (Winter).

Part II

Theoretical Classifications and Monetary Matters

Chapter 4

Keynes's, Keynesian and Monetarist Economics : An Overview

4.1. Introduction

Some recent history of economic theory is a way of presenting the economics of the recent past in a perspective and of introducing numerous topics that are treated in later chapters. Since the early impact of Keynes's General Theory (1936), a convention in any such chronological arrangement has been to treat Keynes's work as a watershed and to contrast it and various interpretations of it with the earlier economics. This objective was in part to reveal the changes that had occurred, to indicate what was new, and thereby to put the more recent work in perspective. This and the next chapter have a similar objective and thus offer a classificatory arrangement of theories within the areas of macroeconomics and money, albeit with special attention to the economics of Keynes and of the post-World War II years. The various bodies of theory that have come forward in this extended period are compared and their attributes are listed. This approach, which is partly in keeping with convention, was selected with the view to simplifying matters later. The next chapter enlarges on some of the topics of the present chapter and, in addition, introduces attributes of the economics thought popular at the time Keynes was writing his General Theory. Keynes called this economics "classical." Others have called it "neo-classical," using "classical" in reference to works appearing much earlier.

This overview of economic theory addresses itself particularly to the impact of the theory on worldly affairs and to its empirical relevance. In fact, the unifying theme for the various topics in this book is that of public policy--forecasting, economic behavior, and control of economic behavior--with the view to achieving national economic goals. Keynes had a similar interest in public policy, as have numerous economists before and since. His General Theory was in large measure a response to the unemployment of the 1930s, the government's failure to control it, and the inadequacies of existing theory in explaining it.

As viewed by Milton Friedman (1953), and others the search in positive economics--the economics of the real world as distinct from some ethical system--is for empirically relevant theory, theory that is consistent in its logic and with observed facts. Indeed, the strong prospect for such a body of economics becomes most viable in the presence of the modern computer for two reasons: first, the computer permitted analyses of more data in more ways, and at considerably lower costs than was ever dreamt possible before; and, second, the presence of the computer made more difficult the avoidance of the challenge that a main corpus of the body of economic theory should be empirically oriented as well as logical. (Frazer 1973) There were numerous players in this drama, but a chief proponent was Milton Friedman with the view that economic theory should serve as a source of fruitful empirical hypotheses and with his work on monetary history and theory and on the consumption function (Friedman 1963; app. to chap. 1, chap. 9, and app. to chap. 16). In addition the actual solution and estimation of parameters for large scale models, with special attention to forecasting (chap. 13), became possible during the initial computer era, designated as approximately the 1960s in the United States.

A crisis in theory occurs under the initial impact of the computer, one might say, symbolized by the incongruencies between the results from analyses of economic data and prevailing theory (Frazer 1973, Hicks 1974). As will be revealed later, the inflationary recessions occurring in 1969-70 and 1973-75 were a dramatic manifestation of the misdirection of policy brought about by bad economic theory. Some new economic theory emerging in the 1960s was advanced to the forefront by such failures of the received economics and by the attention of emerging economics to empirical data.

The classes of theory that are considered here are Keynes's, Keynesian, monetarist, and empirical economics. An additional class, "Cambridge theory," could be added to call attention to the work of some economists (Joan Robinson in particular) with early ties to Keynes and his Cambridge University. Their work has centered on economic problems of monopoly, income distribution, and capital accumulation (Frazer 1976, 1977; Kregel 1976), and has stressed, for the most part, what some call the model of "stationary equilibrium." Although we forego its consideration as a separate body, we will introduce pertinent aspects of it in our discussions of monopoly and income distribution.

The attributes of Keynes's, Keynesian, monetarist, and empirical economics, which are discussed in the present and following chapters, are summarized in table 4-1. The simple listing of attributes leaves much to be explained, so a full understanding of the theories under consideration is not sought in this chapter. The nuances of the theories suggested by table 4-1 and discussed below should serve to introduce the theories, and to elevate the awareness of the complexities involved in the evaluation of positive economic theory. Attention could be given to only the main distinguishing features--say attributes 2, 3, 4, 7, 12, 14, 16, 18, 20, 21, 24, 27, 29, 30, 36, 37-41, 44, 48-53, and 55-58, in table 4-1--and to vagaries and hair splitting to provide added detail. To facilitate this the symbols used in the cells of the matrix are X for a strong emphasis on an attribute, 0 for almost no attention to it, and Ø for some attention to it. The column heads in table 4-1 look beyond chapter 4 and toward much of the text that follows.

4.2. Keynes's Economics

In this text, "Keynes's economics" refers to what Keynes actually said in his works--mainly, A Treatise on Money (1930), and The General Theory (1936) and related papers.[1] Here we rely on various authors, but the distinction between Keynes's work and that of Keynesians is drawn by Leijonhufvud (1968). He suggests that in the hands of American economists who interpreted and studied Keynes's work, a special sort of economics emerged. This parochial view has been labeled "Keynesian." It refers to special attributes of a popular textbook presentation that centered on the income expenditure model and its summary form, the IS-LM model (discussed beginning in chap. 7).

The General Theory appeared in the sixth year of the Great Depression and in the fifty-third year of Keynes's life. Attributes of the economics associated with it may be listed as follows:

1. Keynes perceived of economic theory in terms of its implications for policy purposes. This suggests an interest in the empirical orientation of the theory, in contrast with the existing orientation toward an economic tradition with roots in mechanics. The mechanical approach to knowledge stressed an almost purely deductive approach, a timeless state, and a reversibility of the logical system. It has been characterized by what may be called a Marshallian cross (figure 1-1) in the theory of relative prices and the somewhat related Keynesian crosses of Keynesian economics.

Georgescu-Roegen (1975, 347-48) has described the mechanical tradition of neoclassical economics as follows:

> The greatest ambition of these pioneers was to build an economic science after the model of mechanics--in the words of W. Stanley Jevons --as "the mechanics of utility and self interest." Like most every scholar and philosopher of the first half of the nineteenth century, they were fascinated by the spectacular successes of the

Table 4-1. A Matrix of Attributes

Attributes	Keynes's econ. Col. 1	Keynes-ian econ. Col. 2	Monetar-ist econ. Col. 3	Empirical economics Col. 4
1. Policy implications of a theory, as distinct from simply a mechanical structure	X	Ø	X	X
2. Output adjust ments (sticky prices)	X	X	0	X
3. Price level adjustments	0	0	X	Ø
4. Phillips curve with trade-off irrespective of the state of business conditions	0	X	0	0
5. Phillips curve as covariation in employment and inflation rates rates over the short cycle	0	0	X	X
6. General theory, possible equilibrium at less than full employment	X	X	0	Ø
7. Partial equilibrium, and general equilibrium in the sense of equilbrium in more than one market or sector.	X	X	Ø	Ø
8. Equilibrium as an expotential time path	0	0	X	X
9. Natural rate of unemployment	0	0	X	X

	con't Col. 1	con't Col. 2	con't Col. 3	con't Col. 4
10. Short run, period of constant expectations	X	X	0	0
11. Short run, period of zero time dimension (or with allowances for abstraction from noise)	0	0	0	X
12. Long run, as secular time frame	0	0	X	X
13. Goal of stabilizing the short cycle (trade cycle in Britain), with or without recognition of cyclical time frame	X	X	X	X
14. Disequilibrium, demand price equal to or less than supply price (alternatively, rate of return equal to or less than rate of interest), inequality of foresight	X	X	Ø	Ø
15. Disequilibrium state, shifting liquidity preference demand for money	X	Ø	X	X
16. Disequilibrium (imbalances in "desired" and "actual" money balances)	0	0	X	X
17. Difference of opinion version of liquidity preference	Ø	X	Ø	Ø
18. Pull toward normality version of liquidity preference	X	0	Ø	X

	con't Col. 1	con't Col. 2	con't Col. 3	con't Col. 4
19. Changes in levels in stock and flow quantities (i.e., exclusive of the interest rate, the velocity ratio, and the price level)	X	X	0	0
20. Changes in time rate of change in stock and flow quantities	0	0	X	X
21. Attention to precautionary and speculative motives for holding money	X	0	X	X
22. Announcement effects of policy changes, as under House Concurrent Resolution 133, and ideological shifts, as in political administrations	0	0	0	X
23. The effects of persuasion techniques from the area of social psychology as they may be employed by the President of the United States in the case of the veto, tax and expenditure measures, and by the Chairman of the Board of Governors of the Federal Reserve System in the case of macroeconomic policy generally	0	0	0	X
24. Linkage mechanism for monetary policy, $\Delta M \rightarrow -\Delta i \rightarrow \Delta I$, where i is controlled by central bank	X	X	0	0

	con't Col. 1	con't Col. 2	con't Col. 3	con't Col. 4
25. Weak link, $\Delta M \rightarrow -\Delta i$, due to lack of will by monetary authority	X	0	0	0
26. Weak link, $\Delta M \rightarrow -\Delta i$, due to liquidity trap	Ø	X	0	0
27. Control, $\Delta M \rightarrow -\Delta i$, through open market operations (Δi, a sale, and $-\Delta i$, a purchase)	X	X	X	0
28. Control, $\Delta M \rightarrow -\Delta i$, with trading at the short end of the Treasury's yield curve	X	Ø	Ø	0
29. Inverse variation in i and home construction	0	X	0	X
30. Linkage mechanism $\Delta\dot{M} \rightarrow \Delta\dot{Y} \rightarrow \Delta i$	0	0	X	Ø
31. Interest rate indicator of business conditions, plus attention to inflation rate component	0	0	X	X
32. Easy money ($-\Delta i$), and tight money (Δi)	Ø	X	0	Ø
33. Easy money ($\Delta\dot{M}$), and tight money ($-\Delta\dot{M}$)	Ø	0	X	X

	con't Col. 1	con't Col. 2	con't Col. 3	con't Col. 4
34. Interest induced wealth effect, $-\Delta i \rightarrow \Delta W$, with _ceteras paribus_	X	X	Ø	Ø
35. Interest induced wealth effect, but with _mutatis mutandis_	0	0	Ø	X
36. Money multiplier	0	0	X	Ø
37. Investment multiplier	X	X	0	Ø
38. Emphasis on fiscal policy	X	X	0	Ø
39. Emphasis on monetary policy	Ø	0	X	X
40. Money and finance sectors, including attention to the "crowding out" effect of defict financing	X	0	X	X
41. Two asset model (money and bonds)	X	X	Ø	Ø
42. Four asset model--fixed claim (money and bonds) and residual claim (real capital and equities)	0	0	Ø	X
43. Distinction between human and non-human capital	0	0	X	Ø
44. IS-LM model	0	X	Ø	Ø

	con't Col. 1	con't Col. 2	con't Col. 3	con't Col. 4
45. Structural equations (large scalc models) with emphasis on relative frequency theory of probability	0	X	0	Ø
46. Search for regularity in the data, with reliance upon independent evidence	Ø	0	X	X
47. Simple consumption function, C = f(Y) 0 < dC/dY < 1	X	X	0	Ø
48. Consumption as a function of permanent income (a dynamic case)	0	0	X	X
49. Volatile capital ("autonomous") spending, as source of instability	X	X	0	Ø
50. Faulty governmental policies as source of instability	0	0	X	Ø
51. Control over aggregate demand at a point in time, irrespective of the state of business conditions	Ø	X	0	0
52. Control over aggregate demand within a larger, cyclical time frame	Ø	0	Ø	X
53. Theory of a open economy	0	0	X	X
54. Demand management, and demand side theory of output	X	X	0	Ø

	con't Col. 1	con't Col. 2	con't Col. 3	con't Col. 4
55. Attention to the rationality of expectations with distinction between the "pure" and "general" models	0	0	0	X
56. Forecasting with uncertainty about the parameter values for the forecasting model	0	0	0	X
57. Attention to unidirectional change and the role of non-repetitive events	Ø	0	0	X
58. Some attention to supply side and shortages of mutual resources in analysis of output and prices	0	0	0	X

> science of mechanics in astronomy and accepted Laplace's famous apotheosis of mechanics... as the evangel of ultimate scientific knowledge. They thus had some attenuating circumstances, which cannot, however, be invoked by those who came long after the mechanistic dogma had been banished even from physics....
>
> The latter day economists, without a single second thought, have apparently been happy to develop their discipline on the mechanistic tracks laid out by their forefathers, fiercely fighting any suggestion that economics may be conceived otherwise than as a sister of the science of mechanics. The appeal of the position is obvious. At the back of the mind of almost every standard economists there is the spectacular feat of Urbain Leverrier and John Couch Adams, who discovered the planet Neptune, not by searching the real firmament, but "at the tip of a pencil on a piece of paper."

Georgescu-Roegen (1975, 348) continues his musings with a reference to the stock market:

> What a splendid dream to be able to predict by some paper-and-pencil operations alone where a particular stock will be on the firament of the Stock Exchange Market tomorrow or, even better, one year from now!

2. Keynes reversed the emphasis of neoclassical economics on price adjustments as an equilibrating force to one of adjustments in output (and thus in the employment equilibrium). Keynes stressed the failure of the prices on specific commodities to adjust downward in the presence of insufficient total demand (a concept that Keynesians have come to call "sticky" prices) as a means of stimulating aggregate demand. Wages, as a special sort of price, also failed to adjust downward in the presence of inadequate demand as a matter of empirical reality; hence, they provide another example of the failure of product prices to adjust completely by rightward shifts in the supply curve or to leftward shifts in the demand curve (as introduced in sect. 1.3, and as discussed in sect. 7.1). Keynes simply held that moderate declines in employment were not associated with great declines in money wages. For him there was asymmetry between the respective degrees of upward and downward wage flexibility. although workers might be disposed to resist a reduction in their money rewards, there was no corresponding incentive to resist an increase.

Others have discussed the setting of separate product prices in terms of uncertainty about where to set them (sect. 1.3). In the face of inadequate demand the businessman simply does not have the information necessary to set prices that would achieve the desired goals. This emphasis on price and output adjustments has come up on numerous occasions, such as during the recession of 1973-75.

3. Keynes's price level (or "a mythical price level") in his General Theory entered in the sense of a demand price for capital goods (or investment, to use another term). There he suggests that the demand for capital goods varies inversely with the interest rate, other things remaining the same, such that demand price (or capital value) was more or less than supply price (or cost of the capital goods project). Thus, the inducement for capital spending increases as value exceeds cost, and to invest as cost exceeds value. This inducement to invest (and its absence) may be expressed as an inequality between the rate of interest, as quoted at the bank, and the rate of return on capital spending, as obtained by choosing a discount rate to relate the flow of returns from a capital goods project to its supply price.

This relationship between interest rates and investment demand (as discussed in sect. 8.2) is also found in the work of Irving Fisher, who assumed an inequality of foresight on the part of men in nonfinancial businesses and bankers. The businessmen were quick to anticipate the profitable aspects of inflation (defined as a rise in the price level), while the bankers were slow to introduce an inflationary component into the interest rates they quoted.

This area of theory becomes important as we consider the mechanism for controlling capital spending and the idea of evaluating a theory partly in terms of the validity of its conclusions; particularly, the prospect of an equality of foresight (say, as represented by a simultaneous response of businessmen and bankers to the expectation of inflation) becomes important. Quite possibly the formation of expectations by the public in the contemporary world is different from that in Fisher's day.

4. Keynes proposed a linkage mechanism for the purpose of monetary control based on the third attribute, namely, the inverse between interest rates (negative correlation) relationship and capital spending. This topic becomes important as we consider whether and how (either directly or indirectly) the central bank (that is, the Federal Reserve) influences the rate of interest.

5. In Keynes's work the central bank has control over the rate of interest, though it may be unwilling to take the extreme actions necessary under some circumstances, as in the 1930s in the United States. Most particularly, however, Keynes was influenced by the development of open market operations in the United States. These were formalized in the early 1930s as a part of the Federal Reserve's tools for conducting policy. Essentially, Keynes contended that, through its purchase and sale of short-term government securities, Open Market operations by the central bank could intervene (as defined in chap. 12). A purchase (sale) of short-term securities in the open market would lower (raise) short-term interest rates. The changes at the short end of the curve would then be passed on to the long end of the curve, thus explaining the Federal Reserve's potential control over the long-term rate of interest. This becomes the rate to be considered in the evaluation of capital spending behavior, as in attributes 3 and 4 above.

6. A main economic problem Keynes addressed in writing The General Theory was that of unemployment. Keynes, his students, Keynesian economists and others agree that unemployment is a by-product of declines in real output. The British economy that Keynes observed so closely had been in abysmal condition, even in the 1920s when the United States was so prosperous. Some have pointed to the international economy, and to Great Britain's role in it, in explaining the unique problems accompanying Britian's overvaluation of the pound in the 1920s. However, for the time being we ignore the international implications, concentrating as Keynes did on the causes of unemployment in a closed economy.

In this respect, the late Harry Johnson--of the University of Chicago and the Graduate Institute of International Studies, Geneva, Switzerland--points out the naivete of the concept of full employment as a policy goal. The goal, he says, drawing on Elizabeth Johnson's paper (1974, 106-109), is "intimately related to Keynes's essentially aristocratic Victorian view of the economic requirements of a happy society." He summarizes that view (1975):

> Social happiness consisted of a job for everyone in his appointed place in life--Keynes was little concerned about providing more equal opportunities for advancement within the ordered hierarchy of employments, since in the typical fashion of successful men he believed that society was so organized that anyone of merit if only he exerted himself, could rise to the eminence he had himself attained. Social misery of a severe and completely avoidable kind resulted from the failure of society to keep demand high enough to provide the expected and deserved jobs. (Johnson 1975, 120-21)

This sort of thinking about social mobility leads us to give some attention to inducements and social mobility when we discuss fiscal policy in chapter 11. Of more immediate importance, however, is the recognition that the flaw in the orthodox economics to which Keynes reacted was its inability to explain persistent unemployment, or even the periodic waves of unemployment that accompanied trade cycles in Britain and business conditions in the United States.

7. Keynes's theory was a general theory only up to and including the domestic economy. It was called "general" because it encompassed the unemployment equilibrium. It dealt also with disequilibrium as a dynamic state and related the theory of the real goods sector to that of the monetary (and, some stress, the financial) sector. This separation of the respective sectors had characterized the economic theory before Keynes's General Theory. Keynes attempted to combine the two by emphasizing the motives for holding money. Although the transactions demand for money was generally recognized before Keynes, he broadened the motives for holding money to include the speculative and precautionary motives set out in section 1.2. Keynes was especially interested in speculation concerning bond values and their inverse relation to interest rates, as considered in the liquidity preference demand for money vis-à-vis bonds.

8. In his money and bond model Keynes was inclined to hold expectations constant as interest rates varied. This constancy of expectations was a source of inconsistency in Keynes work, albeit perhaps a minor one. It will be considered in the next chapter, where we consider the liquidity preference demand for money.

Further, the limited scope of speculation in The General Theory failed to encompass speculation with respect to the purchasing power of money and related assets with fixed contractual claims against future income. Some label this speculation "purchasing power risk" to call attention to the risk of holding the latter classes of assets when the level of prices is increasing. The purchasing power of money, we note, varies inversely with the price level.

9. For Keynes, expectations were constant in the short run, even though he admitted to an interplay of changes in expectations in both the short and long run. The constancy of expectations in the short run permitted special attention to this time period and, according to Kregel (1976), "allowed the specification of simple, continuous functional relationships which constantly shifting long-period expectations would have made impossible." Keynes, he says, "could thus 'lock-up'...general expectations and uncertainty without assuming they did not exist." The main simple relationships found in Keynes and considered in later sections are investment demand, liquidity preference, and the consumption function.

Kregel suggests that we could not proceed with a statement of dynamic worldly phenomena (say, with shifting, interdependent, simple relations and dimensions of growth without first having in hand the simple, independent relations of Keynes's short run. This would be difficult to deny. However, questions arise about the role and usefulness of algebraic manipulations of constructions based on the assumption of "constant" expectations when statistical "noise" in time-series data appears to be in response to new information bearing on the future, even over short periods of time. These questions are particularly pertinent if the special time frame for stabilization (control) purposes is that of the short cycle, say as measured from one peak (trough) in business conditions to the next peak (trough).

10. Implicit in the last attribute is the distinction between control in the neighborhood of a point, irrespective of the stage of the business cycle, and control over a larger time frame, as illustrated in figure 4-1, frames a and b, which represent a blown-up portion of figure 3-1.

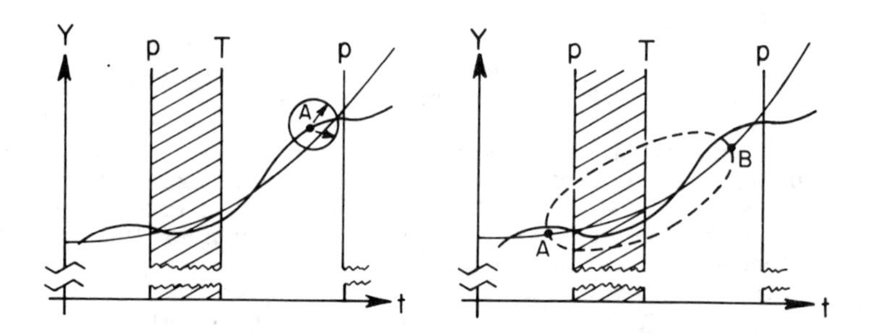

a. Control in the neighborhood of a point

b. Control in the neighborhood of a secular time path

Figure 4-1. Point and Secular Time-Path Control

Attention to control at a point at the expense of control over a longer period, by theorists and the men of affairs they influence, may indeed itself be a source of instability. Further, statistical "noise" may preclude any precise control of an economic system at a point irrespective of a larger time frame as considered on other occasions.

Keynes's theory may be viewed as control at a point, as Keynesian economics seems to attest. Even so, we conclude that cyclical business conditions are an integral factor in Keynes's work. For example, he had considerable background and interest in the so-called trade cycle in Britain; the thoughts of Michael Kalecki (Frazer 1976) that were to have reproduced and paralleled Keynes's were presented under the title Essays in Business Cycle Theory; the book-length work in which Sir John Hicks (1950) presents the summary of the Keynesian model is entitled the Trade Cycle; and, finally, Keynes's policy prescription for smoothing out fluctuations in capital spending (the interest rate control mechanism) suggested control over unstable business conditions.

11. Instability in aggregate demand arose from the investment goods sector in Keynes's economics. He wrote of autonomous investment to suggest a class of spending that was indeterminate within the usual confines of economic theory. However, the role and definition of autonomous spending point out a tradition in economic theory to which Keynes adhered in some respects, namely: the tradition rooted in mechanics as mentioned under attribute 1. The tradition also concerns the role of "ceteris paribus" in economics, whereby certain forces are impounded or held constant, almost arbitrarily so. It permits the construction of the Marshallian cross (fig. 1-1), as well what we call the Keynesian crosses--liquidity preference, aggregate supply and aggregate demand, and investment demand. The use of ceteris paribus in analysis contrasts with that of mutatis mutandis, where variables are allowed to change that do in fact change. This characteristic is important in distinguishing Keynes's and Keynesian economics from monetarist economics. Most notably, Keynesians set special store by the slopes and elasticities implied by the members of their crosses. Monetarists, on the other hand, gave special attention to the shifts in the schedules and thus to a form of dynamics. As we will encounter in the later subject of overshooting (sect. 5.4), there is theory centering about changes in the schedules themselves and thus time paths, disequilibrium states, transitory and permanent (quasi-permanent actually) changes, and damped oscillations.

By the assumption of ceteris paribus, as will be clear later, what Keynes offered with the one hand he took away with the other. His doing this is perhaps best understood by considering his efforts to break with tradition in economics, on the one hand, and to appeal to the professional economists, on the other. An apparent result, as noted by Patinkin (1976), was not to distinguish at all, "between the results due to the properties of a given demand curve and those due to a shift in the curve itself."

12. Keynes's simple consumption function, as noted in section 3.2 was the major specific contribution of The General Theory, apart from and distinct from those aspects of Keynes's work that break with traditional methods of economics. The simple function plays important roles in Keynes's and Keynesian theories, and in more contemporary economic theory. In later chapters on the household sector and consumption, the simple function is given a highly dynamic form.

13. Keynes's theory focuses on levels in the stock and flow quantities and on changes in the levels, as does the Keynesian theory. It contrasts with monetarist economics, in which attention is given to time rates of change. The tendency is toward a highly dynamic and empirically oriented economic theory.

14. Partial equilibrium and general equilibrium both enter in Keynes's economics. The idea of a partial equilibrium is associated with Marshall and refers to an equilibrium in a single market. Thus, partial equilibrium would permit a mathematical solution to schedules such as those depicted in figure 1-1. In this traditional view of Marhsall's economics, equilibrium may also be thought of as a state of equilibrium in the monetary sector of the economy, for example, as distinct from the real goods sector. Milton Friedman, however, was to give a different reading of Marshall (app. to chap. 1, sect. 7.1, app. to chap. 16; and Friedman 1953, 47-99).

The more non-Friedmanesque idea of a general equilibrium is associated with Walras (1834-1910), a Frenchman who taught and wrote at what is now the University of Lausanne in Switzerland. General equilibrium refers to equilibrium (or balance) in many markets, viewed overall. Patinkin extends the idea to Keynes's work, in the sense that Keynes was concerned with equilibrium in more than one sector, and finds in Keynes elements of both partial and general equilibrium (Patinkin 1976, pp. 98-101).

On the other hand, Kregel and Friedman object to some specifications of general equilibrium as applied to Keynes. For example, Kregel (1976) objects to the analogy between the Walrasian notion of general equilibrium and Keynes's specification. Friedman simply does not approve of the distinction drawn between Marhsall and Walras when Walras' system is viewed as one that yields a solution to a large system of simultaneous equation with n variables and n equations (Frazer 1973, 394-95, 462-64). Friedman says that Marshall had his system of n equations and n variables also, but says that the difference lies in Marshall's search for a fruitful empirical hypothesis as opposed to Walras's efforts to simply add more detail. Friedman has attributed this tradition of adding detail to the Keynesians and their large scale econometric models.

Patinkin simply says that Keynes's work can be regarded as "a practical application of Walrasian theory in the sense of reducing Walras's formal model of n equations and n unknowns to manageable proportions." Even so, he does not (as Friedman does not) associate Keynes with the simultaneous method. He does, however, distinguish between Keynes and the Keynesians, saying of Keynes's work, "It was not the general equilibrium IS-LM diagram, with the parallel treatment of the commodity and money markets."

4.3. Keynesian Economics

Although Keynes's writings had great influence on Keynesian economics and public policy in particular, Keynes was not a Keynesian. In the presence of unemployment in the 1930s and apparent failures of British monetary policy, Keynes recommended a fiscal solution--government spending. In the United States, government spending characterized Franklin Roosevelt's New Deal and Harry Truman's Fair Deal, but the U.S. experience with deficit financing cannot be traced to Keynes's influence. Similarly, the Employment Act of 1946--a landmark piece of legislation in prescribing national economic goals for the U.S. economy--was not mainly rooted in Keynes's work. Rather, Congressman Wright Patman in the House and others in the United States Senate provided the leadership for the Employment Act, exclusive of Keynesian thinking. Keynes did not influence American economic policy until almost two decades later.

Alvin Hansen of Harvard was the principal early interpreter of Keynes for the American audience. He had arrived on the Harvard University campus in 1937, and at age fifty assumed a major role in turning out graduate students that were later to have strong influences on economics and, more immediately, on government agencies and financing. Paul Samuelson--the first American Nobel Laureate in economics, the recipient of the second Nobel Prize in economics, and an earlier expositor of Keynesian economics--was strongly influenced by Hansen, although Samuelson had virtually completed his graduate studies at Harvard by the time of Hansen's arrival. The two shared in the development of the interactive multiplier and accelerator model presented in chapter 18.

Hansen was a forerunner to the Keynesian economics we describe, and the principal expositor of the stagnation doctrine. According to this doctrine, a developed economy like the United States was likely to face the long-term economic problem of stagnation; which would result from declining investment opportunities (and thus reduced spending and unemployment) as the market economy engulfed the less developed frontier. The solution or treatment thus called for government intervention and "deficit financing." Eventual and inevitable stagnation did not provide a hopeful outlook for the achievement of full employment without government intervention. Others abroad had stressed the declining rate of return on capital spending and had spoken of the "euthanasia of the rentier": the painless death of the capitalist as industry was nationalized. Their view was a common one of the western economies during the period of the late 1930s and the early post-World War II years, in which the prospect of recovery was uncertain, even in the United States.

The economics of Keynes, or Keynesian economics itself, did not take hold of American officials and national policy until the presidencies of John F. Kennedy and Lyndon B. Johnson, 1960-68. The "new" or Keynesian economics came to Washington most vividly with the astute political economist, Walter Heller, and, as Harry Johnson asserts, won acceptance with the tax cut of 1964 (sect. 11.3). Melville Ulmer (1971, 1) mentions "a new professional establishment" that was gradually assembled and "led by Samuelson, Walter Heller, Arthur Okun, James Tobin, Lawrence Klein, and others."

Some of the attributes of Keynes's economics are also found in Keynesian economics. The Keynesians, even more then Keynes, impounded expectations about prices and other economic magnitudes as they advanced clear statements of the Keynesian building blocks. These were ultimately summarized by the Hicks-Hansen IS-LM model, to which several later chapters in this book are devoted. Eventually, this kind of thinking led to the development of more elaborate structural equations models that emerged in the 1960s, under the impact of the modern computer and in the hands of Lawrence Klein (1950) among others (chap. 13).

For the most part, the Keynesian economics was an economics of abundance in a closed economy. The emphasis was on the inadequacy and the volatility of demand, a theme that is ever-present in discussions of economic stabilization. But attention must also be given to the economics of shortages and the impact of selected prices on the average of prices.

Keynes's definition of the short run was also the Keynesian definition. The focus again was on levels in stock and flow quantities rather than on time rates of change. The linkage scheme whereby the interest rate varies inversely (is negatively correlated) with investment spending was borrowed by the Keynesians, who paid particular attention to the housing sector. There was emphasis as well on Keynes's linkage scheme for the purpose of control over total demand by the central bank, equilibrating adjustments in output rather than prices, and sticky prices. The *ceteris paribus* assumption was generously and more rigorously invoked as expectations about future economic magnitudes were readily impounded.

The Keynesians eventually depart from Keynes, however, and develop a distinct body of economics. The distinguishing attributes of Keynesian economics follow:

1. The Keynesians developed a body of economics in which money and the related finance sectors do not matter. Thus, they separated the economics of money from that of output, whereas Keynes had integrated the two. The means of separating these two were reminiscent of the stagnation thesis and its call for fiscal policy, but they were more formally set out, and had antecedents in Keynes' work as well.

2. The Keynesians formalized the notion of a liquidity trap, and recognized its possible existence under the conditions of the 1930s in the United States. The trap refers to the horizontal segment of a curve relating the rate of interest

(i) to the quantity of money demanded (M), ceteris paribus, as in the liquidity preference construction of the next chapter. This static notion, as in the tradition of mechanics in economics, may be denoted

$$(\Delta M/M)/(\Delta i/i) \rightarrow \infty$$

In words, a very large percentage change in the money stock will all go into the demand for a stock of money balances to hold, and will thus have little or no influence on the rate of interest. In the sense that large quantities of money balances are desired there is no spending; spending results from the public's desire to reduce money balances, at least in relation of current income.

3. The failure of a special class of spending--that for capital goods or investment (I)--to respond to changes in the interest rate is denoted as another static measure, namely, the inelasticity of investment demand,

$$(\Delta I/I)/(\Delta i/i) \rightarrow 0$$

Here the interest rate is said to have no influence on capital spending, based on crude and inadequate observations of the real world (Frazer 1967, chap. 4). This attribute has antecedents in the analysis of the inequality of the rate of interest and the rate of return, as mentioned under the attributes of Keynes's economics and as related to work by Irving Fisher. The investment relation anticipates the Keynesian investment demand building block discussed in chapter 8.

4. Flowing out of the four preceding attributes is the Keynesian linkage scheme,

$$\Delta M \rightarrow - \Delta i \rightarrow \Delta I$$

where the arrows represent the direction of causation. This sequence describes how monetary policy influences spending for real goods and thus leads to an increase in employment, provided that the liquidity trap and the inelasticity of investment demand did not come into play. Thus Keynesians deemphasized the role of money (1) partly because the accepted the unvarified assumption of the liquidity trap, and (2) partly because their view of the linkages was an inappropriate one (at least, as judged from the hindsight of the monetarist research).

5. The foregoing attributes pave the way for a model without money, as in chapter 7, and the manipulation of total demand is left to fiscal policy, as defined and discussed in chapter 11. In the Keynesian model without money, the investment multiplier takes on a special role.

6. The liquidity trap and the inelasticity of investment demand need not always characterize the Keynesian world. Indeed, a negative correlation between the rate of interest and home construction occasionally comes forward in Keynesian economics as an example of how the interest rate influences capital spending. The argument presented in chapter 8 is simply that the financing of capital expenditures by industrial concerns is not analogous to that of spending by households, even for new housing.

7. The Keynesians, like Keynes, neglected money and focused on output adjustments rather than price level adjustments. However, an analysis of the price level was introduced as an appendage to Keynesian economics in the form of the Phillips curve (chap. 19). This curve initially depicted an inverse variation in the rate of change in the price level and the percentage of the labor force that was unemployed. In a ceteris paribus context, there was the idea that through application of policy a point on the curve could be picked and achieved, thus trading off a permanent reduction in the percentage of unemployment for a constant rate of inflation. Time and facts--such as the modern phenomenum of inflationary recession--have not lent much support to this idea.

8. The Keynesians dealt with the inconsistency in Keynes (see attribute 8 above) by suggesting "a difference of opinion" version of the liquidity preference demand for money (sect. 6.3). This version, associated with Tobin, permitted a treatment of expectations as a constant and consequently was consistent with Keynes's definition of the short run as a period of contant expectations with respect to economic magnitudes.

9. Empirical research on the consumption function is a legacy of pre-computer research in economics. This research did not affect the Keynesian theory, nor lead to any adaptation of the Keynesian building blocks to a more dynamic economics. On the other hand, research on consumption as a function of permanent income--conducted by the monetarists and Friedmanian. in particular--lead to the development of a dynamic version of the consumption function (sect. 9.4).

10. A characteristic of Keynesian economics was to ignore troublesome aspects of expectations by invoking ceteris paribus. This applied whether they were considering the liquidity preference demand for money or the expected rate of change in the price level. By such an impoundment and by treating real output (exclusive of the price level) as the central variable to be determined, the Hicks-Hansen IS-LM model became the summary statement of the Keynesian model.

11. The Keynesians operated with the set of relatively simple ideas that are embodied in the IS-LM model, but there was a tendency to add detail without changing the orientation. A result was Keynesian-oriented structural equations models, also called large-scale econometric models because they could incorporate over one hundred variables to be determined (called endogenous variables) and a equal number of non redundant equations. These models, which were such an important part of early empirical work with the modern computer, are introduced in later chapters. An important point about research concerning these models is that they did not measure up to the early claims made for them. Their failure to measure up to early claims (to explain significant aspects of observable reality such as the inflationary recession phenomenum and to provide a satisfactory linkage scheme for guides to policy) is "independent" evidence of the shortcomings of Keynesian theory and the related method of economics.

12. Just as the Keynesians came to neglect the study of money, they also constructed an economic analysis without a financial sector. The exception was the Federal Reserve-MIT an early and major Keynesian-oriented structural equations model, which incorporated a financial sector.

However, complication arises with the financial sector it incorporated--namely, it had the same characteristics that led Keynesian economics to minimize the role of money in the first place. It had a faulty linkage scheme.

13. Some of the early writers, such as Dillard, who analyzed Keynes's writings, discussed the effect on private spending of the financing of a government deficit, but crowding-out effects had no role in Keynesian economics. One dimension of this effect loomed in importance in discussions of national economic policy in 1973-75 as Federal deficits were planned to combat the recession (sect. 12.2).

Essentially, the possibility of a crowding out of private financing by public financing is introduced as a part of the theory of the impact of government spending and financing on the economy. Where banks and other financial institutions have a given capacity for supplying funds for investment purposes, there is the idea that the sale to the public of new issues of government securities may absorb these funds such that few remain for private spending.

4.4. Monetarist and Friedmanian Economics

References to the Keynesian revolution in economics were frequent after the appearance of Keynes's General Theory. It provided the title of an early (and later published) dissertation under Paul Samuelson, The Keynesian Revolution (Klein 1950), which stressed the Keynesian building blocks. Its author, Lawrence R. Klein, was later to become a pioneer in the methodology of large-scale econometric models. His major model, the Wharton Model of the late 1960s, had foundations in Keynesian economics. The label "Keynesian economists" originally referred to followers of Keynes, and only later did "Keynesian economics" come to be used as a label for a special body of economics.

In response to the revolutionary phase, a textbook in principles of economics, Economics, was authored by Paul Samuelson. Its first edition appeared in 1948, with about half of the volume devoted to national income accounting, money and banking, fiscal policy, and the emerging income expenditure model with its several Keynesian building blocks. The first Keynes-oriented principles text had been attempted by Lorie Tarshis, a graduate student at Keynes's Cambridge University and later a professor at Stanford University. But Samuelson was the first to succeed.[2]

As the roles of money and expectations in Keynes's work were minimized, the role of interest rates as the major link with total spending was emphasized. And, as the Keynesian building blocks were given refinement in two-dimensional geometric sketches, the label "macroeconomics" came to apply to the subject matter area, with its counterpart "microeconomics" applying to the traditional theory of price (Friedman 1976), and with Milton Friedman referring to them as a misleading use of scientific jargon. The reason for this reference was that the theory of price also addressed matters concerning the economy as a whole, as should be clear from appendixes to chapters 1 and 16, and from sections 7.1, 9.4, 15.2, and 17.4. In any case, macroeconomic textbooks emerged in the 1960s,[3] and the treatment of "money" and related analysis was removed from the main body of economics as being of little consequence.

In the 1960s--as Keynesian economics reached a zenith--one encountered references to a "Monetarist Counter-Revolution." There were references to a "crisis," to the inability of economic theory to explain observed phenomena and to provide guidance to policy-making officials (sect. 4.1). Joan Robinson, a professor in Keynes's former department, spoke of a second "crisis" in modern economics: the first was the one Keynes addressed; the second crisis was a reoccurrence of the first. In Ms. Robinson's view apparent ingredients of Keynes's work had been overlooked so as to lead to a renewal of the first crisis. Others also wrote on such a crisis, including Sir John Hicks--the Nobel Laureate in economics and a colleague of Ms. Robinson, published his volume, The Crisis in Keynesian Economics (1974).

Filling a void in the recent crisis, and at the same time contributing to it through empirical research, was the emerging monetarist research in the 1960s. Its negative thrust was to question Keynesian orthodoxy; its positive thrust was to reintroduce "money" and related phenomena to the general body of positive economic theory, as Keynes had tried to do in other ways.

Just as the Keynesians had their patrons in Washington, so did the monetarists. Monetarist thinking entered through the executive branch of government in the early years of the Nixon administration as part of the conservative, "free market" -oriented Chicago School. George P. Schultz was a White House advisor and later the Secretary of the Treasury with the broader Chicago view Arthur F. Burns of Columbia University and the National Bureau of Economic Research (NBER) was the Nixon appointee to Chairman of the Board of Governors of the Federal Reserve System in late 1969.

The monetarist thinking of the Chicago School was a rather specialized part. Milton Friedman's Chicago was not synonymous with the larger Chicago view, and the monetarist thinking extended beyond Friedman's, although Friedman stands out among economists of the 1960s and beyond. Friedman, moreover, had strong ties to Arthur Burns and empirical research of the National Bureau (Frazer 1979). He had been a student under the mathematical statisican Harold Hotelling at Columbia, receiving a Ph.D. from Columbia University, and his major works had been published at the NBER.

Upon Burns's arrival at the Board of Governors, the Federal Reserve began quoting monetary policy instructions to the manager of the Federal Reserve's open market account in terms of more specific magnitudes for money and credit aggregates. This was in addition to instructions concerning interest rates and money market conditions, as in the Keynesian linkage scheme.

Monetarist thinking also came to Washington through some democratically controlled committees of the Congress. The Joint Economic Committee had come out strongly for stating monetary policy in terms of the money supply. The Committee's views appeared in a 1968 publication, Standards for Guiding Monetary Actions (U.S. Government Printing Office). To relieve any uncertainty as to the trend of thinking--and partly in response to the Federal Reserve's lapses into a money market, interest rate view--Congress passed a resolution in early 1975 ("House Concurrent Resolution 133"). The resolution of the democratically controlled Congress--though it had no teeth--signaled an abrupt change in the sphere of monetary policy and was later incorporated into the Federal Reserve Act.[4] There were to be sure, problems in the control of aggregates. Hence their arose a need for policy with respect to them to be reaffirmed by the Federal Reserve under Chairman Paul Volcker on the weekend of October 6, 1979 (sect. 6.2).

Monetarist thinking had come to Washington in a conspicious way, although the stronger and broader Chicago view underwent a sharp change in mid-August 1971 when price controls and Keynesian thinking about monopoly pricing exerted a modifying influence (sect. 17.3). A major lesson perhaps of the period about the Chicago view was that the public and elected representatives could not and would not wait for the long-run adjustments of market forces, as encountered in the Chicago view, when faced with current problems.

The attributes of monetarist and Friedmanian thinking may be listed as follows:[5]

1. Much of the monetarist work was a return to Keynes. Some emphasized the role of money in reducing uncertainty about prices, to uncertainty in explaining sticky prices, and to the price system as a communications mechanism, as introduced in section 1.3. Others pointed to the tendency to bring money into general economics. But especially there was objection to the "gap" between economic theory and monetary policy, and to the tendency to add more and more detail to the structural models. There was the idea of bringing the policy and theory closer together (Frazer 1973, 386-93; Friedman 1977, 24-5)--of perceiving the one in terms of the other. Either theory could explain the observed phenomena and serve as a guide to the officials and observers of the economic scene generally, or it was a bad theory. The officials based their policies on some theory, whether conscious or unconscious of doing so.

2. When considering the two-dimensional geometric counterparts to the Keynesian building blocks (and similar static constructions in the tradition of economics), the monetarists held that shifts in the simple relationships (schedules) comprising the constructions may be more important than the movements along the schedules. This becomes, one may say, more of a mutatis mutandis approach to economics than a ceteris paribus one, although both approaches may be employed simultaneously; for example, one may invoke ceteris paribus to identify the structure, and then permit mutatis mutandis to make the economics and its structure more relevant.

3. The monetarist emphasis has been a more dynamic one, with attention to rates of change and differential rates of change rather than to levels of stock and flow quantities. This dynamic view is well exemplified by the use of the liquidity preference construction to illustrate a phenomenon referred to as "overshooting" (sects. 5.4, and 5.5) which introduces rates of change into that construction, and by the dynamic consumption function (sect. 9.4).

Friedman advanced the theory of consumer spending by introducing consumption as a function of permanent income (also variously thought of as the product of wealth and the rate of interest, as income to be received over a lifetime, and as a weighted average of current and past income). This approach has actually come to incorporate a theory of expectations and later, by shifting the weights of the current and past values of income, has permitted a treatment of uncertainty. The effect of all this was an analysis of aggregate consumption, in which the simple Keynesian function is constantly shifting, at faster or slower rates at some times than at others.

4. The attention to rates of change is also illustrated by a different empirical counterpart to the abstract concept of equilibrium. For the Keynesians, with their emphasis on levels, equilibrium was an intersection of two lines, the point of intersection determining the levels of, say, income and consumption. In the Friedmanian approach, equilibrium becomes an exponential growth path when the stock or flow quantity is plotted against time. It was, so to say, the underlying trend line as in figure 3-1, with quantity plotted against a ratio scale on a vertical axis and time on a horizontal axis. Disequilibrium is reflected in departures from the trend path.

5. In the monetarist theory, as characterized by Friedman, there is a so-called portfolio approach. According to this, wealth and asset adjustments work through what has been traditionally called a general equilibrium theory. It is an important part of the foundation of economic theory, and it underlay Keynes's thinking, too. In this framework of what is also called the general theory of choice, economic units are envisioned as making choices to maximize the flow of returns from holding assets. These prospective returns will likely include subjective elements, as well as the returns to wealth or

total assets. Simply stated (as seen in sect. 3.3), the maximum flow of returns occurs when the rates of returns from additions to various classes of assets are equal. Differential changes in the rates of return constitute imbalances, as in adjustments that may occur between the holding of money balances in relation to other assets or income.

6. The theorizing by monetarists, and Friedman especially, has often been ad hoc in character without giving rise to a formal structure. This would be in contrast to Keynesian economics and estimations from data as in their large-scale econometric models. The monetarist approach to empirical data was less formal in two other respects: (1) it was often a search for regularity in the data using a relatively simple statistical method and (2) it often relied on the use of "independent" evidence.

The search for regularity is typified by investigations of cross-sectional data, and time-series data in which series are converted to rates of change and lags are measured from a peak (or trough) rate of change in one variable to a peak (or trough) in another. Among monetarists, Milton Friedman would look to independent evidence to lend support to theories, borrowing results of apparently separate areas of economic research. For example (as will become clearer in later chapters), parallel movements in the income velocity of money (Y/M) and the rate of interest (i) may be generated by manipulations of the Hicks-Hansen IS-LM model. Based on partial evidence, the Keynesians can make a plausible case for a rise in the interest rate as a cause of the change in velocity--all as the rate rises, it induces switching from money balances to bonds. This theory appears less plausible, however, when one considers that the IS-LM model has no allowance for price level changes and when one observes the roughly parallel rising interest rates and roughly parallel movements of estimates of expected inflation, or rising velocity and estimates of expected inflation. In addition, other independent evidence on actual bond portfolios needs to be examined to see whether cash and bond-portfolio adjustments are behaving as the Keynesian theory prescribes.

7. Early monetarists could almost be described as monomaniacs in the singularity of their attention to the money stock as the main policy variable determining total spending. At least the Keynesians viewed them as such in the debates of the 1960s. Friedman initiated this approach in published research, but there were other independent researchers, including Karl Brunner and Allan Meltzer (as a team), and Carl Christ of Johns Hopkins University. In effect, Friedman's approach was to view a time series for the money stock against the background of business conditions (as independently reported by the NBER) and as illustrated in figure 4-2. There the shaded areas signify recessions, as delineated by peaks (P) and troughs (T) in the conditions; peaks and troughs in the rates of change of the money stock are also shown.

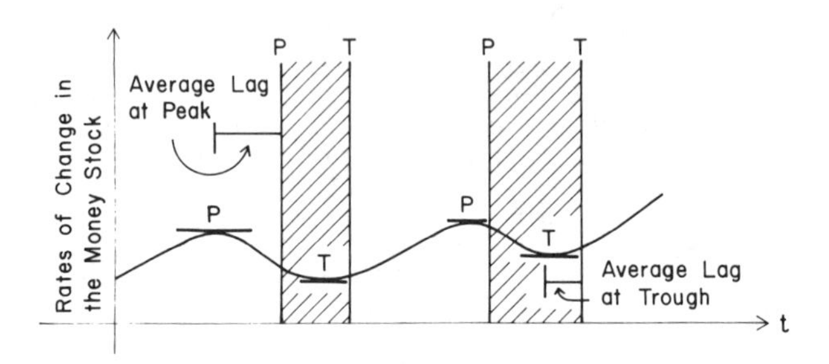

Figure 4-2. Leading Time Rates of Change in the Money Stock

Friedman and his associates measured lags from the peak (trough) of the rate of change in the money stock series to the peak (trough) of business conditions and computed the average lag time; as illustrated in figure 4-2. This approach employed a very simple method in contrast to more sophisticated methods that might have been used (and that were used by some with less success as to the accuracy of the lag times, and especially with respect to the fact that the lag time varied at peaks and troughs).

With reference to a monetary theory of business cycles, Higgins (1979, 13) notes in later review the following two propositions:

> (1) recessions are always accompanied by a "significant" deceleration in monetary growth; and
> (2) "significant" decelerations in monetary growth are always accompanied by recessions.

These are juxtaposed with evidence such as may be summarized by the cyclical patterns of monetary growth in figures 4-3 and 4-4 (source: Higgins 1979). He was especially interested in distinguishing the periods 1867-1913, 1914-51, and 1952-78, and noting the reliance by Friedman and Schwartz (1963) on three basic types of evidence to support the monetary explanation of the business cycle. The three periods single out the pre-Federal Reserve era, 1867-1913, the early years of the Federal Reserve System (or central bank in the U.S.), 1914-51, and the post-accord era, 1952-78. The data for the narrow measure of the money stock (M_1), as used in the figures, only became available after 1913. The post-accord era is a period when the Federal Reserve enjoys a special freedom from

Figure 4.3. Cyclical Pattern of M_1 (demand deposits and currency held by the nonbank public) Growth

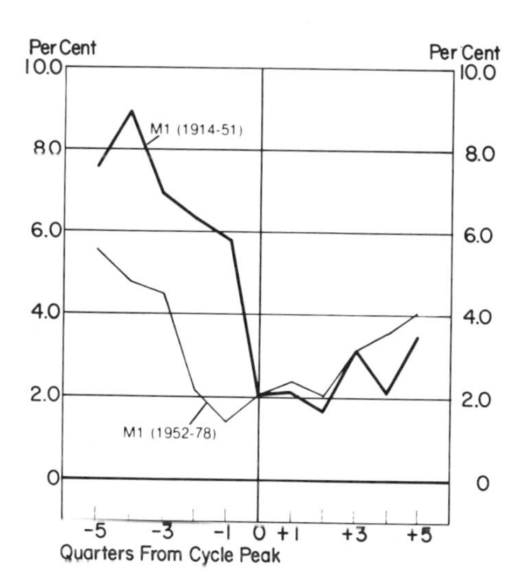

Figure 4.4. Cyclical Pattern of M_2 (M_1 assets plus time and savings at commercial banks) Growth

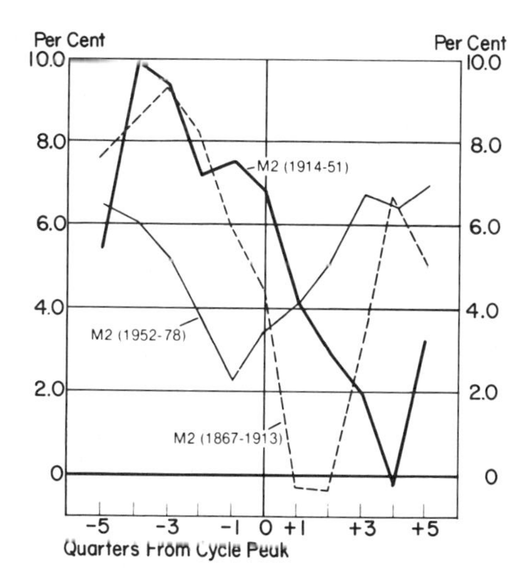

having to support (or peg) U.S. government bond prices. The growth rates for the narrower and broader monetary aggregates, in any case, reveal the leading rates of change patterns, as illustrated in figure 4-2. For the later periods the amplitudes of the growth patterns are more damped. Addition and perspectives on these matters comes later in chapter 6.

The types of evidence offered to support the monetary explanation have included (Higgins 1979, 7) "[1] the pervasive influence of money on other economic variables, [2] the persistance of the association between monetary growth and business cycles, and [3] the observed timing relationship between changes in the rate of monetary growth and changes in other economic variables." With respect to the two propositions about monetary growth and business conditions, Higgins concludes his review of evidence from quarterly data since 1952 thus (1979, 13-14):

> The pattern of monetary growth since 1952 is generally consistent with the view that recessions are always accompanied by "significant" decelerations in monetary growth...
>
> The historical evidence since 1952, however, does not seem to support the view that "significant" monetary deceleration is always accompanied by recession.

Of possible greater importance than the lag time for its practical impact on economic policy research was the attention to the behavior of the money stock in relation to business conditions--namely, that the behavior was largely procyclical or in phase with business conditions. Using the interest rate (i) as an indicator of business conditions (which is shown to be plausible prior to the inflationary recession phenomenon) some explanation of the predominantly procyclical behavior of the money stock (M) is possible using the equality

$$M = M^*_t + h\,(i - i^*),\ h > 0$$

where the asterisk denotes desired (or equilibrium trend) values, and $\underline{h}$ is simply a constant denoting feedback from the business conditions to the officials who have the responsibility for controlling $\underline{M}$. Thus, according to this equation, officials interpret high interest rates (e.g., $i > i^*$) to signal tight money, as would follow from Keynesian theory. The next step, then, would be for the officials to (inadvertently) facilitate monetary growth, in order to satisfy the needs for the growth in output.

8. A practical dimension to the foregoing was for some monetarists to refer to an increase in the growth rate of the money stock as "easy money," even when the faster rate was accompanied by rising interest rates. This, we note, is the reverse of the concept of easy money in the conventional Keynesian orientation.

The monetarists' approach included a treatment of equilibrium in terms of the "actual" stock of money and the "desired" stock. Equilibrium was signified by the equality of desired and actual balances, and the abstraction was given empirical content by reference to the income velocity of money, Y/M, which measured the turnover of the money stock in relation to current spending. Thus, we have another empirical indicator of the disequilibrium state. (It receives special attention in chapter 5.)

9. In the foregoing context of monetarist theory, an acceleration in the growth of the money stock exerts a multiple effect on spending. Rather crudely--in a strictly logical sense--the multiplier could be viewed as the velocity ratio Y/M. This contrasts with the Keynesian view that investment ("autonomous" investment) has a multiple effect on income.

10. Among the simplest aspects of the monetarist approach with its long-run emphasis was that of price level adjustments. Excessive growth in the money stock (i.e., growth exceeding that of real output) went entirely into price inflation, whereas inadequate growth had the opposite effect of price deflation. Thus, economic units adjusted money balances to the "desired" level by raising or lowering prices.

11. Changes in the money stock exert about the same effect on all classes of spending, including spending by households and business organizations alike. This contrasts with the effect of the interest rate on spending in the Keynesian theory, where business investment, exclusive of consumption is affected.

12. According to the monetarists, the main source of instability in business conditions is government economic policy, both monetary and fiscal. The Federal Reserve's premonetarist tradition of focusing almost exclusively on interest rates and related money market conditions was pointed to in this context, as well as the sort of "feedback" mentioned above (as from $i - i^*$ to $M - M^*$). The poor timing of fiscal policy was also considered a source of instability (chap. 10).

4.5. Empirical Economics: A Summary

Common questions elicited by a presentation of Keynesian and monetarist economics are: "What should I believe?" and "Who is right?" Several responses are possible. For example, one may decline a special interest in belief, and stress the task of liberating the mind from the narrow categories of dogma. Or, one may try to reconcile some differences by referring to varieties of evidence--such as observations, results from analyses of data, appeals to facts, and independent sources of evidence--and thus synthesize various attributes of the respective theories into a plausbile body of economics. This plausible body we call "empirical economics" to suggest that it has its roots in varieties of evidence. Even the failures at satisfactory verification of a theory, as in the case of structural equations models of the 1960s and early 1970s vintage, provide a sort of evidence.[6]

The approach of considering conflicting views and dealing with a variety of evidence may give the appearance of uncontrolled rambling in contrast to the neat algebraic sequences the Keynesians first exhibited in the textbooks of the 1960s. Often, for example, instead of one neat statement, one may be confronted with complexities of monetary operations and several, at times inconsistent statements, such as the Keynesian linkage scheme ($\Delta M \rightarrow -\Delta i \rightarrow \Delta I$), the monetarist ($\Delta M \rightarrow \Delta Y$), and empirical evidence showing high positive correlation between interest rates and capital spending by large industrial concerns (chap. 8).

In addition, one, may be confronted with inconsistencies within the separate bodies of theory as well as between them. In chapter 6, for example, two versions of Keynes's and Keynesian approaches to liquidity preference are considered--one is a difference-of-opinion approach with expectations constant, and the other, a pull toward normality with variable expectations. Behavior explained by these approaches cannot coexist in the same world. The one should be subordinated to the other, and this should be made more obvious.

Another inconsistency is immediately apparent when comparing the determinants of consumer spending. In the Keynesian approach the rate of interest has substantial effect on home construction (as in Keynesian attribute 6), while in the monetarist approach the money stock influences investment and household spending without distinction. Moreover, as a strictly factual matter, interest rates and capital spending by business firms vary directly, while the interest rate and housing expenditures vary inversely.

In describing the emerging economic theory (including an economics that extends beyond the monetarist period), the following attributes may be listed:

1. The use of ceteris paribus underlies the static constructions of traditional economics. Much of this structure may be brought forward by recognizing the role of the ceteris paribus assumption, and by simultaneously letting those things change that do in fact change. This enables one to move for example, from a simple consumption function, as in Keynes and Keynesian economics, to a shifting function. Also, we move from the use of the liquidity preference building block to deal with the dynamic phenomenon referred to as "overshooting" (chaps. 5 and 13).

Economists of the Keynesian era were aware of shifting static relations. The difference is that one is now concerned with theory about phenomena relating to the shifts. The exercise is not an idle one, because different conclusions about economic policy emerge, and the differences can be compared with observations as a means of evaluating the theories at hand. As Dillard said of the emphasis on policy in Keynes's approach, "only when we trace the theory to its practical consequences--can we hope to test its validity by an appeal to facts and thus arrive at an evaluation of its probable workability in the actual world" (1948, 53). (See also Frazer 1973, 388-89)

2. What emerges from the observation of data, as in figure 3-1, is that the monetarists' concept of equilibrium growth paths, and divergences from those paths (for money and income, for example), becomes more relevant than levels for the money stock and income as an approach to understanding changes in business conditions in the U.S. economy. The abstract notion of equilibrium thus takes on empirical meaning beyond that of the intersection of two lines in a two-dimensional, and possibly even a larger dimensional geometric construction.

3. The underlying equilibrium framework of the monetarists permits a treatment of a wider range of assets than Keynes dealt with in his two-asset model.

4. The foundations of much of economic theory, which underlay monetarist attribute 5, are preserved. However, the economics that emerges is an economics with money and a theory of output and control in which money, finance, and liquidity play crucial roles. In this respect the traditional Keynesian tendency to deemphasize money and the financial sector is abandoned in lieu of a return to the economics of Keynes.

5. Moreover, the Keynesian linkage scheme is no longer a meaningful assessment of monetary policy in a world where policy is pronounced in terms of time rates of change for money and credit aggregates. Recall, for example, House Concurrent Resolution 133. Under it the Federal Reserve periodically reports its plans for policy in terms of aggregates, and the reporting may be expected to bring further attention to the effect of expected policy.

6. The emerging economics attempts to deal systematically with expectations of economic magnitudes (especially those aspects that can be dealt with most concretely), in lieu of the practice of simply impounding them. Through the empirical success of his consumption function, Friedman has opened the door on a theory of expectations. Further, Irving Fisher's equation relating the nominal rate of interest (i) to the real rate (i_r) plus the expected rate of change in the price level has provided a vehicle for dealing with uncertainty in forecasts. This equation plays a special role in discussions of the control over interest rates in an inflationary recession (which occurs when the price level is rising and output declining).

7. The monetarist places great weight on the determining influence of the money stock, and were successful at reorienting monetary policy. However, there are other sources of instablity in business conditions, other than pro-cyclical monetary policy, that must be dealt with. In particular, we must address the destablizing and volatile dimensions of what has been labeled the "political business cycle." This has been reflected in: (1) the instability in the economy and in expectations resulting from shifts in the political ideologies of parties in power, (2) the tendency of the executive to appeal to the immediate wishes of the electorate through policy changes,

and (3) the prospect for subtle manipulation of business conditions through monetary and fiscal policy to avoid the simultaneous occurrence of a presidential reelection campaign and a recession in the economy. In later chapters, as we get into the subtle influences presidents and chairmen of the Federal Reserve's Board of Governors may have, our discussion extends to the use of announcements and persuasion to influence aspects of economic performance. Here at times we boarder on fields such as social psychology, and independent evidence from a source outside of economics traditionally becomes relevant.

8. In the present, empirical, approach, interest rates are not unimportant, although they do not have the power of influence and policy role attributed to them in Keynesian theory. In spite of this, the emphasis on interest rates as an influence on housing expenditures finds some support. Some classes of spending do behave differently, in contrast to the evenness of the influence of the money stock on classes of spending.

9. The monetarist approach gave special attention to a money stock multiplier while the Keynesian approach stresses the investment multiplier, which includes both business investment and government deficit spending. Simple testing to determine the greater relevance of one or the other theories gave rise to voluminous analyses of data and controversy (Frazer 1973, chap. 5). After reviewing the controversy and the evidence, the conclusion would appear to be that both the monetarist and Keynesian approaches are relevant. However, in contrast to Keynesian economics, this analysis gives special attention to the financing of deficits in the assessment of the impact of deficit financing by the Federal Government and to the "crowding out" of private financing by public financing (chaps. 10 and 12).

10. The monetarists advanced an analysis of price level adjustments, whereas Keynes and the Keynesians advanced the analysis of real output and employment. The present text will deal with both. In addition, attention is given to the apparent phenomenon of "sticky prices," as dealt with by the Keynesians and in more depth by some monetarists. Keynesians have offered as an appendage to the Keynesian building blocks the Phillips curve, which depicts an inverse relation between the rate of change in the price level and the percentage of unemployment. In chapter 17 the complexities of interpreting the Phillips curve are addressed and the entire analysis is extended to incorporate theory about the rationality of expectations.

11. The time dimension over which Keynes and the Keynesians hold expectations constant vanishes in the present version of empirical economics. "Agents" or economic units (households, firms, etc.) use information efficiently, albeit some more so than others, and so the economic outlook is constantly changing in response to new information. (Analyses of expectations comes to the forefront in chapters 5, 6, 14, and 17.)

12. Empirical economics distinguishes between the pure and general models for rational expectations (Frazer 1978). The concept of the pure model is that of the formation of expectations along the lines of predictions that follow from a structural equations model of particular vintage (say, Keynesian or Federal Reserve-MIT), estimated with classical least-squares methods of statistics. This system of structural equations has a solution (Frazer 1973, chap. 14, app.) and the solution yields reduced form equations, as illustrated in chapter 10. This "pure" model is rather strenuous, however, and qualifications are needed to bring it more in line with the worldly phenomena it purports to consider. But the addition of qualifications results in an essentially different model. We call it a more general model because it encompasses a unidirectional role for time, a Bayesian learning process, and interaction between the traditional mechanics of economics and psychological forces (including those of uncertainty). In this model there is evolution and emergence such that, in forecasting, the future cannot be predicted entirely from antecedent conditions. This adds the property that rational expectations must be uncertain expectations. Specifically, there is uncertainty about the parameters of the forecasting model, which is elucidated in chapter 14.

13. The attributes of an emerging empirical economics stated thus far refer for the most part to a closed economy. In later chapters, the attributes will be broadened to include international occurrences that affect the domestic economy. The pricing of natural resources, as introduced in chapter 2, is an example of an international influence on the domestic price level.

14. Natural resources and shortages of them work through the cost (or supply side) of economic analysis to influence prices, unemployment, and output. The present version of an empirical economics gives attention to this supply side of market as well as to total demand. Keynes's and Keynesian economics in contrast, was restricted for the most part to the management of total demand.

FOOTNOTES

1. We are greatly aided in this presentation by the publication of a twenty-five volume collection of Keynes's writings. Two are mentioned in the selected references at the end of the chapter (Moggridge 1973a and 1973b). Patinkin (1976) draws on these volumes and deals with what Keynes actually said; others (Patinkin and Leith 1978) also draw on the volumes in stressing the process of criticism and discussion connected with the development of The General Theory.

2. Sales reached over 2 million copies through its seventh edition (1967).
3. An early text bearing the label was Gardner Ackley, Macroeconomic Theory (New York: The Macmillan Company, 1961). A later one--offer an "unabashed Keynesian" in spirit and coming at the end of the Keynesian era--was Warren L. Smith, Macroeconomics (Homewood, Ill.: Richard D. Irwin, Inc., 1970). Ackely succeeded Walter Heller as Chairman of the President's Council of Economic Advisors. He was a member beginning in 1962, and chairman from 1964-68.
4. Though superficially innocuous the resolution specified a reporting of monetary policy in terms of money and credit aggregates, called for a periodic reporting of monetary policy plans for the forthcoming year, and required a public explanation of departures from announced plans.

    The essence of the latter idea appeared along with other related views in a 1968 publication, Compendium on Monetary Policy Guide-lines and Federal Reserve Structure (U.S. Government Printing Office, pp. 173, 177, 188). The hearing on Resolution 133 and related views were contained in Monetary Policy Oversight (U.S. Government Printing Office, 1975).
5. We have construed this section to encompass monetarists as well as the broader contributions of Friedman to positive economics. Elsewhere, Friedman (1973, 27-29) has a more restricted set of ten monetarist propositions. They deal in some detail with attribute 7, as stated below, and in some degree with attributes 3 and 6.
6. A review of this failure is found in Frazer (1973, chap. 14).

SELECTED READINGS AND REFERENCES

Dillard, Dudley. 1948. The Economics of John Maynard Keynes. New York: Prentice-Hall, Inc.

Fellner, William. 1967. Towards a Reconstruction of Macroeconomics: Problems of Theory and Policy. Washington, D.C.: American Enterprise Institute for Public Policy Research.

Fisher, Irving. 1896. Appreciation and Interest. New York: Macmillan. Reprinted by Augustus M. Kelley (New York, 1961).

Frazer, William. 1967. The Demand for Money. New York: World Publishing Company.

__________. 1973. Crisis in Economic Theory. Gainesville, Florida: University of Florida Press.

__________. 1976. "Keynes and Feiwel's Intellectual History of Kalecki." Southern Economic Journal (October).

____________. 1977. "Income Distribution, Social Utility and Unemployment." Nebraska Journal of Economics and Business (Autumn).

____________. 1978. "Evolutionary Economics, Rational Expectations, and Monetary Policy." Journal of Economic Issues (June).

____________, and William P. Yohe. 1966. Introduction to the Analytics and Institutions of Money and Banking. Princeton, N.J.: D. Van Nostrand Company, Inc.

Friedman, Milton. 1953. Essays in Positive Economics. Chicago: University of Chicago Press.

________. 1973. Money and Economic Development: The Horowitz Lectures of 1972. New York: Praegar Publishers.

________. 1976. Price Theory. Chicago: Aldine Publishing Company.

________, and Anna Jacobson Schwartz. 1963. A Monetary History of the United Sates, 1867-1960. New York: Princeton University Press for the National Bureau of Economic Research.

__________, and ______________. 1970. Monetary Statistics of the United States. New York: Columbia University Press for the National Bureau of Economic Research.

Friedman, Rose D. 1977. "Milton Friedman: Husband and Colleague--(9), Heights and Depths." Oriental Economist (January).

Galbraith, John Kenneth. 1975. "How Keynes Came to America." In Milo Keynes (ed.), Essays on John Maynard Keynes. London: Cambridge University Press.

Georgescu-Roegen, Nicholas. 1975. "Energy and Economic Myths." Southern Economic Journal (January).

Hicks, John R. 1950. A Contribution to the Theory of the Trade Cycle. Oxford: The Clarendon Press.

____________. 1974. The Crisis in Keynesian Economics. New York: Basic Books, Inc.

Higgins, Byron. 1979. "Monetary Growth and Business Cycles, Parts I and II." Economic Review, Federal Reserve Bank of Kansas City (April).

Johnson, Elizabeth. 1974. "John Maynard Keynes: Scientist or Politician?" Journal of Political Economy (January/February).

Johnson, Harry G. 1975. "Keynes and British Economics." In Milo Keynes, ed. Essays on John Maynard Keynes. London: Cambridge University Press.

Kahn, Richard. 1978. Journal of Economic Literature (June).

Klein, Lawrence R. 1950. The Keynesian Revolution. New York: The Macmillan Company. A second edition appeared in 1966 with an additional chapter (IX) on the essential nature of the Keynesian system as a system of simultaneous equations.

Kregel, J.A. 1976. "Economic Methodology in the Face of Uncertainty: The Modelling Methods of Keynes and the Post-Keynesians." Economic Journal (June).

Leijonhufvud, Axel. 1968. On Keynesian Economics and the Economics of Keynes. New York: Oxford University Press.

Mini, Piero V. 1974. Philosophy and Economics. Gainesville, Florida: University of Florida Press. Chs. 1 and 12 through 15.

Moggridge, Donald E. 1975. "The Influence of Keynes on the Economics of his Time." In Milo Keynes, ed. Essays on John Maynard Keynes. London: Cambridge University Press.

__________, ed. 1973a. The Collected Writings of John Maynard Keynes, Vol. XIII, The General Theory and After -- Part 1, Preparation. London: Macmillan.

__________, ed. 1973b. The Collected Writings of John Maynard Keynes, Vol. IV, The General Theory and After-- Part II, Defense and Development. London: Macmillan.

Patinkin, Don. 1965. Money, Interest, and Prices: An Integration of Monetary and Value Theory 2nd ed. New York: Harper & Row.

__________. 1976. Keynes' Monetary Thought: A Study of Its Development. Durham, N.C.: Duke University Press.

__________, and J. Clark Leith, eds. 1978. Keynes, Cambridge and "The General Theory": The process of criticism and discussion connected with the development of The General Theory. Toronto: University of Toronto Press.

Skidelsky, Robert, ed. 1977. The End of the Keynesian Era. New York: Holmes & Meier Publishers, Inc.

Ulmer, Melville J. 1979. "Old and New Fashions in Employment and Inflation Theory." Journal of Economic Issues (March).

Chapter 5

Money, Prices and Income: Some Old and More Recent Exercises

5.1. Introduction

Keynes called all economics that immediately preceded his great work--including the economics of his teacher, Alfred Marshall (1842-1924)--"classical" economics. Others have used the term "neoclassical" in reference to the work from Marshall's time to Keynes's; some even include the work of Irving Fisher (1867-1947) in this category. For the present purpose only limited aspects of neoclassical economics will be reviewed. One finds in monetarist economics and empirical economics some modified neoclassical notions. This chapter draws upon neoclassical economics and selected theories, as outlined in chapter 4, and develops them in more detail. Attention is directed toward monetary aggregates (including the money stock), a reaffirmation of the notion of empirical verification in economics, and a more dynamic approach to economics.

The more dynamic economics is illustrated in this chapter through a consideration of the response of such key variables as the velocity of money (i.e., of money balances in relation to the output of goods and services) and the rate of interest to some common third force; and by the consideration of the changes in time rates of change and of the different rates of change in stock and flow quantities. Viewed overall, the theory set forth in this text is more dynamic in a multifold sense: (1) attention is given to equilibrium time paths, (2) numerous changes are treated as nonreversible ("unidirectional" time), (3) forecasts based on the structure of economic relations are accompanied by uncertainty about the underlying structure, (4) uncertainty is treated as both a probabilistic concept (including actuarial probability and incomplete knowledge) and as a psychological state, and (5) money and liquidity are considered means of dealing with uncertainty from the agent's standpoint.

In the present chapter, attention is also directed toward the way Keynes went about combining the theory of money with that of output and the role in Keynes's economics of the motives for holding money. These motives introduce a psychological or behavioral element into economics, as does a review of Fisher's explanation of on interest rates and the expected rate of inflation. We see that the Keynesians moved away from this concern with psychological notions by impounding expectations in ceteris paribus, and thus reverted back to that view of economics as an allied science of eighteenth-century Newtonian mechanics (Frazer 1978). In empirical economics, we revert to a consideration of money, uncertainty, motives and expectations, à la Keynes and Friedman, with special attention to "rational" expectations.

Some reflections on the roots of a contemporary economics are not idle exercises for two reasons--(1) those of tradition and (2) hypothesis testing. With respect to the first, Adam Smith evaluated physiocratic and mercantilist doctrines in terms of his own "correct" view, and J. M. Keynes (1936, chap. 2) crticially dealt with the postulates of classical economics before setting out his own theory. With respect to the second, we are always testing an hypothesis (i.e., refutable statement generated by analysis) against another for a superior consistency with results from statistical analysis of data, with observations of the real world, and with evidence often extending beyond the scope of the immediate investigation. The question of what ought to be in policy terms becomes one of evaluating one concept of policy against another (say, policy A against B) with the view to getting where we want to be. In broad outline, policy oriented theories are partly arguments for social reform and for predicting the effects of policy. In this activity of selecting among alternatives, we make mistakes and hopefully learn from them. The process of conjecture and refutation goes on (Popper 1965). Pitfalls and misdirection encountered in the past serve as warnings about the future role of economics.[1] As economics evolves toward a stronger empirical focus, some of the extreme shifts in the popularity of one doctrine or another may be constrained, and the misdirection that theory has given at times to national economic policies may be minimized.

5.2. Some Aspects of Neoclassical Economics

The economics before Keynes was characterized by the separation of the theory of output and the theory of money. Output was determined by productive factors including labor. The prices of various goods and services in relation to one another performed allocative functions. They were envisioned as adjusting in such a way as to assure the full utilization of resources, especially labor. The market was automatically self-adjusting. The self-adjusting, full-employment features were envisioned by Keynes as being embodied in J.S. Say's law of markets: Supply creates its own demand; no goods are supplied except to obtain income for spending.

The separate theory of money centered about the equation of exchange. Some have called it the "old" quantity theory, to distinguish it from some of the more modern theories of money demand. Among the old theory's expositors was Irving Fisher who, as it turns out, looms large in modern economics, too. Consequently, we deal with some of his quantity theory views as well as others that emerge in later economics.

The Equation of Exchange

Fisher presented a theory about money and prices, on the one hand, and bank loans and interest rates, on the other. His theory of money and the price level centered on his equation of exchange,

$$MV=PT$$

where $\underline{M}$ is the average money stock in a period, $\underline{P}$ is the average of prices on all transactions, $\underline{T}$ is the total number of transactions in the period, and $\underline{V}$ is transactions velocity (restated, $V = PT/M$). The equation was nothing but an identity for the two sides of all transactions. But there was more. In the short run, velocity was thought to be stable; in the long run, it was thought to be influenced by rather mechanical things such as payment habits and mechanisms.

According to this identity, the average of prices was determined mainly by the money stock, and the analysis of the price level was mainly an analysis of the transactions demand for money (the balances to tide one over from one income receipt to another). The causal mechanism can be seen by rewriting the equation of exchange,

$$M=(T/V)\ P$$

$$\Delta M \rightarrow \Delta P$$

where the arrow represents the direction of causation. Patinkin (1965) has summarized the neoclassical thesis thus: an increase in the stock of money disturbs the relation between the level of money balances and expenditures; this disturbance (a "real balance effect") leads to an increase in spending, which creates demand pressures until the price level has risen in the same proportion as the money balances.

This particular formulation by Fisher and other neoclassicists did not hold up well, as it turns out, as far as the short run (or short cycle) was concerned; however, Fisher said more about prices and related aspects of bank lending and interest rates.

Bank Loans, Prices, and Interest Rates

Fisher noted a lag in the adjustment of prices to changes in the money stock. But the increase in spending reduced inventories and caused a more favorable outlook by businessmen with respect to sales volume. This in turn led to an increase in the demand for loans and bank credit (as on the asset side of a bank balance sheet). The loan demand eventually led to an increase in interest rates, partly because the loan demand exceeded the initial rise in the money stock.

Closely related to this causal relationship was another Fisher thesis, namely: that businessmen were quicker to adjust their expectations about rising prices and the related spending than were the bankers, and the bankers were consequently slow in adjusting their interest rates upward. This meant--as set forth later in the Keynesian context in chapter 8--that the rate of return (r) on capital spending exceeded the rate of interest (i). This imbalance was an inducement to invest. It later became a part of Keynes's and Keynesian economics.

The nominal interest rate (i) as treated by Fisher becomes especially important in the discussion of issues created by the inflation of the late 1960s. The Fisher equation, as it has emerged from Fisher's 1896 statement of it, is

$$i = i_r + (1/P)(dP/dt)^*$$

where i_r is the real rate of interest (the rate after removing the effects of inflation) and where $(1/P)(dP/dt)^*$ is the expected rate of inflation.[3] The idea is that bankers would adjust their interest rates upward to compensate for the prospect of being repaid with lower purchasing power dollars.

Economists in recent years (Carlson 1977; Mullineaux 1977) have examined anticipatory series of inflation rates as one means of dealing with expected inflation, and an adaptive expectations model has been suggested as another means of obtaining a measure for the expected inflation. Part of the former series, known as Livingston data,[4] are introduced in this chapter. The second model is considered more fully in chapter 17, where we introduce influences on expectations that are not always captured by the past. For the present, however, the adaptive model may be set out:

$$\dot{P}_t^e = W_o \dot{P}_t + W_1 \dot{P}_{t-1} + W_2 \dot{P}_{t-2} + \ldots + W_n \dot{P}_{t-n}$$

where $\dot{P}_t^e$ is the annual rate of change in prices expected to occur over the life of the debt instrument in question (i.e., the bank note or a bond), the $\dot{P}$s are rates of change for price levels in current and past periods, and the Ws are weights.[5] The idea is that recent changes in prices have the most influence on expectations and, therefore, the weights for the more distant past are usually smaller.

Of these foregoing ideas, the Fisher interest rate equation has better endured the passage of time. Following the emergence of an inflationary period beginning in 1966, the expectation of inflation became a main explanation for high interest rates. One even encounters a use of persuasive strategies by the chairman of the Board of Governors of the Federal Reserve System in the early to mid-1970s as a means of reducing inflationary expectations and hence interest rates. This topic concerns us later in chapter 12. The dependence of business firms on bank loans--particularly the larger firms with the greatest tendency to plan and form expectations about business conditions--also comes into question in a later chapter. The assumed difference in the sensitivity to information in the formation of expectations on the part of the financial markets, on the one hand, and expenditure units such as large firms, on the other, receives more attention below.

5.3. Keynes's Economics

Keynes (1883-1946) was confronted with a special version of the quantity theory in the lecture halls of Cambridge University. It was characterized by the cash balance approach (Keynes 1923, chap. 3). Using modern parlance and exercising some license in simplification, we can describe this quantity theory as equating the product of income and a factor of proportionality (the Cambridge $\underline{k}$) with to the money supply (i.e., Yk = M). As in Fisher's equation of exchange, changes in the money supply exerted their main influence on the price level ($\Delta M \rightarrow \Delta P$). The orientation in this quantity theory tradition was toward the long run, $\underline{k}$ considered to be more or less constant, depending on habits and practices. Keynes, however, criticized this perspective. We find him, even at this early date, saying (1923, 80):

> But this *long run* is a misleading guide to current affairs. In the *long run* we are all dead. Economists set themselves too easy, too useless a task if in tempestuous seas they can only tell us that when the storm is long past the ocean is flat again. (1938, 80)

So Keynes was to say that large changes in the money supply affected individual fortunes, and that the public, in anticipation of continued changes in prices, would exert efforts in the shorter time span "to make gains and avoid losses during the passage from the equilibirum corresponding to the old value of $\underline{n}$ [the current $\underline{M}$] to the equilibrum corresponding to its new value." The cash balance equation could be written:

$$Y = \frac{1}{k} M \text{ or } \frac{Y}{M} = \frac{1}{k}$$

where $\underline{k}$ (the reciprocal of the ratio of income to the money stock) was beginning to be viewed as a variable, even in the early 1920s. But by the time of the *General Theory* (1936),

Keynes added the precautionary and speculative motives for holding money balances and in effect related these to *k*.[6]

Keynes's approach to cash balances, when combined with the measurement of velocity provided by Fisher's approach, permits us to focus on Keynes's disequilibrium state. His was what has been called in retrospect a "portfolio approach." The motives introduced in the consideration of disequilibrium and the portfolio approach lead to the role Keynes attributed to money and to his liquidity preference model.

The Disequilibrium State

The neoclassical emphasis had been on the transactions demand for money and its use as a medium of exchange for implementing expenditures between pay periods. This turned out to be a long-run view in which a form of equilibrum prevailed (that is, the income velocity of money, Y/M, was constant) at least for a given secular (or long-run) period in which the technology of the underlying payments mechanism and habits in using balances were unchanged. In introducing changes in *k* and the motives for holding money, Keynes in effect did two very important things as far as theory was concerned:

(1) He integrated the theory of money and output.

(2) He focused attention on the short run and the disequilbrium state (as indicated by changes in the income velocity, for example).

Hence Keynes's theory was offered as a more general theory: a theory encompassing the unemployment situation and the disequilibrium state (an imbalance of forces).

Keynes suggested two motives for holding money, in addition to the transactions motive stated in chapter 1:

(1) precautionary motive--the motive to hold balances as a means of dealing with foreseen and unforeseen developments and investment opportunities. Others have labeled the holding of a pool of liquid funds to deal with an anticipated need as a "liquidity motive" for holding assets. Uncertainty (as a probabilistic concept), has also been introduced where liquid balances serve as a source of security and convenience, all as a means of coping with less certain and unforeseen developments.

(2) speculative motive--the motive to hold money (or make adjustments in holdings in relation to other assets or income) as a means of avoiding a loss (or realizing a gain) from changes in capital values.

A Review of Basic Data

Keynes's theory of liquidity preference (as found in the discussion surrounding figure 5-4), and modified versions of the theory are the main pillars of the integrated theory of money and output. These various versions of liquidity preference center on two time series of data, as a first approximation. The first series is that of the income velocity of money. The other is "the" rate of interest.

A contribution of Fisher's formulation of the equation of exchange was that it led to the measurement of the turnover of cash balances. Since Fisher's time and the publication of national income data in the post-World War II years, the equation has been rewritten by substituting output (Q) for the total volume of transactions (T):

$$PQ = MV \text{ where } Y = PQ$$

and

$$V = \frac{Y}{M}$$

(Thus, velocity is equal to the ratio of national income or GNP to the money stock.) Empirical data for the relationship between velocity and designated peaks and troughs in business conditions have indicated several things: (1) the time frame for the short-run disequilibrum is that of the short cycle in business conditions, as illustrated in figure 3-1; (2) the disequilibrium state is predominant, and (3) velocity has tended to move in phase with business conditions, at least for the post-World War II years through 1965, as has the rate of interest. However, after 1965, the velocity ratio and the rate of interest began to drift apart and even to vary immersely, as seen in figure 5-1. The two series of data in figure 5-1 are shown against the background of cyclical phases (as separated by the National Bureau's turning points in business conditions).

The period prior to that shown is the least complicated for pinning down the liquidity preference theory and demonstrating variations in income velocity and "the" interest rate. The 1965-77 period shown in the figure is complicated by the following developments:

(1) The acceleration of inflation from an annual rate (annual data, "all items," CPI) of 1.67 in 1965, to 4.20 in 1968, to 6.23 in 1973, and to a peak of 10.97 in 1974.
(2) The inclusion of the "expected inflation rate" in the nominal rate of interest (Fisher's interest rate equation).
(3) The prospect of not just forecasting an inflation rate, but of doing so with some degree of uncertainty.
(4) A tie between the velocity of money and capital spending, whereby the latter is stimulated by accelerated inflation (as concerns us especially in chapter 8).

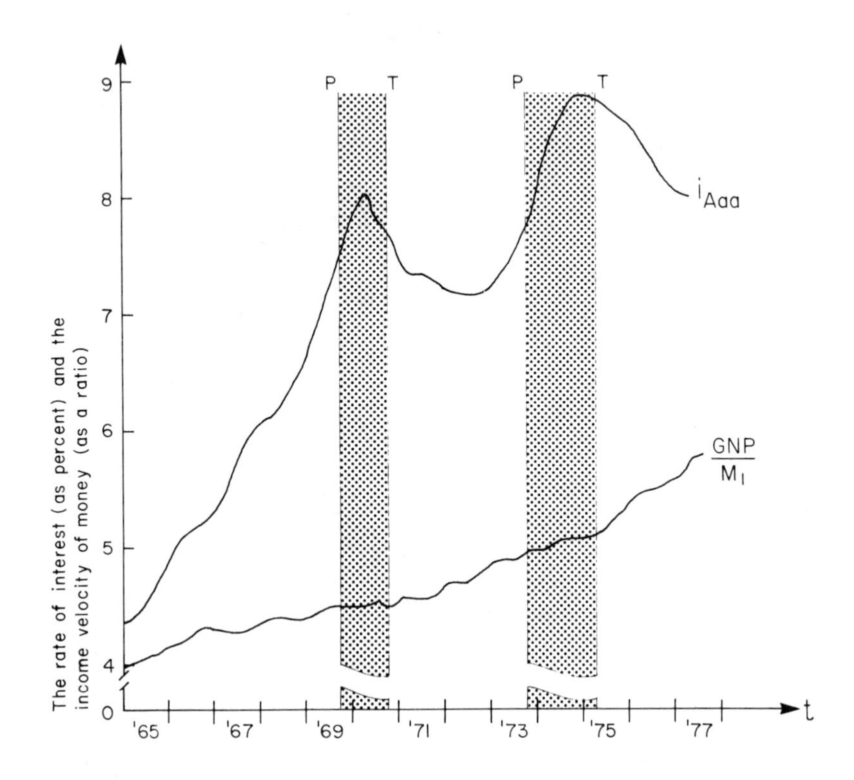

Figure 5-1. Corporate Bond Yields and the Velocity Ratio, 1965-77

Notes on data: All plotted data are quarterly. The yields (as percent per annum) on Aaa rated bonds are averages of daily figures from Moody's Investors Service. The amounts for the narrowly defined money stock, the denominator of the velocity ratio, are averages of daily figures (in billions of dollars) that are reported by the Federal Reserve. The numerator for the velocity ratio is GNP in current dollar (billions) expressed as an annual rate, and reported by the U.S. Department of Commerce.

The peaks and troughs delineating recessions (the shaded areas) are turning points in business conditions as reported by the National Bureau for Economic Research.

(5) A shift from demand to time deposits as proportions of total deposit liabilities during much of the period 1970 through 1976 (as considered in discussion surrounding figure 6-2), even as interest rates declined.
(6) The prospect for changes in the payments mechanism, as introduced by Fisher and as reviewed later in this chapter.

Tying the interest rate to the level of the inflation rate, as in Fisher's interest rate equation, and tieing spending to the acceleration of the inflation rate would lead the interest rate and velocity measure to depart during a secular period of accelerated (decelerated) inflation and, at the same time, set the stage for other possible influences operating via expectations of inflation and uncertainty. Analysis later in the chapter suggests a cost of holding cash balances and foregoing the consumption of some real output in the presence of inflation, resulting in a permanent increase in velocity for any permanent change in the inflation rate. This permanent change in velocity would be some fraction of the interest rate.

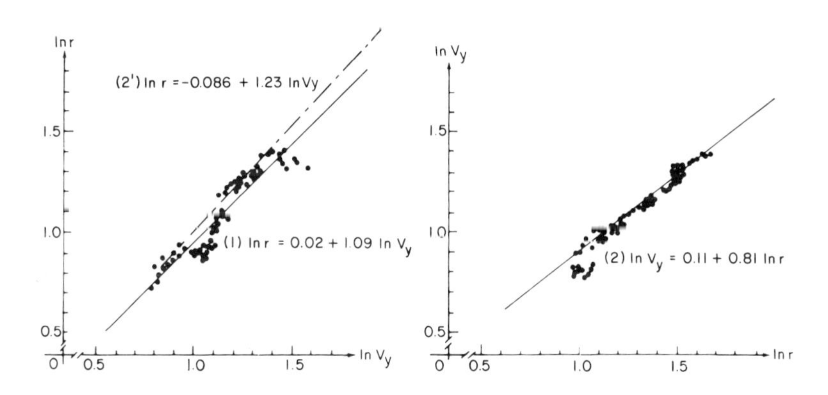

Figure 5-2. The Velocity of Money and the Rate of Interest, 1947-65.

Source: William Frazer, The Demand for Money. Cleveland, Ohio: The World Publishing Company, 1967, p. 38.

For the period 1946 to 1965 the direct variation in velocity and business conditions (represented by interest rate) is illustrated by the scatter diagrams shown in figure 5-2. There we show the results of regressing quarterly data for high grade (Aaa rated) corporate bond yields on the income velocity ratio, and vice versa, after logarithmic transformation of the data. These regressions and results are noted thus:

$$(1) \qquad \ln r = 0.02 + 1.09 \ln V_y, \qquad r^2 = 0.89$$

$$(2) \qquad \ln V_y = 0.11 + 0.81 \ln r, \qquad r^2 = 0.89$$

A variant of equation (2), after algebraic manipulation (Frazer 1967, 39), may also be written:[7]

$$(2') \qquad \ln r = -0.086 + 1.23 \ln V_y$$

The separate interest rate data for the post-World War II years are shown in figure 5-3 as several time series. One part of the figure shows yields on government bonds with different years to maturity, and another part shows yields for different classes of long-term bonds, including corporate Aaa-rated bonds. In the theoretical context we refer to "the" interest rate, but actually there are many rates. The term sometimes means the rate on long-term government bonds (a basic, riskless rental value of money), and a change in the rate means a change in the structure of interest rates. The upward and downward movements in the structure of interest rates are clearly visible in figure 5-3. The differences in the various rates at any given time are thought to reflect differences in risks.

A Portfolio Approach (The Two-asset Model)

Keynes's approach was in fact a portfolio approach to the demand for money and other assets, that is, it envisioned an array of assets yielding various flows of returns and consequently various rates of return. But Keynes focused mainly on two classes of assets: money (including currency, bank deposits, and short-term securities) and bonds (including real capital and equities or the claims of ownership).

The Role of Money (Exclusive of Transactions)

With the motives for holding money and Keynes's cash balance equation in hand, the special role Keynes attributed to money may be illustrated. This calls for the introduction of the capital value (CV) or bond price formula and the liquidity preference model. The formula is as follows:

$$(5.0) \qquad CV = \frac{R_1}{(1+i)^1} + \frac{R_2}{(1+i)^2} + \ldots + \frac{R_n}{(1+i)^n}$$

where the Rs are expected returns per future period (R_1, R_2, ..., R_n) and i is the rate of interest at a current time.

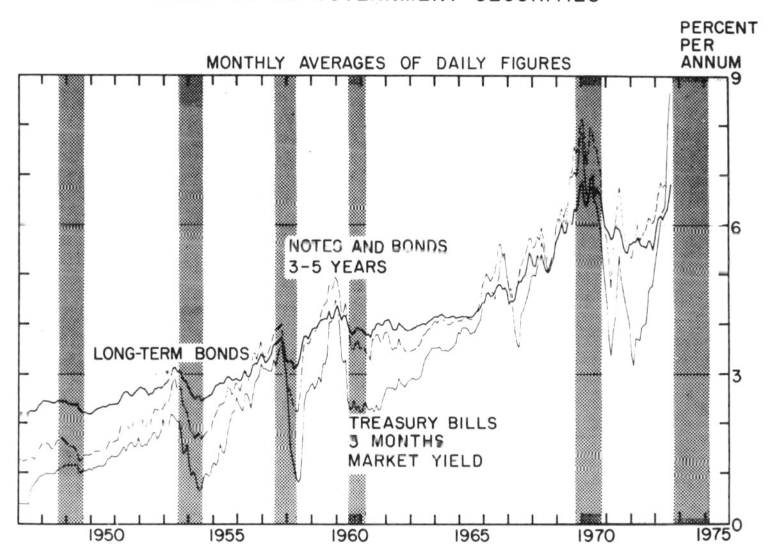

Figure 5-3. Yields on U.S. Government and Other Securities

Source of interest rate data: Historical Chart Book, Board of Governors of the Federal Reserve System.

Note: The shaded areas depict the National Bureau of Economic Research's turning points in business conditions. The Bureau's turning points are November 1948 (peak), October 1949 (trough), July 1953 (peak), August 1954 (trough), July 1957 (peak), April 1958 (trough), May 1960 (peak), February 1961 (trough), November 1969 (peak), November 1970 (trough), November 1973 (peak), and March 1975 (trough).

(cont' fig. 5-3)

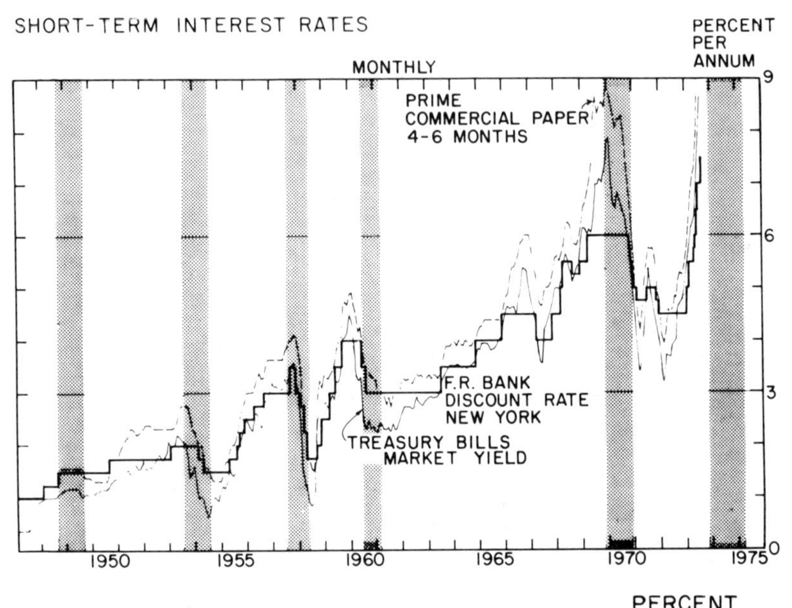
SHORT-TERM INTEREST RATES
MONTHLY
PERCENT PER ANNUM
PRIME COMMERCIAL PAPER 4-6 MONTHS
F.R. BANK DISCOUNT RATE NEW YORK
TREASURY BILLS MARKET YIELD
9
6
3
0
1950
1955
1960
1965
1970
1975

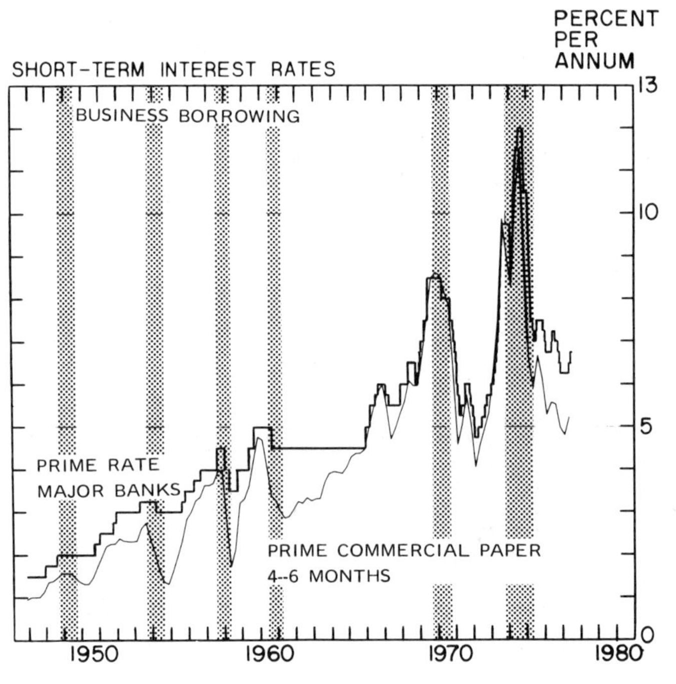
SHORT-TERM INTEREST RATES
PERCENT PER ANNUM
BUSINESS BORROWING
PRIME RATE MAJOR BANKS
PRIME COMMERCIAL PAPER 4--6 MONTHS
13
10
5
0
1950
1960
1970
1980

(cont' fig. 5-3)

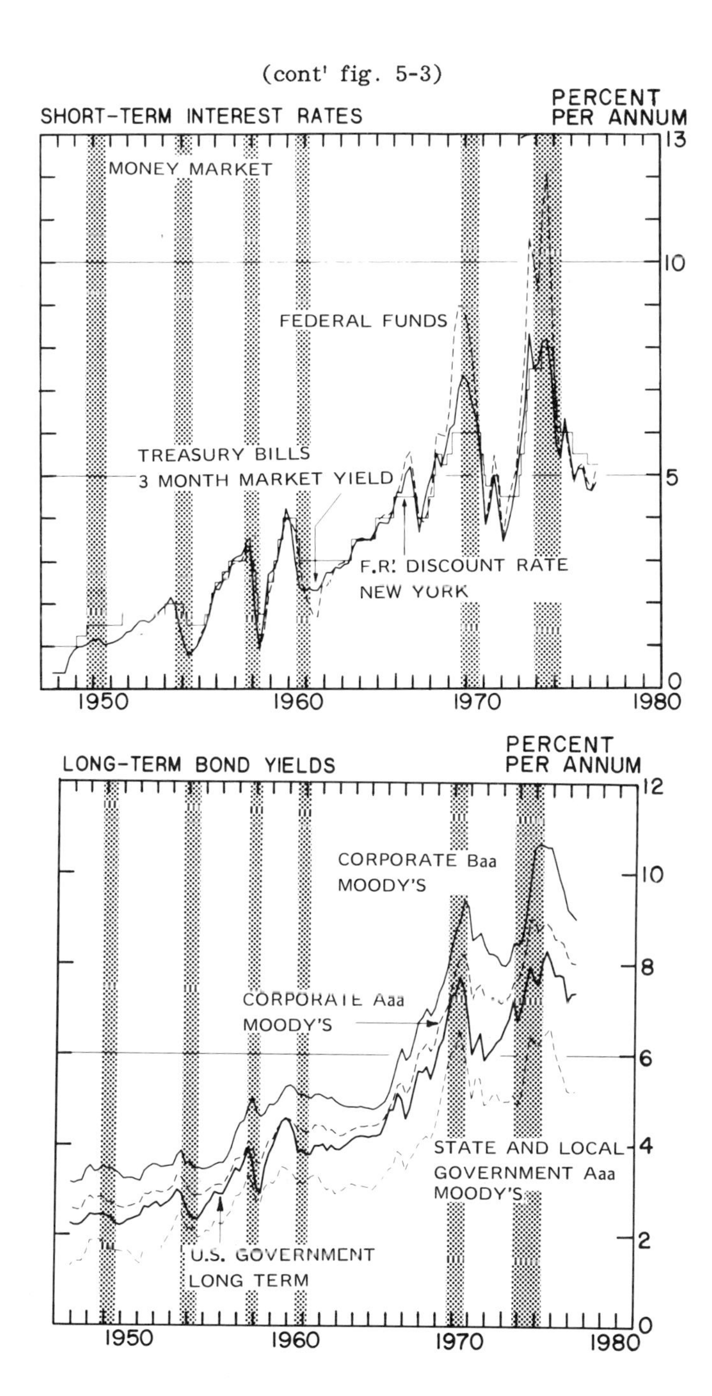
SHORT-TERM INTEREST RATES
PERCENT PER ANNUM
MONEY MARKET
FEDERAL FUNDS
TREASURY BILLS
3 MONTH MARKET YIELD
F.R. DISCOUNT RATE
NEW YORK
13
10
5
0
1950
1960
1970
1980
LONG-TERM BOND YIELDS
PERCENT PER ANNUM
CORPORATE Baa
MOODY'S
CORPORATE Aaa
MOODY'S
STATE AND LOCAL
GOVERNMENT Aaa
MOODY'S
U.S. GOVERNMENT
LONG TERM
12
10
8
6
4
2
0
1950
1960
1970
1980

It is possible that Keynes exaggerated the extent of speculative interest in money and bonds on the part of the mass of economic entities, and it is true that the prospects for speculation and interest rates change when fixed and residual claim assets are introduced. Even so, Keynes's idea centered on a normal rate of interest. As the current rate departed on the downward side from the normal rate, a rise in the rate became more probable. Anticipating such a rise with its stronger probability (or "pull" toward normality), the economic entities strengthened their preference for money balances vis-à-vis bonds as a means of avoiding a loss in bond values. The reverse set of prospects would hold under opposite conditions.

The Liquidity Preference Model

Prospects for speculation led to the liquidity preference model:

$$(5.1) \qquad \text{Demand: } M_d = cY + \frac{b}{i}, \; b > 0$$

$$(5.2) \qquad \text{Supply: } M_s = \gamma$$

$$(5.3) \qquad \text{Equilibrium: } M_s = M_d$$

Equation (5.1) is the equation for an equilateral hyperbola; it depicts a relation between the interest rate (i) and the quantity of money demanded (M_d), with cY and b as constants (actually, they are variable constants, which we will vary at times to simulate certain real world changes). Equation (5.2) depicts the money stock or supply quantity as a control variable along the lines set forth in the next chapter. And, finally, equation (5.3) is simply the condition for a solution to the model (the intersection of two lines). There are three variables (M_d, M_s, and i) and three equations; so, solving for the interest rate, we get:

$$(5.4) \qquad \bar{i} = \frac{b}{\gamma - cY}$$

Actually, this is a relatively static statement, and Keynes and the Keynesians used it in such a form with misleading consequences, as we will see later. Even so, the model and variations of it are not necessarily as static as the solution equation suggests--income certainly changes, and differential changes in spending (income) and the money stock (such as may occur in anticipation of inflation) give rise to changes in velocity. The geometric counterpart to the static form of the model is shown in figure 5-4.

Figure 5-4.
The Liquidity
Preference Model

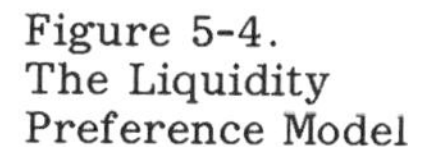

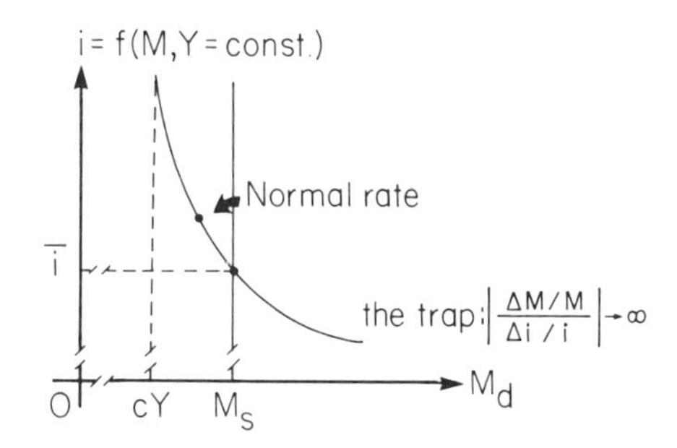

Viewing the solution equation or geometric construction with income held constant, it can be seen that an increase (decrease) in the money supply (M_s or γ) lowers (raises) the rate of interest. This is a part of what we will call Keynes's and the Keynesian's linkage scheme ($\Delta M \rightarrow -\Delta i$). Keynes, however, was very interested in American central banking and the use of open market operations, as stressed in the next chapter, as a means of controlling the interest rate. As a result of his particular view (as well as that of the later Keynesians), an open market purchase, was to increase the demand for bonds, raise their price and lower interest rates (Keynes 1936, 197-8).[8] The cY term of equation (5.1) represents a transaction demand for money, as does the asymptote, cY, of figure 5-4.

For open market purchases to have the envisioned impact, bonds must exhibit three characteristics which they do in fact exhibit: the returns (R's, with the subscripts denoting future time) are contractually determined (as by a bond certificate); the bond is of the marketable type (the interest rate, i, and therefore the value, CV, are determined by the market forces of supply and demand); and, in view of the contractually determined returns, the rate of interest and bond value vary inversely. Indeed, for a long-term bond--as representative of Keynes's two-asset model--a change in the interest rate would have a substantial effect on value, whereas for a short-term bond the effect would be negligible. This is readily seen by taking, say, the first term of equation (5.0) and comparing it with the next-to-the-last term after a given change in the interest rate, e.g.:

$$\frac{R_1}{(1 + i + \Delta i)^1} > \frac{R_{n-1}}{(1 + i + \Delta i)^{n-1}}$$

even with $R_1 = R_{n-1}$. (Note the role of the exponents in the denominators.) The nth term is not considered because it involves the return of the principal as well.

The term b/i in equation (5.1) represents the speculative demand. In the lower segment of the demand curve of figure 5-4 lies the so-called liquidity trap. However, the presence of the trap in the construction is not to suggest the trap as a real world phenomenon or as a condition Keynes thought existed.[9] According to the *a priori* notion of the trap, a large percentage change in the money stock calls forth almost no percentage change in the interest rate.[10] Algebraically

$$\left|\frac{\Delta M/M}{\Delta i/i}\right| \rightarrow \infty \text{ (the trap)}$$

Variations in b/i due to i are actually changes in expectations and the probability of a pull toward normality as one moves along the liquidity preference curve. Keynes also dealt with a difference-of-opinions approach in explaining the demand for money, as set forth later, but his main emphasis was on this pull-toward-normality approach.

Of present importance is the idea of demanding money to hold such that it does not enter the spending stream. With the cY term of figure 5-4 a constant, a strong demand for money vis-à-vis bonds results in a low income velocity (Y/M) as the spending rate is slowed, and a weak demand for money results in a high income velocity as expenditure units attempt to reduce money holdings relative to income. In the one case there is an attempt to reduce the "desired" relative to the "actual" (or controlled) stock of money, and in the other to increase the "desired" relative to the "actual."

What we have now arrived at is one explanation for the roughly parallel movements in velocity and the interest rate that tended to occur before the 1965-77 period. Drawing on the linkage scheme in which a rise (decline) in the interest rate is in effect an inducement to shift out of (into) money balances and into (out of) bonds, the explanation characterizes Keynes's thinking and, to a lesser extent, Keynesian thinking.

In Keynes's model, the treatment of bonds encompasses real capital and leads directly to an explanation of capital spending. For Keynes, the value or demand price of an asset (whether a bond or real capital such as plant and equipment) is controllable just like the bond value. This is juxtaposed against a supply price or cost to yield the investment demand. In contrast, the Keynesian bond category becomes increasingly narrow until there is in Tobin's work a theory of liquidity with money and bonds, as considered in the next chapter, and a separate theory of capital expenditures (Guy 1974).

Structure, Causation, and Statistical Results

To bring out one other dimension of Keynesian thinking and the reverses it was to encounter, some operations may be performed on the simple velocity-interest rate relation using the laws of logarithms (Frazer 1967, chap. 5; 1973, chap. 4):

$$\ln(Y/M) = a + b \ln i$$

Taking the logarithm of the ratio Y/M and rearranging terms, gives:

$$\ln M = b_0 + b_1 \ln Y + b_2 \ln i$$

An early result of using such an equation in the Keynesian period, even among those economists at the Board of Governors of the Federal Reserve System, was to treat the demand for money as determined by income (say, with $b_1 > 1$) and the rate of interest (say with $b_2 < 0$). The Keynesian idea was that the interest rate control variable was a main cause of switching between money balances and non-cash liquid balances (e.g., short-term government bonds). Lagged values were introduced (Frazer 1967, chap. 10) to allow for lags in the effect of monetary policy, which was thought to be reflected in the rate of interest,

$$i_t, i_{t-1}, i_{t-2}, \ldots, i_{t-n}$$

where the sub-scripts denote lagged values.

However, a minority of analysts took issue over the presumption of the interest rate (i) as a control variable and over the idea of fixed lags (say, a fixed lagged structure or fixed weights). In time, the objections of those who dissented were largely justified.

The monetarists had reversed the order of causation found in Keynesian economics and come to consider a different lagged relation, which might be represented:

$$\dot{Y}_t = W_0\dot{M}_t + W_1\dot{M}_{t-1} + W_2\dot{M}_{t-2} + \ldots + W_n\dot{M}_{t-n}$$

There were still those who dissented about the fixed lags (say, a fixed lag structure or constant weights). And, in time, such relations were studied and scrutinized for shifts in the structure.

In line with dissenting opinion, Kopf (1976) reports on a study of the relation between income and current and lagged rates of change in the money stock ($\dot{M}_t$, $\dot{M}_{t-1}$, $\dot{M}_{t-2}$, . . ., $\dot{M}_{t-n}$). He varied the number of quarterly lag terms (i.e., $\dot{M}_t$, $\dot{M}_{t-1}$, $\dot{M}_{t-2}$, etc.), split the sample period (1949:II through 1974:IV) into expansion phases, the first four quarters of each expansion phase, and recession phases.

Kopf's results are instructive with reference to the sorts of theoretical speculations that emerge in this text:

(1) The statistical relations are quite close for periods of contraction and weak in periods of expansion. This is apparently due to the occurrence of more extreme variations in recession phases. (Expansion phases usually proceed slowly, except in their early emergence, while recessionary adjustments occur more rapidly.)

(2) The statistical relations are quite poor in early recovery quarters. This is apparently consistent with a tendency for early recovery from recession to be accompanied by relatively fast growth in output (and thus noninflationary GNP).

(3) There are some changes in the structure of the relations over the entire sample period. For example, the rate of change in the money stock declines less in later recessions. NOTE: All the data analyzed by Kopf are in nominal dollar terms (seasonally adjusted). The strength of his statistical relationships are indicated primarily by the adjusted coefficients of determination, and by the use of other subtle techniques. ("Adjusted" means adjusted for degrees of freedom.)

In directing attention to the implications of his study for forecasting for policy purposes (e.g., projecting the rate of change in GNP on the basis of current and recent rates of change in the money stock), Kopf suggests that, "for policy or projection purposes, separate equations should be used, depending upon the stage of the business cycle, but are likely to detect a long-run shift only with substantial historical perspective." These conclusions and results are of interest in themselves, but also because of the changing structure they suggest. The changing structure is consistent with the view that "outside" forces influence the time series, including those for velocity and interest rates.

5.4. Friedman and Some Monetarist Theory

Milton Friedman, the 1976 Nobel Laureate in economics, is an enigma. Some call him a theorist, and he has referred to himself as an empirical scientist, which may help account for some of the ad hoc character of his approach when viewed as a theoretical system. First, there is a tendency in his work to give the appearance of its having roots in a valid orthodoxy (Frazer 1973, 394-98), in spite of his radical redirection of the theory. The attention to permanent income (expected income over a long period of time or income as an exponential and secular time path) and to rates of change in stock and flow quantities is an example of this redirection. Certainly Friedman's treatment of Keynes's liquidity preference theory, as we introduce it below, is another example.

The notion of underlying trend paths found in Friedman's work may be represented by the equation for a growth curve and, in particular, by the growth curve for the money stock (M):

$$M_t = M_o (1 + g)^t \qquad (5.5)$$

where $\underline{M_o}$ denotes money at the beginning of the base period (or zero time), where $\underline{g}$ is the average growth rate for a period, and where $\underline{t}$ is the number time periods ($t = 0, 1, 2, \ldots, n$)[11]. After a logarithmic transformation of both sides, equation (5.5) becomes:

$$\ln M_t = \ln M_o + \ln (1 + g)t$$

Using this form, the average growth rate for an actual set of data may be readily computed. The latter form suggests a linear regression method for computation. Working back to an equation of the form (5.5), one obtains the following equation for quarterly data for the period 1947-65:

$$(5.6) \qquad M = (107.8)(1.020)^t, \ r^2 = 0.96$$

where M_o is 107.8, the average growth rate per annum is 2.0 percent [(1.020 - 1.00) x 100 = 2.0 percent], and t = 1.00, 1.25, ..., 19.50, 19.75 for seventy-six quarterly observations.

Modified Neoclassical Linkage Scheme

The present part of Friedman's theoretical speculation embraces a neoclassical linkage scheme, as associated with Fisher, with causation running from money to the price level (or to nominal income):

$$\Delta \frac{1}{M}\frac{dM}{dt} \rightarrow \Delta \frac{1}{Y}\frac{dY}{dt}, \ Y = PQ$$

where time rates of change for money and income are noted. In this part of Friedman's work he has been joined by his former student William Gibson. They have also stressed in their separate pieces on this topic the Fisher equation for interest rates and prices, as in the earlier section on neoclassical economics. They deal with the tendency of the economy to generate instability--for spending to overshoot in response to accelerated (decelerated) growth in the money stock, such that income varies about an exponential trend (the equilibrium path).

The tendency toward instability is found in Friedman's and others' empirical investigations and gives rise to the monetarist claim that unstable spending by the government and bad monetary policy are the main sources of instability in the economy. In particular Friedman stressed that the rate of change in the money stock was more procyclical than counter to the destabilizing changes.[12] He pointed to the peaks in the rates of change for the money stock as leading business declines in activity, and troughs as leading recoveries, as illustrated in figure 4-1. And he and others pointed to the fact that the Federal Reserve most often provided a contraction in the money stock during recessionary phases of business from 1921 through 1960 (Frazer 1973, 378-80). The point was that, while, focusing on the rate of interest as the linkage variable, the Federal Reserve thought it was following an easy money policy, even though money balances were actually declining.

For Friedman and some others, demand was the primary determinant of the interest rate, as will be stressed in the next chapter. The analysis proceeds with the Federal Reserve accelerating the growth of the money stock. "Actual" exceeds "desired" balances, and accelerated spending occurs. This rise in income causes the demand curve for money to shift outward. The shift in demand exceeds the initial shift in money, thus overshooting the supply of money. Thus, interest rates rise rather than decline in response to an initial increase in the money stock. This is illustrated in figure 5-5. The linkage scheme is $\Delta M \rightarrow \Delta Y \rightarrow \Delta i$.

This linkage can also be illustrated with a variation of the equation of exchange:

$$\Delta M (Y/M) = \Delta Y$$

where the change in the money stock (ΔM) works through the ratio $\underline{Y/M}$ ("actual $\underline{M}$") to give rise to an increase in income ($\underline{\Delta Y}$). This thrust in income is partly a rise in the price level, which contributes to the expectation of further rise as these expectations are reflected in the nominal interest rate depicted in Fisher's equation and Friedman's linkage scheme.

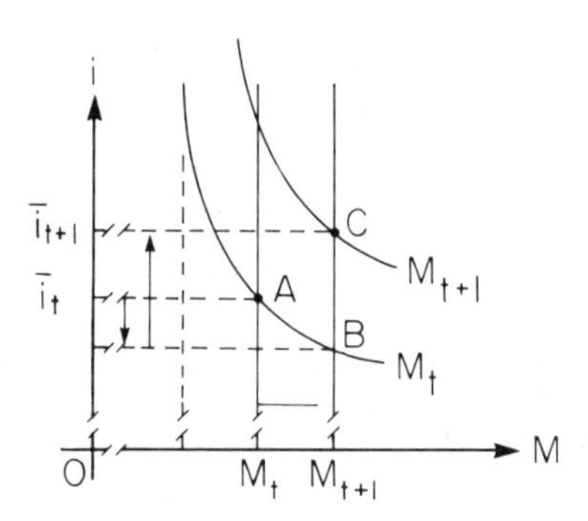

Figure 5-5. Money Stock Growth and Spending

In using the Keynesian construction, as depicted in figure 5-5, Friedman was initially inclined to think of a temporary liquidity effect (a temporary decline in the rate of interest, as a movement along the demand curve from point A to point B). In fact, he and Gibson envisioned an open market purchase of securities by the Federal Reserve as raising bond prices and lowering interest rates, but Friedman also suggested that if the money stock change was announced it would have a more immediate positive effect on rates (moving them up to point C), as if the demand curve in figure 5-5 shifted outward with overshooting. The practice of announcing a monetary policy in advance, as House Concurrent Resolution 133 called for, would become especially relevant at this point.

Time Paths, Equilibrium States, and Damped Oscillations: Hyperthetical Example

Friedman's time paths for nominal income and interest rates may be illustrated further, with reference to time paths and logarithms (Friedman 1968). In these illustrations we proceed with equilibrium time paths for money growth of 3 percent per year, nominal income growth of 3 percent per year, and the interest rate constant at 4 percent per year. At a given time (t_o), the secular time paths for the money stock shifts (without any prior announcement) from 3 to 5 percent, with the consequences depicted in figures 5-6 and 5-7. In the figure for nominal income (5-6), at t_o we note secular time paths C, B, and A. Path C is what would have resulted with continuous monetary growth of 3 percent. Path A depicts a shift upward from path B. Path A is higher because economic entities will hold fewer balances due to an anticipated loss in their purchasing power as the inflation rate increases by 2 percentage points per annum (recall that M increases from 3 to 5 percent). About secular paths A and B are a dotted and broken line respectively. These shown damped oscillations in nominal income that would be cyclical in nature, with nominal income declining in relation to the respective secular paths and then overshooting.

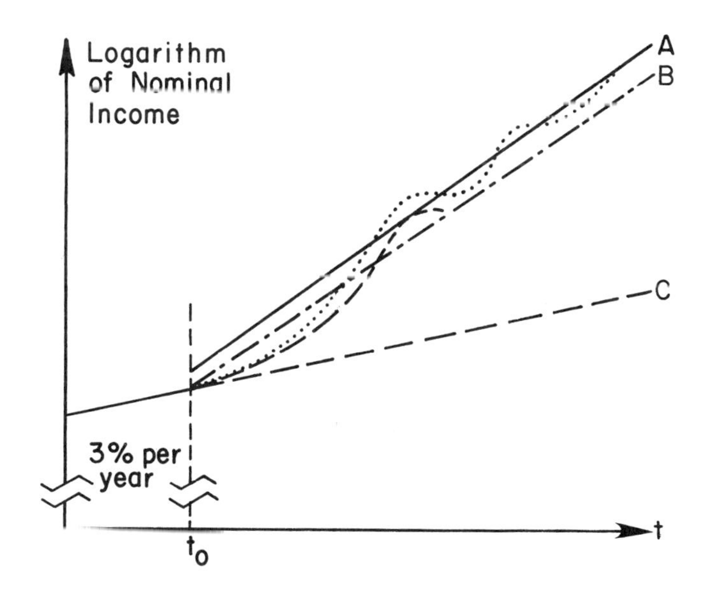

Figure 5-6. Time Paths for Nominal Increase with Monetary Growth Rates of 3 and 5 Percent

Figure 5-7 shows the interest rate changes that would occur under the same conditions. The long-run path for the interest rate at the base time (t_o) shifts from the 4 to the 6 percent level after in response to a rise in the inflation rate of 2 percentage points (as would come about from Fisher's equation for the nominal rate of interest). The cyclical time path initiated by the shift at the base time shows initially the sort of effect depicted in the movement from point A to point B of figure 5-5; namely, it shows a so-called liquidity effect. As income and spending start to rise in response to faster money growth, there is an income effect in figure 5-7 with some overshooting. It is a counterpart to the shift in the liquidity preference curve in figure 5-5.

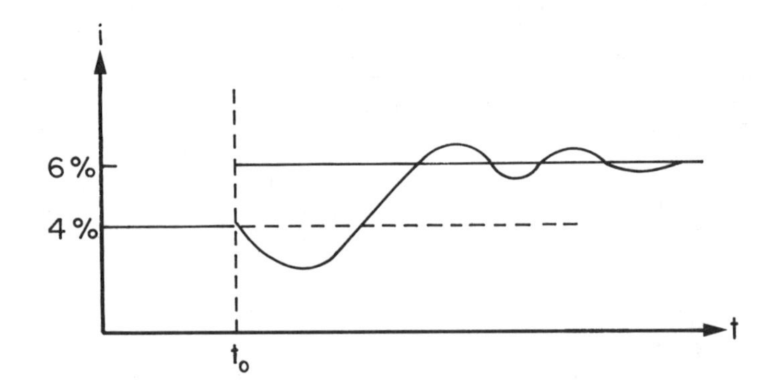

Figure 5-7. Time Paths for the Nominal Interest Rate (Proceeding from i = 4%) with Monetary Growth Rates

In this example the velocity of money (Y/M) and the interest rate (i) would parallel one another as a cyclical matter, but the oscillations would be damped and tend toward new secular equilibria. However, the example would be considered relatively restrictive, because of the following: (1) "actual" equals "desired" money balances at the outset; (2) there is only one discrete (say, quantum) change in the growth for the money stock (as opposed to the pattern of continuous changes in figure 4-1); (3) the monetary policy is not announced in advance, explaining the slow adjustments in expectations; and (4) other complexities surrounding the changes in figure 5-1 are excluded from consideration.

The story of the demand for money, velocity, and interest rate changes is continued in the next section and in other chapters. Only a few additional notes for future reference are considered here.

The monetarists' research had influence. It led to the conclusion: Stabilization is desirable; but, since the interest rate is a measure of business conditions as well as a monetary control, it may be expected to vary with the state of business conditions and expectations about inflation. These expectations may at times become entrenched, complicating the role of monetary policy and the interpretation of the state of business conditions, as during the inflationary recession of 1973-76. Even though interest rates turned upward early in the recovery, they faltered in the fall of 1975 and short-term rates reached the lowest level since late 1972. Apparently this faltering was in response to a more favorable outlook about the immediate control of inflation as the recovery got under way.

Friedman's economics, as just outlined, strongly emphasizes expectations. The Fisher formula says that interest rates reflect expected inflation. Observing the post-World War II secular rise in income velocity, as shown in figures 5-1 and 5-2 and as implied by the faster growth rate for income than for money, Friedman and some others attribute it to greater certainty about the future and an accompanying reduction in the demand for money balances in relation in income. This explanation stands in sharp contrast to the Keynesian explanation of velocity changes, as being caused by the rate of interest, and both explanations contrast with that suggested by reference to figure 5-1, which is discussed in section 5.5.

5.5. Elements of Theory and Empirical Findings: The Velocity-Interest Rate Association

Numerous theories have posited a parallel variation in the rate of interest and the income velocity of money (Frazer 1967; 1973, chap. 14). Keynes's and Keynesian theory especially posited such movement and introduced causation as running from changes in the rate of interest to the velocity ratio, with the rate of interest being viewed in effect as a control variable. Henry Latané in particular was to view the parallel movements almost as an empirical law in a early paper (1954); he later invoked the portfolio theory of James Tobin as an explanation (Latané 1960). For Tobin (1956), a rise in the interest rate induced investors to switch from cash to bonds, thus contributing to a rise in velocity as asset holders attempted to reduce money holdings in relation to income and increase bond holdings in relation to asset size. Later in a Congressional compendium, Latané (1968, 408-9) was to review the entire matter, reassert the hypothesis about the close relation, and update the evidence just as the two variables in figure 5-1 were beginning to depart dramatically.

In contrast to these common interpretations, one opinion (Frazer 1967) held that the two measures (velocity and the interest rates) were responding to the same common force and were in effect being buffeted about by changes in the prospects of inflation. Later, with increasing support for the role of expected inflation as a determinant of interest rates, the position was restated (Frazer 1973): the velocity ratio and the rate of interest are both related to the same force, namely expected inflation. Velocity is tied to a change in the expected inflation rate and the rate of interest to the expected inflation rate. This position with respect to the theory was gleaned from a wide range of evidence (including evidence about the behavior of bonds as a percent of assets and about instability in the structure of a variety of statistical relationships). It was a compact way of stating a crisis in economic theory (Frazer 1973), as indicated by the failure of theory to explain some crucial aspects of economic behavior.[13]

A test of the general notion about the simultaneous response of the key variables that underlie so much of monetary theory follows in this section. The approach in the tests is to allow for the following: the tie between velocity and changes in the expected inflation rate; the tie between the interest rate and the expected inflation rate; and the prospect of forecasting the rate with a varying degree of uncertainty. The goal in so doing is to reestablish parallel movement in the two key variables. Stated differently, the purpose is to reestablish a stable relationship between the key variables, after adjustments, and to offer the achievement as evidence in support of the theory that leads to the adjustments in the respective time series in the first place.

Throughout the rest of this book economic theory is considered partly from the foregoing point of view. One focus is on the control of an economic system that is being buffeted about by changes in the states of expectations. Since the same expectations measure is being related to both velocity and interest rate variables, the actual inflation rate is used as a surrogate for the expected inflation rate. An indicator of uncertainty is used to weight the surrogate for the expected inflation rate, where a change in the indicator is treated as a measure of change in the uncertainty with respect to the forecast for the inflation rate. The standard deviation in the inflation rate forecasts, as obtained from the Livingston survey and as shown in figure 5-8, is used in constructing the uncertainty indicator. It is the ratio of the average of the standard deviation for the period 1966:IV through 1977:II (a constant of 1.35 percentage points) to the standard deviation (σ). As a further adjustment, a factor of 0.80 is used to represent a pull toward normality in expectations and a tendency for forecasts of inflation rates to understate the actual inflation rates over the period in question (Mullineaux 1977). Furthermore, there is an observed tendency for forecasts with a more distant time horizon to be the same as for the eight-month horizon. As reported by Mullineaux (1977, 7), "forecasters seldom envision a significant acceleration or deceleration of inflation when forecasting more than one period ahead."

Results below suggest support for the use of the standard deviation (σ) in inflation rate forecasts as a measure of uncertainty. Further results come later (sect. 18.4). There we find a strong correlation between the standard deviation of inflation rate forecasts and the squared past forecast errors.

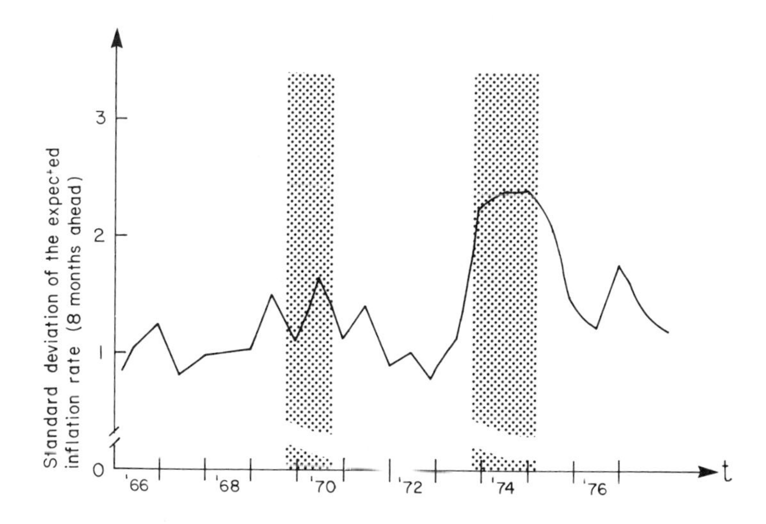

Figure 5-8. The Standard Deviation of the Expected Inflation Rate (forecasts for 8 months ahead), 1964:IV through 1977:II

Notes on the data: The data are Livingston data from John A. Carlson, "A Study of Price Forecasts," Annals of Economic and Social Measurement, Vol. 6 (Winter 1977), Table A1 and from the data bank, Federal Reserve Bank of Philadelphia. The reported data are semiannual, however, and the series of quarterly data has been supplied by taking an average of the data for the beginning and end of each six month period.

The shaded areas are recessions, as indicated by the National Bureau's turning points. The Turning points are shown for November 1979 (peak), November 1970 (trough), November 1973 (peak), and March 1975 (trough).

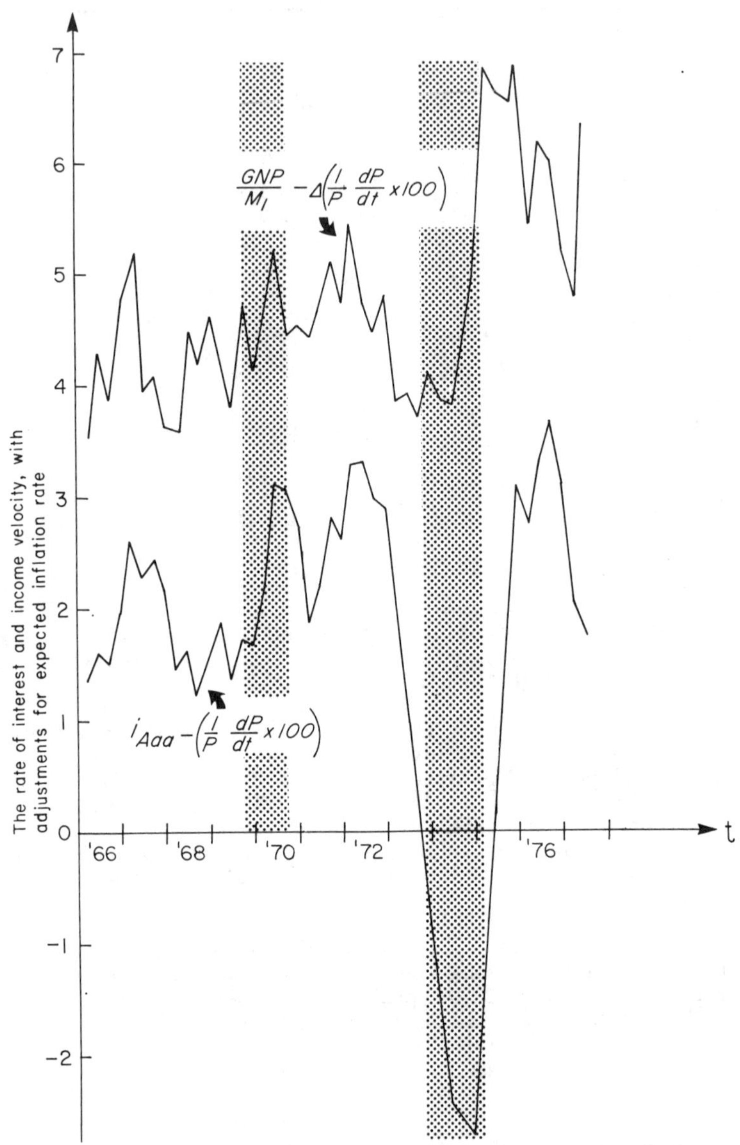

Figure 5-9. The Adjusted Rate of Interest and Income Velocity, 1964:IV through 1977:I

Notes on the data: The interest rate is adjusted for the inflation rate and income velocity for changes in the inflation rate. The inflation rate data are for the GNP deflator as reported by the U.S. Department of Commerce. (Notes from figure 5-8 also apply).

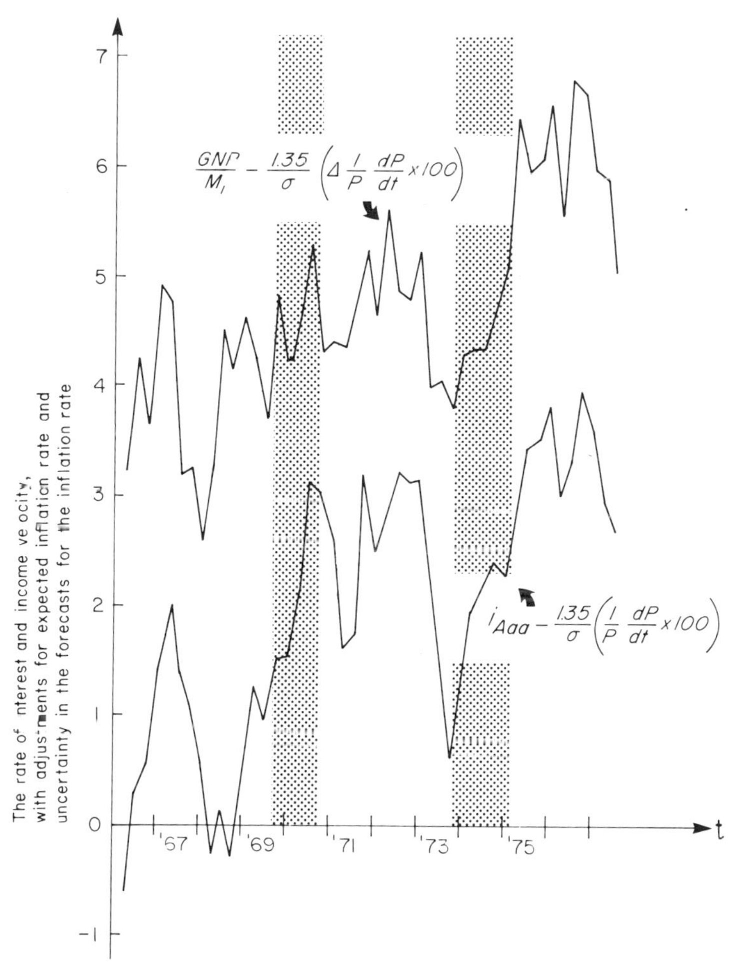

Figure 5-10. The Adjusted Rate of Interest and Income Velocity, 1966:I through 1977:II

Notes on the data: The expected inflation rate and changes in it are adjusted for uncertainty in the forecasts for the inflation rate. The indicator for uncertainty was constructed from the standard deviation in the inflation forecast as shown in figure 5-8. It was constructed thus: by taking the average fluctuation in the forecasts for the period and treating it as a base (1.35 percentage points); by treating the various standard deviations (σs) as the numerator in a ratio with 1.35 as base; and then by treating the reciprocal of these ratios as the uncertainty indicator. (Notes on data in figures 5-8 and 5-9 also apply.)

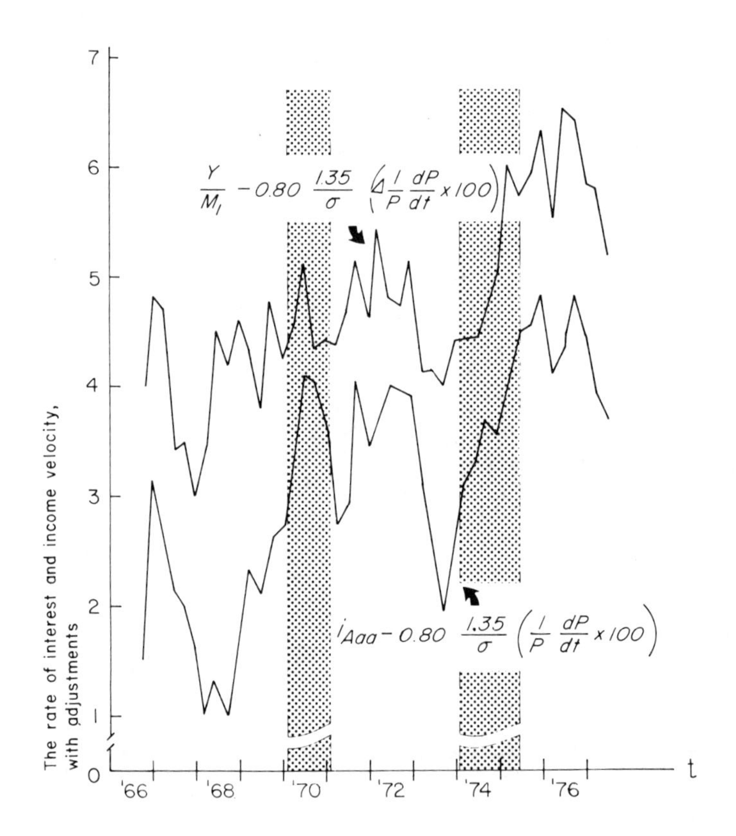

Figure 5-11. The Adjusted Rate of Interest and the Velocity Ratio, 1966:III through 1977:II

Notes on the data: Notes to figures 5-8, 5-9, and 5-10 also apply to this figure.

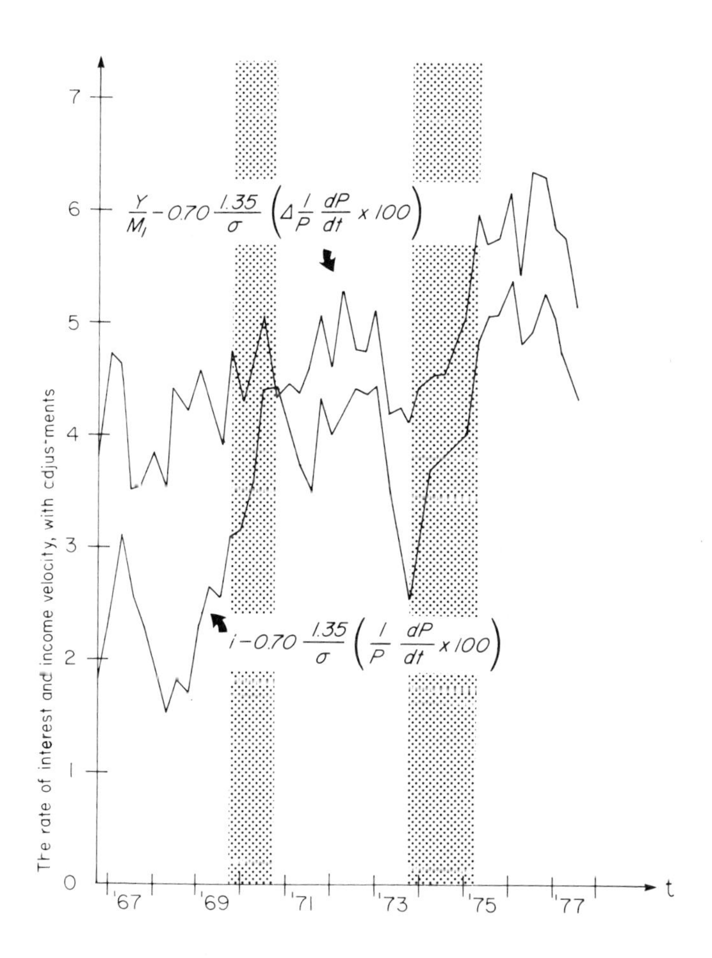

Figure 5-12. The Adjusted Rate of Interest with the Velocity Ratio, 1966:I through 1977:II

Notes on the data: Notes to figures 5-8, 5-9, 5-10, and 5-11 also apply to this figure.

Adjustments in the Time Series

We saw in figure 5-1 that the rate of interest and the income velocity of money drift apart over most of the inflationary period of 1965-77, and even come to vary inversely in the 1974-77 period. However, as shown in figure 5-9, adjustments in the two variables to allow for the expected inflation rate (or the actual inflation rate, viewed as a surrogate for the expected rate), in the one case, and changes in the rate, in the other, tend to reestablish much of the parallel movement once observed for the interest rate and the income velocity ratio. This use of the surrogate is supported by correlations in the inflation rate series for the period 1966:I through 1975:IV, namely:

$$\dot{P}_{CPI} = 0.28 + \underset{(12.14)}{0.90}\,\dot{P}_{GNP},\quad r^2 = 0.80$$

$$\dot{P}_{CPI} = -0.21 + \underset{(10.70)}{1.470}\,\dot{P}^e_{CPI},\quad r^2 = 0.75$$

$$\dot{P}_{CPI} = -0.66 + \underset{(11.00)}{1.52}\,\dot{P}^e_{CPI,\ t-2},\quad r^2 = 0.76$$

(Note: The values in parentheses are t statistics.)

where $\dot{P}_{CPI}$ is the inflation rate for the consumer price index, $\dot{P}_{GNP}$ is the rate for the GNP deflator, P^e_{CPI} is the forecast for the CPI inflation rate eight months ahead (as reported in the Livingston survey, Carlson 1977, and Mullineaux 1977), and $P^e_{CPI,\ t-2}$ is the forecasted inflation rate lagged two quarters.

A major exception to the reestablishment of a parallel movement in figure 5-9 appears for the period 1973:I through 1976:I. This is characterized by extreme changes in the standard deviation for forecasts obtained and reported as a part of the adjusted anticipatory series known as Livingston data, as shown in figure 5-8.

The standard deviation shown in figure 5-8 is for the inflation rate forecasts for eight months ahead. One might presume, however, that extending the horizon for the forecasted inflation rate would not reduce the uncertainty with respect to the forecast. In any case, the widely observed parallel movements in the interest rate and income velocity of the earlier pre-1965 years are virtually reestablished in figure 5-10, where the surrogate for the inflation rate is adjusted for uncertainty. In figures 5-11 and 5-12, the inflation rate of figure 5-10 is further adjusted by factors of 0.80 and 0.70 respectively in order to allow for the tendency to under forecast the actual inflation rate, as indicated by the parameters of the simple regressions above for the inflation rates (e.g.,

$d\dot{P}_{CPI}/d\dot{P}^{e}_{CPI,\ t-2}$ = 1.52) and by the coefficients of determination (r^2 = 0.75 and r^2 = 0.76 respectively).

Some Statistical Results

Statistical analyses of time series for the velocity ratio and the rate of interest (Moody's yield on high-grade corporate bonds) for the period 1966:I through 1977:II, as shown in selected figures, yield the following results.

Unadjusted variables (as depicted in figure 5-1):

$$\ln i = -0.47 + \underset{(8.22)}{1.55} \ln V, \quad r^2 = 60.54$$

$$\ln i = 0.24 + \underset{(0.74)}{1.27} \ln V + a\,t + b\,(t \ln V), \quad r^2 = 85.90$$

Computed F-value for overlapping sample = 37.61
(Note: The values in parentheses are t statistics.)

Variables adjusted for expected inflation, uncertainty in the forecast, seasonality, and 0.80 factor as depicted in figure 5-11:

$$\ln i = -1.89 + \underset{(7.85)}{1.91} \ln V, \quad r^2 = 59.45$$

$$\ln i = -1.71 + \underset{(3.35)}{1.61} \ln V + a\,t + b\,(t \ln V), \quad r^2 = 68.20$$

Computed F-value for overlapping sample = 5.78

These results indicate that the coefficient of determination can be substantially increased (from 60.54 to 85.90) simply by adding time (t and $t \ln V$) as variables. This, together with the large F-value (37.61), indicates that the structure of the relation from figure 5-1 is unstable over time. The results corresponding to series from figure 5-11, on the other hand, indicate that the structure for the adjusted series is more stable.

Furthermore, using varying parameter regression methods, as found in Cooley and Prescott (1976), additional results are obtained. Table 5-1 contains the slope parameters for the series from figure 5-1 for the period 1966:I through 1977:II (with a base of six quarters) and for the model $\ln V = a + b \ln i$, and table 5-2 contains slope parameters that are obtained using adjusted data with the factor 70.0 for the same variables, same period, and same model.

The slope parameters in table 5-2 are more stable than those in table 5-1, as visual inspection indicates. The parallel movement in the series from figure 5-12, however, is brought into best perspective by addressing the slope parameter for a

Table 5-1. The Velocity-Interest Rate Association 1966:I through 1977:II--Varying Parameter Regression (for relation, ln V = a + b ln i, with variables as in figure 5-1)

Slope parameter (vertical least squares fit) Col (1)	Slope parameter (horizontal least (squares fit) Col (2)	Average of data in Columns (1) and (2) Col (3)
0.01	-3.98	-1.98
0.02	3.01	1.52
0.03	2.57	1.30
0.03	2.23	1.13
0.05	2.50	1.28
0.07	2.42	1.25
0.08	2.11	1.09
0.11	2.38	1.25

Table 5-2. The Velocity-Interest Rate Association, 1966:I through 1977:II--Varying Parameter Regression (for relation, ln V = a + b ln i, with variables adjusted as in figure 5-11)

Slope Paramter (vertical least squares fit) Col (1)	Slope parameter (horizontal least squares fit) Col (2)	Average of data in col's (1) and (2) Col (3)
0.54	1.53	1.04
0.58	1.86	1.22
0.52	1.26	0.89
0.61	1.23	0.92
0.69	1.17	0.93
0.81	1.21	1.01
0.97	1.18	1.08
1.15	1.24	1.20

third possible regression line, as in column (3) for the slope parameter.[14] The column (2) parameters become in effect a possible upper limit to the ordinary slope parameters of column (1), with the possible "true" slope parameters falling somewhere in between. The results in column (3) are averages of the results in columns (1) and (2). And, indeed, the average for the slopes reported for the adjusted data in table 5-2 is 1.04. This reflects parallel movement.

The reestablishment of the original, pre-1966 parallel movement in the rate of interest and velocity in more recent data by adjusting for inflation, accelerated inflation, and uncertainty should not be interpreted to suggest that now we have the adjusted variables for tracing causation from one to the other. The present interpretation is that even the adjusted variables are responding to the expectations with respect to inflation. The pre-1966 movements were doing the same thing, but adjustments of the type outlined above were not required to obtain the parallel movements because the inflation was never sustained in a single direction long enough during the sample periods to drive the movements apart.

5.6. The Velocity-Interest Rate Association (The Payments Mechanism)

Since Fisher's time, changes in the payments mechanism have been recognized as a potential source of change in the turnover of money balances. For the 1966-77 period, the payments mechanism was apparently little affected. Before that period cards had become well established (probably in part as a substitute for trade credit, traditionally viewed) and toward the end of that period the prospects for future changes in the payments mechanism loomed much larger. Arthur Burns, reporting as Chairman of the Board of Governors before the Joint Economic Committee in February 1976, could list the following developments as possibly modifying the payments mechanism:

> The spread of overdraft facilities at banks, increased use of credit cards, the growth of NOW accounts in New Hampshire and Massachusetts,[15] the emergence of money market mutual funds, the development of telophonic transfers of funds from savings to checking accounts, and the growing use of savings deposits to pay utility bills, mortgage payments, and other obligations. One very recent development that has had a considerable downward influence on the level of demand deposits was the regulation issued by the banking agencies last November, which enabled partnerships and corporations to open savings accounts at commercial banks in amounts up to $150,000.

All of this means that changes in the statistical composition of money will have to be made at some date to maintain a consistency with the sort of relationships covered in this chapter, and that a different underlying velocity rate may emerge from the changing technology (Commission 1977; Kimball 1978, and Niblack 1976) and the increasing similarities among financial institutions (Lovati 1977).

Of particular importance as one looks ahead is the continuing emrgence of "electronic money," such as under an electronics funds transfer system, or EFTS. As of mid-1976 limited EFT systems included some bank-to-bank systems and a number of local customer-to-bank systems. CHIPS arrangements among commercial banks in New York City are an illustration of the first type, and facilities through which a bank customer may make payments at local stores by presenting a card are examples of the second type. The purpose of the EFT is to permit transfers among deposit liability accounts without the use of checks. In some measure they may enable customers to operate with smaller deposit balances where overdrafts (a use of preauthorized credit) are permitted as a part of the system. The main benefit to the public from such a system is the reduced cost of transferring balances. In 1976 the cost per check for transferring balances was estimated at 32 cents per check; by eliminating the check, EFT was to reduce the cost of paper work.

5.7. Summary

The following characterize chapter 5: the classification of assets; the distinction between the short and long run; and the emphasis on statics, dynamics, equilibrium, the point of monetary intervention, linkage schemes, and the role of expectations. Variation in the velocity of money and the rate of interest in relation to changes in the expected inflation rate and the inflation rate, respectively, have received particular attention.

Consider, first, the classes of assets--money and bonds as fixed claim assets, and real property such as plant and equipment and equities as residual claim assets. The neoclassicists did not say much about this, but their theory of money and that of output were separate and distinct. Much of what they said has been characterized by Say's law. Keynes, in his turn, distinguished money (including some short-term assets) from all other assets (which he treated as bonds). To the theory he contributed dynamic overtones, motives for holding money, the interrelationship of real and monetary sectors; but there were inconsistencies. Depending on how these are resolved, one may move in different analytical directions. In the hands of the Keynesians, Keynes's analysis of expectations was overlooked and expectations were treated as a constant. The stress on the short run was ambiguous. For Keynes it was a period of constant expectations, as it was for the Keynesians, and both were interested in the stabilization of unstable business conditions as depicted by the so-called short cycle (or trade cycle, as known to British writers).

With the short run defined as a period of constant expectations, and proceeding from a static equilibrium in terms of the supply and demand for money, both Keynes and the Keynesians saw the interest rate as being controlled by the central bank. Increasing the supply of money, especially by engaging in an open market purchase, lowered the interest rate; the latter caused the demand price or value of capital goods to exceed the supply price or cost. This set the stage for control over investment spending. The Keynesians, however, introduced weaknesses in their own linkage scheme. Namely, they introduced the prospect of a liquidity trap and the closely related stagnation thesis. Monetary policy was relegated to a secondary role.

The neoclassicists had stressed the long run as the monetarists were later to do in the quantity theory approach. For Irving Fisher, there was the equation of exchange with the velocity of money determined by habit and the payments mechanism in the short run, and with changes in the money stock reflected in price level changes. For Milton Friedman, the long run was a norm or trend where all expectations were realized and about which real world changes occurred, as over the business cycle. For Friedman and monetarists, as for the neoclassicists, the money stock had a more direct influence on spending than in the Keynesian framework. The neoclassicist's effect was a real balance effect with more wealth resulting in more spending. The Friedmanian effect operated via an imbalance in desired and actual money balances, proceeding from equilibrium, where desired equal actual balances. The indicator for the imbalance (or balance) is the income velocity of money, which increases when actual balances exceed desired money balances, and vice versa. Further, Friedman's and other modern analysts' treatment of stock and flow quantities has been more dynamic in that it stresses rates of change and differential rates of change rather than levels and changes in levels.

Using a variation of Keynes's and the Keynesians liquidity preference model, Friedman and Gibson also added a note on the tendency of the reaction to rates of change in the money stock to cause overshooting, and instability in spending. This note altered the Keynesian linkage mechanism so that accelerated growth in the money stock caused interest rates to rise rather than decline, as in Keynesian analysis, and incorporated Fisher's interest rate equation with inflation expectations.

Fisher had a theory of demand for bank loans that entailed expectations and an analysis of the short cycle. As sales by business firms increased their expectations about future returns became more buoyant and raised the rate of return on capital spending relative to the interest rate. The imbalance led to a greater loan demand. This theory was a forerunner to aspects of Keynes's and the Keynesian linkage scheme, namely: that the rate of interest influences spending when it is below the rate of return on capital outlays.

Fisher also defined the nominal rate of interest as the sum of the real rate and the expected rate of change in the price level. This in conjunction with the procyclical nature of the rate of interest was to suggest to later theorists that the Federal Reserve did not control the rate of interest directly from the supply side of the market; demand side influences came forward especially.

Keynesians, monetarists, and others have noted a tendency for the velocity of money and the rate of interest to move together over the short cycle and in other instances, too. The Keynesians read causation into this. For them, the interest rate changes induced switching from money into (out of) bonds, and thus caused the holdings of money to change in relation to income. One dissenting view, however, questioned the Federal Reserve's precise control over the rate of interest from the supply side of the money market. According to this view, the rate of interest and velocity respond more to the same sets of forces, with the income velocity of money being tied to changes in the expected inflation rate. Uncertainty in the forecast enters into the theory, and strong changes in the payment mechanism can play a complicating role.

The forces impounding on expectations enter in as an adjunct to the usual theory. They may include announcements, exhortation by a central political figure, news events, and more or less certainty about the future (and hence faster or slower turnover of money balances).

Fisher's interest rate equation especially becomes useful in dealing with aspects of an unusual phenomenon of the early 1970s, called "stagflation," a term that refers to the tendency for the price level to rise even during recessions. A continuing rise in the price level during a recession may be related to the failure of the rate of interest to adjust downward as rapidly in an inflationary recession such as that for 1973-75. This is the concern of a later chapter on deceleration and unemployment.

In the following chapters, certain parts of these foregoing theories and approaches will come forward in a positive, empirical approach to economic study. There is more attention to the dynamics of the theory (differential rates of change in stock and flow quantities), for example. The older Keynesian model gets remodeled. Equilibrium is treated as the long-run, sustainable growth path about which changes occur. A greater awareness of the roles for expectations and uncertainty emerges. A treatment of bank loans and equality of foresight by bankers and businessmen also receives attention. We will note a tendency for the changing rate of inflation to have a stimulating or damping influence, and society's ability to adjust to any constant rate. This will mean that the precise level of inflation is of no consequence as far as serving as an economic stimulus. A zero rate is as good as a double digit rate. Uncertainty, as in the next chapter, introduces the subject of probability in greater detail. Later we will consider learning on the part of economic entities and a host of topics pretty much obscured by the economics in the precomputer era of economic analysis.

FOOTNOTES

1. One may recall George Santayana's widely quoted dictum (Life of Reason I): "Those who cannot remember the past are condemned to repeat it."
2. Say's law symbolized features of classical economics extending beyond a formal statement of the law. The law,

nevertheless, may be formally stated as a zero sum of excess demands for all commodities exclusive of money. In symbols,

$$\sum_{i=1}^{m-1} p_i E_i = 0,$$

as discussed in the appendix to chapter 1.

In these statements the reference is usually to all goods and services--exclusive of money balances in the one case and inclusive in the other. In the present and later chapters, however, sets of prices corresponding to different sets of goods and services are recognized. PT will stand for the product of the average of prices on all goods and services entering into transactions and the total number of transactions. PQ will stand for the product of the average of prices on the current output of goods and services and the output itself. The latter set of prices is the one in which Keynes had a main interest in discussing the ability of the economic system to adjust to a full employment output (Q_f).

3. The notation is actually that for a time rate of change in prices. In actual computation

$$\frac{P_t - P_{t-1}}{P_{t-1}} \approx \frac{1}{P}\frac{dP}{dt}$$

If the time period (t, t-1) is one year, then (1/P)(dP/dt) = dP/P, and multiplying by 100 yields a percentage rate of change.

4. Livingston data are so-called after their originator, Joseph A. Livingston, a prominent economic journalist from Philadelphia. Livingston started collecting his data by means of a semiannual survey of fifty economists in the business and academic community. In the early 1970s, research economists became interested in the series and in 1978 the Federal Reserve Bank of Philadelphia entered into arrangements with Livingston to maintain the series after his death.

5. The equation is not ready for actual estimation in the form shown, but is made ready by substituting the right-hand member in Fisher's interest rate equation, such that

$$i = \text{const.} + w_o\dot{P}_t + w_1\dot{P}_{t-1} + \ldots + w_n\dot{P}_{t-n}$$

6. Keynes's criticism of the old quantity theory has been stated by Patinkin (1976, 119):

> The quantity theory holds only on two conditions: first, that the speculative demand for money "will always be zero in equilibrium"; second, that the level of output will always be constant at full employment.

Keynes's argument in the latter case was that with no speculative demand and with the assumption of full employment, output and velocity would be constant and that "the wage-unit [a special price] and the price-level will be directly proportonal to the quantity of money." (1936, p. 209).

7. Due to the option of fitting least squares regression lines by minimizing vertical or horizontal differences between the line and the observations, two equations such as (2) and (2') are possible. The true regression line would lie somewhere between the two lines shown in the left-hand part of figure 5-2. This manipulation for obtaining the second line, however, does not alter the correlation coefficient ($r^2 = 0.89$). It reads that the variation in either one of the two variables accounts for 89 percent of the variation in the other variable in a strictly computational sense.

   Many have dealt with the covariation in the income velocity of money and the rate of interest, as reviewed elsewhere (Frazer 1967; 1973, chap. 4), some going back to pre-World War II periods.

8. Forwarding notes on the proofs of the General Theory in 1935, D. H. Robertson also considers "open-market purchases, designed to lower the rate of interest." (See Moggridge 1973a, p. 499) Writing to R. K. Harrod in 1937 on Harrod's The Trade Cycle, Keynes again refers to open market operations. This time the comment is with reference to purchases in the short-term vis-à-vis the long-term sector of the market (Moggridge 1973b, p. 153).

9. The evidence has not supported the prospect of a trap situation in the 1930s. (Frazer 1967, chap. 4; 1973, chap. 11.)

10. Keynesians seemed influenced by the idea of a liquidity trap as an explanation for the failure of monetary policy to bring about spending and high level employment during the years of the Great Depression. At the time, in the early emergence of Keynesian theory, the discussion of the trap was reinforced by the "stagnation thesis" (Scaperlanda 1977), which stated that capitalism had run its course, that intensive capital development had pushed the rate of return on real capital spending too low to attract new private spending, and that government spending (the socialization of investment, the euthanasia of the rentier) must take its place. These alleged failures of monetary policy and the system of private capital spending paved the way for the Era of Fiscal Policy and the Keynesian interest in that policy, somewhat to the exclusion of monetary policy.

11. The computations for equation (5.5) with a 5 percent annual growth rate may be illustrated:

Period	Money Supply	
$t = 0$	M_o	$= M_o$
$t = 1$	$M_o \times 1.05$	$= M_o\ (1+g)$
$t = 2$	$(M_o \times 1.05)\ 1.05$	$= M_o\ (1+g)^2$
$t = 3$	$M_o\ (1.05)^2\ 1.05$	$= M_o\ (1+g)^3$
.	.	.
.	.	.
.	.	.
$t = n$	$M_o(1.05)^n$	$= M_o\ (1+g)^n$

12. The work of Karl Brunner and Allan Meltzer focused on this point, too, as reviewed in Frazer's Crisis in Economic Theory, chapter 10. It was of considerable influence. Some point out that the notion of a procyclical change in bank credit (and/or money) is found in the work of Knut Wichsell, a Swede. It Is interesting to note, however, that the notion had no influence on Federal Reserve policy until the empirical work of Friedman, Brunner and Meltzer, and others.
13. One insightful review of this book stated the relevant conclusion bluntly:

> "For Frazer, the crisis in current monetary theory stems from an erronous explanation of the synchonous relationship between interest rates and income velocity.... Frazer [he continues] proposes an "alternative" approach in which both interest rates and velocity react simultaneously to changes in expectations [especially with respect to inflation]." (Laurant 1975, 1299-1301)

The reviewer may have added that this simultaneity would come about after some abstraction from the noise (Frazer 1973, 398-406), after recognizing some differences in the degree of planning and in the sensitivity with respect to the future by economic agents (468-84), and after some smoothing of the data to allow the Federal Reserve to control monetary aggregates (as discussed in the next chapter).

Other reviewers include Stanley R. Johnson's review in the October 1976 Southern Economic Journal, pp. 1188-89, and a review article by Charles J. Woelfel in the December 1974 Wall Street Review of Books, pp. 322-26.
14. Given the simple regression line for the variables $\underline{V}$ and $\underline{i}$ in case one, and $\underline{i}$ and $\underline{V}$ in case two, a third slope parameter is possible (Frazer 1967, pp. 34-39). Notably, it is the slope parameter obtained by implicit differenti-

ation (dV/di) of the regression equation for the second regression line (e.g., i = a + bV). This slope may serve as an upper limit on the slope of the "true" regression line.

15. NOW accounts refer to interest bearing checking accounts, called Negotiable Order of Withdrawal accounts. This literal payment of interest on checking accounts was initiated on an experimental basis in 1974, but ultimately was to be permitted nationwide.

    Some economists have historically considered the difference between the production costs per dollar of deposit and the service charges per dollar of deposit as an implicit interest payment on checking accounts.

SELECTED READINGS AND REFERENCES

Carlson, John A. 1977. "A Study of Price Forecast." Annals of Economic and Social Measurement (Winter).

Commission. 1977. Final Report of National Commission on Electronic Fund Transfers, EFT in the United States: Policy Recommendations and the Public Interest. Washington, D.C.

Cooley, Thomas F., and Edward C. Prescott. 1976. "Estimation in the Presence of Sequential Variation." Econometrica (January).

Frazer, William. 1967. The Demand for Money. Cleveland, Ohio: The World Publishing Company. Chapters 4 and 5.

__________. 1973. Crisis in Economic Theory. Gainesville, Fla.: University of Florida Press.

__________. 1978. "Monetary Policy, Rational Expectations, and Evolutionary Economics." Journal of Economic Issues (June).

Fisher, Irving. 1896. Appreciation and Interest. New York: Macmillan. (Reprinted by Augustus M. Kelly. (New York 1961).

__________. 1911. The Purchasing Power of Money, rev. ed. New York: The Macmillan Company.

Friedman, Milton. 1968. "Factors Affecting the Level of Interest Rates." In Donald P. Jacobs and Richard T. Pratt, eds., Savings and Residental Financing: 1968 Conference Proceedings. Chicago, Ill.: United States Savings and Loan League.

Friedman, Milton and Ann Jacobson Schwartz. 1970. Monetary Statistics of the United States. New York: Columbia University Press for the National Bureau of Economic Research.

Guy, Charles Eugene. 1974. "Liquidity Preference Theory: Its Relation to Manufacturing Corporations." An Unpublished Doctoral Dissertation, University of Florida.

Hicks, John R. 1974. The Crisis in Keynesian Economics. New York: Basic Books, Inc.

Hunt, W. H. 1974. The Rehabilitation of Say's Law. Athens, Ohio: Ohio University Press.

Keynes, J. M. 1923. A Tract on Monetary Reform. London: Macmillan and Co., Limited. Chapter 3.

__________. 1936. The General Theory of Employment, Interest, and Money, New York: Harcourt, Brace and Company.

Kimball, Ralph C. 1978. "The Maturing of the NOW Accounts in New England," New England Economic Review. Federal Reserve Bank of Boston (July/ August)

Kopf, David H. 1976. "Money and Income in the Postwar Period: An Analysis by Stage of the Business Cycle." Reserve Paper No. 7602, Federal Reserve Bank of New York (March).

Latané, Henry. 1954. "Cash Balances and the Interest Rate: A Pragmatic Approach." Review of Economics and Statistics (November).

__________. 1960. "Income Velocity and Interest Rates: A Pragmatic Approach." Review of Economics and Statistics (November).

__________. 1968. "Income Velocity and Interest Rates: Policy Implications." In Compendium on Monetary Policy Guidelines and Federal Reserve Structure, Subcommitte on Domestic Finance of the Committee on Banking and Currency, House of Representatives. Washington, D.C.: U.S. Government Printing Office (December).

Laurent, Robert. 1975. "A Review of Crisis in Economic Theory by William J. Frazer, Jr." Journal of Political Economy (December).

Lovati, Jean M. 1977. "The Growing Similarities Among Financial Institutions." Review, Federal Reserve Bank of St. Louis (October).

Moggridge, Donald, ed. 1973a. The General Theory and After, Part I Preparation: The Collected Writings of John Maynard Keynes London: The Macmillan Press, Ltd.

__________. 1973b. The General Theory and After, Part II: The Collected Writings of John Maynard Keynes. London: The Macmillan Company, Ltd.

Mullineaux, Donald V. 1977. "Inflation Expectations in the U.S.: A Brief Anatomy." Business Review, Federal Reserve Bank of Philadelphia (July/August).

Niblack, William C. 1976. "Development of Electric Funds Transfer Systems." Review, Federal Reserve Bank of St. Louis (September).

Patinkin, Don. 1965. Money, Interest, and Prices: An Integration of Monetary Value Theory, 2nd ed. New York: Harper & Row.

__________. 1976. Keynes' Monetary Thought: A Study of Its Development. Durham, N.C.: Duke University Press.

Popper, Karl R. 1965. Conjectures and Refutations. New York: Harper and Row, Publishers.
Richardson, Dennis W. 1970. Electric Money: Evolution of an Electric Funds Transfer System. Cambridge, Mass.: MIT Press.
Scaperlanda, Anthony. 1977. "Hansen's Secular Thesis Once Again." Journal of Economic Issues (June).
Sowell, Thomas. 1972. Say's Law: An Historical Analysis. Princeton, N.J.: Princeton University Press.

Chapter 6

Money Stock and Money Demand

6.1. Introduction

In the 1960s, economists and Federal Reserve officials came to focus their attention on monetary aggregates as well as credit and money market conditions (as indicated by rates of interest). Different groups of monetarist researchers placed more or less emphasis on the money base (bank reserves plus currency held by the public) and the money stock (demand deposits net of interbank and government deposits, plus currency held by the public). The emphasis, however, was to bring attention to the monetary aggregates viewed broadly and including bank reserves, bank credit (the total of loans and investments extended by commercial banks), and the money stock (Frazer 1973, chap. 2).

At the policy level, an outgoing chairman of the Board of Governors chaired his last meeting in January 1970, at which a new form of directive to the manager of the open market account was adopted (Pierce 1979, 486; Poole 1979, 475). In it the aggregates were to receive more attention, with a short-term market rate of interest being viewed as an instrument to facilitate the control of the money stock. The change was perhaps inevitable in the light of foregoing research and economic persuasion and, in any case, the new chairman was to foster the transition towards attention to the monetary aggregates broadly viewed, but with a good bit of abstraction from the day-to-day detail of control over the money stock. In that short-time frame, attention was still to be focused on money market conditions, because of some combination of traditionally held views within the Federal Reserve System and views on the part of the new Chairman (sect. 12.5, and Hass 1979). In time, as introduced in section 6.2, the lingering focus on money market conditions, even for operational purposes was to cause further trouble and to undergo further change of landmark proportion on a Saturday night, October 6, 1979.

In particular, under the leadership of Carter appointee G. William Miller from March of 1978 to August 1979, the Federal Reserve found itself (1) going through and partly supporting an accelerating inflation, from a 9 to a 13 percent neighborhood (as measured by the CPI, on a quarterly basis, at an annual rate), and (2) setting a stage for the rate to reach an 18 percent neighborhood in the first quarter of 1980. Indeed, the mid-summer 1979 conditions contributed to a crisis state in White House policy matters and cabinet-level changes, with the "team player" William Miller being transferred from the Federal Reserve to the Treasury, and with the appointment of Paul A. Volcker to the Chairmanship at the Federal Reserve. At the time, Volcker was President of the Federal Reserve Bank of New York (and, as such, also vice-chairman of the Federal Reserve's Open Market Committee). He was known to favor a "disciplined" monetary policy in order to achieve a sense of stability. As we will note from time to time, foreign exchange and free gold markets reacted to the changes (sects. 14.4, 17.3, 19.1)--initially favorably in the Volcker case, from an anticipated, inflation-rate standpoint. However, by October of 1979, reactions against the dollar were continuing at record proportions, and the money supply was accelerating faster than had been expected. Hence, the October 6 actions (Announcements 1979, 830). As dealt with in section 6.2, a primary action was to place "greater emphasis in day-to-day operations on the supply of bank reserves and less emphasis on confining short-term fluctuations in the Federal funds rate.

As stated, matters were drastically changed in 1970, further formalized in 1975, and dramatically altered on October 6, 1979, as far as the indicators of monetary policy were concerned. Results during the 1970-78 era may have been different, as some speculate (Poole 1979, 474-79), but several developments emerge from the new attention to monetary policy: the personality and orientation of the chairman is predominant in policy matters; the political aspects of monetary policy must be confronted both in terms of the success of the chairman and in terms of the Federal Reserve's maintaining independence within the framework of government; and precise control over any single monetary aggregate within less than a period of a few months is impossible under the institutional and operational arrangements that have characterized the system. These larger political matters are addressed much later (sects. 10.3 and 12.5). The control mechanism itself comes up shortly.

The Federal Reserve actions with respect to the move toward a regime of monetary and credit aggregates, as we may call it, are of historical importance. However, they and related matters, such as Federal Reserve appointments and Presidential influence on policy for political ends (nay the political business cycle, as defined and dealt with on other occasions), all become a part of a class of events that bear on economic performance during and beyond the political administrations of the 1970s. The strict economics and the politics of economic stability, instability, and control are inseparable in the world we seek to understand, explain, and possibly control within limits. The broader notions, extending to the political business cycle and the formation of expectations about the future in reaction to government (sects. 17.3, and 17.4) are especially germane as to "what is" (positive economics) and "what is called for" (normative economics).

In this chapter attention will be directed to all of the money and credit aggregates. In section 3.2 the role of banks as financial intermediaries and as suppliers of credit to users of funds was mentioned as a part of the saving and investment process. In supplying credit, commercial banks commonly create money balances. The two aggregates--bank credit and the money stock--have slightly different roles and influence interest rates and spending in different ways. For this reason, attention is directed presently to these and other monetary aggregates (including the narrowly defined money stock, M_1 and more recently M-1A) and to the techniques of policy implementation. The techniques of policy implementation are important in themselves, but they are of added importance because of the implications they hold for selected aspects of the economic theory of the real world.

In the long established tradition of economics there have been efforts to actually identify a supply function (or schedule) for money and a demand function (Frazer 1967, 39-42; Teigen 1976; Gibson 1976). There were selected, and presumably independent, variables in each function. A problem has been the lack of independence in the schedules and the variables. But Milton Friedman provided a different focus to the analysis. Within this context, the money stock can be taken as being determined or controlled exogenously, with the demand side of the market simply adjusting its spending to achieve a "desired" stock. If the stock is more than desired, adjustment occurs through greater spending (and therefore a rise in the velocity of money) and a possible rise in prices; if the stock is less the opposite occurs. In some respects this approach may be viewed as another of Friedman's ways of getting at measurement in an indirect way (sect. 1.3 and app. to chap. 1)--say in this case, without actually confronting the possibly unachievable task of actually identifying supply and demand schedules for money with a preciseness that will serve as a guide to monetary policy.

The point is that we have a stock or supply quantity, not a supply function. Given this the theory focuses on demand phenomena, but recognizes that demand is not independent of the stock. There are, nevertheless, determinants of the monetary aggregates in the accounting and control senses. These are treated in the section 6.2. A following section deals with the theory of the demand for money and various classes of assets. The foundation of money demand is that of utility analysis, and the use of probability enters as a means of treating problems of risk and uncertainty. At times one is confronted with holding more (or less) cash with certainty and less (or more) of alternative risky prospects. Consideration of such adjustments, money demand, and inflationary leads to an introduction to indexation in section 6.4.

6.2. The Control Mechanism

A good bit has been said about the money stock and its control, so let us examine the framework of monetary control and review the techniques of policy implementation. There are related complexities. In this process of going behind the scene, discussion of other monetary aggregates and credit and money multipliers arises. The aggregates include member bank reserves, bank credit, and various measures of the money supply. Each has a different multiplicative relationship to reserves.

Bank Reserves

The bank reserves equation is

$$R + G + C_T - C_S - T_C - F - R_M = 0 \tag{6.1}$$

where

R = Federal Reserve Credit

G = monetary gold stock and its substitute [including monetized special drawing rights or SDRs of the International Monetary Fund (IMF)] since 1970

C_T = Treasury currency

C_S = currency in circulation exclusive of vault cash (i.e., exclusive of currency held by commercial banks as reserves)

T_C = Treasury cash

F = foreign and other Federal Reserve deposits and miscellaneous accounts

R_M = member bank reserves inclusive of vault cash, prior to 1980 legislation (and more inclusive measures since).

The accounts with positive signs are on balance sources of reserves and those with negative signs are on balance uses. Federal Reserve credit is credit temporarily extended through the Federal Reserve's discount windows and more permanently extended through open market operations.

Rearranging the terms of equation (6.1),

$$R_M = R + G + C_T - C_S - T_C - F$$

or

$$R_M = \text{residual} + R + G - C_S \tag{6.2}$$

R, G, and C are singled out because they are of major importance in their influence on member bank reserves (R_M).

The bank reserve equation is actually an accounting identity.[1] In that sense it has some of the aura of soundness that usually accompanies double-entry bookkeeping. However, it is especially useful in stressing that monetary policy may include either policy actions or inactions. For example, on the one hand, the Federal Reserve mainly influences through its actions Federal Reserve credit (R), and, on the other, an inflow of monetized gold or SDRs from foreign trade increases reserves and an increase in the public's currency holdings reduces reserves, and changes in either of these accounts may be offset, reinforced, or accepted as desirable changes by the policymakers. The policymakers and their staffs in effect forecast and monitor the variables other than Federal Reserve credit and then seek to achieve target values, say, for member bank reserves or the monetary base, which is shown in figure 6-1 for the years 1973-79. The policy, at this reserve level of control, may be stated in terms of changes in member bank reserves and/or changes in the monetary base (actually, changes in rates of change in the more dynamic and operational case).

Controlling Reserve Aggregates--Some Statistical Results

The argument for "controllability" of reserve aggregates has been around for some time (Frazer and Yohe 1965, chap. 9), but gains special importance with the renewed interest in monetary aggregates. Rutner (1977) considers the matter with attention to statistical analyses. These are conducted within the context of the bank reserve equation and with attention to the Federal Reserve's open market operations such that the following emerge:

Changes in the member bank reserves

= open market operations
+ other factors affecting member bank reserves.

Changes in the reserve base

= open market operations
+ other factors affecting the base.

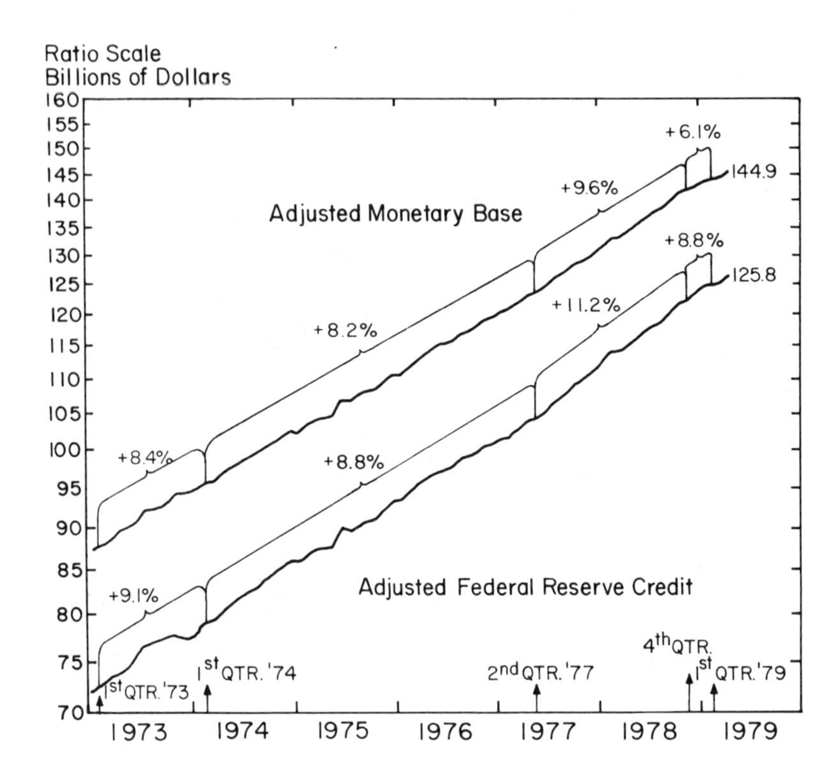

Figure 6-1. Adjusted Federal Reserve Credit and the Monetary Base

Notes to figure: 1. Uses of the monetary base are member bank reserves and currency held by the public and nonmember banks. Adjustments are made for reserve requirement changes and shifts in deposits among classes of banks. Data are computed by this bank. 2. Federal Reserve credit consists of Federal Reserve holdings of securities, loans, float and other assets. Adjusted Federal Reserve credit is computed by substracting treasury deposits at Federal Reserve banks from this series, and adjusting the series for reserve requirement ratio changes and shifts in the same type of deposits between banks where different reserve requirement ratios apply. The data are computed by the Federal Reserve Bank of St. Louis.

Percentages are annual rates of change for periods indicated.

Rutner's method is that of correlation analysis, both simple and partial. The simple analysis provides the straightforward correlation between the two variables (ranging from the extremes of +1 for perfect positive correlation to -1 for perfect negative or inverse correlation). The partial correlation analysis considers the correlation of one variable with another, holding any other factors constant (for example, those in the above equations). The method of holding one variable constant is still to impound it in ceteris paribus. (It is not equivalent to the mathematical technique of taking partial derivatives, since function-of-a-function rules do not come into play, as where two so-called independent variables are not independent). Further, the partial correlations are of two types, since they are obtained by using two different forms of the regression equation:

Y = f(past Y, current X, past X, error term) (Type I)

Y = F(past Y, current X, error term) (Type II)

The type I set of partial correlations takes account of the impact of past movements in both the dependent and independent variables in each regression. Type II takes account only of past movements in the dependent variables, as readily seen by observing the two forms of the regression equation.

The period for which Rutner analyzed data is January 1959 through December 1974. (Over most of the early years of this period there were no formal policy commitments to control reserve aggregates, as distinct from the interest rate targets.) The basic data are logarithmic transformations of weekly, 4-week averages (termed "monthly"), and 13-week averages (termed "quarterly"). The changes being considered in the variables are thus changes in rates of change. This is consistent with attention to rates of change in monetary and credit aggregates rather than to levels for the variables.[2]

A summary of Rutner's correlation results is reproduced as table 6 1. It shows simple and partial correlations for the so-called dependent variables with the respective independent variables and for open market operations (OMO) with other factors. "Other factors" are more highly correlated with member bank reserves than are OMO, but OMO are more highly correlated with the money base. In all cases OMO and "other factors" are negatively (inversely) correlated, "suggesting that simultaneous but opposite movements in the base's two determinants offset some of the partial impact of each determinant." However, "the finding that the correlation between the base and open market operations increased while the correlation between the base and other factors declined as the length of the time period increased [from a weekly to a quarterly period]...suggests that it was open market operations which offset other factors, rather than the other way around." That control may occur along such lines was considered earlier (Frazer 1973, chap. 2) to be controversial. By 1980 the acceptance of the Federal Reserve's technical capability of control on a long-term targeting basis had become widespread.

Table 6-1.

Correlation of Open Market Operations, Reserve Aggregates, and Other Factors

Correlation of	Simple Correlations				Partial Correlations Type I Account Taken of Past Movements in Both Dependent and Independent Variables		
	Weekly	Monthly	Quarterly		Weekly	Monthly	Quarterly
	Member Bank Reserves				Member Bank Reserves		
Member bank reserves with:							
OMO*	.38	.54	.47		.42	.50	.59
Other factors	.74	.73	.49		.72	.49	.63
OMO with other factors*	-.34	-.18	-.54	A#	-.32	-.57	-.53
				B#	-.32	-.55	-.49

		Partial Correlation Type II Account Taken of Past Movements in Dependent Variable		
		Weekly	Monthly	Quarterly
		Member Bank Reserves		
Member bank reserves with:				
OMO*		.29	.50	.36
Other factors		.72	.62	.68
OMO with other factors*	A#	-.25	-.53	-.50
	B#	-.04	-.53	-.48

Source of table: Jack L. Rutner, "The Federal Reserve's Impact on Several Reserve Aggregates," Monthly Review, Federal Reserve Bank of Kansas City, May 1977.

Correlation of	Simple Correlations				Partial Correlations Type I Account Taken of Past Movements in Both Dependent and Independent Variables		
	Weekly	Monthly	Quarterly		Weekly	Monthly	Quarterly
	Monetary Base				Monetary Base		
Monetary base with:							
OMO*	.51	.62	.66		.40	.42	.49
Other factors	.25	.19	.11§		.40	-.08§	-.04§
OMO with other factors	-.71	-.65	-.68	A#	-.78	-.89	-.92
				B#	-.78	-.90	-.90

Correlation of		Partial Correlation Type II Account Taken of Past Movements in Dependent Variable		
		Weekly	Monthly	Quarterly
		Monetary Base		
Monetary base with:				
OMO*		.34	.40	.52
Other factors		.23	.10	.15§
OMO with other factors	A#	-.50	-.86	-.83
	B#	-.73	-.88	-.94

*OMO refers to open market operations.

#In the case of the partial correlations between open market operations and other factors, the value of the correlation coefficient was estimated in two ways. The first correlation given in the table, and denoted by A, was derived under the assumption that other factors determine open market operations. The second, denoted by B, assumes that open market operations determine other factors.

§Indicates correlation is not significantly different from zero (5 per cent level).

Some Complicating Facets of Analysis

Bank reserves, which are basic to our fractional reserve system of credit, money, and banks, have been called high-powered because of the multiple effects they have on the money supply and bank credit. The money supply prior to 1980 (M_1) was usually considered to include the currency held by the public and deposits at banks payable on demand (exclusive of government and interbank deposits). This statistical category was sometimes broadened, however, to include time and savings deposits at commercial banks (the M_2 definition of money) and similar liabilities of other financial institutions. Moreover, the magnitude of bank credit (B_C) as it has appeared on the asset side of the balance sheets of commercial banks need not be exactly matched by the demand deposits on the liabilities side.

Considering bank reserves (R_M) in relation to bank credit (B_C) and the M_1 and M_2 definitions of money, we may note several multiplers, which we will call (m_c, m_1, m_2: $B_C = m_c R_M$, $M_1 = m_1 R_m$, and $M_2 = m_2 R_M$. Others may be denoted for the M_1 and M_2 measures in relation to the nonborrowed part of the monetary base (B^a), notably:

$$M_1 = m_1 B^a$$

$$M_2 = m_2 B^a$$

Actual values for the latter two multipliers for the 1969-76 period are shown in figure 6-2, where the larger values for m_2 (read off of the right hand scale) reflect the broader range of deposit liabilities when time and savings deposits are added. The general downward drift for m_1 and upward drift for m_2 reflect changes in the multipliers in response to various factors (Hoffman 1977) that will be described shortly.

The multipliers may be denoted as sums of infinite geometric progressions (also as taken up later in section 7.2 in considering Keynes's investment multiplier). This may be illustrated by letting ρ (Greek rho) represent the legal reserve ratio (the ratio of required reserves to deposit liabilities) and ΔR_M, an addition to reserves brought about through the Federal Reserve. In this case,

$$\Delta\, DD = \Delta\, R_M \frac{1}{1-(1-\rho)} \tag{6.3}$$

or

$$\Delta\, DD = \Delta\, R_M \underbrace{\frac{1}{\rho}}_{\text{money multiplier}} \tag{6.4}$$

Figure 6-2. Money Multipliers for M_1 and M_2

Source: Hoffman, Stuart G., "Component Ratio Estimation of the Money Multiplier," Working Paper Series, Federal Reserve Bank of Atlanta, August 1977.

where Δ DD is an increase in demand deposits and $1/\rho$ is the money multiplier. The right hand member of equation (6.3) may be written,

$$(6.5) \qquad \sum_{n=1}^{n} \Delta R_M(1-\rho)^{n-1} = \Delta R_M + \Delta R_M(1-\rho) + \Delta R_M(1-\rho)^2 + \Delta R_M(1-\rho)^3 + \ldots + \Delta R_M(1-\rho)^{n-1}$$

In words, the right hand member is the sum of an infinite geometric progression ($\rho<1$). If $\rho = .30$, the money multiplier in equation (6.3) or (6.4) is 1/.30 or 3.33, indicating that demand deposits may increase up to 3.33 times the amount of the increase in reserves.

With profits from increasing bank credit (total loans and investments) in mind, commercial bankers may be expected to react to an increase in reserves just about as depicted, that is, by expanding loans and investments and therefore the money supply. The process works as follows: commercial banks find themselves with extra reserves and see the opportunity to expand loans and/or investments as a means of increasing bank earnings. Credit is granted more freely. When a borrower signs the note (the loan instrument), the bank credits the borrowers' demand deposit accounts. The result is an expansion of bank credit and the money supply, and this may go on until the initial increments in reserves are only a fraction of the new bank credit and the newly created money.

These bank credit and money multipliers can be obtained from algebraic manipulations, but they can also be derived from actual data. For example, quarterly data for ΔDD could be regressed on ΔR_M to obtain a multiplier. This sort of statistical analysis depends on other underlying influences staying the same, while in fact they may not.

The money multiplier, as in equation (6.4), may differ slightly depending on a number of things, such as:

(1) a change in reserves originating through the Federal Reserve vis-à-vis a change resulting from the public electing to hold less currency;

(2) a change in bank holdings of excess reserves, possibly because they are uncertain about future developments, possibly because of an anticipated rise in interest rates (and thus a decline in the value of their bond portfolio), possibly because of diminished inducement to expand credit (as when interest rates are low), and so on;

(3) A switching on the part of the public from some demand to some time deposits (as when the yields on deposits at commercial banks exceed those on shares);

(4) Changes in the reserve requirements set by the Federal Reserve for reserve city and other banks, and for different classes of deposits. (These requirements have been stated as percentage requirements and differ for reserve city and other banks, and by deposit class such as demand and time deposits.)[3]

The subject of fractional reserves and the creation of bank credit and money through such a system is further complicated by a consideration of individual banks vis-à-vis the commercial banking system, by static and dynamic considerations, and by the introduction of the methods by which bank reserves get distributed in our economic system. In the first place, reserves for the system as a whole are given as in equation (6.2). There is little that commercial banks can do to influence them, although they can compete with one another and pass the reserves around.[4] From the individual bank's point of view it may appear that it can influence reserves, but actually one institution can gain only at the loss of another.

The major source of reserves is the accumulation of purchases of securities in the open market. These transactions and policy decisions are made by the Federal Open Market Committee of the Federal Reserve System (the Central bank or bankers bank in the United States). This committee is composed of members of the Board of Governors and the presidents of regional Federal Reserve banks. The open market operations take place over the trading desk at the Federal Reserve Bank of New York, with all regional banks participating in the ownership of the securities. The purchases in question are made mainly through major government securities dealers (including some banks), primarily in New York. This means New York banks get most of the initial increments in reserves. However, as they purchase securities elsewhere, the reserves get passed around. As a check drawn on a New York bank gets deposited in Jacksonville, Florida, for example, the effect of clearing the check is a movement of reserves from New York to Florida. One method of moving the reserves around in the banking system, then, is simply the sale of securities by some banks to other banks.

Other methods include borrowing the excess reserves of other banks (that is, trading in "Federal funds"), a system of interbank deposits, increases in bank capital, and, in the late 1960s (under very tight credit conditions), trading in Eurodollars and the creation of one-bank holding companies. The Federal funds market is a prominent way of moving the reserves through the banking system, but the trading is on a very short-term basis, usually overnight. The system of interbank desposits and correspondent banking is an older methods of moving balances about. In the early history of the United States (and still today), some banks in agricultural regions had a seasonal need for reserves, so they made deposits in other banks (their correspondents) at times and withdrew them when they were needed. As the deposits got moved about through the clearance of checks, the reserves got moved about also.

The sale of capital stock by commercial banks is another means of obtaining reserves, provided the new stock issue is not purchased by the bank's current depositors. As the check payments for the stocks clear, the bank issuing the stock receives credits for reserves.

The origin of the Eurodollar market goes back to the late 1950s, but the development of extensive trading in Eurodollars occurred initially in the late 1960s under very tight credit (high interest rate) conditions in the United States. This trading emerged into one of the world's largest money markets and into a Eurocurrency market, as considered more fully in chapter 19.[5] Eurodollars are dollar deposits that are held by European banks. They arise as Americans, foreigners, international businesses, and foreign governments deposit large balances denominated in dollars in the European banks. These deposit liabilities of European banks are of the nature of time deposit, in that they pay interest and are deposited for a specified time period (as short as overnight, but ordinarily for longer). American banks have become able, under the foregoing conditions, to acquire extra reserves by borrowing Eurodollars. But this is really no different in its affect on reserves than moving reserves about through Federal funds borrwoing in the domestic money market.

The one-bank holding company was a similar construction that enabled individual banks to obtain reserves from other banks; it similarily complicated the achievement of targets for the monetary aggregates. In the holding company case, a nonbank entity would own a major share of a commercial bank, and the nonbank entity could sell commercial paper (i.e., its own notes) to obtain funds for deposit at its banking subsidiary.

Since the initial emergence of the Eurodollar market and the one-bank holding company, both have been made more subject to regulation by the Federal Reserve. However, the Eurodollar market is a relatively free, world-wide market that has spread from its centers in London and on the continent of Europe to the Caribbean, the Mideast, Singapore, Hong Kong, and Tokyo. The Federal Reserve's sole means of regulation is "a reserve requirement against the borrowings of domestic offices of U.S. banks from their foreign branches and from foreign banks. When first imposed in October 1969, it was 10 percent, and it has been varied on occasions since with the view to equalizing the cost to U.S. banks of obtaining funds domestically and abroad."

The subject of bank credit and money multipliers is indeed complicated in its detail.[6] This we leave as subject matter for others, and continue instead in the broad framework.

Some Static and Dynamic Considerations

The public has a seasonal preference for currency (paper notes and coins) as a proportion of the money supply, with the strongest preference coming during the Christmas season. The reason is fairly obvious. But the bank system is generally growing with the economy and income, so that overall currency withdrawals absorb reserves.

Sometimes a very static analysis proceeds this way: some currency is deposited in bank A, raising the bank's reserves. A fraction of these must be kept as reserves against the new deposit, but the excess reserves can be loaned out. So a loan is made. The recipient of the loan then spends his balances, which then get deposited in bank B. The extra reserves move to bank B and the process is repeated, except that the amount of the loan is diminished in each step. The result is a step for each term in the infinite geometric progression, equation (6.5).

The difficulties with this step-wise progression are twofold: (1) some deposits never leave the initial credit granting institution; and (2) other institutions are simultaneously engaging in the process of making loans and/or investments, so that the general thrust in the totals for bank loans and investments is upward as revealed by the data in figure 6-3. At the level of the banking unit all sorts of clearings are taking place, mostly so as to offset one another. Some banks face more adverse clearing balances than others. Even so, operating bankers acquire experience in these things and tracing out the effects of any single transaction is not very useful to them or to economists with interest in the credit creating process.

Another sort of dynamic consideration comes into focus when we consider disequilibrium as depicted in chapter 5 (say, with actual M_S > desired M_d balances, or $M_S > M_d$, as indicated by a rise in income velocity) and, simultaneously, an increase in expected inflation (ΔP^e). Here the economic entity may desire a bank loan to provide "funds" for the purchase of some real goods, for example, some inventories. These may be expected to appreciate in value under the impact of inflation. With inflation there also is the prospect of repaying the loan with low purchasing power dollars. The inducement is clear and the loan is sought.

At the same time this loan expansion is going on, however, velocity is rising to indicate a weakened demand for money (M_s>M_d). This is such that the spenders desire less rather than more money balances. So what do they desire? The answer is bank credit, but in the process an increase in the money stock will come about anyway. This is coincidental to what is desired. The idea then is that bank credit and money may play different roles.

One may of course wish to abstract from day-to-day detail, as just described, and examine the pro or countercyclical thrust of policy, but one should also beware of disguised attempts to treat bank credit and money only as money, and to focus only on the stock of money and its demand in the exposition of the theory. We presently consider money in both static and dynamic contexts. Bank credit enters separately as a part of the flow of saving into investment.

This supply of and demand for funds, including bank credit, constitutes a so-called loanable funds model. Both this model and the liquidity preference demand that follows enter simultaneously into the Keynesian IS-LM model of chapter 13.

The Money Base and Other Aggregates

Experimentation with the bank reserve equation and the process of money creation led Karl Brunner and his former student Allan Meltzer to a discovery (Frazer 1973, chap. 10): namely, that the most stable relationship between changes in the money supply (ΔM) and changes in components of reserves was with changes in the money base, ΔB (i.e., with changes in currency held by the public plus vault cash and deposits at the Federal Reserve). Here currency changes appear on both sides of the regression of ΔM on ΔB and yield higher and more stable correlations.[7] This was no big thing, but the money base has been pointed to as the best control variable for the Federal Reserve, and the best means of controlling the money stock.

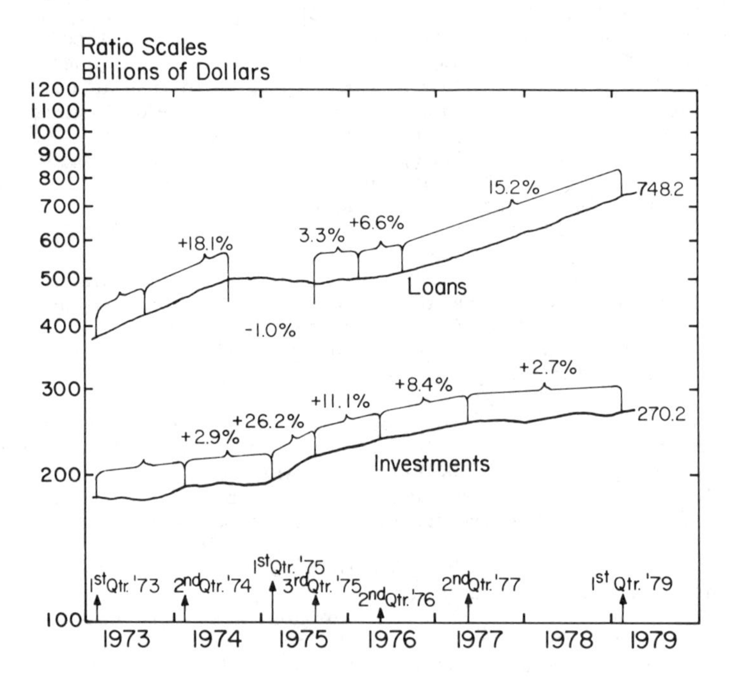

Figure 6-3. Bank Loans and Investments

Source of figure: Federal Reserve Bank of St. Louis.

Despite the foregoing, when the Federal Reserve first shifted its emphasis to money aggregates, partly in response to monetarist research of the 1960s (as reviewed in Frazer [1973]), the new and additional guide to open market operations became member bank reserves available for private nonbank deposits (RPDs); only later was official attention given to the monetary base. Furthermore, the Federal Reserve (or more specifically, the Federal Open Market Committee) was careful to avoid strong emphasis on the money stock as a single control variable for a variety of reasons: its difficulty in measurement on a short-term basis, the erratic behavior of the money stock that results from switching between time and demand deposits, and so on.

The shift of attention to monetary and credit aggregates took on even firmer dimensions, as noted earlier, with a formal request from Congress on March 24, 1975, in the form of

House Concurrent Resolution 133, with the subsequent experience of operations under that resolution (Jianakoplos 1976; Burger and Mudd 1977), and with the action of October 6, 1979 (Announcement 1979, 830). The resolution called for the reporting of policy in terms of the aggregates and for the announcement of the plans for monetary policy for one year in advance. This reporting of the long-run (one-year) plans gives attention to growth rates for the aggregates and takes place on a periodic basis. The operating instructions from the FOMC to the "account manager" at the Federal Reserve Bank of New York are given on a shorter period basis.

In March 1976, the FOMC reported an understanding that several reserve aggregates should receive attention in the formulation of instructions to the "account manager." These included: total reserves, nonborrowed reserves, and the monetary base (total reserves plus currency held by the public) (Burger and Mudd 1977). The monetary aggregates that came to receive attention under House Concurrent Resolution 133 are:

M_1--currency outside of banks and demand deposits (checking accounts) held by the nonbank public.

M_2--M_1 plus commercial bank savings and time deposits except CDs (negotiable certificates of deposit) of $100,000 or more issued by large banks.

M_3--M_2 plus deposits of mutual savings banks, savings and loan association shares, and credit union shares.

M_4 and M_5 are derived by adding CDs to M_2 and M_3, respectively. In late 1978, M_{1+} (M_1 plus prearranged automatic transfers) was added as a sixth monetary aggregate, because of the uncertainties associated with the introduction of prearranged automatic transfers from savings to checking accounts (ATS). The introduction of ATS and the development of other means of making transactions outside the commercial banking system are factors that lead to proposed redefinition of the monetary aggregates (Laporte 1979; Simpson 1979), and later to their redefinition (Simpson 1980).

The Federal Reserve's redefined aggregates (Simpson 1980) are shown in table 6-2, and a comparison of the old and the new is shown in table 6-3. The new measures are labeled M-1A, M-1B, M-2, M-3, and L. The old M-1 corresponds closely to the new M-1A. The difference is simply that demand deposits of foreign commercial banks and other official institutions are netted out of the old M-1. Further, the M-1B measure adds to M-1A the interest-earning checkable deposits at all depository institutions, namely (Simpson 1980, 97-98): "NOW accounts, automatic transfer from savings (ATS) accounts, and credit union share draft balances--as well as a small amount of demand deposits at thrift institutions that cannot, with present data sources, be separated from interest-earning checkable deposits."

Table 6-2. New (1980) Measures of Money and Liquid Assets[1] (billions of dollars, not seasonally adjusted, November 1979)

Aggregate and component	Amount
M-1A	372.2
Currency	106.6
Demand deposits[2]	265.6
M-1B	387.9
M-1A	372.2
Other checkable deposits[3]	15.7
M-2	1,510.0
M-1B	387.9
Overnight RPs issued by commercial banks	20.3
Overnight Eurodollar deposits held by U.S. nonbank residents at Caribbean branches of U.S. banks	3.2
Money market mutual fund shares	40.4
Savings deposits at all depositary institutions	420.0
Small time deposits at all depositary institutions[4]	640.8
M-2 consoldiation component[5]	-2.7
M-3	1,759.1
M-2	1,510.0
Large time deposits at all depositary institutions[6]	219.5
Term RPs issued by commercial banks	21.5
Term RPs issued by savings and loan associations	8.2
L	2,123.8
M-3	1,759.1
Other Eurodollar deposits of U.S. residents other than banks	34.5
Bankers acceptances	27.6
Commercial paper	97.1
Savings bonds	80.0
Liquid Treasury obligations	125.4

[1]Components of M-2, M-3, and L measures generally exclude amounts held by domestic depositary institutions, foreign commercial banks and official institutions, the U.S. government (including the Federal Reserve), and money market mutual funds. Exceptions are bankers acceptances and commercial paper for which data sources permit the removal only of amounts held by money market mutual funds and, in the case of bankers acceptances, amounts held by accepting banks, the Federal Reserve, and the Federal Home Loan Bank System.

[2]Net of demand deposits due to foreign commercial banks and official institutions.

[3]Includes NOW, ATS, and credit union share draft balances and demand deposits at thrift institutions.

[4]Time deposits issued in denominations of less than $100,000.

[5]In order to avoid double counting of some deposits in M-2, those demand deposits owned by thrift institutions (a component of M-1B), which are estimated to be used for servicing their savings and small time deposit liabilities in M-2, are removed.

[6]Time deposits issued in denominations of $100,000 or more.

Table 6-3. The Relation between New (1980) and Old Monetary Aggregates
(billions of dollars, not seasonally adjusted, November 1979)

Aggregate and component	Amount
Old M-1	382.6
Less demand deposits of foreign commercial banks and official institutions	10.4
Equals: New M-1A1	372.2
Plus other checkable deposits	15.7
Equals: New M-1B	387.9
Old M-2	945.3
Plus savings and time deposits at thrift institutions	664.2
Equals: Old M-3	1,609.5
Plus overnight RPs and Eurodollars	23.4
Plus money market mutual fund shares	40.4
Plus demand deposits at mutual savings banks2	1.0
Less large time deposits at all depositary institutions in current M-3	151.2
Less demand deposits of foriegn commercial banks and official institutions	10.4
Less consolidation component3	2.7
Equals: New M-2	1,510.0
Plus large time deposits at all depositary institutions	219.5
Plus term RPs at commercal banks and savings and loan institutions	29.8
Equals: New M-3	1,759.1

1Also includes a very small amount of M-1-type balances at certain U.S. banking offices of foreign banks outside New York City which were not in the old M-1 measure.

2Demand deposits at mutual savings banks were not included in any of the old monetary aggregates.

3Consists of an estimate of demand deposits included in M-1B that are held by thrift institutions for use in servicing their savings and small time deposit liabilities included in the new M-2.

Source of tables 6-2 and 6-3: Federal Reserve Bulletin, November 1980, pp. 98-99.

As Thomas Simpson points out (1980, 102-104), the growth rates for the old M-1, the new M-1A, and the new M-1B show close parallel movement, in the respective measures except that the growth rate for M-1B has tended to be above the growth rates for the other measures in the 1978-79 period. In particular in 1979, there were "shifts in holdings of monetary assets in response to the availability of new deposit services," in particular in NOW accounts in New York State and in ATS accounts nationwide. With new legislation in early 1980 authorizing NOW accounts nationwide for all insured banks, credit unions and savings and loan associations, the difference between M-1A and M-1B should persist for some time. Also, of special interest for the discussion in section 5.5, the income velocities of money, for the old M-1 and the new M-1A and M-1B for the years 1960 through 1979, rise and fall together (and, thus, parallel one another).

With reference to the new measures M-2, M-3, and L, Simpson (1980, 98) proceeds thus:

> The new M-2 measure adds to M-1B overnight repurchase agreements (RPs issued by commercial banks and certain overnight Eurodollars held by U.S. nonbank residents, money market mutual fund shares, and savings and small-denomination time deposits at <u>all</u> depositary institutions. Also, in order to avoid double counting of some deposits in this aggregate, the construction of the new M-2 involves subtracting a consolidation component--an estimate of those demand deposits used by thrift institutions in servicing their savings and time deposit liabilities included in this aggregate. Redefined M-3 is equal to new M-2 plus large-denomination time deposits at all depositary institutions (including negotiable CDs) plus term RPs issued by commercial banks and savings and loan associations. Finally, the very broad measure of liquid assets consisting of other Eurodollar holdings of U.S. residents other than banks, bankers acceptances, commercial paper, savings bonds, and marketable liquid Treasury obligations.

On the comparison of the old M-2 and the new M-2 and M-3 measures, Simpson (1980, 99) proceeds thus:

> New M-2 is closer in concept to old M-3, which included savings and time deposit liabilities of all depositary institutions (other than negotiable CDs at large commercial banks), than it is to old M-2, which excluded the public's holdings of these liabilities of thrift institutions. The major differences between the new M-2 and old M-3 measures are that new M-2 includes money market mutual fund shares, overnight RPs, and overnight Eurodollars--none of which appeared in any of the old monetary aggregates--and

that it excludes all large-denomination time deposits. The only class of large-denomination time deposits not included in the old M-3 (and the old M-2) measure was negotiable CDs at large commercial banks.... By including all large-denomination time deposits at all depositary institutions, the new M-3 is closer in cncept to the old M-5 measure than to the old M-4.... Of course, the new M-3 aggregate is more inclusive than the old M-5 since it contains RPs, certain overnight Eurodollar deposits, and money market mutual fund shares.

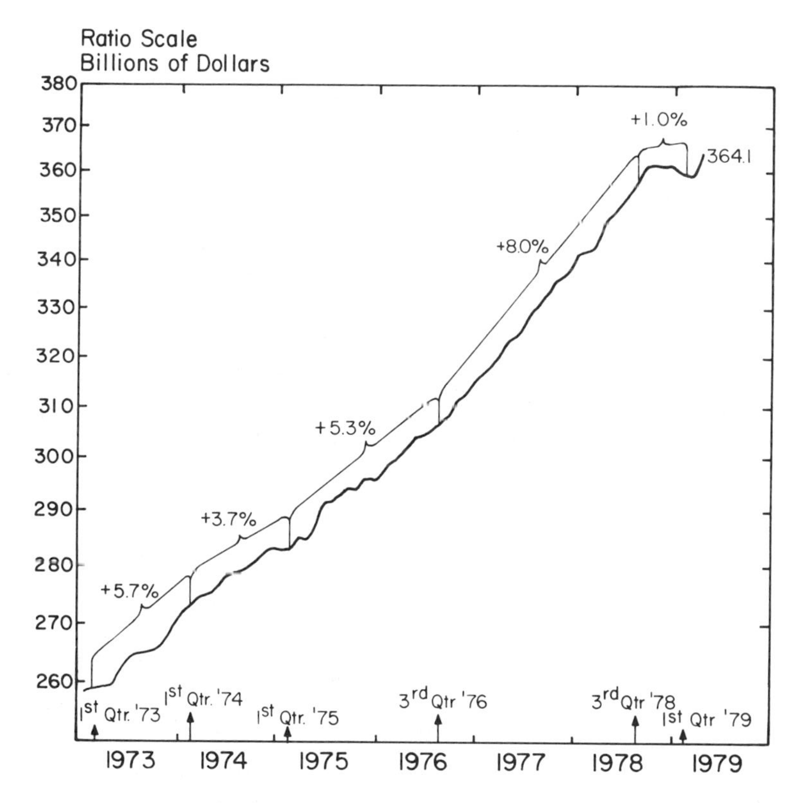

Figure 6-4. The Money Stock (M_1)

Source of figure: Federal Reserve Bank of St. Louis.

The whole array of money and credit aggregates is considered important, for two main reasons: first, because the broader aggregates indicate additions to liquidity ("near money") held by the nonbank public and, second, because the consideration of the complex deviations within the array of aggregates provides relevant information. However, M-1 has been the variable most considered by constructions bearing on economic theory. In 1976 almost every financial report and the bulk of congressional testimony on monetary policy were directed toward movements in M-1,such as those depicted in figure 6-4. The attention to M-1 (and M-1A as its substitute beginning in 1980), and to rates of change in it in particular, is in contrast to the earlier attention to interest rates as the control variable, as under the Keynesian view in section 4.3. Even so, one may encounter statements by congressional figures, the press, and some Federal Reserve officials to the effect that the Federal Reserve sets the interest rate in some very direct way. These sorts of statements have arisen, despite the plethora of evidence that the expected inflation rate is a major component of interest rates and a source of volatility in them (as figures in chapter 5 indicate).

Complexities and FOMC Operating Ranges

With the attention to monetary aggregates in the early 1970s and beyond, some discoveries were made that were only hinted at earlier (Frazer 1973). Notably, it was found that there is no simple and direct link between open market operations, changes in the rate of interest, and changes in the money supply, as some theorists had suggested. Even Milton Friedman, whose work offers so much insight and redirection for economics, had posited that in the short run an open market purchase (sale) of securities raised (lowered) the security prices and thus lowered (raised) the rate of interest. This was reinforced by the thinking about the liquidity effect of a change in the money stock within the context of discussion about the liquidity preference construction (fig. 5-5).

The difficulties with Friedman's simple, short-run (period -of-constant-expectations) links were several. First, the money market in which the FOMC trading desk intervenes to purchase (or sell) securities is continually reacting to new information about the future, to changing underlying conditions, and to the intentions of the Federal Reserve in the first place (Frazer 1973; Jianakoplos 1976; Davis 1977; Holmes and Sternlight 1977). Intervention to buy may at times actually parallel a rise rather than a decline in interest rates.[8] Next, since the latter linkages within the short time frame cannot be relied upon as operating guides to achieving interest rate and money stock targets, and since changes in bank reserves are affected by variables in the bank reserve equations other than Federal Reserve credit, the manager of the open market account has no highly reliable techniques for the implementation of policy in the short period in terms of rates of change in the money stock or any other of the monetary and credit aggregates. Further, the manager's task (and hence the FOMC's task) is complicated by the fact that monthly data on the aggregates are reported with some lag behind the operations themselves.

By 1979 innovations in the payments mechanism (sect. 5.6) and the Federal Reserve's tendency toward using the Federal funds rate as a part of its control mechanism both became complicating factors in the conduct of monetary operations. At the time of the Federal Reserve's October 6 actions, for example, the Federal Reserve announced technical adjustments in its target ranges for M_1, M_2, and M_3 for the earlier midyear 1979 date. The M_1 target had initially assumed a shift of 3 percent of demand deposits to automatic transfer service (ATS) and negotiable order of withdrawal accounts (NOW) accounts, but the October-6 action reset the change at 1½ percent and thus raised a 1½ to 4½ percent target range for M_1 to a range of 3 to 6 percent. The developments in the payments mechanism and apparent difficulty in controlling the intermediate monetary variables, furthermore, had paralled proposals for redefinition of money stock measures and for reliance upon the monetary base as the Federal Reserver's intermediate control variable (Davis 1980; Gambs 1980; and Laporte 1979. In addition, with all these changes going on in the payments mechanism the Federal Reserve had also requested of Congress that all banks and savings and loan associatons be required to keep reserve requirements with the Federal Reserve. The Federal Reserve had had jurisdiction over only its member banks up until this time.

The two technical arguments advanced for the base as the intermediate target (say, intermediate between Federal Reserve operations and the ultimately sought control over GNP) are: (1) that the data on the base become available before those on the money supply, and (2) that they are less subject to error and revision. The less narrowly technical points offered as favoring the base include: that the base is about as closely related to aggregate demand (GNP) as the money supply measures; that the changes in the payments mechanism have tended to weaken the relationship between the money supply measures and aggregate demand, and that the base is more amenable to Federal Reserve control than the money supply measures.

Reacting to such arguments about the base, Davis (1980) and Gambs (1980) both present analyses as "in-house" Federal Reserve economists and conclude that the innovations in the payments mechanism are a sorce of difficulty in setting targets for the base as well as for the money supply measures. Gambs, going a bit further says, "the monetary base does not appear to be as closely related to GNP as is M-1." Continuing, he says, that the largest portion of the base is in the form of currency, the demand for which is poorly related to economic activity. It may be noted, however, that alternative measures for the monetary base are available and have come to be published by the Federal Reserve (Barger 1979). Starting in 1979, the Federal Reserve came to published these including a growth rate series which incorporated adjustments for changes in reserve requirements.

As requested by the Federal Reserve, Congress passed legislation in 1980 (effective September 1) extending reserve requirements to all banks and savings and loan associations for checking-type deposits. This requirement was to equal 15 percent of the increase in assets from a base date. The priviledge to borrow reserves through the Federal Reserve's "discount window" was also extended to the wider range of financial intermediaries. Although M. Friedman had not thought this extension of Federal Reserve control necessary, (Newsweek, 4/14/80) for the control of the policy variables, the Federal Reserve saw it as giving them greater control over the variables.

The foregoing complexities reflect in some measure the procedures that the FOMC intially adopted for reporting policy plans one year in advance to the Congress, in one case, and for providing instructions to the manager of the open market account for the implementation of policy within approximately a one-month period, in a second case. The FOMC came to report its plans to Congress in terms of ranges (a spread between upper and lower annual growth rates) for the rates of change in the aggregates, expressed as percentages. These yearly ranges, as illustrated in figure 6-5, are on the quarterly average (again, a procedure to remove statistical "noise" from the data) for the most recent quarter and the targeted range of quarterly averages for one year in the future. The figure also shows the levels for the monthly money stock (M_1) that were actually achieved for the period 1975:IV to 1976:IV. The range for one year hence may be revised, as the Federal Reserve's chairman reports to committees of the Congress from quarter to quarter.

In the case of instructions to the manager of the account, the FOMC came to provide short-run tolerance ranges at its regularly scheduled meetings (Lang 1979, 2-24). Tolerance ranges were also given by the FOMC for the interest rate on Federal funds, at least before the October 6, 1979 action, cited earlier. Specification of the Federal funds rate did not necessarily indicate a reversion to the old policy of viewing "the rate of interest" as a control variable, but rather the recognition may have indicated that the Federal funds rate served a useful function. First, data are generated immediately and on a day-to-day basis for this rate. Second, the Federal Reserve has often made defensive maneuvers in the money market to balance temporary adjustments occurring in other quarters, and the Federal funds rate is thought to be helpful in that respect.

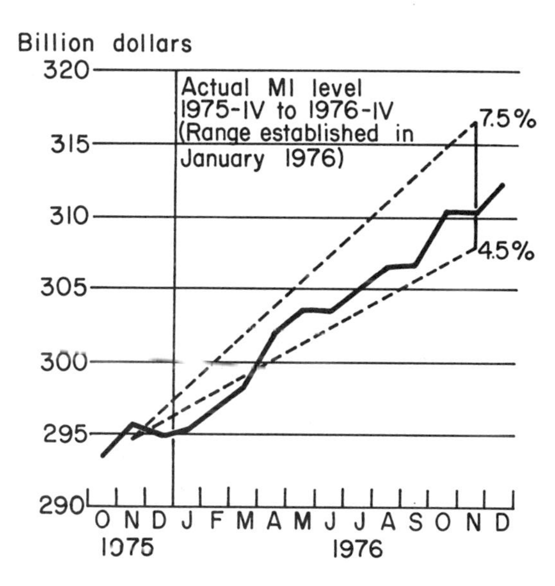

Figure 6-5. The Money Stock (M_1) Relative to Projected One-Year Range

Source: Quarterly Review, Federal Reserve Bank of New York, Spring 1977.

These foregoing apologetics aside, however, Roos (1979, 12-15) took a strong view on the use of the Federal funds rate. He saw the open market actions in practice as tending to stabilize the Federal funds rate more often than the targeted growth in the money stock. Further, he saw this tendency in practice as being more often a reversion to the bias toward interest rate control with its concomitant procyclical effects on interest rates. With such a view, Roos argued strongly against the bias of interest rate control, and for the need to distinguish between the credit market aspects of monetary control and the money stock aspects (later elucidated in chapter 13 as loanable funds aspects and money demand aspects). On the interdependence of all markets and money and credit markets in particular, Roos said:

> Monetary policymakers frequently go astray when they assume their policy actions affect only one specific market [say the Federal funds market] without affecting all markets....
>
> If it were only understood that monetary policy is a powerful tool in the stabilization of general economic activity and the price level, but a weak and very costly tool for the stabilization of individual economic sectors and markets, perhaps the bias toward interest rate control would go away. (Roos 1979, 14)

The Burns Years (Reactions and Introduction)

Arthur Burns, the astute academic economist and Federal Reserve chairman from January 1970 through March of 1978, is critically evaluated and given poor marks by some (Jordan 1979, 496-98; Mayer 1979, 501-04; Pierce 1979, 485-96; Poole 1979, 473-84) for his performance in the first eight years of monetary policy with official attention to monetary aggregates. Against a background of operations and procedures as introduced thus far, one encounters statements such as the following:

> [1] Over the eight Burns years M_1 growth [nominal amounts] was 1.3 percentage points higher and M_2 growth 1.8 percentage points higher than during the preceding eight years. (Poole 1979, 474)

> [2] The first period of cyclical expansion under Burns is bound by the growth cycle dates November 1970 and March 1973 [NBER turning points]. Over this subperiod the M_1 and M_2 growth rates were both 1.2 percentage points higher than their respective average growth rates over the eight Burns years. During the... expansion of the Burns year [from March 1975 to February 1978]... the M_1 and M_2 growth rates... were 0.2 and 0.9 percentage points higher than their respective averages over the eight-year Burns era.
>
> For comparison purposes we may note that the rates of growth of M_1 and M_2 for the growth cycle expansion from October 1967 to March 1969 were 7.4 percent for M_1 and 8.6 percent for M_2. There two growth rates are substantially above the average growth rates for the eight-year period preceding Burns, but the 1967-69 period of monetary acceleration was of shorter duration than the two major periods of monetary acceleration during the Burns era. (Poole 1979, 474)

---

[3] During the subperiod [March 1973 to March 1975] growth rates were 4.9 percent and 7.7 percent, respectively, or 1.0 and 1.3 percentage points respectively, below the average M_1 and M_2 growth rates over the eight Burns years. (Poole 1979, 475)

---

[4] The real problem with monetary policy during the Burns' years was not that money growth fluctuated quarter to quarter but that its average rate was too high and fluctuations around that average were procyclical. (Poole 1979, 475)

---

[5] It is widely understood that a major reason for procyclical monetary growth is the Federal Reserve's efforts to control interest rates in the short-run. This situation did not change under Arthur Burns. (Poole 1979, 476)

---

[6] He [Burns] knew the difference between money and credit, he often lectured Congress that the relation between money growth and interest rates was opposite in the longer-run than in the shorter-run, and he persistently repeated that the only way to achieve and maintain a lower trend rate of inflation was to achieve a lower trend rate of growth of the money supply. (Jordan 1979, 496)

Now, though accurate, the first statement above is possibly biased by the comparison of rates of change in nominal magnitudes during the eight preceding years with the Burns years, since the rates of inflation at the outset of the respective periods (and consequently the real magnitudes being compared were quite different). In fact, the inflation rates were 1.15 and 5.92 percent respectively in terms of the consumer price index. And the rate for the year ended December 1976 (President Ford's last year), was 4.8 percent. Attention to the difference in the nominal and the real magnitudes for monetary growth is important, because the different rates of growth indicate the extent to which inflation is being accomodated (and possibly gradually decelerated) and the extent to which change in the money stock takes place in order to accommodate the expected, secular trend rate of growth in output.

Points (2) through (6) appear accurate enough as to factual content. Furthermore, pre- and post-1973 performances by Burns are in effect set in contrast by statements (2) and (3). The expansion period from November 1970 to March

1973 coincided with an imposition of wage and price controls in several phases after mid-August 1971 (Frazer 1973, 408-09). The first phase was a mandatory wage-price freeze, the second was more flexible, and the third (beginning in January 1973) was voluntary. Details need not be labored, but a major objective of the policy was to "break the inflationary psychology gripping the nation (sects. 12.5, and 17.3). Burns, as Poole recognizes (1979, 480-81), had supported such a policy, and his and Lanzillotti's interpretations are not dissimilar. As set forth at greater length in section 17.3, Lanzillotti comments thus:

> The logic for Phase II [of the early 1970s] was to provide the policy "cover," or diversion, for stimulative fiscal and monetary actions to facilitate economic recovery. Although this strategy contained an obvious economic policy contradiction, the official policy expectation was that if a controls program could even temporarily calm public anxiety and thus alter inflationary "expectations," while economic output increased, a firm base could be established for employment gains with further endogenous stimulus to business activity.

The interpretation attributed to Burns in this early 1970s period was in three parts: (1) that the controls could hold down the cost-push induced part of the inflation rate (as defined fully in sects. 17.1 and 17.2); (2) that the latter would permit a greater expansion than otherwise of monetary growth rates that would stimulate spending; and (3) that the former two parts would permit reductions in the unemployment rate which was high by standards of the early 1960s. Early in his 1970-78 tenure, Burns was concerned with the inflationary expectations aspects of interest rates, "excessive expectational reactions" on the part of the public, public "confidence" in programs, as Poole recognizes (1979), but no special attention is given to this strategy of Burns by the critics. Moreover, Burns was later to give special attention to lowering the natural rate of unemployment (Frazer 1977, 48-57)--defined presently as simply the rate consistent with a constant inflation rate, possibly zero or negative. Next, Burns early concern over inflation was to intensify and as treated later (sect. 12.5), the expectations aspect of his approach was its most predominant part.

Finally, the politics of the business cycle, "the political business cycle" (sects. 10.3, 12.5), can hardly be ignored in the interpretation of policies associated with Burns before and after the presidential reelection of 1972. As addressed later, there are questions about the true independence of the Federal Reserve in a regime of monetary and credit aggregates, and about whether the switch in policy under Burns after 1972 was a recognition of permanent changes in the economy. To be sure, Burns had been close to Richard Nixon from the early Eisenhower years, and Nixon had extended the Federal

Reserve appointment to Burns even before "Inauguration" day 1969 (Viorst 1971, 309-26).

In going over matters of policy as summarized above, Lombra (1979, 498-99) says the following:

> If we start from the premise that policymakers do not pursue procyclical policies intentionally and thus do not intend to destablize the economy, we ought to search for a "reasonable" explanation of why things turn out as they do.

The explanations we consider on later occasions center about:

1. Control at a point vis-à-vis control over a cyclical time frame (sects. 4.3, 8.4, and on other occasions).
2. The political business cycle (sects. 10.3, 12.5, 17.3).
3. Underestimation of the natural rate of unemployment (sects. 8.4 and 11.5, and chap. 17).
4. The failure of the professional literature, until quite recent times, to address the strong expectational component in business conditions matters, both in relation to cyclical and evolutionary, nonrepetitive matters (chaps. 16 and 17, and sect. 21.3).

Lombra (1979, 498-01) mentions, along such lines as considered later, "short-run political ramifications." He says, "The often critcized short-run focus of the Fed would appear to be the product of political pressures which severely circumscribe their independence...." He also mentions the skeptical view of forecasts of 6 months to 2 years in the future, and the "paramount significance accorded incoming data...." With the Fed's short-run focus, "it is not hard to see why the monetary aggregates are not accorded to attention Monetarist think they deserve." Continuing, Lombra says:

> Interest rates (i.e., nominal interest rates) can be observed without error each day and in a superficial sense can be controlled. Data on the money stock on the other hand are subject to frequent revision (e.g., when the seasonals are revised or the data are benchmarked to the quarterly call reports), and seem to display considerable irregular variance.

In the light of present and later analysis, it would appear (1) that a full monetary aggregates approach was not clearly stated without money market ramifications until the October 6, 1979 episode, and (2) that a fully independent Federal Reserve (i.e., independent within the framework of government) is more an illusion than a reality. As considered later, independence as known since the Treasury-Federal Reserve Accord of 1951 was independence over interest rates (Frazer 1973, 196, 254, 264, 270, 372). Independence with respect to the control over aggregates may turn out to be a different issue. This is in part because of analysis concerning the Government Budget Constraint (sect. 10.3), since it presumes a lot more power on the Federal Reserve's part than the Congress may yield. Further, as we see later in chapter 12, President Carter was able to turn monetary policy to his changing goals by the removal of Arthur Burns and the appointment of G. William Miller and others during 1978 and 1979.

6.3. The Demand for Money

Different theories of the demand for money as a part of an asset structure abound in the post-World War II years. All of them have some tie with the work of Keynes. To begin with his was an asset or portfolio approach. The label "portfolio" commonly implies a sheath of securities, but in economics it has come to mean an array of assets as well, including cash (money) holdings and other assets with risky prospects of yielding returns. In some modern instances liability-side management is also readily introduced. The present discussion is restricted to the assets. The aggregates dealt with have included:

(1) Keynes's two asset model--money and bonds (with bonds including real capital and common stocks).[9]

(2) The Keynesian two asset model--money and bonds (with equities and real capital excluded).

(3) Friedman's two asset model--nonhuman and human wealth (with implied distinctions between equities and bonds). These are implied because Friedman denotes a demand function with stock market yields and bond yields.

(4) A two asset model with subcategories (as introduced in sect. 3.3)--

(a) Fixed claim assets	money bonds
(b) Residual claim assets	real capital (e.g., plant and equipment equities

In the most general case--as where one wants to think of both the certain and uncertain prospects of realizing the returns from the assets--one may also think of adjustments at the margins for the various categories of the latter asset model where the alternatives include holding a cash sum with certainty or holding some set of more risky assets (risky with respect to the realization of the returns). The sum of cash (money) that may be exchanged is called the "certainty equivalent" to the additions to assets. The term is given a more formal definition in the appendix A to chapter 6.

The role of expectations, and expected inflation (P^e) in particular, becomes crucial. The first two models impound it, and have the central bank controlling the interest rate without influencing prospects for the future. Sometimes the often-asserted inverse relation between money and interest rates is presented within this framework, and the purchase and sale of securities for the Federal Reserve's open market account are introduced in an ad hoc way.

When expected inflation is impounded, the discounting of income streams for marketable bonds and stocks (equities) operates in the same way. A reduction (rise) in the interest rate results in an increase (decrease) in value.

In contrast, when expected inflation is introduced or the control of the interest rate is not so naively envisioned, radically different adjustments can occur at the margin of the asset accounts. For example, differential changes in the possible income streams from bonds and equities imply differential changes in values and yields (as rates) and call for adjustments at the margins for bonds (fixed claims) and equities (residual claims).

The Baumol-Tobin transactions demand for money and, in particular, Tobin's treatment of the liquidity preference demand for money are brought forward below as Keynesian models. Their impact on economics textbooks has been substantial. Friedman's demand function is presented as well, although the ad hoc character of Friedman's theorizing should again be pointed out. This is possibly due to his focus on empirical study, but, in the present context, it takes the form of his combining Tobin's liquidity preference model (a difference-of-opinion model) and Keynes's model (a pull-toward-normality model). Furthermore, the models he groups together differ in that the one has a relative frequency theory of probability as its foundation (repeated sampling from the same universe) while the other has a subjectivist approach (possible sampling over time from a changing universe).[10] We know from other contexts that Friedman's is a personalistic approach to probability (app. A to chap. 6).

In the cases considered below, utility theory is introduced. Utility analysis may be of the ordinal variety (the ranking of preferences) it may be a cardinal utility (measurement, as illustrated by reference to a thermometer in recording temperature). The utility analysis in Tobin's construction is assumed to be of this second variety. It has a more detailed set of assumptions (app. A to chap. 6). The consideration of probability axioms facilitates a discussion of the marginal utility of wealth (and attitudes toward risk).

In utility analysis with uncertainty, the objective is the maximization of utility (after allowance for attitudes toward risk) subject to a constraint, usually income or assets (or wealth). In the following instances the constraint is assets or wealth. Such an analysis generates rates of return on the additions to the separate categories of wealth. This is more carefully illustrated in section 8.3, but, for the present, we will discuss simpler situations, for example, money holdings with a yield (possibly nothing more than security and convenience) and other assets with yields (including allowances for risk); and money holdings with an opportunity foregone (foregone by not holding bonds or real capital).

In order to understand complex behavior and theory, it is often useful to examine the parts separately and to see whether they can be grasped individually, while keeping the parts in their proper context. Examples of such complex matters include the behavior of decisionmakers in the management of portfolios and Tobin's liquidity behavior toward risk, as presented below.

Tobin's theory entails a consideration of securities as found in Markowitz. Their approaches are emphasized here, in part because of the professional attention given to them, and in part because of their apparent status as landmarks in the development of portfolio behavior in the presence of risk and uncertainty.

The salient parts of Tobin's thoery are his difference-of-opinion approach to liquidity preference, its Keynesian linkage scheme, his diversified portfolio à la Markowitz, his reliance upon a relative frequency approach to probability as a means of dealing with uncertainty, and--probably a corollary of the latter--his reliance on axioms of cardinal utility. These parts are considered later.

The introduction of probability into economic theory can be viewed as a means of making economics more relevant by including analysis of the more common case, namely that of uncertainty. Two strands of reasoning stand out: (1) the mean variance analysis and (2) the modern or neo-Bayesian analysis. The first, introduced by Markowitz and used by Tobin, draws on a relative frequency or classical approach to probability.[11] The second combines utility analysis with the modern theory of subjective (personalistic) or Bayesian probability. The utility analysis itself may be ordinal or cardinal, as dealt with in the appendix to this chapter. The axioms of ordinal analysis, as pointed out there, are less restrictive, and encompassed by the cardinal utility axioms.

The Baumol-Tobin Transactions Demand

Reading through the Baumol and Tobin papers, one might wonder how the theory set forth in them ever came to be invoked as an explanation of observable changes in the income velocity of money or in the sales-to-cash ratio for industrial corporations. In point of fact, however, the models did posit a reduction in transactions balances (i.e., a reduction in balances in relation to income) as interest rates rose. The marginal adjustment was to favor an increase in bond holdings. In Tobin's explanation, this occurred because of certain economies or reductions in the brokerage cost of transactions in bonds per unit of bonds purchased, particularly as the asset size of the unit making the purchase increased. According to Baumol, velocity (or sales-to-cash ratio) rose as the rate of interest exceeded the brokerage cost, thereby inducing a shift into bonds.

These ideas came to be thought of as economies of scale and as being the cause of a rise in sales to cash ratios for firms in particular (Frazer 1967, chap. 8). (For the nonfinancial business sector, sales are a surrogate variable for GNP, whereas the cash balances held by this sector are the counterpart to the money balances held in the overall economy, often with the exception of interbank balances.) Despite the narrowness of the works and the prospect of other important factors, the Tobin and Baumol ideas came actually to be offered as explanations for two tendencies: (1) an observed tendency for sales-to-cash ratios to rise as the size of the firm increased (sect. 8.3) and (2) the tendency for the income velocity of money to rise in the United States over the post-World War II years (fig. 5-2).

As matters have turned out there are several strong bits of evidence that conflict with the Baumol-Tobin ideas as they came to be used by economists and to be presented in college textbooks, namely:

1. As manufacturing corporations increase in asset size, their government bond holdings and related sources of liquidity increase more than in proportion to asset size, but this is not economical (an economy of scale); the liquidity actually costs a great deal, especially when considering the opportunity cost of being liquid rather than investing in plant and equipment. There is, apparently, a security and convenience associated with non cash forms of liquidity, and large firms are willing to pay for it. In particular, noncash liquidity balances are apparently related to the financial planning of large firms. (Sect. 8.3)

2. Over the post-World War II years, the noncash liquidity of firms has declined rather than risen in relation to asset size, while interest rates have risen. Some have attributed this decline to greater certainty about future business conditions or inflation.

The Liquidity Preference Demand for Money (Tobin's Theory)

In his presentation of liquidity preference demand for money, Tobin was reacting to some criticisms of Keynes's theory. As reviewed in section 5.3, Keynes gave special attention to the pull-toward-normality approach. This approach is based on an assumption of the varying probability of an expected return to normality, while at the same time defining the short run of the analysis as a period in which expectations are constant. When this inconsistency was pointed out, Tobin set about a reconstruction that relied upon a difference-of-opinion approach in which expectations were constant. This approach offered no explanation of diversification between money and bonds (as should become clear below), so Tobin introduced Markowitz's mean-variance analysis into the theory of liquidity preference as a means of explaining diversification of the money-bond portfolio.

The difference-of-opinion notion proceeds by recognizing that different individuals share different opinions about the future of interest rates. When individual A's prospective rate is above the present rate (as controlled by the Federal Reserve), individual A's portfolio will consist entirely of money balances, in anticipation of a decline in the price of bonds. When individual B's prospective rate is below the present rate, all his speculative money balances will go into bonds in anticipation of a rise in the price of bonds. This may continue for individual C, and so on. When taken together, the various expectations and the resulting behaviors yield a smooth aggregate demand curve for money balances, as in figure 6-6.

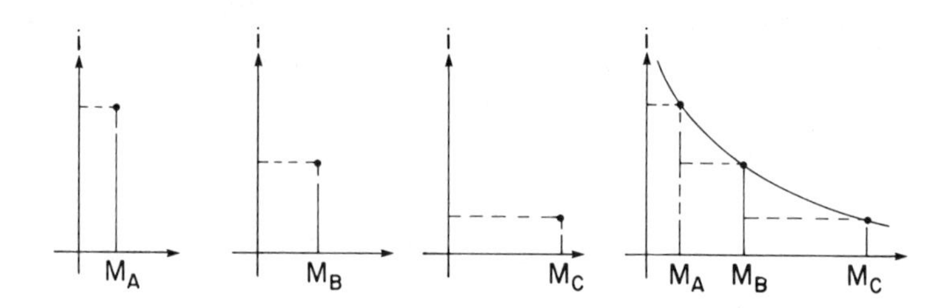

Figure 6-6. Speculative Demand for Money: Difference of Opinion Approach

The criticisms of the Tobin approach are varied. For one, the Federal Reserve controls the rate of interest through the same linkage mechanism as that found in Keynesian economics (i.e., $\Delta M \rightarrow -\Delta i$). Expectations are impounded and other prospects are ruled out, such as:

$$\Delta M \rightarrow \Delta Y \rightarrow \Delta i$$

$$\Delta M \rightarrow \Delta P^e \rightarrow \Delta i$$

where the change in the money stock (ΔM) is influencing spending (ΔY) and/or expected inflation (ΔP^e) and then the interest rate, but with reverse sign ($-\Delta i$).

To say it differently, the possibility that monetary policy may influence demand conditions and then interest rates is ruled out.

Tobin has also been criticized for his way of dealing with diversification. Further, his critics point out that the prospect of differences of opinion is not ruled out by the pull-toward-normality construction, which states that the strength of the prospective pulls change as the interest rate changes about the norm, even though opinions may differ. Under dire circumstances the subjective norm also may change, and in this case there may be no liquidity trap nor simple construction as in figure 5-4. The reader should note that the trap discussed in section 5.3 depends on the pull toward normality.

The Diversified Portfolio: Mean-Variance Analysis

In section 8.3 we consider the discounting of prospective returns (flows of utility) and derive a rule for maximizing this flow of utility; namely: utility is maximized when the rates of return on additions to the various classes of assets are equal. These returns may be weighted to adjust for subjective elements such as risk or liquidity. If we combine the weighted flows of utility, the expected total of the addition to utility (EU) can be denoted:

$$EU = p_1U\ (R_1) + p_2\ U\ (R_2) + \ldots + p_n\ U\ (R_n)$$

$$= \sum_{i=1}^{n} p_i\ U(R_i)$$

where the ps are probabilities and the U(Rs) are utilities. This is one way of introducing a consideration of risk or uncertainty. Another is to use the probability concept of variance in reference to prospective returns as a measure or risk. Such a variance may be denoted for a particular project,

$$\text{var} = \sum_{i=1}^{n} P_i\ (R_i - R)^2$$

where P_i is the probability of the ith return from the project, and R is the mean return.

As one proceeds from these measures of probability, one should distinguish between the relative frequency approach to probability and the subjective, or modern, approach mentioned in notes 10 and 11 above and in appendix A to chapter 6. There are possible situations where the use of one or the other makes little difference, but in the presence of underlying changes in the sampling universe the modern notion is more relevant. To put it differently, the modern notion lends itself to the analysis of more dynamic situations, with evolutionary and nonrepetitive changes as may result from political administrations (sects. 10.3, 12.5, and 17.3) and energy shortages (chap. 16). Nevertheless, we suspend this distinction for the moment, and proceed by following Markowitz and Tobin.

Markowitz developed a decision rule that depended upon the measure of variance, the rule was a prescription for minimizing risk and maximizing return. But it was Tobin who brought the approach into positive economics (i.e., the economics that seeks to explain observable behavior). In this contribution he also introduced cardinal utility analysis, or the axioms of the theory of games and economic behavior, as reviewed in appendix A. He did this because of a particular concept of rationality, and because the relative frequency approach to probability was tied in with the cardinal analysis. So be it, for the time being. The Markowitz mean (expected value) variance rule is as follows:

> The investor should want to select a portfolio that gives rise to some combination of the expected value or mean (E) and variance (V) such that variance is a minimum for a given expected value, and expected value is a maximum for given variance.

Although expectations are introduced they are taken to be invariant during the period the rule is applied. The relative frequency approach to probability requires that the sampling universe remain unchanged as the variance is computed from a large sample.

Figure 6-7. Utility as a Function of Return

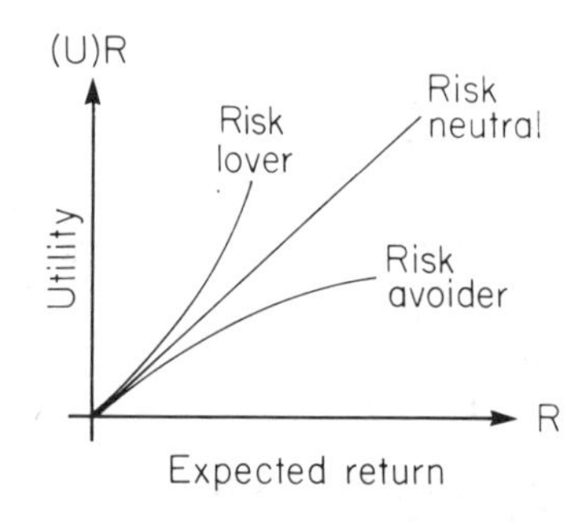

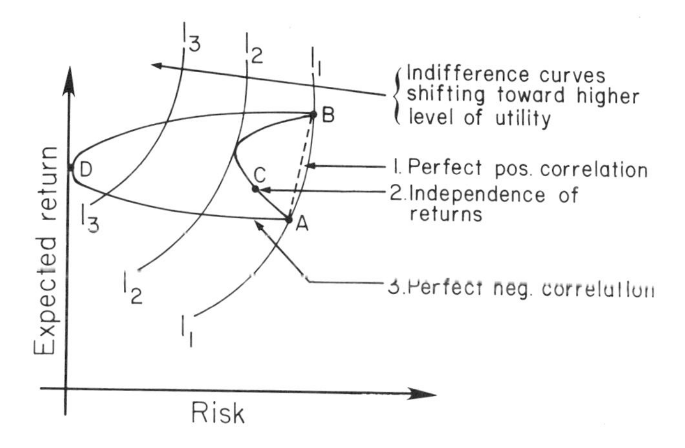

Figure 6-8. Risk Reduction through Diversification: Two Investment Projects

It is common in this analysis to recognize that risk reduces utility, and that different individuals vary in their attitudes toward risk. As developed in appendix A to this chapter and as shown in figure 6-7, risk lovers tend to get more utility from a given addition to wealth than risk averters. The idea, as represented in the figure, is that the utility of extra wealth is increasing at a greater rate for the risk lovers. Consequently, different individuals will have different portfolio objectives, although all may wish to reduce risk for a given return. This preference for a reduction in risk is illustrated in figure 6-8, where three indifference curves (I_1 I_1, I_2 I_2, and I_3 I_3) are superimposed. As the sketch suggests, a higher level of utility is reflected in a leftward shift in the utility curves. We say "superimposed" because the figure itself does not represent a utility space.

We now consider two investment projects, A and B, and so-called opportunity frontiers AB, ACB, and ADB. If the returns from the two projects are perfectly and positively correlated, then there is no reduction in risk by diversification. The frontier is the broken line AB. If the returns from two projects are independent of one another, some diversification may reduce risk because of the prospect that the random nature of the returns will not always work against you. This frontier is the line ACB. But if the returns from the two projects have perfect negative correlation, then the risk can always be reduced by diversification. The opportunity frontier is illustrated by the line ADB. For the risk averter the "efficient portfolio" is always the diversified portfolio. The risk taker, in the extreme, will simply take the highest yield regardless of its accompanying risk.

Figure 6-9.
The Interest Rate,
Risk and Return

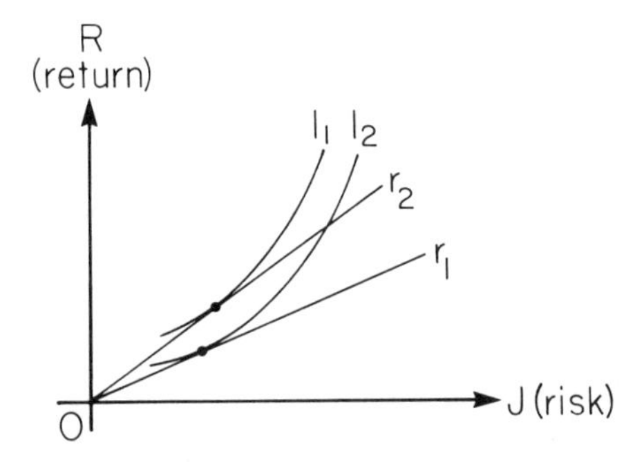

The special nature of the risk--with constant expectations and with independence from the interest rate--in Tobin's theory is illustrated in figure 6-9. The return (R) shown there is equal to the product of the rate of interest and the dollar value of the bonds owned (rB). Each dollar's worth of bonds has j units of risk (expressed as a rate), so that total risk (J) is the product of the risk units and the dollar value (jB). From this information we see that:

$$\frac{R}{J} = \frac{r}{j}$$

and

$$R = \frac{r}{j}\,(J)$$

This defines the straight line emanating from the origin in figure 6-9, the slope of which is

$$\frac{dR}{dJ} = \frac{r}{J}$$

This means that if risk is constant, a rise in the rate of interest increases the slope of the line, e.g., from line r_1 to r_2 in the figure. With indifference curves I_1 and I_2 imposed on the figure, we can see that the increase in yield moves the entity to a higher level of utility without incurring additional risk. The shape of the indifference curves in the construction suggests the entity is risk averse, demanding that risk (J) must increase less than in proportion to return (R) as return increases.

The central feature emerging from Tobin's difference-of-opinion approach (fig. 6-6) and contrasting with the pull-toward-normality approach is that risk is independent of the interest rate. In the pull-toward-normality approach the probability of a loss from declining bond values increases as the rate of interest falls further and further below the normal rate of interest.

Friedman's Approach

Friedman outlined his approach to the demand for money in the mid 1950s and resketched it in the early 1970s (Frazer 1973, 314-17). He does not formally introduce probability, although risk and uncertainty come in various ad hoc ways, such as when he draws on Tobin's difference-of-opinion approach and when he introduces greater certainty as an explanation for the post-World War II rise in velocity of money (chap. 5). Friedman's approach was couched in a general equilibrium context, as have been similar approaches. In these approaches, the theory of general equilibrium is intended to bridge a gap between the study of the behavior of the economy as a whole and the study of separate units. In the one instance, there are index numbers and aggregates, while in the other there are separate entities (individuals, firms, and groups). The theory of choice here envisions a maximization of returns from wealth or total assets, with imbalances resulting from differential changes in the rates of return.

Friedman wrote his demand for money function in the early 1970s thus:

$$\frac{M}{P} = f(y, w; r_m, r_b, r_e, \frac{1}{P}\frac{dP}{dt}; u)$$

where M is the stock of money, P is the price index implicit in estimating national income in constant prices, and y is nominal income in constant prices. The other variables are defined as follows:

w is the fraction of wealth in nonhuman form (or, alternatively, the fraction of income derived from

> property); r_m is the expected nominal rate of return on money; r_b is the expected nominal rate of return on fixed valued securities, including expected changes in their prices; r_e is the expected nominal rate of return on equities, including expected changes in their prices; (1/P) (d P/dt) is the expected rate of change of prices of goods and hence the expected nominal rate of return on real assets; and u is a portmanteau symbol standing for whatever variables other than income may affect the utility attached to the services of money. (Friedman 1970, 204)

Viewing changes in the distribution of income and wealth or their effects as constant or nearly so, it is possible to apply Friedman's demand function to the community as a whole, with M and y referring to per capita amounts. As the term implies, the portmanteau variable is a catchall, used to incorporate much of what one wishes to analyze (changes in the degree of certainty about anticipated returns and business condition).

In applying the demand function to business enterprises, u represents for a "set of variables other than scale affecting the productivity of money balances." Friedman says, "At least one of these--namely, expectations about economic stability--is likely to be common to business enterprises and ultimate wealth holders." The current statement of the function departs from an earlier one in that Friedman has called the yields "expected" yields. Friedman, however, does not explain this change, but study of him indicates that his views evolve with further study and reflection.

In some respects Friedman's function may be viewed as simply a way of listing factors affecting the demand for money. As one can see, it is not likely to be definable by a least-squares, multiple regression equation because the variables in the function are probably interdependent. For example, if the expected price level changes, the expected nominal rate of return on fixed valued securities will change.

In empirical studies the fraction of wealth in nonhuman form (w) in Friedman's function has not been shown to vary in such a way as to make it a significant determinant. But there is the idea that the larger this fraction of wealth, the less the demand for money because of the reduced need for money balances as a means of dealing with emergencies and other unforeseen developments. Friedman conveys this belief by citing "greater certainty" as a cause of the reduction in desired money balances held in relation to income (i.e., as a cause of the rise in velocity) over the post-World War II years (fig. 5-2).

Liquidity Preference and Assets

In using one or the other liquidity preference constructions as a part of one's theory of economic behavior, due attention should be given to assumptions, if for no other reason than the avoidance of inconsistency in the thinking. The role of expectations and the classification of assets are especially complicating. These can be illustrated with reference to the two- (four-) asset classification. This classification is possible without abandoning the notion of the liquidity preference construction with a pull-toward-normality and variable expectations. In such a model, the rise in interest rates (viewed as a rise in the yield on real capital) may still reflect a rise in income in relation to the money stock; only in this case, the inducement may be for adjustments out of both money and bonds.

Recall that in chapter 1 liquidity was defined as the ease of disposal of an asset without expected loss of principal or purchasing power. Recall, next, that all assets can be ranked according to their degree of liquidity (sect. 3.3).

What then do we mean by liquidity preference? We mean a preference for some assets possessing a high degree of liquidity in relation to other assets. Liquidity preference is exhibited in terms of the need for money balances to make transactions, but it takes on speculative dimensions as well. The two types of speculation considered concern changes in interest rates (and therefore bond values) and changes in the price level. In the first case, there is the possibility of a loss or gain from changes in bond values. In the second, there is the possibility of a loss or gain from changes in the future purchasing power of money balances, including money balances to be received in the future as a result of a contractual claim fixed in dollar terms (such as a bond).

In inflation, as we have stressed, the claims of residual claim assets are enlarged. An anticipated increase in the inflation rate then causes adjustments in classes of asset holdings, namely, increased holdings of residual claim assets in relation to total assets. Interest rates rise. The related prospect of a rise in interest rates and a decline in bond values reinforces the notion of a shift out of bonds (and into money, but only momentarily so). What occurs, in effect, is a reduced demand for money in relation to enlarged spending, especially for real (as distinct from financial) assets.

Figure 6-10.
Anticipated Increases in the Inflation Rate: Pull-toward-normality Approaches with Two (Four) Classes of Assets

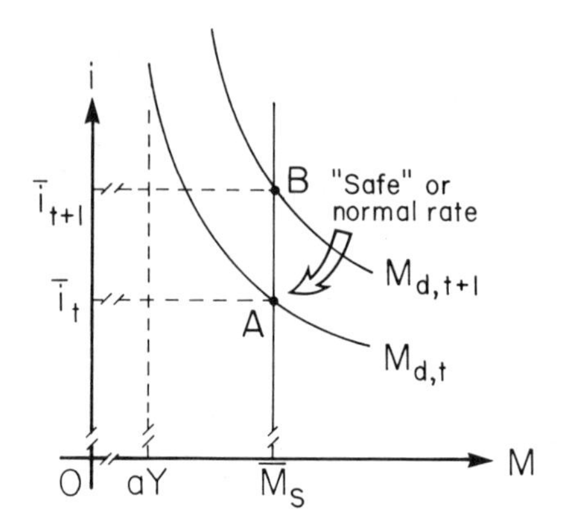

The aspects of the forgoing statement of the theory are illustrated in figure 6-10. What we have is a more rapid outward shift in the demand curve than in the money stock line. Recalling equations (5.1) through (5.4) of section 5.3, we have $i = b/(\gamma - c\,Y)$. The enlarged Y (i.e., enlarged in relation to γ) raises the interest rate.

Working with elements of such a theory, some researchers have reduced the theory to a linear regression model:

$$i = \text{constant} + \beta_1 \frac{1}{M'}\frac{dM'}{dt} + \beta_2 \frac{1}{Y'}\frac{dY'}{dt} + \beta_3 \frac{1}{P}\frac{dP}{dt}$$

where

P = price level

M' = M/P

Y' = Y/P

(1/P)(dP/dt) = rate of change in the price level.

They found the βs to be positive, and β_2 and β_3 to be significantly so. Further, 72.8 percent of the variation in the interest rate was accounted for by variation in the right hand members of the equation (Frazer 1973, chap. 13).

This idea of the foregoing adjustments over the entire range of the asset classes suggests that households and firms may hold such a range of assets. Large manufacturing corporations do, as discussed in chapter 8, but banks, on the other hand, are restricted to trading mainly in loans and investments in the form of financial assets such as bonds and mortgages. Their adjustment to accelerated inflation may simply be a tendency to set higher interest rates on loans to compensate for the prospect of repayment with lower purchasing power dollars. Fisher's interest rate equation, as in chapter 5, may come in here.

Equilibrium Time Paths (More Review)

The theory just reviewed can be considered with respect to the meaning of equilibrium in a dynamic context. In this form we have equilibrium time paths, which are also referred to as exponential time paths in stock and flow quantities. To illustrate such paths, as a first approximation, think of the liquidity preference model with its safe or normal rate of interest as in figure 6-10. Then, consider the following: If we double the stock and flow quantities (M and Y), or let them change at the same rate, what happens to the velocity ratio (Y/M), the rate of interest, and the safe or normal rate (i.e., the expected trend rate in the mind of beholder or by analogy the collective mind of the market participants, as shown in figure 6-10)?

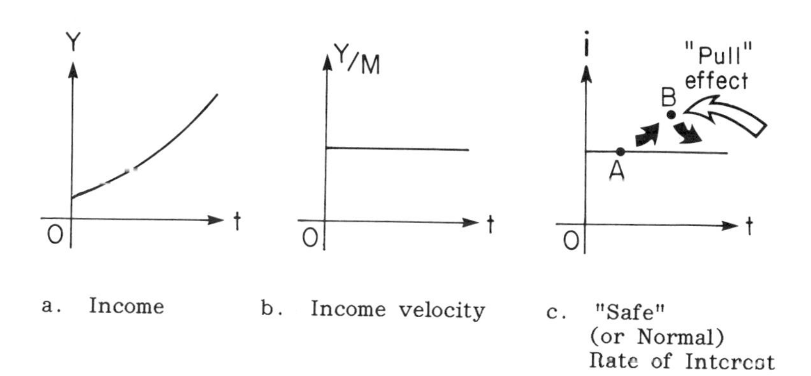

a. Income b. Income velocity c. "Safe" (or Normal) Rate of Interest

Figure 6-11. Equilibrium Time Paths

First, the stock and flow quantities will show exponential growth as in figure 6-11a, although observed values for income may be scattered about this path. Next, the velocity ratio and the rate of interest will show a given level over time (figure 6-11b). The same will be true of the "safe" (or normal), as illustrated in figure 6-11c. Observed values may be scattered about the normal rate. The pull toward normality has been stressed, however when there is movement away from the equilibrium paths, there is an extrapolative push effect as well. There is a momentum. Less has been said about this push effect , but it will receive some consideration later. In this context, Friedman has referred to a tendency for the economic variable to "overshoot" (Friedman 1968; Goldberg and Thurston 1977).[12]

6.4. Indexation

Clauses in contracts that tie expected returns to real returns, through the introduction of an adjustment to compensate for inflation, for example, are called "escalator clauses" (sect. 17.2). And they can address deescalation as well. A general system of escalator clauses, which protects all income recipients against inflation, has come to be called "indexation." The idea of such a comprehensive system has become of increasing interest in a world that has experienced the post-World War II rises in prices.[13] (These are shown for the United States in figure 1-2.)

Forms of Income

The introduction to indexation is closely allied with a consideration of distinct asset classes (sect. 3.3), the effects of inflation on the proceeds from them, and the rule generating exponential time paths of the last section. First, we recognize that assets, as described above, and human capital are the sources of all income.

Income received (as in the introduction to the national income accounts in section 3.2) can take the form of interest, rent, wages and salaries, some tax matters, and profits. Of these, all but profits are for the most part set forth in a contract: the bond certificate, the wage agreement between unions and management, and tax laws. If these contractual claims are fixed in nominal dollar terms, and if the purchasing power of dollars declines and the nominal gross income rises (as in a period of inflation), then the residual part of the income increases and its share of gross income in real terms increases. This can become a basis for speculation over prospective changes in purchasing power and for adjustments in asset holdings. Monetary claims loose liquidity and wealth holders tend to hold real estate and related assets in greater proportions. In a sense real production forces are channeled into "concrete gold," and some of the economies from holding an adequate stock of money balances are lost (sects. 1.1 and 1.2).

In this context, indexation (the conversion of contractual claims in nominal terms into claims in real terms) protects the real income of certain groups. The holders of bonds, for example, can be protected. Instead of specifying a nominal interest rate of, say, 11 percent (a 3 percent real rate plus an 8 percent inflation component), only the "real" rate is settled as a fixed component. The idea is to get parties to the financing of capital expenditures to evaluate the prospects as if the value of money were stable. It is said that this practice protects society partly or as a whole from the instability generated by the prospect for speculative gains arising from inflation, and thereby reduces the instability caused by spending to produce real goods in response to the inflation rate.

Indexation as it relates to the payment of taxes, monetary policy, and wage contracts is discussed in section 17.2. Whether a comprehensive system would be beneficial on balance for the society, and what the implications are for national economy policy, cannot yet be determined. The pros and cons are more complex than indicated thus far.

The Money Illusion

The term "money illusion" has been used in some instances to apply where economic agents--such as consumers, households, and firms--incompletely anticipate changes in the value of money, as during periods of inflation. This means that they respond more to changes in nominal values than to changes in real values. For example, higher (lower) nominal wages are reacted to as higher (lower) real wages to some degree. As an empirical matter, over- and under-reactions to nominal values and anticipated nominal values are thought to occur in the short run (sect. 17.4). Until a given rate of inflation persists and becomes adjusted to, however, a more proper term for this short run behavior might be an "inflation illusion." Regardless of what it is called, the implication is clear: namely, contracts quoted in fixed nominal terms are not completely anticipated in equal real terms.[14]

Quoting contracts for wages, interest, rent, and so on in real terms is one solution for reducing the degree of money illusion. However, instability in business conditions may still exist as economic entities vie for their shares of real income, and profits as residual claims may still exist, too.

6.5. Summary

Consider the schedules for money supply (M_s) and money demand (M_d), both as a function of the rate of interest (i) and some variable constants:

$$M_s = f_1 \text{ (i, variable constants)}$$

$$M_d = f_2 \text{ (i, variable constants)}$$

One of the schedules may be varied (say, via a variable constant) so that a locus of points is traced out and such that this locus is the other schedule (as initially illustrated in appendix to chapter 1). This approach to identification implies that the two schedules are shifted independently of one another. A problem emerges, however, (and it is common to this approach) because of a lack of independence in the movements of the schedules. The "trick" is using such schedules in a valid, empirically verifiable theory, then, is to understand the interrelationships in the schedules so that those things can be changed that do in fact change.

In the case of the money stock and its demand, Friedman poses an approach different from the foregoing traditional approach. The money stock is simply treated as a given, whereas the demand or public side of the market for money balances is assumed to adjust its spending, thereby raising or lowering the average of prices or output until the stock is at the desired level. And, indeed, changes in the stock may influence the demand for money via an increase in money and prices. There may be overshooting in terms of spending (and hence rising velocity) and the changes in the money stock may influence expectations about future prices and income also. The money stock is determined by the Federal Reserve and the public can only adjust its spending as it attempts to reduce or hold more balances.

As to the control of bank reserves and other monetary aggregates in multiple amounts, there is a tradition in economics that only the banking system can create additional credit and money in response to additional reserves. Individual banks in this tradition do not create credit and money. Clearly, though, if the banking system as a whole experiences accelerated growth in bank credit and money, then the banking units comprising the system must participate by experiencing the growth to the extent that they maintain their relative position in the banking community. By this approach, as a first approximation, the theory is moved in a more dynamic, *mutatis mutandis* direction.

The Federal Reserve creates reserves, and bank credit and the money stock (narrowly or broadly viewed) may be related to these reserves via multipliers. The multipliers may vary, depending on the breadth of the aggregate being considered and some other factors, such as more or less certainty about the future on the part of the commercial bankers.

The control of the monetary and credit aggregates, however, is even more complicated than suggested by the changes in the multipliers. The manager of the Federal Reserve's open market account must try to achieve target values for various reserve measures without knowing with certainty the extent of other influences on reserves. Further, there is no precise, reliable guide to the link between money and credit aggregates and the Federal funds rate, which until October 6, 1979 was frequently used by the manager in executing the FOMC's directives for monetary policy. One reason for the lack of a definite link is that the money market may react to the FOMC's interventions or to other information and events bearing on the future and on the demand for bank credit. Roos sees this interrelationships of markets as a problem in monetary control, along with the failure to distinguish credit market and money demand aspects of Federal Reserve policy. The control arrangement at hand lends itself to support of the old bias toward interest rate control.

The FOMC in any case has come to recognize the complexity of trying to control monetary aggregates in any precise way in the short run. This recognition is demonstrated in part by the prescription of ranges for the money and credit aggregates. These occur on a month-to-month basis, and ranges are also used in announcing plans for policy for one year in the future.

The acceleration or deceleration of monetary aggregates and a host of governmental or business actions and inactions may give rise to changes in the confidence with which views of the future are held and to changes in expectations as well. Prospective returns and utilities may be probabilistically weighted. Moreover, interest rates may depart from normality with a varying probability for the regressive pull toward normality.

The presence of this variation in the pull toward normality concerns the pull toward normality approach to liquidity preference, an approach based on the assumption (by Keynes and the Keynesians) of a constancy of expectations. However, the inconsistency of this assumption with the change in the strength of the prospective return to normality as the interest rate changed led Tobin to construct a difference of opinion approach to the demand for money. His approach is still characterized by Keynesian attributes. For example, expectations are constant, and the Federal Reserve manipulates the interest rate with an explicitly stated inverse relation with the money stock. In the difference-of-opinion approach the assets held are either money or bonds. To explain the diversification of asset holdings to conform more closely to observed holdings, Tobin introduced Markowitz's mean-variance analysis. This approach has traditionally assumed a cardinal rather than ordinal utility analysis, and has called for a larger set of utility axioms. There is no doubt merit in the idea of reducing risk through Markowitz diversification where yields on the respective assets are not perfectly positively correlated.

Perspective is given to Tobin's difference of opinion approach by noting certain prospects. Notably, the Federal Reserve does not control the rate of interest as assumed in the approach, and a presumed switching from money to bonds (both in relation to total assets or income) may not occur as interest rates rise. The latter prospect may hold mainly for the monetary aggregates and for business firms. The alternative possibility is that the interest rate is a measure of the return on capital (similar and almost identical to the rate of return) and that a possible rearrangement of assets to favor real capital i an eminent one. Examination of empirical evidence may shed some light on the velocity of this explanation.

A liquidity preference approach to the demand for assets may consider changes in holdings of a wide range of assets in response to a varying prospect of a return of interest rates to normality and in response to the prospect of purchasing power risks. The short period of Keynes's theory may be treated as approaching zero (short run approaches zero at the limit) and the pull toward normality approach may be retained and re-couched in a Friedmanesque, quasi-permanent magnitude time frame. In this the equilibrium is a time path.

A broader set of asset classes may include fixed claim (money and bonds) and residual claim (real capital and equities) assets. Keynes had a two-asset model, comprised of money and bonds (with bonds including real capital and equities). The Keynesian model includes money and bonds, but with equities and real capital excluded from consideration. Friedman considers rather loosely a wide range of assets classified as human and nonhuman.

The expectation of a greater rate of inflation gives rise to accelerated spending on real assets with a residual claim against future income for those economic entities that may hold such assets. Some holders of debt instruments may simply expand holdings and adjust nominal interest rates upward to protect themselves against anticipated losses of purchasing power due to greater inflation. Indexation has been suggested as another means of minimizing inflation-generated losses to the holders of debt instruments. It is suggested as a partial means of stabilizing inflation induced spending by getting parties to the financing of capital spending to figure prospects as if the real returns per unit of monetary assets were fixed.

In the Keynesian tradition and in the banking view, the rate of interest was the control variable for the Federal Reserve, as variously considered in chapter 4 and above. Monetarist research, on the other hand, had impact and called for the treatment of time rates of change in the money stock (or money and credit aggregates broadly viewed) as the indicator for monetary policy. In the Keynesian view, the procyclical nature of interest rates appeared to signify a countercyclical monetary policy. The monetarist work, however, indicated that in chasing interest rates up and down, the money and credit aggregates were in fact behaving procyclically for the most part and thus were destabilizing. The Friedmanesque approach indeed called for an awareness of cyclical time frames and underlying trend paths with singular attention to the aggregates (or time rates of change in the money stock).

The impact of the monetarist/Friedmanesque approach was formalized by the change in the directive for the manager of the Federal Reserve's open market account in January 1970, by the incorporation of House Concurrent Resolution 133 into the Federal Reserve Act, and by announcement on the part of the Board of Governors on October 6, 1979. Under the new directive and since, greater attention has been given to the money and credit aggregates. The Federal Reserve's affair with the Federal funds rate started out under the aggregates regime as a secondary one but became more than that. Since interest rate data are readily available and of high quality, and since interest rates are important in their own right, they have been used by the FOMC and the account manager in attempts to achieve target rates for money and credit aggregates. However, the arrangement lent itself to the notion of interest rate control rather than that of money and credit aggregates and thus on October 6, 1979 the Board came to the position of having to proceed more directly to the control of the money and credit aggregates.

The first eight years of experience under the new approach coincided with the tenure of Arthur Burns as the Federal Reserve's chairman. Much progress may be observed in the changes in the directives and in the reporting of policy in this period. Critics of Burns years in the Federal Reserve, even so, point out that the time rates of change in the money stock narrowly and broadly viewed were still procyclical.

Perhaps more can be achieved and explanations for the FOMC's behavior under Burns are called for. These would appear to focus on control at a point vis-à-vis control over a cycle, the political aspects surrounding the matter of the independence of the Federal Reserve (the political business cycle), the failure on the part of officals and advisors to estimate correctly and grasp the significance of the natural rate of unemployment, and the failure of professional literature to address the strong expectational component in business conditions matters (both with respect to cyclical and evolutionary, nonrepetitive changes) until quite recent times. In fact, up until these times, economics has assumed the independence of the Federal Reserve within the framework of government (and/or separated economic theory and policy in presumed convenient ways), and failed to address correctly or grasp the significance of the natural rate of unemployment, on the one hand, and economics has tended to impound troublesome expectational matters, in ceteris paribus, and to emphasize levels in stock and flow variables rather than time rates of change, on the other.

FOOTNOTES

1. The derivation of the bank reserve equation from balance sheet items may be found in Frazer and Yohe (1965, 215-221).
2. The reason offered by Rutner for taking the logarithmic transformation of the data is that of removing heteroscedasticity from the regression results. The transformation contributes to this elimination and facilitates the analysis of rates of change. Heteroscedasticity refers to a change in the variance of the error term as an independent variable increases, whereas one of the assumptions of the least-squares regression method is that of homoscedasticity (i.e., the variance of each u_j is the same for all j (j = 1, 2, ..., n) and the independence of the variance from the so-called independent variable x_j.
3. The detailed information is available in current issues of the Federal Reserve Bulletin under "Member Bank Reserve Requirements."

4. As a whole commercial banks simply grow with the growth of reserves, bank credit, and deposit liabilities. Though some may grow faster than others, they may be viewed as participating in a process that permits them to hold some relative position in the overall picture. This view is partly reinforced when we realize that the total number of commercial banks in the United States has only varied from 14,181 at year-end 1947 to 14,171 at year-end 1973.
5. The extensive literature on the Eurodollar market is reviewed by Karlik (1977).
6. We could construct a system of equations as found in Frazer and Yohe (1965, chap. 4), and obtain solutions that yielded different multipliers depending on the public's preference for currency, for time deposits, and so on. And simplified balance sheets or T-accounts could be used to illustrate specific aspects of numerus transactions (Balbach and Burger 1976).
7. The Federal Reserve Bank of St. Louis would add an "adjustment" to the changes in the money base (Burger and Rasche 1977), referred to as the reserve adjustment magnitude (RAM). The purpose of this adjustment can be illustrated with reference to the relation between the base (B) and the money stock (M):

$$M = mB$$

where

$$m = \frac{1 + k}{r(1 + t + g) + k}$$

As mentioned above the multiplier may be influenced by on several factors. In this formation, $\underline{r}$ represents the reserve ratio (consisting of legal reserve requirement ratios plus an excess reserve ratio and a nonmember bank vault cash ratio), $\underline{t}$ is the ratio of time deposits to private demand deposits (reflecting any change in deposits), $\underline{g}$ is the ratio of government demand deposits at commercial banks to private demand deposits (reflecting any disproportionate changes in government held and privately held demand deposits), and $\underline{k}$ is the ratio of currency held by the nonbank public to private demand deposits (reflecting any disporportionate drain of currency).

Now, the money stock may change because of a change in the base or because of a change in the multiple in response to the factors just indicated. The St. Louis Bank's adjustment magnitude (RAM) is in effect a means of relocating the impact of any reserve requirement ratio changes from the multipler (m) to the money base (B). In this way, Federal Reserve actions to change the legal reserve requirement ratio as well as to influence the money base can be summarized in a single measure (B). Burger and Rasche (1977) address themselves to the method of computing the summary measure (B).
8. The short-term rate was at times before October 6, 1979, set as a target at times by the FOMC, with the view to

supporting the achievement of targets for monetary aggregates.

The complexities of the FOMC's operations are illustrated by a Citibank review of market interventions in July of 1978 and in late 1977:

> "When ever long-term interest rates take an upward jump, the Fed takes the rap. But as the recent behavior of long rates demonstrates, the money markets work in mysterious ways. To blame the Fed for a rise in long rates is to be taken in by a case of mistaken identity. It just doesn't work that way.
>
> "When the Federal Reserve's Open Market Committee decided to increase the cost of credit in the middle of July, it raised the federal funds target rate to 7 7/8%. But the securities market reacted to this intended tightening move in a somewhat perverse way--by rallying. Intead of rising, yields dropped sharply. The two-year note that was auctioned to yield 8.61% when the Fed made its tightening move ended up trading nearly 30 basis points lower by the end of July. Long-term bonds dropped by a similar amount, after having reached a cyclical high of 8.74%.
>
> "So, once again, the market's reaction has refuted the charge that the Fed is responsible for high interest rates. It is true that the federal funds rate--the Fed's main instrument for setting policy--is an important determinant of short-term rates. The reason is that the funds rate sets the level of financing costs. But for longer-term maturities, it is the public's perception of future economic growth and inflation that determines interest rates. Thus, it's the public and not the Fed that decides whether rates rise or fall.
>
> "The market also disregarded Fed action--or inaction--during the latter part of 1977. The funds-rate target, which had been raised to 6.50% in October, was virtually unchanged until January of this year. But during that period, long rates rose by about 20 basis points. It was about that time that the public's attitude changed. The economy broke out of its slump and started to work up some steam, while the outlook for inflation was becoming more ominous. Then, too, money growth was still robust; in fact, it was running above the

Fed's target ranges. Rates had nowhere to go but up.

"The recent decline in long rates is the result of the same force--a change in expectations on the part of the public. The economy's strong second-quarter performance is being undercut by uncertainty." (Monthly Economic Review Letter, August 1978, 5.)

9. Patinkin (1976, 81-2) speaks of Keynes's model in The General Theory as a two-stage, three-asset model. First, he has the money an bond model with the monetary authority varying the interest rate to cause imbalances in the rate of interest and rate of return (or marginal efficiency of capital, in relation to capital goods) as discussed under Keynes in chapter 4. Second, he has the liquidity preference block of chapter 5 with the pull toward normality (the expected rate), whereby one is choosing between money balances and bonds. If Patinkin's distinction is accepted, then the latter two-asset model is the one under consideration in this chapter.
10. This aspect of Keynes work has been variously pointed out (Frazer 1973, chap. 8). Weintraub (1975) views it as an innovation in Keynes's work, but Paul Davidson (1972) views Keynes as restricting uncertainty to actuarial, classical probability.
11. The relative frequency approach may be illustrated by denoting the probability of successes (H for heads) thus:

$$\text{Prob (H)} = \lim_{n \to \infty} \frac{m}{n}$$

where m is the number of successes and n is the number of drawings or sample size. The ratio m/n coverges and approaches its limit as the sample size approaches infinity. The analogy is made to standard processes such as coin tossing, drawing cards from a deck, throwing dice, drawing marbles from a jug (with replacement), spinning a roulette wheel, and so on.

Modern Bayesians, on the other hand, define probability not as a relative frequency, but as a degree of belief, allowing for continuous learning and reevaluation of the situation, as under changing conditions.
12. Goldberg and Thurston (1977) modify the economic analysis of overshooting somewhat. They do so by considering the pro-cyclical nature of velocity, as in chapter 5, and by relating the percent change in income to current and past monetary growth rates with a distributed lag model (such as attributed to Koff in chapter 5). The distributed lag model comes up frequently, and a pattern of coefficiencts relating current and past values for monetary growth to capital spending is reviewed in chapter 8. What one finds for the historical periods studied is a pattern of positive coefficients that decline and become a damped oscillation about zero.

From such a pattern of coefficients obtained from the analysis of quarterly data for the 1953-1973 period, Goldberg and Thurston concluded: (1) that the "overshooting" is temporary, (2) that the long-run effect of a change in the growth rate for the money stock is .79 times the change in M, and (3) that the procyclical movements of velocity are primarily the result of the historical pattern of monetary change rather than of overshooting that results from monetary change.

The difficulties encountered by Goldberg and Thurston in their economic analysis are fourfold. First, the historical pattern of changes in the growth rate for the money stock is not that of a one-shot permanent increase in M. Rather it is a procyclical accelerating growth rate for the money stock as illustrated in figure 4-1, such that the effects of an increase in M are cumulative.

Second, they explain a continued rise (after the initial damped effect) in the velocity ratio (Y/M) as due partly to the denominator of the ratio decelerating in relation to the numerator. This is done without recognizing that the continued procyclical rise in velocity, following the peak rate of change in the money stock, signifies an excess of "actual" over "desired" money balances and, hence, continued "overshooting."

Third, Goldberg and Thurston are apparently still influenced by the assumption that a rising interest rate activates "idle" balances by causing some switching from money balances into bonds, as in the Keynesian position outlined in the present chapter. They see the cyclical conformity of interest rates and velocity as _prima facie_ support for the Keynesian point of view, but still fail to take into consideration whether velocity and the rate of interest are responding to some third force (as indicated in section 5.5) or whether bond portfolios are rising in relation to income and assets. For manufacturing corporations, as reviewed in chapter 8, the evidence on portfolio behavior has not supported the Keynesian point of view.

Finally, Goldberg and Thurston appear to be applying an economic analysis of changes at a point, even as they consider cyclical patterns. At such a point, an increase in the time rate of change in the money stock or the interest rate would have effects, possibly with lagged patterns. This is in lieu of an unfolding sequence within a cyclical time frame.

13. Milton Friedman reviews the origins of the escalator clause in an essay reprinted in Giersch et al. (1974). In its earlier form it was called the "tabular standard," and discussed by writers such as Alfred Marshall and Irving Fisher. The early proposals dealt especially with bonds (borrowed capital extended for long periods of time), long leases, and mortgages.

14. The term "money illusion" has been traditionally used to apply in the area of the theory of prices as determined by Marshallian crosses (app. to chap. 1). In that theory if all prices and income change by the same proportion, ceteris paribus, the quantities demanded do not change. There is the empirically testable idea that the consumer will not behave as if it were richer (poorer) when the prices rise (decline), so as to leave real income unchanged as nominal income rises.

SELECTED READINGS AND REFERENCES

Announcements. 1979. Federal Reserve Bulletin 65 (October).

Balbach, Anatol B., and Albert E. Burger. 1976. "Derivation of the Monetary Base." Review, Federal Reserve Bank of St. Louis (November).

Baumol, William J. 1952. "The Transactions Demand for Cash: An Inventory Approach." Quarterly Journal of Economics (November).

Bazdarich, Michael. 1978. "Inflation and Monetary Accommodation in the Pacific Basin." Economic Review, Federal Reserve Bank of San Francisco (Summer).

Brunner, Karl, and Allan H. Meltzer. 1967. "Economies of Scale in Cash Balances Reconsiderd." Quarterly Journal of Economics (August).

Burger, Albert E., and Robert H. Rasche. 1977. "Revision of the Monetary Base." Review, Federal Reserve Bank of St. Louis (July).

Burger, Albert E., and Douglas R. Mudd. 1977. "The FOMC in 1976: Progress Against Inflation." Review, Federal Reserve Bank of St. Louis (March).

Burns, Arthur F. 1973. "Letter from Chairman Burns to Senator Proxmire," Monthly Review, Federal Reserve Bank of New York (November).

Committee. 1976. "Report of the Advisory Committee on Monetary Statistics." Improving the Monetary Aggregates. Washington, D.C.: Board of Governors of the Federal Reserve System.

Davis, Richard G. 1977. "Monetary Objectives and Monetary Policy." Quarterly Review, Federal Reserve Bank of New York (Spring).

___________. 1980. "The Monetary Base as an Intermediate Target for Monetary Policy." Quarterly Review, Federal Reserve Bank of New York 4(Winter).

Davidson, Paul. 1972. Money and the Real World. New York: Halsted Press.

Fellner, William. 1965. Probability and Profit. Homewood, Ill.: Richard D. Irvin, Inc.

Frazer, William. 1967. The Demand for Money. Cleveland, Ohio: The World Publishing Company.

__________. 1973. Crisis in Economic Theory. Gainesville, Fla.: University of Florida Press.

__________, and William P. Yohe. 1965. Introduction to the Analytics and Institutions of Money and Banking. Princeton, N.J.: D. Van Nostrand Company, Inc.

Friedman, Milton. 1968. "Factors Affecting the Level of Interest Rates, Part I." Savings and Residential Financing--1968 Conference Proceedings. Chicago, Ill.: United States Savings and Loan League.

Frydle, Edward J. 1980. "The Debate over Regulating the Eurocurrency Markets." Quarterly Review, Federal Reserve Bank of New York 4(Winter).

Gambs, Carl M. 1980. "Federal Reserve Intermediate Targets: Money or the Monetary Base?" Economic Review, Federal Reserve Bank of Kansas City (January).

Gibson, William E. 1976. "Demand and Supply Functions for Money: A Comment." Econometrica (March).

Giersch, Herbert, Milton Friedman, William Fellner, Edward M. Bernstein, and Alexander Kafka. 1974. Essays on Inflation and Indexation. Washington, D.C.: American Enterprise Institute for Public Policy Research.

Goldberg, Matthew S. and Thomas B. Thurston. 1977. "Monetarism, Overshooting, and Procyclical Movements of Velocity." Economic Inquiry (January).

Hoffman, Stuart G. 1977. "Component Ratio Estimation of the Money Multiplier." Working Paper Series, Federal Reserve Bank of Atlanta (August).

Holmes, Alan R., and Peter D. Sternlight. 1977. "The Implementation of Monetary Policy in 1976." Quarterly Review, Federal Reserve Bank of New York (Spring).

Jianakoplos, Nancy. 1977. "The FOMC in 1975: Announcing Monetary Targets." Review, Federal Reserve Bank of St. Louis (March).

Jordan, Jerry L. 1979. "Discussion." Journal of Finance (May).

Karlik, John R. 1977. Some Questions and Brief Answers about the Eurodollar Market, A Staff Study Prepared for the use of the Joint Economic Committee, Congress of the United States. Washington, D.C.: U.S. Government Printing Office.

Lang, Richard W. 1979. "The FOMC in 1978: Clarifying the Role of the Aggregates." Review, Federal Reserve Bank of St. Louis (March).

Laporte, Anne Marie. 1979. "Proposed Redefinition of Money Stock Measures." Economic Perspectives, Federal Reserve Bank of Chicago (March/April).

Levy, H., and H. M. Markowitz. 1979. "Approximating Expected Utility by a Function of Mean and Variance." American Economic Review (June).

Lombra, Raymond E. 1979. "Discussion." Journal of Finance (May).

Maisel, Sherman J. 1973. Managing the Dollar. New York: W. W. Norton & Company, Inc.
Markowitz, Harry M. 1976. "Portfolio Selection." Journal of Finance (March).
Mayer, Thomas. 1979. "Discussion." Journal of Finance (May).
Morgenstern, Oskar. 1976. "The Collaboration Between Oskar Morgenstern and John von Neumann on the Theory of Games." Journal of Economic Literature (September).
Morgenstern, Oskar, and Gerald L. Thompson. 1976. Mathematical Theory of Expanding and Contracting Economics. Lexington, Mass.: Lexington Books.
Pierce, James L. 1979. "The Political Economy of Arthur Burns." Journal of Finance (May).
Poole, William. 1979. "Burnsian Monetary Policy: Eight Years of Progress?" Journal of Finance (May).
Roos, Lawrence K. 1979. "Monetary Targets--Their Contribution to Policy Formation." Review, Federal Reserve Bank of St. Louis (May).
Rutner, Jack L. 1977. "The Federal Reserve's Impact on Several Reserve Aggregates." Monthly Review, Federal Reserve Bank of Kansas City (May).
Simpson, Thomas D. 1979. "A Proposal for Redefining the Monetary Aggregates." Federal Reserve Bulletin (January).
__________. 1980. "The Redefined Monetary Aggregates." Federal Reserve Bulletin (February).
Tatom, John A. "Money Stock Control Under Alternative Definitions of Money." Review, Federal Reserve Bank of St. Louis (November).
Teigen, Ronald L. 1976. "Demand and Supply Functions for Money: Another Look at Theory and Measurement." Econometrica (March).
Terrell, William T., and William Frazer. 1972. "Interest Rates, Portfolio Behavior, and Marketable Government Securities." Journal of Finance (March).
Tobin, James. 1956. "The Interest-Elasticity of Transactions Demand for Cash." Review of Economics and Statistics (August).
__________. 1958. "Liquidity Preference as Behavior Towards Risk." Review of Economic Studies (February).
__________. 1965. "The Theory of Portfolio Selection." In F. H. Hans and F. P. R. Brechling, eds. The Theory of Interest Rates. New York: St. Martin's Press.
Viorst, Milton. 1971. Hustlers and Heroes. New York: Simon and Schuster.
Weintraub, E. Roy. 1975. "'Uncertainty' and the Keynesian Revolution." History of Political Economy (Winter).
Wenninger, John, and Charles M. Sivesind. 1979. "Defining Money for a Changing Financial System." Quarterly Review, Federal Reserve Bank of New York (Spring).

Part III

Demand Management: The Income and Expenditure Model (with and without Financial Trappings), Statics and Dynamics

Chapter 7

Methodology, Aggregate Demand, and Basic Mechanics

7.1. Introduction

Karl Marx and Frederick Engels (1848, 469-500) issued the Communist Manifesto, which considered, among other things, unemployment. The unemployed--"the industrial reserve army"--were to overthrow the capitalists' system with some improvements in the "army's" organization. In 1936 Keynes's General Theory portrayed a more modest view. He sought as an economist, and one sympathetic to the traditions of Great Britain, a monetary theory of production that would lead to better control over employment in a capitalistic system and, hence, to a "full employment" level of production.[1]

In even more modern times the unemployment rate has been viewed as an important variable affecting the election and reelection of presidents and members of Congress in the United States. It is the ratio of unemployment to the total civilian labor force, which includes the employed and the unemployed members of the civilian noninstitutional population, that is, "all persons 16 years of age and older who are not members of the Armed Forces, members of penal or mental institutions, sanitariums, or homes for the aged or infirm." The employed includes those household members who report at all for pay or profit during a designated week of the month, with due allowance for illness, vacation, strike, or various personal reasons. The unemployed includes persons without work during the designated week of the month, but who are available for work and have been actively seeking work at some time during the four-week period prior to the designated week.

The Data

Time series data on the employment and unemployment variables are shown in figure 7-1 for most of the 1970s. We will turn our attention to such data on later occasions, when we consider them in other context, including against a background of expansion and recession phases of business conditions.

The data underlying the adjusted series shown in figure 7-1 are provided monthly by the Bureau of the Census for the Bureau of Labor Statistics. They are obtained by means of a monthly survey of approximately 50,000 randomly selected households. The Census Bureau data are generally regarded as reliable in a statistical sense, with some allowance for sampling error. For the overall national unemployment rate, in order for a change in the rate to be considered significant (i.e., not attributable to sampling variability), it would have to vary by at least 0.2 percentage points on a monthly basis. Larger errors may occur in the unemployment rates for separate groups comprising of the labor force, such as in the teen-age unemployment rate and the black unemployment rate.[2]

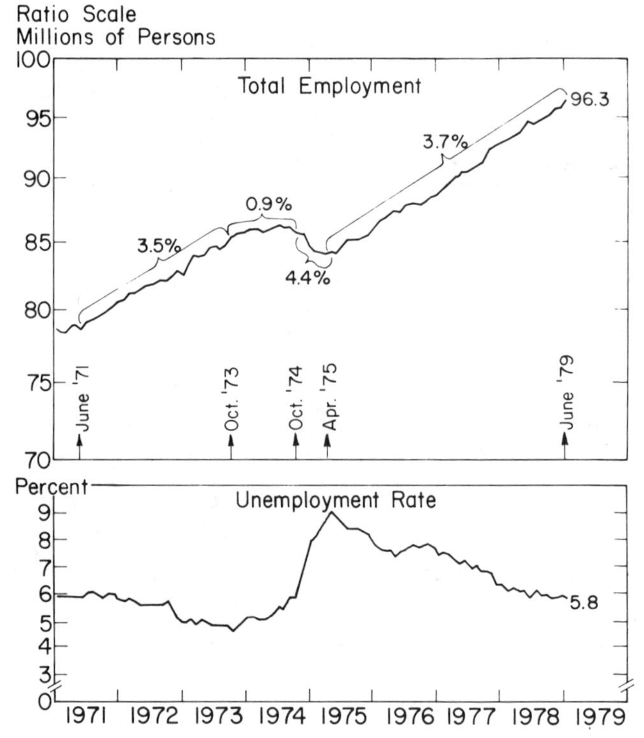

Figure 7-1. Total Employment and the Unemployment Rate

Source of figure: Federal Reserve Bank of St. Louis

The Theory

A central consideration in Keynes's theory of employment was that of aggregate demand. It was viewed as a relation between total spending and output, with output (Q) and employment (N) covarying in the short run, e.g.,

$$\underset{0}{\rule{10cm}{0.4pt}}\; Q \; (Y = PQ,\ P = \text{const.})$$

$$\underset{0}{\rule{10cm}{0.4pt}}\; N \; (\text{labor units})$$

The relation is recognized in books today (Patinkin 1976, 88) as a part of the "diagonal cross" diagram (figure 7-2). The diagram represents the basic income-expenditure building block of Keynes's and Keynesian economics; it also represents one of the great creative episodes in economics (Patinkin and Leith, 1978) in its departure from the way of thinking about demand prior to Keynes.[3] The almost singular custom before this was the demand relation illustrated by one arm of Marshall's cross (figures 1-1 and 2-5), with income (payments for the current output) impounded in ceteris paribus. "How then," Patinkin asks, "could one vividly speak of a demand function for the aggregate of all goods taken together?" (1976, 83). The answer was found in the "diagonal-cross" diagram, in which income (Y = PQ) became the principal variable, free of its impoundment in ceteris paribus, and prices tended to be treated as sticky (P = constant).

The Mechanics

This chapter considers the mechanics of the basic income-expenditure block. It was a contribution of Keynes and the Keynesians. As introduced in chapter 4, they saw instability in total spending, and in investment spending in particular, as the main source of instability, as distinct from supply conditions and shortages of natural resource. Their analysis from a policy point of view with the objective of stabilization gave rise to what may be called the management of aggregate demand.

The basic income-expenditure building block has been referred to as a Keynesian two-sector (without money) model. As presented here the model is highly simplified, as indicated in part by the emphasis on only two sectors: the household or consumer sector and the nonfinancial business or investment sector. The two-sector emphasis may be broken down to include government spending and net foreign investment as well. And the decomposition of spending may be carried even further and, in addition, money--or what is sometimes called the money sector--may be added, as indeed, it will be later.

Certainly Keynes would want us to consider the narrower model as little more than an algebraic exercise, possibly as a preamble of things to come, because money played an essential role in his theory, as did events occurring outside of the mechanical apparatus. In fact, in the early stages of statistical estimation of parameters, Keynes held what may appear as relatively contemporary views from the perspective of the present work, namely: (1) The period for estimation should be split into sub-periods in order to "consider what concordance appears between the different results" (Moggridge 1973, 295 and in general 285-321). And (2) "The object of statistical study," he said, "is not so much to fill in missing variables with a view to prediction [à la Henry Schultz (1938) and Jan Tinbergen (1968), he had in mind], as to test the relevance and validity of the model" (Moggridge 1973, 296). Although Keynes did not specify what he had in mind by testing the entire model, it could appear very much along the lines attributed to M. Friedman below. In any case, continuing, Keynes said (Moggridge 1973, 296-97):

> Economics is a science of thinking in terms of models joined to the art of choosing models which are relevant to the contemporary world. It is compelled to be this, because, unlike the typical natural science, the material to which it is applied is, in too many respects, not homogeneous through time....
>
> Good economists are scarce because the gift for using 'vigilant observation' to choose good models, although it does not require a highly specialized intellectual technique, appears to be a rare one.

Keynes theory was called "general" because it permitted equilibrium to occur at less than full employment as well as at full employment, although it has been pointed to as "a special theory" by some (Ulmer 1979, 2) because of its brilliant but still narrow attention to unemployment in the 1930s (sect. 4.2). The concept of equilibrium, in any case, was that of an intersection of two lines that form a cross. It is essentially that of Keynes's teacher, Alfred Marshall (1842-1924). Keynes, writing against the background of no growth in output and persistent unemployment in Britain, thought the condition corresponded to what he observed. But, despite his attempt to move economics in a dynamic direction, Keynes was imprecise about results due to properties of a given curve and those due to movements in the curve itself (Patinkin 1976, 103-104, 111-14). It remained for the Keynesians to move Keynes's speculations backward, more in the tradition of Marshall and static elasticities, rather than forward toward a more dynamic theory with a treatment of uncertainty, specific time frames, and the like. In some measure this chapter is presented more in a Keynesian mold, but including an introduction to the acceleration principle. This serves two purposes: It offers a mechanical explanation of instability in capital spending, the sort of instability Keynes was concerned with, and it anticipates a later consideration of turning points in business conditions and the interaction between the accelerator and the Keynesian investment multiplier.

The economic theory before Keynes's time was viewed mainly as the theory of relative prices and real output, on the one hand, and the theory of money, on the other. The first explained relative prices and Keynes's attack on it has since been symbolized by his attack on Say's law, which, as viewed by Keynes, implied a full-employment equilibrium level of output. The separate theory of money was mainly viewed as explaining the average of prices for the output of goods and services. Broadly viewed, Keynes's contribution was to introduce motives for holding money--mainly the speculative and precautionary motives--in such a way that variations in the strength of the motives (as reflected in the demand for money) could influence the output or real side of the economy. In a world where empirical investigations cannot avoid the interactions of money demand and real output in studies of the two, any practical theory of the economy must allow for the interaction between the real and monetary aspects of economics. In this chapter, however, we partially "suspend disbelief" and discuss output exclusive of the demand for money. Aside from some commentary about future discussions, we proceed with exercises.

The mechanics considered in this chapter are not themselves a theory. A theory in positive economics is an explanation of real world phenomena, and a good theory is thought to serve as a guide to economic policy as well. A theory consists of the following: (1) its underlying definitions, axioms, and undefined terms; (2) a logical structure or internal consistency that may follow from them (bodies of mathematics such as probability and calculus may enter to ensure consistency); and (3) the conclusions, statements of relationships between variables, and hypotheses that may emerge. A good theory will have the most valid and/or acceptable set of axioms and statements of relationships. In addition, a good theory will be accepted on empirical grounds. In economics especially, several different theories may appear consistent with the same body of evidence on the surface. With such theories there is prudence in seeking a consistency with a wider range of empirical evidence from closely related subject matter. This type of evidence may be called "independent evidence," to suggest that it has been obtained independently and perhaps even for other purposes.

Keynesian and other statements of liquidity preference theory as covered in chapters 5 and 6 are good examples of this latter point. All are consistent with parallel movements in the velocity of money and interest rates. But when one considers differences in assumptions and inconsistencies in aspects of their predictions about the behavior of bond holdings and other assets, then differences in degrees of relevance are more apparent. A good theory is one that best fulfills the standards of positive empirical economics--internal consistency and consistency with the relevant range of observations and results from statistical analyses of data.

What is covered in this chapter as the Keynesian two-sector model is but an exercise in some of the mechanics of economics. The particular ones considered have evolved as part of Keynes's and Keynesian economics. The use of mechanics is dated (like classical mechanics as distinct from statistical mechanics) when attention is given to them as part of a theory with such characteristics as the following: a static form (e.g., emphasizing levels rather than rates of change and differential rates of change), either minimal or no consideration of the dynamics of inflation and little attention to the price level, and the idea of a full-employment equilibrium level without allowing for growth and a natural rate of unemployment. On the other hand, the mechanics (as distinct from the theory) set forth may be carried forward to other discussions and given a modern dress. Keynes's simple consumption function, as used in this chapter and introduced in chapter 3, is shown in chapter 9 to be a part of a more dynamic statement of the response of consumption spending to a weighted average of current and past incomes. The simple function is constantly in motion. The mechanics may be modified in other ways also, as we will begin to demonstrate in this chapter.

Notes on Methodology

Just as we consider partially distinct bodies of economic thought (neoclassical, Keynes's, Keynesian, Friedmanesque) we also encounter different strands in the methodology of economics (of the method of arriving at some understanding of the world). At times these overlap and at times the distinctions one draws between the methods are clear. Especially, as we noted in sections 1.3 and 4.4, Milton Friedman was to give new direction to the subject in the more recent times.

One of Friedman's teachers at Chicago in the early 1930s, Frank H. Knight, had confronted neoclassical economics and, later, in some measure Keynes's economics. In doing so, he tended to see economic behavior and economics as highly complex and thus he backed away entirely from the prospect of economics being an empirical science. Knight, one might say, was indeed adamant about the inability of economists to measure utility, to verify such "economic man concepts" directly, and to distinguish and get at the motives for holding money in any direct way (Henderson 1976). Thus viewing economics, he was to move it toward what others have called an "assumer" science (i.e., being based on assumptions and deductive propositions that make no pretense of dealing with empirical reality). (Hirsch 1976)

M. Friedman, on the other hand, had come into economics with unusual and strong background in mathematical statistics and data analysis. He thus was to combine--in a sense and as a part of his distinct contribution to economics--economic theory, statistics, and data analysis, and in so doing he was to shift economics in the direction of positive economics, empirical economics to be sure. In doing this, Friedman was fully aware of the complexities that drove Knight in a different direction, including towards an interest in ethics (Knight 1935). So, as Friedman brought the theory ("constructions," mechanics) in an empirical direction, he moved to avoid rather than abandon recognition of the problems Knight saw. Friedman thus proceeded to advance a method of getting at fruitful empirical matters indirectly, by asking about the implications of the "theory," of the motives, and so on, and by introducing special time frames (permanent and transitory components of time series, as we will encounter them, and turning points in business conditions). Two specific examples of the difference in the way Friedman is to treat the matter came out below: (1) when we recognize early controversy about the identification of Keynes's simple consumption function, and (2) when we treat the "assumer" method of getting a so-called equilibrium value as distinct from statistical, secular time paths that Friedman addresses.

Furthermore, as already stated, Keynesians moved the work of Keynes back into a neoclassical mold--back along the lines of the common concepts of Marshallian equilibrium (as a solution value yielded by the intersecting arms of a cross) and the distinction between Marshall's theory as one of partial equilibrium and Keynes's as one of general equilibrium. Thus, Friedman came to view Marshall differently (1953b, 47-99). He was, to be sure, to view Marshall, Keynes, and himself as searching for a fruitful empirical hypothesis, as using a total body of economics ("an entire economic model," as it were) to generate some fruitful empirical hypothesis (app. to chap. 1; Boland 1979; and Friedman 1972, 908-920). Examples of this approach would include: (1) the notion that a main thrust of Marshall's work was that prices would adjust in response to inadequate demand rather than output, and (2) the notion that Keynes reversed all of this by generating the hypothesis centering about output adjustments (and hence employment) rather than price adjustments).

On the other hand, Friedman came to view the Keynesians as Walrasians (Frazer 1973, 394-398; Friedman 1955), as seeking to just add detail, say, as distinct from abstracting the common and crucial events from the mass of complex detail and circumstances. This approach he sees as being characterized by the early structural equations models of the Keynesians (chap. 13). To oversimplify but still illustrate the approach one may think of the following: one behavioral equation in a model with a large number of equations, and in the one equation, variables are simply being added on the right-hand side of the equation to improve its fit to the data and presumably explain the single variable on the left-hand side of the equation.

So the above strands of methodology are present--as we encounter the use of an entire model to approach some aspects of reality along Friedmanian lines, and as we encounter the Keynesian mechanics and their much later tie to forecasting (chap. 13). Although we proceed in this chapter with simple mechanics, in anticipation of later topics, both the Friedmanesque and Keynesian approaches will appear at times and be offered as filling possibly complementary functions. There is some ideal to be fulfilled somewhere on the horizon (sect. 14.2) as Friedman would recognize (1951), where the "true" model (the model of the real world) would resemble structural equations models of sorts and would encompass the cases of certainty and uncertainty and of repetitive and nonrepetitive (including so-called outside) changes encountered in the real world, as the more recent generations of forecasting models are beginning to recognize (Eckstein 1978, 185-205).

In particular, the large structural equations models are encountered in the discussion of forecasting (chap. 13). Questions about the instability in the parameters of models bear on evolutionary, nonrepetitive events and the formation of rational expectations (the use of the best economics and information in forming views of the future). Though a lot of simple method gets employed, the philosophical foundations of its use are sophisticated. There are details about time series, governmental policies and institutions, other institutions, forecasting, leading and lagging indications of business conditions, and the like that get complicated in their detail. An initial, pre-publication title to Friedman's major early piece on methodology (Friedman 1953a, 3-43) was "The Relevance of Economic Analysis to Prediction and Policy." The combination of theoretic abstractions, and of attention to empirical data and economic policy was to characterize the monetarists of the post-Keynesian era (Frazer 1973, chap. 18), as it does the present work (as summarized in chapter 20).

7.2. Aggregate Income and Aggregate Demand

An important and possibly unsettled problem of analysis has been that of distinguishing consumption from investment expenditures. There have been several classificatory schemes. According to one, consumable goods and services are short-lived, whereas investment goods have longer lives. They are utilized in the production of other goods and services, and may be called instrumental or real capital to distinguish them from the capital funds supplied through the sale of stock in the new issues market for securities. Keynes accepted this distinction in his time, and it is still accepted.

Another view of the distinction between consumption and investment has been advanced by Friedman. Drawing on Keynesian analysis and the consumption function notion as posited later, he said that consumption was the spending that was correlated with income and that investment was autonomous spending. But there were difficulties in defining "autonomous spending" and controversy ensued (Frazer 1973, secs. 5.1, 5.2).

What emerged out of the controversy were alternative views. Meiselman, for example, said, "Autonomous spending is understood to originate outside of the usual economic calculus--a Vietnam, or perhaps a burst of spending for capital goods following technological innovation, or a change in tax rates following a conversion to a new economic ideology." This view was framed in a statistical context. It held that: in any equation defining spending, the autonomous spending would be that part of the so-called independent variable that was uncorrelated with the error term, such as:

$$E = a + b\,[C(Y) + A] + u$$

where E is total spending for current output, [C(Y) + A] is consumption as a function of income (Y) plus autonomous spending (A), C is the portion of income spent on consumption and u is the random error term. The function C(Y) has to be independently estimated or else income is correlated with itself.

Another view for distinguishing consumer spending from investment calls for identifying the sector doing the spending. The threshold of the household becomes a dividing line. Household spending, with the exception of housing expenditures, is defined as consumption, whereas business firms engage in investment or capital spending. The households retain some of their income as savings, and thus set aside funds that ultimately get channeled into investment by the business firms. Government spending and net foreign investment may also be considered. This latter approach emphasizes the separation of the behavioral groups that account for saving, on the one hand, and investment, on the other. Keynes saw this separation as having a potential for instability in investment spending. In earlier times, saving and investment were performed by the same groups. Later however, financial institutions such as banks, savings and loan associations, and insurance companies enter as financial intermediaries, maintaining an intermediate position between the savers and the investors as introduced in chapter 3.

Ingredients of both the first and last methods of distinguishing consumption and investment receive the greatest emphasis in most discussions of the Keynesian model. The distinct contributions of Keynes, with reference to the income-expenditure model are his consumption function and his definition of saving. The consumption function, as introduced earlier may be restated:

$$C = f(Y) \quad , 0 < dC/dY < 1$$

or, as defined by a linear approximation,

$$C = a + b\,Y, \; 0 < dC/dY = b < 1$$

where, in addition to the symbols defined earlier, dC/dY is the marginal propensity to consume. Keynes thought this function depicted an observable regularity and called it a fundamental psychological law.

Adding investment to consumption yields aggregate expenditures or aggregate demand (E),

$$E = a + b\,Y + I, \; dE/dY = b \qquad (7.0)$$

where investment (I) is a constant. The idea is that investment is less dependent on income in the immediate future or past. The autonomous emphasis, mentioned earlier, has suggested that $\underline{I}$ is rather volatile--a variable constant--especially in relation to what Keynes and Keynesians considered a relatively stable consumption function.

Saving, on the other hand, was simply a residual, composed of that portion of income (Y) not spent on consumption:

$$S(Y) = Y - C(Y)$$

Aggregate Income was thus:

$$Y = S(Y) + C(Y) \qquad (7.1)$$

$$\frac{dY}{dY} = \frac{dS}{dY} + \frac{dC}{dY} = 1$$

where a derivative with respect to itself is equal to one.

Three conditions are possible with respect to the income-demand relations as defined by equations (7.0) and (7.1): the relations parallel (no solution to the equations), coincide (an infinite number of solutions), or they intersect (a solution). The assumption about the consumption function and the definition of saving guarantee the solution (i.e., guarantees intersection):

$$Y = E$$

substituting

$$Y = a + bY + I$$

and rearranging terms

$$Y - bY = a + I$$

$$Y(1-b) = a + I$$

yields (solution or reduced form) $$\bar{Y} = (a + I)\left(\frac{1}{1-b}\right)$$

where 1/(1-b) is the investment multiplier.

Here the solution (or equilibrium) value $\underline{\bar{Y}}$ is specified in terms of the parameters of the model. Such an equation in the econometric work of the 1960s came to be called by economists a reduced form.[4]

There is another feature about the solution that may further clarify the role of saving and investment. From the income and demand relations it may be stated,

$$\underbrace{S(Y) + C(Y)}_{\text{Income}} = \underbrace{C(Y) + I}_{\text{Demand}}$$

or

$$S(Y) = I$$

The model as set forth thus far may be depicted as in figure 7-2. There in the upper part of the figure (a), income and demand are shown on the vertical axis, and income is shown on the horizontal axis. The income line is drawn with a slope of one (recall $dY/dY = 1$), or at a 45° angle.[5] The demand line has the intercept $\underline{a}$ and the slope $dC/dY = b$. The lines intersect at the solution $\bar{Y}$. In part (b) of the figure, the saving line is drawn and investment is again shown to have a constant relation to income. The variable $S(Y)$ simply measures off the distance between the consumption line and the income line. The solution value $\bar{Y}$ is again shown.

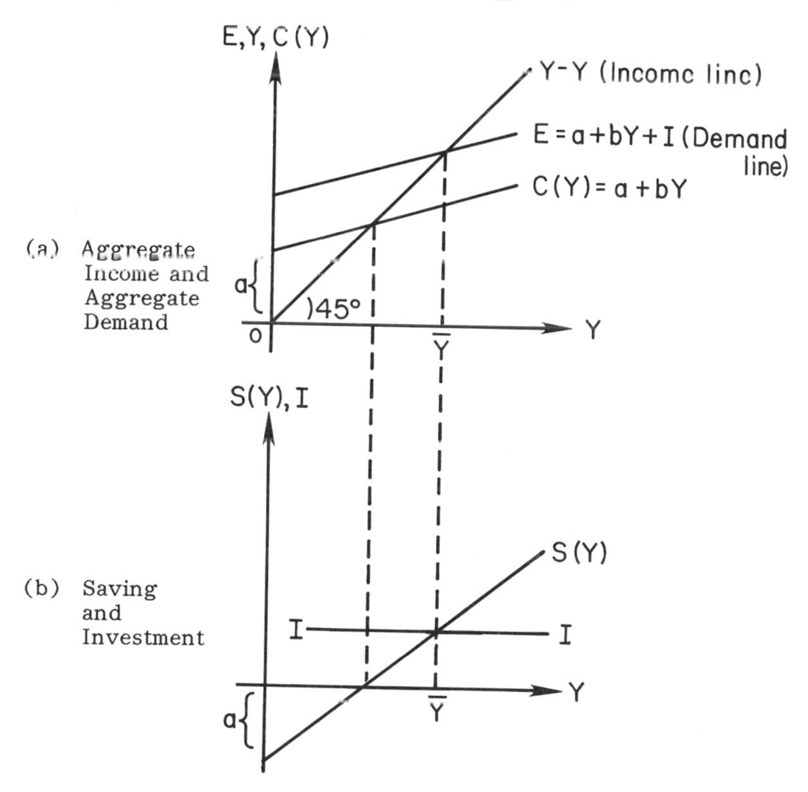

Figure 7-2. Two-Sector Keynesian Model

The Investment Multiplier

Now we come to a very important feature of the model, the investment multiplier which denotes a change in the solution value $\bar{Y}$ with respect to a change in $\underline{I}$:

$$\frac{d\bar{Y}}{dI} = \frac{1}{1 - b}$$

But this multiplier is simply the formula for the $\underline{n}$th partial sum of a converging geometric series,

$$\frac{1}{1 - b} = 1 + b + b^2 + \ldots + b^{n-1} + \ldots$$

where $\lim_{n \to \infty} b^n = 0$ and the series converges.

This is simply R. F. Kahn's famous employment multiplier (Kahn 1931, 173-98). He was applying a geometric series to Britain's unemployment problem of the 1920s and early 1930s. However, the way the multiplier simply drops out of the above model, with a little bit of help from differentiation, was left unmentioned by Keynes and his contemporaries. Keynes had apparently intended to suggest (in a coauthored 1929 pamphlet) a process of "primary" and "secondary" employment generated by public works expenditures, and he was later to draw on Kahn's formulation in the highly original context of the effective demand diagram [part (a) of figure 7-3]. The foregoing exercise came later, as did sketches of the type shown in figures 7-2 and 7-3.[6]

The multiplier was to play a crucial role. In light of the failures of monetary policy, misconceptions of the policy linkage to total spending, and the depressed state of private spending, the multiplier provided a powerful argument for government spending as a means of overcoming stagnation and unemployment. The existence of the multiplier meant that extra spending no longer had just a pump priming effect. Indeed, its effect would balloon into a larger effect, as may be denoted by the terms of the series,

$$\Delta\bar{Y} = \Delta I \; [1 + b + b^2 + \ldots + b^{n-1} + \ldots]$$

$$\Delta\bar{Y} = \Delta I + \Delta Ib + \Delta Ib^2 + \ldots + \Delta Ib^{n-1} + \ldots$$

The multiplier, one might say, set the stage for the Age of Fiscal Policy, roughly the period from the late 1940s through the 1960s. In the empirical work since the sixties, the multiplier has not been abandoned, but subsequent and renewed attention has been given to the financing of government deficits, to the prospect of "crowding out" private spending, and to the government budget constraint (chaps. 10 and 11). An especially dynamic and empirically oriented sort of economics evolves. It gives attention to a world and circumstances quite difference from those Keynes confronted in Britain in the 1920s and '30s.[7]

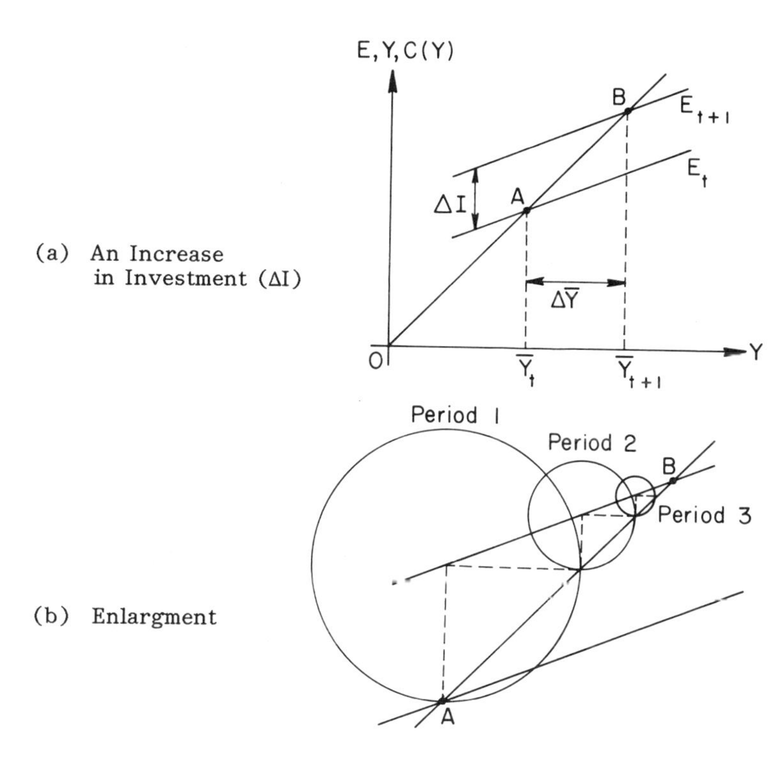

Figure 7-3. Autonomous Investment and the Multiplier

Figure 7-3 illustrates the multiplier. Part (a) of the figure shows an increment in investment, ΔI, and the resulting increment in income, ΔY, as the solution shifts from point A to point B. The lower part (b) is a blow-up of part (a) in the neighborhood of the points A and B. The various steps in the movement from point A to B may be depicted as the products of the increment of investment and the separate terms of the geometric progression. With the slopes of the lines indicated the multiplier process is shown as working itself out fairly rapidly, after only a few periods of spending.

The multiplier in combination with autonomous or unstable investment provides a simple explanation for fluctuations in income. Although figures 7-3(a) and (b) are gross simplifications of the process, they illustrate an important point made by Keynes and later by the Keynesians: that investment is more volatile than consumption, and an important goal of national policy should be to stabilize investment at a full-employment level of spending, or to compensate for irregularities in investment through government spending. Keynes and Keynesians had the greatest hope for the latter. Complexities concerning the financing of a government deficit and the role of monetary policy are considered in chapters 10 and 11.

Full-employment Equilibrium

Variations in the level of income (or real income, Y/P) were expected to parallel changes in the level of employment in the income expenditure building block. There was a full-employment equilibrium level of income. Looking somewhat beyond the Keynesian period as we did in chapter 4, we noted the consistency of a rate of change in income with a given level of employment and hence a rising per capita income as a basic underlying state. But this need not distract us at this point.

At the full-employment level of income there would still be some unemployment. Numerous determinants of it are considered in chapter 11, such as frictional unemployment (unemployment resulting from technological change and growth as displaced workers search for new jobs that give rise to a larger income) and structural unemployment (unemployment due to the mismatching of job skills with job vacancies). To be counted as a part of the labor force for purposes of GNP accounting, one must have a recognized job or be actively looking for work. Unemployment--the difference between the labor force and the number employed--is usually expressed as a percentage of the labor force as in figure 7-1.

The size of the labor force and the unemployment rate both may vary as new workers enter the labor force and as some withdraw. A reduction in the percentage of unemployment and the availability of jobs for women and minorities usually brings new workers such as blacks, poor whites, housewives, and others who were previously not seeking employment) into the labor force, and thus has some offsetting impact on the decline in the rate to begin with. An increase in the unemployment rate may have the reverse effect.

In the early 1960s the Keynesians adopted a 4 percent unemployment rate as the full-employment rate. With the passage of time this was to be revised downward, perhaps resulting from increased worker mobility and better preparation for specific jobs for which demand could be anticipated.

As the 1960s and '70s evolved the unemployment target of 4 percent seemed to be unreasonable. Indeed programs of the 1960s and efforts to achieve a given percentage of unemployment by stabilization policy measures (as distinct from measures to reduce frictional and structural unemployment) possibly gave rise to the rapid inflations of the late 1960s and the early- to late-1970s. This in turn gave rise to what we consider later as inflationary recession (stagflation).

The notion of a natural rate of unemployment has come more to the forefront, as elucidated in section 11.5. The idea is that some percentage of unemployment is consistent with price level stability (i.e., a zero or constant rate of price level change) and average wage increases of a given percent annually (namely, the percentage growth in output per worker). Efforts at achieving other than the natural rate of unemployment through fiscal policy or other government intervention leads to economic instability and possibly to a rise in the unemployment rate.

The natural rate may of course be influenced by measures to reduce frictional and structural unemployment. It is increased by the government raising the minimum wage so that certain sorts of labor are priced out of the market, and by labor unions acting to restrict the entry of nonunion workers to certain jobs, which results in excessive wage increases for the organized segment of the labor force. Also, changes in the distribution of national income among income classes, such as can result from the shaping of expenditure and tax measures by the government, alter the natural rate of unemployment. For instance, measures that reduce after-tax income of mid-range income recipients in relation to the after tax income of lower-range recipients may have several results, such as altering spending habits with respect to certain goods and services and causing certain services of lower income recipients to be priced out of the market. These and other topics relating to unemployment, government, and output come up on later occasions.

7.3. Output, Price-Level Adjustments, and the Velocity of Money

The model presented thus far is commonly considered to be a model for the determination of real income (Y/P) or of output (Q). The average of prices (P) for the output of goods and services, however, has been introduced in various ways--either by introducing the Phillips Curve as an appendage, as done later, or by expressing an income identity (PQ = MV), or by relying on ad hoc techniques.

A major contribution of Keynes, as noted earlier (sects. 1.3 and 4.2), was to shift the emphasis in economics from price adjustments, as in Alfred Marshall's approach, to output adjustments. Prices tended to be "sticky" or, in more modern parlance, there was uncertainty and inadequacy of information about where to set them in order for the goods and services to clear the market. The price level was emphasized, nevertheless, by the early and later quantity theorists. The latter focused on an income identity,

$$MV = PQ$$

where M is the money stock, V the income velocity of money, and the product PQ is income, and where again we have different labels for the two sides of a set of transactions. All the shifts in demand described above can be translated in terms of this identity. For example, if they all occurred with the price level as constant and with money given (M = constant), then all the foregoing adjustments in output also imply changes in the income velocity of money.

One may wish to speculate about how money influences prices. Marshall, other pre-Keynesians, and even post-World War II monetarists recognized that in the long run excessive changes in the money stock went into price level changes. The monetarists of the post-World War II vintage were especially interested in the long run. Keynes and Keynesians, however, were more interested in the short run. They focused on quantity adjustments with, as stated, some ad hoc

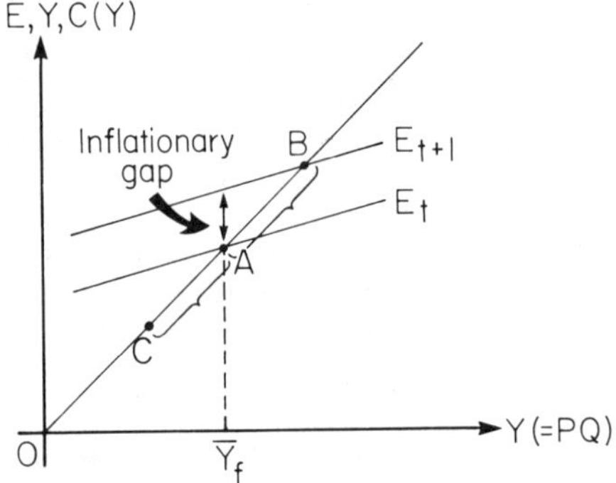

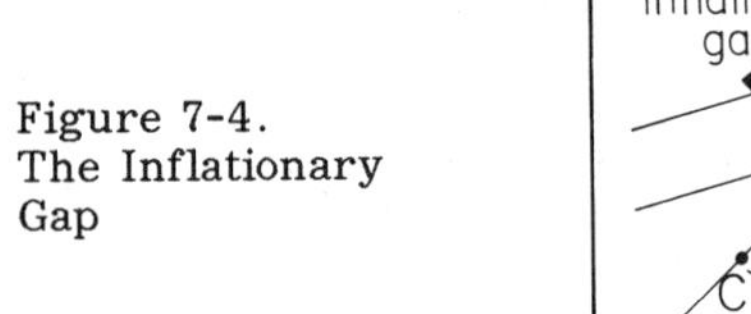
Figure 7-4. The Inflationary Gap

references to prices. These have sometimes been brought into focus by reference to inflationary and deflationary gaps (Ulmer 1979, 3). Inflation here simply means a rise in the average of prices and deflation, a decline. The first is the more common experience, for a host of reasons brought out later.

The inflationary gap is shown in figure 7-4, where demand has shifted from E_t to E_{t+1}. If the economy were already producing a full-employment level of output, then prices (mainly) would rise to bring about a new equilibrium at point B. Some changes might also occur in the full-employment income, $\overline{Y}_f$, because additional housewives, minorities, and others are drawn into the labor force when unemployment conditions improve.

A shift in the downward direction in figure 7-4, as from point A to a lower point C, would reveal a deflationary gap. The idea is that there would be downward pressure on prices (including the prices of services), but the adjustment to a new equilibrium point would occur mainly through output changes, especially if prices were slow to adjust. This sequence of first output and then price changes occurred in the automobile and electrical equipment industries in early 1975. Following sharp reductions in output in 1974, the major auto makers (following the leadership of Chrysler) announced rebates to new car buyers of up to $600 on certain models. A few weeks later General Electric announced rebates by mail on 39 small electrical appliances, subject to demonstrating proof of purchase.

Soon the rebate practice became quite widespread in an effort to lure reluctant households into the market place. This rebate craze was a dramatic emergence of some price flexibility. It reemerged on a less widespread basis in November 1976, following two months of decline in leading economic indicators, as defined and described in section 18.1. And it may be expected to emerge again at comparable times in the future.[8] Rebates, it would seem, have apparently gained in popularity with manufacturers because they are temporary price reduction and removing them is not viewed as raising prices by consumers.

Prices in the service trades such as auto repair were less flexible in the 1974-75 period. As real income declined in that period and as a backing up along the consumption function occurred, do-it-yourself car garages began to appear around the country. Some white and blue collar workers who could no longer afford repair service were simply performing it themselves.

Sticky wages or prices lead to phenomena of the foregoing type during periods of declining or slow growth in real income. Especially in the service trades there may also be some changing demand because of income redistribution effects resulting from the shaping of governmental expenditures and revenues.

Keynes, writing in the times of depression, focused on output. In the more typical times of post-World War II years--the Korean episode, the wars on poverty and in Vietnam, the Energy Crisis--the more appropriate emphasis is on both price and output changes.

7.4. Investment--A Volatile Variable

Investment has been pointed to as being a relatively volatile variable, yet it was presented as having no relation to income (or only a secondary relation to consumption). Some may find justification for its having an upward slope ($\underline{I} = \underline{u} + \underline{vY}$, $dI/dY = \underline{v} > 0$) or even a slope that prohibits a solution for the income-expenditure model, as in the case of the E_{t+1} line in figure 7-5.

Considering only positive values for the stock and flow quantities, there is no solution or intersection shown in the figure for $\underline{E}_{t+1}$. The rationale for a positive relation between investment and income and even for the indeterminate solution depicted in figure 7-5 goes back to the acceleration principle as introduced by J. M. Clark (1917), and the interacting accelerator-multiplier model as inspired by Alvin Hansen and as developed by Paul Samuelson (1939).

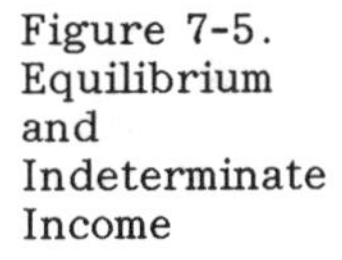
Figure 7-5. Equilibrium and Indeterminate Income

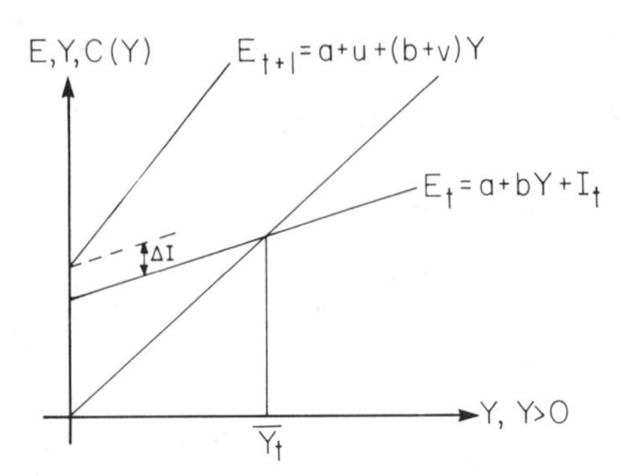

The early justification for relating investment to total income (or sales) centers on the acceleration principle. A common form of the principle derives from two basic relationships:

$$I(t) = \frac{dK(t)}{dt} \tag{7.2}$$

$$g = \frac{K(t)}{Y(t)} \tag{7.3}$$

Equations (7.2) simply states that investment (I) is the addition to capital stock (K), where both are noted as functions of time. Equation (7.3) is called the capital-to-sales or capital-to-output ratio. Real capital is what we usually think of as plant, equipment, and inventories. The idea embodied in the equation is that businessmen will strive to maintain the stock of capital in some constant relation to sales or output.

To combine equations (7.2) and (7.3) multiply each side of (7.2) by the opposite of (7.3) to get

$$I(t)\,\frac{K(t)}{Y(t)} = g\,\frac{dK(t)}{dt} \tag{7.4}$$

Next, divide both sides of (7.2) by K(t)/Y(t):

$$I(t) = g\,\frac{dY(t)}{dt} \tag{7.5}$$

This result embodies what has been called the acceleration principle. It is illustrated in figure 7-6, with presumed variation in income, Y(t), shown in the lower part of the figure and investment shown in the upper part. The model is sometimes more readily intuited if one thinks of the sale of final products as income and increases in inventories as investment spending. In this case, constant sales means no derived demand (that is, only replacement demand) for inventories; an increase in sales initially means an accelerated change in inventories to bring them in line with current sales (treating

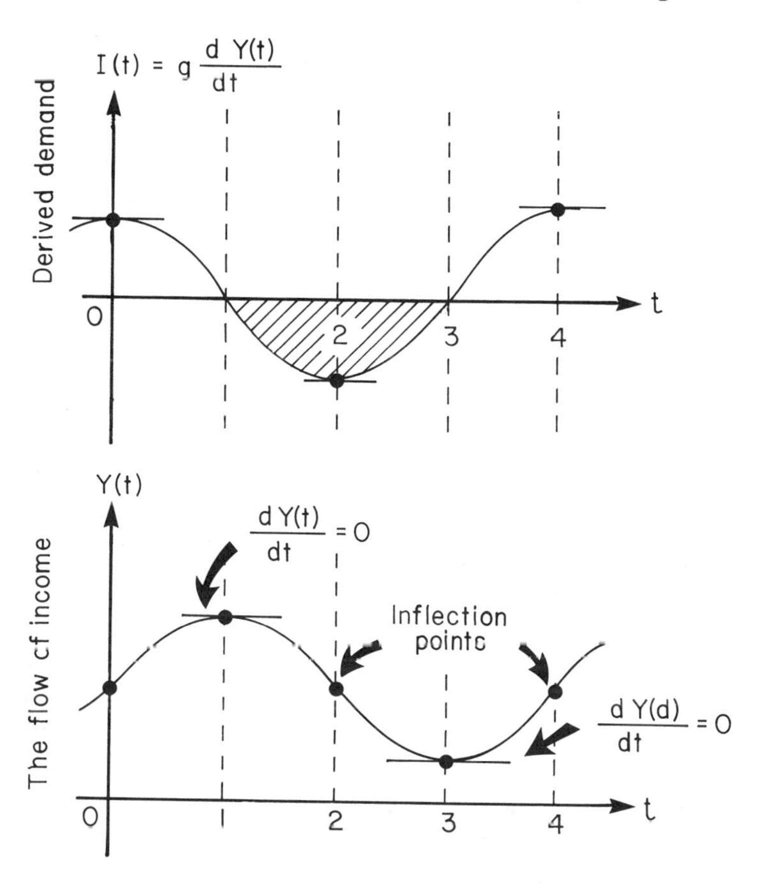

Figure 7-6. The Acceleration Principle

inventories as a constant proportion of sales); and a decrease in sales initially means an accelerated liquidation of a portion of inventories (and hence negative derived investment). In the special sales/inventory case as well as in the more general case, there is the idea that a variation in income causes a disproportionate change in investment. In the time interval from 3 to 4, for example, investment increases more than in proportion to income. This would be consistent with the indeterminancy line in figure 7-5. Using modern terminology, one can say there is some "overshooting" depicted in figure 7-6. That is, once investment is turned in a given direction, as at $t = 1$ it over-reacts and becomes negative, and disinvestment continues until income turns upward again. Note that if the flow of income simply levels off, $d\,Y(t)/dt = 0$, then investment is zero, $I(t) = 0$, and if the flow of income declines, then investment is negative, as in the case of depreciation of capital without replacement. For the flow of investment to decline, all income must do is to simply experience a slower rate of growth.

The sort of causation depicted in figure 7-6 is reversed from that depicted in the Keynesian cross with investment changing and working through the investment multiplier. There,

$$dI(t) \rightarrow d\,Y(t)$$

and hence spending over-reacts to a change in investment,

$$\Delta I \text{ (multiplier)} = \Delta Y$$

and $\Delta Y > \Delta I$

Samuelson's contribution (1939) was to combine the acceleration principle and the investment multiplier in a single framework provided by elementary difference equations.[9] With the assignment of certain parameter values the framework provided certain conclusions about whether the economic system was characterized by perfectly periodic fluctuations, damped oscillatory movements, explosive oscillatory movements, or expansive ever-increasing movements (as dealt with in section 18.2). It is this sort of thing that also suggests the indeterminancy of income in figure 7.5. The interacting multiplier and accelerator models provide one explanation of turning points in business conditions. The topic will interest us more later.

There are of course questions: (1) about the essentially mechanical nature of the periods generated by the interacting multiplier and accelerator, (2) about whether businessmen respond in such routine ways to sales changes, as assumed in the accelerator principle, or whether they show great sensitivity (as addressed in chapters 14 and 17) in the formation of expectations. Even though these may be essentially empirical matters, to be worked out through empirical work, the multiplier and the accelerator are suggestive of matters calling for further consideration. The multiplier appears to describe how spending circulates in the system with increasing linkages into savings as the circulation continues and income expands at a decreasing rate. The acceleration principle may explain why investment spending is highly volatile in relation to other forms of spending. Autonomous investment, as mentioned earlier (sects. 4.2 and 7.2) and later in chapter 8, is also suggestive of topics to be treated later, such as instability in the parameters of equations and forces operating outside of the usual economic construction.

7.5. Summary

A contribution of Keynes's work was setting up the cateogories for saving and investment, as he did, and stating their equality. The categories represented nonfinancial business and household sectors with possible divergences in their behavior. Accordingly, investment was treated as a wellspring of unstable income. Consumption (and thus saving) was more stable. The consumption function was a major contribution and the assumption about its slope was the key to a solution for the income-expenditure model. This solution furthermore is illustrative of the Keynesian notion of equilibrium, as distinct from a secular time path.

Keynes had said a lot about money, the motives for holding and spending it, and the interaction of the real output and monetary sectors. However, he was skeptical of the workings of monetary policy (or interest rate changes as he viewed it) in the 1930s, the sensitivity of business investment to interest rate changes, and in general the will to enterprise on the part of business. Further, his theory had stressed adjustments in output and employment in response to demand changes rather than price-level adjustments. The level of employment was determined by level of output. The Keynesians especially deemphasized money, and consequently stressed the investment multiplier and governmental means of economic stabilization. For this reason salient features of Keynesian economics emerge with the mechanics set forth in this chapter. These mechanics with modifications endure still as a part of Friedmanesque economics, because Friedman does not reject them in his various statistical endeavors. Instead he reorients the mechanics, introduces special time frames, equilibrium time paths. Indeed, Friedman seeks the use of an entire model to generate some fruitful empirical hypothesis.

The Keynesian also got into the use of an entire economic model, but their method, Friedman charged, was that of simply adding detail. In any case, the method associated with the Keynesians comes forward later in our forecasting models. At some ideal state, the "true" model (the model of the real world) and the Friedmanesque and Keynesian approaches may come together. Addressed by us later, however, is the role of nonrepetitive events, and thus speculation about the possible inability to ever forecast and know the future with certainty (i.e., to ever know about the stability of the the parameters of economics traditionally viewed).

Autonomous spending is just such an activity, of change coming from outside the scope of the economic model traditional viewed. In its presence, the Keynesian multiplier supplies an explanation for instability in income, and it provided as well a strong argument for the use of governmental spending and tax measures to attain full employment. The Keynesians took as their policy guide a full-employment target. Friedman challenged the latter, he and others shifting the analysis of stock and flow quantities from one of levels to rate of change, and money and prices were again integrated into the analysis.

A natural rate of unemployment may be defined as one that occurs along with sustainable (or equilibrium) growth paths in the stock and flow quantities. It will coincide with a stable price level also and, as we see later, any constant rate of change in prices may coincide with stability. The present point is that efforts to stabilize unemployment at other than the natural rate will contribute to instability in spending, output, employment, and prices. The initial pursuit of an unemployment target below the natural rate will result in an accelerated rate of change in prices. This sort of statement about dynamic analysis is more an assertion at this point than a conclusion of a theory.

FOOTNOTES

1. The notion of Keynes's having offered a challenge to the Marxist view of the breakdown of the capitalist economy runs throughout Keynesana. Lorie Tarshis, a student of Keynes from 1932 to 1935, however, reports on the challenge, as he recalls it, in the early 1930s. See Tarshis's comments (Patinkin and Leith 1948, 51-52).
2. For more detail on the unemployment rate, see Lovati (1976).
3. The crosses characterizing Keynes's General Theory do not appear as drawings in The General Theory. Even among those who took lecture notes as Keynes lectured from the proofs of the General Theory in 1934-35, there is some question about his use of them (see Patinkin and Leith 1978, 72, 78). Tarshis recalls formulations on the blackboard of such concepts as the "Propensity to Consume" and the "Liquidity Preference Function." The diagrams that presently appear as figures 7-2 and 7-4 were first encountered in the early editions of Paul Samuelson's Economics.
4. Ideally, the parameters of the behavioral equations of a model (i.e., the equations other than identities) could be estimated empirically, and the same sort of estimations could be made independently for the reduced form equations. In this ideal case, compatible estimates for the two sets of equations should be obtained. However, the estimating technique of classical least-squares regression analysis depends on special assumptions, e.g., that conditions underlying the estimate from period to period are stable (or, in other words, the sampling from one sample period to the next is from the same universe).

   These are rather ideal conditions, so a good bit of the art of economics is making adequate judgement about changing the parameters that represent the underlying conditions.

5. This 45° line has on occasion been called the supply line; hence intersecting supply and demand lines. Tarshis however, addresses the importance Keynes attached to the aggregate supply function. He notes an attempt by Keynes to demonstrate its linearity and then concludes thus:

   > "Insofar as the modern treatment makes use of the intersection of the aggregate demand function and the well-known straight line from the origin to determine output or income, we either have no aggregate supply function--in the sense of a behavioral function--but merely a neat way of showing the solution to an equation for aggregate demand, or we have suppressed some of the really interesting insights about the price-output responses of profit-seeking firms." (Patinkin and Leith 1978, 60-62)

   We agree, but the sorts of questions Tarshis raises about profit-maximizing firms and marginal and average costs curves are probably better handled in a different and more dynamic context (and will be handled in the later chapters on these cost curves, the value of the marginal product of labor, the Phillips curve, and rational expectations).
6. The multiplier shown is a multiplier that follows from a sustained increase in investment (i.e., the increment WI is maintained), though in a more dynamic analysis there may be an interplay of a volatile I working through the multiplier and giving rise to movement from one solution point to another. Patinkin would simply say in 1976 (1976, 70-71) that Kahn's multiplier was a dynamic one, "showing in terms of a declining geometric series the sequence of 'secondary employments' generated by a once-and-for-all increase in investment." He was to repeat this later (Patinkin and Leith 1978, 18-19) in stressing the genre of the multiplier and its connection with Keynes's work. Samuelson also addresses the multiplier in the same volume (Patinkin and Leith 1978, 83-85).
7. Keynes's specific and original contribution in the present context and in the setting in which he wrote was to direct attention to the concept of effective demand and to provide a theoretical basis for fiscal policy with which to approach the problem of dire depression. As often repeated, and as repeated again in Patinkin and Leith (1978, 44-47), others had advocated public works and public spending as a cure for depression and unemployment, but Keynes offered a counter-theory to the prevailing economic theory. We quote Walter Salant:

   > "The point is in the statement "it takes a theory to kill a theory." Facts are not sufficient, at least not until they become overwhelming. The proponents of established

theory are skillful at ignoring facts that conflict with it. You need a theoretical refutation of established theory to make acceptable a policy that flies in its face." (Patinkin and Leith 1978, 47)

8. Another--slight variation of the rebate form of price adjustment, in effect--has been the use of the warranty in the automotive industry as a disguise form of price adjustment and competition. In the later 1960s, Chrylser introduced a broad five-year or 50,000 mile factory warranty war in the industry that lasted five or six years. As repair costs escalated in the early 1970s, warranty converage was scaled back to the original 12-month or 12,000-mile standard. However, in early 1979, as forecast of declining growth rates for production began to appear, GM began adding a 36-month or 36,000-mile mechanical insurance policy to its list of options that could be purchased. Ford quickly followed, and speculation soon centered about a spring promotion by Chrysler of a free five-year, 50,000-mile extended warranty.
9. The Academy of Sciences of the Nobel foundation pointed to Samuelson's work on the interacting multiplier and accelerator, among other things, in awarding him the second Nobel Prize in economics in 1970.

SELECTED READINGS AND REFERENCES

Boland, Lawrence R. 1979. "A Critique of Friedman's Critics." Journal of Economic Literature (June).

Clark, John Maurice (with an introductory essay, "Some Documentary Notes on the Relations among J. M. Clark, N. A. L. J. Johannsen, and J. M. Keynes," by Joseph Dorfman). 1970. The Costs of the World War to the American People. New York: Augustus M. Kelly (Originally published in 1931).

Clark, John Maurice. 1917. "Business Acceleration and the Law of Demand: A Technical Factor of Economic Cycles" The Journal of Political Economy (March). Reprinted in 1944. Readings in Business Cycle Theory. Philadelphia: Pa.: The Blackiston Company.

Duesenberry, James S. 1952. Income, Saving, and the Theory of Consumer Behavior. Cambridge: Harvard University Press.

Eckstein, Otto. 1978. The Great Recession. New York: North-Holland Publishing Company.

Frazer, William. 1973. Crisis in Economic Theory. Gainesville, Fla.: University of Florida Press. Chapter 5.

__________. 1979. "Positive Economics, the Axioms Controversy, and Methodology." Journal of Economic Issues 13(December).

Friedman, Milton. 1951. "Comment on 'A Test of an Econometric Model for the United States, 1921-1947'." In Conference on Business Cycles. New York: National Bureau of Economic Research.

________. 1953a. "The Methodology of Positive Economics." In Essays in Positive Economics. Chicago: University of Chicago Press.

________. 1953b. "The Marshallian Demand Curve." In Essays in Positive Economics. Chicago: University of Chicago Press.

________. 1955. "Leon Walras and His Economic System." American Economic Review 45(December).

________. 1972. "Comments on the Critics." Journal of Political Economy (September/October).

Hansen, Alvin H. 1953. A Guide to Keynes. New York: McGraw-Hill Book Company, Inc.

Henderson, John P. 1976. "The History of Thought in the Development of the Chicago Paradigm." In Warren J. Samuels, ed. 1976. The Chicago School of Political Economy. East Lansing, Mich.: Association for Evolutionry Economics.

Hirsch, Eva and Abraham. 1976. "The Heterodox Methodology of Two Chicago Economics." In Warren J. Samuels, ed. 1976. The Chicago School of Political Economy. East Lansing, Mich.: Association for Evolutionary Economics.

Kahn, Richard F. 1931. "The Relation of Home Investment to Unemployment." Economic Journal (June).

________. 1978. "Some Aspects of the Development of Keynes's Thought." Journal of Economic Literature 16 (June).

Knight, Frank H. 1935. The Ethics of Competition and Other Essays. Second impression 1951, by Augustus M. Kelley, Inc., New York.

Leijonhufvud, Axel. 1968. On Keynesian Economics and the Economics of Keynes. New York: Oxford University Press.

Lovati, Jean M. 1976. "The Unemployment Rate as an Economic Indicator." Review, Federal Reserve Bank of St. Louis (September).

Marx, Karl, and Fredrich Engels. 1848. Communist Manifesto. London (February). Reprinted with editorial comment in Tucker, Robert C., ed. 1978. The Marx-Engels Reader. New York: W. W. Norton and Company.

Moggridge, Donald, ed. 1973. The General Theory and After, Part II, Defense and Development. In the Collected Writings of John Maynard Keynes. London: St. Martin's Press for the Royal Econometric Society.

Patinkin, Don. 1976. Keynes' Monetary Thought: A Study of Its Development. Durham, North Carolina: Duke University Press.

________. 1978. "The Process of Writing The General Theory: A Critical Survey." In Don Patinkin and J. Clark Leith, eds. 1978. Keynes, Cambridge, and the General Theory. Toronto: University of Toronto Press.

__________ and J. Clark Leith, eds. 1978. Keynes, Cambridge, and the General Theory--The process of criticism and discussion connected with the development of The General Theory. Toronto: University of Toronto Press.

Samuleson, Paul A. 1939. "Interaction between the Multiplier Analysis and the Principle of Acceleration." Review of Economics Statistics, (May). Reprinted in 1944. Readings in Business Cycle Theory. Philadelphia, Pa.: The Blackiston Company.

Schultz, Henry. 1938. The Theory and Measurement of Demand. Chicago, Ill.: University of Chicago Press.

Tinbergen, Jan. 1968. Statistical Testing of Business-Cycle Theories. New York: Agathon Press. Includes series of League of Nations Publications 1938-1939.

Ulmer, Melville, J. 1979. "Old and New Fashions in Employment and Inflation Theory." Journal of Economic Issues 13 (March).

Chapter 8
Investment and the Nonfinancial Firm

8.1. Introduction

In Keynes's and Keynesian theory, autonomous spending--especially as it works through the investment multiplier--was the main source of instability in the economy (sects. 4.2 and 4.3). Money and the financing of expenditures were relegated to a relatively minor role by the Keynesians. In contrast, and in reaction to the Keynesians, monetarists of the 1960s stressed that the money stock and certain aspects of government financing were the main sources of instability (sect. 4.4). Moreover, they later considered the financing of a government deficit to have a "crowding out" effect on private financing and spending. Fiscal policy as considered in chapter 10 was pointed to as an offender, but monetary policy with its Keynesian linkage scheme was also singled out.

A controversy between Keynesians and monetarists ushered in the 1960s and centered on whether autonomous spending or the money stock accounted for more of the volatility in income. As the controversy raged, studies were presented as evidence of both as sources of instability (Frazer 1973, chap. 5). A difference was that monetary policy as a destabilizing force could be controlled and thus reoriented in response to the findings, volatile investment might continue as a source of instability until more can be learned about its control. Moreover, even as the Keynesian-monetarist controversy subsided, others came along to point to interactions between politics, the electorate, and economic conditions as further sources of instability in the economy. Studies of these latter interactions come under the heading "the political business cycle."

Whether instability arises from the private sector or from the political business cycle, one is back to viewing capital spending as a separate category of spending requiring further understanding and stabilization. It may occasionally be called upon to provide faster growth in output and to improve the competitive position of the U.S. vis-à-vis the rest of the world. In these cases, selected tax measures, considered later in this chapter, become relevant.

Empirical works on the consumption function have been more satisfactory in isolating and identifying consumption relations than investment functions. This is suggestive of the greater difficulty in treating and understanding investment spending, as considered in this chapter. The extra difficulty appears to arise from various sources: (1) the sophistication of large firms in forecasting and planning, especially financial planning as a means of avoiding some of the effects of disturbances, (2) the greater amount of financial resources for implementing financial plans by large firms, (3) systematic differences in the entities comprising the business sector, especially differences relating to asset size, and (4) a high sensitivity to announcements and new information about such diverse prospects as product changes and modifications, business conditions, and government actions and inactions.

When one attempts to identify the group of economic entities engaged in the activity of investment spending, the tendency is to think of industrial concerns, mainly firms manufacturing products. Due to the variety and sheer number, there is certainly no "typical" concern. Even so, when one thinks of the firms accounting for most of the products and real capital investment as a proportion of total spending (GNP), one is consistently led to the 500-1000 or so largest manufacturing corporations, listed year after year in Fortune magazine.[1]

Their shares are listed on the New York Stock Exchange, for the most part, and their sales grow very much as GNP grows.[2] Their managerial functions are separate from stock ownership. However, some evidence presented later (sect. 14.4) suggests that: (1) the managers and the shareholders react to much the same information that permeates business conditions, and (2) they react as if the managers were representing the stockholders (that is, as if control and ownership were not distinct functions).

The large part of these firms' capital spending is financed by saving, as introduced in chapters 3 and 7. Some of this is internal, in the form of retained earnings, but outside financing is also utilized, especially during periods of sustained capital spending at high levels. Such firms, as stated, are characterized by planning, including capital budgeting and financial planning for future capital expenditures, as well as planning to avoid the disruptive effects of tight credit, which may be more typically felt by households.

Some analysis and description are called for to deal with the behavior of the firms just characterized. First, because of their influence on current output of goods and services, we will examine capital budgeting and capital spending. Next, we will introduce the subject of maximizing returns from the production of output. Here the firms are shown to have a financial structure that occasionally requires borrowing from banks and from the capital markets. There is the associated problem of minimizing the cost of producing a given output. The emphasis is on selecting the best labor and capital combination, given technical efficiency (chap. 2, n. 9, and sect. 15.2). (The achievement of this efficiency is left by economists to the engineers.) Although much of this is static analysis, it may be cast in a dynamic framework.

8.2. Capital Investment

The Keynesian investment demand building block may serve as an introduction to the determination of capital spending. The formal capital budgeting procedures utilized by a number of large industrial firms coincides very much with the notions attributed to the capital investment process by the Keynesian model. An introduction to this technique may offer insight into some real-world phenomena that are presumed to be captured by the investment demand model.

There are two immediate and interrelated notions that underlie Keynes's investment demand model (Keynes 1936, 135-37), and other related notions found in the respective works of Irving Fisher and Knut Wicksell (sect. 9.1). The immediate concepts are those of the demand price (or current value, CV) and the supply price (or cost, C) of a given project:

$$CV_o = \frac{\pi_1}{(1+i)^1} + \frac{\pi_2}{(1+i)^2} + \frac{\pi_3}{(1+i)^3} + \ldots + \frac{\pi_n}{(1+i)^n}$$

$$C_o = \frac{\pi_1}{(1+r)^1} + \frac{\pi_2}{(1+r)^2} + \frac{\pi_3}{(1+r)^3} + \ldots + \frac{\pi_n}{(1+r)^n}$$

The π's are the extra returns generated by the project on an annual basis, net of all financing costs. These returns are only prospects and consequently are dated with subscripts for future periods. The $\underline{i}$ is the cost of borrowing expressed as a rate. It simplifies the discussions to assume that the rate is controlled in a very direct way by some all-powerful authority. We may call it the Federal Reserve. Now, with the expectations given and the interest rate a controlled variable, the current value of the project clearly varies inversely with the rate of interest.

The cost (C) or supply price may be readily obtained from a supplier or contractor for example. Once the cost is estimated, the rate of return (r) for discounting the future inflows is computed. This rate (r) and the rate of interest (i) are variables for the present time period, with $\underline{r}$ depending on the investment outlay and the future prospects and with $\underline{i}$ depending on the hypothetical, all powerful Federal Reserve. The exponents on the factors (1+i) and (1+r) reflect preference for present over future funds, so that returns received in the more distant future are discounted the most, as elucidated in sections 9.4, and 16.6.

As the interest rate declines, $r_o > i_o$ and $CV_o > C_o$, clearly providing an inducement for increased capital spending, ceteris paribus. An increase in the rate of interest has the reverse effect in this framework. The sort of questions one may raise about this analysis are: Is the interest rate actually controllable in such a fashion, and does the outlook really remain constant? Does the result simply depend on the excessive arbitrariness of what has been impounded in ceteris paribus?

The answers to these questions would lie in the sorts of evidence taken up in chapter 5 primarily. Additional evidence on the nominal interest rate comes up on other occasions, including in chapter 12.

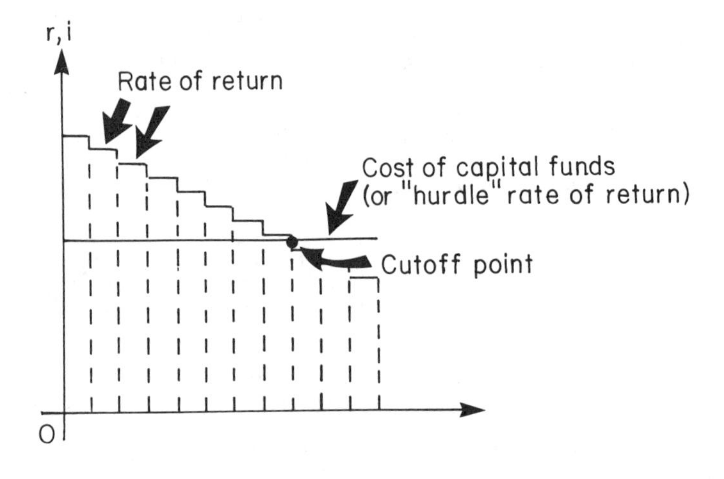

Figure 8-1. Illustrated Budgeting Procedure

Capital Budgeting

A procedure for allocating the capital funds in a firm is to have departments submit spending proposals in which their contribution to future returns or profits are estimated, along with each project's rate of return. Projects are then ranked in the descending order, as determined by their rates of return, as in figure 8-1. Management then selects a rate, designated as the cost of capital (or the "hurdle" rate of return), that provides a cutoff point--a point below which projects will not be considered. This point as measured on the horizontal axis then determines the level of capital spending.

A backlog of such projects may be formally approved and scheduled for implementation. This backlog will be added to at times and decreased by cancellations and by the implementation of plans. The New York-based National Industrial Conference Board has reported quarterly since the 1950s on capital spending plans for the thousand largest manufacturing corporations; in more recent years this reporting has included data on capital appropriations (funds set aside in the corporate budgeting and planning process for new plant and equipment).[3] Because these appropriations are eventually paid out for planning, contracting, and the construction or delivery of the new plant or equipment, they are viewed by the Conference Board as a leading indicator of capital expenditures (Grossman 1975).

The Keynesian Investment Demand Model

Theoretically, a downward-sloping line could be fitted to the midpoints of the histograms representing projects in figure 8-1 and, by aggregating the separate investment amounts of individual firms, an aggregate investment demand schedule could be constructed. However, the Keynesian investment demand schedule is not so readily obtained empirically, and instead arises from a priori reasoning. Keynesians have called the downward-sloping schedule the marginal efficiency of capital (MEC) schedule, because it embodies the rate of return on capital or its marginal efficiency.[4]

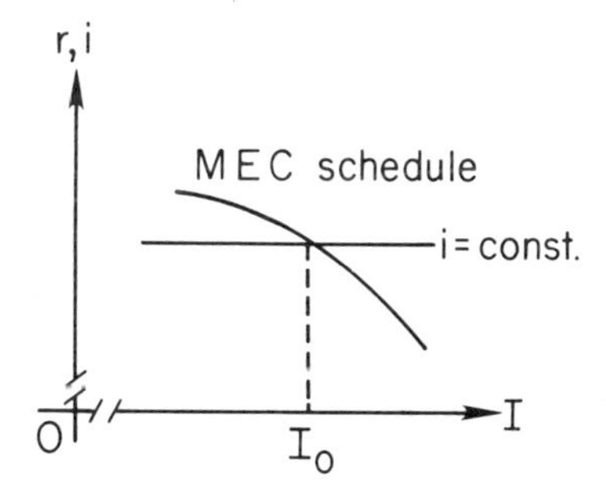

Figure 8-2.
The Investment
Demand Model

In the aggregate, the rationale for the downward slope is that, as investment increases, the profitability of the separate units comprising the enlarged flow declines because of increasing costs and the possible need to price the increased output at a lower price to stimulate sales. The interest rate is external to this particular construction (as shown in figure 8-2) and thought to be determined by the Federal Reserve in the liquidity preference segment of the larger Keynesian model (sects. 5.3, 6.3, and 13.1).

According to the static interpretation (in which the Federal Reserve sets the interest rate), a rise (decline) in the rate means less (more) investment. In chapter 7, we noted that an increase (or accelerated rise) in investment leads to an increase (or accelerated rise) in income, which leads to an increase in saving. Thus, in the controlled ceteris paribus context, a lower interest rate means more investment, more income, and more saving, all such as to maintain the saving-investment equality. This inverse variation between interest rates and investments, when combined with analysis in the form of the Keynesians two-sector model leads to the investment-saving (IS) leg of the IS-LM construction in chapter 13. These relationships are summarized in figure 8-3.

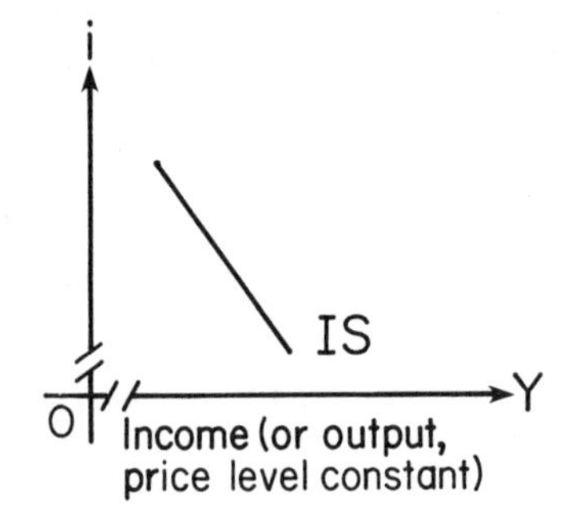

Figure 8-3.
The IS Curve

Dynamic Considerations, Inflationary Expectations, and Monetary Policy

In Keynes's formulation of investment demand some central features stand out. They emerged to plague the theory in more modern times in which two changes have occurred, namely: (1) a reorientation of the monetary policy stance from one of control over the interest rate in a fairly direct way through open market operations to one with attention to control over money and credit aggregates and demand side influences on the rate of interest (as elucidated in chapter 6); and (2) the recognition that the rate of interest is adjusted for the expected inflation rate, with some possible uncertainty in the forecast (sect. 5-5).

The central features of Keynes's theory of investment demand are: (1) a tie between movements in the investment demand schedule and the expected inflation rate, and (2) a presumed absence of any effect on the interest rate from inflationary expectations (1936, 141-42). Indeed, Keynes recognized outward shifts in the MEC schedule as the prospect of inflation exerts impact upon the flows of returns (π_1, π_2, ..., π_n), on the one hand, and then strove to deny the appropriateness of Fisher's interest rate equation ($i = i_r + (1/P)(dP/dt)^*$, on the other.[5]

On inflationary expectations, Keynes said there will be no effect on current affairs if inflation is unanticipated,

> whilst, if it is foreseen, the prices of existing goods will be forthwith so adjusted that the advantages of

> holding money and of holding goods are again equalized, and it will be too late for holders of money to suffer again a change in the rate of interest which will offset the prospective change during the period of the loan in the value of the money lent. For the dilemma is not successfully escaped by Professor Pigou's expedient of supposing that the prospective change in the value of money is foreseen by one set of people but not foreseen by another. [Note: This foresight attribute would be as in Fisher's view of bank loans and interest rates, sect. 5-2].

"The mistake," Keynes said, "lies in supposing that it is the rate of interest on which prospective changes in the value of money will directly react, instead of the marginal efficiency of a given stock of capital." Continuing, he said the following:

> The prices of existing assets will always adjust themselves to changes in expectations concerning the prospective value of money. The significance of such changes in expectations lies in their effect on the readiness to produce new assets through their reaction on the marginal efficiency of capital. The stimulating effect of the expectation of higher prices is due, not to its raising the rate of interest (that would be a paradoxical way of stimulating output--in so far as the rate of interest rises, the stimulating effect is to that extent offset), but to its raising the marginal efficiency of a given stock of capital.

In these passages, Keynes came close to dealing with his own dilemma--as viewed with the hindsight of modern times. First, we might recognize that when the prospect of inflation impacts upon a firm's prospective returns from new capital outlays (pure speculation in property values aside), the only way for the higher flows of returns on the new capital to be realized is for the new capital to be brought into place. This takes time. These manufacturing firms are specializing in production, and the enlarged portion of production must be produced in order to realize the enlarged flow of returns from the new production. Next, financial markets can adjust yields (as rates) quite readily to the prospect of inflation, and this is the troublesome point. Keynes simply cannot bring himself to deny the role of interest rate as a control variable.[6]

The simple difficulty is that redirection of the theory is called for in light of evidence about the rate of interest and its inflation rate component and the evidence on monetary operations (sect. 6-2). For the stimulating effect of expected inflation, we must look elsewhere than to the impoundment of the interest rate (i) as a control variable and the contemporaneous inequalities ($MEC_t > i_t$, and $i_t > MEC_t$). In looking elsewhere, there are several interrelated prospects in the presence of accelerating inflation. First, in contrast to the contemporaneous inequality, there is the prospect of MEC_t < MEC_{t+n} and $i_t < i_{t+n}$. The MEC on plant and equipment being put in place today reflects the current prospects for inflation (deflation), but still it may not do so to the extent of the MEC two years hence, when the prospect is for accelerated inflation (deflation, $MEC_t > MEC_{t+n}$).

Next, from the point of view of a producer of capital goods (say, a construction contractor), labor costs enter as the major cost for the most part. The producer cannot realize the fruits of production and labor the fruits of employment without production taking place. Where such argument about the stimulating effect of inflation on production and employment comes up later, in discussion of the Phillips curve (sect. 17.4; and Frazer 1978, 354-356), there are two routes to go. More elaborately stated later, one is that a money illusion may exist on the part of workers for some time following the acceleration of inflation and that as a consequence their services are offered at less than what would otherwise be the case. Labor costs do not catch up immediately with the rising product prices. A second argument is that employment may expand because jobs are available irrespective of any money illusion and an increase in real wages for some time to come. The impact of wages upon the labor supply does appear to have diminished over time, and in the case of union contracted wages contracts are not negotiated upward immediately.

Revealed Interest Rate and Investment Behavior

In the investment component of the Keynesian model, one might admit autonomous spending and outside influences on anticipated future developments. For example, the prospect of accelerated inflation proceeding from a zero or low rate and working through the expected flow of returns (π_1, π_2, ..., π_n) would be represented by a shift to the right (or a faster shift, as the case may be) in the MEC schedule. Referring to the liquidity preference construction in sections 5.3 and 6.3, this would mean influence on the demand side of the market for funds (money and bank credit), causing the interest rate to rise. One may say with reference to the investment construction (figure 8-2) or the liquidity preference construction (figure 5-5) that the demand side of the market for real capital or for funds dominates in the more common of the post-World War II booms, all such that the MEC schedule shifts more than the interest rate, and investment increases even while interest rates are rising.

Only after the foregoing shift has continued for some time--probably at an unsustainable rate as far as secular trend is concerned--does it slow down, perhaps in response to an overwhelming pull toward normality (the sustainable trend line for capital spending). When deceleration occurs, movement along the downward-sloping demand schedule comes into play, and at this unusual time capital spending may decelerate as the interest rate holds firm and possibly even declines.

The predominance of a direct variation in the rate of interest and capital spending would be in accord with what one observes in the more common cases--for example, as depicted by a tendency for capital spending to rise at a more rapid rate during a boom, at the same time interest rates are rising.[7] As reported by the Department of Commerce (1976), turning points in interest rates and business investment expenditures both coincide at the peak of general business conditions and both lag business conditions somewhat at the trough. This relationship between high-grade (Aaa) corporate bond yields and gross private domestic investment is shown in figure 8-4 for the more common experiences from 1952 through 1975, and for the less common experience from 1969 through 1975 in the insert to figure 8-4. The less common experience, as from 1969 through 1975, may be identified with two interrelated tendencies: (1) that of strong inflationary expectations, even in recession, and (2) that of greater uncertainty about the expected flows of returns [i.e., probabilistically weighted returns, $(Pb)_1\pi_1$, $(Pb)_2\pi_2$, ..., $(Pb)_n\pi_n$] because of greater uncertainty about the future of business conditions in the presence of accelerated inflation and familiarity with the destabilizing consequences of excessive inflation. From the vantage point of early 1978, the prospect of accelerating inflation from an already high rate during the 1969-75 period quite possibly injected uncertainty that reduced the value of long-term capital (and thus the rate of return), even as inflation increased the "hurdle" rate of return and sales continued at a growing rate.

The predominance of the direct variation in the variables of figure 8-4 need not lead to an outright rejection of the capital budgeting process as summarized in figure 8-1. One may still view that earlier process as going on, but more as an iterative part of a larger budgetary process. In the larger process the budgeting would continue as in figure 8-1, but the budgeting committee would be varying the "cut-off" rate of return to align with its perception of the present vis-à-vis the future, and new projects with newly evaluated rates of return would continually alter the line suggested by the histograms of figure 8-1.

Tax Measures and the Marginal Efficiency of Capital

Exclusive of the presence or absence of control over the rate of interest, there are several tax measures through which the government can directly affect the rate of return on capital (that is, can shift the MEC schedule or, in dynamic terms, shift it at a faster or slower rate). These measures for providing more (or less) inducement for capital spending primarily include accelerated depreciation, the income tax credit, and the corporate income tax rate itself. In addressing the tax incentive to investment and assessing tax credits and cuts, Abel concludes from his MIT dissertation (1978, 54-66) the following: (1) "That an investment tax credit can lead to a

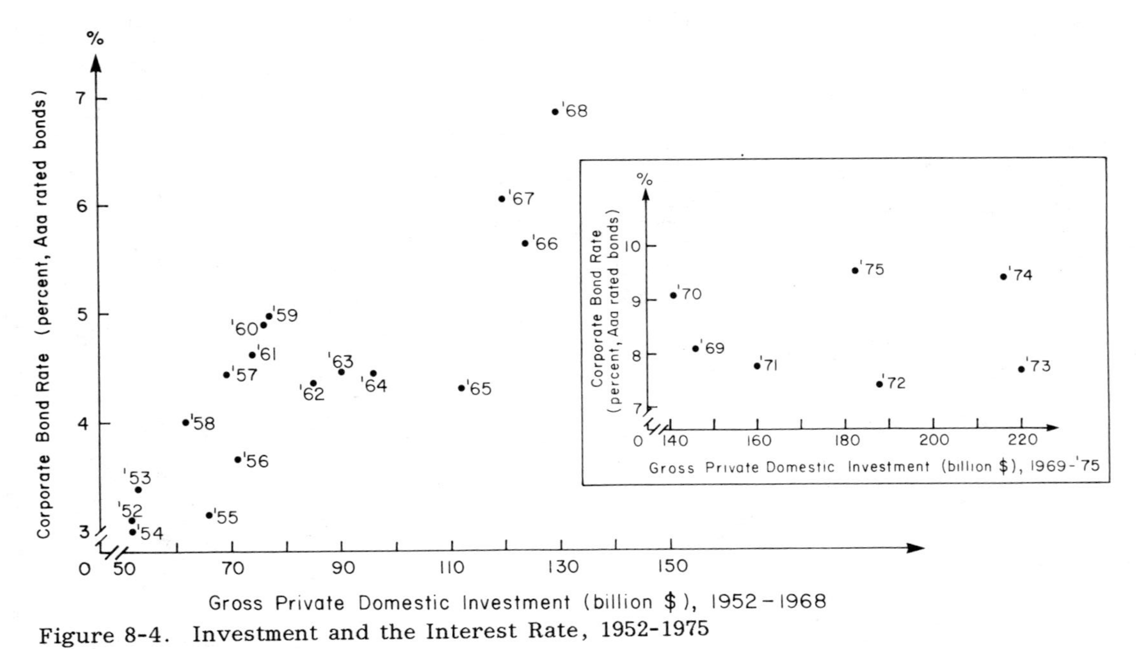

Figure 8-4. Investment and the Interest Rate, 1952-1975

Sources of data: The interest rate data are Moody's Aaa corporate bond yields and the investment data are from National Income Accounts as compiled by the Department of Commerce. Both sets are found in the Federal Reserve Bulletin, and in the U.S. Department of Commerce's Handbook of Cyclical Indicators.

given increase in capital formation at a smaller cost to the Treasury than can a cut in the corporate tax rate...." (2) And that "the efficacy of a corporate tax cut as an investment stimulus is considerably weakened by highly accelerated schedules of depreciation allowances and by the sensitivity of the after-tax cost of capital to the corporate tax rate." (One may recall that the costs of debt expressed as interest is deductible in computing taxable corporate income.)

The tax credit for machinery and equipment was first introduced in the United States in January 1962. An initial 7 percent credit stayed in effect until April 1969, with a seven and one-half month suspension in 1966-1967. In 1975, during the recession of 1973-75, the credit was raised to 10 percent, and in early 1977 President Carter proposed giving corporations a choice of taking a 4 percent credit on payroll taxes (primarily the social security levy) or having the 10 percent investment credit raised to 12 percent. This proposal was never implemented, however, and in his 1978 tax message Carter proposed reducing the corporate income tax. The resulting 1979 tax bill included the following: an extension of the 10 percent credit to apply to certain buildings (along with other minor changes) and a reduction in the top rate on corporate income from a time-honored 48 percent to 46 percent rate, with slightly lower but progressive rates for each of four $25,000 brackets up to $100,000. Even with high inflation rates, these 1979 tax measures must have contributed to planned increase in investment spending by the nation's businesses of nearly 13 percent (or 4.5 percent after discounting for inflation) for 1979, as reported in mid-1979.

All three of the tax measures reviewed work through the flows of return ($\pi_1, \pi_2, \ldots, \pi_n$) in exerting impact on either the current value of capital assets or on the rate of return from additions to capital assets. For example, reduction in the corporate income tax raises the flow of returns, and it does so on both the old and new stock of capital, and changes in accelerated depreciation and the tax credit affect the rate of return on additions to the stock of capital.

These last two measures may be illustrated by proceeding with three assumptions: (1) the corporate income tax rate is 50 percent; (2) the rate of return on capital expenditures under an ordinary depreciation method is 5 percent; and (3) the net return from a capital outlay tapers off in succeeding years. Under these assumptions, a $1,000 investment with a ten-year life may appear as follows:

$$\$1,000 = \frac{\$184}{(1+0.05)^1} + \frac{\$171}{(1+0.05)^2} + \cdots + \frac{\$46}{(1+0.05)^{10}}$$

The net returns sum to $1,242. A switch to accelerated depreciation--a faster write-off of investment expenditures for corporate income tax purposes--would instead cause the investment to appear:

$$\$1{,}000 = \frac{\$234}{(1+0.056)^{1}} + \frac{\$202}{(1+0.056)^{2}} + \ldots + \frac{\$46}{(1+0.056)^{10}}$$

The returns in the early years are higher under the accelerated depreciation, such that the rate of return increases from 5.0 percent in the first computation to 5.6 percent in the second.

A tax credit has very special effect in that it is not simply a write-off from the tax base. In effect the Treasury shares in meeting the cost of new capital equipment for the private sector. The credit takes the form of an allowable deduction (a credit) from a portion of the tax payment itself. A 7 percent credit increases the first year's cash returns by $70 (to continue the above example) and increases the rate of return on the capital outlay to 7.6 percent:

$$\$1{,}000 = \frac{\$304}{(1+0.076)^{1}} + \frac{\$202}{(1+0.076)^{2}} + \ldots + \frac{\$46}{(1+0.076)^{10}}$$

In this example the rate of return is increased from 5.0 percent to 7.6 percent by allowing a tax credit.

The capital gains tax is another tax that can affect the return on investment, working through the taxation of individual incomes as far as the availability of risk capital to business is concerned. In general a gains tax provides for a preferential tax treatment of income realized from the sale of capital assets, other real property, homes, or stocks that have been held for longer than six months. Prior to the 1979 tax bill the law allowed corporations paying the top 48 percent rate on corporate income to pay an alternative rate of 30 percent for capital gains. In addition, part of a corporation's gains were subject to a 15 percent minimum tax, which could raise the top rate on corporate capital gains to 31.125 percent. The 1979 bill reduced the alternative rate from 30 to 28 percent, and set the maximum rate at 29.67 percent.

Some further attention to capital spending by the federal government, along the lines of the 1979 tax bill appears called for, in view of problems addressed later. These include a declining share of income to capital (sect. 15.3) and declining productivity of workers such as may be partly attributed to insufficient capital (sect. 17.1).

8.3. Maxima and Minima of Firm Behavior

Firms may be viewed as doing a lot of maximizing and minimizing, and liquidity and risk elements (the inverse of liquidity) enter into the exercise, as formulated against the background of the extreme value problems concerning the Lagrangian function (sects. 3.3 and 17.6, and apps. to chaps. 9 and 16). Keynes hinted at the existence of these liquidity elements in chapter 17 ("The Essential Properties of Interest and Money") of the General Theory (Frazer 1958).

Against this background of the extreme value problem, firms may be viewed as maximizing the following:

(1) the flow of returns, given total assets

(2) production, given cost

(3) profits

and minimizing:

(1) the cost of funds expressed as an outflow of funds, given total assets

(2) costs, given the production process.

The numbers (1) in each group are different sides of the same activity, as are the numbers (2). The first activity leads to a maximum profit position, after allowances for risk factors, as does the latter when the analysis of production is combined with that for revenue and cost functions. In this section we deal with the first activity. The discussion of production functions and the labor market comes in chapters 15, 16, and 17.

Maximization of Returns

Consider first the asset side of a balance sheet--particularly key assets such as cash (money, M), government and similar type securities (G), and real or instrumental capital (such as plant and equipment, P)--and consider as well the maximization of returns over costs, subject to constraint. The constraint is

$$g(M,G,P) = P_M M + P_G G + P_P P = 0$$

where the Ps are prices per units and P_M is the special price of money in terms of itself (P_M - 1). The Lagrangian function (i.e., the function to be maximized subject to constraint) is

$$L(M,G,P,r) = f(M,G,P) + r[g(M,G,P) - P_M M - P_G G - P_P P]$$

where f(M,G,P) is the utility function and r is the Lagrangian factor of proportionality. One statement of the first order conditions for an extreme value that follows from this function is

$$\frac{\partial U/\partial M}{P_M} = \frac{\partial U/\partial M}{P_G} = \frac{\partial U/\partial P}{P_P} = r$$

This says that the rates obtained by dividing the extra or marginal utilities resulting from additions to the various classes of assets by their prices are equal, as introduced in section

3.3. In other words, after an allowance for risk or liquidity premiums, the rates of return on the various classes of assets should be equal if the overall flow of returns is to be maximized. In the case of cash balances there is little or no dollar return per se, but rather the security and convenience from having liquid balances. This conforms to the usual ranking of asset accounts on a balance sheet in descending order of liquidity (the inverse of risk).

In the minimization case, the objective is to minimize the cost of financing expressed as an outflow of funds on key accounts. The resulting conditions for an extreme value are that the interest rates on additional funds from the alternative sources are equal. The Lagrangian multiplier turns out to be the rate of interest in this case. As presently expressed, it too contains an intangible liquidity factor, only as a drain against the firm. It conforms to the listing of liability-side accounts on a balance sheet, where the accounts are listed in the decreasing order of the liquidity drains against the firm.

Where the inflows of funds expressed as rates consist of returns less carrying cost (q-c) plus a liquidity premium (l), and the outflows concern tangible costs plus a liquidity drain, we have key asset-side and key liability-side accounts shown thus:

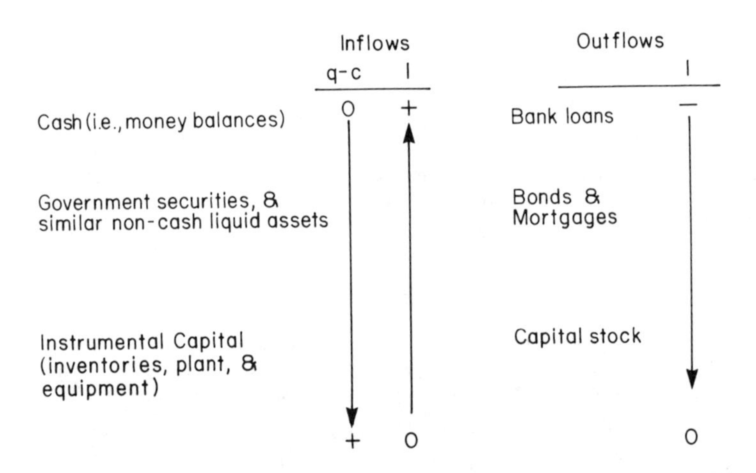

Now, the allocative mechanism for uses and sources of funds as introduced in sections 3.2 and 3.3 is intact. But there are two other analytical matters to be introduced. One concerns specifically the equality of the rate of return and the ratios of the marginal utilities to the prices of the various classes of assets, e.g.,

$$\frac{\partial U/\partial P}{P_P} = r$$

or, re-arranging terms

$$\frac{\partial U/\partial P}{r} = P_P \quad \text{(Supply price)}$$

This is the perpetuity form of the demand and supply price formulas introduced earlier in the chapter (i.e., formulas for CV_o and C_o in section 8.2). It is obtained from those formulas as the time horizon for the $\underline{n}^{th}$ return approaches a distant future (say 30 years). This is acceptable as a first approximation because we are concerned with higher or lower values rather than the exact magnitudes of differences.

Adjustments

The last analytical matter, whereby the rates of return on additions to the various assets are equal, concerns the impact of accelerated inflation, asset adjustments, and the two-way classification of assets (and thus liabilities, too, since every item on the liabilities side of the balance sheet is some other entity's asset) as introduced in section 3.3 and on other occasions; namely: assets have fixed or contractual claim against future income (e.g., money and bonds) or a residual claim (e.g., instrumental capital and its ownership counterpart, capital stock). To illustrate once again the importance of this classification, one may think of the expected rate of change in the price level, $(1/P)(dP/dt)^*$, as a measure of expected inflaton or as a surrogate for business conditions (a rise indicating expansion and a constant or declining magnitude, recession). We ask: What sorts of marginal adjustments occur in the Lagrangian, fixed-claim, residual-claim context as the anticipation of inflation increases?

To answer this latter question, other questions and their possible answers may be called to mind, namely: What happens to the rate of interest? Recall,

$$r = i_r + (1/P)(dP/dt)^*$$

Clearly, if expectations are not impounded, the interest rate rises. Further, if the firm can obtain financing (an increase in a bank loan, for example), then how does the bank compensate for the anticipated loss through repayment of the loan with low purchasing power dollars? The answer is through an upward adjustment in the interest rate. Next, another question might be: Why doesn't the bank invest in residual claim assets? The answer is that banks and some other financial institutions are constrained from doing so by regulations and the specialization of their functions.

We have now, set forth the background for answering the larger question, namely: What sorts of marginal adjustments occur for nonfinancial business firms and the Lagrangian, fixed-claim, residual-claim context? The answer is that the flow of returns on residual claim assets increase and thus the rate of return:

$$C_o = \frac{R \text{ (including increment because } 1/P\ dP/dt)}{r}$$

where r increases to equate the flow to C_o (a constant). The higher rate of return brings about equilibrating adjustments in the asset and liability structures. From the nonfinancial firm's point of view, there is little incentive to invest in debt-type securities because these returns offer less purchasing power and because they are not primarily in the business of lending funds. Consequently, changes are set in motion to increase outlays on real capital (to adjust residual claim assets upward), and to increase borrowing, possibly we will see shortly with the view to temporarily increase liquidity.

We have now created the situation where firms are expanding plant and equipment in the face of rising interest rates closely related and rising inflation rates, and lagging increases in costs (C_o). The capital-goods costs, as noted and addressed much later (sect. 17.4), are lagging behind the other adjustments. Indeed, the labor-cost component of the capital-goods cost is lagging for various reasons: a temporary money illusion on the part of labor, contracts with labor are not immediately renegotiable, and/or the expansion of production and hence employment may proceed for some time without concomitant increases in real wages.

This analysis must be set against the more static analysis focusing on imbalances between the rate of return and the interest rate. Imbalances, such as $\underline{r} > \underline{i}$, could be viewed as representing the excess of a future rate of return (or future interest rates) over a present interest rate. The future rate of return, however, is actually the rate for relating the expected flow of returns at a future date to the forecasted cost of some capital project at the future date. If the present is 1980 and the cost of the capital project is forecasted for January 1, 1984, then

$$C_{1984} = \frac{R_{1984}}{(1+r)^1} + \frac{R_{1985}}{(1+r)^2} + \frac{R_{1986}}{(1+r)^3} + \ldots$$

where r is the rate of return thought to prevail on January 1, 1984.

The present theory differs from the statement of static theory in the last section. It predicts increases in rates of return, interest rates, and the flow of capital spending, as in figure 8-4. It relaxes the assumptions of constant or given values. Results from analyses of data appear to be more in accord with the latter theory. The behavior of interest rates has been shown before (figure 5-3), and the behavior of capital spending is suggested by the covariation in the interest rate and capital spending in figure 8-4. The investment schedule and the constant interest rate in figure 8-2 can be shifted to accomodate this observed behavior.

a. Cash Balances with Respect to Asset Size

b. Bank Loans with Respect to Asset Size

c. Government Securities with Respect to Asset Size

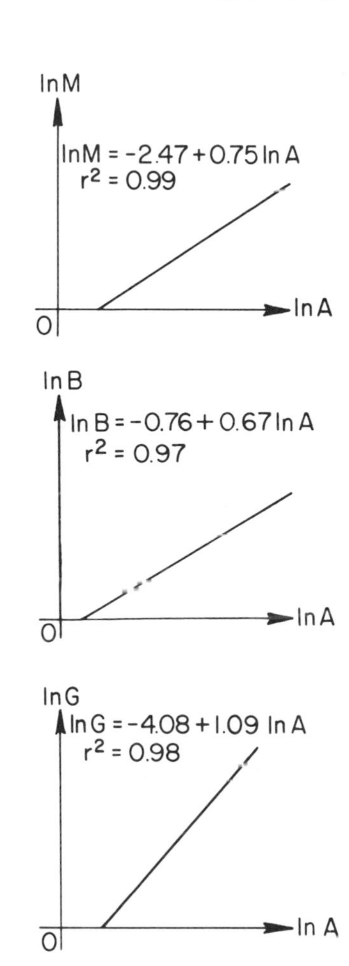

Figure 8-5. Changes in the Liquidity Structure of Manufacturing Corporations as they vary by Asset Size

Note: The data are pooled, cross-section data for manufacturing corporations on a per-firm basis for 1974:IV, 1975:IV, 1976:IV, and 1977:IV. The data for firms by asset-size groups are converted to a per-firm basis and limited to corporations with assets of $10 million and over since the data for firms in this range are for a complete canvas of firms.

Source of data: Federal Trade Commission, as reported in their Quarterly Financial Report.

Analyses of the type we have engaged in apply to matters of instability in business conditions, but there are secular patterns to be explained also. Some of these will be dealt with in later chapters.

The Planning of the Financing

As the backlog of planned expenditures builds up, the chief financial officers of the major firms may be expected to plan for the provision of funds. A conventional way of doing this is to employ expertise in the management of cash, using proceeds from this and other sources to build up liquidity by (1) increasing noncash liquid assets and (2) working down bank indebtedness in relation to asset size. A possible alternative that has opened up since the mid-1970s is trading in futures contracts for securities, as reviewed in section 12.3. The conventional route, as far as marketable liquid assets are concerned, gives rise to a practice of purchasing liquid assets with maturity dates that coincide with the anticipated need for funds and to a liquidity hedging hypothesis (sect. 12.4).

Statistical results concerning the conventional method of building liquidity have appeared for many quarters in a number of sources (Frazer 1973, chap. 15). They are further illustrated by the results for pooled, cross-section data for 1974:IV, 1975:IV, 1976:IV, and 1977:IV, and by the diagrams in figure 8-5. In summary, the results for cash (M), bank loans (B,) and government securities (G), each with respect to asset size (A), are:

$$\ln M = -2.47 + 0.75 \ln A,\ r^2 = 0.99$$

$$\ln B = -0.76 + 0.67 \ln A,\ r^2 = 0.97$$

$$\ln G = -4.08 + 1.09 \ln A,\ r^2 = 0.98$$

"cash balances" (M) includes specifically cash and demand deposits in the U.S., "government securities" is a generic term referring to U.S. government and other liquid securities, and "bank loans" stands for the short-, intermediate-, and long-term indebtedness of the firms (manufacturing corporations in this case) at banks.

The statistical results and figures show that government securities increase more than in proportion and bank loans less than in proportion to asset size. Some of the funds for the resulting buildup in liquidity may come from internal sources, namely depreciation as a tax write-off and retained earnings. Any sizable backlog of planned capital ventures, however, will also require outside funds, obtained from the capital markets (the long-term bond market and the equity market).

The tendency for nonfinancial firms to obtain funds from the capital markets in anticipation of future needs and on relatively favorable terms is reflected in figure 8-6 by the ratio of funds raised from long-term sources (equity issues, bonds, and mortgages) to total net funds raised in financial markets. As the figure shows, a reduction in liquidity accompanies the shift to short-term financing during an expansion phase, and especially during the final stages of an expansion phase.

Financial planning assures some independence from tight credit conditions (as indicated by higher interest rates) that usually develop during expansionary phases, when most firms undertake increased capital spending. As that time approaches the firms will be in relatively sound financial condition (and thus credit worthy from the bank's point of view), probably with commitments from the banks where they do business. The banks, for their part, may be faced with decelerated growth in reserves and strong loan demand. In such a setting the interest rate rises, not just as a reflection of inflation, but as a means of rationing scarce bank funds to the most credit-worthy borrowers. These rates are best known to readers of the financial press as "prime" lending rate. In the 1975-80 boom, under conditions such as those just described, the prime loan rate reached a record 19½ percent.

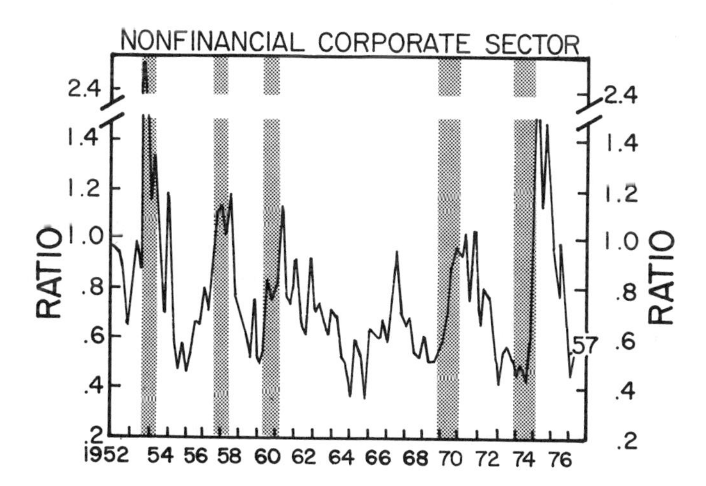

Figure 8-6. Ratio of Funds Raise from Long-Term Sources to Total Net Funds Raised.

Source of figure: Federal Reserve Bank of St. Louis

Note. Long-term sources of funds are equity issues, bonds, and mortgages. Shaded areas represent periods of business recession.

At this latter phase the boom is cresting and the reverse credit conditions will follow. Banks will have an abundance of funds to lend. If one can judge from history, this results from reduced loan demand and secondarily from growth in bank reserves. The firms, for their part, will be cutting back and rebuilding liquidity as funds flow in from retained earnings and depreciation.

8.4. Lagged Relations, Capital Spending, and Capacity Utilization

In view of what has been said in this chapter, and earlier in the case of the money stock (narrowly defined), we would expect leading indicators of capital spending (and, therefore, business conditions) to include the liquidity of nonfinancial corporations, the money stock (its time rate of change), capital appropriations, and contracts and orders for plant and equipment. Said differently, we would expect capital spending to lag behind the leading indicators. These indicators are considered below. Also introduced are measures of capacity utilization in manufacturing. They play an important role in the analysis of economic activity, particularly near peaks in business conditions when these measures serve as leading indicators.

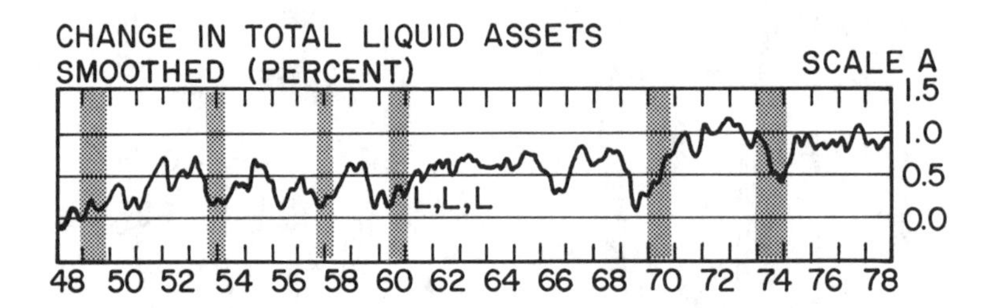

Figure 8-7. Changes (percent) in Total Liquid Assets

Source: U.S. Department of Commerce, Business Conditions Digest (1976).

Total Liquid Assets

The tendency described in the last section for the liquidity of firms (especially large ones) to be related to future capital spending means that liquidity may serve as a leading indicator of business conditions. Indeed, the Department of Commerce series (1976) for changes in total liquid assets shows this to be the case. As reproduced in figure

8-7, percent changes in total liquid assets are shown with the designation L, L, L. The first L signifies that the series leads at peaks, the second that it leads at troughs, and the third that the series has been selected for consistency of its timing at both peaks and troughs.

Capital Spending and the Money Stock

Distributed lag models are commonly brought forward for the purpose of considering time lags in a relationship between one variable and another (Frazer 1973, app. to chap. 15). Using the level of capital spending (I) and the money stock (M) for simplicity of notation, a distributed lag model might appear:

$$I = \text{const.} + \beta_o M_t + \beta_1 M_{t-1} + \ldots + \beta_n M_{t-n}$$

The lagged coefficients (β's) for such a model can be plotted to reveal the lagged pattern. Figure 8-8 provides an illustration.

Smoother patterns can be obtained (as in figure 8-8), by applying the technique of the Almon lag (named after the author of a main paper on the technique). This technique eliminates some of the irregularity in the coefficients that may result from multicollinearity or interdependence between the lagged variables. Moreover, the magnitude of the regression coefficients (β's) in a distributed lag model may be constrained

Figure 8-8. A Pattern of Coefficients for Distributed Lag Model

to sum to one; in this case the presumed impact of the lagged variable can be described as a percent of the total impact (1 x 100 = 100 percent).

The theory introduced along with distributed lag models traditionally assumed fixed lag patterns, or stable parameter values. This was in the 1960s when they were first widely used and when the parameter values were first being estimated empirically. Eventually economists realized that even these relatively dynamic models were too static, in the sense that the lags themselves were not fixed lags. The lags could vary with phases of business conditions or under changed secular conditions, for example. This added dynamic feature and the concomitant attention to forces outside the theory was readily brought out (it comes up again in section 17.4).

One method for estimating variation in the parameters is that of variable parameter regression estimation (Cooley and Prescott 1976). A more traditional method for revealing changed lagged patterns is that of splitting the sample. Here, estimates for parameter values are obtained for data for a given sample period. Estimates are also obtained for separate parts or subperiods of the sample, or simply for a later period. When this is done, the result is not uncommonly a significant difference in the estimated parameter values for the separate periods.

In other words, the lagged relations themselves may vary. The possible causes of this are worthy of consideration. The lagged relationships may reflect different political administrations, periods of different degrees of social and political awareness, or periods of different degrees of certainty about the future economic and social conditions (Frazer 1973).

Another possible cause of variation in effects resulting from changes in monetary and credit aggregates is House Concurrent Resolution 133, which calls on the Federal Reserve to give advance notice of its plans for monetary and credit policy. Thus, the announced policies (say M*), rather than the actual policies (say M), may be responsible for the observed effects. This would shorten the lag time as some have recognized (sect. 18.5). The degree to which the announced plans for policy influence the lag will depend on the credibility of the announcement. With the passage of time this should depend on the spread between the announced plans and the actual, *ex post* changes; that is, $M_t - M_t^*$, as $t = 0, 1, 2, 3, \ldots, n$.

Capital Appropriations

Using the Almon lag technique the National Industrial Conference Board has specified a lag relation between capital expenditures and capital appropriations for the 1,000 manufacturing firms in their canvas of such firms (Grossman 1975). Specifying a distributed lag pattern for quarterly data for the 1960:I to 1974:II period the Board concluded:

> Our data indicates that only 10% of appropriations are spent during the same quarter. By the end of two quarters fully 42% of appropriations are converted to capital expenditures; 71% are spent after four quarters, 80% after five quarters, and 90% after two years.

Considering further some of the possible determinants of capital appropriations themselves, the Conference Board offers another model. It relates appropriations to corporate profits after taxes (deflated by the GNP deflator), the monetary supply (also deflated), a measure of capacity utilization, and the effective level of the investment tax credit. Dummy variables are included to account for effects of the so-called energy crisis and increases in appropriations for pollution control equipment. These variables are intended to capture the changing lag patterns over time (as mentioned in describing the method of splitting the sample).

Contracts for Orders

Contracts for orders of plant and equipment (1972 dollars) is another leading indicator of business conditions, reported by the Department of Commerce (1976). Their graphical presentation of it is reproduced in figure 8-9, where orders (in billions of 1972 dollars) are plotted against a logarithmic scale, as introduced first in section 3.1. This means that changes in the time series reflect percentage changes. One can also discern a secular growth pattern in the data in addition to the cyclical patterns. The shaded areas are delineated by National Bureau turning points. The three L's (L, L, L) in the figure signify that the series leads at peaks, troughs, and overall.

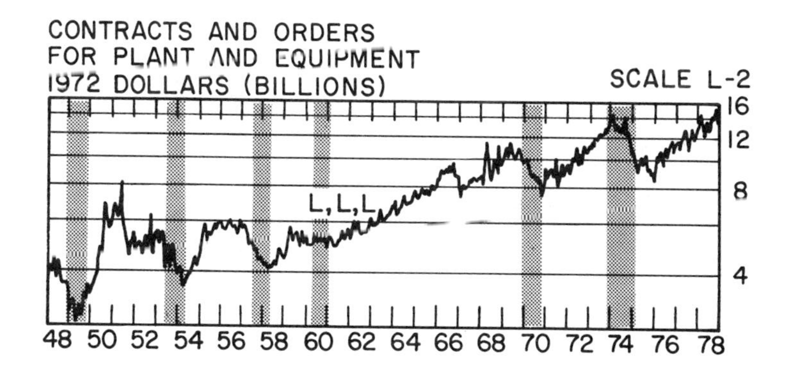

Figure 8-9. Contracts and Orders for Plant and Equipment (1972 dollars in billions)

Source: U.S. Department of Commerce, Business Conditions Digest (1976).

Capacity Utilization in Manufacturing

There are four principal measures of capacity utilization in manufacturing as critically evaluated by Ragan (1976). These are provided by Wharton Econometric Forecasting Associates, McGraw-Hill Publishing Company, the Department of Commerce Bureau of Economic Analysis (BEA), and the Board of Governors of the Federal Reserve System (FRB).[8] The BEA and FRB measures are more frequently employed and shown in figure 8-10. The designation L, C, U indicates that the measures tend to lead at cyclical peaks (L), roughly coincide at troughs (C), and are unclassified otherwise (U). Although the two measures tend to behave very similarily, Ragan says "the FRB utilization rate probably reflects current utilization of capital stock most accurately, provided that the statistical relationships on which it is based are kept up to date."

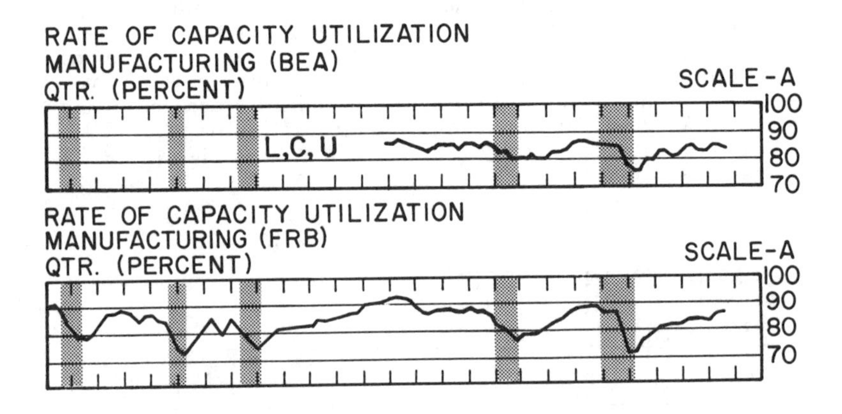

Figure 8-10. Capacity Utilization in Manufacturing

Source: U.S. Department of Commerce, Business Conditions Digest (1976).

The utilization of capacity in the manufacturing sector, as indicated by the FRB measure, is addressed in more recent studies by Bisignano and McElhattan. The former (1978, 6-19), addresses uncertainty with respect to anticipated inflation and finds that it reduces the demand for investment goods in manufacturing, and increases labor demand and the rate of capacity utilization. Using Livingston data, as introduced in chapter 5, Bisignano deals with errors in the inflation rate forecasts of the wholesale-price index and relates these to uncertainty in the inflation rate forecasts and consequently to a firm's future output prices. Such uncertainty after the early-1975 trough in business conditions, he finds, leads to a substitution of some additional labor for capital and to a higher utilization rate. The idea is that the firm minimizes the costs of its forecast error in this regard by using less of the factor that is more permanently committed.

McElhattan (1978, 20-30) addresses permanent magnitudes and uses a cyclical time frame, as found in the work of Milton Friedman (sect. 4.4). In particular she studies the full capacity utilization rate in relation to the "natural rate of unemployment." As with setting target and actual rates of unemployment below the natural rate, attempts to maintain a capacity utilization rate above the estimated natural-capacity utilization rate lead to a steadily increasing inflation rate. Such analyses with the Friedmanesque time frame come up in greater detail when we consider both a variable natural rate of unemployment (sect. 11.5) and the short- and long-run Phillips relations (sect. 17.4).

Some economists have treated the historical peak of capacity utilization ("the 87-to-88 percent level of the 1973 period") as the level beyond which inflation accelerates, as would be consistent with the Keynesian view of control over business conditions at a point (sect. 4.3). McElhattan, on the other hand, reported from her findings that a "natural rate" of capacity utilization fell in the 80 to 83 ½ percent range, much below the peak level. She concluded thus:

> Inflation tends to accelerate when the operating rate surpasses 82 percent--or more generally, the range of 80 to 83½ percent. Once beyond that range, excess demand generates inflationary pressures as less efficient labor and capital resources are called into use. Thus, since utilization rates recently have approached 85 percent, we could expect mounting inflationary pressures from the domestic, nonfarm business sector of our economy.
>
> Once capacity utilization exceeds the range indicated, the increased inflation tends to become imbedded in future inflation, with the current period's higher prices being reflected in the next period's expectations. Our analysis suggests that when the operating rate rises above the full-capacity range, its return to that range will be accompanied by a higher rate of inflation. For the inflation rate to decline, therefore, capacity utilization would have to fall below its equilibrium value, such as generally happens in a business recession.
>
> ....The important policy task, therefore, is to steer a steady course which does not permit output growth to exceed its long-run potential. Under such circumstances, a stable rate of inflation can be maintained with both capital and labor at their full ["natural"] utilization rates. (McElhattan 1978, 27)

8.5. Summary

1. Large firms are characterized by the planning and financing of capital expenditures. The practice of capital budgeting embodies the planning of expenditures. Considering this practice we see one way of rationalizing a downward sloping demand curve for capital goods. Another is to consider diminishing returns from additional spending as prices are lowered to sell more output and as the cost of producing more rises. Both rationalizations are highly static (ceteris paribus) in character, and thus may not explain the phenomena that predominate with respect to changes in business conditions.

2. The static characterizations of the investment demand curve in conjunction with historic views about the Federal Reserve's control of the interest rate leads to the prediction of an inverse variation in capital spending and the rate of interest. However, this is inconsistent with the observed variation over most of the post-World War II years. Even so, this does not mean that the interest rate (an occasional useful indicator of business and credit conditions) does not play a key role in constraining and otherwise influencing capital expenditures.

3. The apparent foregoing inconsistency may be rectified by making the analysis more dynamic and by modifying of the Keynesian view of the link between the rate of interest and capital spending by business firms, such that we see the interest rate as being determined more by the expected rate of inflation and demand side changes rather than say open market operations by the Federal Reserve. Later the Keynesian link between the rate of interest and capital spending is shown to relate more to housing expenditures than to industrial-sector expenditures.

4. In dynamic analysis we are concerned with shifts in the schedules obtained under static conditions and with allowing those things to change that do in fact change. In a period of accelerated growth in capital spending, for example, the investment demand schedule is shifting outward and the interest rate is rising, as observed to be the more common condition for the post-World War II years. However, the slope property of the downward sloping MEC schedule may come into play in response to an overwhelming pull toward normality, as may occur at the peak of business conditions, following upward shifts in the schedule.

5. The government has several tools for influencing capital spending, including changes in the corporate income tax rate, accelerated depreciation, and the tax credit. A reduction in the corporate income tax rate normally raises the flow of returns (other things being equal) and the rate of return in the supply price (or cost) expression. A faster write-off for depreciation can alter the distribution of future returns and therefore raise the rate of return, while a larger tax credit increases the return during the first year of the life of the new asset. All of the measures shift the marginal efficiency of capital schedule outward (or outward at a faster

rate). Abel concludes in such matters that an investment tax credit can lead to more capital spending at a smaller cost in revenue to the Treasury than a cut in the corporate income tax rate.

6. Uncertainty about the future flow of returns from a capital goods project may also enter the analysis of capital spending via the supply price (cost) expression. This uncertainty can be a general uncertainty about the future, and it can be uncertainty about the inflation rate forecast. Either sort of uncertainty can be expressed in the present context by assigning weights or probabilities to the prospective returns. Greater uncertainty, as may be engendered by the prospect of a renewal of the inflationary recession phenomenon in a near future, would lower the rate of return on capital expenditures. It would show up as a restraint to the outward movement of the MEC schedule. In closely related analysis, Bisignano reports that uncertainty with respect to anticipated inflation reduces the demand for investment goods in manufacturing, and that it leads to a substitution of some additional labor and utilization of existing productive capacity.

7. The theory treats firms as maximizing the flow returns (net of all costs, except the cost of borrowing), after allowing for subjective elements such as uncertainty. In one case, the maximization analysis leads to a rule: for maximum returns, the rates of return on additions to alternative classes or assets should be equal. A similar rule applies for the cost of financing and interest rates. These rate of return and interest rate rules hold as first approximations, even in a dynamic context. However, there are real-world complications: the interest rate is not simply controlled by the Federal Reserve, Fisher's equation may be introduced, and rates of return and interest are not independent of one another, since both may respond to the prospect of inflation.

8. In the dynamic analysis that more nearly grapples with observable phenomena, we encounter rates of change in stock and flow quantities. To arrive at this point we do not abandon static methods, but rather alter the use and treatment of them.

9. Even the treatment of lagged relationships between variables calls for more dynamic consideration. There is the fundamental question of whether lag patterns are fixed. Statistical results have suggested variation in lag patterns and a change in the structure of relationships over time. Sources of structural change may encompass different social and political trends and different phases of business conditions. In statistical estimation of parameters, these structural changes are not viewed as the behavior of a random variable, but rather they are seen to be more permanent changes.

10. Anticipated effects of monetary policy may have a more immediate effect (less lag time) than unexpected effects. For example, the announcement of monetary policy plans, as under House Concurrent Resolution 133, may be expected to alter the lag time between changes in monetary and credit aggregates and their influences. The extent of announced

effects, with the passage of time, may depend on the Federal Reserve's credibility, based on the difference between previously announced policies and the actual, ex post value for the monetary aggregate.

11. Examination of notions of liquidity, financial planning, and the money stock and budgeting in light of the investment demand building block suggests that liquid assets, the money stock, capital appropriations, and contracts for new orders are leading indicators of business conditions. Measures of capacity utilization also occasionally lead changes in the business cycle.

FOOTNOTES

1. The predominance of the large firms in the total picture of manufacturing firms is partly indicated by the following facts: In the U.S. in the final quarter of 1977, the 174 largest manufacturing corporations owned 62 percent of the assets of all manufacturing corporations with assets of $10 million and over, whereas 4,993 manufacturing corporations with assets below $10 million owned only 19 percent of the amount of the assets owned by the 174 largest. See Federal Trade Commission, Quarterly Financial Report for Manufacturing, Mining, and Trade Corporations, Fourth Quarter 1977.
2. In the detail provided by overall and split sample periods, the relationships between sales of manufacturing and trade ($S_{M\&T}$) establishments and GNP in current dollars (after a logarithmic transformation of the data) are as follows:

Period 1954:I through 1975:IV

$$\ln S_{M\&T} = 6.54 + \underset{(99.21)}{0.89} \ln GNP, \quad r^2 = 0.99$$

Period 1954:I through 1960:IV

$$\ln S_{M\&T} = 7.17 + \underset{(21.35)}{0.80} \ln GNP, \quad r^2 = 0.94$$

Period 1961:I through 1970:IV

$$\ln S_{M\&T} = 6.66 + \underset{(86.38)}{0.87} \ln GNP, \quad r^2 = 0.99$$

Period 1971:I through 1975:IV

$$\ln S_{M\&T} = 3.83 + 1.28 \ln GNP, \; r^2 = 0.98$$
$$(33.77)$$
(t-values in parentheses)

The coefficients of determination (r^2) indicate that from 94 to 99 percent of the variation in sales is accounted for by variation in GNP per quarter at an annual rate for the periods covered. (Source of data: The two series of data are numbers 56 and 200 from Handbook of Cyclical Indicators: A Supplement to Business Conditions Digest, U.S. Department of Commerce, Bureau of Economic Analysis, May 1977.)

3. The Conference Board's time series for newly approved capital appropriations (1,000 manufacturing corporations) and for capital appropriations appear (as series 11 and 97 respectively) in the U.S. Department of Commerce's Handbook of Cyclical Indicators (see note 2).

4. By the rate of return on capital we mean the rate for relating the prospective flow of returns (net of all costs except interest cost) from capital outlays to the cost (or supply price) of the capital outlays. In the case of a perpetual flow of returns of a given magnitude ($R_1 = R_2 = R_3 = \ldots = R_n$, $n \to \infty$ or 30 years), this rate will be the Lagrangian multiplier, initially shown in section 3.3. Some writers prefer to distinguish between the rate of return on capital and the marginal efficiency of capital (or investment in capital), where the rate of return refers to the rate in the context of a single firm's capital budgeting, and where the marginal efficiency of capital (MEC or MEI), refers to the rate for capital outlays for society as a whole (i.e., for total capital spending). The latter is then said to be embodied in the schedule (or function) relating "the rate" to total dollar amount of capital spending. However, we do not try to make such distinction for the rates. In addition, in aggregating firms' schedules to get a total investment demand, we would not be altering the rates of return usually depicted on the vertical axes. Note:

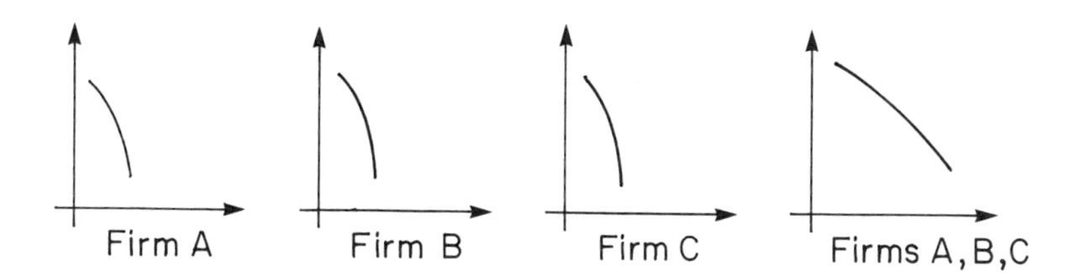

Irving Fisher used "rate of return" and Keynes, "marginal efficiency of capital" to refer to the identical substantive phenomenon.

5. Keynes was especially interested in the long-term interest rate as it may be controlled through open market operations by the Federal Reserve, and there was in his day no attention at all given to the prospect that anticipated growth in the money stock would influence inflationary expectations and hence interest rates. The liquidity preference construction in Keynes's work envisions an open market purchase (sale) that raises (lowers) bond prices and hence lowers (raises the market rate of interest in a very precise way (Keynes 1936, 197-98). Forwarding notes on the proofs of the General Theory in 1935, D. H. Robertson also considers "open-market purchases, designed to lower the rate of interest" (Moggridge 1973a, 499). In writing to R. F. Harrod about Harrod's The Trade Cycle, Keynes again refers to open market operations, with reference to purchases in the short-term vis-à-vis the long-term sector of the market (Moggridge 1973b, 153).

   Mullineaux (1977, 3-12) presents results which suggest that anticipated growth in the money stock has become more a determinant of expected inflation since widespread attention in the financial press has been diverted to it. In his day, Keynes (1936, 198) gave attention to the effects of news about policy, only he had the news working directly on the interest rate via expectations of future changes in the interest rate.

6. Sir Roy Harrod, Keynes's biographer (The Life of John Maynard Keynes, 1951), was to recognize over thirty years later how crucial Keynes's point was about not having anticipated inflation's impact on both the nominal rate of interest and the relative value of contractual and residual claim assets (as introduced in section 3.3 earlier). Harrod was to say:

> "What the new-found anticipation does is to change the relative values of money-denominated assets on the one side and equities and real estate on the other...
>
> "The idea that a new-found expectation can alter the relative value of two money-denominated assets is logically impossible, and must not be accepted into the corpus of economic theory....
>
> "The occurrence of a new-found belief firmly held, that a certain rate of inflation will occur, cannot affect the rate of interest. But the growth of uncertainty about what rate of inflation, if any, is in prospect, can send up the rate of interest." (1971, 62)

In contrast to this last statement, increased uncertainty about the inflation rate was shown to reduce the interest rate rather than raise it (compare figures 5-9 and 5-10).

7. The tendency for capital spending to vary roughly in phase with business conditions is also reflected in a tendency for expenditures on new plant and equipment (for all domestic private business except farming, real estate, the professions, and non profit membership institutions) to vary directly with GNP.

   Period 1961:I through 1970:IV

   $$\ln GNP = 3.63 + \underset{(36.6)}{0.74} \ln I, \quad r^2 = 0.97$$

   Period 1971:I through 1975:IV

   $$\ln GNP = 2.76 + \underset{(17.82)}{0.96} \ln I, \quad r^2 = 0.95$$

   Both of the series are provided by the Department of Commerce and reported as series 200 and 61 respectively in the May 1977 Handbook of Cyclical Indicators.

8. The term "capacity" may be defined as "the quantity of output that can be produced in a fixed period of time, given the existing stock of capital." In the case of an engineering interpretation there is the idea that production occurs around the clock, seven days a week. The most common interpretation about the period of utilization, and the one used in reference to the BEA and FRB measures, is that of normal, average, or typical conditions. The utilization rate (percent of total capacity) provided by BEA is based on a survey of the percentage of capacity at which firms report they are operating. The FRB uses this and additional information. For further discussion of measurements of capacity and utilization rates, see Ragan (1976) and Raddock (1979).

SELECTED READINGS AND REFERENCES

Abel, Andrew B. 1978. Tax Incentives to Investment: An Assessment of Tax Credits and Tax Cuts. New England Economic Review (November/December).

Bisignano, Joseph. 1978. "Inflationary Expectations and Factor Demands in Manufacturing." Economic Review, Federal Reserve Bank of San Francisco (Fall).

Commerce, U.S. Department of. 1976. Business Conditions Digest, new Revised Edition (November).

Cooley, Thomas F., and Edward C. Prescott. 1976. "Estimation in the Presence of Stochastic Parameter Variation." Econometrica (January).

Fisher, Irving. 1896. Appreciation and Interest. New York: Macmillan.

Frazer, William. 1958. "Some Factors Affecting Business Financing." Southern Economic Journal (July).

__________. 1967. The Demand for Money. Cleveland, Ohio: The World Publishing Company. Chapter 7.

__________. 1973. Crisis in Economic Theory. Gainesville, Fla.: University of Florida Press. Chapters 5 and 15.

__________. 1978. "Evolutionary Economics, Rational Expectations, and Monetary Policy." Journal of Economic Issues (June).

Grossman, Elliot S. 1975. "Getting a Better Bead on a Leading Indicator." The Conference Board Record (March).

Harrod, Roy. 1911. "Discussion Paper." In J. C. Gilbert and R. Sedgewick, eds. Monetary Theory and Monetary Policy in the 1970's. Oxford: Oxford University Press.

Keynes, John Maynard. 1936. The General Theory of Employment, Interest and Money. New York: Harcourt, Brace and Company. Chapters 11 and 17.

McElhattan, Rose. 1978. "Estimating a Stable-Inflation Capacity-Utilization Rate." Economic Review, Federal Reserve Bank of San Francisco (Fall).

Moggridge, Donald, ed. 1973a. The Collected Writings of John Maynard Keynes, Volume XIII. London: Macmillan, St. Martin's Press.

__________. 1973b. The Collected Writings of John Maynard Keynes, Volume XIV. London: Macmillan, St. Martin's Press.

Mullineaux. 1977. "Inflationary Expectations in the U.S.: A Brief Anatomy." Business Review, Federal Reserve Bank of Philadelphia (July/August).

Raddock, Richard. 1979. "Revision of Capacity Utilization Rate." Federal Reserve Bulletin (August).

Ragan, James F. 1976. "Measuring Capacity Utilization in Manufacturing." Quarterly Review, Federal Reserve Bank of New York (Winter).

Wonnacott, Paul. 1974. Macroeconomics. Homewood, Ill.: Richard D. Irwin, Inc. Chapters 4 and 14.

Chapter 9

The Household Sector: Home Construction and the Dynamic Consumption Function

9.1. Introduction

In chapter 8 we considered the market rate of interest ($i = i_{real}$ + const./σ 1/P dP*/dt) and the equality/inequality of the rate of interest and the rate of return ($i = r$). In doing so, we touched upon a crucial point about the received economic theory and the control mechanism found in that theory. And, in touching upon the crucial point, we indicated the significance for redirection of the theory, by having the rate of interest and the rate of return tied to some common force (the inflation rate). Now, both of these formulations that were considered earlier (the market rate and the equality/inequality of i and r) have a long history in economic theory with considerable struggle and vacillation as to the appropriate formulation (Keynes 1950a, 155, 197, 207, 212; Keynes 1950b, 206-07; Keynes 1936, 242-43; Moggridge 1973a, 253-54, 479; Moggridge 1973b, 431n; Patinkin 1965, 581-97; Patinkin 1976, 36, 47-9; Patinkin and Leith 1978, 5-6, 136). First, i_{real} = i - const./σ 1/P dP*/dt and this real rate (i_{real}) turns out to be roughly equivalent to what has historically been treated as the "natural rate of interest," namely: the natural rate is equivalent to the market rate, given constant relative prices (including the purchasing power of money), where the rate of interest is defined as the rate of exchange between any good now and the same good a year later. Further, changes in relative prices were treated in the appendix to chapter 1 (figure A1-2) and related to price indexes and the inflation rate there and in section 6.4.

Next, Keynes, at times with antecedents sometimes associated with the Swedish economists Knut Wicksell (1851-1926), almost equated the "natural" rate with the rate of return on capital. Specifically he (1950a, 154-155) called the natural rate the rate that would preserve the equality between the flow of saving and the flow of investment.

As it turns out, in this history of theory, three things happened:

1. The natural rate and consequently its equivalent (the real rate) may be drawn from relatively pure exercises in the theory of consumer behavior.

2. Milton Friedman originally introduced that theory in the framework of his permanent income determinaton of consumption (Friedman 1957).

3. An affinity is established between the natural rate of interest and the natural rate of unemployment (Frazer 1977, 54-57).

The natural rate of unemployment has been defined as the rate of unemployment conducive to price level stability. In some measure, Friedman backs into the definition of the natural rate of unemployment, without clearly establishing the basis for his doing so, as found in the work of Wicksell. However, what emerges from the sort of approach found in Friedman's work, with reference to these "natural" concepts, is a far more dynamic and extended treatment than the forebears had in mind. For one thing, the natural magnitudes are themselves variable (say, quasi-permanent), and subject to control by government (sect. 11.5), apart from the Keynesian control through demand management. Keynes (1936, 242-243) had recognized this variability and indeed it can in fact be seen in figures 5-10, 5-11, and 5-12. Only now, in the dynamic context, something is added, notably: the idea of the natural magnitudes as smoothed (quasi-permanent), secular time paths. These secular time paths can be altered, as noted and as considered in later chapters with attention to detail. Even so, adding the new dimension offers new insights and control prospects.

This foregoing alteration in approach is readily seen from the following exercise. First, note Frisch's restatement of Wicksell's use of the term:

> So long as the market rate of interest is maintained at a level below the natural rate, the general price level will be increasing all the time, and the increase will be faster the greater the difference between the market rate and the normal rate. (Frische 1952, 690)

Next, recall

$$i_{real} = i - const./\sigma \ 1/P \ dP/dt$$

and

$$i = i_{real} + const./\sigma \ 1/P \ dP/dt$$

Now, in the presence of inflation, there is no way to reduce the market rate of interest below the "natural" (the real) rate. Indeed, the inflation raises the market rate above the natural rate, and the entire control mechanism in the history of modern economic theory is altered.

From the control point of view, the control is shown to operate via its influence over the outlook for business conditions (and inflationary prospects in particular) and to impinge upon the demand side (and expectations aspects) of the markets for goods and services primarily ($\Delta\dot{M} \rightarrow \Delta\dot{Y} \rightarrow \Delta i$ as well as $\Delta\dot{M} \rightarrow \Delta i$, where $\Delta\dot{M}$ is announced in advance and $i = i_{real} + const./\sigma \ 1/P \ dP/dt$). This is in contrast to the Keynesian linkage $\Delta M \rightarrow -\Delta i \rightarrow \Delta I$, but there are some special aspects of home construction that should be singled out. Further, the control time frames are different too. The Friedmanian one is control within an extended time frame, and the Keynesian one is control at a point (fig. 4-1).

This traversing to get at the current theoretical framework is not entirely as laid out by Friedman. Friedman comes to contribute to redirection, and, in this chapter, one encounters the crucial function, $C = k \ Y_p$, where Y_p is permanent income and k is a factor of proportionality. A main theme is that the ratio C/Y_p is predominantly constant (quasi-permanent), but the factor k can vary. One also encounters Friedman's use of Fisher's theory of the rate of interest that is at the same time compatible with notions about the permanent magnitudes, the non-inflationary rate of interest, and the economic theory of exhaustible resources (sect. 16.6). One factor contributing to the variation in k, $C = k \ Y_p$, is the rate of interest. The rate introduced by Friedman, however, is more of a rate of interest that induces switching between present and future consumption in a secular time frame, as elucidated in section 9.4. This is quite different from but not unrelated to the market rate found in the shorter time frame and treated along with the liquidity preference demand for money with overshooting (sects. 5-4 and 6-4).

The foregoing topics about interest rates and consumption have until recent times been topics of relatively pure economic theory. In what follows, nevertheless, some somewhat less pure topics in the area of consumer behavior precede the final consideration of the consumption function, the permanent income hypothesis, and the time preference theory of the rate of interest.

9.2. Secular Change, Household Spending, and Home Construction

Keynes's consumption function was introduced earlier (sect. 7.2). As discussed by Keynes, its non-axiomatic and behavioral nature was mentioned. Among other things, the problem of distinguishing consumption and investment expenditures was mentioned along with that of distinguishing sectors along behavioral lines (sect. 7.2). In this chapter, these problems are dealt with by considering consumption as a part of households' spending patterns. Both consumption and capital expenditures play important roles in the Keynesian economics of post-World War II years, and both are brought forward as a still relevant part of economic theory.

In dealing with spending by the household sector on either strictly consumerable items or on housing with its consumerable services, one could note its dependence on a whole host of variables at both the micro- and macro-economic levels such as average age of the population, family composition, location of resident whether (urban or rural), education, and distribution of income. However, some simplification is necessary, in useful and relevant theory, and especially at the macro-level at which we proceed. With this in mind, we abstract from most of the detailed considerations and emphasize primarily income, the interest rate, and some aspects of expectations. In the later sections of the chapter, we proceed with wealth (permanent or, actually, quasi-permanent income), interest rates, and expectations as a part of a more highly dynamic theory about consumption. The theory there falls under the classification of wealth theories of consumer behavior.

The study of spending behavior [and, therefore, saving behavior, since $S(Y) = Y - C(Y)$] by households in relation to income was among the first topics in Keynesian economics to undergo widespread and intensive empirical study. As a persual of Thomas Mayer's book (1972) indicates, the consumption function has been one of the most extensively studied relations in economics. Although most of this early study pre-dates the research undertaken since the widespread use of the modern electronic computer, particularly in the 1960's, it retains its relevance and viability. This would be true especially when the consumption function is recast in a more general setting of household spending and in its subsequent dynamic form. Both facilitate a way of thinking about household behavior. And, in addition, as brought out in chapters 10 and 11, traces of reasoning about the simple consumption function still enter into thinking and policy matters concerning tax cuts, the progressive feature of the tax structure, and government induced changes in the distribution of income.

A review of some aspects of short-run changes, secular trends, household spending on durable and non-durable goods, and home construction provides background with which we may view in better perspective some aspects of economic behavior and the consumption function in particular. As on earlier occasions, we proceed by emphasizing an underlying time path, departures from it, and by establishing a tie with the basic mechanics of economics.

Short-run Changes and Secular Trend

In chapters 5 and 6, attention was directed toward rates of change in stock and flow quantites, and the idea of an underlying growth path for such aggregates as money, bank reserves, assets, and income. Such a trend path was first shown for income (in constant prices) in figure 3-1, and it may be viewed as the trend path for a locus of solution values for the small equation system comprising the Keynesian two-sector model from chapter 7. Such a trend path is also a solution to the Domar model (Domar 1946, 137-47) of three equations and three unknowns:

$$\bar{S}(t) = k\,\bar{Y}\,(t)$$

$$\bar{I}(t) - g\,\frac{d\bar{Y}(t)}{dt}$$

$$\bar{S}(t) = \bar{I}(t),\ k > 0,\ g > 0$$

where the earlier equilibrium values for saving ($\bar{S}$), income ($\bar{Y}$) and investment ($\bar{I}$) are denoted as functions of time.[1]

The solution is

$$\bar{Y} = ae^{k/g\ t}$$

where $\underline{a}$ is $\bar{Y}_o$ (or initial value for income) and $\underline{e}$ is the calculus constant (2.7) for growth. Taking the logarithm of both sides of the latter growth equation,

$$\ln \bar{Y} = \ln a + \ln e^{k/g\ t}$$

$$= \ln \bar{Y}_o + k/g\ t \ln e$$

$$= \ln \bar{Y}_o + k/g\ t$$

This is the same form as found in the growth equations in chapter 5 and in discussion surrounding figure 3-1,[2] where in the present case k/g is the growth rate (x 100, for percentage).

By varying the parameter values relating to income and to the rate of change in income (i.e., by varying k and g) fluctuations about the trend path in figure 3-1 may be generated. Thus clearly, the treatment of income as an equilibrium (Y) in the two-sector model with levels (rather than rates of change) for flow quantities cannot represent any balancing of forces as the term "equilibrium" was originally used in mechanics. When we begin to change the earlier stock and flow quantities at constant rates, however, we do get trend paths about which the changes in business conditions occur. These have been called equilibrium time paths or sustainable growths paths. The switch from the discussion of levels to rates of change makes the basic theory more relevant in a sense but it also advances the subject in a more dynamic direction.

Referring back to the two-sector model of chapter 7, we would have the aggregate demand line of figure 7-2 shifting upward by larger and larger amounts to generate the locus of equilibrium points in figure 3-1. Changes in the rate of change in the expenditure line of figure 7-2, such that it accelerated and then declerated, would cause fluctations in output about a trend line as in figure 3-1. One idea is for these changes to reflect a greater volatility in investment and total spending than in the consumption function such that the ensuing changes in income in turn cause some changes along Keynes's consumption function. Even so, shifts in the consumption function are possible also and indeed typical in the dynamic version of the model.

One way of considering the shifting, simple function is in terms of an adaptive expectations model. What the adaptive expectations model does, as set forth in a later section of this chapter, is to focus on a constantly shifting Keynesian consumption function. What we add is variation in income and only lesser variation in the function line, such that the retardation of income leads to a slower decline in consumption. When this happens in actual practice, empiricists tend to distinguish between non-durable and more durable sorts of goods such as household appliances and automobiles. Such a distinction in the empirical data reveals that the durable goods are most sensitive to income changes than retail sales generally. Durable goods may be postponed more readily, and repairs can be made to render the existing appliances and the transportation equipment usable for a longer period of time.

Durable Goods and Installment Debt

The tendency for durable goods purchases to be volatile and postponable is reflected in time series for new orders placed with durable goods industries, as shown in figure 9-1a. There we see that the new orders decline ordinarily long before a recession (as delineated by National Bureau turning points) and well into a recession. This would usually be true in nominal terms, but the distinction between nominal and real (or constant dollar) terms becomes important at times, especially in the presence of an inflationary recession such as that of 1973-75 (as dealt with in later chapters). For the present, no stress is placed on the distinction between nominal and real income as it may exist in the minds of consumers.

The tendency for durable goods orders to vary as just described--even while serving as a leading indicator of business conditions--reveals even more than indicated, when considered along with consumer installment debt and the interest rates in figure 5-3. The consumer installment debt is of the type used to finance the purchase of durable goods. A time series for it (as plotted against a logarithmic scale) is shown in figure 9-1b. It too serves as a leading indicator and, at the same time, reveals largely pro-cyclical characteristics. What this behavior signifies in conjunction with interest rate behavior for most of the post-World War II years, prior to the unusual interest rate behavior of the 1970s, is that the contraction (expansion) of the debt leads the decline (rise) in interest rates and that it tends to expand most when interest rates are rising.

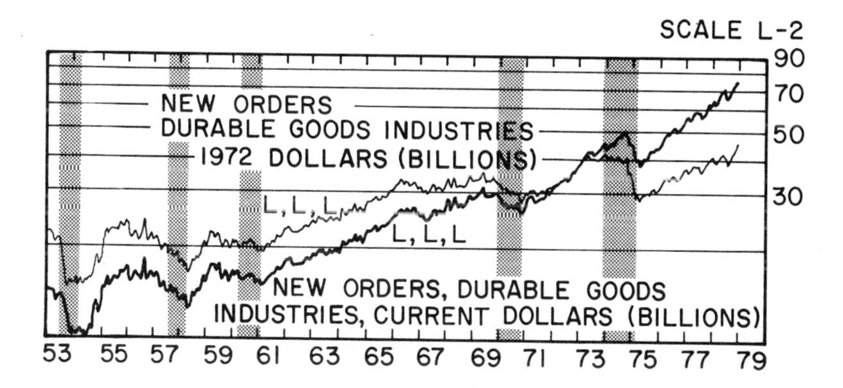

Figure 9-1a. New Orders, Durable Goods Industries

Source: U.S. Department of Commerce, Business Conditions Digest (1976).

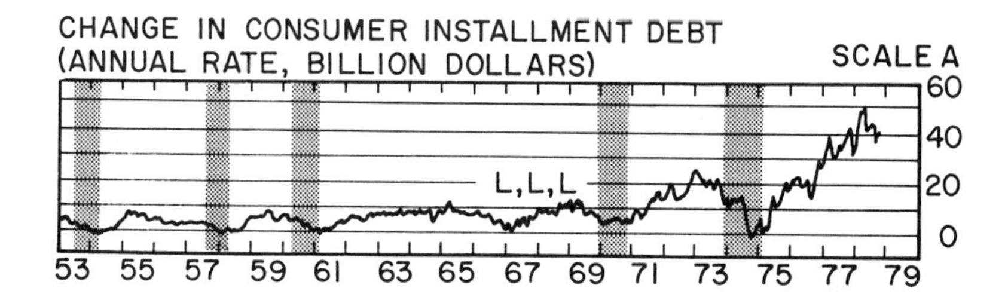

Figure 9-1b. Changes in Consumer Installment Debt

Source: U.S. Department of Commerce, Business Conditions Digest (1976).

Home Construction

The purchase of housing for the vast majority of households is the largest single outlay they make, and the debt instrument involved (the mortgage) has a longer time to maturity than installment contracts for durable goods purchases. This means--as earlier mechanics of interest rate changes suggest--that a given change in the interest rate on a new mortgage increases the monthly payments considerably more than for a short-maturity instrument of the type that may be used. Consequently, we may look for different effects of interest rate changes in this sphere of economic behavior. Further, inflation and rising energy cost (chap. 16) hold implications for the housing market, as they may work through the interest rate, the Federal capital gains tax as it relates to housing, and the cost and value of housing. This would be especially true when one considers tax measures and features of the progressive income tax (chaps. 10 and 11).

In some respects, a home purchase is like a capital expenditure by a firm, and in both cases the interest cost of debt financing is deductible for income tax purposes. Important differences center about (1) the tendency for government to stress the welfare aspects of decent housing and to give a high priority to it as a part of other social programs, (2) the strong tendency toward the financial planning of capital expenditures by large firms (sect. 8.3), (3) the progressive feature of the personal income tax, and (4) the treatment of realized capital gains from the sale of housing. On occasions the government programs in conjunction with special features of financial markets have actually contributed to instability in housing expenditures. Housing industry spokesmen have said after such occasions that the government uses the housing industry as a means of trying to stabilize other dimensions of business conditions. Such government programs are mentioned below, along with other features about the financial markets and the purchase of housing.

The instability of home construction has been an incontestable feature of it. There has been a tendency for it to move out of phase with business condition (say, as indicated by the rate of interest prior to the dominance of the inflationary recession phenomenum in 1969-70 and 1973-75), and to serve as a major leading indicator of recovery from a recession.

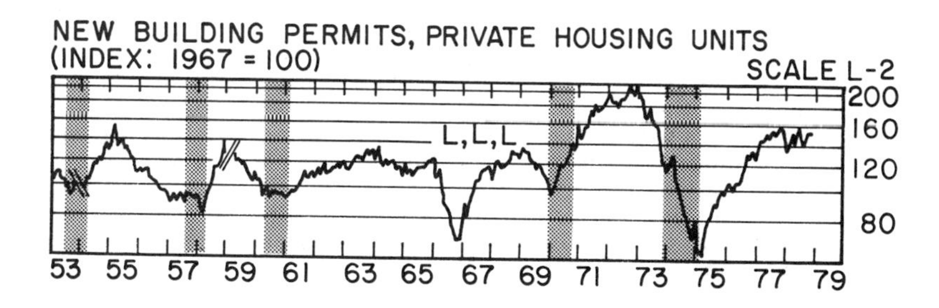

Figure 9-2. New Building Permits, Private Housing Units.

Source: U.S. Department of Commerce, Business Conditions Digest (1976).

The tendency for home construction to pull the economy out of recession and then to level off as interest rates rise is reflected in another leading indicator--namely that for new building permits--as shown in figure 9-2, for most of the post-World War II years. A perverse behavior appears in the presence of the unusual inflationary recession of 1973-75. Two conclusions are suggested, namely: (1) home construction fairs poorly in the presence of a recession with inflation, probably because of a sizable inflationary component in the interest rate; and (2) home construction will for the most part vary inversely with the interest rate over the cycle.[3] This is consistent with the variation depicted in a static Keynesian investment demand relation.

This tendency toward an inverse variation in interest rates and home construction led Keynesians to point to housing as the example of the influence of interest rates on capital spending--all as in Keynes's two asset model and in the closely relation Keynesian investment demand model. As one will recall from chapters 4, 5, and 8, the Federal Reserve raised and lowered the rate of interest at its pleasure and, other things being equal, capital spending varied inversely in the Keynesian view. The relationship is possibly more complex in its detail. Even so, an immediate reaction may be to question why the Keynesians went to the extreme of choosing such a welfare oriented class of capital spending to illustrate what was essentially to be a control over spending by firms with a relatively free market orientation.

Background on Home Financing

Home financing as we know it today (with small downpayments and long maturity dates on the mortgages, i.e., on the financial instrument) evolved mainly out the 1930s. Savings banks were an early source of funds for home construction in the North Eastern region of the United States, but Savings and Loan Associations (S and L's) evolved as the most specialized source of funds for home construction. Commerical banks have entered the field to some extent, home improvement loans have become widespread, and one has encountered proposals about extending to S and L's the unique money and credit creating features of commerical banks. In March 1980, Congress in fact passed a bill allowing all insured banks, credit unions, and savings and loan associations to offer checking accounts that earn interest. The bill, effective at year-end 1980, blurred even further the historical distinction between S and L's and commercial banks.

In addition, to the new issues mortgage market, there has evolved a secondary mortgage market. The government has guided the development of this market with the view of facilitating trading in mortgages to help make them more liquid, and to indirectly supply new funds to the institutions originating mortgages such as the S and L's. This active support of the mortgage market was first undertaken through the reorganization of the Federal National Mortgage Association ("Fannie Mae") in 1954 and later in 1968 through the Government National Mortgage Association (GNMA). GNMA secures funds through the sale of its own securities, and supports the mortgage market by supplying funds to it and hence increasing the liquidity of mortgages. In 1975 a futures market, of the type considered later in chapter 12, was inaugurated for the financial instruments of GNMA, with the idea of attracting even more investors to the financing of housing (Froeuiss 1978).

The special features of governmental regulation in the mortgage, home financing area that one needs to mention, as background for some history of the interest rate linkage mechanism, include FHA insured and VA guaranteed mortgages, as well as the Federal Reserve's Regulation Q. Under these government insured and guaranteed mortgage programs, as they emerged from the 1930s and World War II respectively, the government set the ceiling on the interest rate for financing. Similarily interest rate ceilings for savings deposits and share accounts at selected classes of financial institutions were set also. This has been under Regulation Q. However, effective over a six-year period beginning in 1980, banks, credit unions and savings and loan associations have been freed to pay savers whatever rate of interest they want to pay.

Against the historical background, before the change just mentioned, an inverse relation between the interest rate and home construction may be explained. Market interest rates, including that on conventional (as opposed to FHA insured and VA guaranteed) mortgages, would start to rise. Two related changes would follow: (1) credit granting institutions would reduce the purchase of the relatively low yield mortgages, and (2) a shift from savings type deposits to higher yielding means of savings on the part of the depositors would reduce the flow of funds for home construction. For this S and L segment of the financial markets we have an example of what was called disintermediation in chapter 3.

Originally the ceilings on deposit interest rates were intended as a means of regulating competition between selected financial institutions. In the 1960s, in any event, the ceilings were varied and a greater flexibility emerged as a means of coping with what we have just outlined (Frazer 1968, 182-184). Despite the foregoing, however, the roughly inverse relation between the interest rate and new housing units has still persisted in some measure. Only now the reasoning is different, it centers about market rates irrespective of the ceilings, and occasionally active support in the secondary market has added influence. In this new explanation, as in the past, a rise in interest rates adds a considerable amount to household's monthly payment on a new house,[4] and its income becomes an effective constraint on the house the average family can purchase. The added feature for accounting for a different capital spending pattern for households, as distinct from large industrial concerns, however, is the recognition of the absence of planning, especially planning to avoid the constraining effect of rising interest rates. The role of liquidity and financial planning with respect to this objective was reviewed in section 3.2 (note 7).

Some of what we have said about housing, social programs, and the role of housing as a leading indicator of business conditions reflects a conventional orientation toward the matters in the post-World War II years through the early 1970s. This is quite adequate for appraising the behavior and theory about the interest linkage, but the conventional orientation may be misleading as an aid to formulating a perspective on the future in some crucial respects. Namely, the old patterns and optimistic social goals are complicated by the phenomenum of an inflationary recession, by the energy crisis, and by the phenomenum of the monetization of housing. The presence of inflation in a recession means that interest rates do not adjust downward in the degree attained in ordinary, more historical recessions. This slowness in adjustment means that home construction cannot be relied upon to help pull the economy out of recession, as in the non-inflationary recession, and inflation in recession contributes to a prolonging of recession.

The energy crisis (sect. 2.4, and chap. 16) heralded a new era--a change in the more secular outlook for housing as well as for other aspects of spending for household operations and maintenance. It meant an erosion of the standard of living that was based on low-cost energy, and gave rise to the prospect that the average American family could no longer look forward to the ownership and operation of a single family home.

The monetization of housing, as described below, comes about in a world that may be characterized by accelerating housing costs, inflation generally, and a tendency for income taxes to rise more rapidly than income. The combination means appreciation in housing values, on the one hand, and gives advantage to having an income tax deduction in the form of large interest payments, on the other. Ordinarily, as interest rates would rise, as in 1978, the home construction business would fare poorly, but with the combination of circumstances just mentioned, speculation in home purchases becomes a good deal for those who can afford it.

The Monetization of Housing

The secular rise in inflation after 1965 contributed to both the rise in the monthly interest payment on new home mortgages and to the purchase price of old and new housing, and it ultimately led to a peculiar phenomenum, namely, a tendency toward the monetization of housing. The monetization works as follows. The inflation raises the value of existing homes, such that they may be sold to yield a cash sum to the home owner that is above the sum of the owners payments toward an equity in the new house. A sale will monetize (yield cash sum of) this equity plus appreciation. A fraction of the equity and the realized appreciation (a capital gain) may be used as payment on a more expensive home, and a liquid balance remains for other use, although there has been a Federal tax (at a preferential rate) on a capital gain from a housing sale unless the full proceeds of the sale are reinvested in other assets.[5] The new mortgage payments are now larger, of course, but the larger payments (especially, in the early years of a new mortgage) are deductible from income for tax purposes. The benefits of this deduction, moreover, increase as two other changes occur: (1) as a rising nominal income places the homeowner in a higher income tax bracket, and (2) as government makes and proposes the extension of the progressive feature of the income for the middle class through tax cuts and proposals (as in 1964, 1975, and 1978, as considered in chapter 11).

The inflation, rising costs, and tax features have other interrelated effects that extend to a consideration of "Proposition 13" of section 10.3. Single family housing gets priced out of the market for low income families, and the mix in the construction of single family and multi-unit housing changes.

As a part of a response to the taxpayers revolt described in section 10.3, including with national dimensions, the Federal government's tax bill for 1979 increased the preferential treatment on the taxation of the capital gain from home sales. There were some complexities and lower rates, but the 1979 bill reduced the top rate on individual capital gains (profits from the sale of stock, real estate and other capital assets) from 49 percent to 28 percent. The bottom rate on gains was cut from 7 percent to 5.6 percent and there were rate cuts in between the top and bottom rates. Next, the 1979 bill contained changes that permitted a person 55 years of age and older to avoid capital gains taxation up to $100,000 of gains on the sale of an owned home, occupied for 3 of the past 5 years. The provision was retained that has permitted the avoidance of capital gains taxes all together where someone buys a new home within 18 months and pays as much as he obtains from the sale of the old home.

9.3. The Consumption Function

The consumption function is difficult to write about for several reasons: (1) partly because so much has been written on the subject; (2) partly because of at least some instability in most of the mechanical relationships in economics, even after numerous additional variables are added; (3) partly because of a tendency to introduce a psychology of spending ("habits," adaptation," "emulation") in the tradition of Thorstein Veblen (1899; and Duesenberry 1952); and (4) partly because of the role of both cross-section studies and time-series studies in economics. In the history of economics there has been a rationale for using statistical results from cross-section studies as if they suggest long-run relations. Even so, sometimes the cross-section studies may have bearing on the long run (as in the case from section 8.4), and sometimes they may not have a direct bearing (as in the case of the simple consumption function). In addition, in the case of consumption function studies one encounters an admixture of thinking: (a) about households with more of less income on a cross-section basis, (b) about households with incomes changing over time, and (c) about changes in aggregate consumer spending and income over time.

Several hypotheses about consumption abound. These include the absolute income hypothesis and the relative income hypothesis, and the permanent income hypothesis. These hypotheses are not inconsistent with one another, and indeed tend to salvage Keynes's original statement and make the whole subject more dynamic.

The Absolute Income Hypothesis

Keynes referred to his basic consumption relation as a fundamental psychological law (sects. 3.2, and 7.2). With some embellishment, it goes as follows: As income increases (decreases) consumption increases (decreases), but less (more) than in proportion to income. There is the idea of habits and a standard of living such that as income temporarily declines, consumption continues at a level that consumer units have become accustomed to. The maintenance of this previous standard may be financed in some measure by increasing consumer debt and/or by drawing down on savings that have been accumulated from previous income. Milton Friedman adds to the prospect of the workings of this law in strictly empirical terms by noting that some income recipients may not be "permanently" high or low, and indeed may be temporarily experiencing extra large income. Some writers, actors, actresses, TV personalities, movie producers, professional athletes, football coaches, promoters of new ventures, corporate executives at the higher eschelon, casino gamblers, pornographers, wildcatters, and risk takers generally may be among these.

As we have seen, Keynes's function may be stated

$$C = f(Y),\ o < \frac{dC}{dY} < 1$$

and the slope of the saving function is

$$\frac{dS}{dY} = 1 - \frac{dC}{dY}$$

In early empirical studies, the saving function as a complement of the consumption function often received attention. One form of representing the absolute income hypothesis was

$$S = a + bY + cZ + u$$

where, in addition to variables defined earlier, Z is a conglomerate of other variables, u is the random error term, and

$$\frac{dS}{dY} = b = 1 - \frac{dC}{dY}$$

The less the slope of the consumption function, the greater the slope of the saving function, and vice versa. Saving as a proportion of income and as a function of income was studied as well, e.g.,

$$\frac{S}{Y} = a' + b'\ Y + c'\ Z + u$$

In studying these relationships both cross-section (budget) and time series data have been used. As empirical study evolved, the main observations calling for explanation were as follows:

1. In the studies of cross-section data and social groups, the low income households consume more in relation to their income group than do high income households.

2. Over long periods of time the saving income ratio (S/Y)--and therefore the consumption income ratio (C/Y), in view of the definition of saving as that part of income not spent on consumption--is constant. Another way of saying this is that within the secular time frame the income elasticity of consumption is unity.

The former evidence on households and the latter evidence on national savings--as derived by Kuznets, the 1972 Nobel laureate in economics, and others--seemed to contradict the absolute income hypothesis. The absolute income hypothesis had in a sense forecasts an increasing saving to income ratio. This would be in the tradition that cross-section evidence may indicate secular trends, although cross-section evidence may yield other relevant information as well.

A tendency to rely upon the reasoning about the simple consumption function in the late 1930s and well into the 1960s on the part of some, lead to depressing forecasts about the market economy, as in the United States. The reasoning suggested an excess of saving (capital accumulation in financial terms), and less than adequate consumer spending for the maintenance of a full employment economy. The persistence of spending as reflected in the data over long periods brought out the inadequacy of the reasoning about the simple function as it may relate to changes over time.

The Relative Income Hypothesis and Permanent Income

The relative income hypothesis helped explain the cross-section evidence above and provided some explanation for the constancy of the saving to income ratio over long periods of time. The introduction of consumption as a function of permanent income, in the next section, and the use there of an adaptive expectations model to estimate permanent income helps reconcile aspects of both the simple Keynesian function and long-run behavior. In that formulation one encounters both "pull" effects and "push" effects on expectations. The "pull" effect is a regressive pull toward normality, as toward a secular trend of past incomes as the trend is extrapolated into the future. The "push" effect refers to the effect of recent changes in income on expectations about future income. In that analysis greater certainty means a greater influence of the more distant past as it is extrapolated into the more distant future. Greater uncertainty means an enlarged influence of the present as where, at the limit, there is only the present with no yesterday and no tomorrow.

The Relative Income Hypothesis

Two early post-World War II writers stated the relative income hypothesis thus:

$$s/y = a + b\ (y/\bar{y})$$

where s and y represent individual saving and income, and $\bar{y}$ represents average income. In words, they reasoned that the saving rate depended not on the level of income but on the individual's relative position on the income scale. Duesenberry varied the expression for the hypothesis somewhat:

$$S/Y = a + b\ (Y/Y_o)$$

where Y_o represents a prior peak level of income after adjustment for price and population changes.

Duesenberry in effect transformed the relative income hypotheses into an expression for the aggregate saving to aggregate income ratio as a function of the ratio of current income to the highest prior level of income. The idea again was that saving and therefore consumption depended on the standard of living to which the behavioral units had been accustomed. In the secular time frame that standard, Y_o, could increase as habits adapted and thus keep the saving to income ratio (S/Y) from rising.

In Duesenberry's formulation low income itself does not make a household save less than a high income household. Instead, households are influenced by other households through an emulation effect as found in the work of Thorstein Veblen. This emphasis on "emulation" does no harm to the "habit persistence" notion found in Keynes ($dC/dY < 1$), and, at the same time, there is no reason to expect the average of the propensities of different households to consume to fall as income rises secularly and as the more persistent psychological propensities adapt to changes. The "habit persistence" notion was formalized by Duesenberry by introducing lagged income as a determinant of consumption, and thus what has since been called a "pull" effect.

Wealth Theories

Wealth theories have been the main ones offered as an explanation of the constancy of the saving to income ratio in the secular time frame. They include the life cycle hypothesis[6] and the permanent income theory of Friedman. A host of variables and motives influencing consumption are considered. Many of these are introduced as authors consider the existence of plans for spending which extend over the lives of individuals. Further complications arise from reliance on a combination of seemingly incompatable approaches. In both cases there are elements of metastatics, including the desire for future consumption as a motive for saving and the extension of the assumption of perfect market information to a consideration of changes over time. In metastatics implications of time differences are introduced but outside influences and changes resulting from uncertainty are impounded. A theory employing metastatics is not a fully dynamic theory (i.e., fully *mutatis mutandis*). In the life cycle hypothesis work one encounters effort and proposals to add more and more variables in order to discover stable relations between the time series.

The motives for saving (refraining from consumption) in Modigliani and Brumberg (1954) concern the bequeathing of assets, the maintenance of a smooth stream of consumption with an irregular income, the accumulation of assets to meet emergencies, and funds for purchasing equity in consumer durables prior to acquiring their use. Uncertainty about the economic future centers about some of the motives, but then a satisfactory theory is said to be offered by Modigliani and Brumberg without coming to grips with the formidable problem of uncertainty.

Some of the characteristics of the life cycle hypothesis are incorporated in Friedman's Theory, but the adaptive expectations model emerges as a central part of the study of time series. For this reason Friedman's approach is stressed. It treats consumption as a proportion of permanent income and treats that proportion mainly as a function of the rate of interest and the ratio of non-human to total wealth. The first moves the theory of consumption in a very dynamic direction, when aided by adaptive expectations models, and at the same time helps reconcile the constancy of the saving-to-income ratio over time with cross-section data from household budget studies. In a sense, though, what Friedman advances in the one case, he detracts from in the other. The theory of interest in question is most compatible with Friedman's long-run emphasis; it does not explain the behavior of interest rates as in the case of liquidity preference (sects. 5.4 and 6.4) and hence households spending and saving behavior. Indeed, the interest rate theory reviewed comes from a relatively static treatment with indifference curve diagrams (initially as introduced in sect. 3.3), although it has a compatibility with the dynamics of exhaustible resources (sect. 16.6), as initially encountered by Friedman in the 1930s. The Fisher theory, as some would view it (Mini 1974, 253-255), is more an explanation of the existence of interest rates than of the behavior of interest rates. In other words, it is not the theory of interest in the liquidity preference context with overshooting.[7] However, we recognize below the prospect that in the secular time frame an increase in the real rate of interest (as defined below) will reduce consumption in relation to permanent income at a present time, other things being equal.)

9.4. The Permanent Income Hypothesis

After dealing with separate behavioral units, Friedman (1957) introduced aggregate consumption (C) as being some constant proportion (k) of aggregate permanent income (Y_p)

$$C = k\,(i,\ Wnh/W,\ u)\ Y_p$$

where k is mainly some function of the following: the rate of interest (i), used as a symbol for a complex of interest rates; the ratio of non-human to total wealth (Wnh/W), as may be compared with Friedman's approach in sections 5.4 and 6.3, and u is the portmanteau (or catch-all) variable. The observed values were viewed as consisting of a permanent component (Y_p) and a transitory component (T), for income (Y), e.g.,

$$Y = Y_p + Y_T$$

and as shown in figure 9-3. The transitory part of income turns out to be another name for the business cycle.

To allow for both a trend value for income (i.e., for a constant percentage rate of growth) and for a weighted average of adjusted deviations of past values from the trend, Friedman defined permanent income in a simple form:

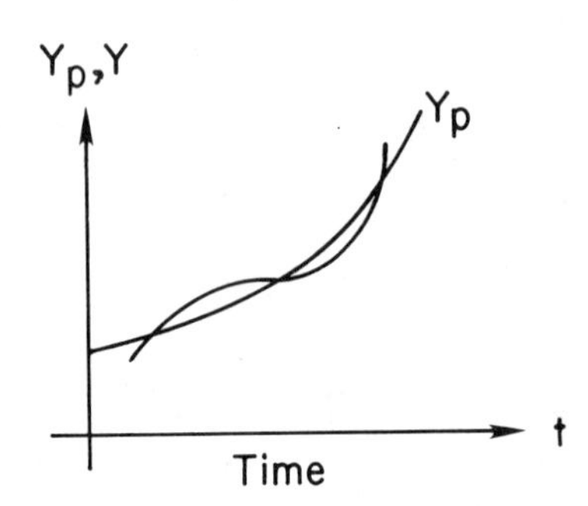

Figure 9-3.
Permanent and Transitory Components of Income

$$Y_p(T) = \beta \int_{-\infty}^{T} e^{(\beta - \alpha)(t - T)} Y(t)dt$$

where

T is time for expected income,

t is time of observation being weighted,

e 2.7 (from the calculus constant),

and

$e^{(\beta - \alpha)(t - T)}$ is the exponentially declining weight.
With this definition the function to be fitted to aggregate data became

$$C = k\, \beta \int_{-\infty}^{T} e^{(\beta - \alpha)(t - T)} Y(t)dt$$

Friedman noted, of course, that this equation cannot be fitted directly to data for discrete time units such as a year. The method of fitting the equation to data involved an adaptive expectations model and evolved separately from the initial statement of the consumption theory (Friedman 1957).[8]

A special form of the adaptive expectations model may be denoted

$$Y_{pt} = \beta Y_t + \beta(1-\beta)Y_{t-1} + \beta(1-\beta)^2 Y_{t-2} + \dots + \beta(1-\beta)^n Y_{t-n}$$

where $C = \alpha Y_{pt}$

Here the weights for the earlier years income rapidly diminish so that beyond some point in time the observed income values have a negligible effect. Further, last years permanent income can be denoted

$$Y_{pt-1} = \beta\, Y_{t-1} + \beta(1-\beta)\, Y_{t-2} + \ldots + \beta(1-\beta)^{n-1}\, Y_{t-n} + \beta(1-\beta)^{n}\, Y_{t-(n+1)}$$

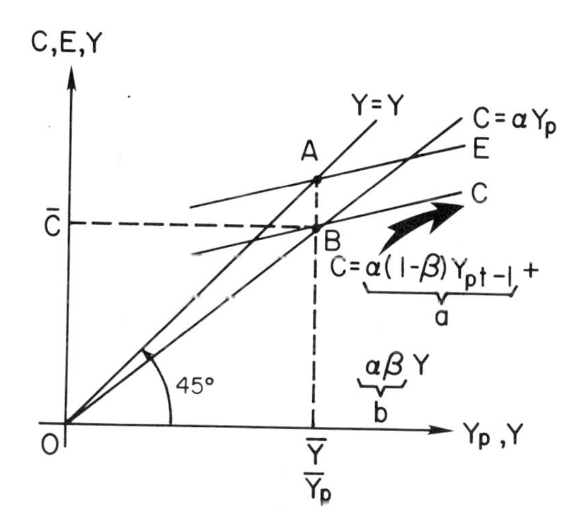

Figure 9-4. Long- and Short-Run Consumption Functions

Using this and substituting in the former expression we obtain another expression that can be approximated thus:

$$Y_{pt} = \beta Y + (1 - \beta)\, Y_{pt-1}$$

If measured income (Y) is above last year's permanent income then permanent income will rise, but by a smaller amount than current income. Even so, the idea of declining weights is that current values have more influence.

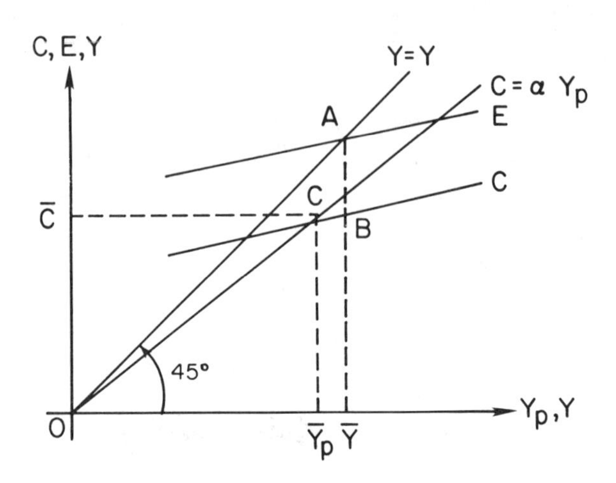

Figure 9-5. Long- and Short-Run Consumption Function with Volatile Investment

Using this last result and substituting in $C = \alpha Y_p$

$$C = \underbrace{\alpha(1 - \beta)Y_{pt-1}}_{\substack{\text{intercept} \\ \text{parameter a}}} + \underbrace{\alpha \ \beta}_{\substack{\text{slope} \\ \text{parameter b}}} Y_t$$

or $$C = a + b\ Y$$

This expression is the simple static consumption function (sect. 7.2). The permanent function and the short-run (or static) relation are shown together in figure 9-4, against a background and coordinate system comprising the aggregate expenditure (E), aggregate income (Y) block of the Keynesian system. The same variables are denoted on the vertical and horizontal axes, as in figure 7-2, except that permanent income (Y_p) is shown on the horizontal axis as well as current income (Y). As drawn, the distance between the 45° line and the permanent consumption line ($C = \alpha Y_p$) is saving. This depicts the growth state, and a long-run secular time frame. In this state and time frame the simple expenditure line (E) and the simple consumption function are shifting upward at constant rates, and the points A and B are moving outward along the 45° line and the permanent consumption line respectively.

Different rates of spending for consumption and investment from those ordinarily depicted by secular time paths for the expenditures variables themselves will give rise to two kinds of additional changes that may warrant attention: (1) fluctuations in current income (Y) about the permanent income line (Y_p), and (2) possibly movements along the simple consumption function. The fluctuations have already been illustrated in figure 9-3. The other sorts of movements are illustrated in figure 9-5, by permitting investment expenditures to shift upward at a faster rate than the simple consumption function. Current income (Y) exceeds permanent income (Y_p), and there is in effect forward movement along the simple function. When total spending returns to its equilibrium trend paths, the points B and C in figure 9-5 will again merge.

A possible virtue of the permanent income hypothesis about consumption is that in empirical estimation of parameter values and in the prediction of consumption from sample period to sample period, the permanent relationship is a more stable one. It has been Friedman's thesis in his empirical work, that he was seeking stable relationships, regularity in the data. But even in the Friedman model, as income accelerates (decelerates) its effect on consumption is restrained by the past values. This would be such that acceleration (deceleration) in income leads to a less than proportional increase (decrease) in consumption. Friedman's function in effect retains and complements the Keynesian function.

Transitory Spending

As stated, Friedman's has been a long-run emphasis that abstracted from transitory income or spending. This may be discussed with reference to the difference between points B and C in figure 9-5, where current income exceeds permanent income at a given time $Y > Y_p$). Consumption spending at point B is what would follow from current income and a movement along the simple consumption function with slope dC/dY or b. The spending at C is what would follow for permanent income Y_p. The difference in current income Y and permanent income (Y_p) that results from spending (E) is transitory spending, but within the framework giving rise to figure 9-4, change comes about to move the short-run function along the 45° line.

This short-run volatility calls for more attention. This would especially seem so in a world where economics may be expected to serve as a guide to national economic policy and where politicians are sensitive to the electorate and the achievement of stabilization goals in the short run and impatient about waiting as Friedman's early policy prescriptions for economic stabilization called for.

Some of the volatility in question may be expected to occur in a world where there has been the following: a secular increase in the proportion of household expenditures that may be postponed, such as those for durable goods, and the commensurate changes in the means of financing these expenditures. Indeed, the practice of granting installment credit has grown since the 1930s. A rule of thumb often governing the

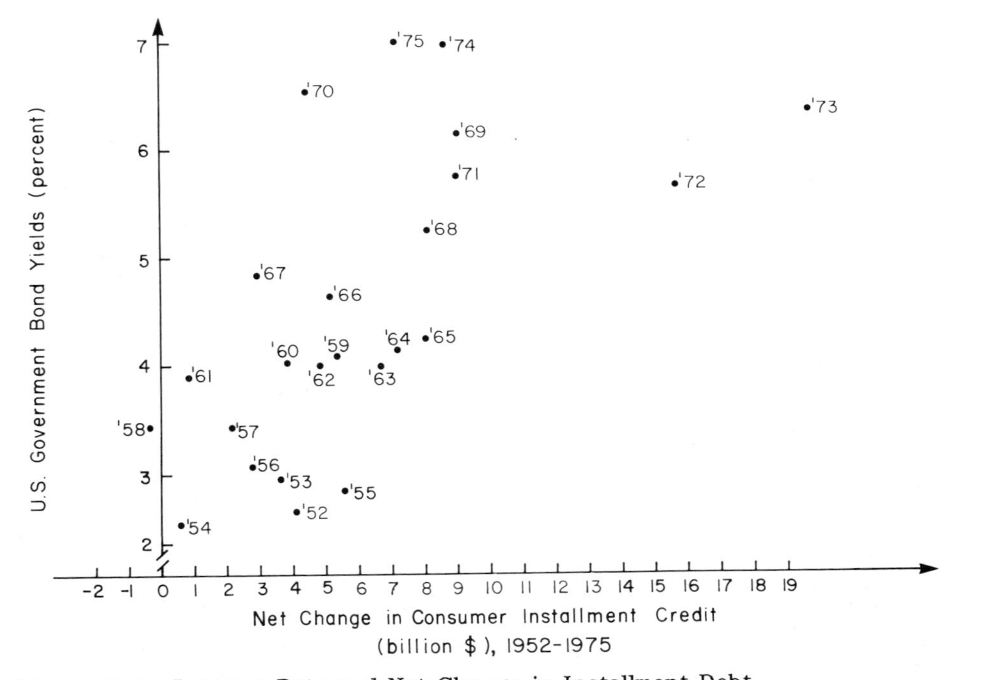

Figure 9-6. Interest Rate and Net Change in Installment Debt.
Note: The long-term rate is that for U.S. Government securities. Data for it and for installment credit appear in the Federal Reserve Bulletin.

granting of that credit is germaine, namely: the maturity of the installment contract may vary with the life of the good being purchased as long as the unpaid credit balance does not exceed the value of the good at any time in the life of the good.

The practice of granting installment credit widens the range of potential sources of funds for making expenditures. Credit may be used as well as current income and past savings. When an expansion phase of business conditions is in progress and when there is a thurst and buoyancy in household spending the dollar volume of installment credit extended may grow at a faster rate than repayments, and when the reverse conditions prevail the growth of installment credit extended in relation to repayments may decline. As this analysis suggests, using the rate of interest as a measure of business conditions (exclusive of rates during inflationary recessions such as in 1970 and 1974), we may observe positive covariation for the interest rate on long-term government bonds and net changes in installment credit outstanding, as in figure 9-6.

A positive net change in installment credit is one indication that desired spending for installment-financed goods is greater than warranted by current income. Using it as in figure 9-6 and viewing the interest rate as a substitute variable for business conditions suggests that desired spending tends to be greater than warranted by income in an expansion phase of business conditions and tends to be less than warranted in a recession phase.

Consumption, Permanent Income, and the Time Preference for Income

The relationship between consumption and permanent income, as just posited, is influenced by the variable proportionality factor k, which Friedman has stated as a function of the ratio of non-human wealth to total wealth (Wnh/W), and the rate of interest (i), and other things (u). The ratio Wnh/W is intended to reflect mainly the importance of liquid assets as a means of dealing with uncertain situations and meeting emergencies. These assets of course are the easier to convert into needed cash, so where they were relatively abundant in family budgets Friedman was inclined in expect more consumption in relation to permanent income. The interest rate, however, received more attention as a factor, especially where viewed as a payment for foregoing present consumption for future consumption, as dealt with by Irving Fisher (1930), as couched in geometric terms by him (1930, chaps. 10 and 11), and as later couched in the static indifference curve approach.[9] It gives rise to what has been called the natural rate of interest (sect. 9.1).

The static interest theory in question centers about what has historically been called the time preference for money, but what is actually an expression of the preference for income (or consumption) today over income in the future. The common capital value (CV) expression in pure mathematical form contains a form of this time preference, e.g.,

$$CV = R_0/(1 + i)^0 > CV = R_{20}/(1+i)^{20},$$

where $R_0 = R_{20}$.

In the static/indifference curve form associated with Fisher but not as found in its exact modern form, the interest rate is said to be determined by the impatience of behavioral units to consume at the present rather than to forego present for future consumption and by the opportunities for production with accumulated capital (Fisher 1930).[10]

The static analysis of interest and its influence on consumption proceeds within the framework of utility analysis at the so-called microeconomic level. Two classes of goods are considered--future (F) and present (P) goods. There is one income (Y_0) to be spent by the individual over the two periods, this year and the next. The choice considered is that of spending on present consumption (C_0) or next year's consumption. Saving is that part of income not spent ($Y_0 - C_0$), and because of the increment in capital there will be slightly more in the way of future goods, as well as in the way of income for spending next year. The amount for spending is Y_0 but if it is spent on future goods the total spent would be $(1 + r) Y_0$, where <u>r</u> is the rate of interest. A two-dimensional sketch with budget line imposed is shown in figure 9-7. The Point A consists of coordinates C_0 and $(1 + r) (Y_0 - C_0)$. The slope of the budget line (recall rise over run) is $-\Delta F/\Delta P = (1+r)(Y_0 - C_0) / (Y_0 - C_0)$ or the negative of $(1 + r)$. This ratio $-\Delta F/\Delta P$ or the factor $1 + r$ is also the rate at which future goods can be obtained per unit of sacrificed present goods, given constant taste, expectations, and other prices. This exchange between money now and money a year hence is what Sir John Hicks notes to be the market rate of interest in his addressing the temporary equilibrium method. With the condition that money prices are unchanged, this market rate is equated with Wicksell's "natural rate" of interest (Hicks 1965, 59).

The economic agent in question is thought to prefer present over future consumption, as stated above, and to prefer more rather than less of the goods. Hence the indifference curves have a greater negative slope and are convex to the origin. Such curves are shown in the P-F plane in figure 9-8, where the curves U_1 and U_2 are cut by a 45° line. If there was no preference for present over future goods or vice versa the slope of the indifference curves would be minus one at the points cut by the 45° line. The slopes of the curves are denoted $- \Delta F/\Delta P$ or $-\Delta P(1 + t) /\Delta P$, or more accurately,

$$\lim_{\Delta P \to 0} \Delta P(1+t)/\Delta P,$$

where 1 + t is the negative of the slope and where t (the time preference counterpart to the rate of interest) is the marginal time preference.

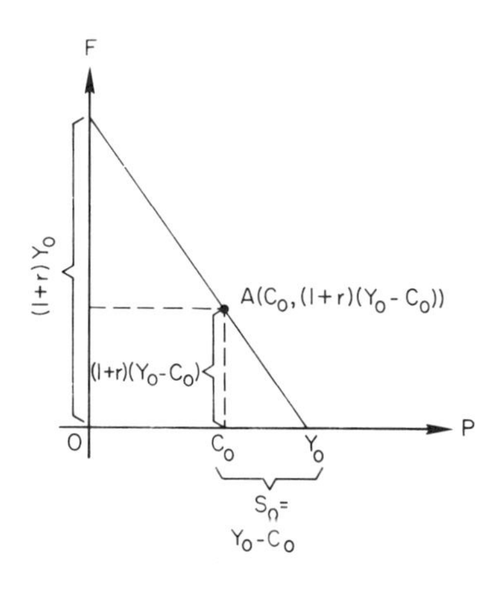

Figure 9-7. Budget Constraint Encompassing Two Distinct Time Periods

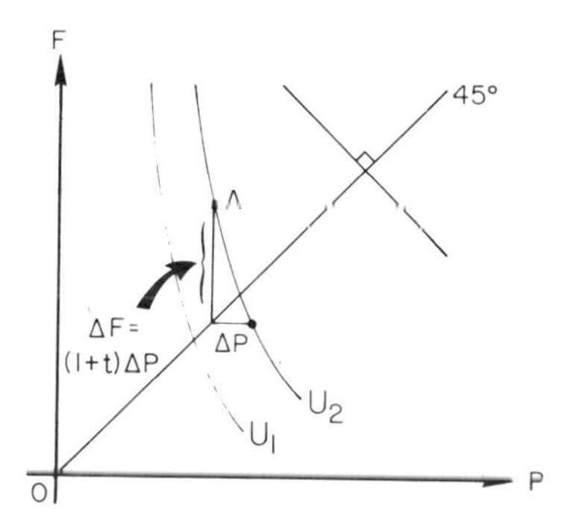

Figure 9-8. Indifference Curves for Two Discrete Time Periods

The first order condition for utility maximization is that the slope of the budget line and the slope of the indifference be equal at the point where the highest attainable indifference curve touches the budget line. Point A in figure 9-9 is such a point and there (1 + r) = (1 + t). This figure combines the budget and indifference curves from figure 9-7 and 9-8 respectively. (The first order conditions of figure 9-9 are considered further, along with second order conditions, in appendix to chapter 9. Though treated in the appendix, second order conditions are assumed satisfied throughout the text.)

Now we wish to raise the rate of interest (Δr). To the individual it may now appear that he (she) can obtain the same present consumption (C_0) and more future consumption, ΔP(1

+ r_o + Δr). But for individuals as a whole the production possibilities are fixed. There are then no income effects (as shown in a similar construction, figure A16-1), only substitution effects. These are readily distinguishable in the utility framework, as illustrated in figure 9-10. There the apparent income effect of the rise in the rate of interest is to move the intersection of the budget line along the vertical axis from $\Delta P(1 + r)$ to $\Delta P(1 + r + \Delta r)$. But since there are no income effects, the new and apparent income line is shifted back (while maintaining its slope) to a point of tangency with the original indifference curve (U_2 in this case). This substitution effect of the interest rate change may then be noted in terms of the changes occurring in present and future goods as one moves from point A to point C. Consumption declines ($-\Delta P$) and saving increases (ΔP).

Figure 9-9. Maximum Utility from Consumption and Saving

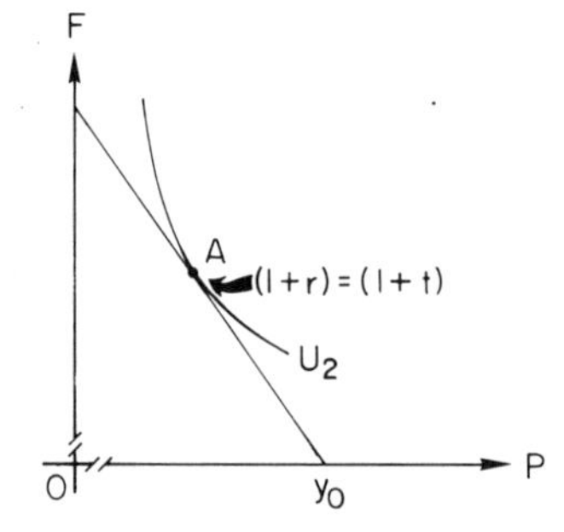

Hence the basis for a possible change in consumption,

$$C = k\,Y_p,$$

where k(Wnh/W, i). The static analysis with taste, expectations and other prices constant would appear to suggest that a rise in interest rates increases saving and decreases consumption at the given level of income. The causal sequence would be

$$\Delta i \rightarrow -\Delta k \rightarrow -\Delta C$$

This reduction in consumption ($-\Delta C$) would lower the slope of the $C = \alpha Y_p$ line in figure 9-5. It could feedback to raise permanent income in the long run.

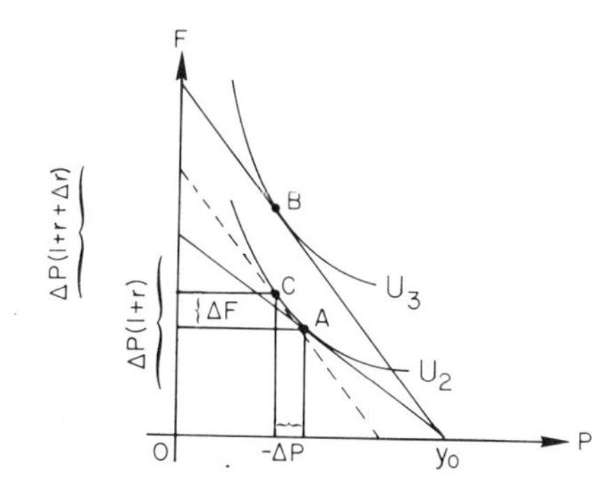

Figure 9-10.
Substitution
Effect

Transitory/Dynamic Considerations

What brings about the change in the interest rate, however? Suppose it is dominated by forces operating on the demand side of the market for consumer and commerical credit generally. Suppose there is the expectation of inflation instead of an arbitrary increase in the rate of interest. In this case, the preference may favor more strongly present over future consumption or upward adjustments in interest rates as a means of compensation for the prospect of a loss in purchasing power.

The causal sequence just depicted with the Fisher interest theory in mind would be at variance with the control linkage attributed to Friedman and as introduced earlier (sects. 5.4 and 6.4), namely:

$$\Delta\dot{M} \rightarrow \Delta\dot{Y} \rightarrow \Delta i$$

In this linkage scheme, the impact of the accelerated growth in money was upon consumption and investment spending equally. The explanation for this apparent inconsistency in the linkage is that Friedman's consumption function work deals with permanent magnitudes, and his liquidity preference with overshooting involves transitory as well as permanent changes and the expectation of inflation.

In the earlier theory (sects. 5.2, and 5.4), accelerated growth in the money stock causes accelerated growth in spending ($\Delta\dot{M} \rightarrow \Delta\dot{Y}$), with some extra push effect, and the expectation of inflation may act to raise the interest rate, as rates are adjusted upward to allow for the expectation, and as households reduce money holdings in relation to income. Using the adaptative expectations notion ($Y^e_t = W_0 Y_t + W_1 Y_{t-1} + W_2 Y_{t-2} + \ldots + W_n Y_{t-n}$) to depict the push effect, the weights to the more recent magnitudes (i.e., W_0, W_1, W_2, and so on) are greater (increasing) in relation the weights for the more distant past (W_{n-2}, W_{n-1}, W_n, and so on). The influence of the more distant past values increases as the "pull" effect of normality takes over.

In the presence of great uncertainty about a turn in expected income, the push effects of recent changes in income dominate the pull effects. As a greater certainty about a change in the direction of income movements takes over, the weights of the more distant past (the "pull" toward normality) takes on a greater influence. In this way, consumption spending may respond to changes in expectations about future income. The shifts in the simple consumption function in figure 9-4 may occur at different rates as expectations about income vary, as in the present context.

9.5. Summary

Key points in this chapter include the following:

1. We have presented a sketch of an exponential time path with total spending varying about it, such that in the long run, the ratios of consumption to income and saving to income most accurately approximate constants rather than declining and rising ratios. Initially, however, there is an exercise in the form of the Domar model and a consideration of relatively static concepts--the simple Keynesian function, and an inverse variation in interest rates and home construction, as depicted by Keynesian investment demand relation.

2. Some dynamics of leading indicators are introduced--new orders placed with durable goods industries and changes in consumer installment debt. The latter reflects more of a procyclical than countercyclical sort of behavior, say as suggested by a Keynesian, interest rate, spending relation.

3. Keynes's simple consumption function imparted some psychology and behavior into a traditionally dismal subject. Following this lead, Duesenberry introduced more psychology whereby households are influenced by one another through an "emulation" effect. This helped explain the cross-section evidence whereby lower income households consume more in relation to their income (social) group than do higher income households in given social groups.

4. In Duesenberry's formulation there is also the possibility of households adjusting spending habits to income, in the secular time frame, so that the saving to income need not decline in that time frame.

5. Keynes's law, as embodied in his consumption function may be rescued by rendering the theory more dynamic, and by introducing more, rather than less, psychology into an otherwise dismal subject. The rescue may be made by treating consumption as a function of permanent income, as in the next chapter, and by using an adaptive expectation model to define permanent income. "Push" and "pull" effects may be introduced along with varying degrees of uncertainty about the economic outlook.

6. Housing expenditures play a rather special role in macroeconomic theory. The purchase of a housing unit is an unusually large outlay for a household. The financial instru-

ment involved has a long time-to-maturity feature. These characteristics taken together mean that a change in the interest rate has a substantial effect on the size of the monthly payments required to service the mortgage. This--in turn and in combination with a lack of planning by households to avoid tight credit conditions--means that income has a substantial restraining effect on housing expenditures, the monotization of housing aside. Expenditures on new housing units have varied inversely with the rate of interest in the early post-World War II years. When the rate moves strictly in phase with business conditions, as before the inflationary recession phenomenon, housing expenditures serve as a leading indicator of business conditions.

7. The future role of housing expenditures is complicated by prospects for the inflationary recession and a continuing high cost for energy. The first means that the home construction industry will not serve to an earlier degree to help pull the economy out of recession. The second means that many of the optimistic goals for single-family home ownership will not be realized.

8. Persistent and often rising inflation rates have contributed to a high and often rising cost of housing, interest rates (and thus interest payments on newly purchased homes). This along with inflated personal incomes, tax cuts that make the income tax a more progressive tax, and the practice of treating interest payments as a deduction from taxable income have contributed to what some economists refer to as the monotization of housing. This includes: selling housing by the home owner at an inflated price and with the receipt of a cash balance in excess of previous downpayment and payments towards principal; purchase of new home with larger monthly payment (mainly interest payment in early years of the new mortgage) and through use of only a fraction of recently received cash balance (hence the resulting monotization); and finally the deduction of inflated interest payment from inflated taxable income (often taxable at a higher tax rate).

9. Short- and long-run consumption functions are readily distinguishable, when the measure of permanent income is treated as being obtainable with a form of an adaptive expectations model. Keynes's short-run function drops out as a continuously shifting function.

10. The difference between current income, as in the argument for the short-run function, and permanent income is transitory income. Conceptually, this turns out to be another name for the business-conditions deviations of income from some secular or trend line for income.

11. The short-run function is volatile. Several features of household spending practices help explain this, including the role of installment financing of durable goods purchases. These purchases can be postponed as the simple consumption undergoes a reduced forward momentum. Under more buoyant and exhilarating conditions, the forward shift may be accelerated beyond what might be called for. Desired spending exceeds income; installment credit extended exceeds repayments.

12. One of the factors Friedman introduced to explain shifts in the parameter (k) relation consumption to permanent income ($C = kY_p$) was the rate of interest. The role for this rate is couched in a review of the static difference curve approach to the theory of interest. The main feature of a high rate in the theory is to bring about a substitution of future consumption for present consumption. Such does not occur in the case of ordinary consumer spending.

13. The latter is not exactly what the static, indifference curve approach to the interest rates conveys. Even so, it seems reasonable to view interest as a payment for postponing consumption, when the objective is to explain the existence of interest rather than its behavior and when we seek later to deal with the pricing of an exhaustible resource. The theory is simply not very predictive of household spending and behavior under changing business conditions. In the more dynamic case with expectations entering it--especially the expectation of inflation--the preference may shift to favor present spending on residual claims against future income such as real goods and property. If this is called saving, then expected inflation encourages it and higher interest rates too. From the creditor's side of the market, the nominal interest rate may be adjusted upward in the face of inflation to compensate for any loss in the purchasing power of a dollar stream of fixed contractual returns. This suggests the equation showing the nominal interest rate as the sum of the real rate plus the expected rate of change in the price level with a factor for uncertainty.

14. Static analyses about interest rates aside--as in the view of interest as a payment for the postponement of consumption--the consumption, current and lagged income relaton may be used to deal with dynamic phenomena such as uncertainty about changes in future income. In the presence of uncertainty about future changes, the influence of current and recent values for income have a strong "push" effect on expectations. Greater certainty, on the other hand, suggests more of a "pull" toward normality, an extrapolation of the more distant past into the future.

FOOTNOTES

1. There are several methods of solution to this model. One is found in the Frazer and Yohe (1966, 223).
2. The laws of logarithms used here are $\ln (M \cdot N) = \ln M + \ln N$ and $\ln M^r = r \ln M$

   In the special case of natural logrithms,

   $\ln e = 1$, where e is the growth constant 2.7 from the calculus.

3. We say "over the cycle" because over a longer post-World War II time (say, the secular time frame) the volume of home construction in either current or constant dollar terms may be expected to grow exponentially even with interest rates unchanged. In some respects this complication about the dollar volume (in current of constant dollars) and a secular time frame is minimized by the use of the data underlying figure 9-2. There we have changes in an index concerning permits for private housing units rather than a dollar volume that may be expected to grow more over time with the wealth of society.
4. To approximate the effect of a change in the interest rate for the monthly payment on a mortgage the table below may be used. It gives the monthly payment for borrowing $1,000, for the different rates and maturities shown.

RATES OF INTEREST

YRS.	(Mos)	7	7½	8	8½	9	9½	10
5	(60)	19.81	20.04	20.28	20.52	20.76	21.00	21.25
10	(120)	11.62	11.87	12.13	12.40	12.67	12.94	13.22
15	(180)	8.99	9.27	9.57	9.85	10.14	10.44	10.75
20	(240)	7.76	8.06	8.36	8.68	9.00	9.32	9.65
25	(300)	7.07	7.39	7.72	8.05	8.39	8.74	9.09
30	(360)	6.66	6.99	7.34	7.69	8.05	8.41	8.78

Now assume the home buyer needs $30,000 for the purchase and assumes a 25-year maturity date on the mortgage at 8 percent. The monthly payment is $231.60 per month (i.e., $7.72 x 30). If the interest rate goes to 10 percent, then the payment is $272.70 per month (i.e., $9.09 x 30), an increase of $41.10 per month.

5. In July of 1978, the House Ways and Means Committee amended President Carter's tax-cut bill of that year to entitle homeowners to a tax-free profit of up to $100,000 on the sale of a house. This was to be a one-time-only escape from the tax. As we consider in chapter 14, however, the bill had previously been amended to cut the capital gains tax from the 49 percent rate to 35 percent, and to eliminate the tax on any capital gains caused by inflation.
6. The life cycle hypothesis is found initially in the work of Franco Modigliani and Richard Brumberg, and in that of Franco Modigliani and Albert Ando. References on this are found in Mayer's book (1972, 27 n. 29).
7. The static case below, employs the sort of effort found in pre-Keynes's economics to explain the existence of interest in constrast to behavior, as Mlnl (1974, 253-255) would suggests. According to his review, Keynes tended to take the existence of interest for granted, as an observable fact of life, and sought to explain its behavior. He says that Keynes is not inclined to accept reason as the only source of knowledge. Continuing he says of Keynes:

> "He was concerned with explaining movements in the rate of interest, movements that he finds caused by the usual elements of uncertainty, expectations connections, mass psychology... This is why he called the interest rate a highly psychological phenomenon."

8. Marcelle Arak (1978, 945-951) reviews the past use of the geometrically weighted average of past incomes as the standard proxy for permanent income. In addition she treats consumption as a function of permanent income ($C_t = \alpha P_t + \varepsilon_t$) and deals with the <u>ex post</u> prediction (as defined later in section 13.5) of consumption for the period 1949-1973. She notes [as in her equation (1) of the subsequent section 14.2] that "the 'rational' forecast of a variable is that forecast based upon the same mechanism that is known to generate outcome." After allowance for "any unexpected change in the anticipated receipt stream" to obtain her alternative to the standard proxy for permanent income, she appears to have in mind, an improvement in the prediction of consumption as it would appear in the FMP model (i.e., the Federal Reserve, M.I.T., Univ. of Pennsylvania model, an updated Fed-MIT model of about 1968 vintage as mentioned on later occasions). To past income, in the adaptive expectations model contex, Arak adds past levels of consumption to derive a better measure of past savings, since "all saving [$S_t = Y_t - C_t$] tends to increase permanent income."

   Permanent income P_t is defined in the ordinary way, namely as equal to the product of the rate of interest and wealth (rW_t). Moreover, with the rate of interest constant, $1/P\ dP/dt = r\ (1/W\ dW/dt)$.

   The geometrically weighted average Arak maintains, "omits that saving which results from a negative disturbance in the consumption function and that dissaving which results from a positive disturbance." Consequently, Arak presents permanent income (P_t) as being equal to "the difference between two geometrically weighted averages with identical rates of decline: (1) a geometrically weighted average of past income levels and (2) a geometrically weighted average of past consumption function disturbances."

9. Fisher makes due asides in <u>The Theory of Interest</u> (1930) to the antecedence of his exposition, as found in.. the work of John Rae (1796-1872) and Eugene Von Bohm-Bawerk (1851-1914). The static indifference curve approach in the present text, however, is mainly associated with Sir John Hicks's <u>Value and Capital</u> (1939), and the approach has its foundations in Lagrangian methods, as considered in the appendix to chapter 16. Hicks's 1939 work is said to represent the best modern exposition of the static theory of value.

10. In using this approach Friedman (1967,7) cites the following sources: Irving Fisher, <u>The Rate of Interest</u> (New

York: Macmillan, 1907), especially chapter VI, pp. 87-116 and 387-392; Irving Fisher, The Theory of Interest (New York: Macmillan, 1930, especially chapters X and XI; and Kenneth E. Boulding, Economic Analysis, Revised ed. (New York: Harper, 1948), pp. 734-741.

Samuelson (1976, app. to chap. 30) also offers an exposition of the indifference curve approach drawing on Fisher.

SELECTED READINGS AND REFERENCES

Arak, Marcelle. 1978. "The Geometrically Weighted Average of Past Incomes as a Representation of Permanent Income: A Reconsideration." Southern Economic Journal (April).

Commerce, U.S. Department of. 1976. Business Conditions Digest, New Revised Edition (November).

Domar, E. D. 1946. "Capital Expansion, Rate of Growth, and Employment." Econometrica (April).

Duesenberry, James S. 1952. Income, Saving, and The Theory of Consumer Behavior. Cambridge, Mass.: Harvard University Press.

___________. 1958. Business Cycles and Economic Growth. New York: McGraw-Hill Book Company, Inc.

Ferber, Robert. 1962. "Research on Household Behavior." American Economic Review (March).

Fisher, Irving. 1954. The Theory of Interest, As Determined by Impatience to Spend Income and Opportunity to Invest It. New York: Kelly & Millman, Inc. Originally published by Macmillan, 1930.

Frazer, William. 1968. In Compendium on Monetary Policy Guidelines and Federal Reserve Structure. Washington, D.C.: U.S. Government Printing Office (December).

___________. 1977. "Income Distribution, Social Utility, and Unemployment." Nebraska Journal of Economics and Business (Autumn).

___________. 1973. Crisis in Economic Theory. Gainesville, Fla.: University of Florida Press. Chapter 8 and Appendix to Chapter 15.

___________, and William P. Yohe. 1966. Introduction to the Analytics and Institutions of Money and Banking. Princeton, N.J.: D. Van Nostrand Company, Inc.

Friedman, Milton. 1957. A Theory of The Consumption Function. Princeton, N.J.: Princeton University Press for the National Bureau of Economic Research.

___________. 1976. Price Theory, revised edition. Chicago: Aldine Publishing Company. Chapter 17.

Frische, Ragner. 1952. "Frische on Wicksell." In Henry William Spiegel, ed. The Development of Economic Thought: Great Economists in Perspective. New York: John Wiley & Sons, Inc.

Froevis, Kenneth C. 1978. "GNMA Futures: Stablizing or Destabilizing?" Economic Review, Federal Reserve Bank of San Francisco (Spring).

Guttentag, Jack M. 1961. "The Short Cycle in Residential Construction, 1946-59." American Economic Review (June).

Keynes, John M. 1950a. A Treatise on Money: Vol. I, The Pure Theory of Money. London: Macmillan and Col., Limited. Originally published in 1930.

__________. 1950b. A Treatise on Money: Vol. II, The Pure Theory of Money. London: Macmillan and Col., Limited. Originally published in 1930.

__________. 1936. The General Theory of Employment, Interest and Money. New York: Harcourt, Brace and Company.

Mayer, Thomas. 1972. Permanent Income, Wealth and Consumption. Berkeley, Cal.: University of California Press.

Mini, Paul V. 1974. Philosophy and Economics: The Origins and Development of Economic Theory. Gainesville, Fla.: University of Florida Press.

Modigliani, Franco, and Richard Brumberg. 1954. "Utility Analysis and the Consumption Function: An Interpretation of Cross-Section Data." In Kenneth K. Kurihara, ed. Post Keynesian Economics. New Jersey: Rutgers University Press.

Moggridge, Donald, ed. 1973a. The Collected Writings of John Maynard Keynes: Vol. XIII, The General Theory and After, Part 1, Prepartion. London: The Macmillan Press Limited.

__________, ed. 1973b. The Collected Writings of John Maynard Keynes: Vol. XIV, The General Theory and After, Part II, Defense and Development. London: The Macmillan Press Limited.

Patinkin, Don. 1965. Money, Interest, and Prices, 2nd edition, An Integration of Monetary and Value Theory. New York: Harper & Row, Publishers.

__________. 1976. Keynes' Monetary Thought: A Study of Its Development. Durham, North Carolina: Duke University Press.

__________, and J. Clark Leith, eds. 1978. Keynes, Cambridge and The General Theory, The Process of Criticism and Discussion Connected with the Development of The General Theory. Toronto: University of Toronto Press.

Samuelson, Paul A. 1976. Economics, Tenth Edition. New York: McGraw-Hill Book Company. Appendix to Chapter 30.

Veblen, Thorstein. 1934. The Theory of the Leisure Class. New York: The Modern Library. Originally publshed in 1899.

Chapter 10

The Government Sector

10.1. Introduction

Chapter 7 introduced the elementary mechanics of the income expenditure approach to income determination, and chapters 8 and 9 elaborated on additional detail with the view to moving toward a more dynamic (time-rate-of-change, secular/short-cycle evolutionary) theory of economic behavior. Chapter 8 expanded on the income expenditure model by giving attention to Keynes's investment demand block, the planning of capital outlays, their financing, the planning of their financing, the role of liquidity in the financial structure of industrial corporations, and leading indicators of business conditions. Chapter 9 gave further consideration to the simple consumption function, to the financing of durable goods, expenditures, and housing, and to the latter's behavior in relation to interest rates, business conditions, and expected inflation rates. In particular, attention was directed to a tendency towards the monetization of housing in a world characterized by high inflation rates, and disproportionate increases in personal income taxes beyond minimum taxable income levels.

Chapters 10 through 12 further expand on the income expenditure model by taking a more in-depth look at the government sector. Chapter 10 moves along these lines by introducing the theoretic and legislative background of fiscal policy, fiscal concepts and trends, the Proposition 13 phenomenum, the political business cycle, the Laffer curve, inflation as a tax, structural equations with special attention to the Keynesian mechanics, and by attaching the government budget constraint to the Keynesian concepts. Chapter 11 introduces the spector of government induced income redistribution, reviews a tendency for government to set its target rates of unemployment below the "natural rate" and to thereby induce economic instability, and it introduces the "natural" rate of unemployment as a variable. Control over the natural rate is distinct from control over the unemployment rate through the management of total spending via fiscal and monetary policy.

Chapter 12 returns to a consideration of the financing of government deficits, and to the possible "crowding out" effect of such financing. It also introduces the management of the federal debt (the tailoring of interest coupons and the time to maturity of the debt), the Treasury yield curve, theories of the term structure of interest rates (as indicated by the Treasury yield curve). There is further consideration of the political business cycle, as we encounter an example of the use of "persuasive" strategies as a means of influencing interest rates.

Fiscal Policy

Fiscal policy, as defined shortly, evolved mainly from Keynes's and Keynesian economics as a part of the income expenditure model, as the review of attributes in sections 4.2 and 4.3 suggests. That part of economics may be brought forward as a legacy of the Keynesian period and combined with some economics of money and finance to move the theory in a more viable direction. Aspects of Keynesian economics, then, move into the category of empirical economics. Some traditional Keynesians refered to themselves as "eclectic Keynesians," as they moved in this direction.

In reviewing the literature on the measurement of fiscal influences Blinder and Solow (1973) recognize its development on the basis of important Keynesian attributes: an emphasis on fiscal policy; a tendency to ignore price level changes or to treat them independently of fiscal policy; a tendency to omit any consideration of monetary influences; a tendency to focus on changes in the level of aggregate demand; a tendency to ignore influence of relative price changes and transfer of wealth problems (in the sense that the consumption function and the slopes of the tangents would be unchanged by the policy operations directed towards changing income); a tendency to rely on the interest linkage $+ \Delta M \rightarrow - \Delta i \rightarrow + \Delta I$; and a tendency to rely upon econometric models of the whole economy as the source of the empirical foundation for rational fiscal policy. Against this background, there will be in the present chapter some asides to price level changes and inflation, some introduction of monetary and financial influences through a consideration of "the government budget constraint"; some asides to rates of change rather than levels in stock and flow quantities, and recognition of the hopeful and idealistic nature of structural equation models for the whole economy (the entire domestic economy in its international setting).

Structural Equations Models

In essence a large structural equations model develops as variables and equations are added to a relatively small scale structural equations model (say as might depict the essence of the more limited Keynesian income expenditure model). In the presence of unstable parameters, as introduced in section 5.5, the idea is to add variables and equations to account for some of the instabilitiy in the initially simple relationships. In the tradition of the classical, least squares method of estimating coefficients there is the notion of sampling from an unchanging universe over a long period of time and then proceeding with control measures over the economy in the next period as if no structural changes had occurred, as initially considered in chapters 5 and 6. The practical and methodological problem has been that the structural models become unwieldy in size, even without achieving the stable relations. Even so, in the late 1970s a new generation of these models was recognizing expanded roles for the possible historical sources of instability in the structures, i.e., for expanded treatment of financial factors, expectational matters and uncertainty, inflation forecasting, and the presence of major exogenous elements (say, the presence of instability in the parameters).

In contrast to the structural equations approach, monetarists of the 1960's proceeded with more simple method and, as characterized by Milton Friedman's leadership, searched for regularity in observable data. They were pessimistic about the capability of economists to develop the promised structural equations models. Even so, there is a sense in which some "true" ideal, large-scale, structural equations model lies in the background of logical speculations about the functioning of the economy. In the contex of such an ideal there are reduced form (solution) equations, as illustrated shortly. Such an equation may be said to be implied by monetarist work. As an example of this work, one may envision the rate of change in the money stock as a control variable in a reduced form equation, with impact on GNP (an endogenous variable, with equilibrium value defined by the reduced form equation).

The more ideal attainments aside, the present approach is to stress foundations and fundamentals rather than elaborate structures. This is partly a means of bringing the subject matter to an introductory level, partly a recognition of the need to give attention to fundamentals, as a means of achieving insights into economics and the behavior of the economy, and partly a concession to the indirect use of economic constructs and simple method along Friedmanesque lines (sect. 7.1) The concept of an ideal specific model of the economy in its open setting is used, however, because discussions of some simple procedures suggests it and because the "ideal" emerges in section 14.2, as we define "rational expectations."

10.2. Fiscal Policy and the Congress

The idea of a fiscal policy, consciously thought out and pursued by the government as a means of stabilizing the economy, finds early embodiment in the Employment Act of 1946 (Joint Committee 1977). It has developed since then with increased recognition being given to the need for the coordination of government policies and the control of separate budgetary actions of Congress. Coordination is complicated where the central bank (or Federal Reserve in the United States) is alleged to be independent within the framework of government, and where it could as a consequence of actual independence reinforced, neutralized, or offset fiscal policy. Moreover, the expenditures, revenues and hence budget surpluses or deficits coming from the Congress have been the result of numerous separate spending and taxing measures, often studied and considered by separate and distinct committees. This was such that the control over any spending and taxing measures, as required by a fiscal policy and its adequate timing, were almost impossible.

Two important congressional actions emerged in the mid-1970s to deal with the problems of coordination and control. Considered separately or together they changed radically the framework for governmental policy with respect to economic stabilization. One--House Concurrent Resolution 133 (First Meeting 1975, and First Report 1975, and since incorporated in the Federal Reserve Act)--was introduced in section 6.2, as it related to monetary and credit policy. For one thing, it called for periodic statements of the Federal Reserve's plans for the monetary and credit aggregates for one year in advance. This mean planned monetary and credit policy are known and can be taken account of in forecasts for the economy and in the formation of a fiscal policy. The second important congressional action was the Congressional Budget and Impoundment Control Act of 1974. Its highlights are considered below.

Both the move toward money and credit aggregates (sect. 6.2) and the budget-setting process adopted by Congress in 1974 were still alive in 1980, and both held promise of continuing so, with some qualifications. First, as we encounter later (sect. 12.5), true independence on the part of the Federal Reserve is said to have been compromised in some quarters. There is especially some question of whether the Federal Reserve can truly be independent of Congress under a regime of money and credit aggregates, in view of potential power to offset the wishes of Congress. The government budget constraint (sect. 10.5) provides one leg of the analysis for questioning true independence. Next, as we will see on subsequent occasions (chap. 17, and sect. 18.5), the history of stabilization policy on the part of Congress as well as the Federal Reserve, since the adoption of the 1974 budgetary device leaves much to be desired. Along Friedmanesque lines, as considered below and later (sects. 10.5, 17.2, and 18.5), the Senate Budget Committee actually voted 8 to 9 in March of 1980, in support of a constitutional amendment to limit Congressional spending.

Congressional Budget and Impoundment Act of 1974

Fiscal policy may be broadly defined as the shaping of government revenues and expenditures and thus surpluses or deficits, with the view to achieving national economic goals. The Congressional Budget and Impoundment Act of 1974 recognizes this and requires the Congress to establish overall Federal budget targets--for receipts, expenditures, and the resulting surplus or deficit--that appear to be consistent with the broad requirements of national economic policy. Important features of the Act called for budget committees in each House of Congress, a separate Congressional Budget office, and a new timetable for the formation of the budget. The new committees of the congress are charged with the task of formulating a congressional budget appropriate to the requirements of economic stabilization. The new budget office parallels the Office of Management and Budget in the Executive Office of the President, but it assists the Congress in making forecasts for the economy and in specifying the necessary fiscal policy. The new budget timetable changed the fiscal year for the government so that it now begins on October 1 instead of July 1, as has been traditional, and it lengthens the time span devoted to the budget process among other things.

The Budget Timetable

A consideration of the budget timetable, as in table 10-1, provides some insights into the budget process. The process, as outlined, may be viewed as occurring in four stages. In the first stage Congress considers the President's "current service budget." It is a statement of projected receipts and outlays for the coming fiscal year. The projections are based on the assumption of no change in programs and tax laws, and on an economic forecast provided by the President's Council of Economic Advisors. This early statement provides a base for use by the Congress in evaluating the President's February budget proposal, mainly a statement incorporating a forecast of ongoing programs and proposed changes in programs and tax measures.

The second stage involves the formation of the initial congressional budget. In the new Act this budget is termed the first concurrent resolution on the budget. It is a working budget and later may be made to mesh with the fiscal policy requirements of the new budget committees.

In the third stage Congress acts on budgetary measures through the usual procedures, moving from subcommittees to full committees, then to actions by the House and Senate, and finally to conference resolution. Final passage of bills at this stage is held up until a summary of legislation overall is prepared. Final action must clear Congress no later than the seventh day after Labor Day.

The final stage in the process is a review of all spending, revenue, and fiscal policy measures. They must mesh, so

Table 10-1. Congressional Budget Timetable

On or Before	Action to be completed	
Nov. 10	Presidential submission of "current services budget" that includes expectations for next fiscal year-given current economic forecasts and an assumption of no further legislative action on spending programs	First Stage (Nov. through Jan/Feb.)
15th day after Congress convenes.	President submits his budget proposal for the next fiscal year	
Mar. 15	Congressional committees and joint committees report to the budget committees on the President's budget and the economic outlook.	Second stage (mid-March through mid May). Preliminary working budget phase.
Apr. 1	Congressional Budget Office submits report to budget committees recommending requisite budget totals.	
Apr. 15	Budget committees report to their respective Houses the first concurrent resolution on the budget establishing key budget totals.	
May 15	Committees report bills and resolutions authorizing new budget authority, and Congress passes the first concurrent budget resolution.	
7th day after Labor Day	Congress completes action on all bills and resolutions from legislative and appropriate committees providing new budget and spending authority.	Third stage (mid May through mid September). The usual procedures phase for appropriations measures.
Sept. 15	Congress completes action on a second concurrent resolution of the budget.	
Sept. 25	Congress completes action on a reconciliation bill or resolution implementing the second concurrent resolution on the budget.	Fourth stage (mid September through October). Review phase for budget as a whole.
Oct. 1	Fiscal year begins.	

Source: "Recent Trends in Federal Budget Policy," Federal Reserve Bulletin, July 1975.

programs and targets for expenditures and revenues may be adjusted. Also, the economic forecast may have changed. The budget process is concluded with the enactment of a reconciliation bill. It adjusts separate committee actions on expenditures and revenues to the overall budget targets affirmed by Congress.

10.3. Fiscal Concepts and Trends

In the early development of a fiscal policy literature, a budget deficit was to be expansionary and a surplus restrictive, in part, because government spending in excess of revenue increased total demand and revenues in excess of expenditures reduced income at the disposal of non-governmental spending units. Since Keynes's and Keynesian economics, these deficits and surpluses were to have a multiplier effects as first mentioned in chapters 4 and deduced in section 7.2. As shown in the next section, however, the multiplier for spending was larger by one than that for an increase in revenue (or a decrease, as the case may be). Thus, even in the presence of a balanced budget with increases in both spending and revenues, there was some impact on GNP.

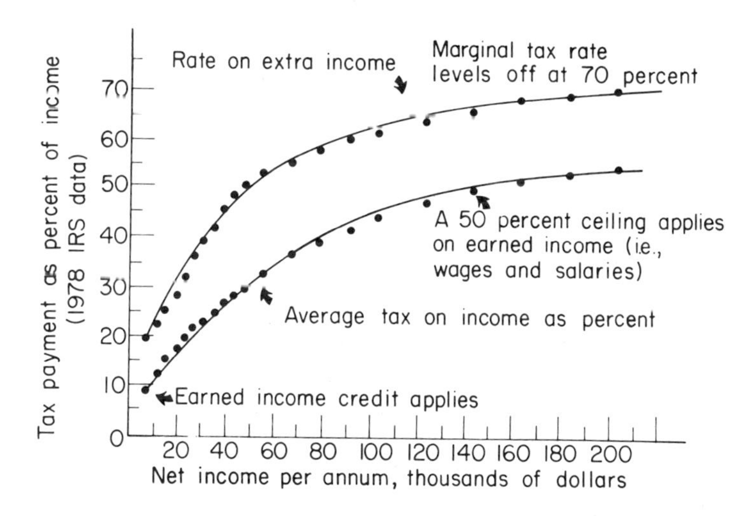

Figure 10-1. Income Tax Rate Schedule for Married Taxpayers Filing Joint Return (1978 income, before exemptions, but after deductions)

Still later the measurement of "fiscal impact," as on GNP, was complicated by the realization of the role of the progressive income tax. For example, as formalized in the next section, an increase in nominal income contributes automatically to a more than proportional increase in revenue and thus alters any initially planned deficit. This progrssive feature of the personal tax is illustrated in figure 10-1. There data are plotted for the marginal tax rate (i.e., rate on extra income) and for the average tax rate, both as percentages and for 1978 taxes (married taxpayers filing joint return). The data are for taxes after deductions but before exemptions. Some of these would be for expenses in earning the income and some would be for what we call "loopholes" below.

As noted, the marginal rate increases rapidly, up to an income of about forty thousand for a joint return (say, from 25 percent at $15,200 to 45 percent), and then it starts to level of at 70 percent at an income of $200,000. Thereafter the rate is a flat rate; it is not a progressive rate. At the lower end of the income scale, we note the earned income credit.[1]

A question raised in the presence of the progressive income tax was what would be the budget state of fiscal actions that brought the economy to full employment. The concept of the "full employment surplus" (FES) emerged, as dealt with more fully in the next section. It was popularized by Walter Heller of President Kennedy's Council of Economic Advisors. It has since been called the "full employment balance" and the "high employment budget," and it expands the host of budget concepts. These may be viewed as including the historical administrative budget, the unified budget, the national income accounts (or GNP accounting) budget, and the "high employment" budget, as explained and illustrated in the appendix to chapter 10. In fiscal year 1969 the unified budget replaced the administrative budget as the government's basic planning document. The difference was the inclusion in the former of receipts and expenditures of funds owned by the government, as well as receipts and expenditures of trust funds.

Under Heller's definition, fiscal policy was restrictive if the budget was in surplus at full employment. It was expansionary if the budget was in deficit, as shown figure 10-2. A chief difference between the FES and the ordinary budget was that the former called for a distinction between discretionary changes in fiscal policy (changes in tax schedules and spending) and changes that would occur automatically (i.e., given income changes and existing programs and the tax structure). The FES budget had the distinction of specifically allowing for automatic changes and others required to achieve the full employment goal.

Much of this is very idealistic, but the concepts of fiscal impact and FES are basic to a potentially viable theory. "Fiscal impact" precisely equals the product of a suitable budget measure and a multiplier. Viewed differently, the ratio of the impact to the budget measure will equal the multiplier. In the early Keynesian without-money model these would be known quite simply. On the other hand, quite the contrary

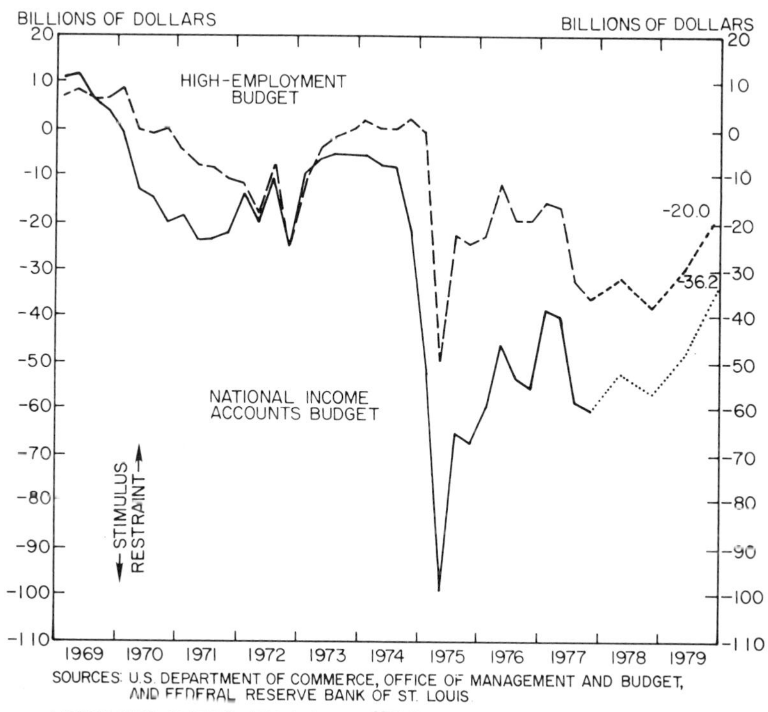

Figure 10-2. Fiscal Measures: Surpluses (+); Deficit (-) (quarterly totals at annual rates, seasonally adjusted)

Sources: U.S. Department of Commerce, Office of Management and Budget, and Federal Reserve Bank of St. Louis

Prepared by Federal Reserve Bank of St. Louis.

became the case with the state of economics in the 1970's. Estimating the budget measure at full employment came to depend on the art of forecasting. Furthermore, knowledge of the impact of a suitable budget measure depends on an empirically satisfactory and combined theory of money, finance, and output. These stringent requirements may ultimately be met by some generation of structural equations models.

The Automatic Stabilizers

The distinction between discretionary and automatic changes has run throughout the post-World War II fiscal policy literature. The automatic (or "built-in") stabilizers are the taxes and programs that yielded changes automatically as the state of the economy changed. According to the definition they caused an automatic return of funds to the private sector during a recession phase of business conditions. The automatic stabilizers tended to improve the timing of fiscal policy because of their tie to business conditions. Sensitive ones were the corporate and personal income taxes and the payroll taxes in combination with unemployment compensation.

Two trends in the economy, however, worked to complicate their role. One has been the growth in social programs and outlays. In the area of social outlays, expenditures for income security have come to include (with reference to functional categories) social security and unemployment insurance

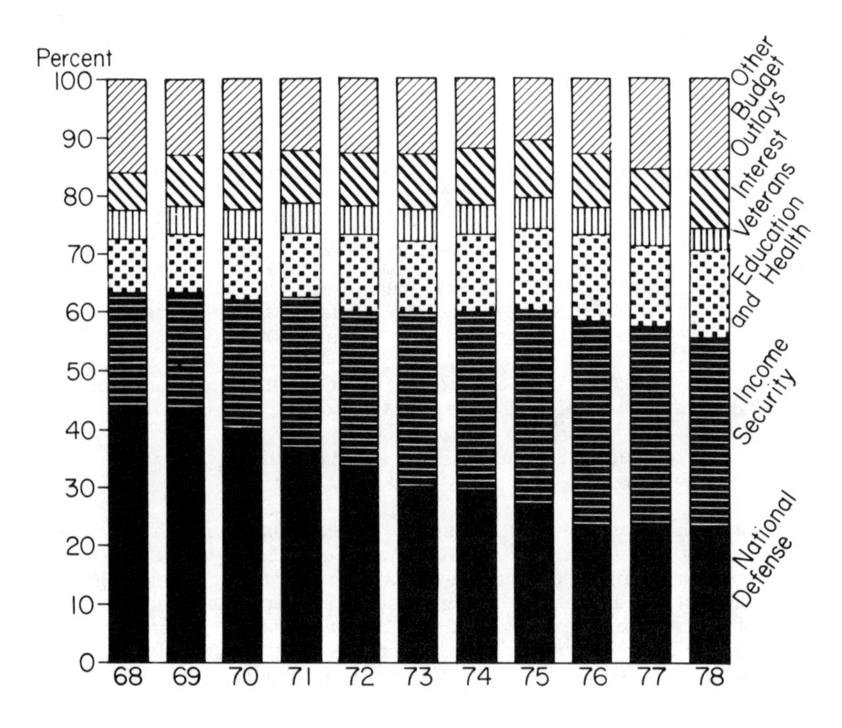

Figure
10-3. Functional Classification of Budget Outlays

programs, public assistance, and supplements to low-income families for food and housing. These programs introduce problems for control because they are open-ended in character, inacted under a so-called "entitlement authority." As eligibility requirements are met under these programs, spending increases automatically. Spending under these programs has sometimes been described as "uncontrollable."

The other complicating trend affecting spending for social programs, and automatic stabilizers as well, is that of secular inflation, and especially the inflationary recession. In the presence of inflation Congress tended to respond by liberalizing benefit payments. Moreover, Congress has tended to turn to indexation, as defined in section 6.4, as a means of keeping benefit payments more current with rising prices. Still another complication has been the occasional presence of rising nominal income and declining real income, as in 1973-75, so that the income tax with its progressivity withdraws funds from the private sector during recession. In these cases, the so-called "automatic"stabilizers no longer stabilize.

Budgetary Trends (Mid 1960s Through Mid 1970s)

In some measure Congress has itself contributed to the inflation that complicated its controls. In the ten years 1965-75 Federal outlays increased 175 percent or at an average annual growth rate of about 11 percent. In contrast, revenues increased only 140 percent over the ten year period. The large and persistent deficits, one may say, added little to our nation's capacity or product, but they added substantially to aggregate monetary demand for goods and services. They were no doubt directly responsible for much of the accelerating inflation of the 1965-75 decade.

Other trends in Federal Budget outlays that complicated fiscal policy concern outlays for income security and for national defense. Those for income security as a proportion of total outlays increased from 22 percent in fiscal 1965 to 33 percent in fiscal 1975, while the proportion for national defense declined from 42 to 27 percent over the same period. These trends have continued since, as shown in figure 10-3 for the decade 1968-78. In addition, Federal outlays as a percentage of GNP also increased from the early- to mid-1970s, but especially in the decade 1968-78, social programs increased as a percentage of GNP and national defense spending declined, as shown in figure 10-4. However, the invasion of the U.S. embassy in Tehran and the seizure of hostages by Iranian students on November 4, 1979, and the invasion of Afghanistan by Soviet troops on December 30, 1979, both promised to alter the foregoing trend in defense spending under the budget for the fiscal year 1981.

As a part of these overall budget trends the share that fell in the "uncontrollable" category grew from about 65 percent to 75 percent in the first half of the 1970s. It then continued in that neighborhood and stood at 76.6 percent of Federal expenditures in the 1981 budget initially proposed by

President Carter. Interest payments on the public debt are entirely a part of "uncontrollables," since they vary with financial markets conditions, but in contrast only about 40 percent of defense-related outlays are a part, in that they do not require new congressional appropriations each year.

Impoundment of Funds

In the presence of inflation and the growth of "uncontrollables," the administration in the early 1970s began withholding funds from programs for purposes of managerial efficiency and as a means of implementing an anti-inflation policy. The authority for the former had an earlier history, but the latter was more recent and questionable. The wishes of Congress were in some measure being circumvented. It was this as well as other deficiencies in the budget control process that led to the Congressional Budget and Impoundment Control Act of 1974.

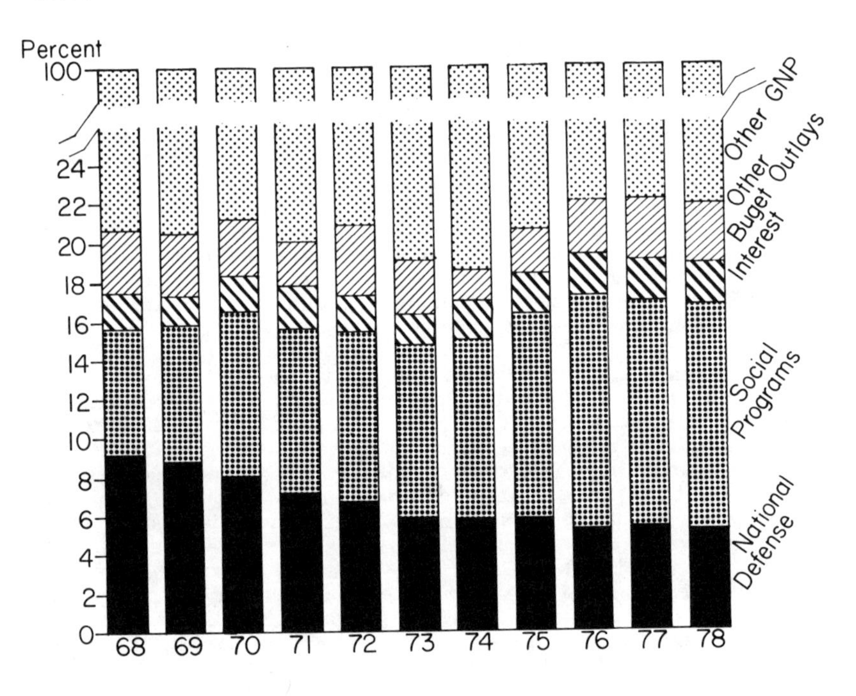

Figure 10-4. Federal Outlays as Percent of GNP

A section of the Act deals with impoundments. They are classified as a deferral of spending to a later date or as a recommended cancellation of budget authority. The cancellation is defined as a recision. To override a presidential deferral only a simple majority vote in either the house of the senate is required. In the case of a recision a new enabling law must be passed with 45 days of the presidential request. Without such a bill the President must disburse the funds.

Even the Budget Control Act should make clear, however, that the President can influence the timing of government spending within limits. This--along with some authority over appointment to the Board of Governors of the Federal Reserve System[2]--may be seen as giving him some control over the timing of turning points in business conditions (sects. 12.5 and 18.5). Hence, a dimension is added to what has historically been referred to as the political business cycle.

The Political Business Cycle

The term "the political business cycle" was coined by Kalecki (1943), and has taken various related meanings. Kalecki saw the political business cycle as instability in the economy that would be caused by shifts in political administrations and the economic policies their varying ideologies would give rise to. Fair (1976) indicated changes in the elected officials that would coincide with the public's dissatisfaction in economic performance (as indicated by inflation and unemployment rates), and MacRae (1977) indicated that economic instability could be generated by having the President attempt to maximize his appeal to the voters by reacting to their particular economic concerns of the moment (say, with alternating attention from unemployment to inflation and vice versa).

In addition, from the control side of business conditions, attention has been directed to the President and other highly placed leaders being able to influence subtle changes in business conditions through the impoundment of funds and through the use of persuasion. This may be with the view to implementing a more politically acceptable program or with the view to avoiding such calamitous circumstances as the coincidence of a recession and a reelection campaign. Here, in the area of persuasion techniques (as reviewed in the appendix to chapter 12), we encounter the officials using subtle, persuasive messages in order to gain support for a particular program and thus accelerate its implementation, or to change belief, say about the future outlook, or the urgency of the problem at hand. Examples of such strategies and stances by officials have included in modern times one adopted by Arthur Burns, as Chairman of the Board of Governors, 1970-78 (sects. 6.2, and 12.5), and another adopted by President Carter in the case of a voluntary wage and price program with respect to wage and price guidelines (sect. 17-3). The latter program, undertaken in mid-1978, was extended to include the support of William Miller (Testimony before the House Banking Committee, 7/25/78), Carter's replacement for Arthur Burns.

In some measure, in late 1978, we saw President Carter switch the concern early in his administration from unemployment to inflation and unemployment, and to concern with the Proposition 13 phenomenum started in California. This switch occured as the unemployment rate declined from 8 to 6 percent and the inflation rate rose from 6 percent to over 10 on a per annum basis in the second quarter of 1978, and as the public came to express more concern over inflation. That concern appeared to reach crisis proportions in early 1980, as the inflation rate reached 18 percent and the prime loan rate 18¼ percent. The Carter response in these instances was so sensitive, that on Friday, March 14, he announced a revision of his proposed 1981 budget. The revision followed by only six weeks, the original proposal to Congress. The new proposed budget was to achieve the first balanced budget since 1969.

Proposition 13 (Jarvis-Gann Amendment)

Proposition 13 was presented to and passed by the voters of California on June 6, 1978, as an amendment to the state constitution. It passed by a margin of almost 2 to 1, and symbolized what has been referred to as a taxpayers revolt. The proposition limited annual property taxes to 1 percent of market value, in effect called for a cut in property taxes of 57 percent, placed a 2 percent ceiling on increases in assessments so long as the property is not sold, and imposed added difficulty in raising taxes from other sources. Although the California initiative was directed at the property tax, the message its passage sent was thought to be a more general one, with other states following suit by limiting tax revenues in other ways, and with impact at the Federal level. Following the passage of Proposition 13, a Gallup poll showed 57 percent of the general public favoring a Jarvis-style tax cut (Newsweek, June 19, 1978). In fact, the tax cut under Proposition 13 was apparently so successful (say, in terms of reducing taxes without catastrophically reducing services from the public's view), that by early 1980 the Howard Jarvis of Proposition 13 was back with Proposition 9. The new proposition, known as Jarvis II, was scheduled to appear on the ballot at the June 3 date for the state's presidential primary. It called for a 50 percent cut in the California income tax.

The reaction by the California voters to the Jarvis-Gann constitutional amendment was apparently in response to inflation induced increases in property values and taxes, and growing dissatisfaction with ineffiency in government services. The Proposition was a crude but potentially effective way of expressing dissatisfaction, and the reaction reflected by it soon spread to other states and to Washington, D.C.. At the national level, Congress voted cuts in corporate and capital gains taxes (sects. 8.2 and 9.2 respectively), initiated the first cuts in the personal income tax rates since the introduction of progressive taxation that did not make the tax structure more progressive (sect. 11.3), and passed a proposal that offered further tax cuts in the long run if the Federal government limited spending in accordance with a specific rule. The latter proposal, however, was dropped by Senate-House conferees in the final stages of agreement with respect to the 1979 tax package.

In theoretic terms, the proposition and the apparent voter preferences had several dimensions. From governments point of view, there was added constraint on spending and hence a fiscal impact on employment. From the public's point of view, there was to be adjustments in the costs (prices) of government services but with minor impact on the services provided by the government. The latter issue, one might say in theoretic terms, was one of price adjustments versus output adjustments, as in the difference between classical economics and Keynesian economics.

Such a public initiative, as suggested by Proposition 13, could go a long way towards fulfilling broad stabilization and employment objectives of government, if made effective and properly directed. For one thing, by adding downward flexibility to price and wage adjustments (or to their accelerated rise) it could give effect to the sorts of adjustments envisioned by neo-classical theory in response to insufficient aggregate demand (sections 1.3, 4.2, and later in chapter 17) and hence to shortening the duration of a recession or to avoiding recession all together. For another thing, an effective and properly guided initiative, could possibly reduce the natural rate of unemployment, as elaborated upon in the next chapter, and hence widen the scope for reductions in the unemployment rate through demand management. To be sure, as described mainly in section 17.3, President Carter's voluntary approach to the control of wages and prices during the 1977-79 period, with some assistance from persuasive strategies, could be viewed as trying to get classical, price sorts of adjustments, as a tradeoff for Keynesian, output sorts of adjustments.

The Laffer Curve

Against the background of rising government expenditures and deficits, the rising tax revenues generated by unlegislated inflation taxes, and Proposition 13, one encountered on the national scene in 1978 the Laffer curve (Newsweek 6/26/78; Wall Street Journal 10/1/78). It summarizes some features of revenue yields to the government as tax rates vary and as the uses of revenues by government vary. It also entails matters of public response to government and inefficiencies caused by the transfer of activities from the monetary economy to a barter sector of such an economy. The monetary economy is one with production and exchange for an indirect satisfaction of wants. The barter economy is one with the less efficient production and exchange for direct satisfaction of wants (sects. 1.1 and 1.2).

The Laffer curve is named after Arthur B. Laffer, a White House assistant in the early 1970s (Frazer 1973, 225-27), Stanford Ph.D., a formerly tenured professor at Chicago, and more recently a professor of business and finance at the University of Southern California. It would appear that Laffer had spurned professional writing for larger media events. The attention brought to his curve and its implications would appear in part attributable to the timing of the message. According to Laffer's reading of the U.S. position on the curve, it called for massive tax cuts that would actually increase revenues, and it addressed aspects of the Proposition 13 phenomenum. Senator William Roth of Delaware called him "the new guru, an economic genius." Harvard's and the National Bureau's Martin Felstein is said to have called the curve "something a Congressman can digest in about 30 seconds and then talk about for months."

On the occasion of initiating the curve, Laffer noted (Wanniski 1978, 97-103), "There are always two tax rates [the two fixed points] that yield the same revenues." These he said occur when the tax rate is zero and 100 percent respectively. At 100 percent, when all fruits of labor in the "monetary economy" are confiscated by the government, people will not work in the monetary economy, although this does not preclude their doing so in the "barter economy."

The monetary economy for Laffer is essentially that of production and exchange in a market for indirect satisfaction of wants. There is then a division of labor with workers specializing according to their comparative advantage, with a resulting increase in production from their doing so. The barter economy, on the other hand, is one of production, do-it-yourself work, and exchange as for a direct satisfaction of wants. It is chiefly, in the Laffer context, a way of continuing some production, albeit without the advantages of the efficient use of labor, and at the same time avoiding the payment of taxes. "The worst mistakes in history," Wanniski says (1978, 102), while drawing on Laffer, "are made by political leaders who, instead of realizing that rates could be lowered as a means of gaining revenues, become alarmed at the fall in revenues as citizens seek to escape higher rates by bartering, and do-it-yourself work." The impulse of the leaders, he says, "is to impose taxes that cannot be escaped, the most onerous of which is a poll tax or head tax, which must be paid annually for the mere privilege of living."

Continuing, Wanniski notes (1978, 103), that since modern governments have abandoned the notion of a poll tax to get revenues from the barter economy, they do other things instead. For one, they admit activities not previously admitted to the public market place such as gambling and pornography. For another, they resort to the "timeless remedy of governments that find revenues falling in the face of rising tax rates [namely, to increasing the number and powers of the tax collectors]."

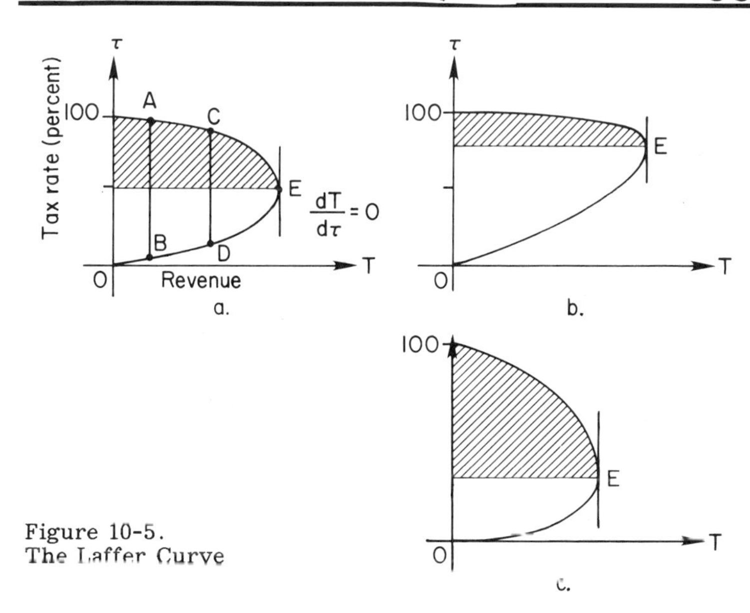

Figure 10-5.
The Laffer Curve

The curve Wanniski addresses is shown in the a-part of figure 10-5. The fixed points are at the origin and at 100 percent, and beyond them there are always two tax rates that will yield the same revenues. These are illustrated in the a-part of figure 10-5 by the tax points A and B and C and D, respectively. Starting at the origin in the a-part, as the tax rate (τ) rises revenue (T) rises up to the extreme value $dT/d\tau = 0$. Beyond the point of the extreme value, further rise in the tax rate will no longer increase revenue but does instead decrease it. There are two associated developments, notably: there is a shift of activity from the market economy where revenues are obtained by the government to the barter economy; and pari passu there is less production than would otherwise be attained because barter-economy activities are less efficient (without division of labor and indirect production to satisfy wants).

The shaded area of the Laffer figure indicates the prohibitive range for the tax rate. Rates in the range indicated are unnecessarily high, and can be reduced with gains in both output and revenue. As indicated, moreover, the curve and location of the extreme value (and hence the range for prohibitive tax rates) are not fixed, except for the origin and 100 percent rate. The point of tendency ($dT/d\tau = 0$) is the point at which the electorate desires to be taxed and it may vary, as indicated by the b- and a-part of figure 10-5. As Wanniski says (1978, 99) of the siege of Leningrad in World War II, for example, "the people of the city produced for 900 days at tax rates approaching 100 percent." He says (1978, 99):

> Russian soldiers and civilians worked to their physical limits, receiving as pay the barest of rations. Had the citizens of Leningrad not wished to be taxed at that high rate in order to hold off the Nazi army, the city would have fallen, with many citizens paying the ultimate tax rate.

Such an attitude toward taxation would be reflected more accurately by the b-part than the a-part of figure 10-5.

Moving in another direction the electorate may reveal a different shaped curve with a different location for the extreme point ($dT/d\tau = 0$), such as shown in the c-part of figure 10-5. The use of the revenues by the political leaders will influence the acceptible tax rates on the part of the electorate. In rejecting a school-bond issue, at the local level, for example, the electorate is sending the message that "the price in tax rates is too high in terms of the goods and services offered by the government." On such matters, Wanniski says (1978, 98-9), "It is the task of the political leader to determine point E [$dT/d\tau = 0$] and to follow it through its variations as closely as is possible."

Another example of a reduced willingness on the part of the electorate to pay taxes with targeted expenditures in mind would follow along the lines of the proposition 13 phenomenum. In its national dimension, we encounter increased unwillingness to pay taxes on the part of the electorate, and hence an enlargement of the shaded area in relation to the unshaded area in the c-part of figure 11-5. Also, for the c-part of the figure, the "money economy" is more likely to suffer at the expense of higher tax rates, and the government is quite likely to resort to efforts directed toward expanding taxable activities and enhancing the powers of tax collectors (the IRS, at the national level).

The curve has had its supporters, and detractors, and funds have been granted to test notions that are associated with the curve. Some have questioned the sorts of taxes Laffer had in mind. On the one hand, he has appeared to stress taxes that thwart incentive, production, and the employment of capital in productive areas. Capital gains taxes have been pointed to ("Ideological Tic," Wall Street Journal, 6/23/78) and indeed the Laffer curve was associated with the move to cut capital gains taxes in 1978. On the other hand, Laffer has apparently not spurned the support that would come from arguments for a Keynesian/Kennedy style tax cut (sect. 11.3) and the full employment surplus argument below (sect. 10.4), and some journalist have confused the latter with the Laffer argument.

Tax Limitation and Inflation as a Tax

Milton Friedman the political economist appeared on commercial television in support of Proposition 13 in 1978, and helped find the National Tax Limitation Committee with efforts directed toward tax limitation through a constitutional amendment (Newsweek, 6/19/78, 26; and Friedman 1978, 14-21), partly to limit "the unlegislated rise in taxes produced by inflation." The prospects looked good for the matter to succeed, Friedman asserts, until California's Governor Jerry Brown propelled the issue into national politics and helped make it partisan political issue (Newsweek, 3/26/79, 87). The philosophy of the constitutional amendment strategy, as expounded much earlier by Friedman was nonpartisan, "the problem of getting them [people] to give up what they see as in their special interest." On the idea of a flat rate income tax, for example, Friedman had proposed achieving a concensus through getting the right wing to give up tax loopholes (deductions for charitable contributions, interest payments, real-estate taxes, special treatment of capital gains, oil depletion allowances and all the rest, except strictly occupational expenses) and the left wing to give up the higher rates. He argued that very few in the higher brackets pay taxes because of the loopholes and that besides "the graduated tax protects rather than redistributes wealth" (Playboy 1973, 60, 65).

In any case, the draft of the constitutional amendment that was to be proposed by Friedman's National Tax Limitation Committee in 1979, was directed towards limiting spending rather than taxes directly (Newsweek, 3/5/79, 87). The draft amendment proposed in broad outline a two-part limit on Federal spending --"one to apply if the Humphrey-Hawkins inflation goal of 3 per cent is attained; the other if inflation is higher than that."[3] At or below the 3-percent level, the amendment would permit

> Federal spending to rise by the same percentago as dollar gross national product.... If spending rose by the maximum permitted amount, it would remain a constant percentage of GNP... In addition, if a thrifty Congress held spending below the maximum for any year, so that spending went down as a percentage of income, that lower level of spending would be the base for spending limits in future years. The result would be a permanent reduction in spending as a percentage of income. (Newsweek, 3/5/79, 87)

If inflation of greater than 3 percent, the limit on spending under the draft proposal would be a tighter one, the higher the inflation the tighter the limit.

In defense of the draft proposal, Friedman argued thus

> Deficits have occurred and grown primarily because there has been political pressure on Congress to increase spending but not taxes. A firm cap on Federal spending would relieve that pressure. The deficit would disappear as economic growth raised tax receipts as a fraction of income, while the amendment kept spending constant or declining. Soon

> Congress would have the pleasant duty of reducing taxes in order to keep down the surplus. (Newsweek, 3/5/79, 87)

As stated by Friedman (1978, 16), the defect in our political and constitutional structure that calls for spending limits "is that we have no means whereby the public at large ever gets to vote on the total budget of the government." Instead, "for any single spending measure... there is always a small group that has a strong interest in that measure." Furthermore, none of us are "too strongly opposed to any one small measure that will benefit someone else." The purpose of the limitation (or a limitation on spending, as Friedman sees it, Newsweek 3/5/79, 87), is to remedy the defect brought about by vocal special interest, on the one hand, and the passiveness of opponents when the special interest measures are many in number and individually of little consequence, on the other.

"As long as high government spending remains," Friedman says (1978, 18), "we shall have the hidden tax of inflation." This would be partly as the tax works through the income tax by pushing households into higher effective tax rates ("bracket creep") without legislation (Newsweek, 4/14/80, 90). It would also include, as addressed by Friedman at an earlier date (1973, 40-41; 1975, 16-23), the hidden tax on the holding of cash balances.

The hidden tax brought by inflation is a source of inconvenience when it contributes to a reduction in cash holdings below those that may otherwise be held (sects. 3.3 and 6.3), and it is a tax on the remaining balances that are held. The tax base in this latter regard is most vividly expressed as a value equal to a percentage of annual income. The tax rate in effect is the inflation rate, and the revenue loss is the product of the tax base and the tax rate. In the United States in the first quarter of 1979, the money stock (M_1, average of daily figures, seasonally adjuted) was equal to 57.85 days of annual income, and the inflation rate (say, the added tax rate imposed by inflation) was over 10 percent. Inflation alone at this time then was equivalent to an added tax amounting to approximately 5.8 days of income.

10.4. The Keynesian Model

Several ideas converge as we consider some views of the fiscalist of the 1960s: the idea of a control mechanism such that some variable such as government spending (G), in the reduced form equation of the Keynesian three sector model, can be manipulated to achieve some target value for income (Y); the idea that employment will vary directly with income in the neighborhood of the equilibrium value Y, at least in the short run before technological change and accompanying increases in the output per worker cause income to grow too much, even with a constant labor force; and the idea that tax revenues will increase, indeed even at a faster rate, as income increases because of the nature imparted to the tax structure by the corporate and even more progressive personal income taxes. This automatic rise in revenue has been called "fiscal drag" because, Heller said (1966, 64-67), it siphons too much of the economic substance out of the private economy and thereby chokes expansion. In its presence tax cuts are called for.

The Three Sector Model

Once we add government spending (G), and tax revenues (T), the two sector model of chapter 7 is slightly modified. The new construction is shown in figure 10-6, where total income received is denoted Y ($Y \equiv Y_d + S_b + T$). Treating consumption as a function of disposable income (Y_d) or income after business saving and taxes ($Y - S_b - T$), however, the structural form of the model is as follows:

(Demand relation) $E = C(Y_d) + I + G,$

where $C(Y_d) = a + bY_d$

(Income) $Y = Y_d + S_b + T$

where $Y_d = Y - S_b - T$

and where tax revenues are a function of income and a tax parameter (think of it as a tax rate), i.e., $T(Y, \tau)$. In addition--anticipating discussions of the "crowding out effect" of deficit financing--the difference G-T represents roughly a deficit by government to be financed, and the difference $I - S_b$ depicts in some measure the capital spending of business firms that will require external financing (where S_b represents earning retained by business and funds from the tax credit and depreciation of real capital). We say "roughly" and "in some measure" because other sources of funds are sometimes available, such as reductions in cash accounts.

Figure 10-6. Three-Sector, Income Expenditure Model

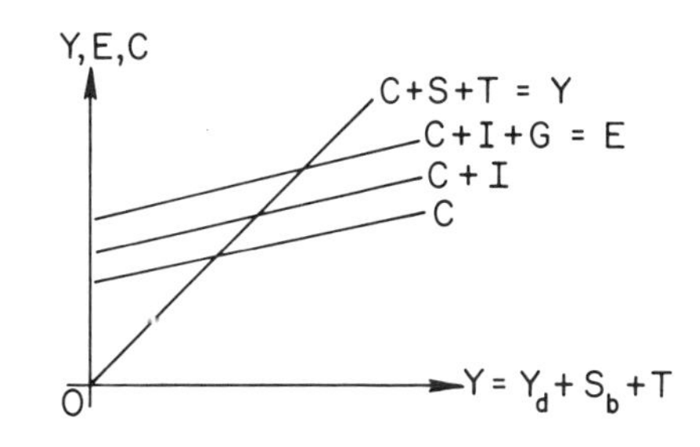

The variables treated as constants in the model are:

$T = \bar{T}$

$S_b = \bar{S}_b$

$I = \bar{I}$

$G = \bar{G}$

(Equilibrium) $E = Y$

Furthermore, consumption is a function of disposable income in the algebraic model even though total income is denoted on the horizontal axis in figure 10-6, and, in addition, taxes enter in a very special way as absolute tax yields, given the generally progressive rate structure whereby tax liabilities increase more than in proportion with income. Given the structure, as income (Y) increases tax yields (T) increase at a faster rate and disposable income at a slower rate. This means that the consumption function has less of a slope (smaller b) than it would in the absence of a progressive tax structure. A change in the progressivity of the structure, as in the tax rates, then may affect the position of the function through its slope, but a parallel shift may occur too in the presence of across the board changes in rates for different income classifications (i.e., changes that affect the tax liabilities of each income class by the same percentage). The parallel shifts would be noted as a change in the intercept parameter a. This will be illustrated with reference to the reduced form equation for the model.

Setting the demand relation equal to income, the reduced form equation follows:

$$Y_d + \bar{S}_b + \bar{T} = a + b\,Y_d + \bar{I} + \bar{G}$$

$$(Y - \bar{S}_b - \bar{T}) + \bar{S}_b + \bar{T} = a + b\,(\bar{Y} - \bar{S}_b - \bar{T}) + \bar{I} + G$$

$$Y = a + bY - b\bar{S}_b - b\bar{T} + \bar{I} + \bar{G}$$

$$Y(1 - b) = a - b\bar{S}_b - b\bar{T} + \bar{I} + \bar{G}$$

$$\text{(Reduced form)} \quad \bar{Y} = \left(\frac{1}{1 - b}\right)(a - b\bar{S}_b - b\bar{T} + \bar{I} + \bar{G})$$

The solution value for income $(\bar{Y})$ is given in term of constants, otherwise there is no single solution. This is why the variables T, S_b, I, and G were denoted as constants (i.e., with bars over them). This special sort of solution equation is called a reduced form in economics where the constants can be viewed as exogenous variables (i.e., as variables outside of the model itself, or as policy or control variables).[4] With reference to this form and an increase in government spending and therefore income and tax revenues,

$$\underbrace{\Delta\bar{Y}}_{\text{Fiscal Impact}} = \underbrace{\left(\frac{1}{1-b}\right)}_{\text{Multiplier}} \underbrace{[(\Delta\bar{G} - \Delta T)}_{\text{Actual Budget Deficit}} \underbrace{-b\Delta\bar{T}]}_{\text{Reduction in spending due to increase in tax revenue}}$$

The warning about consumption as a function of disposable income comes into play when we consider changes in the underlying conditions giving rise to the curves described by the model. For example, an across the board cut (increase) in income tax rates that leaves the progressivity of the tax structure unchanged means an upward (downward) shift in the consumption function. As it turns out, the extent of the cut at a given income level may be denoted

$$(-b)(-\Delta T),$$

where ΔT is the change in the dollar amount of tax yields for a given change in income. Even so, an across the board cut in tax liabilities that leaves the progressive feature of the tax unchanged is properly a change in the intercept, i.e., $\Delta a = (-b)(-\Delta T)$, and an increase is $-\Delta a = (-b)(\Delta T)$. The effect of such an increase in taxes on Y is $(1/1\text{-}b)(-b\Delta T)$ or $(1/1\text{-}b)(-\Delta a) = -\Delta Y$. These changes are shown in figure 10-7. They are not changes in the actual term for taxes as seen in the right hand member of the reduced form equation.

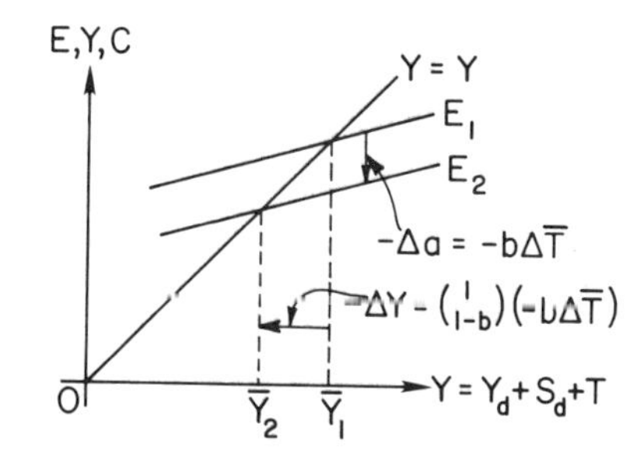

Figure 10-7.
An Increase in Taxes

Income and Tax Rate Induced Changes in Tax Revenue

Tax revenue (T) has been introduced as a function of tax rates and income (τ, and Y respectively). In the simple model, however--and one might add, in the analysis of worldly phenomena as well--we must distinguish between two different kinds of tax rate changes, namely: those that leave the progressiveness of the structure unchanged and those that alter it. The first appears as a parallel shift in the simple function, and the second appears as a change in the slope (in the parameter b). In the presence of actual tax cuts, as on occasions since 1964 (and as considered in section 11.3), these latter two changes occur simultaneously along with revenue changes resulting from income changes. As considered in the next chapter, changes in the progressive feature of the tax structure further concern the following: incentives for work and the movement to higher income brackets; and the permanency (or lack of income and social mobility) of income earning units in the different income brackets.

In the simple model depicted in figure 10-7 and in the matters just introduced, one encounters some of the complexities centering about the interdependence of economic variables when that interdependence is free to operate. We have to comprehend, in economics, in other words, both the results obtained through the practice of simplification by impoundment of complexities in ceteris paribus, and the complexities introduced when interdependence is free to operate outside of its impoundment in ceteris paribus.

The Balanced Budget Multiplier

When we consider an increase in government spending (ΔG) with a balanced increase in taxes (ΔT), the parameter b is seen in an even further role. First the balanced budget effects on income (Y), where $\Delta G = \Delta T$:

$$\left(\frac{1}{1 - b}\right) \Delta G = \Delta G + \Delta Gb + \Delta Gb^2 + \Delta Gb^3 + \ldots$$

$$\left(\frac{b}{1 - b}\right) \Delta T = \Delta Tb + \Delta Tb^2 + \Delta Tb^3 + \ldots$$

Difference = ΔG

In government spending there is a first round effect of ΔG, but with an increase in taxes (ΔT) the first round of effect is ΔTb, instead of ΔT, because there is some presumed leakage from the first round effect into saving.

The result just outlined gives rise to the balanced budget multiplier of one. Some have dignified the exercise by calling the result the unit multiplier theorem. In words, if government spending and the amount of taxes collected change by the same amount, the resulting change in income will equal the change in government spending.

The idea underlying the balanced budget multiplier of one is that the taxes take away from the enlarged income but not by the amount injected through expenditures. Some of what is withdrawn in tax revenues comes out of saving or what would otherwise be leakages from income into saving, e.g., as any enlarged flow of spending proceeds through the various terms of the geometric progression in section 7.2.

Fine Tuning and "The Full Employment Balance."

The ideas listed at the beginning of this section led the astute political economists Walter Heller to formulate the concepts of fine tuning and the full employment surplus. He reasoned that a budgetary figure could be obtained by which to gauge fiscal policy. This was not just in terms of fiscal action and inactions, but in terms of a full employment surplus --"The excess of revenues over expenditures which would prevail at 4 percent unemployment (as a percentage of the labor force)." The 4 percent figure was to be set at a lower level following improvements in the matching of the labor skills of the unemployed with the job vacancies (i.e., following a reduction in "structural unemployment").

These fiscalist notions have also been embodied in Okun's Law,

$$Y_f - Y = 0.03\ (U - 4)Y$$

where $Y_f - Y$ is the GNP gap, U is the unemployment rate, 0.03 is a production factor, and 4 is the full employment goal for the unemployment rate (U). (Note that there is no gap when U = 4.0.) The late Arthur Okun (1928-1980) had been with the White House's Council of Economic Advisors in early 1960s and was the Council's Chairman in the late years of the Johnson administration. Okun later served as an outside consultant to the Carter White House.

The foregoing concepts merited the label "fine tuning" because they suggested a high degree of refinement in the control mechanism, all without reference to the state of the business cycle or the larger goal of smoothing it out. Further, the notion of a full employment target as it prevailed in the early 1960s must be juxtaposed with the notion of a natural rate of unemployment, as defined in section 9.1 and elucidated in the next chapter. Aspects of the present Keynesian approach also emerge later in chapter 17 in our consideration of the prospect of selecting precise unemployment and price inflation percentages, as for a point on the Phillips curve, without considering the broader nature of instability.

As matters have evolved, the attainment of full employment has not always been accompanied by a budget surplus. The concept has been rechristened "the full employment balance." Further, there has been recognition of a need to consider a broader set of developments. Even so, there is the prospect in these exercises that at times an increase (decrease) in government spending contributes to a reduction (increase) in unemployment. A broader set of notions about policies and stabilization emerge below and in the next chapter and the present notions may be brought forward at the appropriate time.

The tendency for the economy to generate a budgetary surplus (or a smaller deficit) as income rises is shown by the upward sloping line AA, with a given tax structure (i.e., with given tax rates and degree of progressivity) in figure 10-8. A reduction in the income tax rates across the board may change the structure, e.g., as represented by a downward shift in line AA. The reduced taxes appears to reduce the surplus at the unemployment level Y_u. The reduced taxes, however, would increase income Y, say via an upward shift in the consumpton function. Following out the analysis there, income would increase and tax revenues also. The degree of the increase in the revenues from a given tax cut would depend on the degree of progressivity in the tax structure.

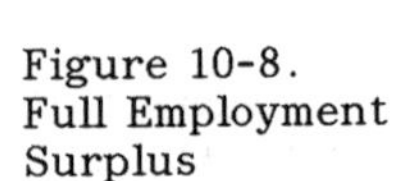
Figure 10-8.
Full Employment
Surplus

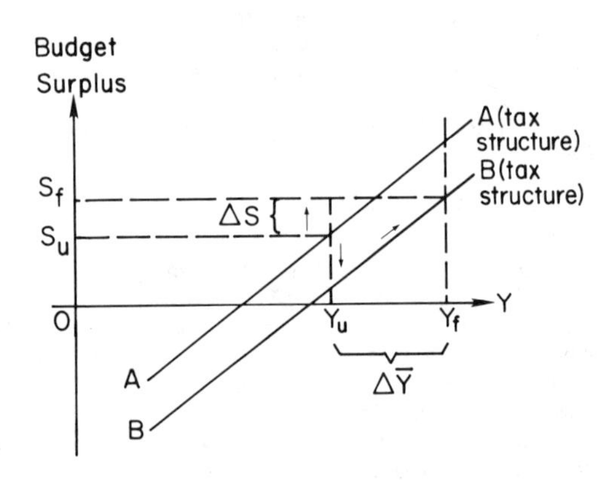

In figure 10-8, the tax structure change is shown as a shift from line AA to BB. But income Y increases, as revenue increases, as shown by the arrow along the line BB. At the full employment income Y_f the surplus in the budget has actually increased from the initial S_u to S_f.

This sort of reasoning was first presented as the basis for an actual tax program to overcome fiscal drag due to the tendency for income tax revenues to rise more than in proportion to income, in the presence of a progressive income tax. The tax program emerged in 1964 under a Democratic administration. The employment part of the program, if not the budget surplus part, underlay proposed actions of a Republican administration in early 1975, and the Carter administration in 1978. The 1975 tax cut and its extension for the first six months of 1976, as well as the Carter proposal, come up in chapter 11.

10.5. The Government Budget Constraint

The Keynesian model just outlined proports to show the impacts of a change in government spending and tax revenues on income. It says nothing about the possible effect on private spending that may result from the financing of a government deficit and there is no allowance for the role of monetary policy in the assessment of the net impact of the deficit. Allowing for these the Keynesian multiplier may be overstated. Such an allowance was a part of Keynes's economics, and it reemerges under the monetarist influence, as a part of empirical economics ("soft monetarism" or "eclectic" Keynesianism, Blinder and Solow would say). The formal treatment of the subject has come up under the label "government budget constraint."

This section considers initially some informal views of the financial effects of a deficit and the monetary policy role (actually the credit policy role since the concern is with bank credit, the total of loans and investments of the commercial banks). It finally considers the government budget constraint.

The Crowding Out Effect

In early consideration of Keynes's work, possible effects of financing a government deficit were considered. There was the possibility that in financing a deficit (as through the sale of bonds) "funds" may be diverted from the private sector and thus have adverse effects on private spending. A net result consequently could be a lower investment multiplier.

The institutional groups that typically hold the marketable portion of the Federal debt are commercial banks, nonfinancial corporations, insurance companies, general funds of states and local governments, savings and loan associations, mutual savings banks, pension and retirement funds, and "all others." These groups also hold other debt-type instruments or securities, as may arise when the private sectors of the economy originate new issues to obtain funds for their spending. On the sources-of-funds side, a given amount of funds flows to the groups mentioned, partly from households, as they purchase insurance and the like. The question then arises as to whether the sale of additional bonds by the government may "crowd out" the issues of the private sector. It would of course do so, where the funds are limited and are being sought by the private sector. There would be no obvious crowding out, as in a depression, if funds were available in sufficient amount, including in excess of amounts held for speculative and precautionary purposes. Further, there would be no crowding out if newly issed government bonds were acquired by commercial banks in response to increase in reserves above the legally required amounts and above those amounts held for speculative and precautionary purposes, and above the amounts called to support sustainable growth in bank loans to the private sector. The Federal Reserve could provide the extra reserves.

At other times, funds may be less readily available and the Federal Reserve less willing to supply them. An example of the unwillingness of the independent Federal Reserve occurred in early 1975 when a congressional committee was considering a proposed budget. The deficit in President Ford's budget at that time was a record amount and the democratic controlled Congress was moving toward an even larger deficit than proposed. Testifying before the committee the Federal Reserve's Chairman said the Board would not permit an explosion of money and credit to help finance public and private financing demands. This was a warning to the Congress about enlarging the 1975-76 deficit.[5]

Possible Interest Rate and Price Induced Effects

In a Keynesian framework with some price level changes introduced ad hoc, Blinder and Solow consider some fiscal policy induced changes that might reduce the size of the Keynesian multiplier. For example, increased government spending and real output call for more money balances. Where these are not forthcoming interest rates may rise and partly reduce the effect of the increase in government spending. Further, there will be other so-called "monetary snubbing" effects if prices rise as real demand increases:

1. The real value of unchanged nominal money stock will be lower and thus have further constraining effect.

2. Higher prices for goods and services lower the purchasing power of proceeds obtained from the government securities held by the private sector, and thus there is a possible wealth effect that may reduce spending.

3. Tax receipts will rise and reduce private spending in real terms under a progressive tax system legislated in money terms.

4. Higher prices in an open economy will depress exports and thus reduce investment spending.

These effects would serve to reduce the size of the fiscal policy multiplier.

The Government Budget Constraint

The government budget constraint, as it has appeared most commonly, consists of the constraint imposed on the financing of a deficit in nominal dollar terms--denoted P[G -

T(Y, τ)]--by the need for a change in high powered money (dR/dt) (the monetary base or "outside money")[6] and/or by the need for additional borrowing from the private sector through the sale of bonds (dB/dt). An equation may be written:

$$(1) \qquad \frac{dR}{dt} + \frac{dB}{dt} = P[G - T(Y, \tau)]$$

Blinder and Solow would alter equation (1) slightly to recognize the need to pay interest on the Federal debt, and others would allow for the change in the Treasury's cash account as a means of financing some part of a deficit or as a means of absorbing a surplus. In any case excluding these allowances as being of minor importance, equation (1) is adequate. In the static case, as where levels are being dealt with rather than rates of change, the so-called long-run equilibrium is denoted dR/dt = dB/dt = 0. (Blinder and Solow recognize the possibility of a dynamic statement with rates of change in stock and flow quantities).

The idea is that the deficit will be financed by the sale of bonds to the Federal Reserve (in which case an increase in reserves) or by a sale of bonds to the household or business sectors. (The Federal Reserve of course does not buy new issues from the Treasury in the conduct of open market operations, but instead buys outstanding issues from private dealers.) The requirement that the Federal Reserve buy the bonds will be recognized as being satisfied in any case, where the Federal Reserve buys an amount in the market equivalent to some amount sold to the business, private financial, and household sectors. The reader should recall (sect. 6.2), however, that an open market purchase will increase reserves and hence bank credit (the total of loans and investments) by a multiple amount. In addition, in the context of the bank reserve equation of chapters 6, changes in reserves may occur from sources other than open market operations.

Now, in the context of the bank reserve equation it becomes clear why the monetarist may claim, as reviewed by Blinder and Solow, that a change in high powered money (dR/dt) to finance a deficit is a change in monetary policy and not fiscal policy. Namely, it is because a change in bank credit and monetary aggregates (actually a change in the rate of change in the dynamic case) is what we have defined as a change in monetary policy. On the basis of operational considerations and criteria for a satisfactory policy measure, a change in a deficit would go entirely into bond holdings by the household and business sectors if monetary policy did not allow for the change in bank reserves.

Blinder and Solow (1974, 57) quote the monetarist thus.

> Deficit spending carries with it either creation of new high-powered money [in which case they call it monetary policy] or new bond floatations [in which case they deny that it will be expansionary].

Then, Blinder and Solow, say that their version of equation (1) above does not take side in doctorial disputes. It may read, they say, "you cannot increase the high-powered money stock without either deficit spending or bond retirement." There is some truth in this statement but with a major exception: open market purchases (sect. 6.2) are a main source of reserves in the fractional reserve system, and on their base banks may create multipler increases in bank loans and investments, all such that the open market purchase results in an expansion of the symbolic bonds held outside of the government. Thus, contrary to the Blinder and Solow statement, high powered money may be increased, as through open market operations, without deficit spending by the government and without the net retirement of bonds.

The Blinder and Solow view of open market operations as simply swaps between R and B is an inoperative view of monetary policy and the money and credit system. To consider "swaps" of R for B (or B for R) as open market operations and as "strictly monetary policies" is to ignore the essence and uniqueness of banks as financial institutions and of the Federal Reserve's control mechanism. A purchase of securities in the open market is no way a swap of R for B. Indeed a purchase will have the effect of expanding money and credit aggregates by multiple amounts (sect. 6.2).[7] In essence R increases such that the loans and investments of commercial banks may increase by some multiple amount, in the presence of the credit multiplier. A part of these investments may be holdings of the government's bonds so that B can increase even as and by a larger amount than R increases. The credit mechanism is unique in this respect.

In addition, open market operations were not originally and need not be currently confined to government securities. In the early years of open market operations commercial paper was purchased and today negotiable certificates of deposit (CD's) could be purchased just as easily. This aspect of operations would be such that the Federal Reserve could accomodate through an expansive policy the sale of new issues of government securities to commercial banks without themselves purchasing the securities, and such that the Federal Reserve's policy does not depend on any federal deficit or fiscal policy. The reverse would not be true that the government could finance a deficit without either "crowding out" private financing or relying on the credit and monetary policies.

Finally, the Federal Reserve is an independent agency within the framework of government. As such, the Federal Reserve becomes responsible for either supporting the financing of a deficit (as through expansion of bank credit) or for permitting the financing of a government deficit to crowd out other financing. But once again, the reverse is not true for fiscal policy.

10.6. Summary

Fiscal policy as indicated by some budgetary measure such as a deficit and the analysis surrounding its impact on total spending via a multiplier is mainly a legacy of Keynesian economics (sect. 4.3). In a broader sense it may be defined as a shaping of government revenues (including specific tax measures, as considered in the next chapter) and expenditures with the view to achieving economic goals, all after allowance for a host of indirect possibilities (including the prospect of "crowding out"). As introduced by Keynes and as later introduced by the monetarists in the late 1960s through the mid-1970s, the theory may be expanded to include financial, credit and monetary considerations, especially as embodied in the consideration of the government budget constraint.

In the 1960s we get the concepts of a "full employment" balance in the budget and of "fiscal drag." In the former case, there is the idea about what the state of the budget will be at full or "high" employment. A surplus in this state suggests that fiscal policy is contractive and a deficit that it is expansive. Fiscal drag is the drag on spending by the private sector that is created as income in nominal dollar terms increases in the presence of a progressive tax structure. This structure implies that spending power is progressively withdrawn from the household sector. Consequently, to reduce drag on the economy, tax cuts that leave the slope of the simple consumption function unchanged are called for. Other tax cuts may have effect on spending, but these are compensating for the drag rather than removing it.

In more common parlance, a simple deficit is expansive and a surplus contractive. And further, in the tradition of early Keynesian economics, an increment in spending with no increment in revenues (hence, a deficit) has a multiplier effect, and an increase in government spending with equal increase in revenues (i.e., a balanced budget in common parlance) yields a balanced budget multiplier of one. In the analysis of the impact of these measures today, allowances for the financial side effects of fiscal policy, traditionally viewed, are known to reduce the traditional Keynesian expenditure multiplier.

In the simple three sector Keynesian model--with consumption as a function of disposable income and without monetary policy and the complexities of deficit financing--one encounters tax revenue as a function of the tax rate (say on personal income) and income. Even in this simplified context, some tax rate changes shift the simple consumption function through its intercept parameter, others change the slope of the function (and hence the value of the Keynesian multiplier), and some may change the function in both ways. As elucidated in the next chapter, there are the related and additional complexities bearing on incentives for work, government induced redistribution of income, and the permanency of income earning units in the difference income brackets.

Interrelationships between fiscal policy, on the one hand, and credit and monetary policy, on the other, come into focus on two levels. At a formal level one encounters the government budget constraint, namely--deficits must be financed by the sale of bonds to the private sector or by the Federal Reserve's increasing high powered money. In the one case, there is the likely possibility of "crowding out" private financing and, in the other, the deficit financing becomes dependent on the credit policy of the Federal Reserve. There is no use trying to consider "swaps" between bank reserves (R) and government bonds (B) as open market operations, and then to consider bond or high-powered money financed deficit spending as fiscal policy. This ignores the Federal Reserve's ability to expand high-powered money independently of a government deficit, and it ignores the unique credit and money creating powers of open market operations in a fractional reserve system, and hence the more indirect ways in which the Federal Reserve allegedly may support Treasury financing as through the expansion of credit at commercial banks. In addition, the Federal Reserve has some independence in the decision to offset or reinforce fiscal policy. The reverse is not the case with fiscal policy.

At a statutory level the need to allow for an interrelationship between fiscal and monetary policy is brought into focus through Congressional actions of the mid-1970s--namely, House Concurrent Resolution 133 and the Congressional Budget and Impoundment Act of 1974. Under the first action, the plans for monetary and credit aggregates are known periodically for one year in advance. These, in the light of recognized monetary influences, become a part of the input in forecasting economic conditions, and/or in forecasting any budget surplus or deficit that will exist under a host of different conditions.

In the concept of a "high" employment budget surplus (or deficit), a distinction is drawn between so-called "automatic stabilizers" (those that change automatically with changes in the state of business conditions and inflation) and the discretionary stabilizers (those that require a decision by the Congress). Traditionally the automatic stabilizers were so-called because of their behavior in relation to the phases of business conditions. This traditional behavior, and the stabilization role of the progressive income tax, however, are complicated by the presence of inflation during recession. The progressive income tax overall and especially in such instances leads to higher effective tax rates without those rates requiring the historically expected legislative attention and to a withdrawal of funds from the private sector during a recession when income in nominal dollar amounts is rising.

Forecasting the state of business, budget measures, and their impacts is an important part of the work of the Congressional Budget Office. It extends to the budgetary work of the Congress under the budget control law. Such forecasting suggests a rather idealistic structural equations model but, at the 1980 state of the methodology of such models, a good bit of judgment, experience, and simple study of empirical evidence enters into forecasting, as indicated later. The degree to which these matters enter into forecasting increases as the effort to establish causal linkages in the models increases. Strict forecasting--as a simple projection of the past into the future--is less complicated.

The 1974 budget control law was a response to a recognized need to improve on the budgeting process in the Congress, especially as it related to fiscal policy, and a response to selected budgetary trends and the exercise of executive powers by the President. In the first place, before the new law, there was insufficient constraint on all the separate expenditure and revenue bills of Congress as far as fiscal policy was concerned. In the second place, social programs and so-called "uncontrollable" expenditures grew into sizable proportions of federal spending in the 1965-75 period. These, in combination with the presence of inflation and the inflationary recession phenomenon, had led to the Presidential impoundment of funds for some programs authorized by the Congress. The Congress itself wanted greater control over the President's impoundment of funds. The 1974 act, however, establishes procedure for the impoundment of funds by the President, and recognizes the President's role in the impoundment of funds. Through impoundment and through other means the President may be recognized as having possible influence over the timing of government spending and thus possibly over the timing of turning points in business conditions.

The role of government with attention to fiscal policy may be a stabilizing one, but it may be a destabilizing one as well, as recognized by references to the political business cycle. There ideological shifts, say at times of election, may be a source of instability, and over-reaction by the President and elected officials in the Congress to the current economic concerns of the electoriate may be another. Especially, there is also the prospect for the President to influence the timing of business conditions to avoid having recession coincide with a reelection year.

The spending, taxing, and inflationary policies of governments in the 1960s and 1970s led to something of a tax payers revolt in 1978. At the state level, California's Proposition's 13 amended the state's constitution and thereby both reduced and placed a ceiling on property taxes. The taxation matter spread nationally as a political issue and coincided with reductions in capital gains taxes by the Congress of the United States. At this time also, one encounters public interest in Arthur Laffer's curve which summarizes some features of revenue yields to the government as tax rates vary and as the uses of revenues by the government vary. There are matters of public response to the government, disincentives for productivity activities, and a transfer of economic activities from the monetary economy to a barter sector. Laffer's use of his curve suggests a public response such that reductions in tax rates on productive activities will generate more rather than less revenues. The argument parallels the Keynesian argument for tax cuts in some measure but with notable differences, namely: the former addresses incentives and activities and the latter addresses tax cuts that result in spending with multiplier effects that generate extra revenue in the presence of a progressive income tax. Cutting taxes in the latter context is said to reduce fiscal drag on spending.

In the inflation era from 1965 to 1980, Milton Friedman especially comes to address the role of inflation as a tax. In the presence of the progressive income tax, with a role for vested interest, and in the absence of incentives for government to curb spending, he sees accelerating government revenues and spending. The defect of the system he says "is that we have no means whereby the public gets to vote on the total budget of the government." The aggregate of special interests dominate and none are "too strongly opposed to any one small measure that will benefit someone also." Friedman envisions constitutional limits on governmental spending as a means of reducing inflation, limiting taxes, and restricting the growth of government. The constitutional approach is that of getting a large consensus by having special interest yield to their own and larger interest.

Inflation as a tax is also vividly dealt with by Friedman, when he notes cash holdings as a percentage of income and deals with the loss of purchasing power from this source in the presence of inflation. The inflation tax on cash balances is the product of the inflation rate and the tax base (the value equal to a percentage of annual income).

FOOTNOTES

1. This credit was introduced in a 1975 tax act. Under the 1975 act a cash rebate or credit is possible. It amounts to 10 percent of wages and salaries earned up to a maximum of $400 at $4,000 of income, and the credit diminishes for incomes of over $4,000 until it disappears at $8,000. The earned credit is token recognition of the negative income tax concept that was initially proposed by Milton Friedman (1968).

   Effective in 1979, the maximum value of the Earned Income Credit was raised from $400 to $500, and the old upper limit of $8,000 was raised to $10,000.

2. The appointments for the seven members to the Board of Governors of the Federal Reserve System are for fourteen year terms and they are staggered with one new appointment coming up every two years as far as expired terms are concerned. Resignations, however, are frequent, and the chairman of the board is appointed by the President. He may have special influence as the main spokesman for the Board. At other times, it may require strong leader-

ship and/or the passage of time before the President can stack the board membership to favor a particular policy or point of view.

3. The essence of the Humphrey-Hawkins Act is set forth and placed in perspective by President Carter (1980), as he reviews long-term economic goals:

   "In 1978 the Humphrey-Hawkins Full Employment and Balanced Growth Act was passed with the active support of my Administration. The general objectives of the act--and those of my Administration--are to achieve full employment and reasonable price stability.

   "When I signed that act a little over a year ago, it was my hope that we could achieve by 1983 the interim goals it set forth: to reduce the overall unemployment rate to 4 percent and to achieve a 3 percent inflation rate.

   "Since the end of 1978, however, huge OPEC oil price increases have made the outlook for economic growth much worse, and at the same time have sharply increased inflation. The economic policies I have recommended for the next 2 years will help the economy adjust to the impact of higher OPEC oil prices. But no policies can change the realities which those higher prices impose.

   "I have therefore been forced to conclude that reaching the goals of a 4 percent unemployment rate and 3 percent inflation by 1983 is no longer practicable. Reduction of the unemployment rate to 4 percent by 1983, starting from the level now expected in 1981, would require an extraordinarily high economic growth rate. Efforts to stimulate the economy to achieve so high a growth rate would be counterproductive. The immediate result would be extremely strong upward pressure on wage rates, costs, and prices. This would undercut the basis for sustained economic expansion and postpone still further the date at which we could reasonably expect a return to a 4 percent unemployment rate.

   "Reducing inlation from the 10 percent expected in 1980 to 3 percent by 1983 would be an equally unrealistic expectation. Recent experience indicates that the momentum of inflation built up over the past 15 years is extremely strong. A practical goal for reducing inflation takes this fact into account.

   "Because of these economic realities, I have used the authority provided to me in the Humphrey-Hawkins Act to extend the timetable for achieving a 4 percent unemployment rate and 3 percent inflation. The target year for achieving 4 percent unemployment is now 1985, a 2-year deferment. The target year for lowering inflation to 3 percent has been postponed until 3 years after that."

4. We have here a feature of traditional economic analysis that distinguishes it from ordinary mathematical analysis. Two other distinguishing features in the same class of features include the literal impoundment of some forces in <u>ceteris paribus</u> and the frequent treatment of interdepen-

dent variables and variable constants as if they were independent.

5. A complication (first introduced in sect. 6.2) is that on other occasions the Federal Reserve has shown some strong survival powers in changing with the political climate. To not evidence this flexibility of purpose could over a sustained period incur the ire of Congress. The Federal Reserve is a creature of the Congress.
6. Blinder and Solow (1974) do not speak of "high powered" money or of bank reserves except indirectly in quoting a monetarists position. They use the terms "outside" money and "the money base." According to the terminology an open market purchase of securities increases reserves (a claim against the government, viewing the Federal Reserve as government). John G. Gurley and Edward S. Shaw (Money in A Theory of Finance (Washington, D.C.: The Brookings Institution 1960) are credited with originating the terms "outside" and "inside" money (pp. 72-73). Outside money for them is money issued by the government. It is a claim against the government (against a unit of the private sector) and is a claim held by consumers and firms. Inside money, on the other hand, is the opposite of outside. It is a claim against the private sector in the sense that it is a liability say of commercial banks. Most money in the banking system known in the United States, consequently, is inside money.
7. Possibly Blinder and Solow prefer to disallow these effects, but to do so renders their statement of foundations inoperative as it relates to the banking system of the United States.

SELECTED READINGS AND REFERENCES

Burns, Arthur. 1976. "Statement Before the Joint Economic Committee." Federal Reserve Bulletin (March).

Baird, Charles W. 1973. Macroeconomics: An Integration of Money, Search, and Income Theories. Chicago: Science Research Associates, Inc.

Blinder, Alan S., and Robert M. Solow. 1974. "Analytical Foundations of Fiscal Policy." In The Economics of Public Finance. Washington, D.C.: The Brookings Institution. A section of this paper draws heavily on Blinder's and Solow's paper, "Does Fiscal Policy Matter?" Journal of Political Economy (November).

Carter, Jimmy. 1980. Economic Report of the President together with The Annual Report of the Council of Economic Advisors. Washington, D.C.: U.S. Government Printing Office.

Fair, Ray C. 1978. "The Effect of Economic Events on Votes for President." Review of Economic and Statistics (May).
Frazer, William. 1973. Crisis in Economic Theory. Gainesville, Florida: University of Florida Press.
__________. 1978. "The Government Budget Constraint." Public Finance Quarterly (July).
Friedman, Milton. 1968. "The Case for the Negative Income Tax." In Melvin R. Laird, ed. Republican Papers. New York: Frederick A. Praeger.
__________. 1973. Money and Economic Development: The Horowitz Lectures of 1972. New York: Praeger Publishers.
__________. 1975. Milton Friedman en Chile: Bases para un desarvaollo economico. Santiago de Chile: Fundacion de Estudios Economicos Banco Hipotecario Nacional.
__________. 1978. "The Limitations of Tax Limitation." In Milton Friedman 1978, Tax Limitation, Inflation and the Role of Government. Dallas, Texas: The Fisher Institution.
Heller, Walter W. 1966. New Dimensions of Political Economy. New York: W. W. Norton and Company, Inc.
Infante, Ettor F., and Jerome L. Stein. 1976. "Does Fiscal Policy Matter?" Journal of Monetary Economics (November).
Joint Economic Committee. 1977. Employment Act of 1946, as Amended, with Related Laws (annotated) and Rules of the Joint Economic Committee, Congress of the United States. Washington, D.C.: U.S. Government Printing Office.
Kalecki, Michael. 1943. "Political Aspects of Full Employment." Political Quarterly (October/December).
MacRae, C. Duncan. 1977. "A Political Model of the Business Cycle," Journal of Political Economy (April).
Meeting. 1975. First Meeting on the Conduct of Monetary Policy, Hearing before the Committee on Banking, Housing, and Urban Affairs, United States Senate, First Session on the Conduct of Monetary Policy Pursuant to House Concurrent Resolution 133. Washington, D.C.: U.S. Government Printing Office.
Playboy. 1973. "Playboy Interview: Milton Friedman." Playboy (February).
Report. 1975. First Report on the Conduct of Monetary Policy, from the Committee on Banking, Housing and Urban Affairs, United States Senate A Report filed Pursuant to House Concurrent Resolution 133. Washington, D.C.: U.S. Government Printing Office.
Trends. 1975. "Recent Trends in Federal Budget Policy." Federal Reserve Bulletin (July).
Wanniski, Jude. 1978. The Way the World Works. New York: Simon and Schuster.

Chapter 11

The Government Sector: Income Redistribution, the GNP Gap, and the Natural Rate of Unemployment

11.1. Introduction

Ideological and a few practical matters arise in our consideration of the government's use of tax and transfer payments to redistribute income. This redistribution may be viewed in either of two respects, namely: as an alteration in the flow of income from one group to another, where income groups are expressed in terms of upper and lower quartiles, quintiles, et cetera, as illustrated in section 11.2; and/or as taking from some households a disproportionate share of the values of their marginal products (i.e., values of extra contributions to production) for redistribution to others, where under free market exchange conditions (sects. 1.1 and 1.2) households may be expected to enter voluntarily into exchange and obtain roughly in such exchange the value of their marginal product for doing so. This latter concept awaits fuller elucidation in subsequent discussion of labor markets (sect. 15.2), but it also receives further introduction below (sect. 11.4), as we encounter Milton Friedman's views on voluntary association and the graduated (or progressive) income tax.

The possibly more practical side of these abstract topics comes up below (sects. 11.4 and 11.5) as we consider the government's management of total spending, the natural rate of unemployment, work incentives, minimum wages, social experimentation, and the negative income tax. As we will see, the government may at times pursue national demand management policies that are at variance with its other social policies and that consequently give rise to government induced inflation and an added tax burden.

The distribution of income and especially its redistribution through tax and transfer-payments means has been of reoccurring interests to economists. Especially it seems so in modern times when economies with high rates of capital formation and work incentives, such as West Germany and Japan, have performed so well and when economies that have departed toward Keynesian/socialist orientations, such as Great Britain and the U.S., have performed so poorly (sect. 2.5). The approaches taken by economists to the redistribution of income have usually centered about (1) the compound notions of the optimization of some social welfare function and of the assumption of the declining marginal utility of income (app. A to chap. 6), and (2) personalistic views of equity and justice, as introduced below. Historically, prior to government intervention with the view towards redistribution, the capitalist ethic appeared to hold forth in the traditional market societies as an accepted "absolute," namely: each should be paid according to the value of the marginal product of the labor and capital owned (sect. 15.2). Against this, we encounter in Karl Marx, drawing on the English economists and art critic John Ruskin, the socialist ethic, namely: "From each according to his ability, to each according to his needs!"

Since Marx's time and later Alfred Marshall's, economists appear to have treated one or the other of the foregoing ethics as a social goal, and/or to assume with Marshall the declining marginal utility of income and hence maximum social utility through a more equal distribution (Britain 1976, chap. 1; Friedman 1938, 129-30; Kearl 1979, 28-37; Rivlin 1975).

Milton Friedman, on the other hand, proceeded somewhat differently. First, on grounds concerning probability and the measurement of social utility, he abandons the Marshallian assumption (app. A to chap. 6). Second, he finds no basis for choice between the conflicting ethical principles unless one sets some higher goal (Friedman 1938, 129-30; Friedman 1962, 164-65). The one he then sets is freedom. It depends on constitutional protections from simple marjority rule and on the market (Friedman 1962, chs. 1 and 2). Through a virtual consensus on certain matters, members of society agree on principles of protection of certain basic rights like free speech for everyone.

Moreover, as a practical matter, many decisions in society must be made through the voting of a simple majority, and every decision in society cannot be submitted conveniently to voting. The market, thus, extends the scope of decision making about what, how much, and for whom to produce, and, at the same time, it protects freedom by limiting the scope of government and enlarging that of voluntary association and free choice (including especially the choice of occupation). This choice comes about in an exchange economy where production is undertaken for indirect satisfaction of wants (sects. 1.1, and 1.2). Both government and private monopoly are problems (1962, chs. 2 and 8), and there is the problem of "neighborhood effects" in the presence of free market, voluntary exchange. These effects would encompass pollution of air and water, destruction of the wilderness, and so on (chap. 16). Such effects, in any case, can become a reason for expanding government or limiting it, as the public sees fit. "Voluntary associations" in the exchange market context (sects. 1.1 and 1.2) play a key role in Friedman's system, and they work so as to make the economic system function efficiently and to minimize the use of force in the society. There is freedom of dissent, including in the market place for ideas. Friedman can indeed get quite exercised in discussing the humaneness of the capitalist system (1978a; and 1978b 9-13). "In order for a society to be at once humane and to give opportunity for great human achievements it is necessary that a small minority of people who do not have materialistic objectives have the greatest degree of freedom" (1978b, 12). Continuing, he says (1978a, 4), "Capitalism tends to give much freer rein to the more humane values of human beings. It tends to develop a climate which is more favorable to the development on the one hand of a higher moral climate of responsibility and on the other to greater achievements in every realm of human activity."

These views of Friedman's provide some background for understanding what may appear as rather harsh views on Friedman's part about the graduated income tax, inherited wealth, and government redistribution of income. Income is unequally distributed and inheritance of both human and genetic qualities makes a difference in one's place in both the income and wealth brackets (Brittain 1977; 1978). As a matter of social justice and exclusive of other goals (freedom mainly, but possibly also the functioning of the social system), most would agree that there should be equality of opportunity in the struggle for success as measured by income and wealth though this may not be attainable in the Friedmanesque perspective. Furthermore, many would agree that tax policies can more directly affect environmental transmission of earning capacity and inherited wealth than genetic transmission.

Official targets in the drive for equality of opportunity have included the elimination of discrimination on the basis of "race, color, religion, national origin, sex, age, marital status, personal appearance, sexual orientation, family responsibilities, physical handicap, matriculation, and political affiliation." Often government policies aimed at achieving more equality of opportunity have been aimed at overcoming job discrimination on these bases. The reasons for persistent income differences, however, are thought to be more deeply rooted than suggested by these surface characteristics alone. Beyond surface characteristics, and the explanation of much status in life in terms of inheritance and formal education (Brittain 1977 and 1978), the proper functioning of the economic system depends on the development and existence of motivation, skills, and the willingness of some to accept risk. The major ideas encountered below, such as those of Friedman and John Rawls, are usually thought to apply to a nation. There are some, however, who reflect on them as possibly being extended to a larger world (one encompassing rich and poor nations, and so on). This extra dimension is not further adopted, in the present treatment.

The chapter proceeds with a consideration of government induced redistribution of income,1 as through tax and transfer-payment measures, and its relation to overall economic goals such as low unemployment rates and economic stability.

It also introduces static consumption and utility theory bearing on government policies with respect to income redistribution, and then continues with reviews of notions about distributive justice, work incentives, working to live vis-à-vis living to work, potential and actual GNP, and the GNP gap (the difference between potential and actual GNP). These concepts of potential and actual GNP have counterparts in the "natural" and "target" rates of unemployment, and the natural/target rate gap.

The static notions of consumption and utility theory give rise to the desirability of a more equal distribution of income. A crucial and damaging assumption underlying the static theory is that of the independence of the consumption behavior of households, in the one case, and the utility of households, in the other case. The evidence from everyday life against this assumption, in part, gives rise to an alternative approach to the theory of distributive justice. Here, one encounters Rawls's rules, so-called after their author John Rawls. Rawls envisions an abstract representative man, as contrasted with the presumed independence of the utilities and consumption practices encountered in the traditional economic theory.

A less restricted economic theory than that of utility in the tradition of Marshall does not require the assumption of the declining marginal utility of income (as mentioned in sect. 1.3 and app. A to chap. 6). Rawls's approach, moreover, allows for inequality in the distribution of income, and would appear to support income inequality based on achievement. As such the approach allows for work and creative incentives in the form of inequality. At the same time, however, it places a minimum floor, in the form of basic rights and opportunities for everyone. As a consequence of such a compound of prospects, the approach would be consistent with some degree of upward and downward social and economic mobility. Although Milton Friedman himself (1962, chap. 10) opposes on grounds of equity the use of inheritance taxes as a means of attempting to assure greater social and economic mobility, he has called attention in his consumption function work (sects. 9.3 and 9.4) to the temporary nature of many on the high and low sides with respect to household budgets. Many, who may be viewed as having opted for high risk ventures, get included in this category (e.g., as noted earlier, some writers, actors, actresses, TV personalities, movie producers, professional athletes, football coaches, promoters of new ventures, corporate executives at the higher eschelon, casino gamblers, pornographers, wild catters, and risk takers generally). Even after addressing inheritance and the inequality of material wealth, Brittain (1978, 3, 14-17) surveys articles on the very wealthy from Fortune magazine and notes "that about one-half of the very wealthy have been self-made men."

As will be indicated (Hearings 1979), governmental efforts to moderate the distribution of income and enhance equality of opportunity also impact on the unemployment rate expressed as a "natural" rate. The "natural rate of unemployment" was first casually introduced by Milton Friedman (1968a; Frazer

1973, 6-7; and Frazer 1977) in his 1967 presidential address to the American Economic Association. The introduction was not accompanied by much attention to the formulation of and basis for the concept, except monetary economists of earlier decades would have recognized its relation to the Wicksellian concept of the natural rate of interest (sects. 9.1 and 9.4). Controversy ensued and Friedman later cited the tie to Wicksell. To be sure, however, as has been the case with Friedman on other occasions, a good bit is implied that is not found in Wicksell. First, as follows from Friedman's attention to permanent magnitudes, the "natural" rate is a magnitude similar to permanent income. It is a secular time path for the rate of unemployment that can be sustained without introducing instability into business conditions and price level changes in particular.

Furthermore, in treating the "natural rate" concept in the present work, we recognize three extensions of the concept: First, the natural-rate trend line has a counterpart to potential GNP also expressed as a secular trend line in relation to actual GNP as a time series. The assumption of a low (high) natural rate means a high (low) GNP trend line. Second, imbalances in the actual GNP, as indicated by its relation to the trend line for potential GNP, come about as the Government sets the potential GNP trend line too high and pursues it as if it depicts a locus of target GNP values. Said differently, the pursuit of a target rate of unemployment (N_T) through demand management by means of fiscal and/or monetary policy, that is below the natural rate of unemployment (N_{RU}) gives rise to inflation. The more persistent pursuit of the elusive goal, in the foregoing context, gives rise to even more rapid inflation and ultimately to both inflation and unemployment.

The third extension of the natural rate of unemployment concept is that it is a variable (say, a variable constant or a quasi-permanent magnitude). We will consider the following function:

$$N_{RU} = f(Y_{RD}, Y_{GS}, N_{\Delta C}, N_{Gov}, N_{Reg}, P_{13}, U),$$

where Y_{RD} is government induced redistribution of income, Y_{GS} is income growth as a secular matter (later with special attention to technological change, scarce natural resources, and the possible substitution of labor and capital for scarce energy sources), $N_{\Delta C}$ is change in the composition of the labor force, N_{Gov} is government as an employer of last resort, N_{Reg} is government regulation in the more monopolistic segments of labor and product markets, P_{13} is a Proposition 13 phenomenum, and U is a portmanteau (or catch-all variable).

As may already be suggested by the foregoing formulation, the natural rate of unemployment (and its counterpart, the potential GNP line) is a variable over which the government has some control. The complexities encountered in this control perspective from a policy point of view are severalfold, notably: demand management, as through monetary and fiscal policy can control the unemployment rate until it reaches the natural rate trend line for unemployment, and thereafter the pursuit of low target rates is destabilizing; and the government may vary the natural rate of unemployment (the potential GNP trend path), but by means other than through demand management. The distinction is important and receives consideration.

11.2. The Trend of Redistribution

Government transfer payments and taxes concern the main means by which the government consciously or inadvertently redistributes income. These payments and taxes have distribution effects beyond those called for by market forces, as where shifts in household and business demands occur to warrant faster growth in one product market than in another and thus to warrant faster income growth for the workers in the faster growing market and so on.

Browning (1976; 1979) is one who has reported on the distribution of income after allowing for items of income after taxes and items excluded from ordinary money income. His measures have attracted comment (Smeeding 1979), and this has led to their further defense. He proceeds initially by using data on the distribution of income for five income groups (lowest, 2nd, 3rd, 4th, and highest group)[2] with the shares summing to 100 percent, except for possible discrepancy in rounding.

A simple reporting of the distribution of income for selected years 1952, 1962, and 1972 does not reflect any trend in the redistribution of income. However, by comparison, the data on income distribution after allowances for items of income ordinarily excluded and after allowances for taxes do reflect some redistribution in the decade 1962-72, although in broad outline and over many years inequality of income is known to have persisted through varying circumstances (including "through New Deal, Fair Deal, New Society, Great Society, and the War Against Poverty") (Brittain 1977). The trends in the decades 1952-62 and 1962-72 are captured by Browning's adjusted data in table 11-1. There we see that the distribution in the lowest quintile for family income increased by 1.1 percentage points from 1952 to 1962 and by 3.6 percentage points from 1962 to 1972. This redistribution is also reflected in the larger shares for the second lowest group and smaller shares for the higher income groups.

Browning's approach of allowing for taxes and transfer payments, moreover, is also consistent with Pagan's reevaluation of poverty in the United States (1979), although Pagan deals only with poverty level incomes. The Bureau of the Census definition of what constitutes poverty is not highly dynamic in the sense that the definition does not deal with elevating households to higher income status in relation to other households. However, the poverty standard is defined by a needs-based approach (minimum food and necessities) that makes it free of inflation risk, and it has included only the measure of money income. Using such an approach and measure the performance of the economy and the government's programs in eliminating poverty over the 1967-77 period would be astonishingly poor. Thus, what Pagan reports over a period that encompasses Browning's 1962-72 period is that the programs have been astonishingly successful in moving households above the standard, when transfers-in-kind are allowed for (including food stamps and child nutrition, rent supplements and public housing, medicaid, and so on). Even so, there are adverse effects attributed to high implicit marginal tax rates, inefficiency by the programs in achieving targets, and slowing growth rates in the economy. The work disincentive effects reported by Pagan (1979) are among the major findings of the government's social experimentation, as reviewed in section 11.4.

In the presence of works disincentives broadly viewed, there is further reason why the redistribution of income in the presence of the progressive income tax and transfer payments is no greater than it seems. Namely, in order to get certain jobs done and insure the mobility of human resources, a higher income before the income tax is needed to get the job done with an after tax income. Milton Friedman (1962, 172) says "this is the usual incident effect of taxation" and that it discourages entry into highly taxed activities. In the case of the graduate income tax, he notes the discouragement of entry into "activities with large risk and non-pecuniary disadvantages." Friedman sees this foregoing effect of the incidence of the progressive tax, as the reason for so many "loopholes" in the law. The ones he names are (Friedman 1962, 172) "percentage depletion, exemption of interest on state and municipal bonds, especially favorable treatment of capital gains, expense accounts, other indirect ways of payment, conversion of ordinary income to capital gains."

Table 11-1.
Percentage Income Shares for Family Income Classes (adjusted data)

Quintile	Lowest	2nd	3rd	4th	Highest
Year					
1952	7.8	14.8	18.8	23.3	35.3
1962	9.0	15.1	19.1	22.9	34.0
1972	12.6	16.1	18.4	20.9	31.9

Source of table: Edgar K. Browning, "The Trend Toward Equality in the Distribution of Income," Southern Economic Journal, July 1976, pp. 912- 923.

11.3. The Distribution of Income, Social Justice, and Total Spending

The present topics under consideration that involve some admixture of ethical and economic notions, on the one hand, and some theoretic and empirical matters, on the other, include two main streams of thought about the distribution of income (Frazer 1977). One surrounds Keynes's simple consumption function and the other is found in the theory of utility.

Despite these theories economists as a whole have been unable to say a great deal on entirely scientific grounds about the distribution of income that would be most desirable for society, and yet decisions about the matter are almost routinely made by government. What one encounters are vague and poorly founded expressions about social justice intermixed with humanistic expressions of guilt and emotional feelings, on the one hand, and Milton Friedman's analysis of choice and voluntary exchange, under free market exchange conditions with freedom as a goal, on the other. This section seeks, as a result of the predicament for economists as a group to agree on income redistribution matters, to sort out issues and alternatives. In this sorting out task we are guided in the next section by the catalytic work of John Rawls, a Harvard professor of philosophy, on social justice, and by results from an extraordinarily large, governmentally sponsored research program (costing approximately $112 million) involving experimentation. Especially we have Rawls's rules, and Milton Friedman's notion of inequality as a sign of dynamic change.

The Static Consumption Function

Keynes stated his simple function as a psychological law and recognized factors governing it (including the distribution of income). According to the simple statement consumption (C) increased less than income (Y) and even such that the slope of the function declined as income increased. The weaker statement was required for the solution (a "stability condition," Keynes said) to the basic income, aggregate demand building block, but Keynes thought the second statement held as a rule. In discussions of the distribution of income he thought in terms of a declining marginal propensity to consume, as income increased. Furthermore, he recognized both individual propensities to consume [say, $c = f(y)$] and a collective or aggregate consumption function [say, $C = F(Y)$].

The simple function is sketched in figure 11-1a, with a lower slope for the tangent line at point B than at point A. The idea with respect to income redistribution is that a transfer of income from income groups with low marginal propensities to consume (the counterpart to point B of the aggregate relation) to those with high marginal propensities will increase total spending. Keynes himself, however, through any short-run effect of income redistribution on spending to be unlikely, and he favored such action only as a last resort, only "if there were no productive investment left." In addition, income redistribution to increase spending was viewed very much as a one-shot affair by him. This would be because a moderation of the distribution of income would diminish the slope of the consumption function and hence the multiplier. Kalecki's position, on the other hand and as reviewed elsewhere (Frazer 1967), was a much stronger one. He viewed variations in the distribution as a main source leading to turning points in business conditions, and a more equal distribution led to reductions in otherwise chronic unemployment. However, in contrast, the data he examined "indicated no pronounced changes in the relative share of wages in national income during the course of the business cycle." One encounters Bowley's law: namely, labor gets a constant share of income in the long run. Such a law is also associated with the Cobb-Douglas production function in section 15.2, and with the economic problem of the declining productivity per worker in section 17.1. One encounters one of Karl Popper's "practical technological rules stating what we cannot do." Namely (Popper 1965, 343): "'You cannot, without increasing productivity, raise the real income of the working population' and 'You cannot equalize real incomes and at the same time raise productivity'."

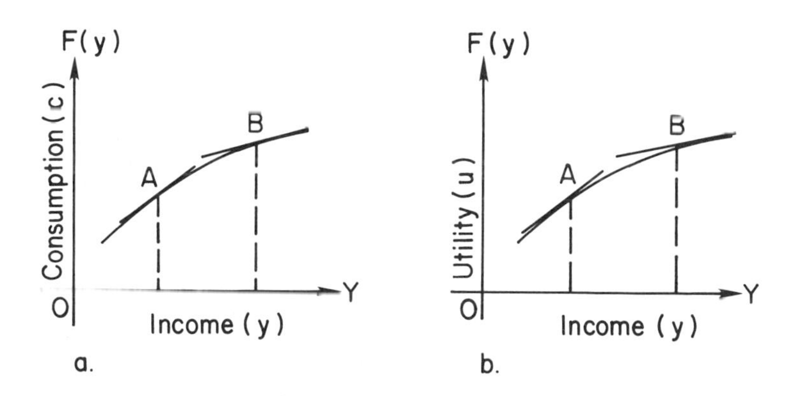

Figure 11-1. The Static Consumption and Utility of Income Functions

The reasoning reviewed about income distribution and the simple consumption function assumes an independence of the spending behavior of households and individuals from one another. In contrast, economists such as Thorstein Veblen (1899), and James Duesenberry (1952) in that tradition, have viewed the spending practices of behavioral units as being interdependent. The notion of interdependence has been signified by such phrases as "conspicious consumption" and "invidious consumption." This in part helps explain the constancy of the ratio C/Y, just as Friedman's notion of consumption as a function of permanent income helps account for it as an empirical observation, all as considered in sections 9.3 and 9.4.

Consumption and Utility Theory

Inadvertent or otherwise on the part of economists, the reasoning about the simple consumption function, income redistribution, and total spending parallels that about the social utility of income U(Y), and income redistribution. Keynes let the matter slip on one occasion by saying income (command over wage units) will "represent different degrees of subjective 'utility' " when discussing "the community's subjective propensity to spend on consumption." The respective functions depicted in figure 11-1 are drawn in identical fashion by different economists functioning independently of one another.

The significance of this parallel quality is considerable. For one thing, the two sets of reasoning tend to reinforce one another in their impact of the minds of economists and policy-makers. For still another, the empirical work on the consumption function may serve as an independent source of evidence on the utility function, U(Y).

Utility Theory

In the static theory of utility one ecounters formal sets of axioms for ordinal and cardinal versions of the theory (apps. to chap. 6). In both versions the assumption of the independence of individual utilities is troublesome, especially when considering the addition of utility and the redistribution of income, and in both versions the individual is choosing so as to maximize utility. One encounters the notion of the utility of income (or wealth, since the two are related) for the behavioral units, and (assuming additive and independent individual utilities) that of a total social utility (or social welfare) for the society as a whole.

Paralleling the reasoning about the simple consumption function, there is a simple utility function as in figure 11-1b. Since the marginal utility of wealth at point A is greater than at point B, in the figure, total social utility is thought to be enhanced by a more equal distribution of income. This appears to be a common view among economists, despite the assumption of non-additive and independent individual utilities, and despite the parallel between the speculation about the consumption and utility functions. Indeed, the economist has tended to think of the related marginal utilities of income and wealth as diminishing for behavioral units as income and wealth increased (i.e., to think of utility increasing less than in proportion to income) and, exclusive of enjoyment from the pure art of gambling, to think of experiments with games of chance as possible confirmation of this. In the appendixes to chapter 6, such experiments were mentioned. There, a subject was neutral with respect to the marginal utility of wealth and rational (in the sense of a consistence with the laws of the pure mathematics of probability), if it were just willing to accept a fair bet with a fifty-fifty chance of winning.

The majority view among economists about the distribution of income (as reviewed by Alice Rivlin, the first Director of Congressional Budget Office, and others [Brittain 1976, chap. 1; Kearl 1979, 28-37]), may have been more determined by empathy for the lower income households (and hence by a parascientific dimension) than by any scientific body of economics. Furthermore, ethical considerations play a big role, say, as in the public's decision to set a minimum floor on household incomes.

The Static Theories, and the Tax Cuts

As reviewed in chapter 10, the progressive income tax is such that individuals with incomes above minimum taxable levels are esculated into higher income tax brackets as they participate in the growth of nominal income even with constant or declining real income (tax loopholes aside). Recognizing that the progressive income tax can cause a drag on spending as nominal incomes rise, Congress inaugurated a tax cut for 1964, in the presence of sluggish growth, and they enacted one again in 1975 in the presence of the inflationary recession. In addition, President Carter proposed a cut in the personal income tax rates in his tax message for 1978. Initially this too was offered as a stimulus to total spending also, but the emphasis shifted to taxation proper following the Proposition 13 initiative in California (sect. 10.3).

In the first tax cut the Keynesian expenditure multiplier as derived from the slope of simple consumption function underlay Congressional committee discussion of the proposed measures, and the enacted tax reduction ranged from 40 percent of an individual's tax liability for the lower tax bracket to about 12 percent for the twenty to fifty thousand dollar income bracket. For the second cut, President Ford had proposed a flat 12 percent cut in an individual's tax liability, up to maximum "rebate" of one thousand dollars, but, Congress countered with a plan that favored the smaller tax payer with a larger total revenue cut and some with an "earned income credit." For the third broad cut in tax liabilities, President Carter's proposed changes would also have made the tax structure more progressive for the income ranges between 25,000 and 50,000 dollar adjusted gross income. However, in this latter case, the taxpayers initiated the revolt described in sect. 10.3, and the final bill left virtually unaltered the extent of the progressiveness in the tax structure.[3]

Explicit in the first case were the ideas underlying the simple consumption function of figure 11-1a, and tacit in the second were the ideas underlying both the static consumption and utility functions. In the second case, moreover, a goal of income maintenance for lower income groups was present. But, in both cases the tax cuts favored redistribution of income toward lower income groups and made the tax structure more progressive in the twenty-to-fifty thousand income range, and in both cases the underlying rationale was Keynesian, consumer spending oriented.

President Carter's proposed tax cut for 1978 would have further increased the progressiveness of the tax structure. An across the board cut in tax liability of 2 percent would leave the progressive characteristic unchanged, but President Carter proposed a 2 percentage point reduction in the tax rate. Thus, the tax structure would have been left more progressive after the Carter tax cut. With reference to figure 10-7, the slope parameter b would have been reduced. At a given income level, there is less spending because of a reduced disposable income, and there is less saving by households at these levels because the government drains it off in taxes. The government may continue to cut taxes in the future and increase the progressiveness of the tax structure in selected ranges and without attention to the loopholes, but in the long-run it may substantially altered the distribution of income by such cuts, and possible reduced the flow of saving out of income (as a proportion) that has traditionally gone from the household to the business sector. Indeed, with the Carter government approaching a reelection year and a crisis state in mid-July 1979, as the onset of the third of the inflationary recessions in little more than a decade was compounded by gasoline shortages at the pump and the OPEC price hikes of June 1979 (sect. 2.4), the President recognized among other things in a major address ("Transcript of address," New York Times, 7/17/79) the following aspect of the consumption/spending syndrome, notably:

> The productivity of American workers is actually dropping and the willingness of Americans to save for the future has fallen below that of all other people in the Western world.

Within the span of as little as thirteen months, from June 1978 to July 1979, an emphasis on the tax cuts of a different kind had been occurring, first with Proposition 13 (sect. 10.3), the wide-ranging cuts in business and capital gains taxes (sects. 8.2, 9.2, 14.4), and then with the mid-year review of the economy by the Congressional Budget Office (Outlook 1979). Ms. Rivlin (1979), the director said at that time, that in confronting the recession that if Congress decides to counter rising unemployment, it should consider tax cuts that would also dampen inflation. She cited possible cuts in payroll taxes, enactment of tax incentives to lower wage demands, and a structuring of business taxes to spur productivity.

In the tax-cut, redistribution-of-income sphere, we start in the 1960s with what we may recognize as one class of tax cuts--those to spur consumer spending and employment. We end in the late 1970s with another class--those to provide incentives for work and innovation, to provide for greater wage flexibility, and to spur productivity and capital spending. Those changes that simply attempt to alter the arithmetic of inflation measurement aside (sects. 17.2, and 17.3), we may summarize four classes of tax rate changes:

1. The demand management, Keynesian, consumption function cuts, tending toward income redistribution as may be recognized in terms of analysis surrounding the simple consumption function (fig. 11-1).

2. Laffer cuts that give the weight of attention to increasing output, expand the exchange economy in relation to the barter economy (sects. 1.1, 1.2, 10.3), expand incentives for work and production, and increase capital spending and saving.

3. Neutral tax changes as where the relative positions of the "agents," the households and the firms, are left unchanged in the redistribution matters.

4. Tax changes undertaken mainly on the grounds of achieving equity and justice in taxation.

All of these classes, as they affect our principle concern, bear on fiscal-policy, inflation, employment, and unemployment-rate matters.

Justice in Taxaton: Two-Adult Households

In the matters concerning justice in taxation, Manson (1979, 222-26) gets into tax and transfer schemes with two-adult households and with simultaneous attention to utility from combinations of work and leisure. Here two important but historically overlooked matters come together. One draws on prior discussion with reference to GNP accounting (sect. 3.1), and the other draws on future discussion of the supply curve for labor in the short run (sect. 15.2). In the earlier case, we noted an implicit income in the form of the services of a housewife (homekeeper, masseuse, and so on) that go unrecorded in GNP accounting and untaxed as income. In the latter case, we review the derivation of the supply curve for labor with reference to a choice between work and leisure. Within a limited time period, the real income required to call forth additional man hours of work is thought to increase at a rapid rate as hours of work increase, as sketched in figure

11-2. This is thought to be because the choice between work and leisure tends to favor leisure as the real income rises.

Figure 11-2.
The Supply
Curve for Labor

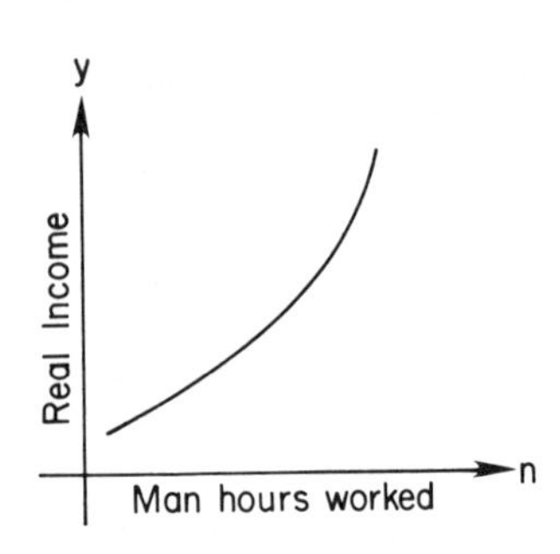

The point of equity with respect to the two-adult household as a decision unit then centers about whether one or both members of the household work. The choice is thought to be equivalent to a choice between additional work in the labor market or additional leisure with a non-working partner revealing an option for leisure. Drawing on work by others, Manser introduces "earning capacity" (EC) for the two-adult household as a measure of well-being of the household, and treats a tax on income at full income (FYT) as the most equitable means of classifying and treating households in the same position. This is possible, regardless of the progressive or regressive nature of the tax system when treating households in unequal pre-tax positions.

Manser (1979, 225) concludes that the idea that income taxation in general violates the utility-based definition of tax equity is not new. "However," she says, "considering the problem of tax equity in the context of households suggests that the distortion of equity caused by falure to tax adult nonwork hours is not insignificant, since a large part of the variation in nonwork hours of two-adult households arises because many women provide little or no market labor, while most of the others work close to full time." Thus, Manser concludes, "Introduction of a tax deduction based on a summary measure of work effort, say on the number of full-time workers in the household, could perhaps improve equity."

Quite obviously, in any case, taxation based on earning capacity and for a tax deduction based on a summary measure of work effort would increase the size of the labor force as defined in section 7.1. It would turn out, in the discussion below (sect. 11.5), to bear on the labor force, the unemployment rate, and stabilization matters.

11.4. Rawls's Work and Some Dynamic and Empirical Considerations

Four means of giving perspective to the static theories of consumption and utility, and to their policy implications are (1) to consider Rawls's rules, (2) recall the discussion of the dynamic consumption function in sects. 9.3 and 9.4, (3) review the effects of broadening the coverage of minimum wage laws to include teenagers, and (4) review results from social experimentation bearing on welfare reform. Rawls's work opens up an alternative to the economist's way of approaching aspects of income distribution, and illuminates some of the problems in the economic method. The discussion of the dynamic consumption function raises the prospect of treating the utility function in the same way, and the parallel in the reasoning surrounding the two static relations in figure 11-1 suggest the possible use of empirical evidence about consumption in dealing with utility. Finally, the extension of minimum wage laws to include teenagers and the resulting increase in unemployment rates for that group of workers in the 1960s and early 1970s provides one clear example of the effects of a more equal distribution of income on unemployment when the skills and potential productivity of labor are overlooked.

Although most of the literature on minimum wages and unemployment, as cited below, is rather recent, Milton Friedman gave attention to the consequences of minimum wages much earlier (1962, 180-81; 1977, 335; and Playboy 1973, 54). In particular, he likes to point out that his own parents may not have had employment and hence opportunity as emigrants to the United States had minimum wages been as high in relation to their day as they have been in his.

Rawls's Rules, Rivlin, and Friedman

Though Rawls was specifically interested in the theory of justice, the institutions of liberty, the operations of the economic order, and the notion of morally right behavior, his work has stimulated interest among economists. According to Rawls (1971), one thinks about rules, as has Friedman, that should govern the choice of a society by people who knew they were going to have to live in it, but at the same time had no knowledge about what their social or economic status would be.[4] There are two rules and the second one has two parts.

1. There are certain basic rights for everyone. They are distributed evenly and cannot be given up for any other benefit.

2. Inequalities are justifiable only on two interrelated grounds--
   a. Income differences must work to the benefit of everyone, including the least advantaged.

b. Advantegeous positions are held only on the basis of achievement with equal opportunity for attaining them.

The determination of the fulfillment of these rules is not easy and without controversy. The first suggests a minimum floor of rights and income. Perhaps a "guaranteed annual income" or a "negative income tax" to use a phrase that has come from suggestions by Milton Friedman (1968b), but the rule does not even say whether this minimum level of income is an absolute one or in relation to GNP. The second possibility suggests that death taxes (estate and inheritance taxes) may be used to assure some equality of opportunity and to discourage the exemption of a special "moneyed class" from productive work.

There are special complications in assuring the equality of opportunity to earn income, as reviewed by Alice Rivlin (1975) and by Milton Friedman. She suggests that the seed to some special advantages may lie in the family unit itself, as does Brittain (1977; 1978). Accordingly, Rivlin suggests, Rawls's rules are either trivial or involve "very difficult decisions about the extent to which the family should be perpetuated as a socializing force..."

Addressing ethical principles along similar lines (1962, 163-164), Friedman encounters difficulty in distinguishing the treatment of initial differences in endowments. He asks rhetorically: "Is there any greater ethical justification for the high returns to the individual who inherits from his parents a peculiar voice for which there is great demand than for the high returns to the individual who inherits property?" He notes wealth can be passed on as a sum of money to finance training and education or as a trust fund yielding property income. He does this even while recognizing that inequalities arising from personal capacities and individually accumulated wealth are generally not considered so inappropriate, as those due to inherited wealth.

Friedman opposes both the graduated income tax, as indicated earlier (sect. 10.3), and inheritance taxes. The first he opposes because it interferes with voluntary associations (in particular payment according to the value of marginal product), fails to generate as much revenue as a flat rate tax of around 16 percent, provides loopholes for those in very high tax brackets, channels productive resources into schemes to avoid taxes, and because the graduated tax protects rather than redistributes wealth (Friedman 1962, 13-4, 166-68; Playboy 1973, 60, 62). The second he opposes because enforcement of it only forces inheritance to take different forms, because he believes the motive to bequeath wealth to be strong, and because he prefers the achievement of equality through bringing low wealth households up (Playboy 1973, 60).

Rawls, Pareto, and the Income Tax

Economists have lived for many years, following the work of Vilfredo Pareto (1848-1923), with a criterion known as Pareto optimality and with Pareto's law. The first is modified in modern times by Rawls's theory and the second by the predominance of the progressive income tax as a source of governmental revenue.

Pareto's criticism concerned the optimum performance of the competitive economic system. If the various assumptions of the economists' competitive model were fulfilled, a result was obtained (a so-called equilibrium) such that it would not be possible to make some people better off without at the same time making others worse off. There was to be no movement from the equilibrium at which everyone was better off. Pareto's law, on the other hand, held that income was distributed the same under a variety of different social, political, and tax systems, and over different periods of time.

Rawls modified Pareto's so-called optimality criterion by referring to it as an allocated efficiency criterion, and by introducing his "difference principle" (1971, 15-78). The efficiency referred to was on two levels. "First," as stated by Phillips (1975), "distribution of commodities is efficient when no distribution could make someone better off without making another worse off." Next, "the organization of production is efficient when no alteration of inputs will produce more of one commodity without reducing the amount of another commodity produced." As pointed out by Rawls these solution points (or efficiency conditions) were many, and the choice among them could be restricted somewhat to obtain a higher level of optimality. The restriction was that other considerations (Rawls's rules, as stated above) must precede those of efficiency.

Rawls says (1971), the difference principle "removes the indeterminateness of the principle of efficiency by singling out a particular position from which the social and economic inequalities of the basic structure are to be judged." Continuing, he says:

> Assuming the framework of institutions required by equal liberty and fair equality of opportunity, the higher expectations of those better situated are just if and only if they work as part of the scheme which improves the expectations of the least advantaged members of society.

Friedman would no doubt argue (1980, chap. 1), inheritance aside, that this aspect of justice on the part of the better situated is precisely what free market exchange conditions and cooperation through voluntary exchange give rise to.

Special Features of Rawls's Work

Rawls's rules apply to abstract representative man (the "least" and "most" advantaged) and to institutions and public rules rather than to individuals. In addition, Rawls's system concerns only two classes of goods--primary goods (rights, liberties, and opportunities for all), in one class, and power, income, and wealth, in the other. In dealing with representative man, Rawls's philosophical system is thought to avoid the problem in utility theory of making interpersonal utility comparisons as mentioned later (and in appendixes to chap. 6).

Once Rawls's first rule is satisfied (and hence equal distribution of primary goods), as judged possible on no more than intuititve grounds, then power, income and wealth, may be distributed, subject only to the rule that the least advantaged benefit. Taxes and transfer payments are features of achieving the distribution of justice, but once the social system is operational the revenues of the government may be based on the benefits received principle of taxation (as distinct from the second common taxation principles, namely, so-called ability to pay). Thus, a flat-rate tax on consumption or income may be acceptable since it interferes less with work incentive.

Friedman, the Flat-Rate Income Tax, and the Value-Added Tax

With all the visible debate about Proposition 13, Keynesian tax cuts versus Laffer cuts, inflation as a hidden tax, and a constitutional amendment to limit government spending (sect. 10.3), Congress came to consider the value-added tax (VAT). In fact, by early 1980, the chairmen of both the tax-writing committees of Congress (Sen. Russell B. Long and Rep. Al Ullman) had come to endorse such a tax for the United States. The tax quite simply is a tax on the value added at the various stages of production, such as found in national income accounting (sect. 3.2). It would be collected from the producing units. Slight variations of its calculation abound, and like the federal income tax the law-makers and administrators may attach exemptions, create loopholes and the like, and thereby increase administrative and collection costs (Hafer, 1980, 3-10). VAT proponents, however, argue for the tax as a way of achieving neutrality toward economic behavior and allocative efficiency within the economic system. VAT is thus seen by some as a way of avoiding the disturbing effects of the existing U.S. tax system on economic incentives and performance. It tends like the sales tax, in any case, to be somewhat of a regressive tax since its economic incidence (i.e., the final burden of the tax) falls on those who purchase goods and services, and since it gets collected at the point of sales. The tax becomes a cost of production, and hence gives rise to leftward shifts in supply schedules (fig. 1-1).

With exemptions for capital expenditures and depreciation allowances for firms (sect. 8.2), VAT could become mainly a consumption tax. For a country concerned with capital accumulation and productivity (sects. 15.2 and 17.1), this feature of the tax could be good. The tax, revenue, and incentive goals of VAT, however, could be achieved without VAT. Questions arise about how such a tax would combine with or substitute for the income tax, with its current strong, built-in, and dampening effects on economic incentive.

Milton Friedman--the proponent of the flat-rate income tax, and the modern guardian of free choice, voluntary association, payment to the factors of production according to the value of marginal product, and the negative income tax--opposes the tax (Newsweek, 4/14/80, 90). He has seen it as a shift in tactics by the government to get revenue and at the same time hide the incidence of the tax to the tax payer. He notes: "Because it would be collected by business enterprise, VAT would be concealed in the total price the consumer paid and hence not perceived as a direct tax burden. That is its advantage to the legislators--and its major defect to the taxpayers."

The Dynamic Consumption Function and Utility

As noted in sect. 9.3, the ratio C(Y)/Y has been constant for long periods of time as a secular matter. This long-run tendency was reconciled with the evidence supporting the simple consumption function through the introduction of consumption as a function of permanent income. In view of the parallel in the reasoning about the static relations in figure 11-1, there is the possibility that the evidence from the consumer spending area has some bearing on the theory of the utility of income. This possibility suggests that the ratio U(Y)/Y may also be constant, and that the static utility of income theory is an inadequate one upon which to base national economic policy with respect to the distribution of income.

Minimum Wages and Unemployment

Broadening the coverage of workers under the minimum wage laws since the 1960s concerns inadvertent efforts at the redistribution of income. The results show that this broadening of the coverage had impact on unemployment. The extensions were to industries with heavy teenage employment such as agriculture, retail trade, and services. On the whole, the increases in the minimum wage standards have not been any more inflationary than wage increases in manufacturing overall, since the early 1960s,[5] but problems are noticeable in the extension of the coverage to include workers who have traditionally earned less than the standard wage. Of special concern have been extensions to those sectors with high teenage unemployment. The increases in the teenage (youth 16-19) unemployment rates that have paralleled these developments are widely discussed.[6]

Articles in professional journals have noted the prevalence of teenage employment and attributed it to the extension of minimum wage coverage.[7] The reasons given are that higher wage rates for unskilled workers lead to the substitution of machines for labor and skilled workers for non-skilled, since the wage rates are not directly affected by the minimum wage. Also mentioned are the costs of training teenagers who have not acquired the basic habits of punctuality and concentration on the job.

The presence of government induced "subemployment" has led to the proposal for differential minimum wage rates for teenagers and an expanded role for the government in the maintenance of high employment. Arthur Burns, in fact, has advanced the proposal for a special minimum wage for teenagers, and referred to the special handling of teenage employment in Japan. "In Japan," he says "teenagers will be paid a rate that is at or below the productive contribution to the firm on the part of these youngsters. In our country, on the other hand, instead of underpricing the labor of the young people or pricing it correctly, we tend to overprice it through a Federal minimum wage law."[8]

Burns (during his active tenure as Chairman of the Board of Governors of the Federal Reserve System) and others have also supported a role for government as "an employer of last resort." This support has been directed toward the employment of the involuntary unemployed" and to anyone "willing to work at a rate of pay somewhat below the Federal minimum wage." Somewhat along such lines, but without the modifications added by Burns, has been the "Humphrey-Hawkins" bill (technically the "Humphrey-Hawkins Full Employment and Balanced Growth Act of 1976"). As placed before Congress in 1976 the bill proposed to establish a process of long-range economic planning to achieve "a full-employment goal... consistent with a rate of unemployment not in excess of 3 percent of the adult Americans in the civilian labor force." The goal was to be achieved within four years after the passage of the bill. Along similar lines, President Carter supported in his 1976 campaign a target rate of 4 percent unemployment by 1980. Later, in November of 1977, he endorsed a watered-down Humphrey-Hawkins bill that set a 4 percent unemployment rate as the goal for 1983, and following the end of the 95th Congress, in October 1978, he signed into law a final Humphrey-Hawkins bill. However, no new programs were mandated by the bill and targets were added for a reduced inflation, a balanced budget, a surplus in the balance of international trade, and higher price supports for farmers. Even in the initial endorsement the president refrained from committing himself to any new programs to reach the target for the unemployment rate.

The Spirit of the Economy

The utilities of households are not independent of one another, and consumption expenditures by households are not independent of one another. The evidence of this is varied, but mostly it is a part of everyday experiences--for the most part individuals and households have established a history of response to style changes and material and non-material things vary in style; firms expect and receive responses by a number of households in varying degrees to advertising; consumers expand and vary the amounts of installment credit in use in common patterns. In view of such interdependence, there is some question about whether total social utility is enchanced by the government inducing greater equality in the distribution of income. Rather it may appear that government induced moderation in the distribution of income (as through the use of transfer payments and the progressive income tax) raises the natural rate of unemployment. Questions of justice in the distribution of income arise, as well as questions about the equality of opportunity, and upward (and downward) social mobility. Rawls's rules provide some guidance on the matter of justice.

The second rule implies that those receiving higher incomes should contribute in tangible, productive ways as individuals and not simply through reliance on inherited capital. The possibility of some measure of equality of opportunity, and the prospect that all will not contribute as outlined, all lead to upward and downward social mobility. Friedman (1962, 171), writing before Rawls, makes the point about social mobility by considering two societies with the same distribution of annual income but two basically different kinds of inequality. These have to do (1) with "temporary, short-run differences in income" and (2) "long-run income status" respectively. According to Friedman: "In one there is great mobility and change so that the position of particular families in the income hierarchy varies widely from year to year. In the other there is great rigidity so that each family stays in the same position year after year." Continuing, he concludes, "in any meaningful sense, the inequality in the first society is a "sign of dynamic change, social mobility, and equality of opportunity," while the other is a status society and a more unequal society.

On the related matters of income differences, motivation, and incentives, the sociologist Max Weber (1930, chap. 2) at an earlier time and Milton Friedman in a more recent time (1976, 12) give attention to the difference between working to live and living to work. In the first case, there is little aspiration to earn income beyond that required for some customary way of living. At this level of attainment, raising income simply increases leisure and reduces work. There is some evidence of this. In the second case, on the other hand, there is a spirit, a force that motivates the economic subjects toward higher attainments. Weber spoke of it at an earlier time as a spirit of capitalism and as the protestant ethic. The proper functioning of the economic system, as in the United States, would appear to require some sort of spirit for work and accomplishment, a work ethic (possibly a protestant ethic minus traditional religious significance), and social mobility. Social mobility in the future, in any case, may be quite different from that of the past in the United States. The past has been characterized by the development of a geographical frontier, large measures of the exploitation of natural resources, and social migration of ethnic groups (Kuznets 1977). In the immediate future and beyond, however, the physical frontier, once California, and the natural resources are more limited. In the future migration into the United States will certainly be different.

Social Experimentation, Unemployment, and the Negative Income Tax

Results from social experimentation on an extraordinary scale bearing on welfare reform (Chapmans 1978; Hearings 1979) have tended to be consistent with the following, as considered earlier, namely: that government transfer payments tending toward a more equal distribution of income do not bring about greater spending and employment; that government transfer payments tending toward a more equal distribution do not lower the natural rate of unemployment; that government transfer payments reduce work incentives in the absence of a strong work ethic ("living to work"); and that an absence of inequality as a sign of dynamic change reduces work incentive. Moreover, the experimental results cast doubt on the use of the negative income tax (or guaranteed income) as a means of welfare reform unless coupled with mandatory work requirements. Such results were being reported, in late 1978 (Hearings 1979), from the use of the technique of social experimentation as a means of getting evidence about economic behavior (Ferber 1978).

The idea in the government-underwritten experiment was to measure the possible effects of the negative income tax (or social maintenance programs) under the conditions of a controlled experiment with the basis for income maintenance involving two variables--a support level (q) and the rate (r) of reduction in benefits as income (y) increases above the support level. The payment receipt (p) from the program thus is the support level less the product of the rate of reduction in the benefits and income; that is

$$p = q - ry.$$

The two most comprehensive of the government research programs were conducted in Seattle, Washington and Denver, Colorado. There, 2,700 families were given direct cash assistance for three- or five-year periods, and an additional 2,000 families served as the control group by remaining on welfare or struggling along on their own. Among the first group, some were on welfare and others classified as "working poor."

There were no job requirements and no strings attached other than researchers being allowed to study their lives.

The results--though supporting some of the notions in this chapter --were very contrary to what was expected on the part of welfare experts at an earlier date with respect to strengthening family ties, and encouraging work and self sufficiency. The plans tested appeared to contribute to family breakup, to substantial reduction in work effort and corresponding increases in dependence on public subsidy. Over the two-year period of the Seattle-Denver guaranteed income experiment, family breakup increased 244 percent for whites, 169 percent for blacks, and 194 percent for Chicanos. Apparently these increases were due to the income guarantee applying separately to husbands and wives and thus having a "liberating" effect on women who may otherwise have remained in unpleasant marriages for financial reasons.

In addition to family breakup, male breadwinners and wives receiving assistance worked an average of 6 and 17 percent fewer hours respectively, and women who headed households worked 12 percent less. In terms of the progressive feature for earned income (i.e., r y), men worked 10.6 percent fewer hours when they lost 70 percent in benefits for every dollar earned and they worked 6.2 percent fewer hours when the rate of the tax was 50 percent. Reflecting possible absence of a work ethic and/or the absence of an expectation of upward social mobility, the disincentive for work was twice as high for blacks and Hispanics as for whites.

Reflecting on the foregoing evidence, Senator Patrick Moynihan, who had been involved for over a decade in welfare reform, said (Hearings 1979): "some of the major findings--first presented to this Subcommittee last spring--raise questions about the fundamental premise of the type of welfare reform proposal that has dominated our thinking." President Carter himself had proposed replacing the system he inherited with a system of direct cash outlays for families below a set income level (suggested as the then $6,200 poverty line). The more money the families earned, the less assistance they were to receive.

Despite the foregoing evidence, Milton Friedman would no doubt still favor welfare reform along the lines of his negative income tax idea and the Denver experiment, because he would not find the receipt of a cash sum as demeaning as welfare in kind. Following Friedman (1962, 16, 111, 113-115, 200), moreover, the appropriate approach to those who do not respond to work incentives may be through the use of persuasion and education with respect to the benefits of work and merits of voluntary association. This would be in lieu of force, as may be encountered under other forms of social organization.

11.5. Natural and Target Rates of Unemployment

As expressed early in chapters 7 and 10, unemployment and the unemployment rate are special variables bearing on output and instability in a mixed regulated-market economy. A practice under Keynesian influence was to consider a desirable policy target for the rate of unemployment, irrespective of consideration for the "natural rate of unemployment" (i.e., the rate compatible with a sustainable rate of growth in output and a zero inflation rate). Now we wish to consider both, and the prospect that setting and pursuing a target rate below the natural rate leads to instability, including recession in the presence of inflation.

First, we recognize that the natural rate of unemployment gives rise to the "potential" (or "maximum potential") GNP, and that both depend upon assumptions about the size of the labor force and the unemployment rate that can be maintained.[9] The natural rate, as stated on other occasions, is the rate that can be sustained as a matter of secular trend, and the maximum potential GNP is the GNP that will accompany the natural rate. The difference between the "actual" GNP and the potential so defined has been called "the GNP gap," and estimates of the potential have come to be presented by such diverse groups as the President's Council of Economic Advisors (CEA), Citibank (formerly the National City Bank of New York), and the Congressional Budget Office. In a mid-1978 comparison of estimates by the former two groups (Citibank, Monthly Economic Letter, July 1978), the Citibank adopted a potential GNP based on an assumed 3.5 percent rate of unemployment for prime-age males (those 25 to 54) and an equivalent natural rate of unemployment of about 6 percent, and they cited the CEA's potential GNP as being consistent with a 4.9 percent unemployment rate. Citibank noted: "these differences in the assumed, natural rates of unemployment markedly affect the size of the GNP gap. The CEA's gap for 1977 was more than $74 billion while Citibank's was only a trifle more than $18 billion.

Continuing Citibank noted crucial differences in the two sets of estimates with reference to policy conclusions:

> For the council, writing in its annual budget report at the beginning of this year, the size of the gap meant that "there are still ample supplies of idle labor and capital resources available. In the period immediately ahead, growth in real output can therefore proceed at a rate above its long term trend without risking a resurgence of demand-induced inflation."
>
> Since the appearance of their annual report in February of this year, the CEA, along with the rest of the Carter Administration, has backed away from its position.

Next, it should be clear, that the gap between actual GNP in constant dollar and potential GNP will be large, if the presumed unemployment rate at full employment is arbitrarily presumed to be low. A sketch depicting "actual GNP" (in 1972 prices) and an arbitrarily derived gap between it and for full employment GNP is shown as figure 11-3. The near-potential zone in the figure is associated with an unemployment rate between 4 and 5 percent, for the undisclosed period shown.

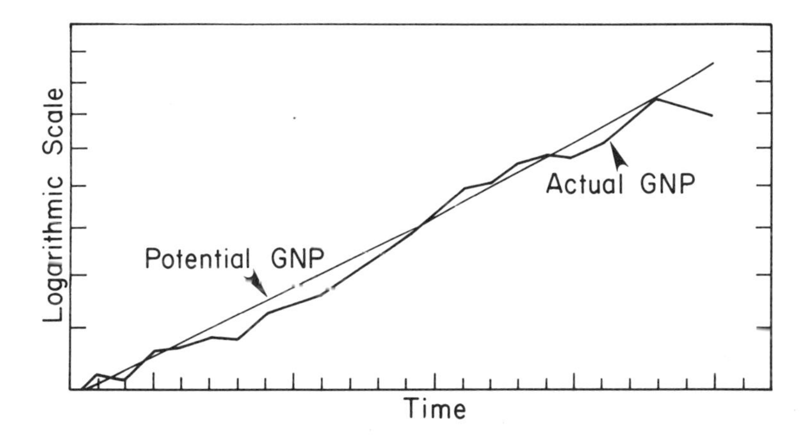

Figure 11-3. Actual and Potential GNP

Finally, Citibank stresses in its review the determinants of the "GNP gap" at a point in time. They do so mainly with attention to demand management, technological change, and incentives thus:

1. The utilization of economic capacity. This would be as suggested by the utilization measures reviewed in section 8.4. They note "that inflation accelerates as economic capacity--the labor force and existing capital facilities--is more fully utilized."

2. The stock of capital invested in productive enterprise. This would simply include investment, as treated in chapter 8.

3. Technology or the advanced knowledge that's embodied in the design of capital equipment. This factor was first introduced in discussion of figure 3-1, and it takes on special dimensions in the subsequent consideration of production functions, and scarce natural resources (chaps. 15 and 16).

4. The ways in which government impinges on the willingness of people to work, save and invest. These topics are the subject matter of work incentives (as in the last section), chapters 8 and 9.

Many factors may be stressed in addressing the central determinants of the GNP gap, at a point in time and over the secular time frame as well. At this stage we may consider factors affecting full employment GNP, mainly as a secular, long-run matter and then we consider separately the stabilization aspect of control (i.e., the matter of setting the target unemployment rate below the natural unemployment rate). Factors affecting full employment GNP are important, first, because they affect real GNP and, second, because they influence the unemployment rate. Partial and interrelated lists of the factors follow:

Policy factors exclusive of monetary and fiscal policy affecting full employment GNP

1) The size of labor force. This may vary inversely with the unemployment rate since at low rates conditions attract new entries (housewives, and minorities) who may not otherwise find acceptance.
2) A heavier (lower) tax burden on middle income recipients may lead to an increase (decrease) in working couples, as a means of maintaining a relative position in the distribution of income among families.
3) Government induced changes in the distribution of income, as may result from transfer payments and taxation.
4) The liberation of women from confinement to the household.
5) The exercise of opportunities for "self betterment" (education and the like) that may follow from changes in

Policy factors exclusive of monetary and fiscal policy affecting the unemployment rate

1) Short-run changes in the size of the labor force, as under factors affecting full employment GNP, such as may occur before the job market can absorb them.
2) Welfare and wealth transfer programs overall that make the employed more selective in their search for a job (and hence lengthen the search time for employment).
3) The provision of more generous social security and unemployment benefits.
4) Disproportionate changes in minimum wages as prescribed by law including changes in to broader or narrower groups).
5) The freedom to search for a job, that may simply follow from changes in real income.
6) Changes in the composition of the labor force with shifts toward (away from) groups with higher or lower unemployment rates. (The female and teenage segments of the labor force have different labor employment rates, e.g., and the mix of labor force

real income and the accumulation of savings.
6) Changes in retirement age, sometimes enforce through law.
7) Frictional unemployment (the movement of workers from one job to another) such as may be influenced by the employment agency means of matching unemployed workers with vacant jobs.
8) Technological unemployment (as where workers are displaced by technological change and where labor skills are outdated).

as to age and sex may change.
7) The role of the government as an employer of last resort.
8) The regulatory arrangements for dealing with excessive wage and price changes, such as may occur in the more monopolistic segments of the labor and product markets (sect. 17.2).
9) The substitution of labor for scarce energy and capital (sects. 15.4 and 17.1), as thought to prevail in 1979 and early 1980.

Variable Unemployment Rates

As the two lists suggest, the size of the labor force (and hence full employment GNP) and the unemployment rate for any given size labor force are not constant. Taking the lists as a clue, one may simplify and define as a first approximation the natural rate of unemployment (N_{RU}) as a function of government induced redistribution (Y_{RD}), the growth in income as a secular matter (Y_{GS}), changes in the composition of the labor force ($N_{\Delta C}$), the government as an employer of last resort (N_{Gov}), the nature of government regulation in the more monopolistic segments of labor and product markets (N_{Reg}), and an effectively directed and broadly bases Proposition 13 phenomenum (P_{13}). Hence,

$$N_{RU} = f\,(Y_{RD}, Y_{GS}, N_{\Delta C}, N_{Gov}, N_{Reg}, P_{13}, U)$$

In the 1960s and early 1970s, the first three of the variables in the function, as discussed above, were doubtless contributing to a rise in the natural rate (N_{RU}), but no attention was given to this variable N_{RU}. Further, we might expect that the last three variables in the function could be used to reduce the natural rate (N_{RU}). One mentioned in the early 1980 presidential primaries was a cut in the minimum wage for workers under 21 years of age, from a full minimum to 85 percent of the minimum set for the labor force as a whole. However, government regulation of labor and product markets and tax incentives for increasing inititive and productivity are not considered further until we take up the more elaborate discussion of wage and price guidelines in chapter 17. The main point presently is that there are prospects for reducing the natural rate. This would permit monetary and fiscal policy to influence aggregate demand so as to move toward a rate of unemployment more in line with a low desired rate, all without possible inflationary and destabilizing consequences.

Inflation and Instability

In a broad outline, as may be shown,[10] the inflation rate was modest in the early 1960s as the unemployment rate declined. It began to accelerate in 1965 as the unemployment rate declined further. Thereafter the acceptance of increasing inflation rates accompanied the efforts to sustain the low unemployment rate as the boom of the 1960s progressed. After that and some abatement in the rate in 1971 and 1972, the inflation rate accelerated even faster through 1974, even as the unemployment rate remained high by the standard of the late 1960s. In 1975, a year of inflation and recession, the unemployment rate jumped to 8.5 percent as inflation continued at a slightly slower rate.

Said differently, as demand management presses for a low target rate of unemployment some progress toward it may follow. However, if this rate is below the natural rate (and the natural rate may even be increasing for other reasons), then greater effort is required to move unemployment toward the target rate. Ultimately, the growth in effort required to achieve the given target rate is limited, and conditions in 1978 and 1979 (as reviewed later in chapter 17) indicate that even sustained effort is inadequate to mitigate against the resulting twin problem of both inflation and unemployment.

The Significance of the Switch on the "Natural Rate"

The significance for economic theory of the shift of attention from "the natural rate of interest" (sects. 8.2 and 9.1) to the "natural rate of unemployment" is substantial. First, drawing on parts of Fisher's work and parts of Wicksell's, Keynes obtains a part of his control linkage by having the interest rate vary vis-à-vis the rate of return (or MEC). This rate of return is in a sense a "natural" or real rate, and setting the real rate below it leads to an enlarged capital spending, and Wicksell would add an increase in the inflation rate. In addition, Keynes would note the volatility of the MEC schedule in response to any expected inflation rate. However, he would do all of this even as he draws on parts of Fisher and even as he denies the prospect of having the expected inflation rate influence the rate of interest (say, viewed as a control variable).

Following Wicksell (sect. 9.1), placing the market rate of interest below the natural rate would lead to inflation. Again, however, this must occur without Fisher's equation for the nominal rate of interest becoming operative.

Finally, following the shift of emphasis from the "market" and "natural" rates of interest to the "target" and "natural" rates of unemployment, there is no such inconsistency as sketched earlier (sect. 9.1) or apparent need to deny the operation of Fisher's interest rate equation (or variations of it, as in sect. 5.5). Indeed, setting the target rate of unemployment is definitely a policy matter, and it need not be tied to the expected inflation rate in the same way the latter is tied to the market rate of interest. Thus, setting and pursuing a target rate of unemployment below the natural rate may lead to inflation and its prospect as sketched earlier all without being influenced by that prospect.

11.6. Summary

Economists have addressed the question of the distribution of income, without reconciling the controversial issues about it, and legislative bodies routinely make decisions bearing on it in exercising taxation powers and in spending proceeds from taxes and debt financing. Common goals for the implementation of tax and expenditure measures have included full employment and social justice.

The main notions involved on the part of economists and philosophers have centered about the capitalist ethic, the Ruskinian premise, the analysis of utility, the simple consumption function, freedom through an extension of decision making to the market of an exchange economy, freedom through voluntary association and entry into exchange so as to obtain one's marginal product, Pareto optimality, Rawls's rules, and the specification of full employment income. The a priori speculation in utility theory (assuming independent utilities for different behavioral units) has drifted toward the notion of a declining marginal utility of additional income. The controversial assumption of independence then permits the conclusion that total social utility is enhanced by a more equal distribution of income, since those receiving government transfer payments have a higher marginal utility than those giving up extra income.

The simple consumption function, as advanced by Keynes, and its counterparts in the case of household budget studies eschewed complexities of utility analysis, since together they were advanced as simple empirical notions. Even so, the reasoning about expenditures and income distribution followed similar lines to those found in utility analysis. There was the idea from the budget studies that spending increased less than in proportion to income (i.e., in Keynes's terms, the marginal propensity to consume declined). Assuming household spending decisions are made independent of one another, total spending was thought to be enhanced by a more equal distribution of income. One economist (Kalecki) made this a part of the theory for achieving full employment spending.

In contrast to these consumption theory notions, the ratio of saving to income has tended to remain fairly constant over long periods of time. (A more elaborable theory of consumption reconciled this fact in chapter 9.) The parallel in reasoning about utility and consumption is suggestive though, namely: the ratio of utility and wealth may not be quite like that suggested by static utility theory.

The theories of an exchange economy with indirect satisfaction of wants and of a competitive market system have long offered notions bearing on efficiency, and specialization that are tangential to notions about the distribution of income. Milton Friedman in particular elevates the importance of freedom and voluntary association in the exchange economy. The reduction in the need for governmental decision making, as provided by extending the scope of the market, protects freedom and elevates the importance of free choice. Constitutional measures, as obtained through an essential consensus, does also, and the market and the constitutional provisions together protect freedom. By producing and entering into exchange on a voluntary basis the agents are free to get the value of their marginal product in the exchange. Governmental intervention as through the graduated income tax, on the other hand, causes the agents to enter into exchange unequally. For such and other reasons bearing on freedom, the scope of government, equity, and efficiency, Milton Friedman tends to favor a flat-rate income tax, but offers the negative income tax as a cushion for low income and as an improvement over welfare in kind.

With respect to efficiency, an optimality criteria is encountered in Pareto optimality, namely: there is an optimum in the sense that the economic system cannot be modified so as to make some people better off without at the same time making others worse off. The specialization idea is that of the division of labor which also leads to efficiency.

Rawls sought to modify the role of the optimality notion by asserting that other considerations must precede it. His rules elevate to a more humanistic level the discussions about the distribution of income, and his approach avoids the assumption about the independence of respective household utilities by referring to institutions and an abstract representaive man rather than to individuals or households. Rawls's system has two classes of goods--rights, liberties and opportunities for all, in one instance, and power, income and wealth, in the other. The first set of goods is to be equally distributed, and the second is to be earned by activities that work to everyone's advantage.

Rawls's system does not preclude work incentives, inducements for capital spending, and inequality in the distribution of income. And it directly calls attention to social mobility. In a society with some degree of equality of opportunity, with advantageous positions, with incentives, and with work ethics, income inequality should appear to be temporary for some households, and to give rise to dynamic change.

Income inequality of course, may exist in a more permanent way, although Friedman stresses the temporary nature of the income positions of many. Characteristics of whether the social movement exist will depend on the opportunity for social mobility and on the difference in the work attitude, a possible difference between "living to work" and "working to live." In the latter case, rising income may simply lead to increased leisure.

In any case, the supply curve for labor is thought to reflect an increasing preference for leisure over work, and Manser relates the concept to the additional matter of justice in taxation and the distribution of income. Most notably Manser finds it unjust to tax a working couple at a higher tax rate than a couple with the same earning capacity but with a non-working (in the labor market, that is) partner. To overcome such inequity she notes earning capacity and treats a tax on income at full income as the most equitable means of classifying and treating households in the same earning capacity position.

Over time, rising incomes have doubtlessly led to some increases in educational opportunities, job search time, and an avoidance of routine, distasteful and dehumanizing jobs on a permanent basis. Further, government efforts at inducing income redistribution and greater equality of opportunity have likely contributed to increased job search time, and to pricing certain age and ethnic groups out of the market, at one end of the income spectrum. The particular reliance on the graduated income tax may also have discouraged entry into "activities with large risk and non-pecuniary disadvantages." Similarily, participation in the labor market may be influenced by the tendency to tax a working couple at a higher tax rate than a couple with the same earning capacity but with a non-working partner.

Alterations in economic incentives and adverse influences on the performance of the economy have come to be associated with the U.S. tax system. These public reactions, as revealed by Proposition 13 phenomenum, and the move toward a constitutional limitation on government spending, have prompted interest on the part of Congress and some others to consider a value-added tax. Clearly it could have desirable effects on economic incentives and performance and it could be just another tax--Milton Friedman would add, another hidden tax. He favors instead openness and simplicity in the means of taxation, and a flat-rate income tax as a means of neutralizing the effects of taxation on economic incentives and performance.

Whatever the ethical basis, government efforts to moderate the distribution of income have on occasion raised the natural rate of unemployment. Governmental social experimentation indicates this, and an example of governmental actions that raise the natural rate of unemployment has been the extension of minimum wage laws to industries such as retail sales that have traditionally employed large numbers of teenagers. The natural rate may be influenced by other measures, however, and some have been considered, including changes in the composition of the labor force, and the government as employer of last resort.

The "natural rate of unemployment" concept comes to us from Knut Wicksell and via other routes. It is presently treated as a permanent magnitude, as an exponential trend line, as a variable constant, and as having a counterpart in potential GNP. As implied by the definition for the natural rate, potential GNP is the secular trend line that can be achieved, maintained, and sustained, all without introducing instability into the economy and into the price level in particular. Actual GNP may vary about the potential GNP line, and hence "transitory" GNP (or the GNP gap).

A source of instability in business conditions comes from the government's setting the potential GNP line too high and then from pursuing it as a target through demand management policies. A result is inflation, an even more illusive target value for demand management, and ultimately both inflation and recession.

As noted, the government may vary the potential GNP line, but not through the use of demand management within its ordinary limits. Seeking out and setting the potential GNP line to accord with "true" potential GNP, gives the maximum scope within which monetary and fiscal policy may operate to raise and lower total demand with the view to achieving national economic goals.

The distinction between the "target" and "natural" rates of unemployment is given impetus by Friedman, and it holds special implications for economic policy and for economic theory. On the policy level, it facilitates a distinction between what may be achieved in the way of a low unemployment rate through demand management as distinct from other policy measures. On the theoretic level, the shift in attention from the "market" and "natural" rates of interest to the "target" and "natural" rates of unemployment permits an analysis of government induced inflation without at the same time having to deny the operation of a Fisher-type phenomenon (i.e., the phenomenon where the market rate of interest contains an expected inflation rate).

FOOTNOTES

1. "Government induced" changes are stressed because changes in the distribution of income may also occur in response to shifts in market forces. These may come about on the product side as a result of shifts in households' demands, and on the side of firms and hence from changes in the composition of the factors of production and in marginal productivities of labor and capital. These market forces are considered on other occasions, and especially we consider factor markets in chapters 15 and 17. An earlier, comprehensive work on income distribution theory is provided by Bronfenbrenner (1971).

2. This format for reporting the distribution of income gives rise to a special measure of median family income. Ordinarily the median value for a variable separates the values assigned to the variable into two equal parts. However, the median measure for group data proceeds by separating the frequency (number of families) into two equal parts, namely n/2, where n is total cumulative frequency. With the groups arranged from lowest to highest and their frequencies computed, the group for which comparative frequencies have come to equal n/2 is selected. The median (Md) is then equal to the lower limit of this income class (L), plus a fraction of the frequency (f) in the median class. That fraction is (n/2 - F)/f, where F is cumulative frequency to up to the lower limit and C is length of the median class. Thus,

$$Md = L + C(n/2-F)/f$$

In 1975, the median family income was $13,720. The mean was $15,546. It is simply the total for family income divided by the number of families. The data for median and mean incomes received special attention in the presidential election campaign of 1976, when Carter said to a reporter he would both lower and raise taxes with the mean or median serving as a dividing line. He knew the concepts, but not the actual measures. Their low values apparently surprised him.

3. Estimates of how the final bill affected typical taxpayers were prepared by staff for the joint conference committee on taxation. To prepare the estimates they assumed that adjusted gross income was entirely from wages, salary or self-employment. Capital gains were excluded, and the staff assumed deductions from adjusted income equal to 23 percent of income. The estimates are not reported below, but were used to obtain tax rates on marginal (extra) income for the 1978 law and the "new" law enacted in 1978. As was noted by comparison of the marginal rates under the 1978 law and the "new" law respectively, the progressive feature of the tax law was altered only slightly for incomes up to $50,000 per year and were left virtually unchanged for incomes between 50,000 and 100,000 dollars.

4. Friedman (1962, 162) makes a similar point about choosing before the fact, by making the analogy of entering upon life's occupations to the choice of entering a lottery with very unequal prizes. An inequality of income is the result of permitting individuals to make the most of their initial equality. To redistribute income after the fact, he says, is equivalent to denying the opportunity to enter the lottery.

He offers in addition (Friedman 1962,163) an interesting exercise bearing on the preference for uncertainty and inequality in the distribution of income. In this, Friedman sees the economic "agents" as entering upon occupations, investments, and the like in accordance with a taste for uncertainty. In the absence of such taste, we would see large diversified corporations and cooperatives of movie actresses. The diversification would combine risky and non-risky ventures. In the case of the movie actresses, they would develop a cooperative through which to share income more or less evenly, if they had a great dislike for uncertainty. The cooperative would in effect provide "insurance through the pooling of risks."

5. Ratios (as percentage) of Fair Labor Standards Act minimum wage to gross hourly earnings of production workers in manufacturing are as follows:

Effective data	Old coverage	New nonfarm coverage	Farm workers
Sept. 1961	50	43	--
Sept. 1963	51	--	--
Sept. 1964	--	45	--
Sept. 1964	--	48	--
Feb. 1967	50	36	36
Feb. 1968	54	39	39
Feb. 1969	--	42	42
Feb. 1970	--	44	--
Feb. 1971	--	46	--
May 1974	46	44	37
Jan. 1975	45	43	39
Jan. 1976	46	44	40

Source: Minimum Wage and Maximum Hours Standards Under the Fair Labor Standard Act, An Economic Effects Study Submitted to Congress 1975, U.S. Department of Labor, Employment Standards Administration, p. 15.

6. Suggestive data for youth 16-19 are as follows:

UNEMPLOYMENT RATE

Year	Male		Female	
	Black	White	Black	White
1960	13.9	14.1	25.1	13.0
1965	23.6	13.1	32.8	14.2
1970	25.4	13.8	34.9	13.6
1971	29.7	15.3	36.1	15.4
1972	30.1	14.4	38.5	14.6
1973	28.4	12.6	34.9	13.3

Source: U.S., Department of Labor, Manpower Report of the President, 1974 Government Printing Office, 1974.

7. These articles are reproduced in Fair Labor Amendments of 1973, Part 1, Subcommittee on Labor of the Committee on Labor and Public Welfare, United States Senate

(Washington, D.C.: U.S. Government Printing Office, 1973).

8. Arthur Burns made such a suggestion during the latter part of his tenure as Chairman of the Board of Governors during the period 1970-77. See Arthur F. Burns, "Statement before the Joint Economic Committee," Federal Reserve Bulletin, March 1976, and Arthur F. Burns, "The Real Issues of Inflation and Unemployment," Address at the University of Georgia, September 19, 1975. Printed in Challenge, January/February 1976. See also Feldstein, Martin S., Lowering the Permanent Rate of Unemployment, A Study Prepared for the Use of the Joint Economic Committee, Congress of the United States (Washington, D.C.; U.S. Government Printing Office, 1973), pp. 22-23.

9. Attention is directed to employment and demographic factors in this context. There are of course many other factors affecting the trend rate of growth in GNP, including technological, natural resources, political, and sociological factors. These are all stressed on other occasions.

The concept of full employment GNP (or "potential GNP," as it was initially called) was first developed by the Council of Economic Advisors in 1962. It was associated in that period with Arthur Okun and the assumption of a 4.0 unemployment rate, as in Okun's Law of the last chapter. Rasche and Tatom (1977, 10-13) review aspects of the development and measurement of "potential GNP."

10.

Year	Percent Unemployment	Percent Inflation	Year	Percent Unemployment	Percent Inflation
1960	5.6	1.58	1970	4.9	5.9
1961	6.7	1.07	1971	5.9	4.30
1962	5.6	1.15	1972	5.6	3.30
1963	5.7	1.23	1973	4.9	6.23
1964	5.2	1.31	1974	5.6	10.97
1965	4.6	1.67	1975	8.5	9.14
1966	3.8	2.91			
1967	3.8	2.88			
1968	3.6	4.20			
1969	3.5	5.37			

The unemployment rate is the percent of the Civilian labor unemployed, as reported by the Bureau of Labor Statistics. The inflation rate is computed from annual data for "all items" in the Consumer Price Index, also as reported by BLS.

SELECTED READINGS AND REFERENCES

Arrow, Kenneth J. 1973. "Some Ordinalist-Utilitarian Notes on Rawls' Theory of Justice." Journal of Philosophy (May 10).

Brittain, John A. 1977. The Inheritance of Economic States. Washington, D.C.: The Brookings Institution.

__________. 1978. Inheritance and the Inequality of Material Wealth. Washington, D.C.: The Brookings Institution.

Bronfenbrenner, Martin. 1971. Income Distribution Theory. Chicago, Ill.: Aldine-Atherton, Inc.

Browning, Edgar K. 1976. "The Trend Toward Equality in the Distribution of Income." Southern Economic Journal (July).

__________. 1979. "On the Distribution of Net Income: Reply." Southern Economic Journal (January).

Canterbery, E. Ray. 1979. "A Vita Theory of the Personal Income Distribution." Southern Economic Journal (July).

Chapman, Stephen. 1978. "Poor Laws." New Republic (December 2).

Cooper, George. 1979. A Voluntary Tax? New Perspectives on Sophisticated Tax Avoidance. Washington, D.C.: The Brookings Institution.

Falconer, Robert T. 1978. "The Minimum Wage: A Perspective." Quarterly Review, Federal Reserve Bank of New York (Autumn).

Ferber, Robert, and Werner E. Hirsch. 1978. "Social Experimentation and Economic Policy: A Survey." Journal of Economic Literature 16(December).

Frazer, William. 1976. "Keynes and Feiwel's Intellectual History of Kalecki." Southern Economic Journal (October).

__________. 1977. "Income Distribution, Social Untility, and Unemployment." Nebraska Journal of Economics and Business (Autumn).

Friedman, Milton. 1938. Studies in Income and Wealth, vol. 2. New York: National Bureau of Economic Research.

__________. 1962. Capitalism and Freedom. Chicago: University of Chicago Press. Chapter X.

__________. 1968a. "The Role of Monetary Policy." American Economic Review (March).

__________. 1968b. "The Case for the Negative Income Tax." In Melvin R. Laird, ed. Republican Papers. New York: Frederick A. Praeger.

__________. 1976. Price Theory. Chicago: Aldine Publishing Company. Chapter 2.

__________. 1977. "The Future of Capitalism." In Vital Speeches (March 15). Reprinted as Chapter 1, in Milton Friedman, 1978. Tax Limitation, Inflation and the Role of Government. Dallas, Texas: The Fisher Institute.

__________. 1978a. "Is Capitalism Human?" The Sohioan (April).

__________. 1978b. The Economics of Freedom. Cleveland, Ohio: Standard Oil Company.

___________, and Rose Friedman. 1980. Free to Choose. New York: Harcourt Brace Jovanovich.

Griliches, Zvi, Wilhelm Krelle, Hans-Jürgen Krupp, and Oldrick Kyn, eds. 1978. Income Distribution and Economic Inequality. New York: Halstead Press, John Wiley & Sons.

Hafer, R. W., and Michael E. Trebing. 1980. "The Value-Added Tax--A Review of the Issues." Review, Federal Reserve Bank of St. Louis (January).

Hearings. 1979. Welfare Research and Income Maintenance, Senate Finance Committee's Subcommittee on Public Assistance. Washington, D.C.: U.S. Government Printing Office.

Intriligator, Michael D. 1979. "Income Redistribution: A Probabilistic Approach." American Economic Review (March).

Kearl, J. R., Clayne L. Pope, Gordon T. Whiting, and Larry T. Wimmer. 1979. "A Confusion of Economists?" American Economic Review 69 (May).

Kuznets, Simon. 1977. "Two Centuries of Economic Growth -- Reflections on the U.S. Experience." American Economic Review Proceedings (April).

Kershaw, David, and Robert J. Lampman. 1977. The New Jersey Income-Maintenance Experiment, vol. 1. New York: Academic Press.

Manser, Marilyn E. 1979. "Comparing Households with Different Structures: The Problem of Equity." American Economic Review 69 (May).

Marx, Karl. 1875. Critique of the Gotha Program." In Robert C. Tucker, ed. 1978. The Marx-Engels Reader, second edition. New York: W. W. Norton & Company, Inc.

Moggridge, Donald, ed. 1973. The Collected Writings of John Maynard Keynes, Vol. XIV, The General Theory and After: Part II, Defense and Development. London: Macmillan, St. Martin's Press for the Royal Economic Society.

Okun, Arthur M. 1975. Equality and Efficiency: The Big Tradeoff. Washington, D.C.: The Brookings Institution.

Outlook. 1979. The Economic Outlook for 1979-1980: An Update. A Report to the Senate and House Committees on the Budget. Washington, D.C.: U.S. Government Printing Office.

Pagan, Morton. 1979. "Poverty in the United States: A Reevaluation." Policy Review (Spring).

Phillips, Samuel T. 1975. "Rawls' Economic Position" Public Finance Quarterly (January).

Playboy. 1973. "Playboy Interview: Milton Friedman." Playboy (February).

Popper, Karl. 1965. Conjectures and Refutations: The Growth of Scientific Knowledge. New York: Harper & Row, Publishers).

Rasche, Robert H., and John A. Tatom. "Energy Resources and Potential GNP." Review, Federal Reserve Bank of St. Louis (June).

Rawls, John. 1971. A Theory of Justice. Cambridge, Mass.: The Belknak Press of Harvard University Press.

Report, Join Economic Committee. 1979. The Effects of Structural Employment and Training Programs on Inflation and Unemployment. Washington, D.C.: U.S. Government Printing Office.

Rivlin, Alice M. 1975. "Income Distribution -- Can Economics Help?" American Economic Review, Proceedings (May).

________. 1979. "Statement of Alice M. Rivlin, Director, Congressional Budget Office, before the Committee on the Budget, U.S., House of Representatives." (July 11).

Smeeding, Timothy M. 1979. "On the Distribution of Net Income: Comment." Southern Economic Journal (January).

Tilman, Rick. 1976. "The New Left and the Libertarian Right: Notes for a Reappraisal of the Convergence Thesis." Nebraska Journal of Economics and Business (Autumn).

Veblen, Thorstein. 1934. The Theory of the Leisure Class. New York: The Modern Library. Originally published in 1899.

Watts, Harold, and Albert Rees, eds. 1977. The New Jersey Income-Maintenance Experiment, vols. 2 and 3. New York: Academic Press.

Weber, Max. 1952. The Protestant Ethic and the Spirit of Capitalism. New York: Charles Scribner's Sons. First published in Great Britain in 1930.

Zell, Stephen P. 1978. "The Problem of Rising Teenage Unemployment: A Reappraisal." Economic Review, Federal Reserve Bank of Kansas City (March).

Chapter 12

The Government Sector: Debt Management, Interest Rates, Politics and Persuasion

12.1. Introduction

The implications of government spending and revenue measures for aggregate demand and the performance of the economy have been variously considered in chapters 10 and 11. In section 10.5 the government budget constraint was introduced but otherwise not much has been said about the financing of the Federal debt, the "crowding out" effect of the deficit financing, and the Treasury's management of the debt. These topics were considered important at an earlier time in discussions of controls over the economy. They reemerge as being of importance in a more contemporary time--as the real and monetary (and financial) sides of economic study are further integrated into macroeconomics, and as discussion is even further extended to include the Treasury's yield curve, and theories of the term structure of interest rates. This importance attributed to the old topics is not because debt management itself is still thought to be a useful tool for achieving economic stability. Rather it is because a consideration of the old topics of "crowding out" and debt management--as they bear on monetary policy linkages, financing, and on the term structure of interest rates (as depicted by the Treasury yield curve)--are instructive about controls, their effects and the behavior of interest rates.

Historically, the construction of the curve from yields on marketable government securities (differing mainly with respect to time to maturity) has been frequently treated as depicting a market forecast of yields on a series of future short-term debt instruments, and it has often been said to behave as if it were a forecast. Here, once again, however, historical data are being studied to deal with expectations about the future, as in the case of studying expected inflation with the use of past inflation rates (sect. 5.5), and, still again, we are confronted with a new potential source of data for studying market forecasts in terms of anticipatory rather than just historical data. These come in the form of yields resulting from trading in futures contracts for three-month treasury bills (Hoel 1977) and long-term U.S. Government bond issues as well (Chicago Board of Trade 1977). Such trading in the T-bills began in January 1976 on the International Monetary Market (IMM), as a division of the Chicago Mercantile Exchange. Other anticipatory series, one may recall, include the expected inflation rate from section 5.5, planned capital outlays from section 8.4, announced monetary policy (as under House Concurrent Resolution 133), and forecasts made by the Congressional Budget Office for the Congress (sect. 10.2).

As the evidence reveals, as early as chapter 5, market rates of interest are among the most psychological of variables. This suggests that they may be influenced by the persuasive strategies of the appropriate officials (for example, a highly respected chairman of the Federal Reserve's Board of Governors), say with some control over real magnitudes, money and credit aggregates. The role of the chairman and an example of the use of persuasion are considered in a final section. Especially, the radical changes in the structure of policy making brought on by House Concurrent Resolution 133 lend themselves to a use of announcement effects and persuasive messages by a strong and highly regarded chairman. Under this resolution, as stressed in sections 6.2 and 10.2, plans for monetary policy are announced in advance.

In considering persuasive techniques and the role of the Chairman of the Federal Reserve's Board of Governors, we are especially interested in the tenure of Arthur F. Burns from 1970 to 1978. We look beyond it, but Burns's tenure has been widely reflected upon (Burns 1978; Hass 1979, 113-130; Lombra 1980, 94-105). As indicated earlier (sect. 6.2), it paralleled the first eight years of policy under a money and credit aggregates regime of sorts. The diversion of control over short-term interest rates, as noted earlier (sect. 6.2), kept arising in this period and beyond until the October 6, 1979 announcement. As noted, Burns has been much criticized by economists. Raymond Lombra has stressed (1980, 103), in reviewing Burns's reflections (1978), "It is unfortunate that Burns's considerable ability, prestige, and powers of persuasion were not used to clarify the role of monetary policy and defend a less politically expedient policy."

The attention among the critics has been on Burns having compromised the historical independence of the Federal Reserve within the framework of government. Burns reflected a lot on this (1978, 379-385, 415-423), but the tendency among the critics as been to think of independence in contradictory ways, namely: to think in terms of a regime of money and credit aggregates, on the one hand, and to tacitly or otherwise reflect on the Federal Reserve's hard-won independence from the Treasury at the time of the Treasury-Federal Reserve accord of 1951, where the issue was one of independence from the pegging of interest rates on the government's securities, on the other.

Burns, as we see (sect. 12.5), moved to address the issues of macroeconomic policy broadly viewed early in his tenure and to have given a remarkable performance from the vantage point of a political and highly persuasive figure (Hass 1979, 113-130). He was above all an astute political economist with strong orientation toward an empirical economics. As if Burns were recalling the government budget constraint (sect. 10.5), Lombra (1980, 97) has quoted him thus: "In pure theory, it would be possible for the Federal Reserve, through its monetary policy, to nullify completely what the legislature does. But in practice, central banks, being a part of the government, having a certain responsibility, and not wanting to nullify the will of the legislature or to produce shocks in the economy, will accomodate what the legislature does."

A lesson from the Burns regime may well be stated thus: The Federal Reserve is not truly our independent policy entity within the framework of government, and independence under an aggregates regime with a government budget constraint is a sort of independence never previously contemplated by the founders of the Federal Reserve System and monetary economists. With the October 6, 1979 action announced by Paul Volcker (sect. 6.2) and with the considerable clout of independence expressed upon his becoming Chairman of the Federal Reserve in July 1979, the independence of the Federal Reserve is yet to be tested against a background, say, of an 8 percent unemployment rate and a 5 percent inflation rate. Burns's spectacular performance aside (sect. 12.5), the Federal Reserve may still be thought of most accurately as part of the instability in the economy that is caused by government. Some viewing such a role on the Federal Reserve's part, may wish to reflect further on Friedman's economic Bill of Rights (Friedman 1980, 298-309). One provision reads thus:

> Congress shall have the power to authorize non-interest bearing obligations of the government in the form of currency or book entries, provided that the total dollar amount outstanding increases by no more than 5 percent per year and no less than 3 percent. (Friedman 1980, 308)

12.2. Financing the Debt

The Federal debt arises from the financing of budgetary deficits. It mostly grew to a large proportion during the World War II years, roughly from year-end 1941 to year-end 1945, until at that time it had become larger than GNP, as shown in table 12-1. By 1960 the debt had declined measurably as a percent of GNP. The decline in the percentage slowed from 1960 to 1964, and then the percentage increased some from 1964 to 68. From 1968 through 1974 gross public debt (GPD) as a percentage of GNP dropped from 52.3 to 35.0. Reflecting a record peace time level deficit for the fiscal year ending in 1976, the percentage increased some by year-end 1975, continued at that level for a few years and dropped in 1978, as nominal GNP accelerated under the impact of inflation. Contemplating such an episode of debt declining in relation to nominal GNP at a time of inflation but using smaller debt figures than those in table 12-1, the Friedmans note (1980, 269-270): "In the decade from 1968 through 1978, the federal government had a cumulative deficit of more than $260 billion, yet the debt amounted to 30 percent of national income in 1968, to 28 percent in 1978."

Table 12-1
Gross Public Debt (dollar amounts if billions)

END OF PERIOD	TOTAL GROSS PUBLIC DEBT (GPD)	MARKETABLE DEBT AS PERCENT OF GPD	GPD AS PERCENT OF GNP
1941--Dec.	64.3	64.7	51.6
1945--Dec.	278.7	91.7	139.9
1960--Dec.	290.4	83.5	57.6
1964--Dec.	318.7	83.9	50.4
1968--Dec.	358.0	66.1	52.3
1974--Dec.	492.7	57.4	35.0
1975--Dec.	576.6	63.0	38.5
1976--Dec.	653.5	64.5	38.3
1977--Dec.	718.9	64.0	38.0
1978--Dec.	789.2	61.7	35.6

Note: Marketable debt includes bills, notes and bonds in the more recent years. Gross Public Debt includes interest bearing public issues (both marketable and non-marketable issues plus a small amount of convertable bonds) and special issues (i.e., issues held by U.S. Government agencies and trust funds and the Federal home loan banks).

Federal debt, of course, is different from private debt in several respects, namely, it has typically been owned domestically (to ourselves) until the energy crisis years (sect. 2.4), and the financial instruments representing it are of the highest quality of risk. When the credit worthiness of the government is questioned, the credit worthiness of other units operating under it is even more questionable. The government's credit worthiness, however, is not unlimited. The size of the debt in relation to GNP is one measure of the country's ability to carry and service the debt, and the soundness and purchasing power of its currency may be cited as another, since inflation (as in the context of chapter 2) means a loss of purchasing power from contractually fixed dollar returns and possible further loss to foreign owners of the debt instruments as the value of the denominating currency falls in the foreign exchange markets.[1]

The instruments representing the marketable portion of the Federal debt include in recent years bills, notes and bonds (32.4, 54.6, 13.0 percent respectively in April 1979). The bills are issued at maturities of three, six, and twelve months in selected denominations. They are issued at a weekly auction conducted by the Federal Reserve Banks for the Treasury, and prices (and therefore yields) are determined by buyers in competitive bidding at the regular auctions. In contrast, yield and maturity features of the other instruments are tailored by the Treasury, with notes having maturities of up to five years, and bonds having maturities of longer direction. The marketable debt instruments of the Government have enjoyed a wide market, with depth, and resilency since the early post-World War II years (Roosa 1956), and, as mentioned earlier, a futures market opened for three-month Treasury bills in 1976 (Hoel 1977).

The "Crowding Out" Effect

A major sort of consideration about the growth of the debt, or large jumps in its size, is that new financing might crowd other sectors of the economy out of the market for funds, along lines introduced in section 10.5. In that case we get a substitution of governmental spending for spending by other sectors of the economy.

At this time, we recall the government budget constraint (sect. 10.5); we also renew the consideration of monetary policy and introduce some empirical considerations.

The empirical considerations concern two important recessions in economic history, the recessions of 1937-38 and of 1973-75. These like other recessions are in a sense--as liquidity preference analysis viewed would suggest--a result of shift in the strength of a preference for liquidity. On the financial side, households and businesses reduce indebtedness at the bank in relation to asset size or income, liquid balances are accumulated, and the extension of new installment credit decelerates as repayments accelerate. On the real goods side, spending decelerates. The recessions of 1937-38 and 1973-75 are not immune to this characterization, though unique features accompany both.

Commercial banks at the earlier time had reserves in excess of legal requirements, the demand for bank loans was negligible, and highly liquid securities such as U.S. Treasury bills were very much in demand by the banks.[2] It would appear that the banks would welcome new securities to the market and that these would have no crowding out effect.

In 1975 a taskforce of the Senate's Budget Committee (Task Force 1975) similarly reported on the liquidity of financial institutions and groups that commonly hold government securities, and similarily concluded that "crowding out" of deficit financing would be unlikely. This would be because industrial concerns were not planning large capital outlays that would require a heavy volume of financing (sect. 8.4). The change in the Treasury's net borrowing and the liquidity shifts by nonfinancial businesses, as events of calendar year 1975 unfolded, are depicted in figure 12-1, as reported by the Federal Reserve Bank of Chicago and as constructed from sources and uses of funds data (sect. 7.2). Exclusive of other changes shown and exclusive of the Treasury's sponsored agency borrowing (largely to support the housing market), the Treasury increased borrowing from approximately $12 billion in 1974 to over $80 billion in 1975, and nonfinancial businesses reduced their net withdrawal of funds from the financial markets from approximately $85 to $34 billion. This latter reduction included a net repayment of short-term debt.

Figure 12-1. Liquidity Shift and Treasury Financing

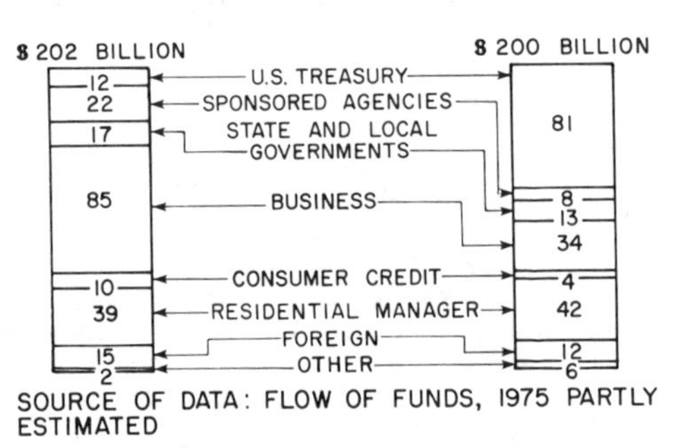

Source of chart: "Financial Market Pressures Ease," <u>Business Conditions</u>, Federal Reserve Bank of Chicago, February 1976.

The Market for Bank Credit

The issue at the time of the 1937-38 recession centered about the metaphor "Pushing on a String," and the issue can be similarly viewed at the later time. Monetary policy was said--in invoking the metaphor--to be like pushing on a string. Monetary polcy could restrain a boom (pull on a string) but it could not induce recovery any more than it could "push on a string." Monetary policy was viewed as working entirely through the supply side of the market for funds, as in the Keynesian theory of section 4.3 (recall $\Delta M \rightarrow -\Delta i \rightarrow \Delta I$). Monetary analysis, as it emerged in the hands of the monetarists, was different (recall $\Delta \dot{M} \rightarrow \Delta \dot{Y} \rightarrow \Delta i$). According to it accelerated growth of money and credit aggregates would work on the demand side of the market for funds.

Thus, taking a monetarist linkage view and recognizing a recession as a strengthened preference for liquidity, spending and "loan demand" from the spending side of the market for goods and services (a policy induced recovery) would come about from satisfying the preference for liquidity as would result from the Federal Reserves conducting any necessary open market operations in securities to achieve the accelerated growth in credit and monetary aggregates. Firms and households may not borrow immediately, but banks can buy securities in the market independently of borrowers coming to them.

In this context, any financing through the sale of long-term debt issues by the Treasury would either "crowd out" private financing and/or call for supportive efforts on the part of the Federal Reserve. The crowding out would occur in either or some combination of two senses: (1) in the sense the Treasury would absorb liquidity that would be needed to have commercial banks and other business-directed financial institutions expand credit to commercial users, and/or (2) in the sense that the Treasury's financing would directly substitute for what would otherwise be an extension of credit to the non-government sector. The other alternative (namely, the supportive monetary policy) would occur in the sense that the Federal Reserve would provide more rapid growth in bank reserves than would be the case in the absence of Treasury financing. In the context of section 10.5 and the government budget constraint shown there ($dB/dt + dR/dt =$ deficit), we have either the crowding out (dB/dt) or monetary policy (dR/dt). The apparent liquidity of institutions in 1937-38 and 1973-75 is simply more apparent than real in relation to the liquidity demanded by the institutions.

12.3. Debt Management and the Yield Curve

The Federal debt, as stated earlier, is represented by securities. In the present case there are government securities that fall mainly into the categories of marketable, non-marketable (e.g., the common series E savings bond), and special issues of debt instruments. We are most interested in the marketable portion, approximately 61.8 percent of total gross public debt at year-end 1978, as shown in table 12-1. It is the negotiable part that is traded by securities dealers. Its management by the Treasury, as far as new issues are concerned, consists mainly of the following: auctioning Treasury bills, gauging the interest rate feature and establishing a time to maturity feature for the numerous other issues of debt, and thus determining an average time to maturity for the outstanding issues. The different marketable debt issues have at times been as large as seventy odd in number, and some are maturing regularly and being refinanced. The debt is being "rolled over."

The management might be with the view to simply getting the market to accept the issues at minimum interest cost and thus with the view to suiting the market, or with some other objective such as the achievement of national economic goals. In the early post-World War II years, debt management by the U.S. Treasury was viewed as an area of policy for the achievement of national economic goals, and economic stability in particular.

There were several aspects of thinking that stood out. One was that a rise (decline) in interest rates automatically contributed to less (greater) liquidity, given an average time to maturity for the marketable debt, and that, as a consequence, it automatically had some stabilizing influence. As may occur in recession (compare fig. 5-3), a decline in interest rates paralleled a rise in bond prices and thus contributed to liquidity. In the expansion phase of business, the reverse occurred, and there would be some "lock-in" effect as the holders of marketable debt instruments exhibited hesitancy to liquidate them and undergo the reporting of losses from their sale. Another aspect of debt management with respect to stabilization was that the average time to maturity of the debt could be varied to influence liquidity and thus spending, say, by moving toward a shorter average time to maturity in recession (or in anticipation of recession) and toward a longer average time in a boom (or in anticipation of a boom). Still another was that the Treasury's yield curve could be twisted (or its sweep altered) through varying the quantity of instruments placed in one maturity segment of the market as opposed to another.

The first two of the foregoing thoughts are still valid, but there is a complication in aggressively pursuing a policy of changing the average time to maturity, as brought out below. The third of the foregoing thoughts depends on invalid theories of the term structure, again as brought out below.

Variation in the Time-to-Maturity Profile

Debt management with the view to varying the average time to maturity of the marketable debt and possibly having some stabilizing influence on economic conditions may be illustrated with the use of time-to-maturity profiles for the debt. These may readily be constructed as the free-hand fit of curves to coordinates consisting of time to maturity for the various issues of the public debt and the respective sums of the par values making up the separate issues as proportions of the total marketable debt. Two such curves depicting distributions of the debt are shown in figure 12-2, where the arithmetic means (or average, m) and model values (m_o) for the distributions are shown.[3] These distributions are similar to probability distributions, and their relative frequencies sum to one.

The mean, one may recall, is to the right of the model value (or mid-point of the class with the largest number of frequencies) as a measure of central tendency when skewness is to the right, as in part a of figure 12-2, and it is to the left of the model value when skewness is to the left.[4] However, the mean is pulled to the right by shifting the large relative frequencies more to the right, as in the case of the Treasury's issuing more long-term debt issues and fewer short-term debt issues, both as proportions of the total debt.

The change in the profile, as from part a to part b of figure 12-2, obtained through debt management would have a restraining influence on total spending and on business conditions during an expansion phase. It would work through the "lock-in" effect and the tendency for a rise in interest rates to have a greater effect on the market values for debt instruments, the longer the time to maturity. The reverse changes in the time-to-maturity profile would contribute to greater liquidity. The extent of such changes in liquidity and interest rates, as during a recession, would depend on the possible presence or absence of an inflationary component in the interest rate (say, as during the simultaneous occurrance of inflation and recession).

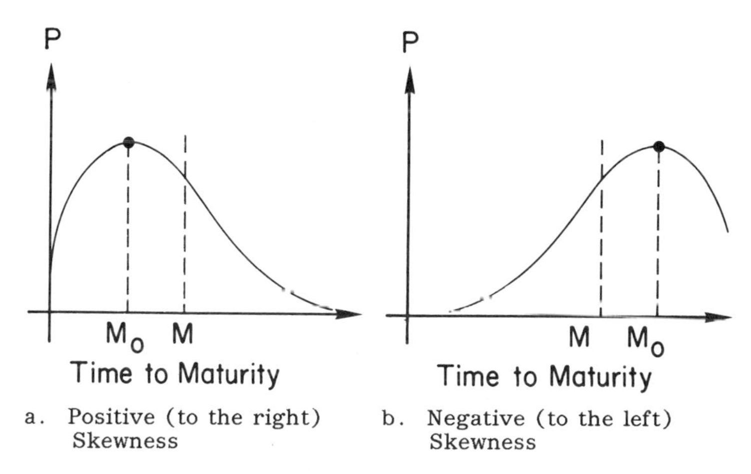

a. Positive (to the right) Skewness

b. Negative (to the left) Skewness

Figure 12-2. Time-to-Maturity Profiles for the Public Debt

The difficulties encountered by the aggressive pursuit of a countercyclical debt management policy are simply stated. First, altering the average time to maturity of the public debt requires more time than is normally available within the time frame of a simple phase of the short cycle. Second, altering the average time to maturity runs counter to notions about tailoring maturities of new issues to suit the market, as brought out below.

The Term Structure of Interest Rates

"Term structure of interest rates" is the structure of yields on financial assets (most commonly government securities holdings) that differ mainly with respect to the time to maturity feature at a given time. Some notion of this structure may be obtained from examining the interest rates for three classes of government securities that differ mainly with respect to the maturity features. These would include short-, intermediate-, and long-term securities as in the upper part of figure 5-3. One would then observe in effect an upward sweeping curve (called a yield curve), if a curve were fit to the rates plotted against time to maturity (a horizontal axis) at a trough of business conditions such as mid-year 1954. The yield curve would be flatter or even downward sweeping, if it were to be fit near a peak of business conditions.[5]

Here we have discussed a yield curve and yields on only three classes of securities. More elaborately fitted curves could be obtained, however, from actual yields (as rates) on many different issues, at various dates, as shown in figure 12-3. Usually the term structure depicts a rather smooth pattern of interest rates, mainly because of the way the values of the separate issues of securities (and therefore their interest rates) are interrelated through arbitrage transactions and by having traders and dealers operating in the relatively free financial markets. The arbitrage transaction in this contex would entail a sale of securities of one maturity along the yield curve and the immediate purchase of other securities of another maturity whose yield may be out of the pattern of yields on the upward side. This sort of transaction permits a sure gain (say, without risk), as would characterize the arbitrage transactions. Other adjustments in prices (and therefore yields) by traders and dealers would include changes in the quotation of selling prices that would simply bring yields more into accord with prevailing views about future yields, all without quantities of securities actually flowing into or out of the markets.

A common feature of the interrelationships has been depicted and verified empirically on repeated occasions. It is, in words, that one plus the long-term rate of interest $(1 + R_n)$ is equal to the nth root of the geometric average of each of the separate yields plus one on n different single period securities, $(1 + r_1)(1 + r_2) \ldots (1 + r_n)$. In symbols,

$$(1 + R_n) = \sqrt[n]{(1+r_1)(1+r_2)\ldots(1+r_n)}$$

An underlying idea is that expected return--including a serialized stream of returns and/or appreciation (depreciation) in value--from an expected single period yield series is derived from a series of single period yield expected to prevail at various times in the future. There is the related notion that the long-term rate (R_n) will be high in relation to expected short-term rates $(r_1, r_2, \ldots r_n)$ if the rates on the short-dated instruments are expected to rise. Or, with reference to the yield curve defined above, the yield curve will have an upward sweeping shape when interest rates are expected to rise, and it will take on a flatter or possibly a downward sweeping shape as interest rates increase and come to reflect the greater prospect of a decline in interest rates.

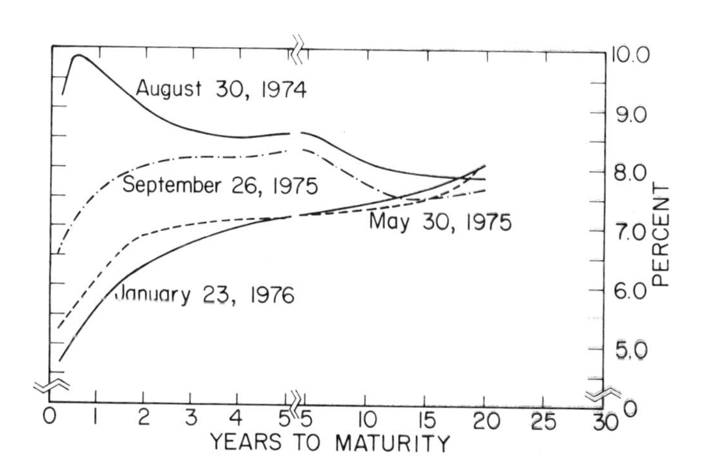

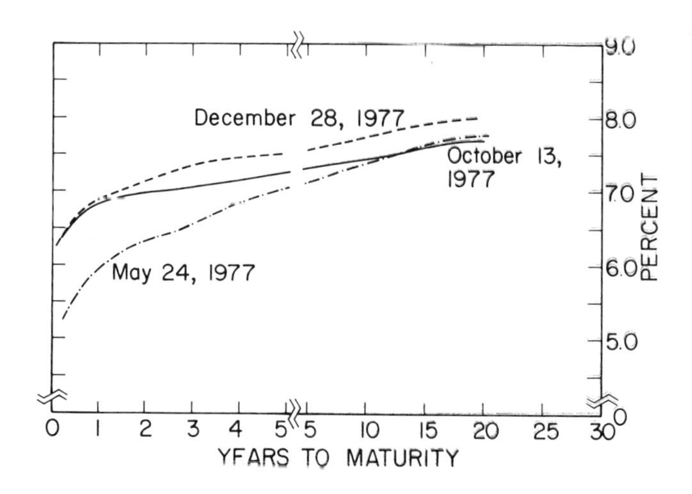

Figure 12-3. Yields on U.S. Government Securities

Source: Federal Reserve Bank of St. Louis

The Futures Markets for Treasury Bills and Other U.S. Government Securities

The Treasury yield curve, as just mentioned, is thought to reflect market forecasts of yields on future issues of short- and intermediate-dated issues of U.S. Government securities, and it has been viewed as such. The relatively new futures markets for these issues are thought to offer further prospects for studying forecasting behavior. In particular, with the passage of time, data should be generated to determine whether the yields on futures in Treasury bills and other U.S. Government securities behave as the yields shown in yield curves predict they will behave, and to help determine whether the yields on futures contracts will be unbiased forecasts of rates observed in the future. The prospect, since the new markets came about, has been positive for the former sort of behavior (Poole 1978).

The first of the interest rate futures contracts was started by the Chicago Board of Trade (CBT) in October of 1975 for Government National Mortgage Association (GNMA) futures (Froewiss 1978). They were first followed by trading in T-bill contracts on the International Monetary Market (IMM) in January 1976, and then trading was extended by CBT to include long-term U.S. Government bonds. All operate in essentially the same way as the traditional commodities futures markets.

The futures contracts for bills as traded on the IMM (a division of the Chicago Mercantile Exchange) are uniform with respect to amount and maturity date of deliverable three-month bills totaling $1 million of par value.[6] There were initially six futures contracts for six different three-month Treasury bills extending about a year and a half in the future, and later the number of contracts was increased to eight. Prices of these contracts are called "futures prices." In contrast, prices of existing Treasury bills are called "cash" or "spot" prices.

As arises later in chapter 19 in further consideration of exchange rates, and rates on exchange for future delivery in particular, there are "spot" and "forward exchange rates." Futures contracts differ from forward contracts in several respects. As listed by Hoel (1977, n1): "(1) forward contracts are generally not negotiable; (2) forward contracts are not standardized; (3) delivery of the commodity is expected on forward contracts unless otherwise agreed upon by the parties involved in the transactions while futures contracts are usually settled by offsetting contracts; (4) futures contracts are made and traded on the floor of futures exchanges and forward contracts are not."

From the point of view of a borrower (user) of funds or a lender (supplier) of funds, the futures market permits a transfer of risk concerning changes in interest rates to a speculator. This transferring of risk is called hedging (Chicago Board of Trade, 1977).[7] As defined by the separate and distinct Chicago Mercantile Exchange, a hedge is "The purchase or sale of a futures contract as a temporary substitute for a merchandising transaction to be made at a later date," and a speculator is "One who attempts to anticipate price changes and through market activities make profits."

As considered in chapter 8, large industrial corporations plan their financing, often with the view to avoiding the uncertainty and likely higher interest costs of the future financing of capital expenditures. There this activity may take the form of selling bonds in the capital market and returning the proceeds to the money and/or credit markets by purchasing short-dated securities in the money market, in the one case, or by reducing indebtedness at the bank, in the other. In any case, there is an increase in liquidity as a potential source of funds for future use. This activity of purchasing a security, particularly one with a maturity that coincides with an anticipated future need for funds, we call below liquidity hedging. In a sense, then, the futures markets in debt instruments provides a possible substitute way of hedging.

Hoel (1977, 23-24) notes that the advantage of a T-bill futures hedge is its lower transactions costs and smaller tie-up of capital than in the case of the Treasury bills market itself. She adds, "Of course, when participants find it less costly and more convenient for them to obtain the desired protection in the market for Treasury bills they will do so instead of using the futures market." She illustrates alternatives available and costs involved. Higgins (1978) goes a bit further and poses the question, "Would it have been better (more profitable) to hedge with T-bill futures than just invest in T-bills at the time money was available [for the period January 1976 through June 1977]?" He concludes that futures were a better buy, but notes that the percentage of transactions comprising hedges and speculation respectively were unknown.

12.4. Theories of the Term Structure

Theories of the term structure of interest rates may be classified as neo-classical, modified neo-classical (possibly including liquidity preference theory with reference to "normal backwardation"), market segmentation theory, and post-computer expectations theories (including so-called variants of preferred habitat theory and efficient markets theory). Some combinations of the latter theories focus on a preference for securities with particular maturities and the prospect that prices (and thus yields) on the short- and long-dated securities are simply responding to the same circumstances efficiently (say, to information efficiently, as later encountered in the efficient markets and rational expectations notions of chap. 14). With one exception (Terrell 1972; and Michaelson 1973, chap. 6), the apparently closely related empirical study of portfolio selection (defined with reference to the composition and the choice of assets) has not been considered simultaneously with the term structure theory for the most part.

Neoclassical Theory

The neoclassical theory has especially been associated with Frederick Lutz (1940), although it did not originate with him. The main point of the theory is that, at any particular time, long-term rates represent an average of prospective short-term rates, as denoted by the formula above for $(1 + R_n)$. There is here an assumed indifference between holding a single contract of long duration or a series of periodically renegotiated, short-term contracts.

Meiselman's Theory

Meiselman's expectations theory (1962) is in strong measure neoclassical, in the sense that follows the indifference assumption about holding a single contracts of long duration or a series of periodically renegotiated, short-term contracts. Meiselman adds to this, however, and his specific contributions have been summarized thus (Frazer 1973, 249): "(1) to assume that a fictional 'forward' interest rate was implicit in the term structure as represented by the yield curve, and to claim that the 'forward' rate is the market expectation of the rate that will prevail in the future; (2) to set forth a known error learning model that was previously thought to explain error learning as a part of the formation of expectations; and (3) to analyze term structure data to determine whether they behaved as if they represented forecasts." Meiselman's tests of the expectations theory showed that adjustments in the yield curve forecast of interest rates followed a pattern similiar to that of known forecasts.

Liquidity Preference Theory (Backwardation)

The liquidity preference theory, as found in Keynes (1930, 142-147) and Hicks (1946, 136-139) and as dealt with by Leijonhufvud (1968, 288-289), asserts a preference for the certainty of capital over the certainty of income, and consequently posits a predominance of an upward sloping yield curve. The tendency for yields on long-dated securities to exceed those on short-dated securities gives rise to the reference "normal backwardation."

There is an additional bit about monetary policy in connection with this theory. It is that the Treasury yield curve can be shifted upward (downward) through open market sales (purchases) conducted mainly in short-dated securities. Through a properly functioning arbitrage and expectations mechanism, the operations in the short-dated securities get transmitted as effects on the long-dated securities.

Market Segmentation Theory

Market segmentation theory is associated with John Culbertson (1957). He argues that choosing financial assets on the basis of expected return is tantamount to gambling (1957, 499). Instead, expectations are treated as being non-operative (or zero elastic), and the interest rate determined in one maturity sector of the market is independent of that in the other. There are separate markets and equilibrium values are determined in each with respect to quantities being brought to and taken from the market. This would be as with the most static use of the Marshallian cross.[8]

Preferred Habitat vs. Efficient Market

As reviewed by Phillips and Pippenger (1976) and elsewhere (Frazer 1973, chap. 13; Terrell 1972), Franco Modigiliani and Richard Sutch offered a preferred habitat theory which reflected a preference (preferred habitat) for particular maturities. Their theory (Frazer 1973, 263-266) has "extrapolative" and "push" effects but remarkably has been described as another name for market segmentation (Kessel 1967). In particular, it appears as a supply side theory, with short- relative to long-term rates being controlled by having the Treasury vary the time-to-maturity composition of the debt.

As opposed to this sort of control, Phillips and Pippenger (1976) offer a simplified efficient markets view (SEM), namely --"For simplicity, the impact of new information on capital markets is arbitrarily divided into three components: the impact of new information that is relevant primarily to the determination of short-term rates x(t), the impact of new information that is relevant primarily to long-term rates y(t), and the impact of new information that is relevant to both rates z(t)." From Phillips's and Peppinger's point of view, "both long-term and short-term rates...are related to each other to the extent that both respond to the same information z(t)."

Although their statistical results do not rule out "extrolative push" and "regressive pull" effects, Phillips and Peppinger find results consistent with their model. Again, however, they do not deal empirically with portfolio preferences.

The Control Mechanism and Alternative Theory

In all of the above theories, except the "naive" efficient markets model, there is either an assumed indifference between holding issues of different maturity and/or the supply of and demand for particular quantities make a major difference in the structure of interest rates. The first assumption can be considered outright by noting whether different time to maturity profiles for different institutional holders of U.S. Government securities exists. The others simply permit the control of interest rates directly through open market purchases and sales or the twisting of the yield curve through manipulations by the Treasury of the time to maturity features of the different debt instruments. This turns out to be at odds with the sort of independent interest rate evidence we have variously considered (including in chapter 5 in particular), and the additional sort we consider below.

Setting aside the prominent features of these foregoing theories, however, is not to set aside all of the features. The term structure of interest rates may still behave as if it were a forecast of future interest rates, "push" and "pull" effects may still operate, and empirically speaking $(1+R_n)$ may still be equal to the nth root of the geometric average of each of the separate yields plus one on n different singe period securities, $(1+r_1)$ $(1+r_2)\ldots(1+r_n)$. In particular, liquidity hedging behavior may be present and yields adjusting to accommodate expectations, but they may be doing so independently of a predominant supply-demand-quantity mechanism.

The problem was not with the behavior of the yields (as rates), but rather it has been with the behavior of groups of holders of securities with respect to a strong preference for selected maturities. Investing institutional groups--such as nonfinancial corporations, commercial banks, savings and loan associations, and life insurance companies--have been shown to prefer certain maturity distribution patterns of securities that matched a future flow of funds against the needs for funds for future outlays, deriving mainly from liabilities. These preferred maturity profiles have been shown to be fairly stable over time. There is a hedging, "a liquidity hedging" against the future need for funds, as illustrated below, that occurs as securities are selected with maturity features that correspond to the timing of the anticipated need.

The alternative means of explaining yield curve behavior centers about a more predominantly expectations approach than Meiselman's early approach. According to the alternative the two sides of market transactions in securities are responding to about the same forces and events and are simply setting yields in accordance with mutual expectations (e.g., as may materialize about the expected rate of change in the price level). Further, there are possible "push" and "pull" effects operating on interest rates as in adaptive expectations models. Short-term rates move upward (downward) the most in a boom (in a recession) because recent changes in rates are in that direction and because of a reduced pull toward normality on those rates. The greater pull toward normality for long-term rates centers about the prospect that market participants look further into the past when determining prospects for a more distant future.

Adaptive expectations models for short-term (i_S) and long-term (i_L) rates may appear thus:

$$i_S = \text{const.} + \beta_o\, i_t + \beta_1\, i_{t-1}$$

$$i_L = \text{const.} + \beta_o\, i_t + \beta_1\, i_{t-1} + \ldots + \beta_n\, i_{t-n}$$

Here the "push" effect of recent changes is working exclusively on the short-term rate. In contrast, the more distant past imposes some regressive "pull" toward normality on the long-term rate of interest.

All the foregoing stress on expectations does not rule out the prospect that simple changes in the quantity of one security in relation to another coming on the market will not have some influence. Rather, as a first approximation, the expectations role is thought to be of special importance in public policy considerations.

The sort of evidence one encounters in the present area of study concerns time to maturity profiles of the holdings of federal debt by institutional groups. These may be obtained in several ways, including: by computing each institutional groups' holdings of specific issues as percentages of their par value dollar's worth of holdings and plotting against time to maturity, or by computing each institutional groups holdings of specific issues as percentages of the par value dollar's worth of total public debt and plotting against time to maturity of the issues in question. The first sets of observations provide profiles that are independent of one another. Institutional shares of the public debt as dependent variables, on the other hand, emphasize interdependent institutional differences.

Maturity profiles emphasizing interdependent institutional differences for institutional shares of the marketable debt are shown in figure 12-4. In the figure, for given dates, each security issue (and no fewer than 65 in all) is shown as a proportion (P) of total public holdings of marketable debt on the vertical axes and the different maturities in months are shown on the horizontal axes.

Profiles of the type illustrated in figure 12-4 have been shown to be fairly stable over time (Terrell 1972). In combination with this the Treasury has been described as following its most typical policy of tailoring the new issues to suit the market. What this has meant is that the maturity profiles were demand-side determined and that the Treasury merely shaped the supply of long- relative to short-dated instruments for the most part. When one considers the movements of the Treasury's yield curve over time in the context of this demand side, tailoring framework, however--as reflected in figure 5-3--it is apparent that significant forces are shaping the term structure other than the quantities of short- relative to long-dated issues coming on and being withdrawn from the market. These other forces would appear to be in the realm of expectations.

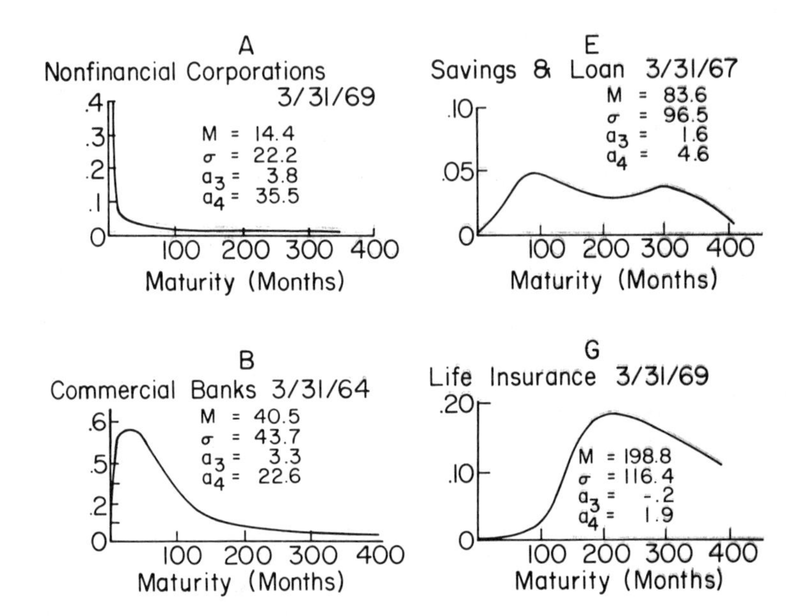

Figure 12-4. Selected Maturity Profiles of Government Security Holdings

Source: William T. Terrell and William J. Frazer, Jr., "Interest Rates, Portfolio Behavior, and Marketable Government Securities," Journal of Finance, March 1972.

Operation Twist

A laboratory experiment of a sort suggesting support for the foregoing view of interest rate behavior is the Federal Reserve's Operation Twist which was undertaken by the Treasury and the Federal Reserve in early 1961 (Frazer 1973, 160, 252, 262-263, 267, 273-274). The conditions were: (1) an early stage of recovery from the 1960-61 recession, (2) losses of gold and a withdrawal of short-term balances on deposit in the United States (as would be revealed by a U.S. statement of the balance of international payments, such as table 2-1), and (3) sluggish capital spending in the United States. Against this background, the Treasury was to have its influence through tailoring the maturities of new issues to obtain the objective, and the Federal Reserve for its part was to twist the Treasury's yield curve by raising short-term rates and lowering long-term rates via open market sales in one instance and purchase in the other.[9] The high short rates were to help retain foreign balances held in the United States, as will be considered in chapter 19, and the low long rates were to help stimulate domestic investment along the lines investment demand as depicted in figure 8-2. However, no visible effects of the operation were detected and statistical methods were unable to facilitate the isolation of any effects. The obvious prospect is the predominance of expectations sorts of phenomena.

The conditions for the twist operation, as just depicted, make it a good example of a laboratory like situation, in part because the natural tendencies favor an upward sweeping curve and the objective was to alter this. Had the conditions been more in accord with a downward sweeping yield curve, as in the later stages of a boom, success could possibly be claimed for the operation even if it were not warranted. This would be because the operation would have been moving with "natural" tendencies, and success could more readily be claimed even where it were not warranted.

On general efforts to twist the yield curve Meiselman has noted with reference to the period 1958-68 a main finding of various independent researchers, namely: "the only dependable way to change the relationship between short-term and long-term interest rates is to change the level of rates." But even here evidence suggests a predominance of demand rather than independent supply side phenomena. What we have in the present consideration of the term structure is further evidence about the importance of expectations in shaping interest rates, evidence about the frailty of any simple linkage whereby the Federal Reserve lowers (raises) interest rates as a means of stimulating (dumping) capital spending, and a need for a theory of monetary control with special attention to expectations and forecasting (Frazer 1978b).

The evidence just reviewed suggests, furthermore, difficulties inherent in the Treasury's attempting to influence the attainment of national economic goals such as the rate of unemployment through debt management. Perhaps the best they can do is to maintain and on occasion lengthen the average time to maturity of the Federal debt. This tends to make the debt less liquid for its holders when interest rates are rising. The effect is called a "lock-in" effect, to suggest some unwillingness on the part of bond holders to dispose of their bonds when bond prices have been declining.

12.5. The Burns's Years and Beyond: The Role of the Chairman of the Board of Governors

Much has been said about the Burns's years at the Federal Reserve by him (1978) and others (sect. C.2). In some measure this comes about because of the turbulence in government, the economy, and in the economics of those years, and in some measure it comes about because of the rising attention to monetary and credit aggregates. A central issue that appears midway in Burns's tenure and continues beyond it is that of the independence of the Federal Reserve within the framework of government. As that issue comes up with respect to Burns and beyond, however, one is taken back by Edward Kane (1974, 743-752) to the early 1950s when the Federal Reserve's issue of independence was last addressed. On that occasion the issue centered about the Federal Reserve's independence from having to support the Treasury's financing and marketing of the Federal debt. From Burns's macroeconomic policy perspective, moreover, he never minimized the importance of interest rates even under the money and credit aggregates approach. This section, thus, proceeds against the foregoing background with attention to the "pegged -rate" episode, Burns's view of policy, and the role for persuasion on Burns's part in his vision of macroeconomic policy.

Pegged Interest Rates, 1946-1950

Following the end of World War II and the growth of Federal debt during the war, there was concern about what would happen to the government securities market (Frazer and Yohe 1966, 574-577). The result was a tacit agreement between the Federal Reserve and the Treasury whereby the Federal Reserve was said to be pegging interest rates. The policy was known--which helped to influence expectations about rates and was thus to achieve pegged rates--and the Federal Reserve stood ready to buy and sell at announced rates. With the hindsight of what we know about interest rates and the focus on open market operations (sect. 6.2), we would expect this task to be difficult, especially in the presence of inflation, and so it was. The task of control under pegged rates may not have been so difficult, of course, had the operations been more along Friedmanesque lines--i.e., more toward changing money and credit aggregates at sustainable rates (fig. 6-11).

Through agreement the rates were adjusted upward in 1947-48, the 1948-49 recession posed no problem as rates adjusted downward, and then in 1950 under renewed inflationary pressure (though mild by the standards of the 1970s) open discord erupted between the Federal Reserve and the Treasury. Ostensibly on the Federal Reserve's part, there was the view that the rates should be allowed to adjust to market forces. Further, under the market pressures developing in the presence of the inflation there was some question about whether the Federal Reserve could in fact maintain pegged rates, although this was not pursued too much at that time. The issue instead became one of the Federal Reserve's independence within the framework of government. An agreement between the Federal Reserve and the Treasury to that effect was announced on March 4, 1951.

The old issue becomes important again, first in 1974 and then in later criticisms that develop around monetary policy and Arthur Burns.

The Burns/Friedman Episode: Federal Reserve Independence

At the 1974 date, criticism emerged in Congressional hearings and in the press over the monetary policy during 1971 to 1973. The issue in the hearings (1974) focused on policy and a conflict between Milton Friedman and Arthur Burns, Friedman's friend since days at Rutgers University in the school year 1930-31. At that time Edward Kane, a money-and-banking economist, wrote of "The Re-politization of the Federal Reserve" (Kane 1974, 743-752). In referring to policy under Burns, Kane (1974, 743) harks back to the period of the accord and immediately beyond by referring to a power "Chairman McCable 'bled' for in 1951 and that over the next two decades, Chairman Martin labored assiduously to consolidate." Later, as program chairman for the 1978 proceedings of the American Finance Association, Kane scheduled a session with papers on the appraisal of Burns's performance as chairman from 1970 through 1978. These papers were those of Burns's critics that were cited earlier (sect. 6.2).

The questions which then come up are: (1) does independence on the Federal Reserve's part mean something drastically difference under an interest rate regime vis-ạ-vis one of money and credit aggregates?, and (2) has the academic economist's view of independence been mostly an illusion?

The first question gets resolved when we focus on the role of the government budget constraint (sect. 10.5). The resolution is that independence in the respective regimes has quite different implications. Interest rates, we see, are highly resilient and much can happen without their nullifying the intentions of the Congress. This is not so with monetary policy as depicted under a government budget constraint.

Next, light is shed on the second question by the earlier introduction to Burns's tenure (sect. 6.2), and by his view of his own job as it emerged in the 1974 hearings. Circumstances at the Federal Reserve and in government since Burns's time further reveal an essentially political role for the Federal Reserve.

The view of the Federal Reserve that emerges from 1974 and beyond, on Burns' part, with respect to independence has two parts: (1) it means an independent platform from which to plead with Congress for a sound macroeconomic policy, and (2) it means a platform from which one may hopefully persuade the public that a sound policy will be followed.

Although Arthur Burns paid great respect to the independence of the Federal Reserve (1978, 379-385 and 415-423) the first of the two parts to independence comes out in an inquiry on Senator Proxmire's part in 1974 hearings and in reflections by Lombra on Burns's Reflections (1980, 94-105). The inquiry by Senator Proxmire in the Friedman/Burns episode proceeds as follows:

> Mr. Burns: You know, Senator, there are some people in this world--and I am not going to refer to anyone by name, it doesn't matter--who

think that it is the business of the Federal Reserve to correct for every mistake that is made by the private sector of our economy or by Congress or by the executive establishment. But Congress has not given the Federal Reserve that power, and I don't think the Congress should give the Federal Reserve any such power.

As for the power that we have, we could stop this inflation in a very few months, and stop it dead in its tracks. We have not done it. And we have no intention of doing it, because the only way we could do that is to bring the distress of mass unemployment on this Nation.

Proxmire probes deeper and brings Milton Friedman back into the picture thus (Hearings 1974, 747):

Senator Proxmire: That may very well be true. Let me ask you if you would agree with this concluding argument of Mr. Friedman:

"There is literally no way to end inflation that will not involve a temporary, though perhaps fairly protracted, period of low economic growth and relatively high unemployment. Avoidance of the earlier excessive monetary growth would have had far less costly consequences for the community than cutting monetary growth down to an appropriate level will have now. But the damage has been done. The longer we wait the harder it will be. And there is no other way to stop inflation."

Do you agree with that rather rigorous insistence on this kind of choice, a choice which I think most of us, many of us at least, would make on the side of saving, if this is the case, then we will have to find some way of ameliorating the consequences of inflation?

Mr. Burns: You are drawing me into something, Senator, that I said I didn't want to do. And I hope we can end this. I don't want to quarrel with my very good friend. You have questions to put to me about economic policy, but let's ...

Senator Proxmire: That isn't the question. It doesn't matter. You and Mr. Friedman highly respect each other, you are both excellent economists. And as I have said, I think you and Mr. Kissinger represent two of the best appointments I have seen in 17 years.

Mr. Burns: Thank you very much.

The discussion with Proxmire tails off thus:

Senator Proxmire: My time is up. But tell us, what do we do without going through an unemployment period caused by tighter money and more restrictive fiscal policy, either/or?

Mr. Burns: Well, the question is not whether we go through an unemployment period. The question is whether we can manage this problem without going through a fairly protracted period of low economic growth and relatively high unemployment. For a brief period I am afraid we will just have to take that.

You know, one can talk about money supply from now until doomsday. But what we have now in our country is not a deficiency of demand, but a reduction in our capacity to produce, because of the sudden and very serious oil shortage. And the effects have ramified--take our automobile factories--over the country. A large part of automobile capacity you can just write off, it is dead. It is dead because people don't want to buy big cars. Now, at a time like this we will have to suffer, I am afraid, some unemployment. But I think the period could be brief. And if we conduct our monetary and fiscal policies prudently, I think we can got onto a track that will gradually diminish the rate of inflation. At the end of perhaps 2 or 3 years we can return to price stability without going through a protracted period of heavy unemployment.

(This last paragraph would have applied in 1980 as well as it did in 1977.)

There is further discussion with other committee members. Proxmire re-enters the picture, and the questioning gets back to Friedman and the independence of the Federal Reserve (Hearing 1974, 755-756):

Senator Proxmire: I am going to do this again.

I apologize for referring so frequently to Mr. Friedman, but he is a very able man, and he puts the case very strongly. And it is a question that I think has to be asked of you, Mr. Burns. I will conclude it this way.

The only justification for the Fed wanting independence is because it enables it to take measures that are wise for the long run even if not popular in

> the short run. That is why it is so discouraging to have the reply consist almost entirely of a denial of the responsibility for inflation and to attempt to place the blame elsewhere. If the Fed does not explain to the public the nature of our problems and the costs involved in ending inflation, if it does not take the lead in imposing the temporary unpopular measure required, who does?

Interest Rates and Burns's Performance

Although acknowledging the money and credit aggregates approach, we find Arthur Burns continuously devoting attention to interest rates as an important determinant of numerous classes of spending. His view of them and his efforts to exert some control over them was entwined with his view of the problem of inflation.

The analysis of the yield curve (sect. 12.4) and the almost purely psychological phenomenon reflected in the interest rates at times provides some further background for Burns's orchestration of macroeconomic policy. Thus far we have noted in section 12.5 in relation to the interest rate phenomenon the common practice by the Treasury of tailoring issues to suit the market, the behavior of interest rates as reflected in the yield curve, the failure of "operation twist," the liquidity hedging hypothesis, and the reported stability of time-to-maturity profiles. Much earlier (sect. 5.5) we recognized uncertainty and inflationary-expectations components in interest rates.

These prospects for interest-rate determination then suggest a consistency with the possibility of influencing interest rates by having some public official in high office, such as the President of the United States or Chairman of the Federal Reserve, act as a masseuse to the public's psyche, say through the use of persuasive messages, as introduced in section 10.3. Arthur Burns--renowned business cycle analyst, respected economist, and Chairman of the Board of Governors of the Federal Reserve System from February 1, 1970 through February 1, 1978[10]--apparently played such a role, leading up to and during a 1975-76 period of unique behavior for interest rates over the post-World War II years, despite the critical assessments about the behavior of monetary aggregates encountered in section 6.2. The unique behavior was the decline in market interest rates, as a whole following September 1975, when ordinarily they should have been rising. After some period of upward movement of interest rates, and during the expansion of economic activity following the recession from November 1973 to March 1975, interest rates behaved as shown in figure 12-5.

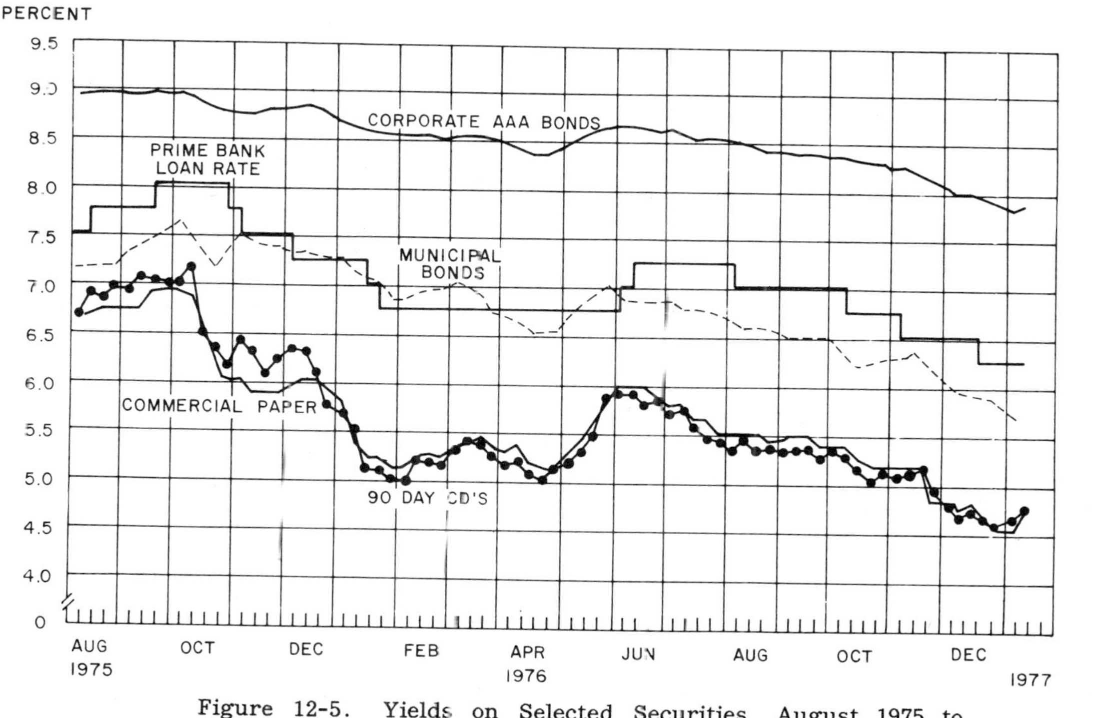

Figure 12-5. Yields on Selected Securities, August 1975 to October 1976

On the unique interest rate movements we quote Burns (1976, 234):

> There is a striking contrast between the movement of interest rates during the current recovery and their behavior in past cyclical upswings. Short-term interest rates normally begin to move up at about the same time as the upturn in general business activity, although the rise varies from one cycle to another. In the current economic upswing, a vigorous rebound of activity, a continuing high rate of inflation, and a record volume of Treasury borrowing might well have been expected to exert strong upward pressures on short-term interest rates. However, after some run-up in the summer months of last year, short-term rates turned down again last fall and since then have declined to the lowest level since later 1972. Long-term rates have also moved down; yields on high-grade new issues of corporations are now at their lowest level since early 1974.
>
> Conditions in financial markets thus remain favorable for economic expansion. Interest rates are generally lower than at the trough of the recession. Savings flows to thrift institutions are still very ample, and commitments of funds to the mortgage market are continuing to increase. Mortgage interest rates are therefore edging down.

Uniqueness of Interest Rate Movements, 1975:III through 1977:I

The methods for supporting the claim for the uniqueness of the interest rate behavior during the period from the third quarter of 1975 through the first quarter of 1977 are twofold. They center about theory and data, in one case, and simply an examination of data, in another.

The theory concerns aspects of the demand for money (sect. 6.3) and the term structure of interest rates (sect. 12.4). In the demand context, accelerating the growth of the money stock leads to an excess of "desired" over "actual" balances, some rise in spending (likely with overshooting and hence a rise in the ratio of spending to the money stock), and most commonly a rise in "the" rate of interest. The alleged tendency for the interest rate to rise may be qualified at times by the prospect of a short-lived liquidity effect. The tendency for interest rates to rise, in any case, may be associated with the nominal interest rate as a sum of the real rate (i.e., the nominal rate less the expected inflation rate) and the expected inflation rate as weighted for uncertainty in the forecast. Added qualifications enter when we consider theory of the term structure whereby the long-term rate is influenced especially by the outlook over a more distant future (usually interpreted as a pull toward normality).

The method of simply examining the data without the added restrictions imposed by theoretical considerations is straight forward. It proceeds first, by recognizing the presence of repetitive behavior in the more common time series for the economy, including the money stock (narrowly and broadly defined), GNP (possibly in constant price terms), and short- and long-term interest rates, and, second, by recognizing deviations from the more common pattern. In the present case, we are concerned with post-World War II data for a particular segment during expansion phases of business conditions, notably: a segment of six quarters duration beginning two quarters after troughs in business conditions. This is the segment where we expect to find unique behavior during the early stages of recovery from the 1973-75 recession.

The data and patterns in question are shown in figures 12-6 and 12-7, for the segment in question following each of the troughs in business conditions for the post-World War II years. Figure 12-6 shows percentage changes in the money stock (M_1 and M_2), GNP in constant prices (GNP_{72}), and the GNP deflator (P_{GNP}). All of these percentage changes are positive, and of such magnitude as to reflect a rise in the income velocity ratio (GNP/M_1). Figure 12-7 shows in addition the data for key interest rates (the three month Treasury bill rate, B_{3M}, the rate on long-term Government bonds, $B_{GOV'T}$, and the rate on high-grade corporate bonds, (B_{Aaa}) over the segment of cyclical up-turn in question.

The behavior of the series is as one would expect from the economic theory for the most part, although the behavior is somewhat more complicated for the last three expansion phases beginning in the early 1960s. In the early 1960s, the upturn was a sluggish one, the business outlook dampted, and the prospects of inflation and dollar devaluation ominous. Hence we see in the D part of figure 12-7 a characteristic rise in the short-term rate over the phase 1961:II through 1963:I but modest declines in long-term rates. This pattern was to persist in some measure in the comparable phase following the 1969-70 recession. By the 1969-70 recession, moreover, the phenomenum of recession and inflation was discernable, with some apparent impact on the up-turns that followed. Even so, the short-term interest rate (with expected inflation rate component) does not decline during the considered segment of the expansion phase until the 1975-77 period. The departure in the interest rate behavior here, in this period, is substantial and unique, extending to the direction and extend of movement.

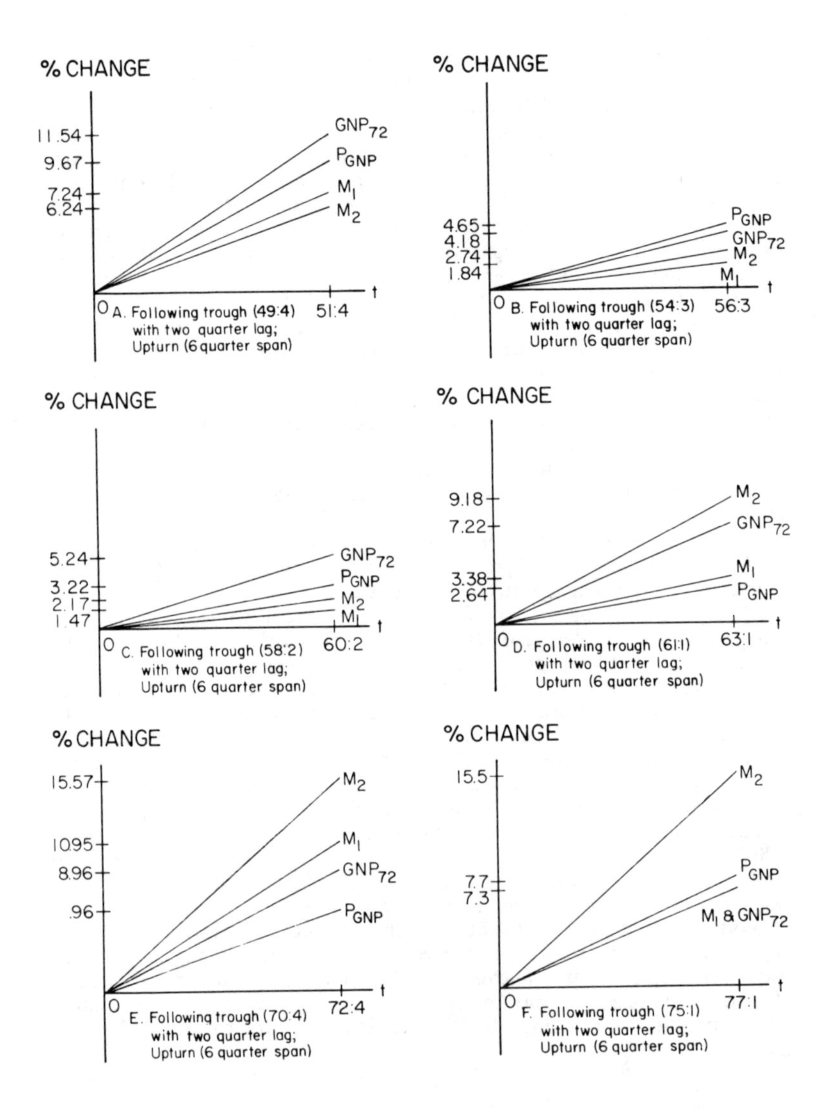

Figure 12-6. Percentage Changes in the Money Stock, GNP (1972 prices), and the GNP Deflator: A Selected Segment of Recovery Phases over the Post-World War II Years

Sources of data: The Federal Reserve System and the U.S. Department of Commerce.

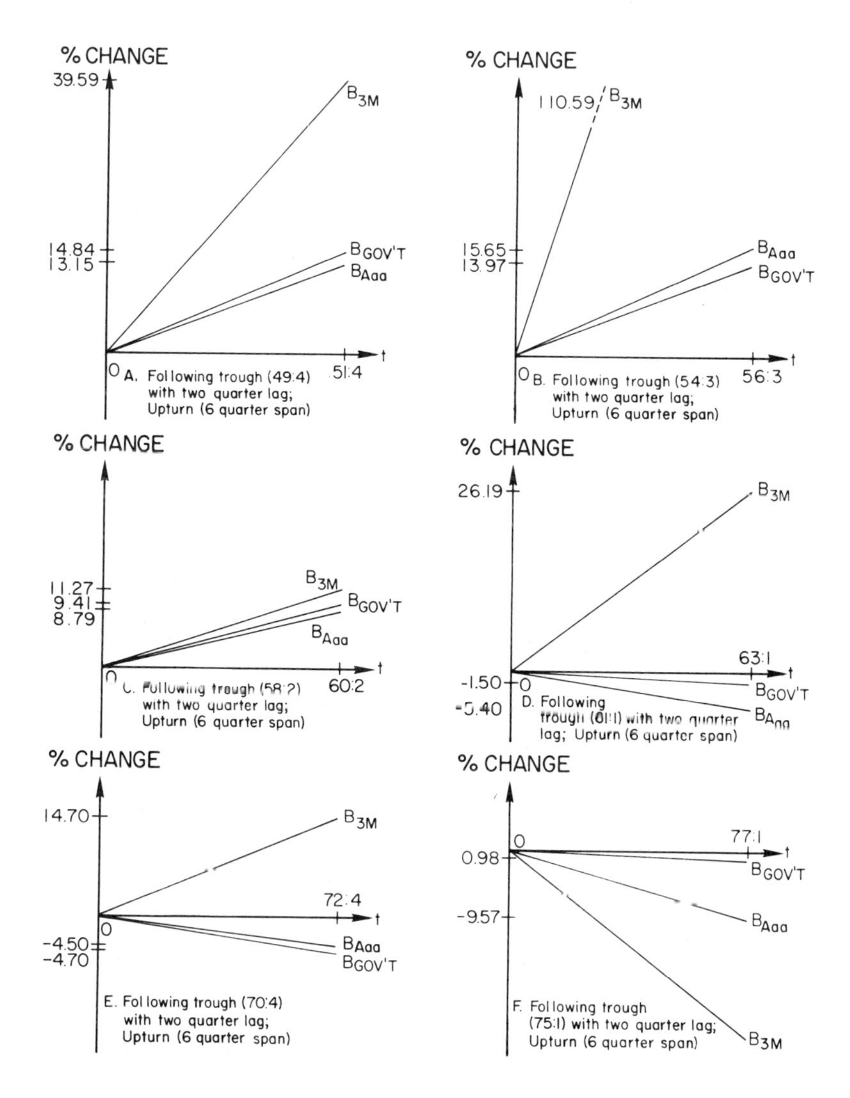

Figure 12-7. Percentage Changes in the Treasury Bill Rate, and Yields on Government and High-Grade Corporate Bonds: A Selected Segment of Recovery Phases over the Post World War II Years

Source of data: The Federal Reserve System and Moody's Investors Service.

Though methods employed by Abrams et al. (1980, 30-42) lack the subtlety to get at the complexities we consider, they nevertheless also reflect a picture that is consistent wth the one we outline in focusing on the inflation-rate component of the interest rate from 1975:III through 1977:I. Notably, using regression methods to obtain Federal Reserve responses to inflation and unemployment goals, and to monetary aggregates versus interest rate targets for the period 1970-1977 and the subperiods 1970:III to 1973:IV and 1973:IV to 1977:III, Abrams et al. (1980, 30-42) report these results indicating the following: a systematic response to both interest-rate and monetary-aggregate targets; and a systematic response to the inflation rate only in the latter sub-period.

The Role of the Chairman

Awareness of the role of the Chairman of the Board of Governors of the Federal Reserve System is especially germane to an understanding of Burns's orchestation of the management of inflation and the unique behavior of interest rates and short-term rates in particular during the recovery from the 1973-75 recession. For this awareness we draw from Maisel (1973, chap. 6), a former member of the Board of Governors, on the sources of power available to the Chairman.[11] These are noted as "extralegal" because legally the Chairman has only one vote in seven as a Board member and there is little difference between the chairman and others in the respect. The five extralegal sources of power are as follows

> First, his appointment makes him the titular head of and the spokesman for the Federal Reserve System. It is assumed that the Chairman's voice reflects System policy. But, even if this were not the case, it is often true in fact because of announcement effects. Second, the Chairman represents the System and he participates in many decisions which never come before the Board. The acts of representation and participation carry power per se. Third, any chairmanship carries certain inherent powers, such as the selection of the agenda and the leadership of meetings, which at times influence decisions. Fourth, the Federal Reserve Board has delegated much of its supervisory power over the staff and the System to the Chairman, thus increasing his actual strength. And, finally a less tangible strength is his ability, because of his other powers, to attract extra votes at Board and FOMC meetings. (Maisel 1973, 123-124)

On the Chairman as official spokesman, Maisel comments thus (1973, 125): "Since the Chairman's views get wide publicity, they may lead to major changes in expectations and, as a result, to changes in actual policy even though they initially reflected a purely personal view point."

On the basis of his experience as a Board member (with tenure, 1965-1973), Maisel (1973, 110) constructs a chart that reflects his assessment of the relative monetary powers of the various groups within and outside of the Federal Reserve. The Chairman stands out with 45 percent of the inside power. The staff of the Board and the FOMC (Federal Open Market Committee) come next with 25 percent, then the other six governors with 20, and the regional Federal Reserve banks with 10.

On Burns in particular, Maisel says (1973, 120), "He has devoted more effort to relations with Congress. His concerns have encompassed the entire scope of the administration's economic problems..." Continuing, he says (1973, 121), "his [Burns's] concern has been with overall macroeconomic policy (including its coordination with other government programs)." Then, "he [Burns] saw the Fed's role as one of innovator, supporter, and public pleader for good macropolicy."

In summary, Maisel stresses the role of the Chairman:

> Much of the public's awareness of the Federal Reserve System comes through the Chairman and his public statements. He personifies the System, and monetary policy is seen as a reflection of his ideas and personality. His role in monetary decisions is paramount. (Maisel 1973, 107)

Burns's Approach, 1970-1976

An apparent persuasive strategy emerges in Arthur Burns's public statements, 1970 76. Through these statements he establishes in the mind of his audience some broadly based notions.12 First, as stressed early in his tenure and reaffirmed later, economic laws are not working the way they used to, namely: expectations about inflation and economic events play a more crucial role in determining business conditions and the effects of monetary and fiscal policies. Next, market interest rates are important variables in business conditions--especially in relation to home construction, municipal financing, and capital expenditure plans--but they may contain a sizable inflation premium. This means partly and at selected times that interest rates cannot be lowered and important segments of business activity stimulated via the interest rate route without reducing the expected rate of inflation. And, third, the releases of projected changes in credit and monetary aggregates have influence that extend beyond the actual changes that may later take place. For example, a projection for the money stock above the actual change may cause bankers and other lenders to make excess loan commitments to business and thus delay the damping effect of an actual change.

As inflation develops in the 1970s, with roots going back into the 1960s, Burns establishes inflation as a secular trend problem, partly distinct from and partly related to shorter swings in business conditions. Inflation, he says, is engrained in the public's expectations and the public has lost confidence in the government's willingness to deal with it. In broad outline, against this background,a part of Burns's strategy was to influence expectations and restore public confidence in the government's willingness to do something about the inflation.

Thus--early on, as introduced in section 6.2--Phase II of Nixon's price control program was supposed to provide a cover and hold down the inflation rate while other policies could proceed to stimulate spending and reduce the unemployment rate. Burns, we see, was a part of this, as apparently was his persuasive strategy to lower inflationary expectations. This early part of his approach, whatever its merits, failed in its avoidance of the 1973-75 recession, although its short-run consequences may have helped in Nixon's 1972 reelection. Burns in any case, over the longer period, did not falter in his approach, and it appears to have been paying off in the 1975-77 period, as far as interest rates and checking the inflation were concerned. The ultimate impact of the strategy is partly symbolized by the uniqueness of the behavior of interest rates following an earlier upturn in business conditions in 1975.

Burns's encompassing macroeconomic approach to policy and the political problems of policy as suggested by the foregoing and other information would not appear incongruous with Raymond Lombra's reflections (1980, 97) as set out thus:

> Burns seems to have a model where there are n causes of inflation, and monetary policy is the nth. Within this model monetary policy is totally endogenous; the nation must first deal successfully with the n - 1 causes of inflation and only then can the nth--that is, monetary policy--be formulated and executed in a manner consistent with long-run price stability. Put more succinctly, although he does not deny money creation played a role in the inflation, he does reject the view that it was the most important factor and that monetary policy <u>by itself</u> could have pursued a course of action that would have altered the inflation rate in any significant way. This contention lies at the heart of the inflation problem.
>
> Many would reject Burns's hypothesis. His view reflects an assessment of the political environment, the constraints imposed by structural relationships in the economy, and what he believes was a generally irresponsible fiscal policy. Inflation in this view is essentially a political problem. Once this is understood, seeming paradoxes in Burns's various statements can be resolved. To illustrate the point, the following expression of intention appears in nearly every statement Burns made on monetary policy: "We have no intention of letting the money supply grow at a rate that will add fuel to the fires of inflation. On the contrary, we are

determined to bring about a gradual reduction in the rate of money expansion to a pace compatible with reasonable price stability."

Formalizing the Role of Persuasive Strategies

Colloquially, Burns's approach may be characterized as "jaw-boning," say, with extra attention to confidence and credibility. Even so, efforts are made in this book and in the appendix to chapter 12 to formalize the role of persuasion. It and political aspects of monetary policy have been dealt with elsewhere (Hass 1979). These efforts at formalizing the role of persuasion include the introduction of evidence on the effects of persuasion from the field of social psychology. The details found there indicate the importance of the following: (1) the credibility of the announcement as indicated by the spread between previously announced plans for policy targets and the targets actually achieved by the monetary authorities for the monetary and credit aggregates; (2) the strength and novelty of the attention-generating persuasive message accompanying the announcement; and (3) the extent of the recognized expertise of the source of the announcement.

The Miller Period, 1978-79

Whatever the critics may say (sect. 6.2) of the Burns's years, his must have been a tough act to follow for William Miller ("Announements" March 1978, 248-49), the Carter appointee following the rejection of Burns. In his brief tenure, his strength as an administrator of the Federal Reserve System stood out, as did three fairly distinct phases of public behavior. First, Miller openly talked of the problem of inflation, even in opposition to the White House. By early 1978, however, he became a part of what has been labeled Phase II of President Carter's voluntary wage and price program (as elucidated in sect. 17.3). There was then to follow a time of apparent subordination by the Fed, and, finally, in the closing phase of the 1978-79 inflation the profile at the Federal Reserve was a political one of avoiding any share in the blame for bringing on recession.

Miller appears in this phase to have hesitated about decelerating money and credit aggregates with the consequence of their actually accelerating in the second and third quarters of 1979. These developments combined with the Iranians attacking the U.S. embassy in Tehran in February, the student invasion of the embassy on November 4, and the Soviet invasion of Afghanistan on December 30--all apparently fueled rising expectations about the inflation rate, and hence rising interest rates (with the prime loan rate reaching 20 percent on April 2, 1980) and thus the postponement of recession from 1979 to 1980.

Reflecting Miller's team-player role, Carter announced plans on July 19, 1979 to transfer Miller to the Treasury post in his Cabinet. Paul Volcker was then named to succeed Miller as Chairman on July 25, 1979. A main switch to a more viable monetary aggregate policy came on October 6, as introduced earlier (sect. 6.2). The new stance was well received. The test for a truely independent Federal Reserve and a money-and-credit-aggregates regime was still to lie ahead for a time of high unemployment rates. The hope may be that the Federal Reserve has learned the lesson, that it should be inconceivable that it would repeat its traditional error of excessive ease in the first years of a recovery.

This view of the Federal Reserve with a strong Chairman and spokesman, with the Chairman serving mostly at the pleasure of the President, and with the Federal Reserve being a creature of the Congress, however, is not an encouraging one. The Federal Reserve is a part of the politics of government on this foregoing view. In its light, some may wish to choose the constitutional option provided by Milton Friedman (sect. 12.1). Others may still prefer the Federal Reserve as Arthur Burns saw it.

12.6. Summary

Two important aspects of the Federal debt concern us as we consider fiscal and monetary controls and the management of debt. The first is that the financing of large jumps in the size of the debt may have a "crowding out" effect, as introduced in chapter 11. Such an effect has not been thought to occur in recession, e.g., as in 1937-38 and 1973-75.

In time of recession the demand for liquidity is large and only reduced amounts of new capital spending by the private sector are forthcoming. A strictly supply side appraisal to the link between monetary policy and total demand suggests in such a setting that no "crowding out" would occur. The Keynesian approach was such an approach. A demand side approach, on the other hand, suggests liquidity is abundant because of the demand for it and the reduced demand for funds by capital spending units. Hence, the way to overcome recession is to first satisfy the enlarged liquidity preference of the financial institutions and non-financial business sectors. As this occurs increased spending also occurs and the loan portion of bank credit expands. In such a setting, government financing (or refinancing) that takes place may soak up liquidity such that "crowding out" may occur, albeit unapparently so. The degree of "crowding out" will depend on the time to maturity of the government's debt financing.

The second important aspect of the Federal debt concerning us is that its management is unlikely to play more than a minor supportive role in the achievement of national economic goals. Variations in the average time to maturity may enter, but even here the Treasury is very limited because the institutional groups holding the debt have rather definite maturity profiles in mind. These coincide with an anticipated need for funds for an uncertain future and for the fulfillment of specific future needs for funds.

The maturity profiles that characterize the respective institutional holders of government securities tend to be fairly stable over time. This stability, a tendency for the Treasury to tailor issues to suit the market, and a volatility in the spread between long- and short-term rates--all of this--suggests that the rates are in a substantial measure floating around in response to changes in expectations about future rates. This would be in lieu of their movement in response to the supply of short- relative to long-dated issues coming on or being withdrawn from the market.

Such a view of the behavior of yields on government securities is contrary to the more traditional theories of the term structure of interest rates. The theories relying primarily on supply-demand-quantity changes imply strongly that the yield curve can be twisted through debt management (possibly with the support of Federal Reserve open market operations) and indeed that yields can otherwise be controlled by the Federal Reserve through open market operations. "Operation Twist" of early 1961 was an action based on conventional theory. The yield curve was not judged to be measurably affected by the operation.

The validity of the spread between the short- and long-term rates can be explained by "push" and "pull" effects. When rates are moving in a given direction, the extrapolative push of the change is predominant for short-term rates. In contrast, an extrapolation of expectations about long-term rates is more constrained by the average of rates for a more distant past. The regressive pull toward normality is stronger for them.

These foregoing remarks are indicative of an almost purely psychological nature of the behavior of interest rates. Further, this view is supported by the various considerations of the nominal rate of interest as the sum of the real rate and the expected inflation rate as weighted for uncertainty in the forecast. All of this--along with the attention to announced policy changes under House Concurrent Resolution 133--is suggestive of the prospect of influencing interest rates in some measure through the use of persuasion by a highly regarded expert with the role and responsibilities of the Chairman of the Federal Reserve's Board of Governors. This suggestion has been formalized somewhat by treating the average lag in the effect of policy changes on interest rate changes as a function of other variables--credibility of announcements, strength and novelty of messages, and the recognized expertise of the source of the announcement. As Chairman of the Board of Governors, Arthur Burns used persuasion to influence interest rates during the 1970-76 period. The unique decline in interest rates in the September 1975 to September 1976 period of business recovery may be cited as an illustration of aspects of the behavior of interest rates in response to persuasive messages.

Burns's performance however, has not received high marks by his critics. Others, such as Senator Proxmire, have referred to him as one of the two best appointments in government over a seventeen year span. In still other quarters, Burns has been known as having compromised the political independence of the Federal Reserve within the framework of government. Even so, there are redeeming possibilities for Burns's performance. First, the notion of the Federal Reserve's independence is dated by the Treasury-Federal Reserve accord of March 1951. It applies to a regime of presumed interest-rate control. The same sort of independence is not likely to apply under a regime of control through money and credit aggregates with the prospect of a government budget constraint. The Federal Reserve emerges in the latter case as less of an independent agent than presumed since 1951, and as more of a political agent within the framework of government. The alternatives appear as the acceptance of such a political role, or as a constitutional amendment along Friedmanesque lines. Accepting the first route as the prospect, Burns's performance would appear superb by most standards. Viewing his tenure in two parts, from 1970 through 1974, and from 1975 through 1977, Burns's appears to have learned much from his earlier experience.

FOOTNOTES

1. The possibility of "hedging" against exchange rate losses of this type from holding short-term debt instruments comes up in chapter 19. In any case, the foreign and international ownership of the total gross public debt held at about 12 percent over the years 1974-76, and jumped to 15.2 percent at year-end 1977 and to 17.5 at year-end 1978. The data on the ownership are published regularly in the Federal Reserve Bulletin.
2. In 1940, negative interest rates were reported on new issues of 3-month Treasury bills. This 1937-40 episode is reviewed in Frazer (1973, chap. 11).
3. The average time to maturity is actually a weighted average (or expected value). It is the sum of each time to maturity when multiplier by the percentage of the total debt in that maturity. The model value is the time to maturity representing the largest percentage (or relative frequency) of the total debt.
4. On measure of skewness is provided by the formula,

$$\text{skewness} = \frac{\text{mean - mode}}{\text{standard deviation}}$$

where the standard deviation is the square root of the variance. Variance was discussed in chapter 6. Not mentioned above, but also discussed earlier (note 2, chap. 11) was the third of the three statistical measure of central tendency (namely, the median value).

5. A sketch depicting such a simple construction may be shown, as follows:

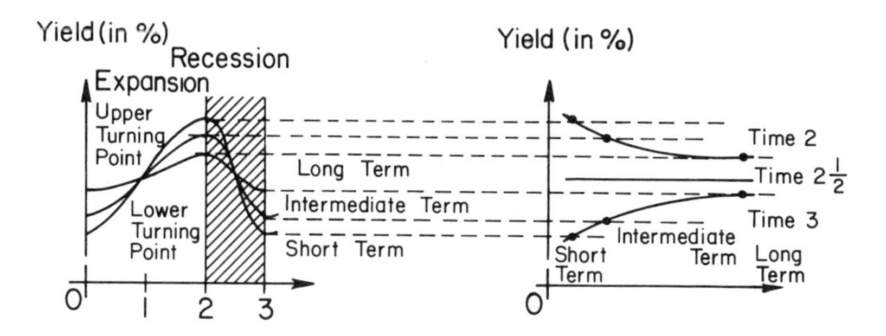

6. Futures contracts are agreements which are standardized with respect to amount, delivery location and procedure. They are described by Hoel (1977,1) as follows: "The contracts, made and traded only on the floor of futures contracts because they provide for both delivery and payment on a future date. However, futures contracts are rarely made for the purpose of actual delivery. Most are settled by purchasing or selling offsetting futures contracts before maturity. A contract to deliver can be settled (or closed) by purchasing an offsetting contract (in effect, to receive delivery) and vice-versa; this is known as the 'right to offset'."
7. Several glossaries of commodity trading terms are available: (Chicago Mercantile Exchange 1977; Chicago Board of Trade 1977; and Hoel 1977).
8. As if to atone for this odd view, Culbertson was later to author one of the first text to deal with Friedman's monetary linkage scheme, namely: Money and Banking (New York: McGraw-Hill Book Company, 1972). Friedman's linkage scheme is clearly present in Culbertson's text, as are waves of optimism and pessimism with reference to business conditions, although he goes astray about stock market prices in Fisher's equation of exchange (sect. 14.3) and vacillates about the determination of interest rates.
9. The Twist concept may readily be depicted thus:

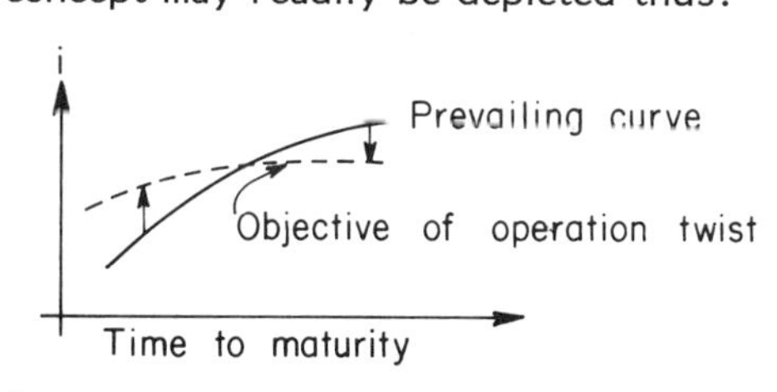

where the solid line is the prevailing yield curve, and the broken lines the position in which the curve was to be twisted.

10. For a polite and courteous account of Burns's suitability for the job at hand, his early background and that just before coming to the Federal Reserve, see Viorst (1971, 309-326). However, the last lines of Viorst essay quote Burns thus: "The responsibility of the Fed is to supervise monetary policy... I don't think it is the Chairman's job to lecture the other branches of government on taxation and spending policies." As matters turned out, Burns approach at the Fed eventually became almost just the opposite from that suggested by the quotation.

    In a statement upon taking office, G. William Miller, Burns's successor said the following (Announcements 1978, 248): "Arthur Burns is a legend in his own time...he has been a great fighter against inflation. His integrity, his intellect, his talents are known, and he is well loved and respected throughout the world.

    In actuality Burns continued to stay on until March 8, as Chairman and until March 31, as a Board member. On February 2, 1978, President Carter designated Burns as Acting Chairman until his succesor as Chairman could be designated. The President had announced his intention on December 28, to appoint Miller as a member of the Board and as Chairman. However, the appointment was delayed by the Senate Banking Committee because of questions about a payment by Bell Helicopter, apparently to get a contract to provide helicopters to the Iranian military. Miller had been Chairman of Textron, Inc., (parent company for Bell), a diversified company headquartered in Providence, Rhode Island, with 180 plants and facilities in the U.S. and in several foreign countries. (The dealings of Textron with Pentagon officials and others during Miller's period as Chairman at Textron was to come up on still later occasions.)

    As an example of a gymnastic in some Federal Reserve matters, Miller was appointed from the San Francisco Federal Reserve District to take the Board position being vacated by David M. Lilly, from the Minneapolis district, while Burns appointment was from the New York district. The opening left by Burns's departure remained unfilled from March 31, until September 18. At that time Nancy H. Teeters, of Indiana, took office to fill the remainder of Burns's term (expiring January 31, 1984).

    The announcement about Miller's appointment as a member and as Chairman of the Board of Governors, his remarks upon taking the oath of office, and a biographical sketch are found in the Federal Reserve Bulletin (Announcements March 1978, 248-249).

    A biographical sketch of Ms. Teeters also appears in the Federal Reserve Bulletin (Announcements, 1978, 777). At the time of her appointment she was serving as chief economist of the House Budget Committee. Prior to that appointment she had been a specialist of the Congressional Research Service, Library of Congress, and from 1970 to 1973 she was a senior fellow at the Brookings Institution.

11. On the responsibilities delegated to the chairman, see "Announcements" (1970, 191).
12. A chronological list of selected statements by Burns over the 1970-76 period may be found in the various issues of the Federal Reserve Bulletin. Specific references include:

Burns, A. F., "Statement before the Joint Economic Committee, February 18, 1970," Federal Reserve Bulletin, March 1970.

______, "Statement before the Joint Economic Committee, February 20, 1973," Federal Reserve Bulletin, March 1973.

______, "Statement before the Joint Economic Committee, February 26, 1974," Federal Reserve Bulletin, March 1974.

______, "Statement before the Joint Economic Committee, February 7, 1975," Federal Reserve Bulletin, February 1975a.

______, "Statement before the Committee on the Budget, U.S. Senate, March 13, 1975," Federal Reserve Bulletin, March 1975b.

______, "Statement before the Committee on Banking, Housing and Urban Affairs, U.S. Senate, November 4, 1974," Federal Reserve Bulletin, November 1975d.

______, "Statement before the Committee on Banking, Housing, and Urban Affairs, U.S. House of Representatives, July 24, 1975," Federal Reserve Bulletin, August 1975c.

______, "Statement before the Joint Economic Committee, February 19, 1976," Federal Reserve Bulletin, March 1976.

Some positions taken by Burns are given added meaning if juxtaposed with two views that prevailed in the 1960s, namely: (View 1) that business policymakers had come to look beyond the troughs of recessions and toward the government's unwillingness to cope with inflation, particularly wage and salary induced inflation (Frazer 1973, 76-77), and (View 2) that the acceptance of higher rates of inflation was a tradeoff for reduced rates of unemployment irrespective of the state of business conditions.

SELECTED READINGS AND REFERENCES

Abrams, Richard K., Richard Froyen, and Roger N. Wand. 1980. "Monetary Policy Reaction Functions, Consistent Expectations, and the Burns Era." Journal of Money, Credit and Banking (February).

"Announcements." 1970. Federal Reserve Bulletin (February).

"Announcements." 1978. Federal Reserve Bulletin (March).

"Announcements." 1978. Federal Reserve Bulletin (September).

Burns, Arthur F. 1976. "Statement before the Joint Economic Committee, February 19, 1976." Federal Reserve Bulletin (March).

__________. 1978. Reflections of and Economic Policy Maker: Speeches and Congressional Statements: 1969-1978. Washington, D.C.: American Enterprise Institute for Public Policy Research.

Burger, Albert E., Richard W. Lang, and Robert H. Rasche. 1977. "The Treasury Bill Futures Market and the Market Expectations of Interest Rates." Review, Federal Reserve Bank of St. Louis (June).

Chicago Board of Trade. 1977. "Hedging Interest Rate Risks."

Chicago Mercantile Exchange. 1977. "Commodity Futures Terms."

Culbertson, John M. 1957. "The Term Structure of Interest Rates." Quarterly Journal of Economics (November).

Frazer, William. 1973. Crisis in Economic Theory. Gainesville, Florida: University of Florida Press. Chaps. 12 and 13.

__________. 1978a. "The Government Budget Constraint," Public Finance Quarterly (June).

__________. 1978b. "Evolutionary Economics, Rational Expectations, and Monetary Policy." Journal of Economic Issues (June).

__________, and William P. Yohe. 1966. Introduction to the Analytics and Institutions of Money and Banking. Princeton, N.J.: D. Van Nostrand Company, Inc.

Friedman, Milton, and Rose Friedman. 1980. Free to Choose. New York: Harcourt Brace Jovanovich.

Froewiss, Kenneth C. 1978. "GNMA Futures: Stabilizing or Destabilizing?," Economic Review. Federal Reser Bank of San Francisco (Spring).

Hass, Jane W., and William Frazer. 1979. "The Political Business Cycle: Adjustments through Persuasion Techniques." Economic Notes (No. 2).

Hearings. 1974. The 1974 Economic Report of the President. Hearings before the Joint Economic Committee of the Congress of the United States, Part 3. Washington, D.C.: U.S. Government Printing Office.

Hicks, John R. 1946. Value and Capital: An Inquiry into Some Fundamental Principles of Economic Theory, 2nd ed. Oxford: Clarendon Press.

__________. 1976. "Some Questions of Time in Economics." In Anthony M. Tang, et al. eds. Evolution, Welfare and Time in Economics: Essays in Honor of Georgescu-Roegen. Lexington, Mass.: Lexington Books, D.C. Heath and Company.

Hoel, Arline. 1977. "A Primer on the Futures Markets for Treasury Bills." Research Paper No. 7702, Federal Reserve Bank of New York.

Huggins, Kenneth M. 1978. "Interest Rate Futures--A Good Hedge?" A paper presented at the Midwest Finance Association Meeting (April 6-7).

Kane, Edward J. 1974. "The Re-Politicization of the Fed." Journal of Financial and Quantitative Analysis (November).

Kessel, Reuben A. 1967. "Comment." Journal of Political Economy, Supplement (August).

Keynes, John Maynard. 1930. A Treatise on Money: The Applied Theory of Money, Vol. II. New York: Harcourt, Brace and Company.

Leijonhufvud, Axel. 1968. On Keynesian Economics and the Economics of Keynes. New York: Oxford University Press.

Lombra, Raymond E. 1980. "Reflections on Burns' Reflections." Journal of Money, Credit and Banking (February).

Lutz, Frederick A. 1940. "The Structure of Interest Rates." Quarterly Journal of Economics (November).

Maisel, Sherman J. 1973. Managing the Dollar: An Inside View by a Recent Governor of the Federal Reserve Board. New York: W. W. Norton & Company, Inc. Chapter 6.

Meiselman, David. 1962. The Term Structure of Interest Rates. Englewood Cliffs, N.J.: Prentice-Hall, Inc.

Michaelson, Jacob B. 1973. The Term Structure of Interest Rates: Financial Intermediaries and Debt Management. New York: Intext Educational Publishers.

Phillips, Llad, and John Pippenger. 1976. "Preferred Habitat vs. Efficient Market: A Test of Alternative Hypotheses." Review, Federal Reserve Bank of St. Louis (May).

Poole, William. 1978. "Using T-Bill Futures to Gauge Interest-Rate Expectations." Economic Review, Federal Reserve Bank of San Francisco (Spring).

Roosa, Robert V. 1956. Federal Reserve Operations in the Money and Government Securities Markets. New York: Federal Reserve Bank of New York.

Task Force. 1975. Seminars, Effects of Fiscal and Monetary Policies on Capital Formation and Economic Growth, Task Force on Capital Needs and Monetary Policy of the Committee on the Budget, United States Senate. Washington, D.C.: U.S. Government Printing Office.

Terrell, William T., and William Frazer. 1972. "Interest Rates, Portfolio Behavior, and Marketable Government Securities." Journal of Finance (March).

Van Horn, James C. 1980. "The Term Structure: A Test of the Segmented Market Hypothesis." Southern Economic Journal (April).

Viorst, Milton. 1971. "Arthur F. Burns: Intellectual as Insider." Husters and Hereos. New York: Simon and Schuster.

Chapter 13

Loanable Funds, Liquidity Preference, and Indeterminancy

13.1. Introduction

Thus far discussion of interest rates has centered about the following: their behavior over time as depicted in figure 5-3; the liquidity preference construction as dealt with by Keynes and others (sects. 5.3, 5.4, 6.3); liquidity elements (and their inverse, risk) comprising the yields on money balances, even in the absence of a payment of interest on demand deposits (sects. 3.3, 8.3); the motives for holding money (sect. 5.2); the interest rate in the capital value, supply price context and in the closely related investment demand building block (sect. 8.2); the interest rate in relation to home construction and installment credit (sect. 9.4); the Fisher equation setting the nominal rate equal to the real rate plus the expected inflation rate, with added allowance for uncertainty in the forecast (sect. 5.5); Wicksell's market and "natural" rates of interest with attention to Keynes and to Friedman's natural rate of unemployment (sects. 9.1, 9.4, 11.5); and theories of the term structure of interest rates and related time-to-maturity profiles depicting preferences for special maturities of debt instruments (sect. 12.3). Obviously, interest rates and related theory are a complicated affair, and much that we perceive with hindsight was not known to Keynes and some others since. Keynes for example, did not have the facts and the statistical results from the computer revolution of the 1960s. Nevertheless, we proceed in this chapter to do a combination of things, namely: on the one hand, to review some matters bearing on crises and redirection in economic theory; and to review some matters bearing on economics as an empirical science; and on the other hand, to introduce the older loanable funds theory of interest that Keynes reacted to, to present a summary statement of the

Keynesian building blocks, to review Hicks's (Hicks 1950) and Hansen's (1953, chap. 7) efforts to tidy up the Keynesian theory with the IS-LM model, and to review the Friedman approach to liquidity preference with overshooting and with modifications focusing upon movements in the income velocity of money and rate of interest (sects. 5.4 and 6.3).

The foregoing topics taken together lead to some reflections and to further prospects: (1) to reflections about the traditional and future role for economic theory, and about adding variables and non-redundant equations to simultaneous equations models, and (2) to anticipation of further consideration of economics in relation to forecasting and thus the formation of expectations.

13.2. Economic Theory, Retrospect, and Forecasting

Dillard (1978) outlines the main revolutions in economic theory in the British tradition from Adam Smith through Maynard Keynes, and inquires about their nature. The theoretical treatises of the revolutionaries, he reports, offer some major new direction to economies and at the same time address a particular problem of the day. This address, he says (1978, 706), is not always found explicit in the treatises alone, and thus one must look into the pamphlets and correspondence of the economists to ascertain their views on policy and reform. Continuing Dillar says:

> The essence of revolutions in economic theory lies in their substance rather than in the invention of new techniques of analysis. Without techniques there can be no economic theory, but economics is more, much more than techniques. The selection of tools and the manner of their use depend on the purpose for which they are intended. All the breakthrough theorist were great technicians even though their tools were sometimes left with rough edges to be polished by their successors.

Keynes himself advanced the view stated by Dillard about the role of economic theory--about its addressing the central problem of the day. One finds this quite explicit, in Keynes's correspondence with Roy Harrod in 1938, concerning an address by Jan Tinbergen entitled "Scope and Method of Economics," and in Hicks (1974, 8). In fact, in Keynes's reaction (Moggridge 1973, 291-301) to Tinbergen on interrelated roles of economic theory presently addressed--that of a simplified abstraction addressing the central problem and that of structural equations models leading to forecasting proper--Keynes says the following in one letter to Harrod (7/4/38):

> It seems to me that economics is a branch of logic, a way of thinking... One can make some quite worthwhile progress merely by using your axioms and maxims [principles, statements of general

> truth]. But one cannot get very far except by devising new and improved models. This requires, as you say, 'a vigilant observation of the actual working of our system'. Progress in economics consists almost entirely in a progressive improvement in the choice of models. The grave fault of the later classical school, exemplified by Pigou, has been to overwork a too simple or out-of-date model, and in not seeing that progress lay in improving the model; whilst Marshall often confused his models, for devising which he had great genius, by wanting to be realistic and by being unnecessarily ashamed of lean and abstract outlines.

Continuing and addressing in the same letter the matter of Tinbergen on the estimation of parameters and statistical verification, Keynes says:

> It is the essence of a model that one does not fill in real values for the variable functions.... For as soon as this is done, the model loses its generality and its value as a mode of thought.... The object of statistical study is not so much to fill in missing variables with a view to prediction, as to test the relevance and validity of the model.

Then, in the letter to Harrod (6/4/38) on the matters of data and observation, Keynes says, "Good economists are scarce because the gift for using 'vigilant observation' to choose good models, although it does not require highly specialized intellectual technique, appears to be a very rare one."

Now, against this preceding background, we may view Keynes's main contribution as focusing on the unemployment problem of capitalism (sects. 4.2 and 7.1) in the 1920s and 1930s in Britain and the early 1930s in the United States. He attacked Say's law as a symbol of classical economics on the negative side, and offered the income-expenditure block centering about the simple consumption function and focusing on the investment multiplier, on the positive side. Monetary policy entered through the liquidity preference demand block and through the theory of backwardation of the last chapter, and the demand for money as a means of speculation and dealing with uncertainty could explain unemployment at less than full employment. The monetary control linkage, nevertheless, was not adequate, as we have noted, and the attention focused instead on government deficits and spending as a means of coping with unemployment (sect. 10.4).

As much as Keynes and the Keynesians contributed, the foregoing is the substance of the Keynesian economics that came to prevail. It seems to serve quite adequately as a guide to policy, in the particular setting of the 1930s, given the inadequacy of the theory of the monetary control linkage. Keynesian economics in the later years, however, has come to be viewed as offering a short-term solution and long-run problems such as further instability and inflation (sect. 11.5; and Skidelsky 1977). It starts, we may conjecture, with good things happening first and the bad things coming later. Initially, with accelerated government spending, budget deficits, and supportive monetary policy, the unemployment rate declines and inflation and interest rates increase somewhat. Later, the inflation rate accelerates, interest rates reflect it, and eventually we end with both inflation and recession. The government deficits may appear small at first and even smaller later as households get moved into higher tax brackets and revenues increase, all without tax rates being changed via the usual routes provided for in the U.S. Constitution.

These economic problems of further instability and inflation, and the problem in theory of an inadequate linkage for monetary control are addressed in a direct way by Friedman. Often, moreover, he sets about (or provides leads to) framing the theory without having to reject a lot of the mechanics inherited from the Keynesians. First, in broad outline, he establishes the time frame with attention to both the short- and long-run and the short-cycle (transitory change) and equilibrium time paths (quasi-permanent trends). Next, in the case of the permanent income hypothesis of consumption, the theory (sect. 9.4) explains the simple relation found in budget studies (cross-section data) and a tendency for the saving to income ratio to be constant in the long run.

Further, after altering the monetary linkage, as found in the liquidity preference construction with overshooting (sect. 6.3) and as reviewed further below, Friedman directs attention towards Fisher's equation for the nominal rate of interest. Rates of change in the money stock and related announcements may influence spending, the prospect of inflation, and interest rates. The presence of an inflationary expectations component in the rate of interest opens the door for a role for persuasion in the economic policy area as it may relate to stability and expected inflation in particular, as considered in the previous chapter. In addition, the perspective on fiscal policy found in Keynesian economics is altered by viewing recession as a response to a strengthened preference for liquidity, by defining monetary policy in terms of monetary aggregates (say, dR/dt as in sects. 10.5 and 12.2), and by recognizing the need to finance government deficits.

Finally, in addressing the control time frame and orientation of Keynesian economics with respect to a target rate of unemployment, Friedman introduces the natural rate of unemployment in the tradition of the natural rate of interest found in Wicksell (sects. 9.1, 9.4). In this tradition, Friedman's attention to the long run adds something, and gives rise to the distinction between actual and potential GNP and an analysis of inflation and control in those terms (sect. 11.5). Of special significance, useful distinction may be made between the use of demand management to achieve minimum sustainable rates of unemployment and policy measures directed toward reducing the natural rate of unemployment.

The inclination thus far is to view both Keynes and Friedman as revolutionaries, in their respective times, having addressed issue of theory and the central problems of a monetary economy in their respective times. However, in passing, we may note at least one big difference in the styles of the respective revolutionaries. Keynes, Carry says (1978, 4, and 26-7), set up quite a "straw man" in his view of the classical economists, and in any case he "laid stress on his own originality and the breaks in his own thinking with the past." Milton Friedman, on the other hand, gave weight to some valid orthodoxy. Even while bringing about change, he seems to have excessively claimed some orthodoxy, perhaps as a way of making the new more acceptable.

In any case, Milton Friedman's work encompasses much that is traditional and much that is new. He comes forward as an empirical scientist in a period when the modern computer was to support the thrust of empiricists in economics. One form the tie with the old takes is the continuous use of schedules and crosses, as in the work of Marshall and Keynes. One form the new takes is empirical estimation with a great deal of attention to data, and in this Friedman recognizes the ideals of structural equations models and the modern literature bearing on forecasting and the analysis of expectations (Friedman 1951). Shortcomings appear in the structural equations methods, however, and we are left with combinations of statistical analyses of data and indirect uses of the constructions fund in traditional economics (sect. 7.1).

Proceeding from the old to structural equations methods, one encounters an effort to make variables determinate within the model, and thus to yield a neat massageable structure. With the proper stroking, the ideal model is to generate linkage schemes, and reveal the impact of a control variable on such key economic variables as GNP, inflation, and/or the unemployment rate. This is to occur as if the parameters of the model are stable from one period to another and as if they continue to be stable on into the forecast period proper. Indeed, the method of parameter estimation is least squares with the presumption of sampling from an unchanged universe. Soon one is into forecasting proper on the basis of such estimation and model construction. The concept of the formation of expectation (forecasts) on the basis of such estimation and model building is treated in chapters 14 and 17 and elsewhere (Frazer 1978) as "pure" rational expectations. A more general concept of rational expectations encompasses the numerous qualifications called for in treating the formation of expectations as they may be encountered in the real world.

Repeated effort at the estimation of parameters and the verification of theory results in experimentation in statistical analyses of data and the direction of attention to "outside" events and nonrepetitive changes. The experimentation gives rise to a lists of principles in chapter 21. These concern the formation of expectations and economic behavior traditionally impounded in <u>ceteris paribus</u> in economics.

13.3. Keynes, Keynesians, and Indeterminancy

Keynes argued (1936, chap. 14) that the classical (or loanable funds) theory of interest was indeterminate and he summarized it. We take "indeterminate" to mean that the rate of interest was insufficiently accounted for (i.e., without exact limits). He had some suggestions and ultimately his liquidity preference demand for money was brought out--together with the other Keynesian building blocks--as more firmly accounting for the rate of interest. In its simplier form--the liquidity block alone--it was not adequately accounted for in the sense that one did not know the rate of interest unless one also knew the underlying income. Hence Hicks and Hansen proceeded to deal with this analytical problem of having income simultaneously determined. The result was the IS-LM model as a summary of the Keynesian system, as presented in this chapter. Hicks--who survived Hansen as an active writer--was later to express regrets about the model in the light of monetarist research (Hicks 1974). Even so, it permeated the textbooks of macroeconomics for two decades and probably is irretrieveably written into the thinking and history of those generations.

The summary IS-LM model was a model for the simultaneous determination of the rate of interest and income, given underlying conditions. It implied a simultaneous system of equations, and in fact the Keynesian system also has been presented as a structural equations system--as a system of simultaneous equations--by one of its early expositors and pioneers in structural equations models (Klein 1966, chap. 9, "The Econometrics of the General Theory"). That particular approach and its relation to Keynesian economics is reviewed. In it, Lawrence Klein is following the tradition in model building established by Jan Tinbergen (Frazer 1973, 391-92; Friedman 1951, 107-08; Moggridge 1973, 291-301), a Dutch economist. For his work, Tinbergen was a co-recipient of the first Nobel Prize in economics in 1969.

Indeterminancy, Structure and Forecasting

Efforts at dealing with the problem of indeterminancy to which Keynes reacted, and then the Keynesians, evolve into large-scale structural equations models, in the tradition of Klein and Tinbergen. There is an ideal, on the one hand, and problems, on the other. According to the ideal, discussions about control variables, multipliers, and impact imply reduced forms. In section 10.4, the government deficit was a control variable impacting on GNP, in a Keynesian tradition.

Such models have not lived up to the claims made for them in the 1960s and indeed, instead of a single forecasting model with the presumption of stable parameters at least three interrelated developments in data analysis and forecasting come out of the 1960s and 70s, namely: (1) programs for obtaining a printout of variations in regression coefficients have come forward (Cooley and Prescott 1973 and 1976), (2) the prospect of uncertainty with respect to non-random changes in the parameters of economic relations has come forward as distinct from uncertainty simply as a random variable in an economic relation (Frazer 1978), and (3) a literature has come about on the evaluation of alternative forecasts (app. to chap. 13). Even so, the frailty of the large-scale structural equations models, as suggested by the evaluation of alternative forecasts, has not thwarted discussion and speculation about the workings of the economic system. Instead, we encounter at times, the notion (but not the reality) of the existence of some ideal structural equations model--one that fulfills early claims for such models, and one that may be used as a standard (as in the case of the definition of rational expectations, in chaps. 14 and 17).

Instead of developing structural equations models in all their formal detail in this text, however, attention is directed toward examination of data, fundamental notions, and the multifold problems of structural equations models of the early vintage (Frazer 1973, chap. 12). Later models move to confront these problems (Eckstein 1978), but the reality that is being confronted by the model builder is revealed by a list of the problems, namely: (1) evolutionary aspects of the economy are not readily manageable on the part of the methods, (2) the economic system is constantly being influenced by so-called outside forces, and (3) the economic theory that leads to the building and acceptance of a particular model is inadequate. In the first case, evolutionary features of the economy concern evolving (ever changing, and not simply repetitive) features of the economy and natural resources, as introduced in chapter 17, and learning on the part of behavioral units and regulatory and control authorities, such that the economist is not sampling from the same universe as he gathers time series data for statistical estimation of coefficients. Some aspects of the learning come up in chapters 17 and 18. In the second case, the economy is constantly being buffeted about by shifts in political administrations, wars on poverty and abroad, crises in credibility and energy, and these too make a difference in the underlying universe from which data are obtained and discussed. And, in the third case, presumably reasonable people confronted with economic theory have not been able to agree about the theory and workings of the economic system. The Friedman, Keynesian episode has been an example.

The lack of agreement on a range of theoretical issues and evidence has characterized the past in economics, though the range of disagreement may be narrowing with the evolution of empirical study and structural equations methods and uses. On the inadequacy of the theoretic/empirical aspect of economics, Milton Friedman himself (1972, ix-x) has observed thus: "most differences about desirable social or economic policy among persons in the Western World reflect different judgements about the ultimate consequences of such policies." Of two policies A and B, in other words, the controversy is an empirical one--one of knowing what policy A or B is going to do towards achieving economic goals such as high employment as distinct from goals for social values (sect. 11.4). Kearl et al. (1979, 34) note evidence in support of Friedman on this.

To say that the early promise, the ideal of large-scale structural equations models, has not been fulfilled should not detract from one use to which they have been put, namely: forecasting, say, as distinct from yielding reduced form equations with adequate control linkages. In the case of forecasting, the large models may be useful as a means of accounting for many possible influences, and as a means of extrapolating much of the past into the future, even with some instability in the parameters. The forecasting emphasis comes up below, exclusive of emphasis on explanations (theories) of observable phenomena.

A Summary of the Keynesian Building Blocks

One summary of the Keynesian building blocks--as reviewed separately in chapters 5 through 9--is shown in figure 13-1. The blocks there are, respectively, the liquidity preference, the investment demand, and saving and investment (or alternatively the aggregate supply, aggregate demand) block. The figure also illustrates the Keynesian linkage scheme whereby a change in the money stock causes an inverse change in the rate of interest, that then causes an inverse change in capital spending (and consequently income). In the first link, an open market purchase of securities by the Federal Reserve was often introduced in lieu of or parallel with a change in the money stock in attempting to illustrate the working of the scheme. The interest rate, one may say, was in effect a control variable working through a reduced form equation to exert impact on capital spending.

The foregoing prospect of a purchase of securities to lower rates, and so on was too simple a view of policy operations as hindsight has revealed (sect. 6.2). There was more to be allowed for, including especially the psychology of the market (underlying conditions) and defensive operations by the Federal Reserve. Even so, an inverse relation between the money stock (or an open market purchase) and the rate of interest was so taken for granted that the interest rate would be treated without examination of the money stock. Indeed, Tinbergen introduced the rate of interest rather than the money stock as the control variable in his Keynesian system.

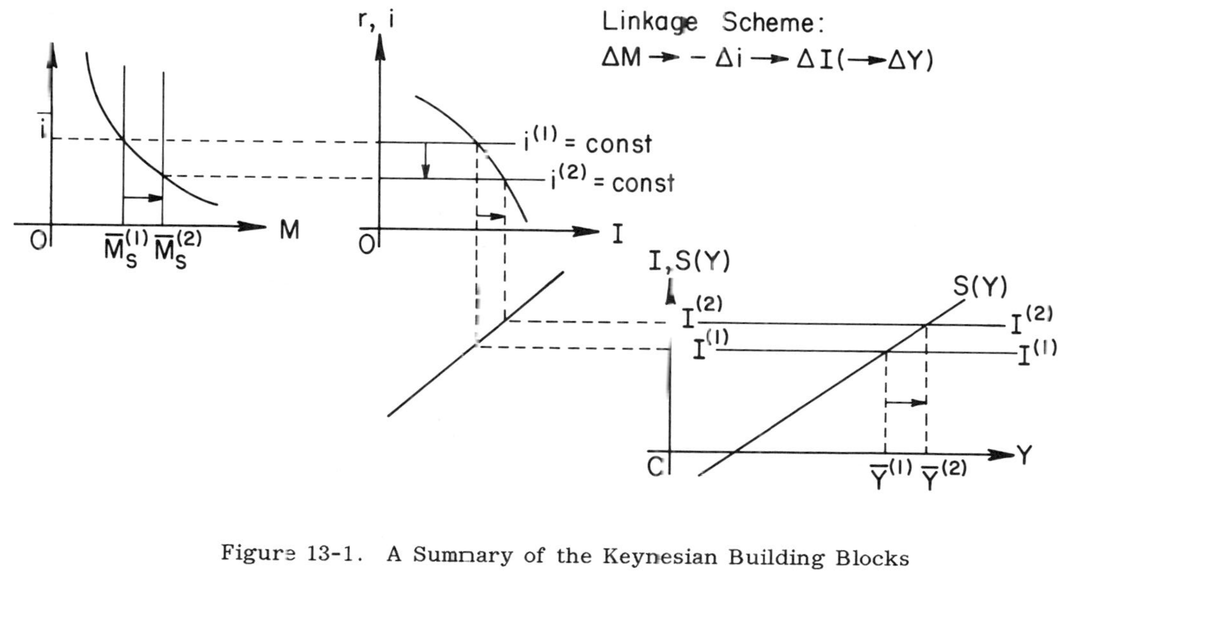

Figure 13-1. A Summary of the Keynesian Building Blocks

As we have seen, underlying conditions rarely are as presumed in the more static economic theory. Expectations about future prices and business conditions (and hence rates of interests) are not constant. The use of the liquidity preference block with the tendency for spending to over react in response to an increase in the money stock is a good example (sect. 6.3). Another prospect that reemerges in this chapter is one in which the influence of the expansion of bank credit (total loans and investment by commercial banks) may be different from that for the money stock. This is complicating in part because in the IS-LM model (as stated below) and the fact that in the Keynesian system no clear distinction is made between the roles for money and bank credit (sect. 6.2; and Roos 1979, 12-15). In the light of such complexities it is not necessary to jettison the Keynesian constructions. Rather they may be modified, or viewed differently (more open ended and flexible, let us say, than in the case of the IS-LM model).

13.4. Flows for Saving and Investment

Keynes described the classical (or what some have described as a loanable funds) theory of interest (Keynes 1936, chap. 14). According to it, there is saving out of current income and there is a demand for these funds for investment purposes. One is an increasing function of the rate of interest and the other a decreasing function. The two relationships intersect to determine the rate of interest and the flows of saving and investment, as in figure 13-2. The rate of interest here is the "price" of investable resources. Saving flows into investment, virtually as described in chapters 3 and 7, where we use Keynes's notions of saving and investment. In these instances, the rate of interest brings the supply of "funds" and the "demand" together, and "funds," as noted earlier (sect. 3.2), are not money balances. From a business firm's point of view the source of funds to the firm from a bank, say, is the firm's liability account for bank loans (i.e., it is the firm's indebtedness at the bank). From the bank's point of view the funds supplied arise from an increase in bank credit (a part of bank assets comparing total loans and investments). It is a feature of the banking system, however, that an expansion of bank credit gives rise to a coincidental expansion of the money stock in most cases, depending on complexities introduced in section 6.2.

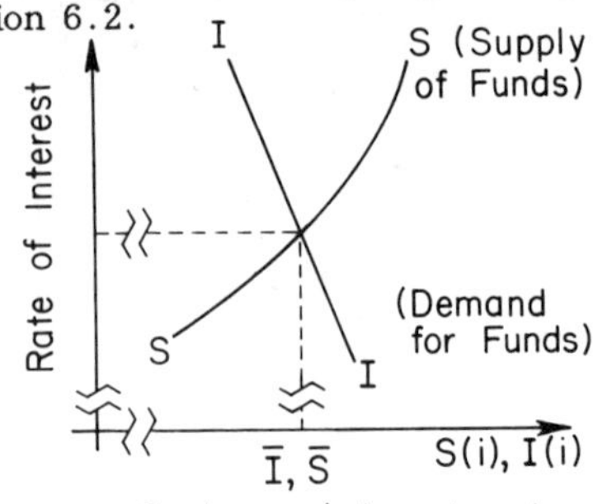

Figure 13-2. Interest as Determined by Saving and Investment

As with most of the other supply and demand crosses we have considered, the respective members of the cross may shift. These shifts could be more important in the determination of the rate of interest than the movements along the respective schedules, especially where both may be shifting or shifting at different rates. Monetarists of the 1960s, among others, stressed this property.

Viewing the saving schedule of figure 13-2 as shifting rightward as income increases Keynes simply said the "schematism" breaks down. Hansen, an early American Keynesian, later said with respect to Keynes's constructions that money is only one determinant of income and the rate of interest. He mentioned others--the investment demand schedule, the consumption function, and the liquidity preference schedule (all as in figure 13-1). What these early economists were doing was adding variables in effect to account for the rate of interest.

Economists as a group were unaware of the practice that became so widespread in the 1960s of adding variables and equations in a structural equations model. The idea essentially was that you had a model consisting of a structure of equations. As in any good simultaneous equations system, the number of variables and non-redundant equations were to be equal. In this case, solutions for any of the variables in terms of the parameters of the system were possible, as illustrated in section 10.4 and on other occasions with a simple model. The economists over the years added the features to this otherwise straightforward mathematical problem. One, the solution equations were called reduced forms, as illustrated in section 10.4; two, a special class of parameters called exogenous variables (or variable constants) was added, and, three, distributed lag relations were added, such as to give rise to a final form equation (sect. 18.5). The variables determined by the model were called endogenous (to denote their being inside the model). The exogenous variables could be controlled, as by an outside authority such as the Federal Reserve or the legislative and executive branches of government. But the point was that for the most part the parameters attached to the endogenous variables of the model would be stable over time.

In statistical parlance, if the parameters had been estimated for one period, then they would remain unchanged when estimated for another sample period.1 Unstable parameters meant that some relevant real world forces were excluded by the theory. To take care of this, the analysts-theorist would add new variables to the system and new equations. The problem arose in this approach that there was no end to the number of variables and equations one could add (Frazer 1973, chap. 14). Operating with an underlying Keynesian approach as we introduced earlier (attribute 45, table 4-1) and discuss later, the Federal Reserve-MIT model of the mid-to-late-1960s grew from sixty-five to over one hundred and fifty equations [and by 1978, Eckstein (1978) had presented a third generation of such a model with 800 equations]. Still there was no adequate stability in the parameters. Something was left out. It has been suggested that omissions had to do with mystifying phenomena, with psychological and socio-economic forces, with learning, changing expectations, changing political administrations, wars on poverty and in Vietnam, the student invasion of the U.S. embassy in Tehran in early November 1979, the later invasion of Soviet troops in Afghanistan, and so on.

In any event, to contribute to understanding and to serve as a guide to policy and control measures, theory must be simple. So we do not quarrel with simplicity itself. A good example was the abstraction from much detail about all the motives governing saving when we considered the dynamic consumption function in chapter 9. We endorse simplicity as essential. As Milton Friedman posited at an early date (1951, 109), "given the existence of economic change the crucial question is whether the theory implicit in the econometric model abstracts any of the essential forces responsible for the economic changes that actually occur." What is suggested with respect to the detail is that students of economics and the economy must give careful attention to fundamentals and to some of the details giving rise to what is being treated as simple. The theory in its present state should not be viewed too firmly as a close-end system (i.e., one with fixed parameters), as is the IS-LM summary of the Keynesian system. In fact, the present conjecture and numerous results suggest (e.g., sect. 18.4 and 18.5) that the forces outside of the more purely mechanical constructs are more important as determinants of economic behavior than those within the constructions.

13.5. Liquidity Preference and Overshooting

Keynes's liquidity preference building block presented a determination of the rate of interest--given income as determined in another block, given Federal Reserve control over the money stock (an exogenous variable). There was also the assumption of a linkage scheme whereby the Federal Reserve controlled the rate of interest in a fairly direct and prescribed way. An increase in the stock of money (say, if one likes, accelerated growth in the stock of money) reduced interest rates. This possibility could be and was often reinforced with the notion that the Federal Reserve increased the money stock through a purchase of securities for its open market account and that a purchase (a quantity demand) raised security prices (bond values) and thus lowered interest rates. The long-term interest rate on government bonds and its direct control as just described were essential features.

As economics became more dynamic--say, in an effort to grapple more adequately with real world forces--some important changes occurred. Notable the liquidity preference schedule was no longer viewed as being independent of the changes in the money stock. Accelerated growth in the latter caused total spending (income) to rise more than in proportion to the money stock (i.e., the ratio Y/M increased) and the interest rate increased rather than decreased. This phenomenum of faster growth in production and the price level (PQ = Y) was called "overshooting," and gave rise especially to price level changes. It was first illustrated in figure 5-5 (now reproduced as figure 13-3b) and is presently illustrated in a different way in part a of figure 13-3.

In part a real money balances (M/P) rather than nominal balances (M) are shown on the horizontal axis. As initially treated by Friedman and Gibson and as reviewed in section 5.4, the idea underlying the construction is that the faster growth of the money stock causes spending and especially the price level (P) to rise. There is overshooting, such that the price level increase causes real money balances to fall, and such that there is a backing up along a more stable demand schedule (namely that for real money balances). The interest rate rises again, as does the velocity ratio.

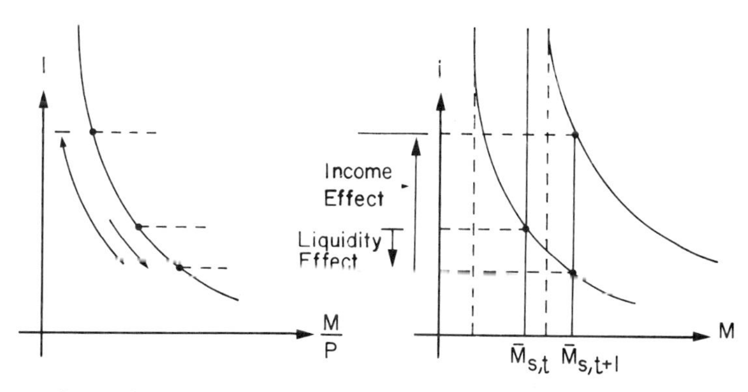

a. Rate of Inflation Effect

b. Liquidity and Income Effects

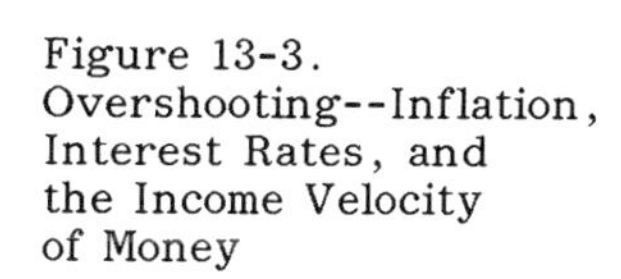
Figure 13-3. Overshooting--Inflation, Interest Rates, and the Income Velocity of Money

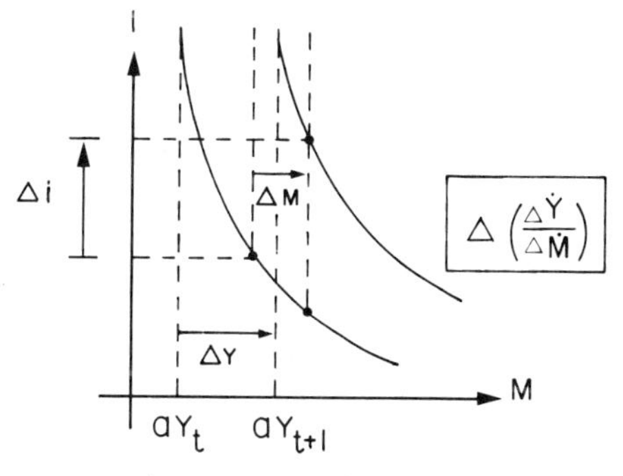

c. Income Velocity Effect

The sketches comprising figure 13-3 are in terms of levels for the stock and flow quantities, but in actuality the analysis should be in terms of time rates of change in these variables. The insert for the velocity ratio in part c of figure 13-3, should remind one of the more dynamic property of the analysis.

The phenomenum of rising velocity, as first shown in figure 5-1, implies an excess of "actual" over "desired" money balances. The adjustment on the demand side of the market for money is occurring as part of efforts to draw down on an otherwise controlled stock of money balances. Such an imbalance ("actual" greater than "desired") is readily illustrated with an expansion phase of business conditions of the 1950s through early 1960s variety (rising velocity of money, and rising interest rates, as treated in chapter 5). However, as the 1960s proceed and usher in the spectra of a secular rise in the inflation rate, and ultimately the inflationary recessions of 1969-70 and 1973-75, and the unique 1975:III through 1977:I period of declining interest rates (figure 12.7)--then, after all this, the earlier common pattern becomes disrupted. It is apparently disrupted by the following: (1) a tie between the interest rate, the expected inflation rate, and uncertainty in the forecast for the inflation rate, and (2) a tie between the velocity ratio and changes in the expected inflation rate, also after allowance for uncertainty in the forecast. Hence, as in chapter 5,

$$i - 0.70\ 1.35/\sigma\ (1/P\ dP/dt \times 100)$$

$$Y/M - 0.70\ 1.35/\sigma\ (1/P\ dP/dt \times 100)$$

Funds and Money Balances in the IS-LM Model

Now--in the present dynamic treatment--an inconsistency emerges in the Keynesian effort to in effect combine in the IS-LM model the classical (or loanable funds) notion about interest rates with the liquidity preference notion. Both notions envision the same interest rate, and indeed it is captured by both notions when one allows for the proper shifts in the schedules.

The inconsistency is this. In the loanable funds theory we are talking about bank credit, a source of funds. The interest rate rises as the amount of credit demanded exceeds that available and as bankers and other suppliers of funds and dealers adjust rates upward. In the liquidity preference block the rate rises as "actual" exceeds "desired" money balances. In other words, from the demand side there is an excess of money balances. A deficiency of bank credit, say, but an excess of money, from the demand sides point of view. Thus, bank credit and money play separate roles. To equate the one with the other and ignore this separation is to distort distinct parts of the analysis. A business firm may go to the bank to make a loan in a boom (rising interest rates) because it desires "funds" (not money balances). In the process of this desire being fulfilled by the banks, new money balances arise as a part of the credit and money creating functions engaged in by commercial banks before 1980, and by these banks and other selected financial institutions since (sect. 6.2). These new money balances, however, are coincidental to the main purpose of the financial action taken by the business firm, namely that of securing a bank loan (not that of securing a stock of money balances).

The IS-LM Model

The IS-LM (for investment-saving, and liquidity-money) model has been viewed as a summary of the Keynesian building blocks. Often it has been said to be essentially a "pedagogial" model--a model to be used in stressing the attributes of Keynesian economics and the related mechanics in the classroom. Some have viewed it as essentially misleading and thus inadequate even for its teaching purpose. It obscures a lot but primarily excludes attention to crucial developments such as liquidity preference with overshooting. Even those most committed to the Keynesian revolution at an earlier time recognize this inadequacy today, and some introduce modifications as we stress later. The model (sect. 18.5) can still play a role, even while addressing mainly the roles of outside forces, such as expected inflation and uncertainty in the forecast.

The IS-LM model as a Keynesian model follows essentially from the analysis surrounding figures 13-2 and 13-3 (or its earlier counterpart, figure 5-5), from the earlier treatment of saving as a function of income S(Y), and from the solution condition for the aggregate supply demand block (namely, saving equals investment, S(Y) = I). The version that follows treats real magnitudes for income (Y/P) and the money stock (M/P), because Keynes and the Keynesians stressed output adjustments. Prices entered in an ad hoc way for later Keynesians, for example, as in the Phillips curve of section 17.4. The emphasis on real magnitudes also calls attention to a limitation of the simple model where money, income, and interest rates might all increase as in figure 13-3.

From figure 13-2 and the other conditions, an increase in income may be viewed as shifting the schedule SS to the right. With both observed saving and investment increasing as income increases and as the interest rate declines we get the IS curve of figure 13-4 (and earlier of figure 8-4). From figure 13-3 (or 5-5), with money constant (M = const.) and real income increasing, the interest rate in the figure rises. In Keynesian terms, a rise in the interest rate causes an attempted shifts out of money and into bonds, such that the velocity of money and hence income rises. Thus we have a liquidity-money curve that increases as income increases (M = const.). This is shown too in figure 13-4, where the interest rate and income are determined at the intersection of the IS and LM curves (price level, P_1). An increase in the money stock would shift the LM curve to the right and lower the rate of interest, as the Keynesians posited, but there is an analytical problem when we introduce the phenomenon of overshooting.

Figure 13-4. Income in Constant Dollars

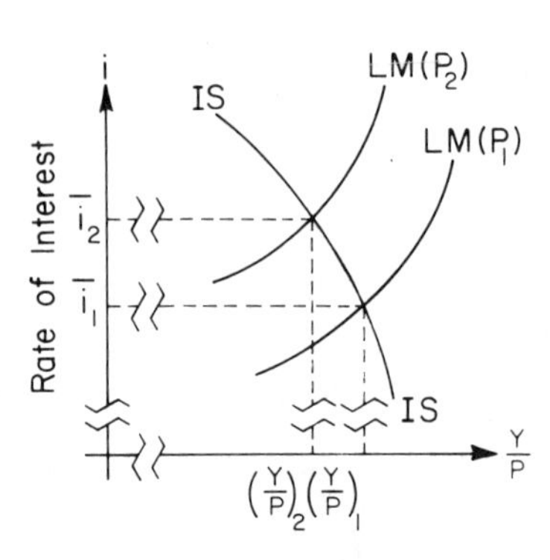

When translated into IS-LM terms, the overshooting phenomena calls for the following: a rise in the price level, from P_1 to P_2; a decline in the real money stock and hence a leftward shift in the LM curve; a decline in real income, from $(Y/P_1)_1$ to $(Y/P_2)_2$; and a rise in the interest rate, from i_1 to i_2. Hence, a faster growth in the money stock leads to a rise in interest rates and a decline in output, which was not what Keynes and the Keynesians posited.

This introduction of the variable price level means that the IS and LM curves are no longer sufficient to determine the equilibrium values of the interest rate and real income. The idea is that you must know the price level from some other source. As shown in a later chapter, Keynesians tended to meet this latter criticism by looking at the labor market. There is the idea that we can determine in part the equilibrium value of real income by looking at the labor market and the economy's aggregate production function (sect. 15.6). The foregoing is the problem of the structural equations model. One tries to add variables and equations to take the place of unstable parameters (the constant price level, in the present case).

13.6. Structural Equations Models

Lawrence Klein (1966) was an early writer on the Keynesian Revolution. He has expessed a view, shared by many, in the early stages of the Keynesian Revolution, that the interrelationships connecting the basic pillars of Keynes's work contained some "profound truths of an amazing sort." Indeed, there were some but perhaps less than originally thought. The saving-investment notion with its ex post equality and the intermediation of the flows of funds into investment must be stressed among these (sect. 3.2). Furthermore, the basic building blocks of Keynes's work still shed much light and expedite the communication of some important ideas, especially when stressed in slightly more dynamic trappings than the Keynesians provided. The pillars of Keynes's and Keynesian analysis have been listed as being those summarized in figure 13-1. Klein stresses too that after interpretation along IS-LM lines the thinking indicated a closed system of two relationships in two unknowns, with an exogenous control over the money stock. The two relationships are:

$$S(r,Y) = I(r,Y) \qquad \text{hence, IS curve}$$

$$M = L(r,Y) \qquad \text{hence, LM curve}$$

where the two unknowns were aggregate income (Y), in real terms, and the interest rate (r).

Klein has stressed even further that the model was too static and unrealistic in its limited detail. He adds detail and stresses the need for a more dynamic orientation. This sort of thing was illustrated in section 9.4, where the Keynesian consumption function gets combined with Friedman's permanent income hypothesis. But mainly Klein's approach was one of adding more detail--more equations and variables--without changing the essential Keynesian nature of the analysis. The present one has been to return to fundamentals, deal with some matters of aggregation and the uses of indexes in relating parts to the whole, and to try to understand the fundamentals and matters of aggregation better, as they may apply in a dynamic setting. Even so, in this section we pursue Klein's approach briefly, and direct attention to the idea of a structure, and to the forecasting of economic conditions and magnitudes. The large models have evolved, as forecasting aids primarily, from earlier ideals about them as abstractions of reality with reduced form equations for guiding national economic policy.

Klein's Extended Model

Klein himself (1966, chaps. 8 and 9) presented an extention of the earlier Klein-Goldberger model to illustrate how greater detail and "realism" may be introduced into Keynesian economics to represent "the (extended) Keynesian system." This early version and the extension used annual data, but Klein recognized that the models would become complicated as more detailed data were used and as disaggregation proceeded. Klein, nevertheless, thought of these early structural models as completing the Keynesian system and as having provided tests of the Keynesian theory. The tests he mentions are those of "simulation" and "forecasting." By simulation he means that the model can be shown to reproduce or trace out the behavior of a variable as indicated by the raw data. Some would call this ex post forecasting, in the sense that an existing, historically generated time series is being forecast (its behavior simulated). This ex post forecasting is carried out by estimating coefficients for the model in question for a sample period, and then by using the model and these estimated values to forecast values for the same sample period. "Forecasting" proper may be thought of as extrapolating values for variables into the future, beyond the same period. The forecasts could then be compared with the actual, subsequent developments.

The extended Keynesian model consisted of 20 equations (sixteen with statistically estimated coefficients and four definitional equations or identities) and 20 endogenous variables (i.e., those "explained" or determined within rather than outside of the model). Apart from detail and added dynamic formulations, the properties one finds in the model are ones we have stressed, notably:

1. The interest rate is a determinant of capital spending. (Sect. 13.3)

2. Imports (exports) are influenced by the price spread as indicated by a domestic and foreign price comparison. (Sect. 2.2)

3. Monetary policy works through the short-term rate of interest. This extends to the long rate and then to the investment. As in the term structure discussion (sect. 12.4), "the long rate is expressed as a moving average of past (expected short rates)." Indeed the short-rate can be viewed as exogenously determined, as an alternative for an exogenously determined money supply.

The problems with the structural equations approach in its initial developments through the early 1970's are numerous. A sense of them may be conveyed, however, by our simply indicating several things: their size seemed uncontrollable, as more and more detail was called for in efforts to achieve stable estimates of parameters; the emphasis shifted from attention to causal linkages and explanations of phenomena to simple forecasting; and many models had fair forecasting records. Important forecasting models of the 1970s that seemed helpful to the forecasters who use them include those of Lawrence Klein's Warton Associates, Otto Eckstein's Data Resources, Inc., Chase Econometrics, and Michael Evan's Evans Econometrics, Inc. (In 1979, McGraw-Hill purchased controlling blocks of stock in Data Resources. They announced at the time of the initial purchase of stock, plans to spend $103 million in the transaction and that Mr. Eckstein would continue as president of Data Resources. Wall Street Journal, 7/16/79).

What arose in response to the foregoing attention to forecasting was an alternative approach, perhaps an intermediate step to the formulation of an improved economic theory and to a future generation of structural models. This alternative may be characterized by several features.

1. There should be a search for regularity in the data, as distinct from a mass of detail.

2. The emphasis should be on "first approximation" to special empirical relationships.

3. One should seek out and use independent evidence in evaluating the economic theory underlying the models.

Two examples of the last feature may be mentioned. For one, in attempting to relate theory to the interest-rate velocity relationship, one could be expected to look at independent evidence on the behavior of bond holdings by crucial sectors as interest rates rose. For another, in evaluating theories of the term structure on interest rates, one might be expected to look at data on the implications for portfolio behavior and not simply examine term structure data. Such consideration was given to porfolio behavior in section 12.3.

Forecasting

In forecasting one may think of the ordinary equations of a structural equations model, and some supportive identities (definitional, non-behavioral equations) and equations that depict lagged relations. The ordinary equations are, in summary: (1) the separate equations of the system, where each endogenous variable of the system is defined in terms of the others, though some may have zero influence on others, and (2) the reduced form equations (one for each endogenous variable). Each separate equation of the equation system proper may be used in the forecasting of its own left-hand member (solution value), and each reduced form equation (one for every solution value) may be used for predicting the impact of a policy or control variable, and, in any case, the former should be supportive of the latter. The forecasting with the separate equations is the most common, and *ex post* forecasting and forecasting proper with simple equations may be illustrated.

Two illustrations of forecasting follow, but with supportive equations. An adaptive expectations model of the type introduced in section 9.4 to deal with permanent income is used. An estimated or simply a computed permanent income could be a variable upon which consumption in a structural equation system depended.

To begin with, permanent income is a set of observations ordered over time

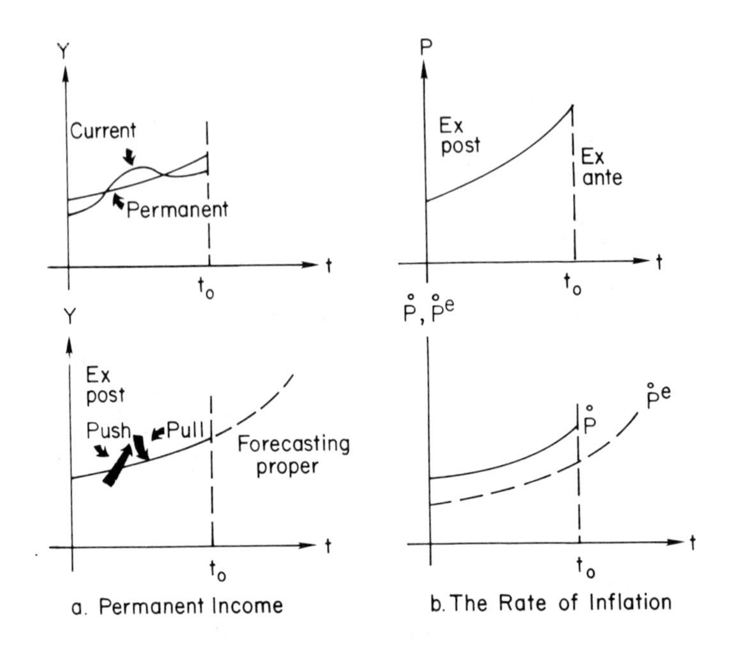

Figure 13-5. Ex post and Forecasting Proper, Using Adaptive Expectations

$$[(t_o, Y_{p,o}), (t_{-1}, Y_{p,-1}), (t_{-2}, Y_{p,-2}), \ldots, (t_{-n}, Y_{p,-n})].$$

The observations for permanent income would have to be obtained by fitting a line to data that are themselves ordered over time. (This exercise would be similar to that for fitting the line to the output data shown in figure 3-1.) Having obtained a series (say Y_{pt}), we could then regress it on current and lagged values for income (Y_t, Y_{t-1}, Y_{t-2}, . . ., Y_{t-n}) using a distributed lag model, for example,

$$Y_{pt} = \text{const} + w_0 Y_t + w_1 Y_{t-1} + w_2 Y_{t-2} + \ldots + w_n Y_{t-n}$$

estimate parameter values

Having obtained numbers for parameter values, the equation could then be used to estimate values for permanent income (denote estimated values,

$\hat{Y}_{pt}, \hat{Y}_{pt-1}, \hat{Y}_{pt-2}, \ldots, \hat{Y}_{t-n}$).[2]

The differences between computed, observed (ex post) values for permanent income and estimated values using the distributed lag model are then forecasting errors, e.g.:[3]

$$Y_{pt} - \hat{Y}_{pt} = \varepsilon_t, \; t = 0, -1, -2, -3, \ldots -n$$

Next, if we were forecasting proper as into the future, say for

$$\hat{Y}_{pt+1}, \hat{Y}_{pt+2}, \ldots, \hat{Y}_{pt+n},$$

then we would not know the errors of the forecast until after the passage of time (i.e., after the fact).

The distinction just drawn between ex post and proper (or ex ante) forecasting is readily illustrated in panel a of figure 13-5. The upper part of panel a shows actual permanent income as the fit of a trend line to actual current income data. The lower part of panel a shows the ex post forecasted permanent income. It will turn out to approximately coincide with the actual permanent income depending on the extent of the lagged time, because of the way permanent income is defined, namely, as a secular trend line. Forecasting proper --say beyond time t_o--is simply a matter of extrapolating the ex post line into the future, as shown by the broken line extending beyond time t_o in the lower part of panel a.

However, the adaptive expectations model can be used in an additional way and this too is illustrated in the lower part of panel a, figure 13-5. First, the most current values for the lagged variable are said, in this additional use, to have an extrapolative "push" effect, i.e., an effect of causing the expected change to continue, say with momentum, in a given direction. And, next, the values from a more distance past have a regressive "pull" effect, i.e., have the effect of pulling the expectation back toward a value for the most distant past. Thus, finally, the weights in the adaptive expectations model may be shifted, first to favor the "push" effect and, then to favor the pull effect. In this way the model may be used to describe forces concerning changes in business conditions, rather than simply having the two effects give smoothness to the trend by offsetting one another. The extent of the lag time too (say, as how far back the term, $w_n Y_{t-n}$, goes in time), will affect the extent to which one is obtaining a smooth trend path or capturing "push" effects.

In another example, we could let the adaptive expectation model be a model for the expected inflation rate (P_t^e):

$$\dot{P}_t^e = W_o \dot{P}_t + W_1 P_{t-1} + \ldots + W_n \dot{P}_{t-n}$$

With a constantly rising price level and an inflation rate as depicted in panel b, of figure 13-5, the actual inflation rate ($\dot{P}_t$) would always be above the expected rate ($\dot{P}_t^e$) obtained with the adaptive model. This is shown in the lower part of panel b, and there also, the ex ante forecasted rate is simply an extrapolation of ex post estimated permanent income. This tendency for the expected rate to always lag behind the actual inflation rate features the fact that the actual price level in the upper part of panel b, was continuously increasing at a faster rate. Had it slowed down, or leveled off, the result in the lower part of panel would have been different. Had the actual price level varied about a given level, the simulation of panel b, would have been more like that in panel a. This exercise comes forward in section 17.4 where we consider the Phillips curve.

With the concept of a structural equations model behind us, as well as the definitions of forecast error, and ex post and ex ante forecasts, some selected conclusions on forecasters and forecasting may be of interest (Zarnowitz 1978):

> The search for a consistently superior forecaster is about as promising as the search for the philosopher's stone.[4]
>
> -------------------------
>
> Of course, competent forecasters use common data and techniques, regularly interact, and are often similarly influenced by recent events and current attitudes and ways of thinking. The genuine ex ante forecasts here considered are all to a large extent "judgmental," and this could well tend to reduce the dispersion among them; there is indeed some evidence that errors of ex ante forecasts with econometric models vary less than errors of ex post forecasts made without judgmental adjustments. While published forecasts by ranking practitioners are often developed with particular skill or care, group average forecasts benefit over time greatly from cancellations of individual errors of opposite sign. At any given time, the deviations between corresponding forecasts from different sources are likely to be reduced by the working of these balancing factors. Thus, it is not surprising that forecasts for the same variable and target period tend to be similar.

13.7. Summary

Key points in this chapter may be listed.

1. Keynes and Friedman offer redirection to economics in their respective eras. Keynes took the more overt stance of a revolutionary, but Friedman offered redirection even while paying homage to orthodoxy. Both as a matter of fact, continue in a tradition of using simple method and having economic theory focus on central economic problems of the day--

unemployment in Keynes's time, and inflation, unemployment, and instability in Friedman's time.

2. Keynes's and Keynesian economics offers a short-run solution but a compound of other problems in the long run. Friedman addresses this time frame without rejecting the mechanics of Keynesian economics. In addition, however, Friedman comes to the forefront as a theoretic/empirical economist and is aided by the presence of the modern computer. We encounter ad mixtures of the old and the new. There is attention to simple method and to the estimation of parameters and to verification of theory. When the problem of indeterminancy is addressed, however, by Keynes and later others, we see it leads ultimately to large scale, structural equations models, to forecasting proper, to the formation of expectations, and to experimentation. The latter are said to lead to a list of principles concerning behavior that was impounded in ceteris paribus by economists prior to the more recent generations of computer modeling (Eckstein 1978).

3. The several Keynesian constructions may be brought together as one summary of the Keynesian system. These remain as a flexible and useful means of depicting and describing some economic phenomena, where the system is not closed in a sense and where some ad hoc introduction of the price level and nominal terms for income and money balances are permitted.

4. The IS-LM model is one summary of the Keynesian system. It is a tightly knit, closed-end summary. There is closely related to it the Keynesian linkage scheme with supply of money balances affecting interest rates inversely. There is also the Keynesian notion of causation whereby the rate of interest induces switching between money and bonds so as to cause the velocity ratio to move parallel with it. And there is the static notion that the role of a change in the money supply is indistinct from that of a change in bank credit. Logic and/or empirical observations may be invoked as a means of questioning the relevance of these attributes to observable phenomena.

5. In the presence of rising velocity "desired" money balances are viewed as being less than "actual" money balances. In this situation there is no motive for borrowing "funds" at the bank. Yet, as an empirical matter, bank loans and credit accelerate at such times. A way out of this confusion is to emphasize the desire for bank credit, and to view money as something that arises as a coincidental part of the credit granting process.

6. The rationale of the downward sloping IS curve is a combination of reasoning about saving as a function of income, about the equality of saving and investment in the aggregate supply demand block, and about the inverse variation in the rate of interest and investment.

7. The rationale about the upward sloping LM curve (M = const.) is that a rise in the interest rate induces switching out of money in relation to income (and into bonds in relation to income).

8. The idea of a close-end system with the interest rate and income determined is suggestive of what came later in the presentation of structural equations models. The variables (actually christened endogeneous variables) were to be determined within the model. This was to be such that parameters of the model could be estimated from analyses of empirical data and that these parameters would be stable from one sample period to another. In the absence of stability in the parameters more variables and equations were to be added. Using Keynesian ideas about the variables and relationships this approach to getting a determinate system seemed endless with respect to the number of equations. A class of variables traditionally excluded from economic theory was left out.

9. The study of structure (and changes in it) is of interest, as evidenced by the attention to investment demand functions, consumption functions, liquidity preference, and the like (and shifts in them), as well as in reduced form equations. Structural changes are changes in the parameters, although the parameters will be more numerous as a system of equations and variables increases in size. The reduced form equations center about the control mechanism by which monetary and fiscal policy (exogenous variables) have impact on the solution values for the variables in the system of equations (endogenous variables).

10. Models as satisfactory abstractions of reality are one thing, and the forecasting performance of them is another. Large scale structural equations models have achieved a capability of improving on the forecasts of forecasters who use them. However, as Christ reports (1975), "they disagree so strongly about the effects of important monetary and fiscal policies that they cannot be considered reliable guides to such policy effects, until it can be determined which of them are wrong in this respect and which (if any) are right.

11. The search in the construction of large scale, structural equations models as abstracts from reality is for equations depicting stable relationships (i.e., stable parameters). These are typically estimated by the use of statistical methods that assume sampling (the collection of data) from the same universe over a period of time. However, changes in political administrations, crises such as in energy, varying degrees in the credibility of leadership, changes in the confidence (or uncertainty) about the future are examples of changes in the universe from which sampling takes place. Hence a central problem in the methodology of the models, namely: there is conflict centering about the sampling from an unchanging universe, and changes that occur in it in fact.

12. Forecasting is of two types--*ex post* (after the fact) forecasting and *ex ante* (before the fact) forecasting--as far as economic models are concerned. The first consist of estimating parameters for an equation over a sample period and then using the equation to forecast values--usually for a variable comprising its left-hand member--by plugging in values for the variables in the right-hand member. The second sort of forecasting is forecasting, proper. In it values for variables

are forecast beyond the sample period (beyond the present time) with the use of the model. In this way the forecasting properties of the model can be tested against data occurring after the building of the model, that is, according to Christ (1975), "after the specifications were decided upon concerning which variables appear in each equation, which variables are endogenous and which exogenous, which is the functional form of each equation, which is the lag structure of each, what restrictions the parameters are to obey, etc."

13. What comes about as an alternative to the structural equations approach has several features--a search for regularity in the data, statements of a "first approximation" to empirical relationships, and a use of wide a variety of evidence (including independent evidence) bearing on theoretical notions. Economic theory becomes most relevant and useful in its dynamic forms, for the present with flexibility to accomodate varying states of uncertainty and expectations about economic magnitudes.

In the background and foreground of this search for regularity are conceptions of some ideal, possible future generation of structural equations model. Attention to simple relations such as the consumption function and investment demand reflects some interest in structure, and the study of policy variables with impact on final target variables is suggestive of reduce form equations (definitions of solution values to some larger underlying structural equations system). Distributed lag relations and "final form" equations come later (sect. 18.5).

FOOTNOTES

1. The sample period is the period over which data are analyzed in the sense that they are used to estimate parameters of a model. The model is presumed to apply beyond the sample period in the classical, relative frequency approach to probability, and it is presumed to have stable parameters in this approach.
2. Here we are predicting a regression line, assuming the use of the classical, least squares regression method.
3. These errors are assumed to be random errors and distributed as in a probability distribution. From the, forecasting ex post, we may obtain standard errors for a regression estimate, and then use the estimate to construct confidence intervals (say 90 or 95 percent confidence intervals). For the 90 percent interval we have an interval that should contain the forecast value 90 percent of the time. Forecasting errors, however, may be systematic (not random) and thus due to forces coming from outside of the model. Further, the estimates for each of

the parameter values (w_0, w_1, w_2, ..., w_n) can be discussed as falling within confidence intervals, with certain assumed random error. But this error too may not be random. It may be due to multicollinearity as mentioned in section 8.4 in relation to the Alman lag technique, and the coefficients may be subject to shifting from one sample period to another in a non-random way, as in response to outside forces.

4. As one may recall, the philosopher's stone was an imaginary substance sought after by alchemists. There was the belief that it would change base metals into gold or silver.

SELECTED READINGS AND REFERENCES

Christ, Carl F. 1975. "Judging the Performance of Econometric Models of the U.S. Economy." International Economic Review (February).

Cooley, Charles Horton. 1918. "Part VII: Intelligent Processes." In Social Process. New York: Charles Scribner's and Sons.

Cooley, Thomas F., and Edward C. Prescott. 1973. "Systematic (Non-Random) Variation Models Varying Parameter Regression: A Theory and Some Applications," Annals of Economic and Social Measurement (July).

__________, and __________. 1976. "Estimation in the Presence of Stochastic Parameter Variation." Econometrica (January).

Corry, B. 1978. "Keynes in the History of Economic Thought: Some Reflections." In A. P. Thirlwall. Keynes and Laissez-Faire. New York: Holmes and Meier Publishers, Inc.

Dillard, Dudley. 1978. "Revolutions in Economic Theory," Southern Economic Journal (April).

Eckstein, Otto. 1978. The Great Recession, with a Postscript on Stagflation. New York: North-Holland Publishing Company.

Frazer, William. 1973. Crisis in Economic Theory. Gainesville, Fla.: University of Florida Press. Chapter 12.

__________. 1978. "Evolutionary Economics, Rational Expectations, and Monetary Economics." Journal of Economic Issues (June).

Friedman, Milton. 1951. "Test of Econometric Model." In Conference on Business Cycles. New York: National Bureau of Economic Research, Inc.

__________. 1972. An Economist's Protest: Columns in Political Economy. Glen Ridge, N.J.: Thomas Horton and Company.

Fromm, Gary, and Lawrence R. Klein. 1976. "The NBER/NSF Model Comparison Seminar: An Analysis of Results." Annals of Economic and Social Measurment (Winter).

Hansen, Alvin. 1953. A Guide to Keynes. New York: McGraw-Hill Book Company, Inc.

Hicks, John R. 1950. A Contribution to the Theory of the Trade Cycle. London: Oxford University Press.

__________. 1974. The Crisis in Keynesian Economics. New York: Basic Books, Inc., Publishers.

Kearl, J. R., Clayne L. Pope, Gordon C. Whiting, and Larry T. Wimmer. 1979. "A Confusion of Economists?" American Economic Review (May).

Keynes, John Maynard. 1936. The General Theory of Employment, Interest and Money. New York: Harcourt Brace and Company.

Klein, Lawrence R. 1966. The Keynesian Revolution, second edition. New York: The Macmillan Company.

__________. 1969. "Estimation of Interdependent Systems in Macroeconomics." Econometrica (April).

Moggridge, Donald, ed. 1973. The Collected Writings of John Maynard Keynes, Vol. XIV. London: The Macmillan Press, Ltd.

Outlook. 1979. The Economic Outlook for 1979-1980: An Update. A Report to the Senate and House Committees on the Budget. Washington, D.C.: U.S. Government Printing Office.

Roos, Lawrence K. 1979. "Monetary Targets--Their Contribution to Policy Formation." Review, Federal Reserve Bank of St. Louis (May).

Skidelsky, Robert, ed. 1977. The End of the Keynesian Era. New York: Holmes & Meier Publishers, Inc.

Zarnowitz, Victor. 1978. "On the Accuracy and Properties of Recent Econometric Forecasts." American Economic Review (May).